The Dictionary of Health Economics, Second Edition

Anthony J. Culyer

University of Toronto, Canada and University of York, UK

Edward Elgar
Cheltenham, UK • Northampton, MA, USA

First Edition © Anthony J. Culyer 2005

Published by
Edward Elgar Publishing Limited
The Lypiatts
15 Lansdown Road
Cheltenham
Glos GL50 2JA
UK

Edward Elgar Publishing, Inc.
William Pratt House
9 Dewey Court
Northampton
Massachusetts 01060
USA

A catalogue record for this book
is available from the British Library

Library of Congress Control Number: 2009941263

Mixed Sources
Product group from well-managed
forests and other controlled sources
www.fsc.org Cert no. SA-COC-1565
© 1996 Forest Stewardship Council

FSC

ISBN 978 1 84980 041 9

Printed and bound by MPG Books Group, UK

CONTENTS

PREFACE TO THE SECOND EDITION

The second edition of *The Dictionary of Health Economics* improves upon the first in what I hope will be agreed to be several respects. Its general purposes remain, however, the same as before: to be as Thomas the tank engine was in the eyes of the Fat Controller – a really useful engine. There is now much greater use to be made of internet search engines than was hitherto the case, so there seemed little point in merely listing what was readily available through that means. What I hope adds value to the *Dictionary* is that I have scrutinized definitions elsewhere and recast them so that they conform better to the idea of 'definition': to provide a definiens for each definiendum that is concise, precise, bounded, and in conformity with (what I perceive as) correct or at least customary usage. The outcome ought to be more reliable definitions and elaborations. In addition, I have selected what I reckon to be good examples from the literature to illustrate the headwords and phrases in, so to speak, action, and I have provided full references for them. The combination of these two qualities of accuracy and example is not readily to be had from the internet – at least not without some fairly extensive searching. It is plain that I have also had to exercise a fair degree of subjective judgment. Being aware of this, and having a reasonable sense of the matters on which health economists (and others) are likely to take up arms, I have tried to be even-handed when it comes to politically loaded notions and to avoid culturally or geographically biased concentrations of empirical interest. The principal changes from the first edition are these:

I have corrected several mistakes and removed as many ambiguities as I could find or that have been pointed out to me.

I have removed a few repetitious entries and edited down some of the verbosity. I have also removed one or two entries whose levity did not serve a serious purpose (while retaining those whose levity did so serve).

I have hugely increased the number of entries – from 1586 in the first edition to 2310 in this. Quite a few of these have been terms that are pertinent but not particular to economics and, as before, I have tried to give the reader a reasonable idea of what the term entails and how it is used without attempting to reach the standard of diligence that might be expected in, for example, dictionaries of accounting, cognitive psychology, epidemiology, ethics, finance or statistics. I trust, as before, that the inhabitants of these foreign but neighbourly terrains will not be offended at this attempt of an alien to explain them to other strangers.

I have provided a comprehensive bibliography of over 1000 published items, with the intentions of both guiding the reader towards the source of a key idea and of providing helpful illustrations of a principle or of an idea as used in a relevant (mostly applied) context. This has also served to rectify what I felt to have been a deficiency in the first edition, namely the absence of explicit mention of many of the household names of health economics. They are now there in abundance, as are the names of many of the aforesaid neighbourly foreigners. I have not gone so far as to provide biographies and only dead people get dates. One cannot help but be astonished at the huge number of people who would now be counted as health economists – and I am sure that I have not used the work of what may well be the majority of those who are active in the field today – in contrast to the (say) couple of baker's dozens of us who were active worldwide when I began to be interested in the subject in the late 1960s.

A consequence of this is that it now seems appropriate to have separate subject and names indices. While I have avoided using the names of drugs, clinical devices, diseases, countries or other jurisdictions as headwords, the subject index picks up any such nouns whether they occur in the definitions or in the bibliography.

I have expanded the number of headwords and phrases that relate to the health economics of poor and middle-income countries, as well as referring to the now more extensive literature that is available.

I have increased the number of cross-references and used them more consistently. Cross-references now exist to most closely related terms, contrasts and antonyms. In the case of synonyms I have given cross-references to a main entry.

In view of the astonishing growth in the number of cost–effectiveness analysis studies, I have provided an appendix listing 100 well-conducted such studies covering a wide variety of conditions and circumstances. Virtually every one of them is a testament to the collaborations that have become possible between economists, clinicians, epidemiologists, biostatisticians, ethicists and others with relevant skills. These are illustrative of the range of application and supplement many references in the main entries to CEA studies that are useful for illustrating a specific issue. They may also be a helpful list for teachers. The list also provides many names that do not appear elsewhere in the *Dictionary* for anyone wishing to make contact with a skilled practitioner in this ambitious combination of applied sciences, economics and social ethics.

I am conscious of a particular bias that is always hard to eradicate, namely that arising from the general character of one's own interests and work in a field. It has not been my intention to emphasize some topics in health economics, or some ways of approaching them, arbitrarily more than others. Some readers may nonetheless detect such a bias. For this reason and many others, and as was the case with the previous edition, I welcome corrections and any other suggestions for improvement. Either of these addresses will serve to find me: tony.culyer@utoronto.ca and ajc17@york.ac.uk.

ACKNOWLEDGEMENTS (SECOND EDITION)

I owe a great debt to those who offered comments on the first edition, who suggested new entries, definitions and references, and to those who read and commented in detail on a draft version of the second edition in whole or in part. In particular, my thanks go to Jo Coast at the University of Birmingham, Richard Cookson at the University of York, Nancy Devlin at the Office of Health Economics, Irfan Dhalla at the University of Toronto, Terry Flynn at the Technical University of Sydney, Jeff Hoch at the University of Toronto, Rosalind Rabin at the EuroQol Group, Tom Rice at UCLA, Rebecca Roberts, and Alan Shiell at the University of Calgary. They must obviously be absolved for not having spotted every omission, error or infelicity.

PREFACE TO THE FIRST EDITION

> Knowledge is of two kinds. We know a subject ourselves, or we know where
> we can find information on it.
>
> (Samuel Johnson, quoted in Boswell's *Life of Johnson*)

This is a book serving the second of these two kinds of knowledge; a
book that I have intended that the reader should be able to dip into
from time to time. It may also serve that other thing with which knowledge is so often mistaken: understanding. If one's appetite is whetted, as
I hope may occasionally be the case, there are loads of decent texts that
provide solid main courses and desserts. The *Dictionary* is not intended
to compete with them. My main wish is that it will be of use to the reader
in a hurry (whether a beginning economist or someone who needs to
understand what economists go on about), who wants a reminder about
a topic or who wants a quick and relatively painless introduction to it. It
would be great if, to borrow from Sir Topham Hat (the Fat Controller
in *Thomas the Tank Engine*), the *Dictionary* were to be a 'really useful
engine'.

Health economists, to a greater extent than most economists, have
engaged in close collaborations with specialists in other fields (not only
other social sciences) and with policy-makers, especially in the area of
health technology assessment. I have intended, therefore, that the book
may be useful to these 'others'. Multidisciplinarity and multiprofessional-
ity also have a consequence for the inclusion criteria used: I have included
many more definitions, particularly in statistics, epidemiology and medicine, than would otherwise have been the case, which may be useful to
health economists without causing outrage to the relevant 'others'. These
are provided, however, strictly on the bikini principle: I have restricted
myself to covering the bare essentials of definition save for cases where
I have judged the other discipline to have become so intertwined with
health economics that it warrants more extended treatment – even explanation. Again, this is not a textbook. I have provided definitions and
occasional interpretational help on non-economic terms on the grounds
that, in multidisciplinary collaborations (whether trans-disciplinary,
cross-disciplinary, interdisciplinary – terms the reader will *not* find in the
Dictionary!) between researchers/teachers who still have a primary single
academic disciplinary base, it is a good thing for each side of the collaboration to have some (even if incomplete) understanding of the concepts
and methods of the others. We economists certainly need such help and

xiii

I have tried to provide it without, I trust, doing too much violence to the meanings of other disciplines' specialized jargon.

Nor is this a general economics dictionary, so I have not included economic terminology that is infrequently used by health economists. There is, for example, hardly any macroeconomics here. The verbal boundaries of 'health economics' are one of the four matters I have wondered more about than about any other inclusion/exclusion criterion. Should it turn out that I have been too stringent in excluding terms, or too lax in including them, I trust my users will let me know.

The second 'boundary' issue about which I have worried concerns the extent to which the *Dictionary* ought to include the names and biographies of significant health economists. I have included people's names only when they have become attached to a headword or phrase requiring an entry (for example, 'Pareto-optimality', 'Altman's nomogram') or where their name has a common adjectival form, as in 'Rawlsian' (none of these three is, of course, a health economist). Only in such cases have I provided some bibliographical information (and occasionally biographical information as well). This is a tough rule and it has produced some odd outcomes. Thus, Kenneth Arrow is in (but not on account of his scientific contribution to health economics) and Alan Williams is in (but on account of his league table and 'plumbing diagram' rather than QALYs or 'fair innings', or. . .). Without explicit mention are Angus Deaton, Mike Drummond, Bob Evans, Martin Feldstein, Richard Frank, Victor Fuchs, Mike Grossman, Bengt Jonsson, Emmett Keeler, Herb Klarman, the two Laves, Harold Luft, Will Manning, Tom McGuire, Gavin Mooney, Joe Newhouse, Mark Pauly, Charles Phelps, Frans Rutten, Frank Sloan, Greg Stoddart, George Torrance, Burt Weisbrod and lots of (mostly younger) others who have played key roles in shaping the discipline. They are there, of course, peering through the undergrowth of the entries but anonymously, just like the 'basic science' giants, many of whom are fortunately still actively with us, on whose intellectual shoulders we all stand: Armen Alchian, Gary Becker, James Buchanan, Milton Friedman, Peter Hammond, John Harsanyi, Werner Hildenbrand, Daniel Kahneman, Ian Little, Paul Samuelson, Joseph Stiglitz, Reinhard Selten, Amartya Sen, Vernon Smith and Vivian Walsh. To venture into list-making exemplifies my problem – where does one stop, how far does one stray into psychology and other related disciplines, and how does one avoid giving offence? So I stopped barely before beginning: the case for inclusion is eponymy. The only exception I have allowed is that of Lionel Robbins, mainly on account of his famous definition of 'economics', because he was *not* a health economist and because he is dead.

A third 'boundary' issue relates to the inclusion or exclusion of organizations. I have included as many official organizations that are substantial users or commissioners of health economics as I can identify and I have also included those health economists' professional organizations of which I know. I have not included any of the many research groups in universities and elsewhere nor have I included the names of government departments and ministries, many of which now have teams of health economists. Where possible, I have included web addresses.

The fourth boundary issue related to references: what to include and what not. I suspect that I have been too strict here in citing only works in which the origin of a headword or phrase is to be found. Providing references on all topics of substance, whether in health economics or one of the 'others', would have been a major additional effort and one whose fruits, moreover, would be doomed to become obsolete relatively early. However, this is a question that might be answered differently should the opportunity arise later.

I have not included obsolete terms, unless I have judged them to have continuing value (as, for example, with 'value in use') but I have left ones in that seem obsolescent until such time as their destiny has become clear.

I have gone well beyond a definition in many cases, especially when I have judged a topic to be a critical element of health economics, one about which there are widespread misconceptions that need putting right, or one where it seemed important to give some insight into the way an idea is used, why it is important or why it is controversial. The aim of these mini-lectures is to help readers to get on track. They are not, however, accompanied by further reading: again, this *Dictionary* is not a textbook and ought not to be treated as though it were. Driving a locomotive demands more than the knowledge that it is merely on the right track.

I have not hesitated to record opinions, sometimes sharp ones, some tongue-in-cheek, where it seemed appropriate. Needless to say, the opinions are mine and there is no implication that they are widely shared amongst health economists. I hope both the explicit opinions and any left implicit will lighten the enquirer's search, even if it does not enlighten it. A dictionary surely need not be entirely po-faced.

I have tried to ensure that the language of the *Dictionary* is inclusive. I use 'they' 'them' and 'their' instead of the tediously repetitive mantra of 'he or she', 'him or her' and 'his or hers' (or 'she or he', 'her or him' and 'hers or his').

Samuel Johnson famously defined a lexicographer as 'A writer of dictionaries; a harmless drudge that busies himself in tracing the original, and detailing the signification of words'. The really significant word in this definition is 'harmless' and I am not sure of his truthfulness in asserting it. Practical lexicographers have the power to confuse, mislead and infuriate, all of which seem to be pretty harmful things to be doing. I have tried to keep my harm as small as possible. At any rate, my risk of doing harm is further reduced by my eschewing any systematic attempts at etymology or word history.

The Dictionary doubtless contains mistakes. I apologize for them now. I would be grateful to hear from readers who want to put me right. My explanation for error is again Johnson's who, according to Boswell, when asked how he came to give a mistaken definition of 'pastern', replied: 'Ignorance, Madam, pure ignorance.' I hope nonetheless that I have hidden most of mine.

My particular hope is that, whatever the imperfections of this *Dictionary*, it will be judged to be of sufficient value for enquirers to want to invest their time in telling me how a recension might make it better. My e-mail addresses are: ajc17@york.ac.uk and aculyer@iwh.on.ca.

ACKNOWLEDGEMENTS (FIRST EDITION)

I am extremely grateful to Ron Akehurst, Werner Brouwer, Adriana Castelli, Li-Jen Cheng, Karl Claxton, Richard Cookson, Roman Dolinschi, Tina Eberstein, Brian Ferguson, Alastair Fischer, John Frank, William Gnam, Clyde Hertzman, Sheilah Hogg-Johnson, Paul Holyoke, Jerry Hurley, Paul Jacobson, Andrew Jones, Robin Kells, Gisela Kobelt, Andreas Maetzel, Evelyne Michaels, Charles Normand, Adam Oliver, Nirmala Ragbir-Day, Sandra Sinclair, Emile Tompa and Adrian Towse for commenting on various definitions and making suggestions for head-words and phrases to include. A particular debt of gratitude is owed to Martin Forster, Desre Kramer, Robin Pope and Tom Rice for their exceptionally painstaking commentaries. All these friends and their many suggested redraftings have enormously improved the *Dictionary*'s amplitude, accuracy and accessibility. I have not always followed their advice so, alas, they cannot be held accountable for the *Dictionary*'s defects. These are entirely my responsibility.

CONVENTIONS

Use of italics
Italicized terms in the text of entries, other than reference titles, are themselves entries in the *Dictionary*. Mention of an entry in another entry is italicized only at the first mention in any entry.

Cross-references
Cross-references are provided at the end of many entries. When there is more than one they are in alphabetical order. These are cross-references to substantive entries and not, for example, to mere synonyms or antonyms. These do not repeat cross-references indicated within the entry by italicized words. Cross-references are not impeded by plurals or other variations to the stems of words that are parts of speech. If a headword is a word in common use with everyday meanings its everyday use in the *Dictionary* will not be cross-referenced to the headword. Thus, 'argument' used in the sense of 'persuasive case' will not be cross-referenced to the headword 'argument'. I have also made quite extensive use of the Latin imperative 'confer' (Cf.) at the end of entries to suggest other entries where there may be relevant comparators and 'See' to draw attention to related ideas.

Order of subject matter
Entries are in strict alphabetical order regardless of their nature.

References and websites
References are as full as it has been possible to make them, though I have eschewed authors' first names. Some names are more complete (for example, in respect of initials) than those given in a cited reference. Websites were current at the time of writing.

A

Ability to Pay

This is not a technical term in economics; it is, however, frequently used as though it were – most frequently as a part of an ethical principle used in connection with an idea of fair taxation, *viz*. that a taxpayer's contribution ought to bear some relation to their *income* or *wealth* (i.e. ability to pay). A strict definition might amount to this: ability to pay is the sum of an individual's tradable *human* and non-human *capital*, i.e. their entire wealth. Some may have in mind no more than the individual's current *budget constraint*. Ability to pay stands in contrast to the *benefit principle* according to which what is paid (e.g. in premiums or taxes) ought to be proportional to the anticipated benefit rather than the wherewithal to acquiring it. This at least has the virtue of making clear that a value judgment is being made.

In the context of taxation, ability to pay is often coupled with the idea that what one pays in (income or wealth) tax ought to be progressive, i.e. that the fraction paid should rise with income or wealth, rather than being merely proportional, let alone regressive. Cf. *Willingness to Pay*. See *Progressivity*, *Regressivity*. See, in the context of health care, Yoder (1989).

Abnormal Profit

Profit in excess of the (so-called 'normal') market rate of return on assets. Some economists term abnormal profit 'profit', effectively treating the 'normal' return as an *opportunity cost*.

Abscissa

The horizontal axis in a two-dimensional diagram. Commonly referred to as the *x*-axis. Sometimes a point on that axis. Cf. *Ordinate*.

Absolute Advantage

This exists when a firm or a jurisdiction can produce a given quantum of a good or service with fewer *inputs* than another. Cf. *Comparative*

Advantage, with which absolute advantage is often confused, even by economists. Call centres are increasingly located in India not because their location there involves fewer inputs for any given number of calls (absolute advantage) but because the lost *output* from using people in this way rather than in another is smaller than it would be in, say, most European countries or North America. Some countries have an absolute advantage in producing nearly everything but it is impossible for them to have a comparative advantage in everything. In matters of efficient resource allocation, absolute advantage is irrelevant and comparative advantage is everything.

Absolute Risk

The probability of an event, such as disease, occurring during a given period of time. Cf. *Relative Risk*.

Absolute Risk Aversion

A characteristic of *utility functions*. It (sometimes referred to as ARA) is a measure of the slope of a utility function and its rate of change. If the measure of absolute risk aversion is unchanged as consumption increases, then there is *constant absolute risk aversion* (sometimes termed CARA). See *Insurance* for an account of how a *diminishing marginal utility of income* generates a form of risk aversion. See *Arrow–Pratt Measure, Risk Aversion*. For the application of ARA in *cost–effectiveness analysis* see Garber and Phelps (1997).

Absolute Risk Increase

The converse of *absolute risk reduction* (ARR).

Absolute Risk Reduction

The absolute arithmetic difference in occurrences of adverse *outcomes* between *experimental* and *control* participants in a *clinical trial*. The reciprocal of *Number Needed to Treat* (NNT). Often referred to as ARR. See *Odds Ratio, Relative Risk Reduction*.

Absorbing State

This is a condition (state) in a *Markov chain* in which the *transition probability* is zero. 'Death' is such a state. Once in such a state, there is no escape from it. See also *Markov Model, Transition Matrix*.

Absorption

A term in *macroeconomics* to describe the major categories of resource use in a jurisdiction other than production. Thus, absorption includes *expenditures* on *consumption, investment*, imports and that by government.

Abuse

There are many types of abuse. Economists have explored aspects of it as an applied topic in health economics, including its *determinants* and *consequences*. An example of an economic study focusing on the social consequences of child abuse, especially sexual abuse, is Currie and Tekin (2006). On drug abuse, see *Addiction*.

Academic Detailing

A method of continuing professional education in which physicians are visited by an expert health professional to discuss prescribing and other aspects of clinical practice. Cf. *Detailing*.

Acceptability Curve

A graphical way of showing more information about *uncertainty* in a *cost–effectiveness analysis* than can be done by using only *confidence intervals* and for comparing more than two interventions, as with *confidence ellipses*. The full name is *cost–effectiveness acceptability curve*. See also *Cost–Effectiveness Acceptability Frontier*.

Access

Access to health care, or its 'accessibility', is often regarded as an important *determinant* of the *equity* of a health care system but the meaning and significance of 'access' or 'accessibility' are nonetheless often left unclear. Insofar as it is important in *equity* it seems that it is cheapness of access that really matters, usually because the writer will have some notion underlying their concern for equity about the importance of meeting *need*, and cheap access seems to be a precondition for having lots of people's needs assessed in order that they might be met. Economists typically treat accessibility as a comprehensive term for 'price'; that is, any user monetary fee that is to be paid plus time and transport costs, waiting, and any other element that constitutes a 'barrier' whether or not that barrier takes a monetary form or can be converted into a monetary form. Barriers may be physical, institutional or social as well as financial. Some may be direct; others indirect. As an example of indirect barrier, access to *insurance* may be the only route to accessing health care itself.

The following have all been found to be important practical barriers: absence of the service; absence of entitlement (e.g. via membership of an insurance plan); absence of translation service; distrust of providers; price (including *deductibles* and *copayments*); gender insensitivity; transport difficulties; inconvenient appointment times; inappropriate language; the existence of the service being unknown; excessive 'social distance' between clients and caregivers; patronising behaviour; waiting lists. Accessibility unimpeded to any significant extent by financial or other barriers is a characteristic of a health care system that is commonly specified or sometimes (as in Canada and the UK) required by statute. See Green (2001), Danzon and Towse (2003) and Holla and Kremer (2009). The access benefits of insurance are analysed in Nyman (1999b). Access challenges in remote areas, especially in developing countries, are formidable. See Ranson et al. (2003, 2006) and Yeung et al. (2008).

Accidents

See *Environmental Health and Safety*.

Account

Either (1) a record of financial transactions covering a period, which is usually a year or (2) an agreement between buyer and seller that the seller will not expect to be paid until an agreed date. See *Balance of Payments, Balance Sheet*.

Accountability

Accountability entails the ability of others to hold someone to account through mechanisms such as minutes of meetings, reporting requirements and audit trails. See Tetlock (1999).

Accountability for Reasonableness

A decision-making procedure that assists agreement on what are legitimate and fair ways of making decisions, without specifying any specific necessary *outcome*. Key elements involve transparency about the grounds of decisions, appeals to rationales that everyone can accept as relevant and fair, procedures for revising decisions in the light of challenges to them and the presence of mechanisms to ensure that the forgoing requirements are met. It goes beyond a requirement that there merely be clear information about options and performance. See Daniels and Sabin (1998).

Accreditation

A process of certification that an organization or individual meets particular quality standards. An example of an organization (US) that provides such certification is the *Joint Commission on Accreditation of Healthcare Organizations*.

Action Research

Action research consists of efforts that are intended to have an impact on the *performance* of an organization. It is often designed and conducted by professionals in order to obtain and use data to improve their own practice. It invariably proceeds by having teams of researchers and research subjects working together. The method generally assumes that complex social processes can be studied best as complete entities (it is thus not reductionist in its philosophy), by introducing changes into these processes (which is where the 'action' bit comes in) and by observing the effects of these changes, which will often be described in the manner of a *qualitative analysis* and from an *idiographic* perspective. See Dick (2000).

Activities of Daily Living

A frequently used set of basic activities of daily life, such as eating, bathing, dressing, toileting, and transferring, each of which can be rated on a simple scale. The activities and their measurements vary according to the groups for whom they are being developed. The scores are sometimes combined in the construction of indices of healthy functioning or to measure changes in response to treatments. The acronym ADL is in common use. See *Barthel Index, Quality-adjusted Life-year*. The pioneering contribution is Katz et al. (1963).

Activity-based Financing

A method of financing public hospitals used in Norway. It uses *diagnostic-related groups* and *block contracts*. See *Payment by Results*.

Actuarial Fairness

An *insurance* premium is actuarially fair when it is equal to the monetary value of the expected loss multiplied by its probability of occurrence.

Act Utilitarianism

Under act *utilitarianism*, it is the *utility* of the consequences of an action that matters in determining whether the action is morally right.

Acute

An adjective used to describe a sudden, relatively brief, occurrence of ill-health or pain, in contrast to *chronic*. Sometimes used to indicate 'severity'.

Adaptive Conjoint Analysis

A form of *conjoint analysis* in which a computer program adapts the range of choices amongst many *attributes* of services to suit the subject doing the ranking. Cf. *Full Profile Conjoint Analysis*.

Addiction

Economists have not always modelled the use of addictive substances in terms of the four common *attributes* of addictiveness: persistence, tolerance, withdrawal and reinforcement. In health economics they have modelled addiction in broadly three ways. The first is in 'imperfectly *rational*' *models* in which individuals effectively have two mutually incompatible but each internally consistent *utility functions* (for example, a farsighted one and a shortsighted one). Second, there are 'myopic irrational' models, in which future consequences are not well-understood or, if understood, are heavily *discounted* or ignored. Finally, there is '*rational addiction*', in which the addictive habit enhances both current and future *utility* sufficiently to overcome the (rationally perceived) negative consequences for the user. The classic economic theory of addiction is to be found in Becker and Murphy (1988). See also Orphanides and Zervos (1995), Ettner et al. (1998), Gruber and Köszegi (2001) and Bernheim and Rangel (2004). See Grossman (2004) on addiction and teen sexual behaviour and Auld and Grootendorst (2004) on milk addiction.

Additionality

The idea that the effects associated with an intervention are additional to other *determinants* and would not have happened anyway.

Addition Rule

A property (also called '*additivity*') according to which the probability of either of two mutually exclusive events occurring is the sum of the probabilities of each occurring.

Additive Model

A *model* in which the combined effect of several factors is their sum. Cf. *Multiplicative Model*.

Additive Separability

A quality of *utility* measurement required also in some measures of *health*. It amounts essentially to the idea that the weights or utilities attached to entities amongst which one is choosing, or which are components of an index of health, can be combined at any point in time and over time by adding without adjusting for any interaction between them that might make the whole more (or less) than the sum of its parts (apart from *discounting*). See *Quality-adjusted Life-year*.

Additive Utility Independence

See *Utility Independence*.

Additivity

A property according to which the probability of either of two mutually exclusive events occurring is the sum of the probabilities of each occurring. Same as *addition rule*.

Adherence

The extent to which the patient follows a clinician's instructions or advice.

Adjacent Complementarity

This is the idea in *models* of addictive behaviour that high previous consumption levels increase the *marginal utility* of current consumption (for example, of cigarettes). This is one aspect of a more general pattern of behaviour characterized by intertemporally dependent preferences. The idea comes originally from Ryder and Heal (1973). See, for a health economics application, Gruber and Köszegi (2001).

Adjusted Odds Ratio

An *odds ratio* that has been corrected for the effects of other variables.

ADL

An acronym for *activities of daily living*.

Administered Prices

Prices set by regulatory agencies (for example, *Medicare's prospective reimbursements* in the US), as distinct from the prices that emerge in the marketplace through the interaction of *demand* and *supply*.

Administrative Costs

Expenditures by an organization on management, administration and associated internal functions like accounting, finance, human resource management, marketing and (sometimes) research. On the relative administrative costs of health care in Canada and the US see Woolhandler et al. (2003).

Administrative Prices

Same as *administered prices*.

Advance Directive

An advance directive instructs doctors and other health care professionals orally or in writing about the kind of care a person wishes to receive in the event of their being unable to specify it in person (as when in a coma). It can specify both what treatments are wanted as well as those that are not. 'Living wills' are instructional advance directives about treatment desired if incapacitated, proxy advance directives designate another person (*agent*) as a surrogate for the *principal*. They are also known as durable (or lasting) powers of attorney.

Advantageous Selection

The absence of a positive correlation between the risk of bad events and *health insurance* coverage has puzzled economists in the past. The explanation seems to lie in the significance for choice of other factors of importance to insurance buyers, which leads to 'advantageous selection' in contrast to *adverse selection* if people who are more risk averse also buy more insurance coverage and actually also have lower risks. See de Meza and Webb (2001) and Fang et al. (2008).

Adverse Event

This usually refers to the consequences of using a pharmaceutical product, medical device or surgical procedure. Serious adverse events might be: death, a life-threatening drug experience, in-patient hospitalization, prolongation of existing hospitalization, a persistent or significant *disability/* incapacity, a congenital anomaly/birth defect, other important medical events that may jeopardize the patient and that may require subsequent corrective medical or surgical intervention to rectify the damage or to prevent future similar outcomes.

Adverse Selection

Insurers tend to set their premiums in relation to the average experience of a *population*. If members of subsets of the population have different *probabilities* of illness (or at any rate they believe they have different probabilities) then those with low probabilities (or low perceived ones) may not buy *insurance* and those with high probabilities (or perceptions) may eagerly seize their opportunity. If this happens, insurers end up with clients who are likely to prove costlier than expected; premiums will have to rise. High-risk individuals tend to 'drive out' low-risk individuals. Cf. *Advantageous Selection*. See *Asymmetry of Information, Equity, Market Failure*. The classic is Rothschild and Stiglitz (1976). See Akerlof (1970), Ettner (1997), Cutler and Reber (1998) and Buchmueller and DiNardo (2002) for applications in health economics.

Aetiological Fraction

The proportion of an outcome that can be attributed to a particular *risk factor*. Also known as the *'etiological fraction'*, *'attributable risk'* and the *'attributable fraction'*.

Aetiology

The study of the causes of disease. Also *'etiology'*.

AETMIS

See *Agence d'Evaluation des Technologies et des Modes d'Intervention en Santé*.

Affine Function

A mathematical function with constant slope and non-zero *intercept*.

Affordability

A term that has no clear meaning in economics, though its one unambiguous possible meaning, *viz.* entities whose purchase price is lower than the value of the purchaser's realizable *wealth*, seems not to be the one people usually have in mind when using the term. It is sometimes taken as a synonym for *budget impact*. Some may have in mind any combination of entities that lies beneath a *budget constraint*. The term is probably best avoided, at least when communicating with economists. However, see Bundorf and Pauly (2006, 2009) and Bradley (2009).

A Fortiori

A Latin tag meaning 'more strongly' or 'even more conclusively'.

Agence d'Evaluation des Technologies et des Modes d'Intervention en Santé

Quebec's provincial agency for *health technology assessments*. Its website is available at: http://www.aetmis.gouv.qc.ca/site/home.phtml (accessed 26 October 2009).

Agency

See *Agency Relationship*.

Agency for Healthcare Research and Quality

A US agency responsible for, amongst other things, *health technology assessments* for the US *Medicaid* and *Medicare* Programs. Its website is available at: www.ahrq.gov/ (accessed 26 October 2009).

Agency Relationship

The relationship between an *agent* and a *principal*. Classically in health care, the role of a physician or other health professional in determining the patient's (or other client's) best interest and acting in a fashion consistent with it. The patient or client is the principal and the professional is the agent. More generally, the agent is anyone acting on behalf of a principal, usually because of *asymmetry of information*. In health care, the situation can become rather complicated by virtue of the facts, first, that the professional thereby has an important role in determining the *demand* for a service as well as its *supply* and, second, that doctors are expected (in many systems) to act not only for the 'patient' but also for 'society' in the form, say, of other patients or of an organization with wider societal responsibilities (like a *managed health care* organization), or taxpayers, or all potential patients. See also *Market Failure, Multi-task Agency, Supplier-induced Demand*. See Arrow (1985), Dranove and White (1987) and McGuire (2000).

Agent

A professional or similar person who acts on behalf of another (the *principal*). See *Agency Relationship*.

Agglomeration

The process by which economic activity becomes increasingly concentrated in a geographical area, like a city. Agglomeration tends to increase when there are beneficial *externalities* for businesses arising from adjacency to other businesses (as in shopping malls) or where skills can be shared, and to decrease when the externalities become negative (as through congestion or pollution, or criminal activity that itself is nurtured by beneficial – to criminals – externalities also arising from agglomeration). See Phelps (1992), Escarce (1996) and Bates and Santerre (2005) for health economics applications.

Aggregation

A process of adding up smaller parts to make a greater whole. For example, aggregate *demand* is the sum of expenditures by consumers, investors, government and net exports and is usually modelled as a function of (aggregate) income and/or the (aggregate) price level.

Aggregation Problem

A difficulty that can give rise to faulty interpretations of events. It arises by using associations that seem to hold at an aggregate level (say, the level of a community) as evidence that they hold also at the individual level. It is also known as the *ecological fallacy*. For example, while the (aggregate) observation that US states with a high proportion of foreign-born residents are also states with high literacy in American English, it does not follow that foreign-born people are more literate in English than the rest. In fact, studies at the individual level have shown that the 'ecological *correlation*' of foreign-born and literacy rates arises because foreign-born people tend to settle in states that already have high literacy in English. At the individual level, the correlation between being foreign-born and ability in English is in fact (as one may expect) negative.

A subtler example arises in the analysis of the causes of differences in the average *population health* and the idea that income inequality may be correlated with (or might even cause) lower average health. If everyone has the same *demand for health* at a variety of incomes and *health* (however measured) rises with income but at a declining rate, then more income inequality implies lower average health (*ceteris paribus*). As income disparities widen, an increase in income for the rich will generate an increase in health that is less than sufficient to compensate for the fall in health generated by an equivalent reduction in income for the poor. Should this be the case, caution is the order of the day in evaluating claims that it is inequality per se that is deleterious to health. Such claims may be right but they are not the only possible explanation: the phenomenon may arise simply because of the underlying *income-elasticity* of the *demand* for health and the non-linear relationship between income and health.

Aging

Aging is commonly cited as one of the main factors underlying ever-growing health care expenditures. The reasons for believing this are, however, not especially obvious and the evidence is virtually non-existent. See Chernichovsky and Markowitz (2004). The evidence is stronger that time to death is an important *determinant* of health care costs. See Coyte et al. (2001), Stearns and Norton (2004), Seshamani and Gray (2004) and Payne et al. (2007).

Agism

Unfair discrimination against old people. A charge against the use of life-years as an outcome measure in *cost–effectiveness analysis* (CEA) and related studies, or life-years weighted for quality (as in the *quality-adjusted life-year,* QALY), is that they discriminate against the use of technologies that are used mainly by the elderly, or indeed any whose life expectancy is shorter than others. The arithmetic is plain: they have fewer years over which to enjoy the better health that is expected to result from the technology in question, so those that are to be used mainly by those with shorter life expectancies will tend to be less preferred if this criterion is used alone and without sensitivity to the potential for what may be deemed to be unfair. In cost–effectiveness analysis, benefit is not, however, the sole criterion on which decisions are (or ought to be) based. So whether a shorter expectation of life prejudices them will also depend partly on the *opportunity cost*, which, other things being equal, will also be less on account of being incurred over a shorter time period, and on the view taken of the role of CEA in public decision-making – for example, whether QALYs, or other time-related *outcome* measures, and associated *cost* information, and the values embedded in them, are regarded as the only relevant data. Most decision-making rubrics emphasize these *algorithms* as aids to decisions not *determinants* of them. Other data are also taken into consideration if CEA is used as a part of a *deliberative process*. For recent vehement denouncers targeting specifically the QALY see Harris (2005, 2006a, 2006b, 2007) and Quigley (2007). Spirited defenders include Claxton and Culyer (2006, 2007, 2008).

AHRQ

Acronym for *Agency for Healthcare Research and Quality*.

AIES

Acronym for *Associazione Italiana di Economia Sanitaria*.

Algorithm

A mathematical procedure or formula for solving a problem in a sequential fashion, with each step depending on the *outcome* of the previous one. Named, in a corrupted 12th-century Latinate version, after the great scholar Mohammed ibn-Musa al-Khwarizmi (780–850 CE) who was born in the ancient Persian empire (in the territory now called Uzbekistan) and spent most of his working life in Baghdad, then arguably the greatest intellectual centre in the world. The root of the word 'algebra' is directly derived from his great work *Kitab al-Jabr*.

Allais Paradox

This is a famous paradox of *expected utility theory* that has caused some to question the validity of the theory and therefore those bits of health economics that use it. Suppose a subject has the following choices under uncertainty:

Gamble A: A 100 per cent chance of receiving $1 million.
Gamble B: A 10 per cent chance of receiving $5 million, an 89 per cent chance of receiving $1 million, and a 1 per cent chance of receiving nothing.

It is a matter of fact that most people choose A over B, even though the expected pecuniary value of B is $1.39 million. Presumably, people have a marked preference for certainty over uncertainty. In terms of expected utility they are revealing (where > indicates preference and U utility) that:

$$U(\$1m) > 0.1U(\$5m) + 0.89U(\$1m) + 0.01U(\$0),$$

and, subtracting $0.89U(\$1m)$ from each side of the inequality, we get:

$$0.11U(\$1m) > 0.1U(\$5m) + 0.01U(\$0).$$

Now present the same subject with a further two gambles:

Gamble C: An 11 per cent chance of receiving $1 million, and an 89 per cent chance of receiving nothing.
Gamble D: A 10 per cent chance of receiving $5 million, and a 90 per cent chance of receiving nothing.

Most people choose D over C. In terms of expected utility, they are revealing that:

$$0.1U(\$5m) + 0.9U(\$0) > 0.11U(\$1m) + 0.89U(\$0).$$

Now, as expected utility theory permits, subtract $0.89U(\$0)$ from each side to get:

$$0.1U(\$5m) + 0.01U(\$0) > 0.11U(\$1m),$$

which is the opposite of what was chosen in the first choice situation. Expected utility theory does not permit of this possibility because preferring A to B implies preferring C over D. Cf. *Bounded Rationality*. See Allais (1953). For a health economics example, see Oliver (2003a).

Alliance

A term used in the pharmaceutical industry to describe the relationship between a pharmaceutical company and its partners in research and development (usually biotechnology companies).

Allocation Bias

A statistical term for *bias* arising from the manner in which subjects are assigned to treatment groups in *trials*.

Allocation Formulae

Public *insurance* for health care commonly implies some commitment to *equity* (not necessarily equality) in the geographical availability of health care services. To this end various formulae are used to distribute budgets from central to lower-tier *commissioners* and providers. These formulae generally seek to find an empirical measure of population *need* for health care and to take account of the existing, inherited stock of resources. See *Equity, Geographical Equity, Inverse Care Law*. See Sutton and Lock (2000) and Hauck et al. (2002), and, for an international perspective and bibliography, Macinko and Starfield (2002).

Allocative Efficiency

A situation in which *resources* are allocated to production processes and the *outputs* of those processes to consumers or clients so as to maximize the *net benefit* to society. *Pareto efficiency* is a specific form of it. Cf. *Efficiency*.

Alternative Hypothesis

A term used in statistical hypothesis testing: a hypothesis about the effect of *interest* that is false if the *null hypothesis* is true (but not necessarily true if the null hypothesis is false).

Alternatives

A feature of all *option appraisals, cost–effectiveness analyses* and *health technology assessments* of decent quality is that various (alternative) interventions are identified and evaluated. For health economics examples see Tappenden et al. (2007) and Kaltenthaler et al. (2008).

Altman's Nomogram

Mathematically it is quite a complicated exercise to calculate the size of a *sample* necessary to achieve a given *statistical power* in *trials*. Altman's *nomogram* is a graphical method of assessing the power and *statistical significance* of a test in a variety of sample sizes. The right-hand vertical axis of the nomogram shows various power values, from 0.05 to 0.995. The left-hand vertical axis represents the 'standardized difference': a ratio that relates the difference of *interest* to the *standard deviation* of the observations. There are two axes within the nomogram, one for a significance level of 0.05, the other for 0.01, with total sample sizes indicated on each. The nomogram can be used to evaluate the optimal sample size once the power is specified, the significance level 5 per cent or 1 per cent is chosen, and the standardized difference is calculated. This nomogram can be found on p. 456 of Altman (1991).

Altruism

In economics this is usually understood as a form of *utility* interdependence in that one person gains utility from the knowledge that another's lot in life is improved. In some versions the utility may come from the act of improving the other's lot rather than the achieved improvement. Where the motive is merely to be seen to be contributing to the improvement, it would seem inappropriate to describe the behaviour as altruistic. Some people have a difficulty in describing any *utility-maximizing* altruism as truly altruistic, though having unselfish preferences seems altruistic enough in so far as altruism can be held to have anything at all to do with preferences (as distinct, for example, from 'doing one's duty'). For a theory based on the idea that individuals have divided utility functions – one self-regarding and the other not – see Margolis (1984). For a philosophical view that altruistic acts flow from compassion (plus a few other conditions) see Nussbaum (2001). See *Caring Externality*, *Utility Function*. See for economics applications Jones-Lee (1991, 1992) and Andersson and Lindberg (2009). On intergenerational aspects see Birchenall and Soares (2009). For an alternative approach based on Sen's (1977) ideas of sympathy and commitment, see Shiell and Rush (2003).

Ambiguity

A term used by decision and game theorists in the context of certain kinds of decisions under uncertainty that, from the perspective of subjective *utility* theory, display a kind of *bias* in the human psyche. This poses problems for users of *expected utility theory*.

Suppose there are two urns, each containing 100 balls, which are either red or black. One urn has 50 red and 50 black balls. The proportion of red and black balls in the other urn is unknown. You can draw one ball from one of the urns, without looking, and if you draw a red ball you win a hundred dollars. Which urn would you choose? Most people choose the 50–50 urn, even though, if we take the view that there are insufficient reasons for discriminating between the two urns, there is no higher probability of getting a red than by picking from the other urn. When offered 100 dollars for a black ball, they also choose the 50–50 urn. They seem to be averse to the 'ambiguity' represented by the other urn and strongly prefer what is apparently clear-cut. This is also known as the *Ellsberg paradox* (Ellsberg, 1961). See Epstein (1999) and Wakker (2000).

Ambulatory Care

Health care provided on an *out-patient* (non-hospitalized) basis. It includes preventive, diagnostic, treatment and rehabilitation services.

Amortization

The accumulation over several years of a fund that enables a *capital* asset to be replaced at the end of its useful life or to repay the debt incurred when it was purchased.

Anaesthesia

Desensitizating to pain, usually through injection or gas. It includes pain management for people with *chronic* painful conditions. The relevant medical speciality is also called 'anaesthesia', 'anesthesia' or 'anesthesiology'.

Analogue Scale

See *EQ-VAS, Visual Analogue Scale*.

Analysis of Covariance

A statistical procedure used to control for the effect of a *covariate* in the relationship between an *independent* and a *dependent variable*. Also known as ANCOVA. Cf. *Analysis of Variance*.

Analysis of Variance

A procedure that uses the *F-test* to test the *null hypothesis* that the *means* of two or more groups are equal. It involves comparison of within and between group *sample* sums of squares (which is where the '*variance*' bit comes in). Also known as ANOVA. Cf. *t-test*.

Analytic Epidemiology

The branch of *epidemiology* concerned with testing hypotheses about relationships between exposures and disease *outcomes*.

ANCOVA

Acronym for *analysis of covariance*.

Andrology

The science of diseases of the male sex.

Anecdote

Same as *case study*. Less politely, 'gossip'.

Annual Equivalent Charge

A constant sum paid annually whose *present value* is the same as (i.e. equivalent to) a *capital* cost.

Annuitized Value

See *Equivalent Annual Cost*.

Annuity

A constant amount of money per year received in perpetuity or for a specified period of time. The *coupon* on a bond is a specific type of annuity.

ANOVA

Acronym for *analysis of variance*.

Antenatal

The period between conception and birth. Same as *prenatal*.

Antitrust

The US term for regulatory policies against *monopoly* and similar practices and for promoting *competition*. For a survey see Gaynor and Vogt (2000).

A Posteriori

A Latin tag meaning 'proceeding inductively', 'inferring cause from effect'. Literally 'from what comes after'. Cf. *A Priori.*

Appraisal

The process of assessing *costs* and *benefits* in relation to a set of objectives and a set of alternative means (options) of realizing them. See *Cost–Benefit Analysis, Cost–Effectiveness Analysis, Cost–Utility Analysis, Option Appraisal, Programme Budgeting and Marginal Analysis*. For health economics examples see Kaltenthaler et al. (2008), Tappenden et al. (2007), and also the Appendix.

Appreciation

An increase in the value of an *asset* or *exchange rate*. It may occur as the result of *inflation* or real factors such as increased *productivity* or greater *demand*. Cf. *Depreciation*.

A Priori

A Latin tag meaning 'proceeding logically from assumption to implication' or, sometimes, 'presumptively'. Literally 'from what is before'. Cf. *A Posteriori*.

AQoL

Acronym for *Assessment of Quality of Life*.

ARA

See *Absolute Risk Aversion*.

Arbitrage

The practice of exploiting price differences between two or more *markets*: matching deals are struck that leave a profit – the difference between the *market prices* minus the *transaction costs*. One who engages in arbitrage is called an arbitrageur.

Arc-elasticity

See *Elasticity*.

Area Probability Sample

A form of *stratified sampling* in which the unit of analysis is a geographical area.

Area Under the Curve

A method comparing two or more *receiver operating characteristic curves* (ROCs). Usually abbreviated to AUC. Roughly speaking, the larger the AUC of a ROC, the better.

Area Wage Index

An index of labour costs used to reimburse hospitals in the US *Medicare* system.

Argument

An *independent variable* that determines the value of a function. For example, in the function $y = a + bx$, the independent variable, or argument, is x.

Arithmetic Mean

A measure of the central tendency of a set of numbers. The *average* of a set of numbers. The sum of the observations divided by their number. Arithmetic mean $= \Sigma X_i/N$, where the X_i are the values of X and N is the total number of observations. The qualifier 'arithmetic' is usually dropped.

Arm

In a *controlled trial* an arm is a group of patients allocated to a particular treatment. In a *randomized controlled trial*, the allocation to different arms is determined by a randomization procedure. Many controlled trials have two arms, one group of patients being assigned to the treatment arm and the other to the *control* arm. Trials may have more than two arms and more than one treatment or *control* arm. See *Control Group*.

ARR

Acronym for *absolute risk reduction*.

Array

Data sorted in order from the lowest to the highest values.

Arrow Award

A prize for health economists awarded annually by the International Health Economics Association for the best published paper in health economics. Its title honours Kenneth Arrow.

Arrow–Debreu Equilibrium

The solution to a set of equations that forms the basis for modern *general equilibrium theory* in economics. The *model* is static but assumes multiple individuals, multiple goods and services and multiple possible states of the world. It specifies the economic environment, a resource allocation mechanism, and a system of property rights. See Arrow and Debreu (1954).

Arrow Impossibility Theorem

One of the astonishing findings of modern economics (moreover from a student's PhD thesis!) is that a set of quite reasonable-sounding requirements about social choice orderings necessarily implies that there is no method for constructing social preferences from *ordinal* individual preferences. In other words, there is no rule, such as majority voting (nor any other), for deriving social preferences from arbitrary individual preferences of the kind commonly assumed by economists. The reasonable requirements (*axioms*) are these:

- *Completeness*: in a choice between *alternatives* A and B, A is socially preferred to B, or B is preferred to A, or there is a social indifference between them.
- *Transitivity*: if A is socially preferred to B and B is preferred to C then A is also preferred to C.
- Non-dictatorship: social preferences should not depend upon the preferences of only one individual – if every individual prefers A to B then socially A should be preferred to B.
- Social preferences should be independent of irrelevant alternatives;

i.e. the social preference for option A compared with B should be independent of the preference for C.

See Arrow (1951).

Arrow–Pratt Measure

A measure of *absolute risk aversion*. Loosely, it is a measure of the curvature of a *utility function*. See Arrow (1970) and Pratt (1964).

Arrow Social Welfare Function

A form of *social welfare function*, specifying how one arrives at social welfare from individual utilities by having various reasonable requirements. See *Arrow Impossibility Theorem, Bergson–Samuelson Social Welfare Function, Pareto Optimality.*

Ascertainment Bias

Same as *detection bias*.

Asociación de Economía de la Salud

The Spanish Association for Health Economics. Its website is available at: www.aes.es (accessed 26 October 2009).

Aspiration Adaptation

An alternative way of doing *decision analysis* for the use of *expected utility theory*. See *Bounded Rationality*.

Assessment of Quality of Life

An Australian measure of *health-related quality of life* having five dimensions (illness, independence of living, quality of social relationships, quality of physical senses, and psychological *well-being*). A website for this instrument is http://www.psychiatry.unimelb.edu.au/qol/aqol/instru ments/AQoL.pdf (accessed 27 October 2009). See *Disability-adjusted Life-year, EuroQol, EQ-5D, 15D®, Health Gain, Health Status, Health Utilities Index, Healthy Years Equivalent, Quality-adjusted Life-year, SF-6D©, SF-8©, SF-12©, SF-36©*. See Hawthorne et al. (1999).

Asset

Any property or entities with marketable worth owned by a person or business. Assets include real property, *human capital*, and enforceable claims against others (including bank accounts, stocks and debts).

Associazione Italiana di Economia Sanitaria

The Italian Association for Health Economists. Its website is available at: www.aiesweb.it (accessed 26 October 2009).

Assortive Matching

The non-random selection of trading partners with respect to one or more *traits* (for example, *productivity*, potential health gain); it is positive when like matches with like more frequently than would be expected by chance (e.g. people with high potential health gain match with effective *health technologies*) and is negative when the reverse occurs (for example, when infectious people match with susceptible people). For an empirical example in health economics see Dow and Philipson (1996).

Asymmetry of Information

The usual asymmetry in health economics relates to the difference in the information known by a patient, or member of the public, and that known by a professional such as a doctor or nurse. While it is sometimes thought that the informational advantage is all on one side (the professional's) this is to take too narrow a view of what the information may be about. For example, while it may be realistic to imagine that a doctor will have more knowledge about the probable consequences of a particular clinical intervention on a person's health, the doctor will usually have less compe-tence in assessing the consequences for that person's home and working life; here the advantage lies with the patient, who will also usually be more competent in judging the value (*utility*) of *alternative* clinical possibilities that the professional may propose (including 'doing nothing'). It would seem to follow that decisions intended to be of real benefit to a patient ought to be taken in a mutual fashion, with professional and patient in effect pooling their respective sets of information and the patient then either reaching the final decision or delegating it to the professional. However, this may not be everyone's experience of the interaction between themselves and their doctor. See *Agency Relationship*.

Another form of asymmetry that is important in health economics is the difference in information available to an insurer and an insured person. The insurer will typically set premia according to broad averages of *probability* and expense to cover the expected liability while the insured person may possess information, for example about private life-style and the risks to *health* that it entails, which is not available to the insurer and that indicates that the probability is higher or lower than the one embodied in the premium calculation. If higher, the incentive to buy *insurance* is, *ceteris paribus*, greater and the risk of financial loss to the insurer is also greater. If lower, it becomes less likely that insurance will be purchased. The use of no-claims 'bonuses' is one way used by insurers to overcome this difficulty, under which a record of low claims in one period is rewarded by lower premiums in a later period. See *Adverse Selection*. See Rothschild and Stiglitz (1976) for a classic article and, in health economics, Rochaix (1989), Phelps (2000) and Cardon and Hendel (2001).

Asymptote

A straight line that is the limiting value of a curve. The asymptote of a curve can be thought of as a line that is continuously approached but never touched by the curve.

Asymptotic Property

In statistics, this usually refers to a property of a statistic that applies as the *sample* size approaches infinity. More generally it is a straight line that is the limiting value of a curve; a tangent to the curve at infinity. See *Asymptote*.

Atomistic Competition

Basically the same as *perfect competition* – very large numbers of sellers each producing identical products.

Atomistic Fallacy

See *Ecological Fallacy*.

Attainment Inequality

A term coined by Sen (1981) to denote a way of looking at inequalities between people in terms of their actual achievements. Cf. *Shortfall Inequality*.

Attention Bias

Same as *Hawthorne effect*. See *Bias*.

Attraction Effect

One of many phenomena that apparently violate the assumption that choices are independent of irrelevant *alternatives*. This one occurs when the introduction of an inferior option influences the relative attractiveness of other alternatives in a choice set. Apparently so-called on account of the 'attraction' that the inferior option can bring to other options. Also known as the '*decoy effect*'. Cf. *Reference-dependent Theory*. See, for a health example, Schwartz and Chapman (1999).

Attributable Fraction

Same as *aetiological fraction*.

Attributable Risk

Same as *aetiological fraction*.

Attribute

This is a generic characteristic of something or someone. In health economics, it is often an aspect of human functioning such as *activities of daily living* that may form components of a measure of *health status*. Sometimes called '*dimension of health*' or '*domain* of health'. In *conjoint analysis*, an attribute may be part of a vignette describing the character of, say, a service that is being valued. In clinical research, the term is used to indicate an *independent variable* that cannot be manipulated by the researcher. Note also the verbal usage: 'to attribute' is to assign a consequence to a cause or an idea to its author.

Attrition

The exclusion or drop-out of individuals for a particular reason after assignment to the *experimental* or *control arm* of a *trial*.

Attrition Bias

Bias caused by non-response in *panel data*. The bias arises if the characteristics of non-responders differ from those of responders.

AUC

Acronym for *area under the curve*.

Audiology

The study of hearing and hearing impairment. In some countries the speciality includes the study of the nature, causes and treatment of diseases of the ear. See *Rehabilitation Medicine* and *Physiatry*.

Audit Trail

A systematic method used in *qualitative research* of documenting the evidence, the phases of research and the decisions taken in interpreting data. In business or public sector accounting, it refers to the documentation of transactions supported by evidence such as ledger entries or minutes of meetings. This documentation may be paper or electronic.

Australian Pharmaceutical Benefits Scheme

This scheme provides access to 'necessary and lifesaving' medicines at subsidized rates under the National Health Act of 1953 and subsequent Australian legislation. There are *copayments* but above an annual expenditure limit, drugs are available either free or at a much reduced price depending on the type of claimant.

Autarky

The state of a non-trading economy or individual. Self-sufficiency. A Latinate derivative not to be confused with the Greek derivative 'autarchy', which means 'despotism'.

Autocorrelation

Autocorrelation occurs when a *variable* is *correlated* with earlier values of itself.

Autonomy

The general ethical principle in medicine of respecting an individual's freedom from external interference and their right to self-determination (subject to like rights for all, and – perhaps – to the individual having a specified set of mental capacities). Along with the principles of *beneficence, nonmaleficence* and *justice*, it completes the so-called 'four principles' of health care ethics. See Beauchamp (2007).

Average

Same as *arithmetic mean.*

Average Cost

As used in economic theory, the average cost is the *total cost* of producing a specified rate of *output* (in the technically most efficient way) divided by that rate of output. Cf. *Opportunity Cost*.

Average Fixed Cost

Total *fixed cost* divided by the rate of *output*. Cf. *Opportunity Cost*.

Average Product

Total product (*output* rate) divided by the amount of *variable factor* used.

Average Revenue

Total revenue divided by the rate of *output*.

Average Total Cost

Total cost divided by the rate of *output*. Cf. *Opportunity Cost*.

Average Variable Cost

Total *variable cost* divided by the rate of *output*. Cf. *Opportunity Cost*.

Avoidable Cost

A *cost* that could be avoided by not producing the *output* of which it is a cost. Many costs are not avoidable – at least not quickly. For example, a contract with a supplier to supply an *input* for three years for an annual payment cannot (without further cost and/or loss) be avoided by ceasing to produce the good using the input. It usually costs something to avoid incurring a cost.

Avoidable Mortality

Deaths from conditions considered amenable to health care, such as treatable cancers, diabetes and cardiovascular disease. One estimate is that approximately 75000 to 101000 preventable deaths could have been averted in the US in 2002. See Nolte and McKee (2008).

Axiom

A primitive assumption or proposition that is taken as given. Theories are built upon sets of mutually consistent axioms and what may be inferred by using them. For the axioms of utility theory see *Utility*. For the axioms underlying the *Arrow impossibility theorem*, see that entry. For an example in health economics see Oliver (2004a).

Axis

A line on a graph along which the value of a *variable* is always zero. Graphs usually have two such lines, one for each of two variables, set at 90° to one another and intersecting at the point at which each variable has a value of zero.

Aziende Sanitarie Locali

Italian local health organizations that commission hospital services on behalf of their local communities. See *Purchaser–Provider Split*.

B

Balance Billing

The practice whereby health care providers collect from patients the difference between the fees they have charged and the reimbursement they receive from insurers. In some jurisdictions (e.g. Canada) it is prohibited by statute. See *Extra Billing*. See McKnight (2007).

Balanced Panel

Opposite of *unbalanced panel*. A research study *panel* in which only respondents for whom the data are complete for all sampling waves are included.

Balanced Scorecard

A tool for measuring organizational *performance*. See Kaplan and Norton (1996).

Balance of Care

The determination of the efficient, or quite commonly, 'appropriate', allocation of clients to types of medical and social care. See *Efficiency*.

Balance of Payments

The balance of payments is the record of a country's trade dealings with the rest of the world. It has two main parts. The *current account* shows the flows of trade in visible and invisible goods (like health services) plus the net effect of interest, profits, dividends and transfers. The *capital account* shows flows of investment and other (financial) *capital* (payment and repayment of debts). 'Official financing', in the form of changes in the central bank's holdings of gold and foreign currency and debt, meets any overall deficit when the current and capital accounts are added together (ignoring statistical errors). By definition the balance of payments must balance. A balance of payments surplus or deficit are therefore slightly misleading terms. A current account balance of payments deficit that is judged to be unsustainable will need remedial action. Although it is often seen as a symbol of a country's economic virility, a balance of payments surplus is not necessarily beneficial since it involves the central bank holding more assets in the form of short-term foreign government debt, and this typically earns a lower *rate of return* compared with other ways of investing taxpayers' contributions to public investment.

Balance of Trade

The value of exports minus that of imports both of goods ('visible' trade) and services ('invisible' trade). A component of the *balance of payments*.

Balance Sheet

A statement at the end of a period (usually a year) of the *wealth* of a person or organization. The balance sheet consists of various *stocks*: assets (cash, bank deposits, stocks of goods and other easily realizable assets; debts owed to the person/organization; investments, for example, other organizations that are owned by the person/organization and fixed assets like buildings less *depreciation*); and liabilities (debts owed to lenders such as bank loans and overdrafts; debts to other creditors, and the shares owned by shareholders). Cf. Profit and loss account, which records *flows*: changes in an organization's net worth or wealth over the period. The basic equation in accounting is assets = liabilities + *equity*, so equity = assets − liabilities.

Bandwagon, Snob and Veblen Effects

These usually relate to occasions when a second person's *consumption* or behaviour directly affects the utility of another, in other words, a form of *externality*. These effects can also be forms of *cognitive bias* encountered in psychological and economic experiments. In health economics, the implications have been chiefly regarding choices of lifestyle. So, for example, the behaviour of binge-drinking teenagers may be interpreted as a 'snob effect' that differentiates them from their more conventional non-boozing contemporaries and also as a 'bandwagon effect' whereby they indentify themselves as members of the group of young bingeing rebels. Thorstein Veblen (1857–1929) was a Norwegian-American sociologist who coined the phrase 'conspicuous consumption'. See Leibenstein (1950).

Bar Chart

A diagram showing the distribution of a non-*continuous variable* (e.g. social class) in which the (usually) vertical height of the equal width columns (bars) above each value is proportional to the relative frequency of observations in that category of the variable. For example, the chart below shows the frequency with which words of various lengths appear in the first sentence of this entry (with 'e.g.' counting as a two-letter word). Same as histogram. Cf. *Piechart*.

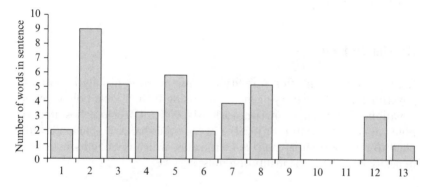

Bargaining in Health Care

In *managed health care* systems and systems where there is a *purchaser–provider split*, bargains need to be struck between the *commissioners* and the providers. Bargaining theory is the general framework in economics used by health economists to analyse such relationships. See, for an example, Barros and Martinez-Giralt (2006).

Barrier to Entry

An impediment to the flow of resources (such as the entry of a new firm) into an industry or segment of a market. It usually refers to human-made impediments (laws, regulations, professional practices, etc.) though many also occur naturally, for example, from *economies of scale*, which might make it very costly for a potential new entrant to achieve a large enough scale that would enable *competition* on similar terms with extant organizations. Barriers include such arrangements as *patents* and *licences*. Many barriers arise through the operation of regulatory agencies. The existence of barriers ought not to lead automatically to the inference that they are invariably undesirable and ought to be removed. Such an inference is best reached (or rejected) after a careful analysis of the *costs* and *benefits* of reducing or removing them. Similar considerations apply to the setting up of new barriers or increasing the height of existing ones. Enormous resources are sometimes devoted to their surmounting by those disadvantaged by barriers, particularly the barriers deliberately created by society to illegal activities like the production and distribution of narcotics. See *Access*, *Contestable Market*. See Morton (2000).

Barrier to Exit

Limits to an organization's ability to cease activity, usually imposed by government or regulatory agencies or arising from a local politically hot situation. For example, it is notoriously difficult to close hospitals for political reasons (central or local). On the other hand, it is much less difficult to replace (senior) management teams, which is a common recourse in health care when the institution must survive.

Barthel Index

An index of the *activities of daily living* on a scale of 0–20. Its website is available at: http://www.strokecenter.org/trials/scales/barthel.html (accessed 27 October 2009). See Mahoney and Barthel (1965).

Base Case Model

A *cost–effectiveness analysis* in which all parameter values have been set at their baseline values.

Baseline

The starting point in a *trial* or *cost–effectiveness analysis* in which the data have not been influenced by the intervention being studied, or the routine, treatment etc. with which other treatments are to be compared.

Baseline Characteristics

Demographic, economic, clinical and other descriptors of the participants in a *trial* or *cost–effectiveness analysis* prior to the intervention, or those descriptors of a *baseline* intervention with which others are to be compared.

Baseline Value

The best estimate of a parameter value in a *cost–effectiveness analysis* (or similar). Cf. *Sensitivity Analysis*.

Base Period

The time period or date at which an index is said to take the value 100.

Base-weighted Index

See *Laspeyres Index*.

Base Year

See *Base Period*.

Baumol Effect

An argument initially promulgated by William Baumol that accounts for the increasing share of service industries (like health care) in *gross domestic product*. The phenomenon is explained in terms of steadily increasing productivity in *capital*-intensive industries, leading to steadily declining relative prices in those industries. The opposite effect occurs in labour-intensive industries like health care. The value (or the productivity) of health care is in general extremely imperfectly revealed in any known markets, even in situations where there are markets for health care, so the story is a bit like Hamlet without the prince – the increasing share is visible but not the slow productivity growth that underlies it. Despite this, and despite the high capital-intensity of some modern medicine, and despite the fact that the *efficiency* of much health care remains untested, many regard Baumol's conjecture as having broad plausibility in health care. See Baumol (1967). Empirical confirmation with respect to the health care sector is in Hartwig (2008).

Bayesian Method

The Bayesian method is a way of revising beliefs about probabilities or the value of a *parameter* as new information is obtained. The old information might, for example, be based on a *systematic review* or a *consensus panel* of experts or a straightforwardly subjective judgment. The *probability* is termed the *prior probability* (or the prior *distribution* within which the true value of a parameter is believed to lie). The new information might be obtained from a recently completed *trial*. The revised probability (or distribution) is called the *posterior probability*. As Rawlins (2008) nicely relates, bookmakers are instinctive Bayesians: a horse's form book corresponds to the prior; the outcome of the last outing on a race course is the trial; the odds for today's race are the posterior odds (Rawlins 2008).

Suppose there is a *population* in which a characteristic (like having cancer) is true for a given fraction and untrue for the rest. It is obviously useful to be able to calculate the *conditional probability* that a particular observation comes from a person truly having the characteristic. This is where Bayesian statistics can help.

The following example is due to Eliezer Yudkowsky on http://yudkowsky.net/bayes/bayes.html (accessed 27 October 2009). It is generally known that 1 per cent of women at aged 40 who participate in routine screening have breast cancer (this is the prior). Eighty per cent of women with breast cancer will get positive mammographies (*true positives*); 9.6 per cent of women without breast cancer will also get positive mammographies (*false positives*) (these all being data obtained from a *clinical trial*). Now suppose a woman in this age group has a positive mammography in a routine screening. What is the probability that she actually has breast cancer? It is not 1 per cent. The correct answer is 7.8 per cent. To see why, these are the steps: out of 10 000 women, 100 have breast cancer; 80 of those 100 have positive mammographies. From the same 10 000 women, 9900 will not have breast cancer and of those 9900 women, 950 will also get positive tests – but falsely. This makes the total number of women with positive (true and false) tests 950 + 80 or 1030. Of those 1030 women with positive tests, 80 will have cancer. Expressed as a proportion, this is 80/1030 or 0.07767 or 7.8 per cent.

This example of *diagnosis* illustrates how Bayesian methods allow a prior belief (in this case about the probability of cancer) to be revised in the light of new information from the test results (probability of a test result conditional on having cancer) to form a posterior belief (the probability of cancer conditional on the test results).

The issues raised in considering the relative merits of Bayesian or *frequentist approaches* to probability arise acutely because of the all-pervading nature of uncertainty in medicine, public health, *population health* and health economics where evidence may accumulate over time from a variety of sources. For purposes of *cost–effectiveness analysis* there is often uncertainty about the detailed natural history of a *disease* (for example, the probability that a breast cancer detected in situ by mammography will progress to invasive cancer is not known and, if it does progress, the time between preclinical detectability and symptomatic disease is also not known). The character of *outcomes* beyond a period of a *clinical trial* is often unknown, along with the distribution across types of patients of beneficial and harmful outcomes and *costs* and whether the way measured outcomes have been defined is appropriate or correlated with outcomes that are appropriate (*construct validity*).

In addition, the use of Bayesian methods enables probability statements to be made in the form of the probability of more general hypotheses being true given the evidence, especially hypotheses that are of direct relevance to policy decision-making. For example, in cost–effectiveness analysis it allows statements to be made about the probability of an intervention being cost-effective given the accumulated evidence. However, the often subjective nature of forming Bayesian priors, which may require judgment or a particular interpretation of existing evidence, means that it is important to consider the *sensitivity* of the posterior results to alternative specification of the priors.

The approach is named after Thomas Bayes (1702–61), an English Presbyterian minister. An amateur mathematician, he was elected a Fellow of the Royal Society in 1742 even though he had no published works on mathematics and, moreover, published none in his lifetime under his own name. For an introduction see Kennedy (2003).

Bayes' Rule

See *Bayesian Method*.

Bayes' Theorem

See *Bayesian Method*.

Beers' List

A list of potentially inappropriate drugs for the elderly. Despite this list at least 8 per cent of seniors in Canada (and doubtless elsewhere too) had long-term prescriptions for one or more of these drugs. Originated in Beers et al. (1991). See Fick et al. (2003) and Canadian Institute for Health Information (2007).

Before and After Study

A study in which *outcomes* are measured before an intervention is implemented and compared with outcomes measured afterwards. Sometimes called a *'pre-post study'*. This form of experimental design is particularly prone to *bias* mainly because of failure to control for potential *confounding* variables. See *Controlled Before and After Study*.

Behavioural Cost Function

In contrast to the *cost function* as normally understood in economics, a behavioural cost function does not assume that the costs associated with each *output* rate are the lowest technically possible. See *X-inefficiency*. The idea is due to Evans (1971). For an application see Bilodeau et al. (2000).

Behavioural Organization Theory

This is an idea that often replaces profit-maximizing theory, namely that organizations are better modelled in terms of the preferences of influential individuals and groups, especially the managers, within them with the general expectation that 'profit' will be but one of the entities they prefer, and not always even one of the preferred entities. The expectation is that the less *competition* there is for the ownership of organizations and the greater the *monopoly* power of the organization, the more discretion there will be for the individuals in question to indulge their own preferences, e.g. for a 'quiet life' or palatial premises. *Non-profit* organizations dominate, of course, in health care, in which the absence of shareholders, whose effective interest in an organization can usually safely be assumed to be the profits it yields them, is the principal characteristic. See, for classics in health economics, Newhouse (1970) and Pauly and Redisch (1973).

Beneficence

The general ethical principle in medicine of trying to 'do good' or be of benefit to another. Along with the principles of *autonomy*, *nonmaleficence* and *justice*, it completes the so-called 'four principles' of health care ethics. See Beauchamp (2007).

Benefit

The gains, before *costs* are deducted, of any particular course of action, therapy, treatment, preventive programme, etc. In standard welfare economics, these gains are to be valued by the total amount that individuals are willing to pay to acquire them (including any externally affected individuals who may not be the direct beneficiaries), or the minimum amount they required to relinquish those they already enjoy. However, individuals are frequently extremely uninformed about what an intervention might do (or even has done) for them, in which case their ability to value it is inherently limited. Moreover, since willingness and *ability to pay* are often correlated (and these are in turn correlated with *health status*) many economists are reluctant to attach any significance to individuals' *willingness to pay*, even if the individuals in question are well informed, though in principle, weighting systems might be adopted to compensate for unequal abilities to pay. Similarly, in principle, weights might be applied to different individuals when adding benefits accruing to different persons. In practice, due to the difficulties inherent in undertaking these tasks, health benefits are left in non-monetized form, especially in *extra-welfarism*, under which health maximization is commonly taken as a proximate social *maximand* for the health care sector. Partly because of these difficulties and partly because of the stated objectives of health policy in many juris-dictions, many health economists have directed their energies to the development of direct measures of *health* without seeking also to assess its monetary value. These factors also doubtless account for the popularity of *cost–effectiveness, cost–utility* and *cost–consequences analyses*. See *Agency Relationship, Assessment of Quality of Life, Disability-adjusted Life-year, EQ-5D, 15D®, Health Gain, Health Status, Health Utilities Index, Healthy Years Equivalent, Quality-adjusted Life-year, SF-6D©, SF-8©, SF-12©, SF-36©*.

Benefit–Cost Ratio

A statistic commonly used to describe the conclusion of a *cost–benefit* study. It is the ratio of the *present value* of *benefits* to the present value of *costs*. Given that the classification of some entities as costs or negative benefits, and benefits or negative costs, is ambiguous, the ratio can be a misleading indicator of *efficiency* and, as a ratio, it gives no indication of the size of the benefits or costs in question. It is usually better to use the dif-ference between the present values rather than their ratio, at the marginal costs and benefits rather than the totals and to use an explicit *comparator*. Cf. *Net Benefit*.

Benefit Principle

This is the idea in the (normative) theory of taxation that what is paid by an individual as tax ought to be related to (even proportional to) the *benefit* derived from the way in which the tax proceeds are used. It is a vir-tually impossible principle to apply consistently or accurately, even when taxes are *earmarked*, especially in the presence of *public goods* and *exter-nalities*, but has been quantified through methods of estimating individu-als' *willingness to pay* such as *conjoint analysis* or *discrete choice analysis*. Cf. *Ability to Pay*.

Benefit Transfer

This term applies to a variety of techniques for transferring the values ascribed to a good, service or *attribute* in one survey or experimental context in relevant ways to another decision or policy context, thereby avoiding the necessity of repeating the experiment or survey.

Bequest Value

Same as *existence value*.

Berenson–Eggers Type of Service Codes

A system of coding types of medical service (e.g. 'surgery', 'MRI scan') used in the US by *Medicare*. Acronym: BETOS. See Berenson and Holahan (1992).

Bergson–Samuelson Social Welfare Function

The original idea for a *social welfare function* is due to Abram Bergson (1914–2003) and was definitively and rigorously developed by Paul Samuelson in his PhD thesis with astonishing virtuosity. Bergson's original idea was extremely general, for the value of social welfare was understood to depend on all the variables that might be considered to affect it. It is usually, however, interpreted as being defined over a particular profile of individual *utilities* and has hence become restricted to those things about which people have *preferences*. This is what is usually meant by the term 'welfarist' – social welfare is deemed to depend on utilities (and not, for example, quantities of goods, characteristics of people, fulfilment of duty, obedience to God, or anything else). See *Arrow Impossibility Theorem, Arrow Social Welfare Function, Pareto Optimality, Social Welfare.* See Bergson (1938) and Samuelson (1947).

Best-evidence Synthesis

Individual research studies rarely provide reliably generalizable and definitive answers to research questions. Best-evidence synthesis is one way of increasing *generalizability*. According to its proponents, best-evidence synthesis couples the statistical rigour of *meta-analyses* in synthesizing quantitative findings with the flexibility of traditional narrative reviews. The method entails having explicit, well-justified and well-described *inclusion criteria* in the review. Unlike meta-analyses, best-evidence syntheses are not limited to statistical *aggregation* and the analysis of quantitative results but supplement these features with a broader literature review that might include *qualitative analysis* and engage in discussion of discrepancies in results that cannot be quantified.

Cf. *Narrative Reviews*. The method was originated by Slavin (1986) in education research.

Best–Worst Scaling

A method of deriving preferences in *discrete choice experiments* that over-comes some of the limitations of other methods by enlarging the choice set confronting subjects. See for examples, Coast et al. (2006) and Flynn et al. (2007).

Beta Distribution

A frequency *distribution* having two *parameters*, usually labelled α and β, mean = $\alpha/(\alpha + \beta)$, variance = $\alpha\beta/[(\alpha + \beta)^2(\alpha + \beta + 1)]$ and that is bounded on the interval 0–1. It is flexible, and can be symmetrical about the *mean* or positively or negatively *skewed*. Cf. *Normal Distribution*.

BETOS

Acronym for *Berenson–Eggers Type of Service codes*.

Between-individual Variability

A variability in *outcome* due to the effects of identifiable sub-groups of individuals differing in age, sex, job and other *covariates*, or who differ in unmeasured differences.

Bias

In *empirical* work, any systematic difference between the empirical results of an analysis and the true facts of the case (e.g. the difference between the *distribution* of *values* in a *sample* and the actual values of the *popula-tion* from which the sample is drawn). In non-statistical areas it is any distorting influence that might systematically lead to wrong or misleading results, for example, a search of the (English language) literature on a subject might lead one to ignore all Chinese contributions (unfortunately, no reviewer knew Chinese) and to conclude something wrong about the results (apart from the apparent fact that Chinese researchers were not working in the field). Research sponsorship (whether by commercial – e.g. industrial – or non-commercial sponsors – e.g. governmental) can lead to pressure on researchers to produce particular results or suppress 'unwanted' results.

Bias is broadly of three kinds: *information* (as when there are systematic coding errors); *selection* (as when there are systematic distortions in the ways that experimental subjects are selected) and *confounding* (as when some *determinants* are not controlled for). More specific common types of bias in empirical health economics, surveys and *clinical trials* include *allocation bias, ascertainment bias (= detection bias), attention bias, cognitive bias, commercial bias, design bias, end of scale bias, exclusion bias, information bias (= observational bias), interviewer bias, justification bias, lead-time bias, length bias, measurement bias, observer bias, omitted variable bias, optimism bias, performance bias, personality bias, publication bias, range bias, recall bias, referral bias, response bias (= sample selection bias), reporting bias, selection bias, spacing out bias, spectrum bias, starting point bias, surveillance bias, therapeutic personality bias, verification bias (= work up bias), volunteer bias* and *withdrawal bias.*

Bias Blind Spot

A *bias* sometimes encountered in psychological and economic experiments whereby subjects fail to compensate for their own *cognitive biases*.

Bidding Games

An alternative to the traditional open-ended questionnaire, which is often used in *willingness to pay* studies. Depending on how a subject responds to a prompted *value*, a search *algorithm* bids them up or down until a final value is settled upon. See, for a health economics application, Frew et al. (2004).

BIE

Acronym for *budget impact analysis*.

Bimodal Distribution

A *distribution* of a *continuous variable* that has two peaks (*modes*), like that of some political opinions in Northern Ireland. For an example from health economics see Brazier et al. (2002).

Binary Variable

A *variable* that can take one of only two *values*: usually 1 and 0 such as 'yes' or 'no', 'well' or 'ill', 'in-patient' or 'out-patient', 'home delivery' or 'hospital delivery'. Some characteristics may be more or less *continuous* (such as degree of ill-health) but the data may be presented in a binary form (sick/not sick). Usually '1' indicates the presence of the characteristic in question and '0' indicates its absence. Same as *dichotomous variable, dummy variable*.

Binomial Distribution

A *distribution* used with discrete random *variables*. When a fair coin is flipped, the *outcome* is one of two mutually exclusive possibilities: heads or tails. If a coin is flipped *n* times, then the binomial distribution can be used to determine the probability of obtaining exactly *r* heads in the *n* outcomes. The formula that is used assumes that the observations are dichotomous, mutually exclusive, independent and randomly selected.

Bioassay

The quantitative assessment of a substance's potency through experimental measurement of its effects on tissue or living creatures.

Bio-equivalence Trial

Same as *equivalence trial*.

Bioethics

A field of applied ethics, usually interpreted (by economists) as concerning ethical issues in medical research (for example, the protection of patients, the experimental use of embryos), health care regulation and health care allocation arrangements.

Biogeneric

Similar to *biosimilar*.

Biologic

Biologics are medicines that are manufactured with biotechnological processes like fermentation, unlike pharmaceutical entities that are chemically synthesized. Examples include human recombinant insulin and growth hormone, biological proteins like erythropoietin, and monoclonal antibodies like trastuzumab. Also known as 'biopharmaceutical agents'. Cf. *Biosimilar*. See, for some health economics of biologics, Grabowski et al. (2007).

Biosimilar

A medicine created through a biotechnological process that is a close copy of an existing off-patent *biologic*. It cannot be identical by virtue of the biological, as distinct from chemical, processes involved in its manufacture. Also known as 'follow-on protein products'.

Birth Rate

See *Crude Birth Rate*.

Birth Weight

An infant's weight as recorded at birth. Low birth weight is conventionally <2500 g, Very low birth weight is <1500 g. Ultra low birth weight is <1000 g.

Bivariate

Data on two (possibly linked) *variables*.

Bivariate Probit Model

A non-linear statistical extension of the *probit model* that has two *binary, dependent variables*. For an example in health economics see Sen (2002).

Bivariate Sensitivity Analysis

A form of *sensitivity analysis* in which two *parameters* are varied at a time. See, for example, Sullivan et al. (2003).

Black Markets

Markets that arise when prices are controlled or other legal regulations are flouted. For example, in health care see Ensor and Thompson (2006) and Szende and Culyer (2006).

Black Report

A report commissioned by the UK Department of Health & Social Security from Sir Douglas Black (1913–2002), the first Chief Scientist at the Department of Health and Social Security, on the inequality of health in the UK. Notorious for being published only in duplicated form for several years in an apparent governmental attempt to hide (or at least not disseminate) bad news. Eventually published as a Penguin. Originally: Black (1980), later Black et al. (1992).

Blinding

Blinding (sometimes called 'masking') refers to a set of techniques designed to reduce *bias* in *trials*. A *double-blind trial* is where neither the patient nor the observer/clinician is aware of whether the patient is in the *control* or *experimental arm* of a trial. A *single-blind trial* is where the patient (or observer/clinician) is aware of which arm they are in but the observer/clinician (or patient) is not. A *triple-blind trial* is one in which subjects, observers/clinicians and analysts are unaware of patient assignment to the arms of the trial. In trials of different styles of patient management or many surgical procedures, full blinding is often, alas, impossible. The seriousness of the potential bias will then depend on the circumstances.

For example, blinding patients to the treatment they receive in a controlled trial matters less when the *outcome* measures are objectively observable events, like death, rather than subjective, like the relief of pain. Even in surgery, patient blinding is possible. For example, in a trial of surgery for osteoarthritis of the knee the controls underwent a sham procedure, having a small slit cut in the side of the knee that was then sewn up again. See Moseley et al. (2002).

Block Contract

A form of contract between health care *purchasers* (*commissioners*) and health care providers, in which a wide range of services is agreed to be provided in exchange for a *global budget*. Cf. *Cost and Volume Contract*. See *Purchaser–Provider Split*.

Blocked Randomization

Same as *blocking*.

Blocking

This is a procedure in *trials* in which subjects are grouped into 'blocks' having the same number of experimental and *control* subjects and blocks are then selected at random. It is a useful method when the numbers of participants in a trial are small. In a large trial simple randomization will tend to give a balanced number of patients in each *arm* but in small studies the numbers may not be so well balanced. In such trials, *blocked randomization* may be used. The order of treatments within the block is randomly permuted.

Bond

A bond is debt issued by a private or governmental corporation. The issuer receives the face value of the bond from its buyer and pays (usually fixed) interest on the debt until 'maturity', when the bond is 'redeemed' through repaying the face value. The buyer can, of course, sell the bond to another buyer at any mutually agreeable price, whatever its face value.

Boolean Logic

The use of the terms 'and', 'or' and 'not' for refining database searches of literature, as in *systematic reviewing*. Named after the English mathematician George Boole (1815–64).

Bootstrapping

A *non-parametric method* of estimating the *distribution* of an estimator or test statistic by 'resampling' the data. The term comes from the old idea that you might be able to lift yourself off the ground by pulling on the straps on the backs of your boots. Suppose you have a *sample* of 20. You 'bootstrap', or recreate, the *population* from which the sample came by duplicating the sample many times over in a computer simulation of the population. Thus, you draw a sample (say of 1) from your sample of 20, record its value, replace it amongst the 20 and draw again. This process is repeated many times. Bootstrapping is particularly useful when data are *skewed* and sample sizes are modest. It is frequently used in estimating probability distributions of *cost–effectiveness ratios*, their *confidence intervals* and *variances*. See Efron and Tibshirani (1998) or Kennedy (2003) for the method. Examples of studies using bootstrapping are Korthals-de Bos et al. (2003) and Kobelt et al. (2005).

Bottom-up Studies

A term used in costing methods for *cost–effectiveness* and similar analyses, according to which data sources for costs are directly obtained from a specific *population* or *sample*. Cf. *Top-down Studies*. For an example, see Renehan et al. (2004).

Bounded Rationality

One usage of this term assumes that individuals behave in a manner that is as optimal with respect to their goals as their resources will allow. Loosely, it means they are content with *outcomes* that are merely satisfactory rather than ideal, operate by rules of thumb, take short-cuts, etc. In essence, this version of the theory recognizes that making decisions is itself a costly exercise and the resources used in weighing up the pros and cons of any choice need themselves to be economized. Another usage avoids entirely the idea that individuals have precisely defined goals that they seek to maximize even if only approximately or by rule of thumb, etc. Instead, people have aspirations that they can adapt up or down according to the ease of realizing them. Both types of bounded rationality relax one or more *axioms* of standard *expected utility theory*. The originator was Herbert Simon. See Simon (1957).

Box Diagram

A diagram used in welfare economics to elucidate efficient resource allocations. See *Contract Curve* for an example to show an efficient allocation of two goods between two people. Similar analytics are used in the case of two goods and two producers (jurisdictions, industries or firms). Also known as the *Edgeworth Box* or Edgeworth-Bowley Box after Ireland's most famous economist Francis Ysidro Edgeworth (1845–1926) and his English popularizer Arthur Lyon Bowley (1869–1957).

Box–Jenkins Approach

One way of doing *time series* or forecasting analysis. A method of extrapolating past data into the future without using *explanatory variables*. See Box and Jenkins (1970).

Box Plot

Sometimes a 'box and whisker' plot. This is a diagram in which the ends of the 'box' indicate the upper and lower values of the *interquartile range* (i.e. the middle 50 per cent) of a *variable*. The ends of the box are called 'hinges'. The distance between the hinges is called the 'H-spread'. The vertical line through the box indicates the *median* value. *Values* one 'step' outside the hinges are called 'inner fences', where a step is 1.5 times the difference between the hinges. Values two steps outside the hinges are called 'outer fences'. In the diagram, the minimum value lies inside the lower inner fence, which is not shown and the maximum value lies inside the upper outer fence, which is not shown. There are one or two 'adjacent values', which are observations just within the inner fences and these mark the extent of the 'whiskers' – the lines extending from either side of the box. Points beyond the extremities of the whiskers identify the maximum and minimum values (in some box plots, the ends of the whiskers are the two extreme values). In *descriptive statistics* the two extreme values, the two limits of the interquartile range and the median are sometimes referred to as the 'five-number summary' of the data. In some versions, the box plot is presented vertically. See Longworth and Bryan (2003) for a practical example.

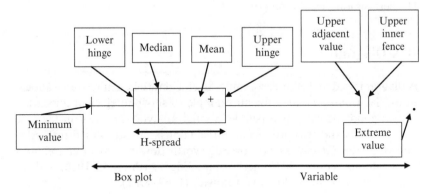

Box and Whisker Plot

See *Box Plot*.

Brand Name

The particular name given to a patented drug. Cf. its *generic* name. For example, Zocor is the brand name for simvastatin and Avastin the brand name for bevacizumab.

Brenner Hypothesis

This is the idea that economic recessions cause both *population mortality* and *morbidity* to rise. The evidence in support of the thesis is not strong. See Brenner (1983) for the hypothesis and Gravelle (1984), Wagstaff (1985) and Laporte (2004) for critical reviews. Also Ruhm (2000).

BSC

Acronym for *balanced scorecard*.

Budget

A statement of planned receipts and expenditures set for a future period – usually a year, though not always a calendar year.

Budget Balance

The difference between the government's current revenue and current expenditure. When they are equal the budget is said to be 'balanced'. When revenue exceeds expenditure there is a 'budget surplus' and when expenditure exceeds revenue there is a 'budget deficit'.

Budget Constraint

Sometimes termed 'budget line'. The limit to expenditure imposed by a cash-limited budget. It is often represented as a straight line in geometrical representations of a consumer's choice possibilities between two goods or services, where it shows the limiting boundary of combinations of purchases that are possible with that budget. Often used in conjunction with *indifference curves* to indicate the choice that would be made by a *utility-maximizing* individual.

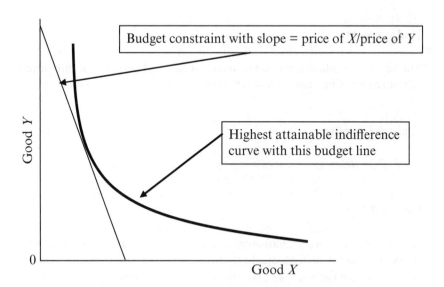

Budget Deficit

See *Budget Balance*.

Budget Impact

Budget impact is a forecast of rates of use (or changes in rates of use) with their consequent short- and medium-term effects on budgets and other resources to help health service managers plan such changes. The estimation of the budget impact of a change in the use of a health care technology (or the introduction of a new one) is a frequent accompaniment to a *cost–effectiveness analysis*. See Mauskopf et al. (2007).

Budget Impact Analysis

The analysis of *budget impact*.

Budget Line

See *Budget Constraint*.

Budget Sets

The sets of 'bundles' (combinations) of goods and services an individual can purchase. The bundles available on or under the *budget constraint*.

Budget Surplus

See *Budget Balance*.

Bulk-billing

Bulk-billing is an Australian term to describe the system under *Medicare* whereby a doctor bills Medicare directly, accepting the Medicare benefits as full payment for a service. The practitioner cannot make any additional charge for a service, nor can any other person or company.

Bundling

This is an alternative method of remunerating providers to *fee-for-service* (FFS) and *capitation* that seeks to overcome some of the disadvantages of FFS (as when patients have to cope with fees due to several providers between whom there may be little coordination) while avoiding the alleged risk, with capitation, of underprovision. Bundled payment systems require a single payment for all services related to a spell of treatment or a condition, possibly spanning multiple providers in multiple settings. They are also known as 'case rates' or 'episode-based payments'. For some feel for the passion the practice evokes in the US see Pennachio (2003).

Burden of Disease

A measure of the total *morbidity* from a particular disease or disease in general, or its impact in terms of unfavourable consequences, or the cost of treating the victims. While such measures have their uses, one common use, which is not recommended, is as an indicator of the pay-off to research (since it takes no account of the probable success of the possible research) and another that is not recommended is as an indicator of priorities for treatment (not recommended as it takes no account of the *effectiveness* of treatments).The burden of disease thus conceived does not measure the real 'burden' (i.e. the *opportunity cost*) of any measures that might be taken to reduce it. A final caution: measures of 'burden' often fail to calibrate *quality of life*. See Mooney and Wiseman (2000) and Andlin-Sobocki et al. (2005). For a third world example of the productivity losses from AIDS/HIV see Wagstaff (2002a) and Fox et al. (2004). For a developed country study on sight impairment see Frick et al (2007); for one on drug misuse see Godfrey et al. (2002).

Burden of Taxation

There are two kinds: the *direct cost* to taxpayers (though this is not a net cost to society as a whole since what some taxpayers lose others gain), and the '*excess burden*' or '*deadweight loss*'. The excess burden is the subtler idea and is best seen in a *demand* and *supply* diagram. Suppose a market is initially in e*quilibrium* at price P and rate of *output*/consumption Q. An indirect tax is then imposed in the form, say, of a constant excise tax that has the effect of vertically displacing the supply curve by the amount of the tax per unit. The new equilibrium price is P_1 and the new output rate is Q_1. The burden is shared (depending on the *elasticities* of demand and supply) between buyers and sellers. The direct cost to demanders is the rectangle labelled *a*, the direct cost to suppliers is *b*. The excess burden for demanders is *c* and that for suppliers is *d*. The excess burdens represent the value over and above their cost of production of goods and services no longer bought and sold that is forgone. Since nearly all health care systems involve a degree (sometimes very large) of government expenditure, it is plain that a part of the price paid for this is the excess burden (which, incidentally, exists also in connection with direct taxes) and not just the proportion of the tax revenue accounted for by public expenditure on health care. See *Excess Health Insurance, Incidence, Shifting*. See Atkinson (1977) for the general case; in health care financing: Feldstein (1973), Feldman and Dowd (1991) and Newhouse (1992).

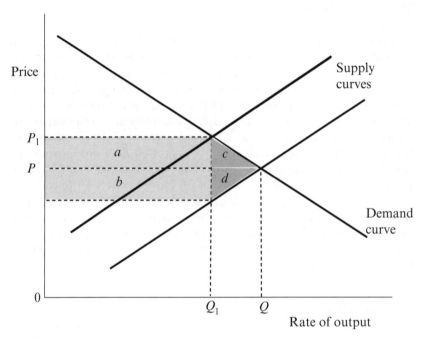

Business Case

An evaluative study done from the (financial) *perspective* of a business.

Business Cycle and Health

Business cycles are the short-term fluctuations around the longer-term trend in *gross domestic product*. Total *mortality* has a procyclical fluctuation, so national health actually improves in recessions. Suicides are an important exception. Smoking and obesity both increase when the economy strengthens, whereas physical activity falls and diet becomes less healthy. See Dockner and Feichtinger (1993), Ruhm (2000, 2006) and Laporte (2004).

C

CADTH

Acronym for *Canadian Agency for Drugs and Technologies in Health*.

Cafeteria Plan

A type of employment *benefit* offered in the US that gains employees partial exemption from *payroll taxes*. They may select (as one does in a cafeteria) a variety of benefits such as *flexible spending accounts* or *medical savings accounts*. See *Consumer-driven Health Care*.

CAHTA

Acronym for *Catalan Agency for Health Technology Assessment and Research*.

Campbell Collaboration

The international Campbell Collaboration (also known as C2) is a non-profit organization similar to the *Cochrane Collaboration*. It aims to help people make well-informed decisions about the effects of interventions in the social, behavioural and educational arenas by preparing, maintaining and disseminating systematic reviews of research studies of interventions. Its website is available at: http://www.campbellcollaboration.org/ (accessed 27 October 2009).

Canadian Agency for Drugs and Technologies in Health

This is a federal Canadian organization conducting *health technology assessments* and *cost–effectiveness analyses* for the information of provincial health ministries in Canada. It was formerly known as the Canadian Coordinating Office for Health Technology Assessment (CCOHTA). The current acronym is CADTH. Its website is available at: http://www.cadth. ca/ (accessed 27 October 2009).

Capabilities

Basic abilities to perform various kinds of function have been proposed as a useful focus in thinking about *equity* both with respect to specific abilities of thought and action and the range of opportunities. Capabilities commonly considered in *health economics* include mobility, being pain-free, being adequately fed, having access to shelter, though in principle the range is much wider than this. Thus, disabled persons are likely to need more resources than others if they are to achieve equal mobility or, more generally, have the same chance of leading a life of quality. The idea originated with Amartya Sen and has since been developed for outcome measurement purposes in economic evaluations. See, e.g., Culyer (1989), Sen (1999), Nussbaum (2000), Coast et al. (2008a, b), Gandjour (2008) and Anand et al. (2009).

Capacity

A measure sometimes of the throughput or *output* of which a hospital or other organization is capable and sometimes of the *stock* of an *input* such as hospital beds, which may determine a limit to throughput or output *rates*. Inevitably, there is an element of arbitrariness in measuring capacity and it will depend on what is taken as 'given'. For example, if single shift-working is taken as given, either the capacity would (other things being equal) be viewed as having increased if there were a move to two-shift working, or the organization would be viewed as operating above capacity. There are also major empirical difficulties in estimating capacity, given the enormous *heterogeneity* of organizations in health care and other industries. See Glazer and Rothenberg (1999). For a study of capacity in the context of managing hospital admissions see Gallivan et al. (2002).

Capacity Building

In some schools of *public health*, capacity building is specifically associated with the creation of sustainable skills, organizational structures, resources and commitment to health improvement in the health and other sectors. Cf. *Capacity*. For an Australian example, see New South Wales Health Department (2001).

Capacity to Benefit

In health economics, this term usually refers to the potential improvement in health an individual or group might achieve through the use of
health services or through the instrumentality of some other *determinant
of health*. It is not always appreciated that there can be a positive capacity to *benefit* even when *health status* is falling over time, provided that
the care in question causes it to fall less than would otherwise be the case.
The relevant comparison is not necessarily '*before and after*' but 'with and
without'. Failure to appreciate this can lead to serious underestimation
of the benefits of some procedures. See *Health Gain, Need*. See, for an
example in health economics, Mooney and Houston (2004).

Capacity Utilization

The extent to which the *capacity* of an organization like a hospital is actually being used. For hospitals, a common measure is the fraction of the
number of beds that are filled (with patients of course).

Capital

Viewed variously as a physical *stock* of *assets* (buildings, land plant, equipment, etc.) that can earn income or generate *utility*, as a stock of financial
assets (government bills, *equities*, bank balances, etc.), or as the *present
value* of the net value of a *flow* of services over time that a particular asset
or programme may yield. Capital (a stock) is measured at a point in time
in contrast to *investment* (a *flow*), which takes place through time. *Human
capital* is the stock of valuable resources embodied in a human being,
not all of which is marketable (or ought, indeed, to be marketed). *Health*
can be seen as an element in human capital that depreciates and may be
invested in. Selling one's stock of human capital (in contrast to selling its
flow) is one way of defining (voluntary) slavery, though this is more commonly called 'indenture' (needless to say, how 'voluntary' such indenture
was is highly questionable). The classic in health economics is Grossman
(1972).

Capital Account

A component of the *balance of payments*.

Capital Consumption

A national income accounting term: the amount by which *gross investment* exceeds *net investment*. Synonymous with '*replacement investment*'.

Capital Cost

The *cost* of acquiring, owning or using an item of capital equipment net of *depreciation*. See *Capital*.

Capital Intensity

A production process (like health care) can be characterized in terms of its *capital* intensity. This is a measure of the use of capital relative to other *factors of production*, such as labour, in the production process. It is usually measured by the ratio of capital to labour or by the share of capital in total factor payments. Health care is relatively labour intensive despite all the fuss made about modern health care technologies. See Baumol (1967) on implications for relative growth rates and *productivity*. For an application to the impact of AIDS see Cuddington and Hancock (1994).

Capital Market

The market for long-term loans.

Capitalized Value

The sum of a discounted *flow* of future *costs* or *benefits*. See *Discounting, Present Value*.

Capitation

A method of paying doctors a fixed fee per period per patient registered (sometimes differentiated according to age or sex of patient) regardless of the amount of service provided. Cf. *Bundling, Fee-for-service*. See Iversen and Lurås (2006).

Cardinal Scale

Ratio scales and *interval scales* are both cardinal scales, in contrast to any scale that indicates no more than the order of entities. Distance and temperature both have several commonly met cardinal scales, for example, kilometres (ratio scale) in the case of distance and Celsius (interval) in the case of temperature. Cardinality is sometimes vulgarly confused, especially when associated with *utility*, with interpersonal comparability, with which, however, it has nothing intrinsic to do at all. Interpersonal comparisons may be made ordinally or cardinally. '*Health*' is commonly measured cardinally or ordinally, according to the instrument used. Cf. *Ordinal Scale*. See *Cost–Effectiveness Analysis, Health-related Quality of Life, Utility*. On converting ordinal measures of health to cardinal measures see Van Doorslaer and Jones (2003).

Cardinal Utility

A characteristic of *utility* measurement. See *Cardinal Scale, Ordinal Scale*.

Cardiology

The medical speciality concerned with diseases and abnormalities of the heart.

Card Sorts

An instrument used in *conjoint analysis*. Combinations of the *attributes* of services are written on cards that subjects are asked to sort into piles indicating their order of preference. For an example see the experiment by Dolan and Green (1998).

Carides Two-stage Method

A method of estimating *cost functions* when the data are censored, typically because of staggered start dates in *trials*. The method involves weighting a cost function by a *survival function*. See Carides (2003).

Caring Externality

A type of *externality* in which one person derives *utility* from the consumption, perceived *well-being*, etc. of another. A caring externality, as is the case with any other kind of externality, is neither a necessary nor a sufficient reason for public intervention via subsidy, tax or regulation, vulgar undergraduate traditions to the contrary. See *External Effects*. See Culyer (1971b, 1991a) and Jacobsson et al. (2005).

Carry Over

The persistence in a *crossover trial* of some of the effects of a treatment applied in an earlier period into a later period of treatment. As an example of a *cost–effectiveness* study in which carry over was modelled explicitly, see Delea et al. (2007).

Cartel

A grouping of producers that acts as a *monopoly*. Suppliers of similar products may coordinate their behaviour implicitly or explicitly by setting common prices, sharing agreed market quotas, or acting in other ways as a single organization might act to increase profit (and prices). Professional organizations in health care often act as though they were cartels through such devices as negotiating a standard fee schedule (per item of service), banning advertising, making particular acts (such as performing injections) legal only for members (and illegal for members of closely related professionals). See *Competition*. Early well-known studies include Kessel (1958) on physicians and Robinson and Luft (1987) on hospitals.

Carveout Firms

Specialized, and specially protected or exempted, health care providers (mostly in mental health care) in the United States. They specialize in *carveouts*. See Frank et al. (1995) and Ettner et al. (1998).

Carveouts

A US term for sub-sections of health care expenditures like pharmacy, mental health, neonatal or substance abuse treatment costs. They may be specifically identified in order to protect them in cost-reducing initiatives or to accord them special subsidies in order to retain their consumers in an *insurance* scheme. See Frank et al. (1995), Ettner et al. (1998) and Frank and Garfield (2007).

Case

A patient having a specified disease or condition who is being investigated or treated, or an example of something investigated, as in '*case study*'.

Case-control Study

A non-experimental study comparing a series of patients with a particular characteristic of interest (the *cases*) with a comparison group of patients (*controls*) who do not have the characteristic in order to determine the effect of exposure to a *risk factor*. Such studies famously provided the first suggestive evidence of an association between cigarette smoking and lung cancer. Such studies are exposed to the risk of *omitted variable bias* from unobserved (or even unsuspected) *confounders*. For a discussion of such possibilities in the case of bicycle helmets, see Curnow (2006) but also MacPherson and Spinks (2008).

Case History

A description of a patient as an individual clinical case. Useful for *audit* purposes but rarely systematic enough or sufficiently controlled for *confounding* for safe generalization. When used as such it is no better than gossip. See *Hierarchy of Evidence*.

Caseload

The number of cases handled in a given period of time by a health care professional or a health care institution.

Case Management

A method of cost control and quality assurance used in many systems of health care that directs individual patients to the most appropriate amount, duration and type of health service and social care and monitors *outcomes*. For an economic evaluation see Gravelle et al. (2007b).

Case-mix

The proportions in the total *stock* or *flow* of patients of the various types into which they may be classified (surgical, medical, for example, or 'complex' and 'simple', urgent or non-urgent). It is often used as a *variable* in hospital cost analysis and in *allocation formulae* to hospitals and regions. See also *Diagnosis-related Group*. For an early and pioneering study see Feldstein (1967).

Case-series Study

A study using patients' accumulated case notes over a period of time. There is no *control group*.

Case Study

A study, often qualitative, reporting on a single organization, event or example thought to be of wider interest than to those immediately concerned with it. An example in health economics is a case study of *NICE*: see Williams et al. (2007).

Cash Terms

Expenditure measured in terms of current (*nominal*) prices. See *Constant Prices*.

Catalan Agency for Health Technology Assessment and Research

CAHTA (in Catalan: Agència d'Avaluació de Tecnologia i Recerca Mèdiques de Catalunya – AATRM) conducts *health technology assessments* and *cost–effectiveness analyses* for use in Catalunya. Its website available at: http://www.gencat.cat/salut/depsan/units/aatrm/html/ca/Du8/index.html (accessed 27 October 2009).

Catastrophic Insurance

See *Catastrophic Payments*.

Catastrophic Payments

People without full health care *insurance* are at risk of incurring enormous *out-of-pocket* expenses should they fall ill. These are what are meant by 'catastrophic'. Catastrophic insurance is a form of health care insurance specifically designed to protect against such eventualities (but not necessarily against lesser financial exposures). In the US, catastrophic health care insurance is usually associated with high *deductibles*. See Gertler and Gruber (2002). On the exposure in the US see Skinner and Feenberg (1994). In low-income countries even small out-of-pocket payments can be catastrophic by crowding-out other essential consumption items such as food, housing and clothing. For a third world case study (where insurance is nearly everywhere very partial) see World Bank (2001) and Wagstaff and van Doorslaer (2003).

Categorical Variable

A variable (sometimes called a *'nominal'* variable) that has two or more categories, but where there is no intrinsic ordering of the categories. For example, gender is a categorical variable having two categories (male and female) and it is not politically correct (nor indeed is it right) to order them intrinsically.

Category Rating Scale

A scale measure of health, or *health-related quality of life*, in which numerals (1, 2, 3, . . .) correspond to states of health (categories) usually having verbal descriptions (such as 'can perform limited *activities of daily living*'). The numerical categories are sometimes assumed to have equal intervals between them (but sometimes not).

Caveat Emptor

A Latin tag meaning 'let the buyer beware!'.

CBA

Acronym for *cost–benefit analysis*.

CCOHTA

Acronym for the former Canadian Coordinating Office for Health Technology Assessment. See *Canadian Agency for Drugs and Technologies in Health*.

CCR

Acronym for *cost-to-charge ratio*.

CDR

Acronym for *Common Drug Review*.

CEA

Acronym for *cost–effectiveness analysis*. Also see *Cost–Effectiveness Analysis Registry*.

CEAC

Acronym for c*ost–effectiveness acceptability curve*.

CEAF

Acronym for *cost–effectiveness acceptability frontier*.

CEA Registry

See *Center for the Evaluation of Value and Risk in Health*.

CED

Acronym for *Committee to Evaluate Drugs*.

CED/CCO

Acronym for *Committee to Evaluate Drugs/Cancer Care Ontario*.

CEDIT

Acronym for *Comité d'Evaluation et de Diffusion des Innovations Technologiques*.

CEESP

Acronym for *Commission d'Evaluation Economique et de la Santé*.

Ceiling Effect

A phenomenon in which a drug reaches a maximum effect. Increasing its dosage further does not increase *outcome*. It may also be the product of a measurement instrument, as when, for example, a measure of health results in a clustering of measures at the top of the permitted range of scores – nearly everyone can score 100 because the top scores possible in a questionnaire are too easily attained. See Brazier et al. (2004).

Ceiling Ratio

The maximum acceptable (to a decision-maker) *incremental cost–effectiveness ratio*. See, e.g. Briggs (2001).

Censored Data

Runs of data, for example, in a *trial*, can be cut off at various points for various reasons. This is called 'censoring'. In some cases, the data become censored because the trial observation period was shorter than *time to event*. Other reasons include *loss to follow-up* and death from some unrelated cause. See Fenn et al. (1995) and Stewart (2001).

Census Tract

A geographical area defined within a *population* census with well-defined boundaries.

Center for the Evaluation of Value and Risk in Health

This centre at Tufts University hosts the CEA Registry – a comprehensive database of *cost–effectiveness* and *cost–utility analyses* in health care. Its website is available at: https://research.tufts-nemc.org/cear/default.aspx (accessed 27 October 2009).

Centers for Medicare & Medicaid Services

The Centers for Medicare & Medicaid Services (CMS) is a federal agency within the US Department of Health and Human Services. Within it, the *Office of Clinical Standards and Quality Programs* evaluates the success of interventions in Medicare, Medicaid and the *State Children's Health Insurance Program*, it identifies and develops best practices and techniques in quality improvement and oversees implementation of these techniques, develops and collaborates on demonstration projects to test and promote quality measurement and improvement and develops, tests and evaluates, adopts and supports *performance* measurement systems (quality indicators). It was formerly known as the *Health Care Financing Administration*. Its website is available at: http://www.cms.hhs.gov/default.asp? (accessed 27 October 2009).

Centile

Also termed '*percentile*'. When a *continuous variable* is split for convenience into 100 equal-sized chunks of data the cut-off points between them are called centiles. See *Quantile*.

Centre for Reviews and Dissemination

This is the largest research group in the world engaged exclusively in high-quality *systematic reviews* that evaluate the effects of health and social care interventions and the delivery and organization of health care. It operates under the auspices of the National Institute for Health Research and is based at the University of York in the UK. Besides its various publications it is home to three major databases: the *Database of Abstracts of Reviews of Effects* (*DARE*), the *National Health Service Economic Evaluation Database* (*NHS EED*), and the *Health Technology Assessment [HTA] Database*. Its website is available at: http://www.york.ac.uk/inst/crd (accessed 27 October 2009).

Centripetal Bias

Same as *referral bias*.

CEPS

Acronym for *Comité Economique des Produits de Santé*.

CER

Acronym for *control event rate*. Also for comparative effectiveness research.

Certainty Effect

The perhaps (or perhaps not) irrational tendency for people to prefer certain *outcomes* over uncertain ones having equivalent *utility*. See Tversky and Kahneman (1981).

Certainty Equivalent

The certain and sure money or *utility* ('sure thing') that a subject would have to receive to be indifferent between it and a given gamble ('uncertain prospect') is called the gamble's 'certainty equivalent'. The certainty equivalent is less than the expected value of the gamble if an individual has a *diminishing marginal utility* of money income and obeys the *axioms* of *expected utility theory*. This indicates a kind of *risk aversion*. In health economics, the usual experiment contains a certain *outcome*, such as five years of healthy life, and an uncertain prospect consisting of the combination of two or more uncertain outcomes such as probability p of having two years of healthy life and probability $(1 - p)$ of having 15 years of healthy life. P is then experimentally adjusted until there is *indifference* between the certain and the uncertain prospects. One purpose of such experiments is to determine the *value* attached to an outcome, given values attached to the others. See *Standard Gamble*. See, for a health economics application, Feeny and Torrance (1989).

Certificate of Need

A method of regulating hospital *capital* developments that requires state (in the US) agencies to review and approve changes in hospital bed *capacity* and major purchases of equipment above certain *threshold* levels. Abbreviated to CON.

CES Production Function

See *Constant Elasticity of Substitution Production Function*.

Ceteris Paribus

A Latin tag meaning 'other things being equal' or (better) 'other things remaining unchanged'. Cf. *Mutatis Mutandis*.

Chaining

A method of reducing certain inconsistencies in the application of methods such as the *standard gamble* and *time trade-off* of eliciting values for health (or, indeed, other) states. See Rutten-van Molken et al. (1995) and Oliver (2004a).

Chemotherapy

The use of chemicals to treat diseases.

Cherry Picking

Same as *cream skimming*.

Child Health

The demand and supply of child health care is partly rooted in the *household production function* and partly in the *industrial organization* of health care and *health insurance*. For a review see Currie (2000). See, for specific aspects, Grossman (2004, 2008) (drugs and teen sexual behaviour, fast food and obesity respectively). On maternal education levels and child health, see Chen and Li (2009).

Child Health Questionnaire

An instrument specifically designed to measure child and adolescent *health status*. Dimensions include general health, physical functioning, limitations in schoolwork and activities with friends, behaviour, mental health, family cohesion, change in health. See Landgraf (1999).

Chiropody

Treatment of the feet.

Chiropractor

A person licensed to practise chiropractic care using manipulation mechanically to restore displaced bones, especially the vertebrae, to their 'proper' alignment.

Chi-squared Test

χ^2 (chi-squared or 'chi-square') is a statistical test of how well sampled or modelled data 'fit' other data sets, for example, data on sickness and data on exposure to a hazard, or data predicted by a *model* and the actual data. The test is based on the chi-square distribution. The latter is a *skewed* distribution obtained from a variable χ having a normal distribution so that the variable's square (χ^2) has a chi-squared distribution. Formally, it is used to test the *null hypothesis* that two or more *population distributions* do not differ. It is the ratio of the sum of the squared differences between observed (O) and expected (E) *values* to the expected value:

$$\chi^2 = \Sigma \frac{[O_i - E_i]^2}{E_i}$$

There are two well-known versions, the Pearson χ^2 test and the *Mantel-Haenszel test*. See *Statistical Significance*.

Choice Experiments

See *Best-worst Scaling, Discrete Choice Experiments, Revealed Preference, Stated Preference*. For a quick review see Burgess et al (2006).

Choice Modelling

A *conjoint analysis* procedure for estimating *willingness to pay* for services using a weighted set of *attributes* of the services in question. See Hall et al. (2004).

Choice Theory

Any theory that purports to explain or account for or to recommend human choices. *Utility theory* and *expected utility theory* are two examples.

CHQ

Acronym for *Child Health Questionnaire*.

Chronic

Long-lasting. The US National Center for Health Statistics defines it as of three or more months' duration. Cf. *Acute*.

Chronic Care Management

Disease management of people with *chronic diseases*. For an economic overview, see Norton (2000).

Chronic Disease

The *long-term care* of people with *chronic* illnesses differs from that for most *acute* care, having a stronger presence of *for-profit* professional providers on the one hand and unpaid armies of volunteer (often family members) on the other. There is little *insurance* for this group of people. For a review see Norton (2000).

Churning

Refers variously to such practices as the transfer of patients between *long-term care* hospitals and co-located *acute* care hospitals simply for financial gain. It is also used as a synonym for staff turnover. The term originates in financial markets (where it is also referred to as 'twisting') – an unethical practice by brokers to increase their commissions by excessively trading on a client's behalf or by convincing policyholders to drop their old coverage and switch to a new *insurance* policy merely to gain the commission. See Klein et al. (2005).

Citizens Council

This council (note the cowardly absence of an apostrophe in 'Citizens') advises the *National Institute for Health and Clinical Excellence* in England and Wales on critical value judgments associated with *health technology assessments* and *clinical guideline* development. Topics addressed have included: factors to take account of in assessing *need*; whether age of patients should be taken into account in deciding what treatments are available in the *National Health Service*; and whether *orphan drugs* ought to be given special consideration. It is like a *consensus panel* or *focus group* and the membership is designed to represent the broad characteristics of the population of England and Wales. Its website is available at: http://www.nice.org.uk/getinvolved/patientandpublicinvolvement/citizens_council.jsp (accessed 27 October 2009).

Citizens' Jury

A *consensus panel* made up of citizens.

Classical Economics

A view (*model*) of the economy in which all *equilibrating variables* like prices, wages, rents and interest rates are perfectly flexible, all resources are perfectly mobile and fully employed. No (sane) economist believes in the descriptive accuracy of such a state of affairs so the challenge (for sane economists), given the analytical tractability of these assumptions, is to exercise judgment wisely in deciding whether any particular instance can be helpfully modelled using such an abstraction. It is contrasted with the Keynesian approach, in which one or more of these assumptions is not maintained and the possibility arises that the economy can settle in an equilibrium state with high levels of resource (especially labour) unemployment. For an economics textbook sticking closely to 'classical' assumptions see Parkin (2008). For neo-Keynesian syntheses, see Mankiw and Romer (1991) and Woodford (2003).

Clinical Budgets

A procedure whereby physicians or teams of physicians in a given special-ity in hospitals are assigned a fixed sum of money for their activity to cover the expenses of, for example, pharmaceutical prescriptions, use of pathology laboratories, or staff salaries. Proposed in the UK by Griffiths (1983) but apparently never evaluated.

Clinical Decision Support

This is usually used to refer to computer-based information systems that alert physicians to irregular prescribing practices, provide technical references to *clinical trials* etc., assist *diagnosis*, and so on, as well as providing solutions to optimizing strategies in complex treatments such as radiation therapy for cancer. For a *cost–consequences analysis* of such a system, see Cobos et al. (2005).

Clinical Effectiveness

Not, so far as one can tell, a technically well-defined term, though it generally seems to imply clinical interventions that have health-improving effects and negative effects that are insufficient to offset the prospective health gain. Sometimes, however, question-beggingly defined as 'doing the right thing in the right way for the right patient at the right time'. Cf. *Cost-effectiveness*.

Clinical Epidemiology

The methods of *epidemiology* applied to clinical matters, especially in determining the *effectiveness* or *efficacy* of clinical interventions in the treatment of medical conditions.

Clinical Governance

The most widely used definition of clinical governance, as used in the UK *National Health Service*, is: a framework through which NHS organizations are accountable for continually improving the quality of their services and safeguarding high standards of care by creating an environment in which excellence in clinical care will flourish. Introduced in 1998, it was a programme to implement extensive culture change: at the professional level, with individual health care professionals adopting evidence-based 'reflective practice' and patients being placed at the centre of professional thinking; at team level, with teams becoming multidisciplinary groups, where understanding about roles, about sharing information and knowledge and about support for each other would become part of everyday practice; and at the organizational level, with organizations putting in place systems and local arrangements to support teams and assure the quality of care provided with commitment and leadership from the Board down. Its website is available at: http://www.dh.gov.uk/en/Publichealth/Patientsafety/Clinicalgovernance/index.htm (accessed 27 October 2009).

Clinical Guidelines

Clinical guidelines are recommendations on the appropriate treatment and care of patients with specific diseases and conditions. They are usually drawn up by multidisciplinary groups of experts and ought to be based on systematic reviews of the literature. Some, such as those developed by the *National Institute for Health and Clinical Excellence*, take account of *cost-effectiveness*.

Clinical Significance

A *treatment effect* that is large enough to be of practical importance to patients and clinicians. This is not the same as *statistical significance* or *cost-effectiveness*. Its assessment takes account of factors like the size of any *outcome*, the importance of the outcome to the patient or clinician, the severity of the condition being treated and the side-effects of the treatment. *Cost* is sometimes also taken into account. It evidently requires a somewhat subjective (but experienced) judgment.

Clinical Trial

Clinical trials are generally tests of the *efficacy* of medical and surgical interventions in which an *experimental* and a *control group* are compared. With pharmaceuticals, trials go through various *phases*, identifying safety and efficacy beyond the *preclinical trial* stage. Trials use samples of patients drawn from a relevant *population* of patients or people at risk and many are multi-centred and international in nature. They vary greatly in their use of *controls* (for example, some compare the procedure being studied with a *placebo*, others with a common practical *alternative*), and in other aspects of their design, their size, duration, choice of *outcome, endpoint*. See also *Phases of Clinical Trials, Pragmatic Trial, Trial*.

Clinimetrics

The science of measuring clinical phenomena such as signs and symptoms.

Closed-ended Questionnaire

An interview schedule or questionnaire in which the respondent has to choose one of a specific set of predetermined mutually exclusive and exhaustive answers. Cf. *Open-ended Questionnaire*.

Closed-panel HMOs

See *Managed Health Care*.

Closed Physician-hospital Organizations

A US form of integration of physicians and hospitals. See *Vertical Integration*.

Cluster

Groupings of events that are thought not to be the product of mere chance.

Cluster Analysis

Statistical methods and *algorithms* used to categorize or group entities that are similar in relevant respects. The term originates in Tryon (1939). For introductory texts see Everitt et al. (2001) and Romesburg (2004).

Cluster Randomized Trial

A *trial* (not necessarily clinical or of a clinical intervention) in which groups (e.g. individuals in clinics, families, geographical areas) are randomized to different *arms*. Cf. *Cluster Sample*. See, for a non-clinical example in health economics, De Allegri et al. (2008). For an example of an evaluation of costs alongside a cluster trial Gold et al. (2007).

Cluster Sample

A *sample* obtained through a two-stage procedure in which the *population* is divided into mutually exclusive and exhaustive groups from which a random *sample* of groups is then taken. If all the observations in the selected groups are used, the procedure is termed 'one-stage' cluster sampling; if a sample from the selected groups is taken, the procedure is 'two-stage' cluster sampling. Cf. *Stratified Sample, Sub-group Analysis.* See Everitt et al. (2001) and Romesburg (2004).

CMA

Acronym for *cost-minimization analysis* (and Canadian Medical Association).

CMS

Acronym for *Centers for Medicare & Medicaid Services.*

Cobb–Douglas Production Function

The Cobb–Douglas *production function* has the form:

$$Y = AK^{\alpha} L^{\beta},$$

where Y is the output rate A, α and β are positive constants; A is a *variable* broadly representing 'technology' and K and L are *capital* and labour services respectively. If there are *constant returns to scale*, then $\alpha + \beta = 1$. With *increasing/decreasing returns to scale* the sum is >1 and <1 respectively. Named after the US mathematician Charles W. Cobb (1875–1949) and the US economist Paul H. Douglas (1892–1976). See Cobb and Douglas (1928).

Cobb–Douglas Utility Function

A utility function taking the form:

$$U = AX_1^{\alpha}X_2,$$

where the X_i are goods or services. See *Cobb–Douglas Production Function*. See Machnes (1979) for an example. Feldstein (1967) Chapter 4 is a classic first application to hospitals.

Cochrane Collaboration

This is an international network of clinicians, researchers and consumers that develops and maintains a collection of *systematic reviews* and *meta-analyses* of the *effectiveness* and *efficacy* of technologies for treating medical conditions. Named in honour of the Welsh epidemiologist Archie Cochrane (1909–88). Its website is available at: www.cochrane.org/docs/siteindex.htm (accessed 28 October 2009). Similar to the *Campbell Collaboration*.

Coding

Assigning numerical values to *categorical variables*, especially in data processing, or text labels for qualitative data.

Coefficient

A value or algebraic expression that expresses the structure of an equation. For example, in the equation $y = c + ax + bz$, a is the coefficient of x and b is the coefficient of z. c is the constant term.

Coefficient of Concordance

See *Kendall's Coefficient of Concordance*.

Coefficient of Determination

Same as R^2.

Coefficient of Variation

A measure of dispersion or variability relative to the *mean*: the *standard deviation* divided by the *arithmetic mean* and multiplied by 100. Usually referred to as CV.

Cognitive Bias

A form of *bias* encountered in psychological and economic experiments. Some of the more common forms include: *bandwagon effect*, *bias blind spots*, *endowment effect*.

Cognitive Psychology

A relatively new branch of psychology (dating from the late 1960s) that theorizes and investigates mental processes, often using formal experimental methods. Of importance for economists is the way in which cognitive psychologists like Daniel Kahneman and Amos Tversky, both of whom are economics Nobel laureates, have investigated decision-making and choice. *Regret* and *prospect theory* are but two of the significant developments. The Bibliography contains several references to the work of these and other cognitive psychologists.

Cohort

A well-defined group of subjects having a common experience or exposure, which is then followed over time.

Cohort Case-control Study

A *case-control study* conducted within a *cohort study*. Also known as a 'nested case-control study'.

Cohort Study

Study of a *cohort*. A study of a group of patients initially with a characteristic of interest (for example, they have been exposed to a *risk factor*) who are then followed over time as various *exogenous* factors have impact. The cohort of interest may be compared with another group, identical as far as possible in all other respects, without the characteristic of interest (i.e. they have not been exposed to the risk factor) each of which is then followed over time. Also called *follow-up study*. Similar to *longitudinal study*.

Coincident Indicator

A statistical measure of events that coincide with other events. Cf. *Lagging Indicator* and *Leading Indicator*.

Coinsurance

Coinsurance is the practice whereby the insured person shares a fraction of an insured loss with the insurer. For example, the *insurance* policy may require the insured person to pay 10 per cent of the expenses of medical care, with the insurer paying 90 per cent. The sum paid by the insured person is known as a *copayment*, so if the expenses are $1000 and the coinsurance rate is 10 per cent, the copayment is $100. Some policies require *deductibles*, sometimes known as the '*excess*', to be paid. Under this arrangement the insured person pays a fixed sum if health care is needed in any given year and the insurer pays all other expenses (usually with further copayments). Thus, if the deductible is $100 and the coinsurance rate 10 per cent, should the event involve an expense of $1000, the insured person pays $190 ($100 plus $90 copayment).

The effects of deductibles and coinsurance can be shown using the figure, which assumes that individuals are *expected utility* maximizers. The vertical axis shows the price of health care P (assumed – perhaps implausibly – to be set equal to *marginal cost*) and the *marginal value* placed upon health care consumption by an individual. The horizontal axis indicates the rate of consumption of health care (so much per day, week, month, etc.). The diagonal curve, roughly equivalent to the *demand curve*, is the marginal value curve and the horizontal line is the (constant, for ease of exposition) marginal cost curve. In a world of no insurance, the individual faces a price $0P$, at which $0C_1$ care will be consumed when ill. Let the individual (while healthy) consider buying insurance. Suppose neither the individual nor the insurer is in any doubt about the *probability, p*, of illness striking in any period (another tall order). Given that the insured, when uninsured, would consume $\$0PaC_1$ the *actuarially fair premium* is p of this amount. We assume also that there is zero *loading* – that is, the insurer adds

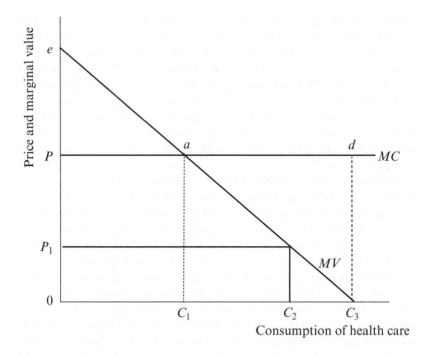

nothing to the premium to cover the administrative costs of operating the insurance service. Now let an individual consider insurance.

They are comparing consumption (if sick) C_1 at a user price P and no premium, with consumption C_3 at a zero price and the payment of a premium. The difference between C_3 and C_1 is due to *moral hazard*. The fair premium payable will be p (the probability of the event occurring) times the cost of care ($0PdC_3$). Given such a premium, whether the individual buys insurance cover will partly depend on whether $Pea > adC_3$. (Note that the individual will definitely buy insurance if the insurer foolishly sets the premium at p times $0PaC_1$, the expense that will be incurred under self-insurance.)

Suppose that cover is purchased: the individual judging that it is worth buying insurance to avoid the financial risk. A policy containing a deductible may still be to the individual's advantage. A deductible does not affect the marginal cost of consumption so, once an individual is insured, they will consume C_3. Suppose there is a deductible of $100. If insurance is taken out, the individual will thus pay $100 and consume C_3 care. If the value of the additional consumption over self-insurance ($C_3 - C_1$) exceeds $100, this will seem a good deal and the care will be purchased. Whether insurance will be purchased, however, depends on the premium combined with the effects of the deductible. The deductible reduces the net benefit of the additional consumption (C_1aC_3) by \$100. So long as the advantage of avoiding the risk of the financial consequences of ill-health remains high enough, the individual will purchase this policy. Plainly, there will be some deductible high enough to overwhelm this advantage and the individual will then self-insure. Deductibles, by reducing the number of small claims (i.e. claims at or below the value of the deductible), may reduce insurance companies' administrative costs and hence enable the *loading* element of the premium to fall.

With coinsurance, the individual pays a percentage of the cost, say $0P_1$, which causes a fall in the amount demanded when insured (from C_3 to C_2) leading to a reduction in the actuarially fair premium as the cost of the care chosen fall. Coinsurance thus can reduce the effect of moral hazard and reduce premiums. Taken to the extreme, let the coinsurance rate approach P. Plainly, at P, there is self-insurance, the premium is zero (and so is moral hazard). The consumer is fully exposed to the financial risk of ill-health. One might expect an optimal coinsurance rate to exist between 0 and P, though it needs to take account of *external effects*. The 'excess' consumption that the coinsurance reduces is in excess only of the optimum seen from the particular individual's viewpoint and, from a wider social viewpoint may not be excessive at all (a *second best* solution is preferable to attempting a first best one). See *Copayment, Insurance*. For effects on utilization and prevention see Ellis et al. (2004) and Trivedi et al. (2008).

Cointervention

In a *randomized trial*, the application of additional procedures to subjects in either *arm* (*experimental* or *control*) of the study.

Collège des Economistes de la Santé

The French health economists' association. Its website is available at: www.ces-asso.org/PagesGB/defaut_gb.htm (accessed 28 October 2009).

Collinearity

This occurs when pairs of *explanatory variables* in a *regression analysis* are correlated. See also *Multicollinearity*.

Comfort Care

Same as *palliative care*.

Comité Economique des Produits de Santé

A committee of the French Ministry of Health responsible for price negotiations with manufacturers of drugs and medical devices.

Comité d'Evaluation et de Diffusion des Innovations Technologiques

CEDIT is a French hospital-based agency for the assessment of medical technologies. Its website is available at: http://cedit.aphp.fr/english/index_present.html (accessed 28 October 2009).

Commercial Bias

A *bias* in some published *cost-effectiveness* research studies that allegedly arises from the source of the studies' research funding. It may also arise from the downright suppression of 'unwanted' scientific results. Cf. *Publication Bias*. See Bero et al. (2007), Bell et al. (2006) and Chalmers (2004). Even thoughtful criticism can provoke storms of antagonistic and strident aggression against the critics from (optimistic) patients and (self-interested) manufacturers. See, for example, the storm over the scepticism expressed over PSA (prostate specific antigen) testing for prostate cancer (Yamey and Wilkes, 2002).

Commission d'Evaluation Economique et de la Santé

A committee of the French *Haute Autorité de Santé* dealing with the *cost-effectiveness* of insured services.

Commissioner

This has a specific meaning in the context of the UK *National Health Service*, where it refers to authorities like *Primary Care Trusts* that are responsible for *commissioning* health care on behalf of local communities. See *Purchaser–Provider Split*.

Commissioning

A term used in the UK *National Health Service* to describe the process through which collective purchasers of health care such as *Primary Care Trusts* reach agreements with providers in an *internal market*. Cf. *Contracting Out*. See Chalkley and Malcomson (2000).

Committee to Evaluate Drugs

An advisory committee to the Ministry of Health and Long Term Care in Ontario, Canada. Its key functions are to evaluate the quality, therapeutic value and cost-effectiveness of drugs for inclusion in publicly funded drug programmes.

Committee to Evaluate Drugs/Cancer Care Ontario

A subcommittee of Ontario's *Committee to Evaluate Drugs* that assesses the cost-effectiveness of cancer drugs.

Common Drug Review

A Canadian organization that is part of the *Canadian Agency for Drugs and Technologies in Health*, which provides participating federal, provincial and territorial drug benefit plans with systematic reviews of the best available clinical evidence, critiques of manufacturer-submitted pharmacoeconomic studies and formulary listing recommendations made by the Canadian Expert Drug Advisory Committee. Its website is available at: http://www.cadth.ca/ (accessed 28 October 2009).

Communicable Disease

An *infectious disease* due to an infectious agent (e.g. bacterium, virus, parasitic worm) or its toxic products that arises through transmission from an infected person, animal, or reservoir (such as swamps, contaminated needles) to a susceptible host, either directly or indirectly through an intermediate plant or animal host, *vector*, or the inanimate environment. See *External Effect*. See R.D. Smith et al. (2004) for an economics application.

Communitarianism

This is the doctrine that individuals' *welfare* cannot be properly understood or measured without regard to their membership of a community and the roles they play in it. Thus, it is not merely the health *outcomes* of, say, care in the community that matter but also the *process utility* of those participating in providing it. Since *extra-welfarism* places no limits on the nature of *well-being* or its sources that are candidates for economic evaluation, communitarian concerns may readily be embraced by it. The principal difference between the two is that communitarianism stipulates the categories of welfare that are to be taken into account whereas extra-welfarism is eclectic as to categories but specific in stipulating an authority (such as a minister of health) to do the stipulating. See Mooney (2005).

Community-based Health Insurance

This includes a variety of *non-profit* health care financing arrangements, including the use of local community health funds, mutual health organizations, rural *health insurance*. See *Insurance*. See Dror and Preker (2002). A review is Ekman (2004).

Community Medicine

The study of health and disease in communities. The underlying discipline to support *public health medicine*.

Community Rating

Setting health care *insurance* premia according to the utilization of a broad population (for example, one defined by employer type or geography). Cf. *Experience Rating*.

Comorbidity

The coexistence in a patient of a disease or diseases in addition to the condition that is the object of study or treatment.

Comparative Advantage

This exists when a firm or a jurisdiction can produce a good or service with less forgone *output* (*opportunity cost*) than another. Cf. *Absolute Advantage*, with which comparative advantage is often confused, even by economists. Call centres are increasingly located in India not because their location there involves fewer *inputs* for any given number of calls (absolute advantage) but because the lost output from using people in this way rather than in another is smaller than it would be in, say, most European countries or North America. Some countries have an absolute advantage in producing nearly everything but it is impossible for them to have a comparative advantage in everything. Conversely, some countries have an absolute advantage in virtually nothing but they too necessarily have a comparative advantage in something. Given certain assumptions, total world production increases, and therefore consumption possibilities increase, if countries specialize according to their comparative, not absolute, advantages. Of course, how these gains from specialization are shared is another matter. Whether the *efficiency* gains exist in practice requires a judgment about *second best*, in view of the prevalence of tariffs and other barriers to trade. Comparative advantage forms the basis of most economic arguments for free trade.

Comparative Effectiveness Research

Another name for *health technology assessment*.

Comparative Health Systems

The general term used to describe studies that compare the various health care systems (though the word 'care' is almost invariably dropped) that exist internationally. On parallel systems within jurisdictions, see Besley et al. (1998) for the UK and Hurley et al. (2008) for Canada. For international comparisons, see Besley and Gouveia (1994), Besley et al. (1998), Evans et al. (2000), Tandon et al. (2000). Culyer et al. (1982) is an early study of some principles for making international comparisons.

Comparative Price Level

See *Purchasing Power Parity*.

Comparative Statics

This is one way of doing economics, which compares states of *equilibrium* that are predicted to come about in response to shocks to (disturbances in) *parameters*. The other main way of doing economics is *dynamics*, in which the focus is on the process of change as people react to disequilibria that arise from such shocks and disturbances. Cf. *Dynamics, General Equilibrium*.

Comparator

One or more alternative options or technologies with which another is compared in *cost–effectiveness analyses* and related methods.

Comparison Axiom

An *axiom* that underpins virtually all economic theories of choice, *viz.* that desired entities can be compared and traded-off. In utilitarian *choice theory*, the axiom is usually represented as 'completeness', that is, one entity is either preferred to another, or the other is preferred to it, or the subject is indifferent between them. See *Indifference Curve, Utility*. Cf. *Protected Values*.

Compensable

An unattractive North American neologism for 'compensatable', chiefly found in research related to workers' compensation and *insurance*.

Compensating Variation

The compensating variation in income is the minimum amount of money that has to be given to an individual *after* a price rise to make them as well off in their own judgment as they were before the change. Similarly, in the case of a price fall, it is the maximum amount of money the individual would be willing to pay after the change that would leave them as well off as they were before the change. It is a measure of welfare change introduced by Sir John Hicks (1904–89) and its main use lies in *cost–benefit analysis* and related techniques for estimating the benefits of public investments. Cf. *Equivalent Variation, Kaldor–Hicks Criterion, Willingness to Accept, Willingness to Pay*. For health economics experiments investigating willingness to pay, see O'Brien and Gafni (1996).

Compensating Wage Differential

The idea that wage differentials compensate workers for undertaking relatively dangerous or unpleasant jobs. See Dorman (1996) for a review of the literature on dangerous work, wage differentials and the implied value placed on lives (by those living them).

Compensation Test

This is a way of measuring the desirability of a proposal for change. If the people who are expected to gain from the change are willing to compensate those who lose (that is, fully compensate them such that they are at the least indifferent between accepting and not accepting the change) then the change is judged to be *welfare* enhancing. An alternative test is to discover whether the expected losers can compensate (just) the potential gainers for going without the proposed change; if so, then the change is not welfare enhancing. Or one might apply both tests. These are ways of trying to identify *Pareto improvements* and *potential Pareto improvements* in *social welfare*. See also *Compensating Variation, Equivalent Variation, Kaldor–Hicks Criterion* and *Scitovsky Criterion*. See Reinhardt (1998).

Competition

In economics, there is a variety of descriptors of types of market competition, most of which relate to competition amongst producers or sellers of goods and services: 'perfect', 'imperfect', 'monopolistic', 'duopolistic' 'oligopolistic' are the five most likely to be encountered. Perfect competition (sometimes 'atomistic competition') is the modelling of a situation in which there are sufficiently large numbers of producers for the activity of any one not to affect the market price. It is sometimes also called *price-taking*. Imperfect competition refers to a situation in which the activity of any one of several producers will affect the price. *Monopoly* stands at the end of the spectrum farthest from perfect competition, and refers to a situation in which there is a single seller. A *duopoly* exists when there are but two producers. An *oligopoly* exists when there are just a few. The idea that there is a direct link between the number of sellers and the 'amount' of competition is not a very good one. It is usually more insightful to consider the nature of the influence that one producer may have on another, or on consumers or employees, and the ease of access to information about competitors' activities and plans, than simply to consider numbers. Nonetheless, within broad bands, numbers of producers in similar fields do form the basis for measuring the *concentration ratio* of an industry. See also *Cartel*.

There can also be degrees of competition between buyers. For example, one of the arguments for concentrating purchasing power for health care in the hands of a *managed health care* organization, or the state at regional or national level, is that this creates substantial influence over the prices that can be obtained from producers and the wages and salaries that must be paid to health service professionals. When buyers are sufficiently large in relation to the market so as to affect price, the condition is termed *monopsony*.

Economists tend to regard competition with favour, though there are some markets in which competition can be extremely damaging, of which the most important is probably the *insurance* market. See *Risk Selection, Yardstick Competition*. For competition studies in the hospital sector see Dranove et al. (1993), Keeler et al. (1999), Kessler and McClellan (2000) and Gaynor and Vogt (2000, 2003). For conditions under which competition may enhance *efficiency*, see Schut and Van de Ven (2005).

Complement

A good or service whose *demand* rises or falls as the price of another good falls or rises is said to be a complement. The *cross-elasticity of demand* is negative. Infliximab and methodextrate, two drugs used in combination in the treatment of rheumatoid arthritis, are an example. So are golf clubs and balls. They tend to be goods that are used together. Cf. *Substitutes*. Examples of empirical studies of unhealthy complementarities are: Dee (1999), Farrelly et al. (2001) and Pudney (2003).

Complete Case Analysis

A method of dealing with *incomplete data*. It involves using only complete cases, with no imputed values to missing data, with the risk of *bias* if the sample with omissions is not representative.

Complete Market

A market is said to be theoretically 'complete' when individuals can obtain *insurance* against any future time and state of the world.

Completeness

One of the standard *axioms* of *choice theory*. It requires that an individual either prefers entity *A* to entity *B*, or *B* to *A*, or that the individual is indifferent between the two. See *Utility*.

Complexity

In *health technology assessments* some technologies may be elusive in their nature (for example, VIHASA: values in health care – a spiritual approach [to staff training]), or multi-institutional (like many public health programmes) or have a pathway from cause to ultimate effect that is tortuous and not well understood, or are such as to engage a less than impartial commitment from analysts. In such cases, and from other sources of complexity as well, health economists have been seeking to develop non-trivial methods for assessing *effectiveness* and *cost-effectiveness*. See, for example, Byford and Sefton (2003) and Shiell and McIntosh (2008).

Compliance

The extent to which patients follow the health advice they receive, despite the fact that in everyday parlance 'comply' is more usually associated with 'instruction' than 'advice'. Yet another form is the extent to which health care professionals follow professional guidelines on best practice. For an economic analysis of the value of devoting resources to improving the implementation of good practice, see Fenwick et al. (2008).

Comprehensiveness

A characteristic of a health care system that is commonly desired or some-times (as in Canada) required by statute. It relates to the range of services that are or ought to be provided, typically including all those deemed 'medically necessary' (which is not equivalent to 'cost-effective'; nor is it an unambiguous idea). It usually covers *in-patient* and *out-patient* care, and community-based services including pharmacy, dentistry and *ophthalmology* services. Cf. *Universality*.

Computable General Equilibrium Models

These *models* are descendants of *input–output models*, based on a *matrix* of the *flows* of goods and services between all the sectors of the economy and all flows of *factors of production*, with *elasticities* that describe the quantitative empirical responsiveness of sectors if any component should change. They have been used in health economics to explore the conse-quences of health care interventions on non-health sectors. See *General Equilibrium*. See, e.g. R.D. Smith et al. (2005, 2009) and Rutten and Reed (2009).

CON

Acronym for *certificate of need*.

Concavity

A property of a *function*. A differentiable function is said to be concave (sometimes 'concave downwards') if, in comparing two points, *a* and *b*, the first derivative is falling. Thus, in the figure, the function relating *health* to *utility* is concave, implying that additional equal increments of health have a decreasing *marginal utility* to whoever is assessing their utility. A function may be convex (or concave upward) when the reverse applies. It may also be initially concave and then convex (or vice versa), when the point at which the change occurs is termed the 'point of inflexion'.

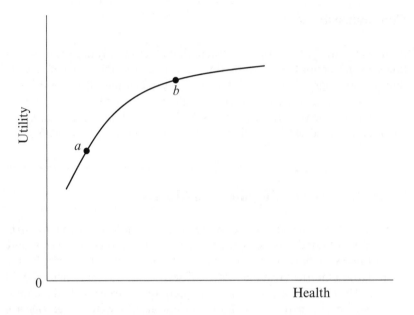

Concentration Curve

See *Concentration Index*.

Concentration Index

In health economics, a concentration index is a means of quantifying the degree of income-related inequality in health. Where there is no income-related inequality, the concentration index is zero. The concentration curve in the diagram shows the relationship between the cumulative percentage of the *population* or *sample* on the horizontal axis, ranked by income and beginning with the poorest on the left, and the cumulative percentage of ill-health (ranked by, say, self-reported *health status*) on the vertical axis beginning with the sickest at the bottom. The concentration index is defined as twice the area between the concentration curve and the line of equality (the 45° line running from the south-west corner to the north-east corner). The convention is that the index takes a negative value when the curve lies above the line of equality, indicating disproportionate concentration of ill-health among the poor, and a positive value when it lies below the line of equality. Cf. *Lorenz Curve*. See Kakwani (1977). O'Donnell et al. (2008) Chapter 7 is an introduction.

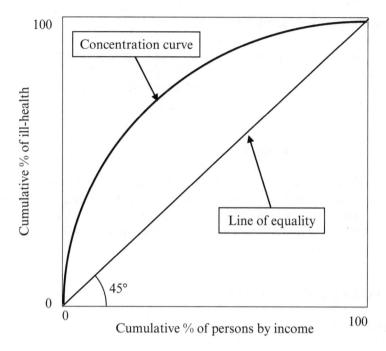

Concentration Ratio

The share of the market (usually by sales or employment) occupied by the largest firms (typically four). An *n*-firm concentration ratio is the ratio for an industry of *n* firms. See also *Herfindahl Index*. See Dranove et al. (1993) for an application to Californian hospitals.

Concept Mapping

A concept map is a diagram for identifying and linking ideas and for gathering and sharing information. It has 'nodes' that contain a concept, activity or question and links to other nodes. The links have descriptive labels and an arrow if there is an obvious direction of flow. It is widely used as a means of brainstorming or creating coherence in managerial teams in health services.

Concurrent Review

A review of a patient's records to determine their *need* for *continuing care*.

Conditional Independence

Two random *variables* are said to be conditionally independent in the presence of another variable when the joint *probability* of the two, given the third, is equal to the product of their individual *conditional probabilities*.

Conditional Probability

The *probability* of an event occurring given that another event has also occurred or a particular state of the world exists. For example, the probability that a person actually has cancer given that they are a member of a *population* group that has tested positive. Cf. *Unconditional Probability*. See *Bayesian Method*.

Condition of the Commons

See *Tragedy of the Commons*.

Confidence Box

A graphical way of representing *confidence intervals* in cost–*effectiveness* or *cost–utility analyses*. Confidence boxes show where a specified percentage (e.g. 95 per cent) of the data in a *scatter plot* will lie. Consider a health care technology that is costlier but also more effective than its *comparator*, so we are in the north-east quadrant of the *cost–effectiveness plane* shown in the figure. The slope of rays such as *a* and *b* show the *incremental cost–effectiveness ratio* ($\Delta C/\Delta E$) of the technology under investigation relative to an *alternative* (*control*). The steeper the ray, the greater the *marginal cost* per marginal gain in *output* compared with the comparator. The upper and lower confidence limits of incremental cost are plotted against the upper and lower confidence limits of the *effectiveness* measure in the form of a box (shaded). Rays *a* and *b* are the outer limits of the confidence interval (usually 95 per cent). Cf. *Confidence Ellipse*. For one of many examples in the cost–effectiveness field, see Joore et al. (2003).

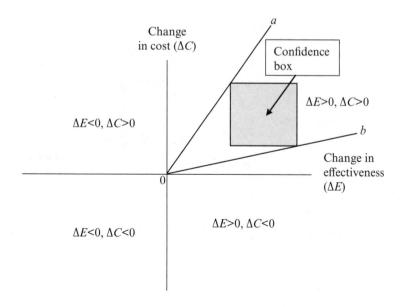

Confidence Ellipse

A graphical way of representing *confidence intervals* in *cost–effectiveness* or *cost–utility analyses*. Confidence ellipses show where a specified percentage (e.g. 95 per cent) of the data in a *scatter plot* will lie. Consider a health care technology that is costlier but also more effective than its (single) *comparator*, so we are in the north-east quadrant of the *cost–effectiveness plane* shown in the figure. The slope of rays such as a' and b' show the *incremental cost–effectiveness ratio* ($\Delta C/\Delta E$) of the technology under investigation relative to an alternative (*control*). The steeper the ray, the greater the *marginal cost* per marginal gain in *output* compared with the comparator. The upper and lower confidence limits of incremental cost are plotted against the upper and lower confidence limits of the *effectiveness* measure in the form of an ellipse (inside the *confidence box*). Rays a' and b' are the outer limits of the confidence interval (usually 95 per cent) and will lie within the rays defined by the corners of the confidence box. Confidence ellipses are visual indicators of *correlation*: they are stretched out from south-west to north-east if there is a positive *covariance* between ΔC and ΔE. The confidence ellipse is more circular when two variables are uncorrelated. For one of many applications see Angus et al. (2003). Cf. *Confidence Box, Cost–Effectiveness Acceptability Curve*.

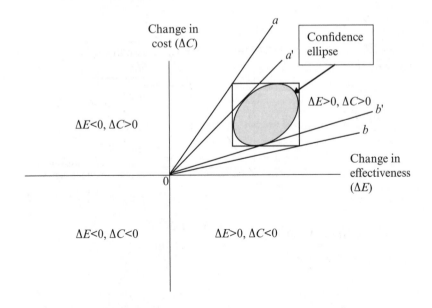

Confidence Ellipsoid

Same (roughly speaking) as *confidence ellipse*.

Confidence Interval

The range of values within which a *population parameter* such as the population *mean* or *variance* is expected to lie with a given degree of confidence. The convention is to set the 'confidence' level at 95 per cent, in the (*frequentist*) sense that, with repeated sampling, 95 per cent of the values will lie in that range. See *Cost–Effectiveness Plane, Confidence Ellipse, Fieller's Theorem*. But see Stinnett and Mullahy (1998).

Confidence Limits

The upper and lower bounds of a *confidence interval*.

Confidence Profile Method

A *Bayesian* type of *meta-analysis*.

Confirmation Bias

A *bias* taking the form of an unfortunate tendency for scientists sometimes to seek to confirm their predictions or expectations rather than refute them.

Confounder

See *Confounding*.

Confounding

Confounding occurs when an effect is attributed to an *independent variable* X when in fact it is due to an omitted (confounding) variable B, which is correlated with both X and the *outcome* (*dependent variable*) of interest. For example, higher socioeconomic status is strongly associated with both more frequent use of hormone replacement therapy and lower risk of coronary heart disease. The association between HRT and lower CHD has been erroneously interpreted as causal (Humphrey et al., 2002). Also known as an '*extraneous variable*'. See *Omitted Variable Bias*.

Conjoint Analysis

A range of techniques used to elicit individuals' *preferences* and *willingness to pay* for health states, health services or particular features of services. Within this range are such methods as *card sorts, choice modelling, discrete choice analysis, hierarchical choice, pairwise comparisons, stated preference* analysis and *trade-off matrices*. A variety of hypothetical questions or vignettes is formulated, each varying in its mix of *attributes* (which have to be considered 'conjointly' by the subject) and subjects are asked to give discrete answer (yes/no or 'I prefer option A', etc.). *Regression analysis* is used to estimate the relative strength of preferences for attributes. In a study of the quality of a fertility service, for example, the attributes to do with quality might include attitudes of staff to the patient (uncaring/unsympathetic; caring/sympathetic), continuity of contact with staff (see same staff; see many different staff), time on waiting list for first IVF attempts (1, 3, 6, 18, 36 months), cost to patient per attempt ($0, $750, $1500, $2500, $3000), chances of taking home a baby (5, 10, 15, 25, 35 per cent), follow up support (yes; no). The resultant scores are usually treated as *utilities*. *Willingness to pay* estimates are also sometimes made. See also

Adaptive Conjoint Analysis, Discrete Choice Analysis, Quality-adjusted Life-year, Utility Measurement. The inventors were Luce and Tukey (1964). See, for examples in health economics, Neumann and Johannesson (1994) and Ryan and Hughes (1997).

Conjunction Fallacy

The error of supposing that a joint *probability* can be higher than the probability of the separate individual probabilities. Tversky and Kahneman (1983) illustrate it thus: Linda is 31 years old, single, outspoken, and very bright. She majored in philosophy. As a student, she was deeply concerned with issues of discrimination and social justice, and also participated in anti-nuclear demonstrations. Which is the more probable:

(1) Linda is a bank teller;
(2) Linda is a feminist;
(3) Linda is a bank teller and is active in the feminist movement?

Tversky and Kahneman (1983) report that 85 percent of respondents indicated that (3) is more likely than (1), thereby assigning a higher probability to the conjunction than its constituents. In describing and explaining behaviour, it seems wise to allow for such widespread departures from '*rationality*'; when prescribing what ought to be done, however, the proper course is less clear.

Consecutive Sampling

Recruiting subjects as they become available. The potential *bias* inherent in this method is plain. Cf. *Convenience Sample, Purposive Sample, Random Sample.* For an example, see Whetten et al. (2006).

Consensus Conference

Similar to *consensus panel.*

Consensus Panel

A panel (sometimes called a consensus conference, focus group or citizens' jury) of people selected for their expertise and other characteristics deemed to be relevant, which is invited to answer one or more questions about which there may be considerable doubt or disagreement on the part of a parent body in order to see if a consensual view can be reached. It is similar to a focus group or citizens' jury, though the achievement of a consensus is not necessarily an intended outcome in these other cases. Panelists will usually have available to them the consensus questions, one or more *systematic reviews*, summaries of the available evidence and the ability to interview invited experts and other stakeholders as witnesses. There may be a facilitator. The conferences usually take place over two or three days. See *Citizens Council*.

Consequences

A term used in *cost–effectiveness analysis* and *cost–consequences analysis* to describe the future effects of a decision. It embraces all the effects that may be deemed relevant, usually classified into *costs* and *benefits*, some being in monetary and others, such as *health* itself, in non-monetary forms. For one of many examples see Lacey et al. (1999).

Consequentialism

The idea that the ethical merit or otherwise of any proposed course of action (for example, changing the financial terms of *access* to health care, or the inclusion of a drug on the list of approved *benefits* in an *insurance* plan) is to be evaluated in terms of its *consequences* (as distinct, say, from the motives of those advocating it, or because one is believed to have a duty to adopt it, or because God commands it). Cf. *Deontology, Utilitarianism*. See Scheffler (1988).

Consistent Estimate

An estimate that converges on the true *parameter value* as the *sample* size approaches infinity.

Constant Absolute Risk Aversion

See *Absolute Risk Aversion*.

Constant Elasticity of Substitution Production Function

Commonly referred to as a CES *production function*. A type of production function having the property that the ratio between proportionate changes and prices and proportionate changes in quantities is constant. In the case of two *inputs*, the form is:

$$Y = A[\alpha K\rho + \beta L\rho]^{(1/\rho)},$$

Where Y is the output rate, A, α and β are constants; A is a *variable* broadly representing 'technology' and K and L are *capital* and labour services respectively. ρ is constant and is a measure of the substitutability of labour for capital services. The *elasticity* of substitution (σ) is $1/(1 + \rho)$. Since ρ is constant, then so is σ; hence the name. If $\rho = 0$ then the function becomes a *Cobb–Douglas production function* and $\sigma = 1$. See *Production Function*. See, in the context of investment in health, Heckman (2007).

Constant Elasticity of Substitution Utility Function

Same as *constant elasticity of substitution production function* with consumption replacing production. See Koç (2004) for an example.

Constant Elasticity of Substitution Welfare Function

Same as *constant elasticity of substitution production function* with *utility* replacing production. For an application in health economics see Dolan and Tsuchiya (2009).

Constant Prices

The use of the prices of a given year in calculating *costs* and *benefits* in other years so as to eliminate the effect of inflation. This is usually done by means of a *price index* or price *deflator*. An example of such an index (deflator) is P_1Q_1/P_0Q_1, where P_1 is a set of prices at date 1, Q_1 is a set of commodities at that date and P_0 is the set of prices for those same commodities at an earlier date. See *Fisher's Ideal Index, Laspeyres Index, Paasche Price Index*. For a review of medical care price index construction see Berndt et al. (2000).

Constant Proportional Time Trade-off

An assumption made in the construction of *quality-adjusted life-years* (QALYs). Subjects must be willing to sacrifice a constant proportion of future years of life for a given QALY gain. First identified by Pliskin et al. (1980). But see Bleichrodt and Johannesson (1997a).

Constant Returns to Scale

A feature of *production functions*. A production function exhibits constant returns to scale if increasing all *factors of production* (*inputs*) in the same proportion increases *outputs* by the same proportion. The way in which output responds to changes in a single *input* is not the same as the response, here described, to a change of scale, where all inputs vary. See *Law of Variable Proportions, Production Function*. For a practical example, see Lohrisch (2006).

Constrained Maximum

The maximum value attainable by a *variable*, like health gain, consistent with satisfying one or more side-conditions, like spending no more than the budget allocated for the purpose.

Constrained Minimum

The minimum value attained by a *variable*, like health care *costs*, consistent with satisfying one or more side-conditions, like maintaining a given level of *health* in the community.

Constraint

The limits (real and imaginary; budgetary, resource, political, etc.) on what it is possible to accomplish. Careful examination of imagined constraints often results in their being seen to be moveable, though usually at some cost. Releasing decision-makers from the curse of unimaginative thinking about constraints is one of the potentially great *benefits* of well-conducted *economic appraisals*. See *Budget Constraint, Health Frontier, Production Possibilities Curve*.

Construct

A notional measure of something that is not directly measurable, such as *'quality of life'* or 'severity of disease'.

Constructed Preferences

Preferences are not always revealed easily through experiments or actual behaviour. In many cases, especially when there is *complexity* of some sort or considerable *uncertainty*, preferences are constructed in the process of their being 'revealed'. In health economics, one situation in which this is likely to occur is when people are weighing up small changes in low probabilities of notable consequences. See Payne et al. (1999) and Brazier et al. (2007).

Construct Validity

A *construct* that correlates well with other conventionally trusted measures of the underlying concept and that discriminates as one would expect (i.e. in ways predicted by theory) between cases having different characteristics is said to have construct validity. For example, a measure of *'health'* that had construct validity would *correlate* inversely with specific indicators of illness and incapacity. The validity of a construct might well vary according to the context in which it is being used. Cf. *Convergent Validity, Criterion Validity, Discriminant Validity, External Validity, Face Validity, Internal Validity, Predictive Validity, Test-retest Validity*. See, for a health economics application, Philips et al. (2006a).

Consultation Fee

A money charge made for consulting a doctor. See *Fee-for-service*.

Consumer

A buyer of goods or services for their own personal satisfaction rather than for use as *inputs* in a household production process. A term better not applied to 'patient' with regard to the latter's use of health services.

Consumer-directed Health Plans

Same as *consumer-driven health care*.

Consumer-driven Health Care

This is care provided under catastrophic *health insurance* plans that allow members to use personal *Health Savings Accounts*, *Health Reimbursement Arrangements* or *Flexible Spending Accounts* to meet their routine health care expenses directly. See Gates et al. (2008) and Rowe et al. (2008).

Consumer Good

An *economic good* used by households for final consumption (i.e. not for selling on or for investment purposes).

Consumer Price Index

A measure of the weighted *price* change over a period of time of a bundle of goods typically purchased by consumers. See *Price Index*.

Consumer Sovereignty

This is not a technical term in economics. It refers to the idea that consumers ultimately determine (often that they ought to determine) the goods and services that are produced, their quantities, qualities and availability in time and space. The nearest idea to it that is used in (welfare) economics is the idea of individual welfare, in which the welfare of all individuals, however (employers, workers, owners, investors, etc. and not just consumers) is taken as comprising the welfare of society, but it is a vulgar error to muddle this concept with 'consumer sovereignty'. It is also sometimes used to mean that consumers are the only (or possibly ought to be the only) judges of their own welfare. See *Pareto Optimality*.

Consumer's Surplus

The difference between what a consumer pays for a good or service and the maximum they would pay rather than go without it. In the first figure below showing a *demand curve* (here linear), it is the shaded area bounded by the demand (*marginal valuation*) curve, the vertical axis and the horizontal line at *P*. Under particular assumptions it is the maximum that someone will pay for the right to purchase the good at price *P* or the minimum they must receive to forgo that privilege. In the second figure, imagine the consumer being constrained to purchase under circumstances where they must reveal the maximum they would pay for a small amount of a good rather than none. This is indicated by the first tall rectangle in the second figure. Then they are asked the maximum they would pay for a second small increment, indicated by the second rectangle, and so on. Now imagine that the increments become increasingly tiny and we consider all such increments up to the marginal valuation that equates to the going price.

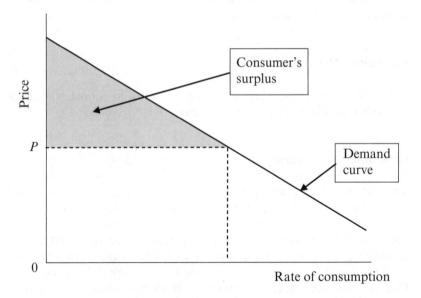

The whole of the area below the demand curve up to that rate of consumption is thus the maximum the individual is willing to pay, the rectangle below the price line is the amount that would actually be paid in a market (price times quantity) and the difference between them is consumer's surplus (shaded in the first figure). Practical estimation of consumer's surplus usually makes the assumption that the relevant section

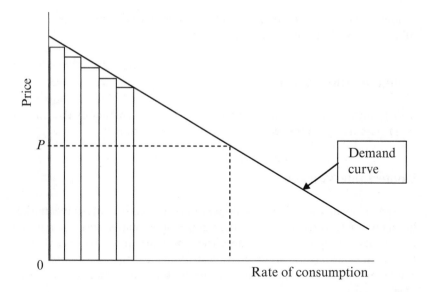

of a demand curve, when one has but two observations, is continuous and linear. See *Compensation Test, Producer's Surplus, Willingness to Pay*. See Keeler (1995) for a health economics example.

Consumption Cost

Usually considered to be the predicted future costs of a survivor's ordinary consumption following a medical intervention. It has been a matter of controversy as to whether such *survivor costs* (and also expected future unrelated medical costs) ought to be included in a *cost–effectiveness analysis* of the initial intervention. See Nyman (2004).

Consumption Rate of Interest

The *rate of interest* at which people are willing to defer present for future consumption after *indirect taxes* on goods have been paid.

Contagious Disease

A *communicable disease* transmitted through physical contact (touching) and infected water droplets. Often used much more loosely as a virtual synonym for '*infectious disease*' and hence inclusive of airborne, insect and other *vectors* of transmission. See *External Effect*.

Contamination Effect

This occurs in *randomized controlled trials* when members of the *control group* gain access to the treatment outside the experiment.

Contestable Market

A market in which *barriers to entry* are low. A perfectly contestable market has a complete absence of barriers to entry: no special *licences*, *patents* or copyrights, no high *fixed costs*, and where no marketing barriers (whether legal or illegal) have been created by incumbent firms. See *Competition*. See Ham (1996) for some reflections on the UK experience with contestable markets.

Context Dependency

The idea that choices are affected by the ways in which they are framed and by the context in which choices are being made. Cf. *Framing Effect*. For a health example see Lacy et al. (2006).

Contingent Trade-off

A contingent trade-off occurs when, in an economic experiment, a subject's *revealed preferences* are dependent (contingent) on the method used to elicit their preferences. It entails a violation of *procedural invariance*, which is a fundamental underpinning of most welfare economics and a good deal of economic experiments for preference elicitation. See Tversky et al. (1988).

Contingent Valuation

Contingent valuation is so called because it is a survey method for eliciting valuations of goods or services by which individuals are asked to state their maximum *willingness to pay* or the minimum *willingness to accept* going without, contingent on a specific hypothetical scenario (like making a market purchase) and a description of options available. It is also known as the *stated preference* method, because the method asks people to state their values directly (and hypothetically), rather than inferring *revealed preference* values from actual choices. A related procedure that depends more on inferring values from the characteristics of services is *conjoint analysis*. Costs are rarely compared with the value of effects. See *Cost–Benefit Analysis, Willingness to Accept, Willingness to Pay*. See Diener et al. (1998), Smith (2003) and Donaldson et al. (2006).

Continuing Care

Similar to *intermediate care*.

Continuity

In general, the idea is of a kind of smoothness in a *function* – no sudden discontinuities. See *Continuous Variable*. More specifically in economics, continuity is one of the standard *axioms* of *utility* theory. It requires that there is an *indifference curve* such that all points to its north-east are preferred to all points to its south-west.

Continuous Time Model

A *model* in which the decision points, *outcomes* or other events occur continuously through time rather than at specific dates, like 'year end'. Cf. *Discrete Time Model*. Examples in health economics include Forster (1989) and Ehrlich and Chuma (1990).

Continuous Variable

A numerical *variable* that can in principle take the value of any real number within an interval. Of course, practical measurement constraints may in practice mean that not all possible values are actually observed. Examples include temperature, blood pressure, cholesterol concentration, labour costs, waiting time. *Demand curves* are generally drawn as continuous or empirically modelled as though they were continuous. Cf. *Discrete Variable*. See *Continuity*.

Contract Curve

A *locus* in an *Edgeworth Box* showing a series of *Pareto-optimal* distributions of a fixed quantity of two goods between two people, each *distribution* being an allocation of the two goods between the two people that can be reached by (assumed costless) contracting (trading). The contract curve is found by connecting the tangencies of the two individuals' *indifference curves*. In the figure, the curve $0_A 0_B$ is the contract curve. Selection of an optimal point on the contract curve requires *value judgments* regarding the distribution of *welfare* between the two individuals.

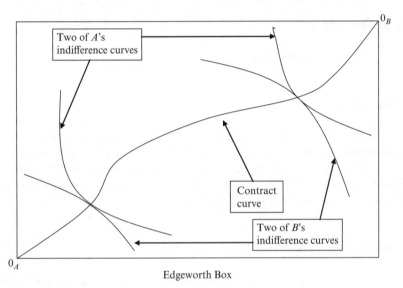

Edgeworth Box

Contracting Out

The sourcing and purchase of a service for an *agency*'s clients from an external organization. Cf. *Health Maintenance Organizations*, *Managed Health Care*. For health economics examples see Chalkley and Malcomson (2000), Duggan (2004) and Chalkley (2006). For some developing country context see Palmer and Mills (2006).

Contracts for Health Care

In several health care systems a distinction is made between community purchasers of health care on behalf of a (usually geographic) *population* and providers in order that they may contract with one another to determine the services to be provided. These arrangements have been most studied in the UK. See Chalkley and Malcomson (2000), Duggan (2004), Chalkley (2006) and Chalkley and McVicar (2008).

Control

In *longitudinal studies* or other kinds of *trial*, a control is an individual without the disease being investigated or one not receiving the treatment whose effects are being investigated, or someone without the *baseline characteristics* of interest being studied in a *cohort study*.

Control Event Rate

The percentage or proportion of events that occur in a *control group*.

Control Group

A group of people acting for purposes of comparison as *controls* in a *trial, cohort study* or economic experiment. Same as control *arm*.

Controlled Before and After Study

A non-randomized *before and after study* having a *control group* with similar characteristics as the *experimental group*. Data are collected for both groups before and after the intervention in the intervention group. See Gravelle et al. (2007b).

Controlled Trial

In *trials*, one group of subjects (the *experimental group* or *experimental arm*) receives an experimental drug, while another group (the *control group* or control *arm*) receives the usual treatment for the disease, another treatment of interest, or a placebo. The control group provides a standard against which the experimental observations may be evaluated and minimizes *bias*. For example, dividing subjects into two groups, the experimental arm and the control arm, means that any *selection bias* will be present in both arms and thus the danger of inferring an effect where there is in fact none is reduced. Randomization in this way ideally means that both arms are subject to the same external *confounding* effects, the only difference between them being the active intervention

Convenience Sample

A *sample* that uses the most readily available subjects and is an easy method for obtaining them (for example, the first 20 patients to enter the clinic on a particular day). Not recommended as the potential *bias* is plain! Also called 'grab' or 'opportunity' sampling. Cf. *Consecutive Sampling, Purposive Sample, Random Sample.*

Convergence

The tendency for different systems of health care, or even whole economies, to become more similar in the challenges they confront and in the ways they solve resource allocation problems.

Convergent Validity

This is an aspect of *construct validity*, whereby a measure is correlated with other measures that are deemed to be acceptable empirical measures of the underlying concept.

Conversion Factor

See *Resource-based Relative Value Scale.*

Convexity

For a general sense, see *Concavity*. More specifically, in economics this is one of the *axioms* of *utility* theory. It stipulates that *indifference curves* are convex (= concave 'upward'). See *Utility.*

Coordinating Centre for Health Technology Assessments

The academic group at the University of Southampton in the UK that manages the *National Health Service*'s *Health Technology Assessment* Programme. The website of its academic parent organization is available at: http://www.netscc.org.uk/ (accessed 28 October 2009).

Cooperative Game

A type of game in *game theory* in which the players may cooperate before choosing what each will do. Cf. *Non-cooperative Game*. See Clark (1995) for one of very few applications in health economics.

Copayment

An arrangement whereby an insured person pays a particular percentage of any bills for health services received, the insurer paying the remainder (Cf. *Deductible*). See *Coinsurance*. For effects on utilization and prevention see Ellis et al. (2004) and Trivedi et al. (2008). It seems that most purchasers of *health insurance* (especially the elderly) are very ill-informed about the size and impact of copayments, which would seem to make them poor instruments for cost control. See e.g. Davidson et al. (1992) and Harris and Keane (1999).

Core

The core of an economy (if one exists) is a state in which (1) no subset of members of the community can improve upon their position (as they see it) through trade or production and (2) which is also a *Pareto optimum*.

Core Services

Although it is not a technical term in health economics, this term is often used to describe the services to which members of a *health insurance* scheme are entitled, or those that are included in a publicly insured bundle of care.

Corner Solution

A corner solution is a choice *outcome* that entails the individual being on a *constraint* such as a *budget constraint* at the point at which the constraint touches one of the axes. It arises from the inability to purchase negative quantities of a good or service or from the absence of negative prices. It is a limiting case in which the usual maximizing conditions, like *marginal value* being equal to price, cannot apply. The *indifference curve* is not tangential to the budget constraint. Similar results can be obtained in labour supply decisions and *production functions*. Cf. *Interior Solution*. See Leung et al. (2004) for an example from health economics where corner solutions are extensively discussed.

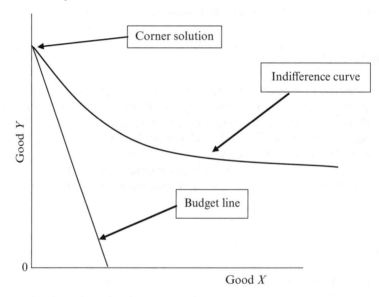

Correlation

The relationship (which may or may not be causal) between two *variables*.

Correlation Coefficient

A linear measure of how closely two *variables* are related. Generally denoted by r, its absolute value provides an indication of the strength of the relationship. The value of *r* varies between +1 and −1, with −1 or +1 indicating a perfect linear relationship, and *r* = 0 indicating no relationship. The sign of the correlation coefficient indicates whether the slope of the line is negative or positive when the two variables are plotted in a scatter diagram. It is also known as Pearson's correlation coefficient after the British statistician Karl Pearson (1857–1936). Correlation does not imply causation. For example, there is evidence that the density of the stork population is correlated with the human *birth rate*. The reason for the relationship is probably that both variables are related to the number of chimney stacks, which are favourite nesting sites for the birds and also an indicator of the size of the human population. Cf. *Spearman's Rank Correlation Coefficient*.

Cost

For the main entry, see *Opportunity Cost*. See also *Average Cost, Capital Cost, Consumption Cost, Direct Cost, Fixed Cost, Indirect Cost, Marginal Cost, Overhead Cost, Productivity Cost, Sunk Cost, Total Cost*.

Cost and Volume Contract

A species of contract between health care purchasers and providers in which the *global budget* is a non-linear function of the number of patients to be treated. Cf. *Block Contract*. See *Purchaser–Provider Split*. See Csaba and Fenn (1997).

Cost–Benefit Analysis

A method of comparing the *costs* and the (money-valued) *benefits* of *alternative* courses of action. It usually requires the calculation of *present values* using a *social discount rate*. It entails the systematic comparison of all those relevant costs and benefits of proposed alternative schemes with a view to determining (1) which scheme, or size of scheme, or combination of schemes, maximizes the difference between benefits and costs, or (2) the magnitude of the benefit that can result from schemes having various costs. The concept of cost or benefit employed is sometimes that of *social cost or benefit*. However, in other cases the scope of the cost and benefit concepts is defined by the interests of the clients for whom the analysis is conducted after discussion between clients and analysts about the options to be considered and the objectives to be sought. This defines what is known as the *perspective* of the study.

The virtues of explicitness (in the objectives postulated, the assumptions and methods adopted) and consistency (the principle that decisions between alternatives should be consistent with objectives) are common to all forms of cost–benefit analysis. Beyond these, however, there are two broad perspectives that analysts may follow: one is often termed the 'social decision-maker's' perspective and the other the 'societal' perspective. Under the social decision-maker's approach, the analyst addresses the question of concern to the decision-maker (which may in practice take considerable eliciting) and adopts the decision-maker's values. This way of approaching the cost–benefit analyst's task is somewhat akin to a consultant's role, the social decision-maker being the client. The other approach involves the analyst in stipulating the social objectives and making the necessary value judgments (or making a value judgment about where they might be obtained other than from decision-makers). In this role the analyst is somewhat distanced from those who make decisions, which may on the one hand have the useful consequence of exposing some choices that a decision-maker may prefer to leave unexposed but, on the other, may result in the fruits of the analysis gathering dust on someone's shelves if the judgments in question prove unacceptable or irrelevant. The former approach is sometimes characterized as being consistent with *extra-welfarism*, perhaps because the client may reject *welfarism*, though there is no particular reason why the analyst adopting the second approach should not also take an extra-welfarist view.

Making *value judgments* explicit is inherent in the practice of cost–benefit analysis. In addition to choosing the perspective, other critical choices, all of which involve making value judgments on behalf of society, usually include: choice of *outcome* measure (and if complex, like '*health gain*', its constituents, reasonable measures of it, its *construct validity*, its scaling and combining with other elements both at a point in time and over time); choice of *cost* measure; and matters concerning the *distribution* and weighting (geographical, between patient or disease groups, ages and sexes, etc.) of *consequences*, whether costs or benefits. To treat these weights as 'equal' is, of course, not to escape making a value judgment: it is to value them equally.

Explicitness in cost–benefit analysis also extends to the treatment of *uncertainty*. It is usually a good idea to identify separately uncertainty in relation to the *parameters* of parts of the analysis and uncertainty in relation to the data themselves.

The usual decision rule in cost–benefit analysis is for the benefit–cost ratio (B/C) to exceed unity or for (B – C) > 0. See also *Benefit–Cost Ratio, Cost–Consequences Analysis, Cost–Effectiveness Analysis, Cost–Utility Analysis, Equity, Extra-welfarism, Shadow Price.* See Drummond et al. (2005) on principles. See G. Hutton et al. (2007) for an example from the developing world. On the differences between cost–benefit and cost–effectiveness analysis see Bleichrodt and Quiggin (1999), Dolan and Edlin (2002) and O'Brien and Gafni (1996).

Cost–Consequences Analysis

A method of assembling the components of the *marginal costs* and the *marginal benefits* of a project or investment *option*, usually in non-comparable units, without any attempt to combine them into a single monetary cost figure or combined artificial *construct*. Thus, the dollar costs of a programme of fluoridation of the water supply may be assembled alongside a qualitative discussion of the negative consequences of involuntary imposition on people who are opposed to the programme. See, as examples, Grant et al. (1997), Lacey et al. (1999) and Rosner et al. (2004).

Cost Containment

Controlling *expenditures on health care* within a predetermined limit or range by such means as limiting budgets (cash limits), imposing or increasing the use of devices such as price controls, *cost-sharing* or *clinical budgets.* See Shen and Melnick (2006) for one of rather few articles on the *effectiveness* of alternative methods of cost containment.

Cost Curve

A graph of *cost* (*average, external, marginal* or *total*) against *output* rate. The cost in question ought to be understood as the lowest possible cost of producing at each output rate, or as the maximum output rate that could be had at that cost.

Cost-effectiveness

In its most general sense, the attainment of a given rate of *output* or *outcome* at the lowest possible *opportunity cost*. Whether the output or outcome in question is worth its cost is another matter, not addressed directly by cost-effectiveness. See *Cost–Effectivenesss Analysis, Efficiency*.

Cost–Effectiveness Acceptability Curve

A cost–effectiveness acceptability curve (CEAC) is a graphical, *Bayesian*, way of showing more information about uncertainty in a *cost–effectiveness analysis* than can be done by using only *confidence intervals*. It can also be used in comparisons of more than two interventions. The curve shows the proportion of estimates of the *incremental cost–effectiveness ratios* (ICERs) that are lower than a variety of possible incremental cost–effectiveness ceiling ratios or thresholds. It thus provides a visual image to aid judgments as to whether a technology actually is cost-effective. The curve typically has a convex section followed by a concave section, with a *point of inflexion*. Introduced in Van Hout et al. (1994). See also, Briggs and Fenn (1998), Löthgren and Zethraeus (2000) and Fenwick et al. (2001). For an empirical example, see Scott et al. (2003).

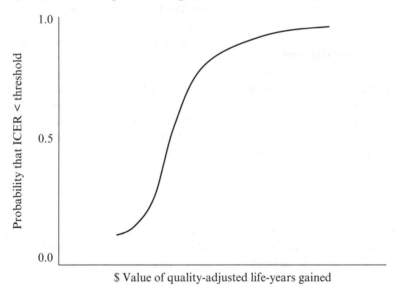

$ Value of quality-adjusted life-years gained

Cost–Effectiveness Analysis

A method of comparing the *opportunity costs* of various *alternative* courses of action having the same *benefit* or in terms of a common unit of *output, outcome*, or other measure of accomplishment. This procedure is used when benefits are difficult to value monetarily, when those that are measurable are not commensurable, or when the objectives are set in terms of health itself. It is similar to *cost–benefit analysis* except that benefit is expressed in terms of a homogeneous index of results achieved rather than in monetary terms (as in cost–benefit analysis) or in terms of several non-commensurable benefits (as in *cost–consequences analysis*). These may be natural units such as the number of lives saved or number of days free from disease, they may be units that are specific to the procedures being compared (like the speed of healing of a wound), or they may be generic (like *quality-adjusted life-years*) thus enabling comparisons of *cost-effectiveness* to be made across many different technologies and patient groups. Many gurus advocate the use of the term *cost–utility analysis* for this latter type of analysis, which in some respects is unfortunate since it seems to imply that QALYs are a measure of *utility* in the customary sense of indicating strength of preferences. It might be more useful, however, to consider them to be a measure of health embodying other – perhaps higher – values than mere preferences – even the preferences of prospective patients and their carers. In truth, QALYs can be both preference based (though there is an issue about whose preferences they should be based on, how they are acquired, and how stable those preferences are – e.g. as between *before and after* treatment) and, say, social value of health based (when there are again issues of whose values and how acquired).

Many of the issues that arise in cost–benefit analysis, such as those of *perspective*, scope of consequences, *discount rate*, *sensitivity analysis*, *modelling*, also arise in cost–effectiveness analysis.

There are literally thousands of empirical cost–effectiveness studies (and the related types) and there is a great deal of quality variation in this corpus, some arising from inherent design problems and others from degrees of expertise in the research team. The Appendix contains a list of studies of acceptable quality (or better) and attempts to indicate the very wide range of topics (diseases, technologies, settings) that have been covered. The criteria used by the *Centre for Reviews and Dissemination* at the University of York, UK, which is the world's major such centre and which has a huge database of evaluated studies, include the following: specification of study question, description of health technology in question, the settings in which it might be used, the population to which it applies, the type of study (CEA, CUA, etc.), perspective of the study (societal, *third party payer*, etc.), sources of data, methods of obtaining data, time period over which data were obtained, measures of benefit, measures of cost, synthesis of benefits and costs, types of modelling employed, currency used, dates of measures, treatment of uncertainty (types of sensitivity analysis), discounting procedure and rates chosen. A good study would be expected to include at the very least a statement about each of these elements. Until relatively recently, most studies were in developed country settings but there is now a good range of studies based in the third world, some of which are listed in the Appendix. An easy introduction is Jefferson et al. (2000). A pioneering empirical study was Klarman et al. (1968). An early methodological classic is Weinstein and Stason (1977). See also Garber and Phelps (1997), Weinstein and Manning (1997) and Garber (2000). For studies of the variability of quality in studies of outcomes see Richardson and Manca (2004) and for one on costing methods Graves et al. (2002). On the treatment of costs in *pragmatic trials*, see Thompson and Barber (2000). On the treatment of *consumption costs* and future unrelated medical costs see Nyman (2004) and Lee (2008). On the differences between cost–benefit and cost–effectiveness analysis see Bleichrodt and Quiggin (1999), Dolan and Edlin (2002) and O'Brien and Gafni (1996). Leading textbooks include Gold et al. (1996) and Drummond et al. (2005). On the specialized sub-field of the CEA of paediatric interventions see Ungar (2006). See the Appendix for 100 illustrative cost–effectiveness studies.

Cost–Effectiveness Analysis Registry

A comprehensive database of over 1700 *cost–effectiveness* and *cost–utility analyses* on a wide variety of diseases and treatments. Its website is available at: http://www.tufts-nemc.org/cearegistry/ (accessed 29 October 2009).

Cost–Effectiveness Expansion Curve

Cost–effectiveness analyses commonly assume that the *incremental cost–effectiveness ratio* (ICER) is independent of the *scale* (or *scope*) of activity or the ordering of patients treated. When these are considered the 'expansion curve' becomes non-linear. The term was coined in Lord et al. (2005).

Cost–Effectiveness Frontier

A *locus* of points showing the cumulative minimum cost of achieving successively larger impact on an outcome such as *quality-adjusted life-years*. Cf. *Health Frontier*. For an exposition, see Lord et al. (2004).

Cost–Effectiveness Plane

This is a diagrammatic way of comparing technologies. A four-quadrant diagram of *cost* difference plotted against effect difference yields: quadrant I, where the intervention is more *effective* and more costly than the *comparator*; quadrant II, where the intervention is more effective and less costly than the comparator; quadrant III, where the intervention is less effective and less costly than the comparator; and quadrant IV, where the intervention is less effective and more costly than the comparator.

In quadrant II, the intervention dominates the comparator and in quadrant IV, the comparator dominates the intervention. Quadrants I and III are the more interesting cases. Here, the *cost-effectiveness* of the alternatives depends upon the size of the *incremental cost–effectiveness ratio* (ICER or $\Delta C/\Delta E$) and on whether the ΔE is positive or negative. Let there be a maximum amount a decision-maker will pay for an increment of outcome (ΔE) indicated by the dashed line λ. Any point to the left of λ indicates that comparator treatment is more cost-effective, while points to the right of λ indicate that intervention is more cost-effective. All points below λ are in the '*region of acceptability*' (note that $\Delta C/\Delta E$ is lower – actually negative – than λ in quadrant IV, but that this quadrant cannot be in the region of acceptability since ΔE is actually negative here). See also *Confidence Box, Confidence Ellipse*. See Briggs and Fenn (1998) and Briggs et al. (2002).

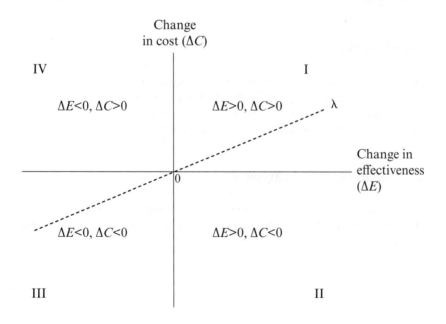

Cost–Effectiveness Ratio

The ratio of *cost* to the *output* or *outcome* in a *cost–effectiveness analysis* or *cost–utility analysis*; or the ratio of the cost difference between two technologies and their outcome differences. See also *Incremental Cost–Effectiveness Ratio*.

Cost–Effectiveness Threshold

The maximum acceptable *incremental cost–effectiveness ratio* acceptable to a decision-maker. Beyond this threshold, health care technologies will not be adopted on *efficiency* grounds alone. See *Cost–Effectiveness Plane*. For a review of the history of a commonly applied threshold, see Grosse (2008). On NICE's notorious threshold, see Appleby et al. (2007) and Culyer et al. (2007).

Cost-efficiency

Same as *cost-effectiveness*. Achieving a given objective at least *cost*, or maximizing achievement at a given cost. A term not much used by health economists.

Cost Function

A function in which *cost* is the *dependent variable* and output *the independent variable*. Strictly, the cost in question is the lowest cost at which each rate of *output* can be produced. Cf. *Behavioural Cost Function*. For an example in health economics see Butler et al. (1995).

Cost-identification Analysis

A term sometimes used to describe the criteria used to select cost categories in decision analytic techniques such as *budget impact*, *cost–benefit* and *cost–effectiveness analysis*.

Cost-minimization Analysis

A primitive form of *cost–effectiveness analysis*, in which cost is the dominant determining factor in a choice between *alternatives* (perhaps because the *outcome* or the *value* of the outcome is the same for each). The valid application of the method plainly depends on establishing the (empirical) truth of the proposition that cost is indeed the dominant *determinant*. For an (almost) comprehensive put-down of the method see Briggs and O'Brien (2001). See Miller (2005), however, for a respectable use of the method.

Cost of Capital

Loosely, the real borrowing rate of interest, i.e. the *nominal* rate of interest less the rate of inflation.

Cost of Illness

A narrow interpretation of the cost imposed by illness focuses merely on the financial consequences of poor health (often misleadingly – and, to economists, offensively – described as 'economic') such as lost earnings from work, expenditure on health services, drugs, etc. Other approaches use an essentially accounting concept of 'cost', that is, the historical record of outcomes (mostly financial) of decisions taken in the past. A wider interpretation seeks to identify the true social *opportunity costs* of being ill with perhaps *shadow prices* being attached to lost working time, informal carers' time spent nursing, health services received, etc. This is essentially forward-looking and predictive. Cf. *Burden of Disease, Disease Costing*. For a well-conducted study, see McKenna et al. (1996).

Cost-per-QALY Analysis

A specific form of *cost–utility* (CUA) or *cost–effectiveness analysis* (CEA) where the decision criterion relates to cost per *quality-adjusted life-year* (QALY). The term appears to have been invented by taxonomizers who are unsure whether CUA is a subdivision of CEA or of *cost–benefit analysis* but it is not clear that a mere renaming resolves that issue. Actually the problem seems to have become worse, for we now have to ask whether cost-per-QALY analysis is a subset of CEA, CUA or CBA. There is also the prospect of there being a new kind of 'analysis' for every outcome measure employed. It is not compulsory, fortunately, to answer this question. See *Cost–Effectiveness Analysis*.

Cost-sharing

Usually used to refer to a method of *financing health care* that involves some portion of the expenditure falling directly on the user. The cost is then shared between user and employer, government, taxpayer, *insurance agency* and so on. This is also sometimes referred to as '*demand*-side cost-sharing'. It is viewed both as a means of deterring relatively 'trivial' consumption (and of course assumes a non-zero price *elasticity* of demand) and as a means of enlarging the financial bases from which health services are financed. What is meant by 'trivial' is anyone's guess. The term '*supply*-side cost-sharing' is a term occasionally used to describe a situation where the provider receives from a *third party payer* less than the full costs of providing a given service. See *Copayment*. See Ellis and McGuire (1993).

Cost-shifting

A loose term used to describe any activity through which *costs* are shifted from one decision-maker to another. As examples, both the activity of health care insurers in increasing *copayments* for insured workers and hospital physicians in prescribing drugs whose cost will fall on community-based practice budgets are ways of shifting costs, in the one case from employers to workers and in the other from *secondary* to *primary care* institutions. In the USA, cost-shifting is said to occur when a hospital charges fees in excess of costs to patients with private *insurance* in order to compensate for losses from patients with government-sponsored insurance or who are uninsured. In these cases, as in many others, it is not necessarily genuine *opportunity costs* that are being shifted, but charges. See also *Incidence*, *Shifting*. See, on workers' compensation, Butler et al. (1997), on service intensity see Rosenman and Friesner (2002).

Cost Sub-group

Individuals who are likely to cause similar costs to be incurred or avoided and may thus be placed in an *experimental group* (as in a *cost–effectiveness analysis* of a clinical technology).

Cost-to-charge Ratio

A term used in the US meaning the ratio of the cost to a hospital of an item of service relative to the charge made for it. Abbreviated to CCR.

Cost–Utility Analysis

A close relative of *cost–benefit* and *cost–effectiveness analysis* but where *benefit* is measured in neither monetary terms nor natural units like 'deaths prevented'. It takes its name from the use of constructed measures of outcome (like *quality-adjusted life-years*), which share many of the characteristics of *utility*, though whether these really are preference-based utilities is a matter of controversy. The attempt to stress a major difference between CEA and CUA seems a somewhat overdone and fruitless bit of taxonomizing as in practice it is often hard to distinguish between the two. See Drummond et al. (2005), Richardson (1994) for principles and the Appendix for many examples.

Cost–Value Analysis

A method of conducting *cost–effectiveness analysis* that embodies societal concerns about fairness. It is an example of the confusing proliferation of names for what might better be simply called 'cost–effectiveness analysis (with better attention than is usual being given to distributional concerns)'. See Nord et al. (1999).

Count Data

See *Count Variable*.

Counterfactual

In economics, the counterfactual is generally taken to be the state of the world as it would otherwise have been, *ceteris paribus*, but for a specific intervention, disturbance or change of some sort that is held to be a cause of the actual (or predicted) state of the world changing. Thus, a rise in a price 'causes' a fall in the rate of use of a resource (*ceteris paribus*) in comparison with either what was previously the case or what would otherwise be the case.

Count Variable

The counted occurrences of an event. Data consisting of integers that cannot take on negative values, such as beds occupied, doctor visits, drug prescriptions. For an introduction see Kennedy (2003). In health economics, see Deb and Trivedi (2006).

Coupon

The annual rate of interest on a *bond's* face value that the issuer promises to pay the bondholder. The term originates from the fact that *coupons* were once actually attached to bonds and had to be cut off or 'clipped' to receive the due interest.

Covariance

A measure of the extent to which the values taken by two *variables* are associated. It is measured as the value of the product of the deviations of the variables from their *arithmetic mean*. The unbiased covariance of a *population* sample is formally defined as:

$$s_{xy}^2 = \frac{\sum_i (x_i - \bar{x})(y_i - \bar{y})}{n - 1}$$

where the (x_i, y_i) are independent, $i = 1 \ldots n$, and the bars over the variables x and y denote sample means. See *Analysis of Covariance*.

Covariate

A *variable* that covaries with a *dependent variable* and that one usually wants to control in order to explore the relationship between *independent variables* and the dependent variable(s). See *Analysis of Covariance*.

Coverage With Evidence Development

The idea that an intervention whose *cost-effectiveness* was unknown or subject to much uncertainty ought to be provided in public health programmes only if accompanied by research designed to reduce the uncertainty. Also known (in the UK) as 'Only In Research'). See J. Hutton et al. (2007).

Cox Proportional Hazards Model

A *semiparametric model* for *duration analysis*. A form of *multiple regression* used in exploring the simultaneous effects of multiple variables on survival. The *model* is 'proportional' because it entails the assumption that the effect of *covariates* is to multiply the basic *hazard function* by a constant. It is named after Sir David Cox; see Cox (1972). For an application in health economics see Basu et al. (2004).

CPHO

Acronym for *closed physician-hospital organization*.

Creaming

Same as *cream skimming*.

Cream Skimming

A practice in private *health insurance* markets by which the insurer obtains a higher proportion of good risks (people with a low probability of needing care or who are likely to need only low-cost care – or both) in their portfolio of clients than is assumed in the calculation of the insurance premiums. Also called 'cherry-picking' and 'creaming'. Cf. *Adverse Selection*. The classic general analysis is Rothschild and Stiglitz (1976). In health economics see Ellis (1998) and Barros (2003).

Criterion Function

Same as *loss function*.

Criterion Validity

The ability of an instrument (like a measure of *health-related quality of life*) to replicate a *gold standard*. Similar to *construct validity*.

Cronbach's Alpha

A measure of how well a set of variables measures a single unidimensional underlying *construct* (such as 'health'). See Cronbach (1951).

Cross-country Comparisons

See *International Comparisons*.

Cross-elasticity of Demand

The responsiveness of the consumption of a good or service to a change in another good's price. See *Elasticity*. A study that examined cross-elasticities between over-the-counter and prescription medicines was O'Brien (1989).

Crossover Design

A type of *trial* design in which each subject receives more than one of the interventions under investigation in random order. It is different from a *parallel groups* design where some subjects receive one treatment and different subjects receive another. The crossover design represents a special situation where there is no separate comparison group, each subject in effect serving as its own *control*. A common procedure for comparing interventions *A* and *B*, for example, would be for the subjects to be randomly allocated to receive them in either the order *A, B* or the order *B, A*, switching from one to the other when the course of treatment ends. It is most often used to study treatments for stable health problems.

Crossover Trial

A trial using a *crossover design*.

Cross-product Ratio

Same as *odds ratio*.

Cross-sectional Data

Data in which each respondent or observation is observed only once, giving a snapshot picture of the *population* at a point in time.

Cross-sectional Study

A study in which the observations of *dependent* and *independent variables*, or exposure and *outcome*, are taken at a single point in time (cf. *Longitudinal Study*). For a health economics example, see Cowing and Holtmann (1983).

Crowding Out

In general, a reduction in private expenditure (especially *investment*) that occurs when a government's expansionary fiscal policy (which may be to the advantage of the health care sector) causes *interest rates* to rise. In health economics, the term has been used to describe the effect that public *health insurance* programmes may have on the *demand* for private health care insurance. See Cutler and Gruber (1996). For an analysis of side-by-side public and private health care see Brekke and Sørgard (2007).

Crude Birth Rate

The number of live births in a year divided by the *population*.

Crude Death Rate

The number of deaths in a year divided by the *population*. Cf. *Standardized Mortality Rate*.

C2

Code name for the *Campbell Collaboration*.

CUA

Acronym for *cost–utility analysis*.

Cue

Any item of information that may be used in making decisions under uncertainty. Some cues can cause bias when questionnaire methods of research are used. See *Implied Value Cue* for an example.

Cumulative Frequency

The number of observations with values below and including some designated value.

Cumulative Incidence Rate

The proportion of an initially disease-free *population* that develops the disease in an interval of time. Also called simply 'cumulative *incidence*'.

Cumulative Meta-analysis

A form of *meta-analysis* in which studies are added one at a time according to a rule such as date of publication. The results are summarized as each study is added. In a graph of a cumulative meta-analysis, each horizontal line represents the summary of the cumulative results up to the point at which the last study was added. See Egger et al. (1997).

Cumulative Prospect Theory

A variant of *prospect theory*. See Tversky and Kahneman (1992).

Cumulative Scaling

See *Guttman Scale*.

Current Account

A part of the *balance of payments*.

Cutoff Value

A point on a continuously scaled diagnostic test beyond which it is judged that the result is a 'positive'. Also known a *'positivity criterion'*.

CV

Acronym for *coefficient of variation* (as well as curriculum vitae).

D

DACEHTA

Acronym for the *Danish Centre for Evaluation and Health Technology Assessment*.

DALE

Acronym for *disability-adjusted life-expectancy*.

DALY

Acronym for *disability-adjusted life-year*.

Danish Centre for Evaluation and Health Technology Assessment

Its key function is to perform *health technology assessments* and evaluations. It also aims to integrate HTA principles into the running and planning of the public health service at all levels. Its website is available at: http://www.sst.dk/English/DACEHTA.aspx (accessed 29 October 2009).

DARE

Acronym for *Database of Abstracts of Reviews of Effects*.

DASH

Acronym for *disabilities of the arm, shoulder and hand*.

Database of Abstracts of Reviews of Effects

A database maintained by the *Centre for Reviews and Dissemination* at the University of York, UK, containing thousands of quality-assessed systematic reviews of the *effectiveness* and *cost-effectiveness* of medical interventions. Its website is available at: http://www.crd.york.ac.uk/crdweb/ (accessed 29 October 2009).

Data Envelope Analysis

A *linear programming* technique that uses empirical evidence of the most efficient producers of *outputs* to locate an *envelope* that predicts the maximum *outputs* achievable with a variety of different *inputs* or *factors of production*. It is particularly vulnerable to *omitted variable bias*. Cf. *Stochastic Frontier Analysis*. See Jacobs and Street (2005) and Hollingsworth (2008).

Data Mining

This has two (altogether different) meanings. The first is overusing data (especially without any theoretical expectation as to what the data might reveal) to draw invalid inferences from apparent correlations obtained by a huge amount of mere number-crunching. The second, more recent, usage is an efficient process of discovering non-obvious regularities in large databases, often using *algorithms* based on *decision trees* or *networks*.

Day Reconstruction Method

A method of measuring *experienced utility*. Invented by Kahneman and colleagues, it involves subjects in detailed descriptions of one day of 'experience', which are then weighted by their duration. Cf. *Experienced Utility, Remembered Utility*. See Kahneman et al. (2004).

DBC

A form of *diagnostic related group* used in the Netherlands. See *Diagnosis Treatment Combination*.

DCA

Acronym for *discrete choice analysis*.

DCE

Acronym for *discrete choice experiment*.

DCF

Acronym for *discounted cash flow*.

DDD

Acronym for *defined daily dose*.

DDMAC

Acronym for *Division of Drug Marketing, Advertising, and Communications* of the US *Food and Drug Administration*.

DEA

Acronym for *data envelope analysis*.

Deadweight Loss

A measure of the loss of *welfare* resulting from misallocations of resources (i.e. inefficient allocations; ones that are not *Pareto-optimal*) or from taxation. For some examples see *Excess Burden, Insurance*.

DEALE

Acronym for *declining exponential approximation to life*.

Debt

A's debt is money (or something else in kind) owed by *A* to *B*. It is a liability. For *B* it is an *asset*.

Decentralization

The policy of delegating some decision-making in health care from high-level authorities like central and federal governments to state, provincial and other regional lower tiers. See *Fiscal Federalism in Health*. See, e.g., Rico and Costa-i-Font (2005) and Costa-i-Font and Moscone (2008) for two Spanish studies.

Decile

When a *continuous variable* is split for convenience into ten equal-sized chunks of data the cut-off points between them are called deciles. See *Quantile*.

Decision Analysis

This typically refers to a formal, essentially *utilitarian*, method for quantifying decision problems under conditions of uncertainty, in which the probability of each event in a chain of events, along with the consequences of such events, is explicitly stated. Some approaches, like *bounded rationality*, do not, however, use quantified probabilities. See *Decision Rule, Decision Tree, Expected Utility Theory, Markov Chain, Multiple Criteria Decision Analysis, Quality-adjusted Life-year*. See Keeney and Raiffa (1976) and Krahn et al. (1997) and, in health economics, Sculpher et al. (2000), Claxton et al. (2004) and Philips et al. (2006b). On decision rules see Johannesson and Weinstein (1993) and on their possible misuse Birch and Gafni (1992, 1993).

Decision Field Theory

A model of decision-making under uncertainty that was invented by psychologists Busemeyer and Townsend (1993). It avoids some of the more restrictive assumptions that underpin most economic theories of choice under uncertainty. See *Decision Analysis*.

Decision-makers' Approach

A method of deriving values for entities not readily measured in other ways for the purposes of public decision-making. It works by assuming that past decisions in the public sector have been consistent and that one may infer from the sums expended that the *benefits* thereby gained must have been valued at least as highly as this expenditure (or, if not expended, then the benefits cannot have been worth this much). For example, if a programme to introduce child-proof bottle caps for drugs at a cost of $50 per expected life saved was not adopted, then it is inferred that the average value of an expected life for children at risk was not greater than $50. Plainly, the method also involves the absence of *confounders* that may have affected the past decisions but that may be irrelevant to the one under current consideration. The method's only advantage seems to lie in exposing apparent inconsistencies in public decision-making! See *Value of Life*. See Sugden and Williams (1978).

Decision Network

Same as *influence diagram*.

Decision Rule

A criterion (or set of criteria) to aid a decision-maker in selecting between *alternative* courses of action. In the context of a *cost–benefit analysis* it may be 'rank all projects in terms of their *benefit–cost ratios* and work down the list until the budget is exhausted'. *In cost–effectiveness* contexts the rule might be 'adopt all projects for which the *incremental cost–effectiveness ratio* lies below a given *threshold* value'. See Johannesson and Weinstein (1993) but also Birch and Gafni (1992, 1993).

Decision Theory

Same as *decision analysis*.

Decision Tree

A diagrammatic representation of a *decision analysis* in which chains of choices are identified, each conditional on a prior choice and with *outcomes* and *probabilities* built in. In the diagram, ■ indicates a decision node, ● indicates a chance node and ◀ indicates an end or terminal node. In this decision tree, the issue is whether to give therapy. If it is given (the *Rx* group), there is a probability *p* of life and of 1 – *p* of death. In the untreated (*control*) group there is a probability *r* of life and 1 – *r* of death. The surviving patients in either *arm* may become *in-patients* or treatment may no longer be needed beyond a certain point. If the costs of the therapy are known, and the probabilities of life or death, and the probabilities that living patients will become hospitalized or no longer need treatment, together with the costs of these options (for both arms), then the (probable) *cost-effectiveness* of the two courses of action may be computed. For an example from Kenya see Kirigia (1997).

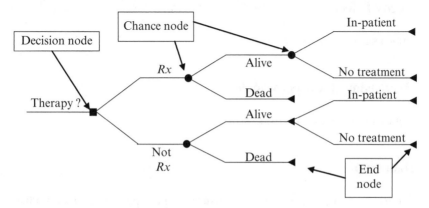

Decision Utility

The *utility* of an *option* prior to experiencing, consuming it, etc. Cf. *Experienced Utility*. The term is due to Kahneman and Tversky (1984).

Declining Exponential Approximation to Life

An *algorithm* for calculating *life expectancy* when death rates are constant. Commonly abbreviated to DEALE. See *Gompertz Function*.

Decomposition

This generally involves the identification of components or correlates of a larger entity in order to understand better the reasons for particular *outcomes*. Thus, inequalities in children's survival are likely to be reflections of other inequalities: for example in income, parental education, *insurance* cover, distance from health care facilities. One method is the Oaxaca decomposition for studying inequalities. This explains differences between groups in terms of differences in the size of the determining *variables* on the one hand and the size of their impact on the other. See Oaxaca (1973) and, for a general introduction, O'Donnell et al. (2006). For empirical examples of Oaxaca decomposition see Ponce et al. (1998) and Wagstaff and Nguyen (2004). For decomposition of the *concentration index*, see Wagstaff et al. (2003).

Decoy Effect

Same as *attraction effect*.

Decreasing Returns to Scale

Same as *diminishing returns to scale*.

Deductible

An arrangement under which the insured person pays a fixed sum when health care is used and the insurer pays all other expenses, subject to a possible *copayment*. It is known as '*excess*' in the UK. See *Coinsurance*. See Manning et al. (1987) and Van Kleef et al. (2008) for US and European studies respectively.

Defensive Medicine

Refers to a style of clinical practice that minimizes the risk of *malpractice* suits, regardless of the value of the services provided to the patient. See Kessler and McClellan (1996), Danzon (2000) and Fenn et al. (2004).

DEFF

Acronym for *design effect*.

Defined Daily Dose

The estimated maintenance dose of a drug used in its main clinical indication.

Deflator

An instrument for eliminating inflation from monetary time series. See *Constant Prices, Price Index*.

Degrees of Freedom

In estimation, the *sample* size minus the number of *parameters* to be estimated. See *Chi-squared Test*.

De-insurance

The removal of a *benefit* from an *insurance* package. For a case study see Giacomini et al. (2000).

Deliberative Process

A process that involves consultation but also engages interested stakeholders in the decision-making process itself. It is characterized by the careful, deliberate consideration and discussion of the advantages and disadvantages of various options in an effort to assist people who are making a decision. The debate is informed by evidence and typically involves all key stakeholders. There are opportunities for participants both to form and to change their opinions. See Culyer and Lomas for an application in health care (2006).

Delphi Method

A systematic method of obtaining a collective opinion, usually of a group of experts, in the absence of more reliable assessments (of, say, *effectiveness* or some other quantitative measure or indicator). The basic method involves a facilitator soliciting opinions, which are then fed back anonymously to the group, whose members may then revise their opinions and feed them back again. After a few rounds, the facilitator usually averages the opinions. For an example in health economics, see Kirigia (1997).

Demand Curve

A two-variable geometrical representation of a *demand function* where the *dependent variable* is rate of consumption or use and the *independent variable* is price. In general, a demand curve shows both the maximum rate of demand for a good or service per unit of time at a variety of prices, and also the maximum price that will be paid for a small additional amount, *ceteris paribus*. Conventionally, the price variable is measured on the *y* axis and quantity on the *x* axis, even when quantity is the *dependent variable*. When price is the dependent variable, the demand curve is commonly referred to as a 'marginal valuation curve'. This is the interpretation showing the maximum amount someone is willing to pay for a small increment in the rate of consumption. Under particular conditions (for example, when the *income-elasticity* of demand is zero) the two curves coincide.

Care needs to be exercised in distinguishing between using the word 'demand' in the sense of a particular rate at a particular price and in the sense of the whole range of rates at a range of prices (a point on the demand curve, cf. the entire curve). It evidently makes (logical) sense to say 'price rose and so demand fell' and also 'demand fell, so price fell', and a little thought reveals that the apparent paradox is resolved once it is seen that 'demand' is here being used in two different senses. Responses to changes in price are seen as movements along the demand curve and responses to changes in other *determinants* such as income are seen as shifts of the entire demand curve.

In most situations in the health field 'demand' is not the demand by traders or dealers, who demand only in order to be able to supply or sell on; it is the demand by users either because it is a *final good* (as in the case of the *demand for health*) or an *intermediate good* or service (as is the case with the *demand for health services*).

Some of the demand-side characteristics that ought always to be borne in mind when using demand curves in the context of health care, especially when making *normative* statements about *welfare*, are the following: uncertainty about the probable *incidence* of disease, its consequences for health and *utility*, the *effectiveness* and likely *cost* of treatments; the (strong?) possibility that the *rationality* assumptions underlying utility theory do not apply when someone is worried, ill-informed, sick, incapacitated or

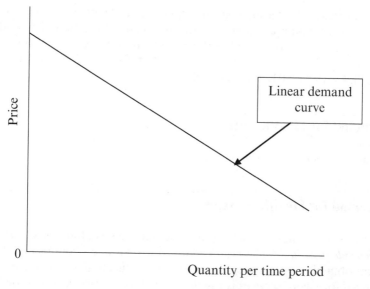

in pain; the fact that there may well be *external* demands for the care of the person(s) whose demand is under consideration in addition to their own demand; and the fact that the price to which a demander is imagined to be responding may not be at all an accurate reflection of the *marginal cost* of providing the care in question. See *Law of Demand*. See Wagstaff (1986). There are many empirical economic studies of demand behaviour that affects health. For some that have bad health consequences see, for example, Ahituv et al. (1996), Cutler et al. (2003), Farrell et al. (2003) and Lundborg (2006). Some examples of how price can deter use of effective health care are Ellis et al. (2004) and Trivedi et al. (2008).

Demand for Health

The maximum amount of *health* chosen as a function of various *independent variables* such as the *rate of return* to investment in health, expected wages from work, the price of health care (not to mention many other variables not often considered by economists such as early parenting, developmental cultural influences, social norms, family circumstances). 'Health' itself can be treated either as a *stock*, which can be invested in and is subject to *depreciation*, or as a *flow*, when it is usually treated as a *construct* such as *quality-adjusted life-years*. The *demand for health services* is a *derived demand* that depends in part on the underlying demand for health. It is a vulgarism to muddle the demand for health with the demand for health services. It is also vulgar to suppose that the only *determinants* of health are economic or pecuniary. See Grossman (1972). Empirical studies include many exploring unhealthy behaviour. For example: Cook and Moore (1993), Mullahy and Sindelar (1996), Buchmueller and Zuvekas (1998), Cawley (2004) and Auld (2005).

Demand for Health Care

Same as *demand for health services*.

Demand for Health Services

The maximum rate of use of health service facilities as a function of various *independent variables* like *health status*, price, distance from facility, time spent obtaining the service, income, wealth, educational attainment. The *demand* for health services is usually treated as a *derived demand* (that is, derived from the *demand for health*).The *income-elasticity* has commonly been found to be around unity, so an increase in income normally leads to a roughly similar proportional increase in the demand for service. The price-elasticity is usually low. The most comprehensive empirical study ever is Manning et al. (1987). Whether it makes sense to view the demand for health care as based on an individual's own decisions is a moot point. The demand for many services depends not only on the perspective of the patients but also on that of the health care professional. See *Agency Relationship, Supplier-induced Demand*. For some of the complexity in unravelling this process see Santos Silva and Windmeijer (2001).

Demand Function

The demand function is a mathematical representation of the maximum rate of demand as the *dependent variable* and its various *determinants*. In a simple example the amount of something demanded is a function of its relative price, buyers' incomes and their 'tastes'. The *demand curve* is a two-dimensional representation of this function in which responses to changes in price are seen as movements along the demand curve and responses to changes in income are seen as shifts of the entire demand curve. See *Demand Curve, Demand for Health Services, Law of Demand*. For an analysis of the demand for grains in the context of tax policies for healthier eating, see Nordström and Thunström (2009).

Demand-side Cost-sharing

See *Cost-sharing, Deductibles, Copayments*.

Demography

The study of the characteristics of human *populations*, such as their size, growth, density, distribution and vital statistics.

Dentistry

The medical speciality concerned with the *diagnosis*, prevention and treatment of diseases of the teeth, gums and related structures of the mouth. For a review of the economics of dentistry see Sintonen and Linnosmaa (2000).

Deontology

Ethical theories broadly based on the idea that what matters (or ought to matter) in moral discourse is categorical – it's either right or wrong. A typical form is any moral theory based on the idea of 'doing one's duty'. This approach is especially associated with Immanuel Kant. 'Lying is always wrong, even if it has good consequences' has characteristic deontological tones. It is very remote from most economic theorizing about what is 'good' for societies, which is generally calculating, *consequentialist* and allows *trade-offs*. The use of '*need*' by non-economists often seems deontological. (Note that the root of the word is the Greek for 'it is binding on' not 'deus', the Latin word for 'god'.) Cf. *Utilitarianism*. See Kant ([1785] 1964).

Dependency Ratio

A measure of the proportion of a *population* composed of people who are too young or too old to work. The dependency ratio is equal to the proportion of individuals aged below 15 or above 64 divided by the proportion of individuals aged 15 to 64, expressed as a percentage. Thus:

$$\text{Dependency ratio} = \frac{(\%\ \text{under } 15)\ +\ (\%\ \text{over } 65)}{\%\ \text{between } 15 \text{ and } 64} \times 100$$

Dependent Variable

A variable (often denoted by y) that is postulated to be determined by one or more *independent variables*. For example, the rate of consumption of a good (dependent variable) may be regarded as behaviourally determined by (amongst other things) its price (independent variable), or the *marginal value* placed on a good (dependent variable) may be regarded as being determined by (amongst other things) its rate of consumption (independent variable). The dependent variable is conventionally found on the left-hand side of a *regression* equation and explanatory variables are on the right. A '*limited dependent variable*' is one that is mostly *continuous* but that also has concentrations of observations at particular *values*. For example, in any period a large number of survey subjects will have made no expenditures on health care, even though expenditure is otherwise a continuous variable. See *Binary Variable, Count Variable, Demand Curve*.

Depreciation

The change in the *value* of a *capital* good over time, usually expressed annually. The value will typically fall due to wear and tear, supersession by other capital items, or through changes in fashion. When the value rises, the term is *appreciation*. The values in question are in *constant prices*: allowance for inflation is a separate matter.

Derived Demand

The maximum the buyer is willing to pay for a good or service as a result of a demand for something else, usually more fundamental. For example, the demand for health care is said to be derived from the *demand for health*.

Dermatology

The medical speciality concerned with diseases and abnormalities of the skin.

Der Simonian and Laird Method

A method of assessing drug *efficacy*. See Der Simonian and Laird (1986).

Descriptive Statistics

The type of statistics in which the emphasis is on describing the principal, or most interesting, features of a set of data. For example, *variables* may be characterized as qualitative or quantitative, or data may be distributed in a particular way around a *mode*, or two sets of data may be related, one rising (or falling) as the other falls (or rises).

Descriptive Study

A study that records a situation or a distribution of data without any analysis of cause and effect or hypothesis testing. Statistical modelling issues are irrelevant: one 'simply' observes that one statistic varies as another varies, for example, health varies as socioeconomic status varies. Cause and effect may not be inferred, even if there have been controls for *covariates*.

Design Bias

Bias in *clinical trials* arising from bad design, such as lack of or poorly chosen *controls*.

Design Effect

A kind of *bias* that arises in taking *samples*, especially in *cluster randomized trials*. An additional observation drawn from the same cluster is likely to be more similar to others in the cluster than if drawn randomly from the whole *population*. The design effect indicates how much larger a sample is needed to achieve the same *precision* as a simple *random sample*. It is the ratio of the true *variance* of a statistic (taking the sampling design into account) to the variance of the statistic for a simple random sample with the same number of cases.

Desmoteric Medicine

Medical practice in prisons. From the Greek for 'prison'.

Detailing

The process by which pharmaceutical companies send agents to doctors to promote their products via information dissemination and the emphasis of positive product *attributes*. The idea is to encourage *prescriptions* rather than directly to encourage purchase. Cf. *Academic Detailing*. See Brekke and Kuhn (2006) for an economic analysis.

Detection Bias

A form of *selection bias* in *trials*. For example, women taking an oral contraceptive will have more frequent cervical smears than women who are not on the pill and so are more likely to have cervical cancer diagnosed (if they actually have it). Thus, in a *case-control study* that compared women with cervical cancer and a *control group*, at least part of any higher pill consumption rates amongst the former group may be due to this effect. Also called 'ascertainment bias'.

Determinant

A factor, characteristic, causal *variable* that affects the character, size, or some other feature of interest in another variable. It has nothing to do with 'determinism' as a philosophical point of view.

Determinants of Health

See *Population Health*.

Deterministic Model

A model in which the *parameters* and *variables* are not subject to random fluctuations. Cf. *Stochastic Model*.

Deterministic Sensitivity Analysis

A *sensitivity analysis* in which single (point) estimates of particular *values*, rather than *distributions* of values, are used. Cf. *Probabilistic Sensitivity Analysis*.

Deutsches Institut für Medizinische Dokumentation und Information

The German federal agency for conducting *cost–utility analyses* and *health technology assessments*. Its website is available at: www.dimdi.de/dynamic/de/index.html (accessed 29 October 2009).

DFLE

Acronym for *disability-free life-expectancy*.

Diagnosis

The attaching of a disease label to a patient's (or family's or larger group's) condition after examining symptoms and performing various tests.

Diagnosis-related Group

Same as *diagnostic-related group*.

Diagnosis Treatment Combination

The Dutch version of *diagnostic-related group*, covering episodes of care.

Diagnostic-related Group

Diagnostic-related Groups (DRGs) are diagnoses grouped according to their clinical similarity and the cost of treatment. Under US *Medicare*, patients are classified according to their DRG, of which there are about 500, and the hospital is reimbursed by a fixed price for the 'standard' treatment under that DRG. Also 'diagnosis-related group', *healthcare resource groups* in England and Australian refined diagnosis-related groups. The inventors were Fetter et al. (1976).

Dichotomous Choice

A questionnaire design principle in *willingness to pay* studies under which subjects can give but two answers. Cf. *Payment Card*. See Ryan et al. (2004).

Dichotomous Variable

Same as *binary variable*.

Difference Principle

This principle of justice is due to John Rawls and states that social and economic inequalities are justifiable only if they are to the advantage of the least advantaged person. See *Fairness*. See Rawls (1971).

Differential Diagnosis

A term that describes a method of reaching a *diagnosis* by a clinician. It consists essentially of creating a broad list of the possible conditions that might underlie the signs and symptoms that are presented and then eliminating the possible conditions individually through further tests, pattern recognition and hypothesis formation through experience.

Diffuse Technology

This term has been used in *cost–effectiveness analysis* to describe complex health care technologies that often comprise combinations of distinct elements having different costs and effects, often across several different services. See, for an evaluation of imaging technology, Keen et al. (1995).

Diffusion

The diffusion of technologies refers to the speed at which new technologies are adopted by professionals in health care. There have been concerns both that the speed is too fast for high-quality care and too slow in bringing more *effective* care to patients. See Smythe (2002). Also Baker and Wheeler (1998) and Ho (2002) for examples in health care (MRI and angioplasty).

DIMDI

Acronym for *Deutsches Institut für Medizinische Dokumentation und Information*.

Dimension of Health

A characteristic, like an *attribute*, but particular to measuring *health*.

Diminishing Marginal Utility

A property of a *utility function*, to the effect that increments of a good or service are assumed to add positive but diminishing additions to total *utility*. It is not to be conceived of as a successive phenomenon, in which the additions take place over time (which is unfortunately how it is often introduced in textbooks) but as an instantaneous characteristic of human preferences. Now largely superseded, save in *expected utility theory*, by the more general (but still 'instantaneous') 'ordinalist' idea of a diminishing *marginal rate of substitution* in consumption or negatively-sloped *indifference curve*. See *Marginal Utility, Ordinal Utility, Utility*.

Diminishing Returns to Scale

A feature of *production functions*. A production function exhibits diminishing returns to scale if increasing all *inputs* in the same proportion increases *outputs* by a smaller proportion. Cf. *Law of Variable Proportions*. For a practical example, see Doherty (1990).

Direct Cost

The internal cost of an activity or decision in terms of the resources used by the agency making the decision in question. It includes the cost of labour, other goods and services, *capital* (usually considered as a rental value) and consumables as incurred by the organization in question. It excludes external costs and *indirect costs* such as *unrelated future medical costs*. See *External Effects, Opportunity Cost*.

Direct Health Care Corporation

A form of US company providing direct health care services to its members and subscribers through contracts with licensed health service personnel and health service institutions. It does not pay cash *indemnity* benefits.

Direct Tax

A tax on income (a *flow*) or wealth (a *stock*). See *Taxes*.

Direct to Consumer Advertising

A controversial alternative promotion used by pharmaceutical companies (where it is permitted) to *detailing* for advertising *prescription drugs*. It involves placing advertisements on television and in general public magazines, newspapers, etc. See Morgan et al. (2003), Bradford and Kleit (2006) and Brekke and Kuhn (2006).

Disabilities of the Arm, Shoulder and Hand

DASH is a self-administered outcome instrument developed as a measure of self-rated upper-extremity *disability* and symptoms for use mainly in studies of occupational health and safety. The DASH consists of a 30-item disability/symptom scale, scored 0 (no disability) to 100. A short form is *Quick*DASH. Its website is http://www.dash.iwh.on.ca/ (accessed 29 October 2009). See Beaton et al. (2001).

Disability

The concept has proved to be controversial by virtue of the fact that some definitions seem to imply unacceptable value judgments about disabled people. In general disability is 'lack of ability'. But how this should be judged (e.g. relative to what level of 'ability') is controversial. A disability may be physical, sensory, cognitive, intellectual and so on; it may be *chronic* or *acute*; and it may have many causes, genetic, environmental, etc. The so-called 'medical model' focuses on medical interventions and their ability to improve 'ability'. A more social type of intervention is also actively pursued in most policy contexts – interventions designed to modify the environment for the convenience of disabled people (e.g. through easing access and mobility) or to change the attitudes of other people. Cf. *Handicap, Impairment*. For a review of the health economics of disability policy see Haveman (2000).

Disability-adjusted Life-expectancy

Disability-adjusted Life-expectancy is a measure of healthy *life expectancy* developed by the *World Health Organization*. Years of expected ill-health are weighted according to severity and subtracted from the expected overall life expectancy to give the equivalent years of healthy life. DALE was developed to facilitate international comparisons of *health* and health *outcomes*. See Anand and Hansson (1997). For a critique see Lyttkens (2003).

Disability-adjusted Life-year

The disability-adjusted life-year is a measure of the burden of disability-causing disease and injury. Age-specific expected life-years are adjusted for expected loss of healthy life during those years, yielding measures of states of health or, when two streams of DALYs are compared, potential health gain or loss by changing from one health care or social intervention to another. Cf. *Assessment of Quality of Life, EuroQol, EQ-5D, 15D®, Health Utilities Index, Healthy Years Equivalent, Quality-adjusted Life-years, SF-6D©, SF-8©, SF-12©, SF-36©*. See *Burden of Disease, Health Gain, Health Status*. See Murray and Acharya (1997).

Disability Days

Days of restricted activity due to disease or injury.

Disability-free Life-expectancy

Disability-free life-expectancy is a health-adjusted life expectancy measure. DFLE defines a threshold of disability. Years lived with health above this *threshold* are counted fully while those below the threshold are not counted. See Robine (1986).

Disability Weight

A weight applied to life-years in the calculation of *disability-adjusted life-years*.

Discounted Cash Flow

A *flow* of money over a time period in which each period's cash is adjusted by an appropriate *discount factor* to represent its (reduced) future value (fundamentally due to *time preference*). The *present value* of the flow is the sum of these discounted values over the period in question. See *Discounting*.

Discounted Utility

It has been common in health economics to *discount* future *health* states, or the *utility* of such states, in much the same way as future consumption has been discounted in mainstream normative economics. However, there is continuing disagreement about the propriety of this, whether discount rates should be constant or vary, whether intertemporal *complementarity* can be adequately represented in discounting procedures, whether *costs* and *benefits* should be discounted at the same rates (constant or otherwise) in *cost–effectiveness analysis* and related studies. See *Discounting*. See Bleichrodt and Gafni (1996), Claxton et al. (2006b, 2010) and Gravelle et al. (2007a). For discounting in clinical decision-making see Höjgård et al. (2002).

Discount Factor

The discount factor for year t is given by $1/(1 + r)^t$ where r is the annual discount rate. Thus, if $r = 0.1$, the discount factor for $t = 1$ is 0.909 and for $t = 5$ it is 0.620. See *Discounting* for a general description.

Discount Rate

The *rate of interest* used to calculate a *present value* or to discount future values. See *Discounting*.

Discounting

A procedure for converting *costs* or *benefits* occurring at different dates to a common measure by use of an appropriate *discount rate*. Thus, with an annual discount rate r (expressed as a decimal fraction) the *present value* (PV) of a cost (C) in one year's time is $PV = C/(1 + r)$. In two years' time, it is $PV = C/(1 = r)^2$. The PV of a stream of future costs is the sum of every year's PV. For a stream, C, that is constant, the discrete time formula is $PV = C(1 - (1 + r)^{-n})P/r$. Of course, the same procedure applies to benefits as to costs. In *cost–effectiveness* and related analyses there is controversy as to whether a common discount rate should be used for costs and benefits and also as regards the use of the general rate used for public sector decisions. See Claxton et al. (2006b, 2010) and Gravelle et al. (2007a). For discounting in clinical decision-making see Höjgård et al. (2002).

Discrete Choice Analysis

Similar to *conjoint analysis*. A procedure used in experimental economics whereby subjects select real or simulated discrete (i.e. 'on' or 'off') options and thereby reveal (or 'state') their preferences. The objects of choice are often combinations of *attributes* of services, often written down on cards, from pairs of which choices are then typically made by the experimental subjects. See *Stated Preference*. Cf. *Revealed Preference*. See Ryan et al. (2001, 2008) and McIntosh (2007). In discrete choice experiments, especially those using *random utility theory*, there has been much discussion of ways of separating the scale of the estimated *parameters* and the magnitude of the random component. See Hensher et al. (1998).

Discrete Choice Experiments

See *Discrete Choice Analysis*.

Discrete Event Simulation

A stochastic method of simulating (modelling) health effects over time based on individual data in contrast to *deterministic models* based on *cohorts*. A health economics application is Campbell et al. (2001).

Discrete Time Model

A *model* in which the decision points, outcomes or other events occur at specific dates, for example, the start or end of a calendar year, rather than continuously. The points are often equidistant from one another. Cf. *Continuous Time Model*. An example of discrete procedures in health economics is Grossman (1972).

Discrete Variable

A variable that is not *continuous* and can take on values only at isolated points, such as the non-negative integers 0, 1, 2, . . . Examples include life, death, discharge from hospital, onset of disease, purchase of *health insurance*.

Discriminant Function Analysis

An alternative to *logistic regression analysis* that is used with *discrete dependent variables* enabling one to allocate entities from two or more populations to the correct one with minimal error. For an example in health economics, see Manning and Marquis (1996).

Discriminant Validity

A measure has discriminant validity when it successfully distinguishes between groups in ways expected in theory.

Disease

The economic *determinants* of specific diseases, the *cost-effectiveness* of strategies for their *prevention* or cure, and the consequences (economic, social and personal) of disease are to be found in innumerable economic research studies. A classic of its kind is Arrow et al. (2004).

Disease Costing

A procedure for assigning the expenditures of a health system or part thereof to the particular diseases for which care is provided. The costs in question tend to be accounting costs, that is historical statements of the outcome of decisions taken in the past, rather than *opportunity costs* specific to a choice context. Accordingly they are not reliable estimates, even in principle, of the likely reduction in 'negative effects' of remedial policies. See *Burden of Disease, Cost of Illness*.

Disease Management

A systematic approach to a health condition or health care intervention that involves organizing preventive, interventional and care approaches across the entire spectrum of the relevant professional groups and that measures *outcomes* in terms of effects on the *population* rather than on an individual. Similar to *chronic care management*. For some economics, see Beaulieu et al. (2006).

Diseconomies of Scale

Opposite of *economies of scale*.

Disinvestment

Reducing one's *capital* stock by, for example, selling capital goods or allowing them to wear out without replacement. In health care it can refer to the process of withdrawing services that have been identified as not *cost-effective*. See, e.g. Elshaug et al. (2007).

Disposable Income

The income left to an individual after payment of *taxes* and receipt of *transfer payments*.

Disposable Personal Income

The share of *national income* accruing to households net of *taxes* and other contractual deductions but including *transfer payments*.

Distribuendum

The good or service that is to be distributed (or redistributed), for example, income, wealth, health or health care.

Distribution

The record of the frequency of occurrence of particular values of a *variable*. It is usually described mathematically or graphically (or both). The distribution records all possible numerical values of the variable and how often each *value* occurs (its *frequency*). The best-known example of a distribution is the bell-shaped curve (the *normal distribution*) shown in the figure for the variable y, where μ is the *mean* (and also the *median*). See *Frequency Distribution, Mean, Median*.

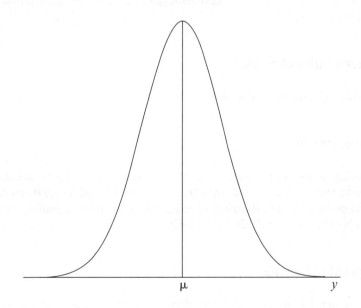

Distribution Function

A mathematical function that gives the relative *frequency* with which a random *variable* falls at or below particular values. Examples include the *binomial, chi-squared, log-normal, normal, t*, and *F*.

Distributional Value Judgments

Distributional *value judgments* are judgments about the desirability or otherwise of various distributions of entities to which moral significance is attached, like health, or health care, or access to health care. They may relate to, or derive from, more fundamental value judgments, for example about the relevance of a person's desert or need. See *Equity*.

Distributive Justice

The fairness (loosely speaking) with which some entity (such as health or health care) is distributed between people or groups of people. See *Equity*.

Disutility

A reduction in *utility*, or a dislike of disagreeable activities, to engage in which requires compensation. 'Work' is commonly so treated by economists.

Divisibility

The idea that *goods* (including *inputs*) do not come in chunks but are usable in infinitely small increments (or decrements). In economics this characteristic (which is useful in mathematical *models*) is often achieved, even when the good in question is manifestly lumpy in physical expression, by investigating rates of use or consumption (since *time* is infinitely divisible). In *cost–effectiveness analysis* the use of combinations of options (e.g. programmes of health care) in identifying those that have *dominance* usually requires programmes to be divisible. Cf. *Indivisibility*. See, for example, Lord et al. (2004).

Division of Drug Marketing, Advertising, and Communications

The branch of the US *Food and Drug Administration* that deals with the economic *appraisal* of pharmaceuticals and medical devices. It licenses drugs, offers guidance to industry, professionals and consumers, and acts as a regulator. Its website is available at: http://www.fda.gov/default.htm (accessed 29 October 2009).

DMF

Acronym for 'decayed missing filled' (teeth).

Domain

In health economics, when not used in one of its mathematical senses, this usually refers to the *attributes* of a health measure.

Dominance

Strong dominance exists when one option, technology or intervention is more *effective* and has lower *costs* than another. Weak dominance exists when one is at least as effective and has costs lower or has the same costs but greater effectiveness. Similarly, a distribution of something (such as mortality in country X) is said to dominate another (say, country Y) if it lies above it at every value or interval. See *Cost–Effectiveness Plane*, *Extended Dominance*.

Donut Hole

This term, coined in the US (where doughnuts have no 'ugh'), refers to an *insurance* plan in which there is a gap within the range of expenditures over which no cover is provided. The *Medicare* prescription drug benefit provides an example. In 2006, enrolees paid the first $250 (US) as a *deductible*, $25 per cent of sums up to the next $2000 in annual covered *prescription drug* expenditures, 100 per cent of the next $2850 in drug expenses and only 5 per cent after their expenditure exceeded $5100 in a year. These dollar amounts are adjusted annually based on the growth in per capita prescription drug spending. The 'hole' in 2006 was the $2251–5100 range. Although donut hole gaps in benefit seem arbitrary, there is political appeal: if the deductible is kept low enough, most people will enjoy at least some covered benefits and costs are lower than if there were no hole.

Dose–Response Curve

This is a diagram in which the *x*-axis plots concentration of a drug (or some other exposure variable, harmful or beneficial) and the *y*-axis plots responses such as secretion of a hormone, heartbeat or health outcome. It is similar to the diagrammatic representation of a *production function* where there is a single variable *input* and a single *output*. The standard dose–response curve has four *parameters*: the baseline response, the maximum response, the slope and the exposure concentration that provokes a response halfway between baseline and maximum. In *meta-analyses*, dose–response can be investigated using *meta-regression*. A typical curve is initially *convex* (from above), followed by a *concave* section, with a *point of inflexion* between.

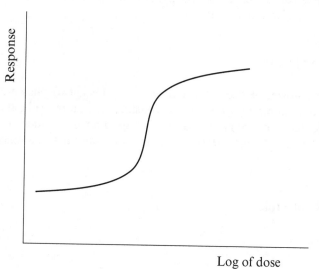

Dose–response curve

Double Blind Trial

A trial in which neither the patient nor the observing/measuring clinician is aware of whether a patient is in the *control* or *experimental arm*. See *Blinding*.

Double Bounded Discrete Choice

A questionnaire design in *discrete choice analysis* that supplements a single option for the subject with a second. See Smith (2000) and Watson and Ryan (2006).

Double Counting

This is a hazard in any method of appraising options. There are three common forms: simple errors due to incorrect arithmetic, suspicious circumstances due to fraudulent accounting practices and subtler forms due to inadequate conceptual clarity, poor administrative records or poor accounting of resource costs.

Double Hurdle

A characteristic of decisions that have, in effect, two phases and two sets of determining *variables* to be considered. For example, there may be a decision to smoke and another regarding how much to smoke. Originated by Cragg (1971). See, for the smoking example, Jones (1989).

Doughnut Hole

See *Donut Hole*.

DQTC

Acronym for the (erstwhile) *Drug Quality and Therapeutics Committee, Ontario*.

DRG

Acronym for *diagnostic (diagnosis) related group*.

DRG Creep

Changes in diagnostic codings by hospitals and other providers in order to take advantage of better remunerated *diagnostic related groups*.

Drug Lag

A term used to describe the slow approval of drugs by the US *Food and Drug Administration* before drugs are permitted to reach the market.

Drug Quality and Therapeutics Committee

A former advisory committee to the Ontario (Canada) Ministry of Health and Long Term Care, which evaluated drugs for provincial formulary listing. Now *Committee to Evaluate Drugs*.

DUKE

See *Duke Health Profile*.

Duke Health Profile

This is a 17-item generic measure of health-related quality of life. There are six components for functional health (physical, mental, social, general, perceived health and self-esteem) and five covering other dimensions (anxiety, depression, anxiety-depression, pain and *disability*). The instrument can be obtained from: http://healthmeasures.mc.duke.edu (accessed 29 October 2009).

Dummy Variable

An alternative name for a *binary variable*, which takes the value 1 or 0. Examples are gender, domicile (home/abroad), pregnancy, liking for Wagner's music. For an introduction see Kennedy (2003). Cf. *Count Data*.

Dumping

A refusal by a health care provider to treat patients whose costs are expected to exceed the compensation payable to the provider. It arises particularly in systems that are dependent on private *health insurance* arrangements. In the US, federal patient-dumping law entitles people in emergency situations to be screened, receive emergency care and to be appropriately transferred to another provider. A hospital must provide 'stabilizing care' for a patient with an emergency medical condition. The hospital must screen for the emergency and provide the care without inquiring about *ability to pay*. Although emergency cover is thus assured (in the US), there is less assurance about non-emergency care for people who lose their jobs or change jobs (and who lose cover that was previously provided through a workplace arrangement). See Ellis (1998).

This is quite different from the usual notion of 'dumping' in international trade: selling goods abroad below their normal market value or below the price charged for them in the domestic market of the exporting country. This form of dumping can be a predatory trade practice whereby the international market, or a certain national market, is flooded with dumped goods in order to force competitors out of the market and establish a *monopoly* position. However, what constitutes 'dumping' in this context is a somewhat subjective and arbitrary judgment and is often a mask for mere protectionism.

Duopoly

A market in which there are but two sellers. See *Competition*.

Duration Analysis

The analysis of the time spent by an individual in a particular state (say, of health). Cf. *Survival Analysis* in medical statistics.

Duration Neglect

A kind of *cognitive bias* that arises in psychological and economic experiments whereby subjects give a disproportionate weight to experiences of short duration or very little weight to the duration of an experience. Cf. *Remembered Utility*. See Fredrickson and Kahneman (1993) and Oliver (2004b).

Durbin–Watson Statistic

A test for *autocorrelation* in residuals (the values predicted by a regression minus the actual values). A *value* near 2 indicates an absence of autocorrelation. See Durbin and Watson (1950, 1951).

DW

Acronym for *Durbin–Watson statistic*.

Dynamics

One way of doing economics, in which the focus is on the process of change as people react to disequilibria arising from disturbances of various kinds affecting a *model*. A common interest in economic dynamics concerns whether and in what way, with what speed, etc., an economy will approach *equilibrium* following a disturbance. The other main way of doing economics is *comparative statics*, which compares the states of equilibrium that are predicted to come about in response to disturbances but not the process through which they come about. For a health economics example of dynamic modelling see Ried (1998).

E

Early Stage Modelling

A method of assessing the likely *effectiveness* or *cost-effectiveness* of a drug or other clinical intervention prior to extensive field *trials*. It typically has four characteristic elements: (1) a *decision analysis* model describing the expected course and management of the disease, (2) a profile of possible *costs* and *outcomes*, (3) an estimated range of possible prices and (4) a *sensitivity analysis*. See Anderson et al. (2004) for an introduction.

Earmarking

Associating particular forms of *tax* with particular forms of expenditure. It is usually seen as a bad thing by politicians, since it reduces their discretion, and a good thing by libertarians, for the same reason. A classic is Buchanan (1963).

EBM

Acronym for *evidence-based medicine*.

ECHE

Acronym for *European Conference on Health Economics*.

Ecological Fallacy

The ecological fallacy consists in thinking that relationships observed for groups necessarily hold for individuals. Thus, while in the aggregate, US states with a high proportion of foreign-born residents are also states with high literacy in American English, it does not follow that foreign-born people are more literate than the rest. For one thing, there may be a large *variance* to which the use of an average gives no clue; for another, there may be many other *determinants* (*confounders*); for yet another, to observe a *correlation* is not to observe cause and effect or the direction of cause and effect. For that one needs a hypothesis. In fact, studies at the individual level have shown that the 'ecological *correlation*' of foreign-born and literacy rates arises because foreign-born people tend to settle in states that already have high literacy. At the individual level, the correlation between being foreign-born and ability in American English is (as one may expect) in fact negative. The *atomistic fallacy* is similar in kind: the fallacy of drawing inferences regarding variability across units defined at a higher level based on data collected for units at a lower level. See *Aggregation Problem* for an economic example. In health economics, see Birch et al. (1998).

Econometrics

The application of statistical and mathematical methods in the field of economics to test economic theories, quantify relationships and other entities of interest, and the methodological development of the techniques for doing these things. For reviews of econometrics as it has been applied in health, see Jones (2000, 2007), Jones and O'Donnell (2002), Jones et al. (2007) and O'Donnell et al. (2008).

Economic Appraisal

A general term for the economic evaluation of options. This can be done from a variety of *perspectives* (social, those of different stakeholders). Some use the term to describe the evaluation of evaluative research studies (for their reliability, generalizability, etc.), as in a systematic review of evaluative studies. See *Cost–Benefit Analysis, Cost–Consequences Analysis, Cost–Effectiveness Analysis, Cost–Utility Analysis, Financial Appraisal*. A gentle introduction is Fox-Rushby and Cairns (2005). See Appendix for 100 examples.

Economic Development and Health

The association between economic development and *health* may be two-way but it is almost certainly even more complex than this suggests. There has been considerable debate as to whether (for example) higher incomes in low-income countries generate better health or higher income inequality in high-income countries generates worse health. For a careful survey, see Deaton (2003). See also Acemoglu and Johnson (2007). On pharmaceuticals and development see Kremer (2002). For a general text: Jack (1999), Witter and Ensor (1997) and Witter et al. (2000).

Economic Evaluation

Same as *economic appraisal*. See *Evaluation*.

Economic Good

A good or service of which more is wanted. It corresponds to the *non-satiation axiom* of economic *choice theory*. It is not necessarily a good or service that commands a market price. In this context 'good' carries no normative baggage and the reasons for wanting the good in question may themselves be good or bad or neither. Health care commonly meets the definition of an economic good or service.

Economics

Economics concerns the study of human behaviour as a relationship between given ends and scarce means having alternative uses. This is the classic (positivist) definition given by Robbins (1932), on which rest claims that economics is a science. Economics also addresses how we (individually or collectively) ought to choose (the normative face of economics) as well as what and why we choose as we do. Even if claims that economics is a science are not entirely sustainable on account of the common infusion of value judgments (often only implicit) and highly imperfect means of hypothesis testing, economics has considerable value in identifying the informational needs of policy and in creating useful categories and perspectives from which to evaluate options. See also *Classical Economics, Health Economics, Neoclassical Economics, Postmodernism.*

Economics of Alcohol

Usually modelled in economics as an *addiction*, with individuals' behaviour being examined under various types of incentive and disincentive, puzzling aspects of their behaviour needing explanation, and the *welfare* consequences of alternative policy options to control excesses. For a review see Cook and Moore (2000).

Economics of Health

Same as *health economics*.

Economics of Hospitals

See *Hospital Behaviour, Hospital Costs, Hospital Economics.*

Economics of Obesity

The economic *determinants* and consequences of *obesity*. Can be modelled as an *addiction*. See Lakdawalla and Philipson (2006) and Grossman (2008).

Economics of Smoking

Usually modelled in economics as an *addiction*, with individuals' behaviour being examined under various types of incentive and disincentive, puzzling aspects of their behaviour needing explanation, and the *welfare* consequences of alternative policy options to control excesses. For a review, see Chaloupka and Warner (2000).

Economics of Substance Abuse

See *Addiction.*

Economies of Scale

This is a result of *increasing returns to scale*: the amount of *resource* used per unit of *output* falls at higher output rates. It implies a falling unit *cost* as output rates increase, as long as *input* prices do not increase so as to offset the scale effect, as they might if the organization in question is a principal user of a resource and there is a degree of *monopsony*. Diseconomies of scale are the contrary phenomenon. In hospitals, it has usually been found that the average cost curve has a shallow 'U' shape with the lowest point around 200 beds. Some studies have found modest scale economies. Cf. *Economies of Scope*. See *Production Function*. See Cowing et al. (1983), Dranove (1998) and Preyra and Pink (2006).

Economies of Scope

Same as '*scope effects*'. Economies of scope enable a firm to produce several goods or services jointly more cheaply than producing them separately. The simultaneous production of hospital care and medical teaching is an example. Cf. *Economies of Scale*. Health economics studies that have estimated economies of scope (as well as scale) include Ullman and Holtman (1985), Granneman et al. (1986) and Preyra and Pink (2006).

ECuity Project

An international research project funded by the European Union whose full title is 'Equity in the Finance and Delivery of Health Care in Europe'. Its website is available at: http://www2.eur.nl/bmg/ecuity// (accessed 30 October 2009).

Edgeworth Box

Named after the Oxford economist Francis Ysidro Edgeworth (1845–1926), this is a diagram showing the possible allocations of given quantities of two goods between two people and how, given conventional assumptions about their preferences, they can achieve a *Pareto-optimal* distribution of the goods between them from any initial starting *distribution*. Sometimes called simply '*box diagram*'. See *Contract Curve* for a figure using the box. The focus is on efficient rather than equitable distributions of goods and services between people but it has been adapted in health economics to enable the simultaneous analysis of both as in, for example Culyer (1971a), Cullis and West (1979), Wagstaff (1991) and Culyer and Wagstaff (1993).

EER

Acronym for *experimental event rate*.

Effect Modification

A change in the size of an effect in a *trial* due to a *variable* that is not an immediate *determinant*. An interaction between the *independent variable* of interest (such as treatment with a drug) and another unrelated variable (such as gender). For example, age is a modifier of the effect of measles infection on the risk of death.

Effect Size

A measure of the difference in *outcome* between intervention groups. The *average* outcome in an *experimental arm* minus that in the *control arm* divided by the *standard deviation* in the control arm. In *epidemiological* studies with *dichotomous* (binary) outcomes and exposures it is often expressed as a *relative risk*, *odds ratio* or risk difference for *binary* outcomes and as difference in *means* for *continuous* outcomes. Same as *treatment effect*.

Effectiveness

A measure similar to *efficacy* except that it refers to the effect of a particular medical technology or procedure on *outcomes* when used in 'actual' practice. It thus differs from *efficacy* in that efficacy concerns only the technical relationship between the procedure and its effects under 'ideal' conditions (in practice, typically the conditions that obtain in a research-oriented teaching hospital or *primary care* practice). 'Actual' practice is thus conceived to be practice as conducted by average professionals working with average resources. In economic jargon, the idea of effectiveness is encompassed within the notion of a *production function*. In *epidemiology*, *clinical trials* are typically designed to generate high levels of *internal validity* (efficacy) and *pragmatic trials* high levels of *external validity* or generalizability. For an introduction to the principles for establishing effectiveness, with lots of examples of ineffective, unscientific and harmful medical practices, see Wootton (2006) and Evans et al. (2007).

Effectiveness Sub-groups

Groups of individuals in a larger *experimental group* for whom the *effectiveness* is expected to be the same.

Effective Patent Life

The effective patent life of a pharmaceutical product is typically shorter than the period of formal protection thanks to regulatory requirements, clinical and other trials. See *Patent*. See Vernon and Grabowski (2000).

Efficacy

The maximum *benefit* or *utility* to the individual of the service, treatment regimen, drug, preventive or control measure advocated or applied under 'ideal' conditions. The *probability* of benefit to individuals in a defined *population* from a medical technology under 'ideal' conditions of use. More generally, the maximum potential effect of a particular medical action in altering the natural history of a particular disease for the better. 'Ideal' might refer to the excellence of the team running the experiment or trial, or to the quality of the establishment in which they are working. Efficacy alone is a poor guide to choice since it takes no account of the other good (possibly better) health outcomes that the same resources could generate, quite apart from the problem that what has efficacy under 'ideal' conditions may not have it (or have less of it) under normal working conditions. For example, Coyle et al. (1999) estimated the efficacy of the hormone erythropoietin (EPO) to reduce patients' exposure to donated blood products in ortho-paedic surgery by conducting a *meta-analysis* of published *randomized controlled trials*. The benefits in terms of life-years gained were small. Relative to orthopaedic surgery without EPO, the benefit was 0.000024 additional life-years and its benefit in augmenting use of the patient's own pre-collected blood was 0.000006 life-years. In short, there was a small expectation of patient benefit. The additional cost per life year amounted, however, to (CAN)$66 million and (CAN)$329 million respectively with the over-whelming implication that many more life-years could be saved by using resources in a different way. Cf. *Cost–Effectiveness Analysis, Effectiveness.*

Efficiency

In a restrictive sense, efficiency is defined either as minimizing the *opportunity cost* of attaining a given *output* or as maximizing the output for a given opportunity cost. The general term used by economists is *Pareto-efficiency*. This is an allocation of resources such that it is not possible to reallocate any of them without imposing uncompensated losses of *utility* on some individual. A variant is *potential Pareto-efficiency*, where it is not possible to reallocate resources without imposing non-compensable losses on someone (i.e. the losses may not actually be compensated). It is common to see the notion of efficiency expressed at three different levels: technical efficiency, where more *inputs* are not used than are technically necessary to attain a given output (there will normally be a wide variety of different combinations arising out of their *substitutability*); cost-efficiency or *cost-effectiveness*, where a given output is produced using the least-cost technically efficient combination of inputs or, conversely, output is maximized for a given level of cost (the combinations of resources here will be a subset of those deemed technically efficient); Pareto-efficiency, where output is not only technically- and cost-efficient but is also set at an efficient rate such that any diminution or increase would cause marginal cost to exceed or fall below the marginal value to consumers. Pareto-efficiency is also termed '*allocative efficiency*' (a somewhat unhelpful term since all three ideas of efficiency are about resource allocation). The first two ideas concern the allocation of inputs to outputs; the third concerns the allocation of outputs to consumers, clients or users.

A variant idea of efficiency arises under what is known as *extra-welfarism*. With this (rather than general utility or welfare) as the framework, the *maximand* may be whatever the analyst or policy-maker selects as appropriate. In health policy, *health* or *health gain* are common objectives. In such cases, health may be set as the maximand and efficiency implies either achieving a given overall level of health in the population at the least opportunity cost or, for a given set of resources, maximizing their impact on overall health. The idea of 'overall' health implies, of course, some means of 'adding up' the health of individual people, which will entail some distributional value judgments concerning the weight each is to have. In extra-welfarism, it seems better not to extend the idea of efficiency to achieve an efficient distribution of outputs to clients, leaving this as a matter of *equity*, to be determined in other ways and by other criteria. Needless to say, equity objectives can themselves also be achieved with varying degrees of efficiency!

It should be plain that 'efficiency' is an inherently *normative* term. It tends to commend itself to economists, who do not always stop to think that whether it is good to be efficient may depend on what it is one is being efficient at doing. An efficiently run torture chamber scarcely commends itself; indeed it were better for such places to be inefficient than efficient. Nevertheless, the economists' concept of efficiency is pretty completely worked out and complements work in related fields such as *epidemiology*. See also *Health Technology Assessment, Interpersonal Comparisons of Utility, Kaldor–Hicks Criterion, X-inefficiency, Utility*.

Effort

Usually applied to the contribution of a team member in the production of a good or service. It is subject to *moral hazard* and *adverse selection* by virtue of it being difficult to observe and calibrate. Not to be confused with *cost*! See Chalkley (2006), Smith and Street (2006) and, for the origins of the idea, Alchian and Demsetz (1972).

Egalitarianism

The political doctrine that ascribes high ethical significance to various types of social equality, for example in relation to the terms of access to health care, the equal meeting of equal needs, or the achievement of an equal distribution of outcomes. It is a common feature of Christian, communist, human rights, Kantian and socialist ethics, and is embodied in the United States constitution. Most concepts of equality are in conflict with one another (e.g. to obtain greater equality of health usually involves greater inequality in the use of health care). It also tends to be the case that moves towards greater equality of something involve the violation of other moral principles, for example, violation of one's 'natural rights'. Note: equality is not necessarily the same as equity. See *Equity*.

Eigenvalue

A measure of the proportion of the total variance accounted for by a single factor in *factor analysis*.

Elasticity

The responsiveness of a *dependent variable* (for example, *output* or *demand*) to changes in one of the variables determining it (for example, an *input*, price or income), *ceteris paribus*. It may be positive or negative. Numerically it is given by:

$$\text{elasticity} = \frac{\% \text{ change in dependent variable}}{\% \text{ change in determining variable.}}$$

Using real variables in the above yields what is known as the arc-elasticity. The limit of this, as the change in the determining variable becomes smaller and smaller, is the point-elasticity, which is not directly observable and must be inferred statistically.

Commonly encountered elasticities are *income-elasticity* (the responsiveness of the consumption of a good or service to changes in income);

demand-elasticity or own-price-elasticity (the responsiveness of the consumption of a good or service to a change in its price), cross (price) elasticity (the responsiveness of the consumption of a good or service to a change in the price of another good or service), supply-elasticity (the responsiveness of the quantity supplied of a good or service to a change in its price), *elasticity of substitution* (the responsiveness of the ratio of two *inputs* to a change in the *marginal rate of substitution*) and elasticity of expectations (the responsiveness of the expected value to a change in its current value).

The largest empirical study ever to attempt to measure the elasticities of demand for health care was Manning et al. (1987). For more recent results that conflict sharply, see Chandra et al. (2007). Critique of the RAND experiment is from Welch et al. (1987) with a reply (Newhouse et al.,1987 and, later, by Nyman, 2007) with a response from Newhouse et al. (2008). See also Wedig (1988). A recent review is in Chapters 8 and 9 of Folland et al. (2010). For a developing country example, where extremely high falls in demand follow even modest *copayments*, see Akin et al. (1998) and Kremer and Miguel (2007). Elasticities of demand have been studied even amongst users of illegal drugs (e.g. Van Ours, 1995 and Bretteville-Jensen, 1999). In preventive care see Ellis et al. (2004) and Trivedi et al. (2008).

Elasticity of Substitution

In *production functions*, a measure of the curvature of an *isoquant*. See *Elasticity*. See, for a health economics example, Grytten and Dalen (1997).

Elective Surgery

Elective surgery is non-emergency surgery, sometimes called 'cold' surgery, that is subject to considerable choice of date of admission to hospital without risk to the patient. Common examples are most surgery undertaken for haemorrhoids or hernias. For an analysis of the *supply* and *demand* for such care see Martin et al. (2007).

Ellsberg Paradox

An awkwardness for *expected utility theory*. In experiments, subjects have displayed an aversion to *ambiguity*, contrary to the assumptions of expected utility theory. See *Ambiguity*. See Ellsberg (1961).

Embodied Technical Progress

Advances in knowledge that are expressed only through investment goods and physical equipment. Disembodied knowledge is knowledge that can be exploited without such investment. For a health economics example see Lichtenberg and Virabhak (2007).

EMEA

Acronym for *European Medicines Evaluation Agency*.

Empirical

Of experience, evidence, observation or experiment as distinct from *a priori* or being based on reason only.

Employee Benefit Plan

A US plan created or maintained by an employer or employee organization that provides benefits to employees. The term may cover retirement pension plans, other plans for life *insurance*, health and dental insurance and *disability* income insurance. A plan's cost may be (nominally) completely paid for by the employer or be shared with employees. In the former case it is unlikely that there would be no wage adjustments, as a result of which the employee will bear at least a fraction of the cost. A plan may also cover such benefits as sick leave, disability, profit-sharing or stock purchasing. See *Incidence*.

Employers' Liability

See *Workers' Compensation*.

Emporiatics

The medical speciality concerned with diseases and treatments of travellers.

Endemic

Disease *prevalences* in a particular location that do not vary much over time.

Endocrinology

The medical speciality concerned with the structure and *physiology* of endocrine glands (glands that secrete directly into the bloodstream).

End of Scale Bias

A form of *bias* found in some instruments for measuring *health status*. It involves a reluctance on the part of experimental subjects to use the extremes of the scale they are offered.

Endogenous

Usually descriptive of a characteristic of a *variable* in an economic *model*. A variable is endogenous if it is a function of other *parameter*s or variables in the model. Cf. *Exogenous*. For a health economics example, see Windmeijer and Santos Silva (1997).

Endowment

In economics this usually refers to the bundle of goods and money that each individual is assumed to hold at the beginning of an analysis.

Endowment Effect

A form of *cognitive bias* encountered in psychological and economic experiments whereby the subject's ownership of an entity affects their valuation of it.

Endpoint

Defines the ultimate *outcome* in a *trial*. Common endpoints are severe toxicity, disease progression or death. These endpoints (other than death) are rarely endpoints of the sort to satisfy economists because they are not easily interpretable in welfare terms and/or because they mark a point in time beyond which further measurement and observation are not done (which may therefore require modelling if there are significant post-endpoint events or trends for *cost-effectiveness* purposes). From such a perspective, such endpoints plainly are not 'ultimate'.

Engel Curve

A function showing the relationship between income and the consumption of a good or service. Named after Ernst Engel (1821–96). See Engel (1895).

ENT

Acronym for ear, nose and throat, the surgical speciality of *otorhinolaryngology*.

Entitlement Theory

This is a libertarian theory holding that a distribution of goods, or income and wealth, is just if it arises in a non-coercive way (for example via voluntary trading between individuals). Cf. *Equity, Fairness, Utilitarianism*. See Nozick (1974).

Envelope

Usually refers to a smooth curve that is tangential to each of a family of curves or a *frontier* marking the boundary between what is possible with given technologies and resources and what is not.

Environmental Health and Safety

A topic on which there is a somewhat patchy economics literature. For principles of evaluating interventions for increasing environmental health and safety see Arrow et al. (1996) and Bosworth et al. (2009). On methods see Loomes (2006). For specific environmental threats to health see, e.g. Jones-Lee (1989) on road traffic safety, Chay and Greenstone (2003) on air pollution and Dolan et al. (2005) on crime. See also *Occupational Disease and Injury*.

Epidemic

A rapid increase in the *prevalence* of a disease. High levels of an infection. Cf. *Endemic, Pandemic*.

Epidemiology

The study of the relationship between *risk factors* and *disease* in human *populations*, including factors that can change the relationship, and the application of such analysis to the design and management of health care systems. Clinical epidemiology is studied in clinical settings, usually by clinician-epidemiologists, and usually with patients as subjects. Experimental epidemiology involves controlled experiments as in laboratory experiments or *randomized controlled trials* (RCTs). Social epidemiology concerns the social *determinant*s of health and its distribution. Epidemiology of any of these kinds may be descriptive (which merely records the facts as they appear to be) or analytic (usually involving the development of and/or the testing of hypotheses). Of the three, social epidemiology can be the most normative and prescriptive. See *Clinical Epidemiology, Population Health, Public Health*. On social epidemiology, see Berkman and Kawachi (2000).

Episode of Care

The course of treatment from a patient's first encounter with a health care provider through to the completion of the last encounter in a sequence of related encounters and treatments.

EQ-5D

EQ-5D is a standardized instrument for use as a generic measure of the quality of health-related life and of health *outcome* (for example in *cost–effectiveness analyses*). It is particularly associated with the QALY (*quality-adjusted life-year*). It is designed for self-completion by respondents and is suited for use in postal surveys, clinics and face-to-face interviews. It is cognitively simple, taking only a few minutes to complete. Instructions to respondents are included in the questionnaire. The EQ-5D has five dimensions: Mobility, Self-care, Usual activity, Pain/discomfort, Anxiety/Depression. The traditional EQ-5D instrument described each dimension in terms of three levels: 1– no problem, 2 – some problem, 3 – extreme problem. More recently, the *EuroQol Group* has developed a five-level version (EQ-5D-5L) and an instrument validated for self-completion by children and young people (EQ-5D-Y). In each case, the instrument comprises two parts: respondents rate their health on the dimensions/levels and record an overall assessment of their health on a *visual analogue scale*, the *EQ-VAS*. See *Health-related Quality of Life*. For general introduction, see Brooks et al. (2003). See also Dolan et al. (1996b). For the UK version see Kind et al. (1998). For the most up-to-date versions, see the EuroQol website http://www.euroqol.org/ (accessed 30 October 2009). For an application in Zimbabwe see Jelsma et al. (2003). For a comparison between EQ-5D and *SF-6D*© see Brazier et al. (2004).

EQ-5D-5L

See *EQ-5D*.

EQ-5D-Y

See *EQ-5D*.

EQ-VAS

Part of the *EQ-5D*. In addition to describing their health on the dimensions and levels of the EQ-5D, respondents are asked to rate their overall *health-related quality of life* on a standard vertical 20 cm visual *analogue scale* (similar to a thermometer) between 100 (best health imaginable) and

0 (worst health imaginable). See, e.g., Whynes (2008) for a comparison between EQ-5D *health state* classifications and EQ-VAS scores.

Equilibrating Variable

A *variable* whose movement tends to eliminate *excess demand* and *excess supply*. See *Equilibrium*.

Equilibrium

In economics, equilibrium is the term used usually to describe the (not necessarily unique) solution to a set of simultaneous *structural equations* that represent the key relationships in a *model* of the economy, or part of it such as a specific market. Thus, the equilibrium price and quantity in a simple three-equation model of a market are those at which *demand* equals *supply*, there being an equation for demand, another for supply and a third, being the equilibrium condition:

$$D = a - bP$$

$$S = c + dP$$

$$D = S.$$

The equilibrium price is thus $(a - c)/(d + b)$. The price at which transactions take place in equilibrium is the same for demanders and suppliers and that the quantity supplied is equal to that demanded. Unless something changes (that is, *the ceteris paribus* qualifier is violated), these equilibrium values will, granted some side-conditions, be stable, so the system as a whole is in a kind of balance that no market participant has any particular reason to want to change. See *General Equilibrium, Equilibrating Variable, Nash Equilibrium, Partial Equilibrium.*

Equipoise

As used, somewhat loosely, in *epidemiology*, a situation in which it is not known which of various treatment options is better. It is a standard ethical requirement of *clinical trials*. The degree of uncertainty regarding each option seems not to come into it.

Equity

This has two quite distinct meanings in economics. One is from account-ing. See *Balance Sheet*. The other is from political philosophy. While *efficiency* is one ethical imperative in the design and operation of health services and other *determinants* of health, equity is another. It is not neces-sarily to be identified with equality or *egalitarianism,* but relates in general to ethical judgments about the *fairness* of income and wealth *distributions, cost* and *benefit* distributions, *access* to health services, exposure to health-threatening hazards and so on. Although not the same as 'equality', equity nearly always involves the equality of something (such as opportunity, health, access). *Horizontal equity* refers to the fairness in the treatment of apparent equals (such as persons with the same income). *Vertical equity* refers to fairness in the treatment of apparent unequals (such as persons with different incomes). A *distribution* of something (such as *health*, income or *health insurance* costs) is said to be horizontally equitable when people are treated the same in some relevant respect. Thus, if the relevant respect (a *value judgment*) is *'need'*, then an equitable distribution is one that treats people with the same need in the same way. A distribution is said to be vertically equitable when people who are different in some relevant way are treated appropriately differently. Thus, if the relevant respect is again 'need', an equitable distribution will accord more (of some relevant entity) to those in greater need of it – how much more will normally entail further value judgments as well, probably, as assessments of the impact of the resources on their relative position in the distribution.

At the risk of some over-simplification: in health and health care, the distribution of health itself is typically regarded as a matter of horizontal equity (i.e. avoidable inequalities are inequitable). The distribution of *transfer payments* and *subsidies*, and *out-of-pocket* payments by people tend to be treated as matters of vertical equity (for example, being equi-tably inversely related to income). Inequalities in health care utilization tend to be viewed as equitable or inequitable accordingly as they support or detract from greater equality in health, with the general (horizontal) presumption that equal health requires equal access possibilities.

For a straightforward introduction see Braveman and Gruskin (2003) and for a general review Wagstaff and Van Doorslaer (2000). On inequal-ity aversion see Wagstaff (1991, 2002b). On equity and QALYs, see Nord et al. (1999), Dolan and Tsuchiya (2006) and Bleichrodt et al. (2008). On equity and equality see Culyer and Wagstaff (1993). On equity and development, see Deaton (2003). On equity in health care and income see Van Doorslaer et al. (1999). On equity and finance see Van Doorslaer et al. (1999). On equity and health see Williams and Cookson (2000, 2006).

On equity and efficiency see Cutler (2002). For a book-length exhaustive treatment of empirical methods see O'Donnell et al. (2008). See also *Concentration Index, Egalitarianism, Gradient in Health, Socioeconomic Differences.*

Equivalence of Numbers

Same as *person trade-off method.*

Equivalence Scale

A scale used in adjusting incomes or expenditures in order to make fair comparisons between households of different sizes and composition. See *Equivalization.*

Equivalence Trial

A type of *trial* where the aim is to establish whether one treatment is as *effective* as (or equivalent to) another. It is most commonly used when the new treatment is expected to be as effective as an existing one but also to have fewer side-effects, a faster recovery rate, lower cost, or other relevant difference. Cf. *Futility Trial, Non-inferiority trial, Superiority trial.*

Equivalent Annual Cost

A constant annual sum of money having the same *present value* as a stream of actual annual costs. Also known as 'annuitized value'.

Equivalent Variation

The equivalent variation in income is the maximum amount of money an individual would be willing to pay *before* a price increase to leave them as well off as they would be after the change. Similarly, in the case of a price fall, it is the minimum amount of money a person would have to receive to be as well off as they would be after the change. It is a measure of welfare change introduced by Sir John Hicks (1904–89) and its main use lies in *cost–benefit analysis* and related techniques for estimating the benefits of public investments. Cf. *Compensating Variation, Kaldor–Hicks Criterion, Willingness to Accept, Willingness to Pay.* See Hicks (1944) for the original analysis, Groot et al. (2004) for a health economics application.

Equivalization

The ugly neologism for an adjustment made to incomes or expenditures to enable fair comparisons to be made between *households* of different sizes and composition. See *Equivalence Scale.* See, for example, Lambert and Yitzakhi (1997).

Ergonomics

The study of the interaction between people, their work place and working environment, including the assessment of the physiological effects on workers of the design of tools, equipment and working methods.

Error Components Model

A regression *model* for *panel data.* See *Multiple Regression.* See Baltagi (2005) for a comprehensive treatment. See Rice and Jones (1997).

Error Term

Consider the following regression *model*:

$$Y_i = a + bX_i + \varepsilon_i$$

where the subscript *i* refers to the *i*th observation. The random error term ε_i (epsilon) captures all the variation in the *independent variable* Y_i that is not explained by the X_i (*dependent*) variables.

Ethics Committee

Ethics committees are agencies (some statutory) that are designed to protect people who are directly or indirectly the subjects of, or might be affected by, research. Committee approval is normally required for research involving patients, relatives or carers of patients; access to data, organs or other bodily material of past and present patients; foetal material and IVF involving patients; the recently dead in hospitals; the use of, or potential access to, health care premises or facilities; health care staff who are recruited as research participants by virtue of their professional role.

Ethnography

The *qualitative analysis* of human races and cultures through extensive face-to-face interviews and interaction with subjects.

Etiological Fraction

Alternative spelling of *aetiological fraction*. Same as *'attributable fraction'*.

Etiology

The study of the causes of disease. Also *'aetiology'*.

European Conference on Health Economics

An annual conference run by European health economists.

European Medicines Evaluation Agency

An agency of the European Union with headquarters in London under the European Commission. It evaluates and supervises medicines for human and veterinary use and authorizes their marketing, an authorization that applies in all countries of the community and also Iceland, Liechtenstein and Norway. All medicinal products for human and animal use derived from biotechnology and other high-technology processes must be approved by the EMEA. Its website is available at: http://www. emea.europa.eu/htms/aboutus/emeaoverview.htm (accessed 30 October 2009).

EuroQol

A term used to refer to the *EQ-5D*. See Brooks et al. (2003).

EuroQol Group

An international group of economists and decision theorists (mainly but not exclusively European) who developed the *EQ-5D* measure of *health-related quality of life* and the index values used in the estimation of a *quality-adjusted life-year*. Its website is available at: www.euroqol.org/ (accessed 30 October 2009).

Evaluation

Determining the value of a procedure, clinical intervention or process through the systematic consideration of its advantages and disadvantages, their distribution, and the probabilities attached to them. For an introduction to clinical evaluation with many examples of what can go wrong in its absence see Evans et al. (2007). See *Cost–Benefit Analysis, Cost–Consequences Analysis, Cost–Effectiveness Analysis, Cost–Utility Analysis, Economic Appraisal*.

Event Rate

The proportion of patients in a group in whom an event is observed. Thus, if the event is observed in 33 out of 100 patients, the event rate is 0.33.

Evidence

This is not such an unambiguous term as may appear. Some take the view that for something to count as evidence it must be scientific, quantitative, free of *confounding* and free of *bias*. Others would admit any asserted 'fact', piece of recorded data, individual 'case', or 'professional opinion' as well as quantitative and qualititive research, the results of controlled and uncontrolled experiments. The dividing line between 'evidence' and 'gossip' is thus not clear. In all cases, judgment needs to be exercised as regards the quality of the evidence, its relevance and applicability in the context under consideration, the degree to which it is contested, its precision, and its sufficiency or completeness – all terms that themselves admit of a variety of definitions. See *Evidence-based Medicine*. On kinds of evidence that may need to be balanced off against one another by decision-makers see Lomas et al. (2005). On harmonizing evidential requirements in formulary-type decisions see Hutton et al. (2008).

Evidence-based Medicine

The practice of medicine informed by the best available evidence of *effectiveness* and other empirically amenable aspects of the clinical management of a patient. There is a lot of argument as to what constitutes *evidence* and the weight to put upon different kinds (for example, evidence from *randomized controlled trials* or from *observational studies*). There is remarkably little evidence that evidence-based medicine (often abbreviated to EBM) leads to better health outcomes for patients, though it must be said that this is absence of (good) evidence rather than (good) evidence of absence of effect. Many people prefer the term 'evidence-informed' on the grounds that there is more to decision-making than mere evidence. An important precursor was Cochrane (1972) but the term was coined by Guyatt (1991). See Guyatt et al. (1992) and Eddy (2005). A useful antidote against the mindless adoption of EBM is Gordon et al. (2003).

Those who attempt conscientiously to use evidence in their decision-making commonly need to confront the following issues: the absence of scientific research (clinical, economic, social) on an important aspect of the matter to hand; a too narrow interpretation of 'scientific' (e.g. to exclude economic and social evidence of a statistical kind); the irrelevance in part or whole of such research as may exist; the need for interpretational skills that they do not have (especially with multidisciplinary material or evidence from disciplines not represented amongst the decision-making group); research of poor quality; research that is dated; research (even high-quality research) whose outcomes are ambiguous and conditional on unknown factors; research that is controversial and contested by expert researchers in the field; research of high quality when judged by a criterion such as *internal validity* but poor when judged by another such as *external validity*; research that is of one level in respect of its clinical or *epidemiological* quality or completeness but of another in respect of its economic or social character; the need to supplement research evidence by the practical experience of clinicians and other professionals either to 'fill gaps' in knowledge or to form judgments about the quality and relevance of such research as exists; non-technical issues as to whether a technology is *sufficiently* effective to warrant recommendation/use; non-technical issues as to whether a technology's probable benefits justify the costs that can be attributed to its introduction and use and the associated risks attached to its use; how much uncertainty to accept and how best to hedge against risks; how best to explain to stakeholders how all such factors have been balanced.

Evidence-informed Medicine

See *Evidence-based Medicine*.

EVPI

Acronym for *expected value of perfect information*. See *Value of Information Analysis*.

Ex Ante

A Latin tag meaning a *variable* as it was before a decision or event, some-times used to mean the planned value of a choice variable as in 'ex ante saving'. Cf. *Ex Post*.

Excess

A term used in *insurance* to mean the sum payable by the insured person, or deducted from the insurer's compensation, in the event of a claim. See *Coinsurance, Copayment*.

Excess Burden

A loss of consumer's and/or producer's surplus. See *Deadweight Loss, Moral Hazard*.

Excess Demand

A condition that exists when the *demand* for a good or service exceeds its *supply* at the prevailing price.

Excess Health Insurance

A much-discussed issue in the US where the excessive use of *health insurance* has been controversially held to account for massive *welfare* losses. Although insurance normally provides *benefits* that exceed its *costs*, through generating a lower price at the point of consumption of health care it also encourages the use of health care beyond the point at which its *marginal value* is equal to its *marginal cost* of production. Whether that is a bad thing is not to be taken as given since it rather depends, amongst other things, on whether there are any relevant *externalities*. Cf. *Moral Hazard*. See Feldstein (1973), Feldman and Dowd (1991) and Newhouse (1992).

Excess Supply

A condition that exists when the *supply* for a good or service exceeds its *demand* at the prevailing price. A condition that is not much met in health care markets but that, when it does occur, can cause enormous political grief for those seeking to eliminate it.

Exchangeability

Sometimes used in a similar way to *generalizability*. In statistics it has a technical meaning: the random vectors $\{x_1, \ldots \ldots x_n\}$ are *exchangeable* if their joint *distribution* is invariant under permutations. In economics it would be understood as implying that the goods in question (or property rights defining how the said goods may be used) were tradable.

Exchange Rate

The number of units of a foreign currency that can be bought with a unit of the domestic currency. A rising exchange rate from the perspective of the domestic economy is, of course, a falling rate from the perspective of the other.

Exchequer Cost

A cost that falls ultimately on taxpayers.

Exchequer Revenue

Revenue that ultimately acts to reduce claims on taxpayers.

Excise Tax

See *Taxes*.

Exclusion Bias

A form of *bias* in a *trial* arising from non-random withdrawals from the trial.

Exclusive Remedy

A concept in *workers' compensation* whereby under the *workers' compensation principle* a worker's right of recovery against the employer is limited to the benefits provided by the workers' compensation law in the jurisdiction in question. Exceptions include cases in which the employer acts with gross negligence, assaults the employee or deliberately engineers an accident.

Existence Value

The value placed upon the continued existence of an asset. In the context of benefits accruing to future generations, it is sometimes termed *bequest value*. Similar to *option demand*. See Weisbrod (1964).

Exogenous

Usually descriptive of a characteristic of a *variable* in an economic *model*. A variable is exogenous if it is not a function of other *parameters* or *variables* in the model. Cf. *Endogenous*. For an example in health economics of the effect on behaviour of exogenous health shocks see Smith et al. (2001).

Expansion Path

A *locus* in a two-*input* diagram that is the set of tangencies between *iso-quants* and *isocost* lines as *output* expands.

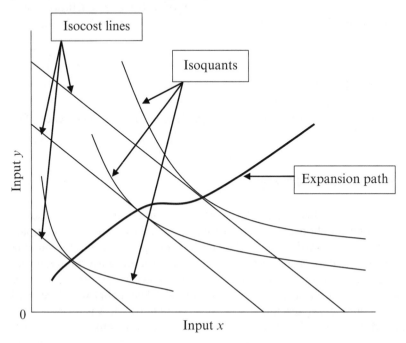

Expectations

Although expectations cannot be directly observed, economists have incorporated them into their (mostly macroeconomic) *models*. Adaptive expectations are ones in which people make adjustments to their expectations in response to a difference between what they previously expected but have now actually experienced. For example, when studying price or *premium inflation* this might be modelled by creating a new expectation consisting of the past expectation of inflation (with a weight) plus the actual inflation experienced (with a weight), the weights summing to unity. Rational expectations are 'rational' in the sense of being consistent with the economic *model* in which they are embodied (for example, if the model predicts that inflation will rise in response to an *exogenous* change, then that will be a rational expectation) and also in the sense that the individuals possessing them will use all the available information in forming their expectations about the future. From another perspective, however, it would seem 'irrational' to ignore the costs of acquiring and interpreting 'information' – so it may not be rational to have rational expectations! In fact, whereas the idea of rational expectations was widely used in *macroeconomics*, in *health economics* it has barely surfaced at all.

Expected Utility

A *utility* number weighted by the *probability* of its occurrence. See *Expected Utility Theory*.

Expected Utility Theory

Expected *utility* theory postulates that a decision-maker chooses (sometimes, ought to choose) between risky or uncertain prospects by comparing their *expected utility* values. Essentially, the approach entails assuming that people maximize a weighted sum of utilities under uncertainty, where the weights are probabilities and choices are between gambles or lotteries containing goods and services of various kinds. The theory was developed in 18th-century Switzerland and became popular after it was formalized in the mid-20th century. There are many alternative formulations but each shares the key features of *transitivity* and *continuity* (common to all utility theories), *completeness* and von Neumann-Morgenstern (vNM) independence. Completeness implies that if lottery x is preferred to lottery y and lottery y is preferred to lottery $z,$ then there is some combination of x and z that will be preferred to y. The vNM *axiom* means, roughly speaking, that adding a third lottery to two lotteries, whose ranking has already been determined, will not affect that ranking. The vNM tag honours those who established the axioms in the last century, John von Neumann (1903–57) and Oscar Morgenstern (1902–76) whose book, *Theory of Games and Economic Behavior* (1944) laid many of the foundations of expected utility theory (though not, oddly that of the axiom bearing their names). This was also the beginning of *game theory* since expected utility theory's axioms were offered (and accepted by many influential scientists) as a justification for the use of expectations in game theory. Cf. *Prospect Theory*, *Regret Theory*. See *Utility*. For both an account and a critique, see Machina (2004).

Expected Value

The weighted average of all possible values of a *variable*, where the weights are probabilities.

Expected Value of Information

The use of *Bayesian* and *frequentist* probabilistic approaches to uncertainty. Thus, decision-analytic methods like *cost–effectiveness analysis* usually build on data that are at best only partially relevant, not completely accurate, whose estimated values have large *variances*, etc. One therefore needs to adjust empirical *distributions*, use explicit judgmental distributions, or collect new data. In determining whether or not to collect additional data, the expected value of information (EVI) approach, as its name implies, invites the analyst to consider the expected value (in the form of a reduction in *opportunity loss*) of additional information and the costs of getting it. EVI comes in two forms: global, in which the reduction in *opportunity loss* from making a decision is estimated across all uncertain *parameters*; and partial, in which the reduction in loss relates to getting additional information about a specific parameter. See *Expected Value of Perfect Information, Expected Value of Sample Information*. Originated by Raiffa and Schlaiffer (1967). For an early example in health economics see Claxton and Posnett (1996). Also Claxton (1999), Coyle et al. (2003) and Eckerman and Willan (2007).

Expected Value of Perfect Information

The quantification of the value of having perfect information about *variables* and *parameters* about whose value one is currently uncertain. See *Expected Value of Information*.

Expected Value of Sample Information

The quantification of the value to a decision-maker of obtaining sampled information prior to the decision. See *Expected Value of Information*. See Brennan and Kharroubi (2007).

Expenditures on Health Care

The total expenditures (public and private) on health care services in a jurisdiction (or on/by a client group) over a period of time. There have been innumerable international comparisons of health care expenditures, often motivated by the false idea that there is a magic benchmark somewhere 'out there' that other decision-makers (can they be politicians?) have got right and that you can use to buttress your case for more (less) spending in your own neck of the woods. The variation in per capita spending (public or private or both combined) and in fractions of *GDP* taken up by health care is substantial.

The most clearly consistent and robust outcome of *econometric* studies is that per capita GDP is a major *determinant* and that the aggregate *income-elasticity* of *demand for health care* is around +1.0 after allowing for *confounders*. See *Aging*. For an authoritative review, with an analysis of *welfare* consequences, see Newhouse (1992); for international comparisons, see Gerdtham and Jönsson (1992, 2000). On the US compared with other countries see Reinhardt et al. (2004), Anderson et al. (2005) and Anderson and Frogner (2008). On aging and health care expenditures see Seshamami and Grady (2004).

Experienced Utility

The experienced utility of an episode of illness or wellness is derived experimentally from real-time measures of the *attributes* of the experience for the subject at the time of the experience. Cf. *Decision Utility, Remembered Utility*. See Kahneman (2000).

Experience Rating

The setting of *insurance* premia where the probabilities used are based on the historical risk, e.g. as revealed by past claims experience. Cf. *Community Rating*.

Experimental Arm

The group of people in a *trial* receiving (or not receiving) a health care technology of interest whose experience will be compared with a *control group*. Also known as 'treatment arm'. See *Clinical Trial*.

Experimental Event Rate

The proportion of patients in an *experimental arm* of a *trial* who are observed to experience the outcome of interest.

Experimental Group

Same as *experimental arm*.

Explanatory Trial

A species of controlled *trial*. Explanatory trials test whether an intervention has *efficacy*; that is, whether it can have a beneficial effect in an ideal situation. They yield understanding of the processes and pathways through which the procedure being tested has its effects. The explanatory trial seeks to maximize *internal validity* by assuring rigorous *control* for *confounding* variables. Cf. *External Validity, Pragmatic Trial*.

Explanatory Variable

Same as *independent variable*.

Ex Post

A Latin tag indicating the value of a *variable* after a decision or event. Sometimes used to denote the *outcome* value of a variable as in 'ex post saving'. Cf. *Ex Ante*.

Expressed Preference

Evidence about preferences gathered by experimental means such as *contingent valuation* rather than being inferred from behaviour. Same as *stated preference*.

Extended Dominance

This is a (treatment, investment) option that dominates another by virtue of its being a linear combination of two other options. *Dominance* means that the combination option is both more *effective* and costs no more than the simple option. See Cantor (1994).

Extensive Margin

A small change in the amount of an *input* used (e.g. number of workers, number of exporters). It is contrasted with the intensive margin: a small change in a characteristic of an input (e.g. hours per worker, exports per exporter). For a health economics example see Ellis (1998).

External Benefit

A benefit falling on others rather than on the decision-maker giving rise to it. See *External Effect*.

External Effect

External effects relate to the consequences of an action by one individual or group as they have an impact on others. There may be external *costs* and external *benefits*. Some are pecuniary, affecting only the value of other resources (as when a new innovation makes a previously valuable resource obsolete); some are technological, physically affecting other people (*communicable disease* is a classic example of this type of – negative – externality; network externality is another kind, referring to any change in the physical benefit that an *agent* derives from a good when the number of other agents consuming the same kind of good changes; antimicrobial resistance is another; *herd immunity* from vaccination is a positive example); some are *utility* effects that impinge on the subjective values of others (as when, for example, one person feels sympathy and distress at the sickness of another, or relief at their recovery). This latter is sometimes known as a *caring externality* (Culyer, 1976). When there are beneficial externalities of this kind, the standard maximizing behaviour assumed for individuals may not result in a *Pareto optimum*, notably if the *marginal benefit* received by the caring person is larger than the net marginal cost of the good or service to the consumer (that is, the *marginal cost* less the *marginal value* to the consumer).

In the diagram, a consumer has a *demand curve* (marginal valuation curve) shown by MV_1 and would, assuming that the price is equal to *marginal social cost* (here assumed constant for convenience) select output rate Q'. However, at that rate of consumption, some other caring individual or individuals also derive *utility* from this individual's consumption, as shown by the height of the curve labelled EMV (external marginal valuation) at this point. The optimal output rate is Q, beyond which the marginal cost to society exceeds the marginal value to society as shown by the vertical sum of the two curves D_1 and EMV. This is a Pareto optimal *equilibrium*, which might be obtained through subsidizing Q consumption, regulating it, or through direct exchange (as in charitable giving) between individuals (note here that in the optimum the marginal value placed by carers (Qa) is just equal to the difference between the marginal cost and the consumer's valuation).

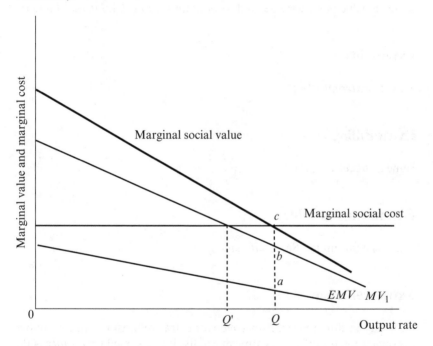

Note also that the mere existence of an externality, even a marginal externality, is not a ground either for predicting *inefficiency* or for subsidizing health care. If the EMV fell to zero at a rate of consumption lower than Q' there is still an externality but it is not 'Pareto-relevant', being entirely *inframarginal*. The analysis of external costs proceeds in a similar fashion but summing internal and external costs vertically rather than the internal and external '*demands*'. See also *Bandwagon, Snob and Veblen Effects, Caring Externality*. The classic piece is Buchanan and Stubblebine (1962). Some illustrative studies follow. On communicable disease see Smith et al. (2004). On an economic scheme to control antimicrobial resistance see Smith and Coast (1998). On the existence of *caring externality* see Culyer (1991a) and Jacobsson et al. (2005). On external effects of managed health care on *health maintenance organizations*, see Chernew et al. (2008). On external effects and hospital location, Escarce (1996) and Bates and Santerre (2005).

External Validity

The extent to which the results of a study can be generalized beyond the setting in which they were derived without misleading. Cf. *Internal Validity*.

Externality

Same as *external effect*.

Extra Billing

Same as *balance billing*.

Extraneous Variable

Same as confounder. See *Confounding*.

Extra-welfarism

As a way of doing *normative economics* extra-welfarism is an alternative to conventional *welfarism*. Conventionally, it is assumed that *utility* is the *maximand*, that sources of utility are goods and services, and that social welfare is derivable from (and only from) individual utilities, and that these utilities depend upon people's *preferences*. Thus, health care constitutes the goods and services that may (amongst other things) enhance *health*. Health, in turn, is a source of utility, both directly and through the effects good health has on one's capacity to enjoy other goods and services.

Extra-welfarism has regard to a potentially wider range of *attributes* than people's consumption of goods and services and might, for example, include changes in consumption or work patterns as direct sources of utility or disutility; or other states and changes in them (for example, being divorced or getting divorced), being 'educated', participating in decisions, sharing sorrows, overcoming difficulties, feeling that one 'belongs', being 'private'. Extra-welfarism is 'extra' not only in enabling the consideration of other things that contribute to human flourishing beyond goods and services and the utility to be had from them, but also the effects on people of the processes and transitions of life. A further distinctive feature is that, in extra-welfarism, the source of the valuation of these *attributes* may not be (or may not exclusively be) people's preferences. The moral authority of extra-welfarism is not asserted *a priori*, but derives from a legitimate authority such as ministers of health, education or housing. The role of economists under extra-welfarism is thus relatively modest compared with standard welfarism and is less overtly political (and 'liberal'). Extra-welfarism has not to date been explicitly applied in several policy arenas to which it appears well-suited (for example, education, one of whose functions entails the change and development of preferences, seems a natural target) and has been principally used in health policy analysis.

In health economics, extra-welfarism commonly postulates health itself as the maximand of the health care sector, rather than the individual utility to which it may give rise. One specific advantage of the approach is that objectives cast in terms of *'health gain'* are commonly set by policy-makers, and this approach fits well with the social decisions approach in *cost–benefit analysis*. Another is that it makes no heroic assumptions about the ability of sick people to make rational *utility-maximizing* decisions on their own behalf, though it certainly assumes that collective decision-making is improved by the use of 'rational' processes like *cost–effectiveness analysis*. Yet another is that indicators of value such as *willingness to pay* may be judged to be too contaminated by *abilities to pay* and imperfections in the *agency relationship* to be relied upon in the construction of health care priorities and the allocation of health care resources. A final claimed advantage is that the method has proved valuable in laying bare the kind of *value judgments* that necessarily inhere in any concept of 'health'.

There is no scientifically 'correct' choice to be made between *welfarism* and extra-welfarism (though the ways in which *costs* and *benefits* are considered might vary radically between them). One's choice between them depends principally on either a direct value judgment or on a judgment about what is the most helpful way of setting up a problem in a particular circumstance. For example, if the agency on whose behalf some research is being undertaken wishes to discover the cost-effectiveness of a new diagnostic procedure, and that agency has clearly espoused 'health' as its *maximand*, it may be most appropriate to adopt an extra-welfarist approach, taking health gain as the maximand and considering pragmatically any other factors deemed significant by the research clients (such as 'ease of implementation', short-term 'impact on waiting times', 'political acceptability' and the costs of achieving political acceptability).

The *quality-adjusted life-year* (QALY) is the most common entity chosen as maximand under extra-welfarism. In this context, however, it is probably best not to view the QALY as an index of (in some sense, average) preferences for health but as a representation of a collectively determined *outcome* measure explicitly posited by an authoritative agency, that is, an agency deemed to be a sufficient authority for the value judgments that are embodied in a QALY. These value judgments may, of course, accord a high place to respecting people's preferences and, if preferences turn out to be all, then the two approaches amount to the same. See *Communitarianism, Welfare Economics*. See Culyer (1989, 1991a) and Brouwer et al. (2008).

Extreme Scenario Sensitivity Analysis

For the main entry see *Sensitivity Analysis*. An extreme scenario analysis involves setting each variable in a *cost–effectiveness analysis* (or similar) simultaneously to take the most optimistic (or pessimistic) value in order to generate a best (or worst) case scenario. Cf. *One-way Sensitivity Analysis, Two-way Sensitivity Analysis*. For an example of the technique in practice see Bhatti and Baibergenova (2008).

F

Face Validity

A judgment about the reasonableness of a measure of something (like *health*) based on its superficial examination by people with relevant expertise/experience, participants as subjects in a measurement exercise or by those seen as clients for the research outcomes.

Factor

In choice experiments such as *discrete choice experiments* the *variables* of interest are often termed 'factors' and the values each can take are referred to as 'factor levels'. A specific factor level is referred to as a 'treatment' and each specific combination of treatments is referred to as either a 'treatment combination' or a 'profile'. See Ryan and Gerard (2003).

Factor Analysis

A *multivariate* statistical method of collapsing many (possibly) correlated *variables* into a smaller number of uncorrelated variables, and of exploring the structure of any relationships between these 'factors' or *principal components*. For an introduction see Kline (1993). An economics application is Kan (2004).

Factor Cost

Gross national product and *gross domestic product* become GNP at factor cost or GDP at factor cost when taxes are subtracted and subsidies added.

Factorial Design

An experimental design when there are several *determinants* (*independent variables* or 'factors') of an *outcome*, each of which may interact with the others, and where each of the determinants can take on several discrete values ('levels'). Thus a 2×2 design (or 2^2) has two factors and two levels. A fractional factorial design economizes on the amount of statistical work required to generate results of a specified quality. See, for a practical health economics example, Carlsson and Martinsson (2003).

Factor of Production

An *input* in the production of goods or services. Factors of production are often classified as land, labour and *capital*.

Factor Substitution

The proposition that one *input* or *factor of production* (like labour) can, given sufficient time for adjustment and sufficient resources to effect the change, be substituted for another (like *capital*) to produce the same *output*. It explicitly denies that, save under special and unusual circumstances, inputs like nurse time and physician time must be in a given *ratio*. See *Isoquant, Substitutes, Substitution in Production*. For a study using the concept in studying *health maintenance organizations* in the US see Okunade (2003).

Factor Taxes

These are taxes on *factors of production*. In health care, payroll taxes are the main factor taxes of interest on account of the fact that they tend to be used as earmarked taxes for health care financing. See *Earmarking, Payroll Taxes, Taxes*.

Fair Chances/Best Outcome Problem

A conflict that has been much debated by medical ethicists. It may be illustrated by a case of two people awaiting an organ transplant. There is no ethically relevant differentiating factor between them and each will live only one week without the transplant. With the transplant, however, one is expected to live two years and the other 20 years. Who should get the transplant: should they have an equal chance (and toss the equivalent of a fair coin) or does the second person's greater gain dominate? Economists tend not to struggle with dilemmas of this sort. See Daniels (1993).

Fair Innings

A term borrowed from cricket but equivalent to the singular usage 'inning' of baseball. It is the name given to the idea that benefits to individuals who have not yet had a 'fair innings' (in terms of length of life in reasonable health) should receive a higher weighting in *cost–effectiveness analyses* than those to people who have had a fair innings (and even higher presumably than those who have already had more than a fair innings). It has proved possible to make empirical estimates of the weights through surveys, but the principle is controversial. See Williams (1997).

Fairness

A general treatment of this topic from an economic point of view is under *Equity*. A famous concept of 'justice as fairness', which has much influenced economists, was developed by the US philosopher John Rawls (1921–2002). The foundation of what is probably the 20th century's most impressive contribution to political philosophy is a *veil of ignorance*. Rawls asks us to imagine ourselves to be the constructors of a just society, but being ignorant of our racial, social, and economic position within that society, on the grounds that these are irrelevant to questions of justice. From this 'original position', he asserts that a rational person would select only two basic principles of justice: first, the *liberty principle*: a schedule of basic rights, including liberty of conscience and movement, freedom of religion, which ought to be equally distributed and as complete as is consistent with each having the same; second, the *difference principle*: social and economic inequalities are justifiable only if they are to the advantage of the least advantaged person. Economists (and others) have struggled to fit health into Rawls' scheme. Rawls himself explicitly excluded health from the operation of the difference principle, arguing that it was a 'natural good' like 'intelligence'. Many economists, philosophers and other analysts think that Rawls was wrong to exclude health in this way. For example, Ronald Green wrote: '[A]ccess to healthcare like all basic primary goods, is important because it is instrumental to the pursuit of whatever other values we might have' (Green, 2001, p. 22). See *Entitlement Theory, Equity, Interpersonal Comparisons of Utility, Utilitarianism*. See Rawls (1971), Andersson and Lyttkens (1999) and Fleurbaey and Schokkaert (2009).

Fairness Gap

A term coined by Fleurbaey and Schokkaert (2009) to describe the gap between an actual *distribution* of health and a hypothetical distribution in which all legitimate grounds for inequality have been removed.

Fair Premium

An *insurance* premium is actuarially fair when it is equal to the monetary value of the *benefit* insured multiplied by the *probability* of successfully claiming that benefit. See Bakker et al. (2000).

False Negative

A test result indicating that a diseased individual is disease-free.

False Positive

A test result indicating that a disease-free individual is diseased.

FCE

Acronym for *finished consultant episode*.

FDA

Acronym for *Food and Drug Administration*.

F-distribution

Used for random *variables* that are constrained to be greater or equal to 0. It is often used in the *analysis of variance* by taking the ratio of the *variance* of the *means* from a number of groups, including random errors, to the variance of the random errors. Also called the *variance ratio distribution*. It is used to evaluate the *statistical significance* of the association between a *determinant* and an *outcome* variable in an analysis of variance. Named after the British statistician Sir Ronald Fisher (1890–1962).

Federal Medical Assistance Percentage

See *Medicaid.*

Fee-for-service

A method of remunerating professionals (especially medical doctors) according to an agreed *fee schedule* specifying what is payable for each item of service supplied. It is to be distinguished from (though it may be used in conjunction with) *capitation* and salaried means of remuneration. Cf. *Bundling.* See Robinson (2001). On the effects of *managed health care* with fee-for-service see Chernew et al. (2008).

Fee Schedule

A list of services or procedures together with the fee for each payable by a *third party payer* like an *insurance* company to a practising clinician.

Fieller's Theorem

A parametric method of calculating *confidence limits* of cost differences and effectiveness differences in *cost–effectiveness analyses.* See Fieller (1954) and Briggs et al. (2002).

15D®

The 15D® is a Finnish generic self-administered instrument for measuring *health-related quality of life* in adults, having 15 dimensions covering almost all aspects of *health-related quality of life* and embodying *utility* or *preference* weights. There are versions also for children and adolescents. See Sintonen and Pekurinen (1993). Its website is available at: http://www.15d-instrument.net/15d (accessed 30 October 2009).

File-drawer Problem

A form of *publication bias* – studies that fail in some respect to meet their author's expectations in respect, for example, of problem solved, or statistically significant results obtained. They are less likely to be submitted for publication than those that are more 'positive'. It is sometimes an indication of a crippling perfectionism on the part of the author. In other cases, extreme perversity can result. For example, suppose that the *null hypothesis* (i.e. that the association being studied does not exist) is indeed the case. But 5 per cent of studies show by chance that a statistically significant relationship exists. These are submitted – and published – leaving the 95 per cent of studies in which the null was not rejected gathering dust in researchers' file drawers and people doing *systematic reviews* concluding wrongly that the null is false. Publication bias occurs whenever the probability of a study being published depends on the *statistical significance* of its results and can have a seriously distorting effect on the conclusions of *systematic reviews* and *meta-analyses*. See Scargle (2000).

Final Good

A good or service that yields direct *utility* to an individual or is not an *input* into the process of making a more ultimate good. Cf. *Intermediate Good*.

Financial Appraisal

A procedure for assessing options that is similar to *economic appraisal* except that only the financial *costs* and *benefits* are considered, rather than *opportunity costs* and a wider set of benefits. See also *Discounting*. It is a vulgar error, and universally offensive to economists, to equate financial appraisal to economic *appraisal*.

Financial Sustainability Plan

A procedure for low-income countries making a transition from dependence upon the *Global Alliance for Vaccines and Immunization* to self-reliance in preventing hepatitis B and Haemophilus influenza type b, diphtheria, tetanus and pertussis. See Lydon et al. (2008).

Financing Health Care

Typical aspects of finance that are examined by health economists include: tax financing, *subsidization* of *access* to health care, income *redistributive impact, insurance* (public and private) and their consequences for *efficiency, equity*, total *expenditure* and patterns of *utilization* of services. See *Equity, Insurance*.

Finished Consultant Episode

A finished consultant episode (FCE) is a period of admitted patient care under a consultant within a National Health Service Trust in England. This is not always the same as a single stay (spell) in hospital.

FinOHTA

Acronym for *Finnish Office of Health Technology Assessment*.

Finnish Office of Health Technology Assessment

The Finnish Office of Health Technology Assessment (FinOHTA) is an independent public assessment agency working as a part of Finland's National Research and Development Centre for Welfare and Health. It produces and disseminates *health technology assessments*. Its website is available at: http://finohta.stakes.fi/EN/index.htm (accessed 30 October 2009).

FIO

Acronym for *fully integrated organization*.

First-copy Cost

The cost of producing an early, experimental version of a drug. See Reiffen and Ward (2005).

First Fundamental Theorem of Welfare Economics

The proposition that, given particular assumptions, competitive markets are *Pareto optimal*. The assumptions include these: markets are *complete*; property rights are well-defined and costlessly enforced, so that buyers and sellers can trade freely in all current and future goods; producers and consumers are selfish maximizers of their benefits and minimizers of their costs; that within these perfectly competitive markets prices are known by all individuals and firms; that the use of the price mechanism does not itself consume resources. Cf. *Second Fundamental Theorem of Welfare Economics*. See, for its originator, Debreu (1959).

First Order Uncertainty

This is the idea in probability theory that, although you may not be in any doubt that a head is a head and a tail a tail, you will be in doubt as to which of them a throw of a fair coin will generate. If you doubt the *fairness* of the coin, then that is a type of *second order uncertainty*. First order uncertainty refers to variability in data and is reflected in the *standard deviation* and *variance*; second order uncertainty refers to uncertainty about *parameter* values and is reflected in the *standard error*. See *Uncertainty*.

Fiscal Federalism in Health

Fiscal federalism concerns the arrangements between the top level of financial management (e.g. central government) and lower tiers (e.g. states, provinces, local authorities). Most publicly funded health care systems combine central powers to determine resource allocation with more locally decentralized powers in various ways. Thus, in the US there are federal health care programmes (for the elderly) and state programmes (for the poor but also with federal support); in Canada health care is a provincial responsibility but governed by federally enforced principles and federal fiscal incentives; in the UK, local health care *commissioners* are funded by a centrally determined budgetary formula but purchase care for local residents according to locally established priorities (within a framework of national priorities). For a general overview see Banting and Corbett (2002). For a study of the central–local interaction in the Italian system see Bordignon and Turati (2009). For a study in South Africa see Okorafor and Thomas (2007). See Rico and Costa-i-Font (2005) and Costa-i-Font and Moscone (2008) for two Spanish studies.

Fisher's Ideal Index

See *Index Numbers*.

Five Number Summary

See *Box Plot*.

Fixed Coefficient Production Function

See *Leontief Production Function*.

Fixed Cohort Study

This is a *cohort study* in which subjects are recruited and enrolled at a uniform point in the natural history of a disease or by some defining event and that does not permit additional subjects to be added subsequently. Cf. *Open Cohort Study*.

Fixed Costs

These are *opportunity costs* that do not vary with *output* rates and that therefore do not form a part of *marginal cost*. Cf. *Sunk Costs* (which are not the same).

Fixed Effects Model

This is a statistical way of controlling for *omitted variable bias* when using *panel data*. The method is so-called on account of the fact that it holds constant ('fixes') the average differences between the *determinants* of a variable by using *dummy variables*. Thus, for example, the effect of geographical location on hospital costs might be controlled by having a dummy variable to represent each hospital's location and this would pick up the (often unobservable) effects of otherwise omitted variables (local wage effects, distance from major suppliers, etc.). The *regression* analysis could then focus on the non-geographical determinants of hospital cost, such as size or ownership, having controlled for the other effects. The method in effect distinguishes between 'within group' variation and 'between group' variation where, in the example just given, the effect of 'group' (i.e. the location of the hospitals) is taken out to enable the analyst to focus on the variations between hospitals in similar locations. Cf. *Random Effects Model.* See, for applications, Rice and Jones (1997), Carpenter (2004) and Newhouse and Sinaiko (2007).

Flat of the Curve Medicine

This refers to a situation in which the impact of additional health care on the health of an individual or a *population* has fallen to zero. The *marginal productivity* of health care is zero. It might arise either through the operation of *diminishing returns to scale* or of the *law of variable proportions*. At the level of population health, it is a consequence of giving priority to patients who are likely to gain most from treatment. See Enthoven (1980).

Flexible Spending Account

A *consumer-driven health plan* in the US by which an employee sets aside a portion of their earnings to pay for medical (and other) expenses and which gains exemption from payroll taxes.

Floor Effect

Opposite of a *ceiling effect*.

Flow

A *variable* having an interval of time dimension: so much per period. Cf. *Stock*, which is the value taken by a variable at a particular date.

Focus Group

A group chosen to discuss and comment on a topic being researched. The group may be informed by relevant witnesses and is usually guided by a facilitator or moderator. Common outcomes are the insights, opinions and conclusions that result from the interaction between the participants. Cf. *Consensus Panel, Citizens' Jury*.

Focusing Illusion

An effect discovered by *cognitive psychologists* when measuring the *utility* of states of *well-being* whereby the act of focusing on an experience leads subjects to exaggerate their significance for their *welfare*. See Kahneman (2008).

Folding Back

The process of 'solving' a *decision tree*, doing all the computations required given the assumptions, *transition probabilities* and so on.

Follow-on Protein Product

Same as *biosimilar* medicine.

Follow-up Study

Same as *cohort study*.

Food and Drug Administration

An organization within the US Department of Health and Human Services with responsibility for the regulation of pharmaceutical and other food and medicinal products. Its home page is available at: http://www.fda.gov/ (accessed 30 October 2009).

Forest Plot

This is a diagram used in *meta-analysis* to show the effects estimated in a variety of *trials* together with their *means* and *confidence intervals*. It provides a diagrammatic representation of the amount of variation between the results of the trials and an estimate of the overall result of the studies as a whole. The results of the included studies are usually shown as squares in a column centred on the point estimate of each study's result. The length of a horizontal line through the square indicates its *confidence interval*. The overall estimate and its confidence interval are shown as a diamond whose centre is the pooled point estimate and whose horizontal tips indicate its confidence interval. It is so-called on account of the 'forest' of lines a typical graph may contain.

This is constructed as follows. The horizontal axis in the figure below measures the treatment effect – for example, the probability of death, so that to the left of the vertical axis death is less likely and to its right it is more likely. Where the vertical axis meets the horizontal corresponds to a probability of 1 (better outcomes are usually but not always to the left). The line *ab* shows the result of a single research study. The square dot in the middle of the line is the point estimate of the mean effect in this study. This is a measure of the effect of the treatment compared with a *control group* and is most often represented as an *odds ratio*. The square is small or large depending on the weight this study is to be given in the combined analysis. The length of the line around the point estimate is the confidence interval for the result. When a study has only a few patients the line will be long and the size of the square in its middle will be small.

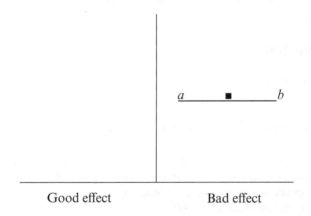

Suppose there are two other studies, shown by the lines *cd* and *ef*. The study represented by *cd* shows the opposite effect to that in the previous study (in this study, the *experimental arm* does better than the *control*) and the confidence interval is narrower and the weight this study receives will be larger. There is a third study also, which has relatively low *statistical significance* and a small weight. Taking all three together, the summary is represented by the diamond, whose height locates the best estimate of effect and whose width indicates its confidence interval. Its position relative to the vertical axis shows what the conclusion is, on balance, taking the whole literature (in this case a forest plot of three items) into account. If the diamond crosses the vertical line, the conclusion is that the literature as a whole does not yield a clear answer about the relative *effectiveness* of the procedure in question (conventionally at the 95 per cent confidence level). The technique originated in the field of education research. See Lewis and Clarke (2001). A typical use is in Renehan et al. (2004) or Moayyedi et al. (2009).

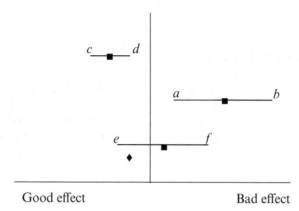

Good effect   Bad effect

Formulary

A list of drugs approved for prescription and reimbursement by a *third party payer*.

For-profit

A motive postulated for much economic behaviour alongside – and partially in conflict with – *utility maximization*. The legitimate role of profit-seeking in health care provision has concerned health economists from the earliest days of the sub-discipline, both in order to understand better why the non-profit organization is so frequently found, even in market-oriented economies, and whether on balance and in what circumstances it can be counted as a good thing. Opinion amongst economists is unlikely, however, to reach a consensus, given the wider political connotations of the issue. The pioneering piece is Newhouse (1970). Some standard references are Pauly and Redisch (1973), Frank and Salkever (1994), Keeler et al. (1999) and Sloan (2000). A discussion in the third world context is in Patouillard et al. (2007). See *Competition, Hospital Economics, Non-profit, Profit*.

Foundation Trust

A type of secondary provider introduced in the English *National Health Service* in 2004 having more local autonomy than other secondary providers. See *Trusts*.

Four-quadrant Diagram

Usually refers to a four-quadrant figure showing the construction of a *health frontier* in a two-person world from a *budget constraint*, two *production functions* and an assumed initial distribution of health. Used to analyse alternative *constructs* of *equity* and how they relate to *efficiency*.

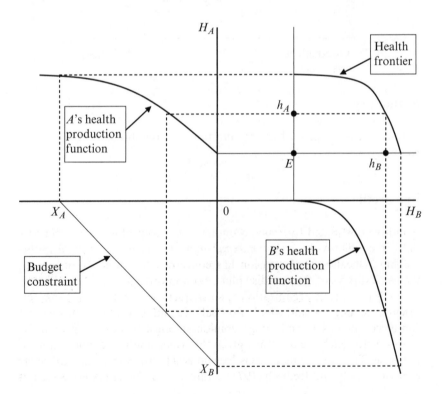

In the figure, a fixed budget for health care is assumed as indicated in the bottom left-hand quadrant, which can be spent either all on A or all on B ($X_A = X_B$) or otherwise divided between them along $X_A\,X_B$. Each individual has an initial endowment of health indicated by E in the top right-hand quadrant (A here assumed initially less healthy than B). The health frontier shows the maximum additional health attainable for either A or B given the health of the other and given the budget constraint, the production functions and the initial endowment. See Culyer and Wagstaff (1993) and Wagstaff (1986) for its immediate precursor.

Fractional Factorial Design

See *Factorial Design, Full Profile Conjoint Analysis.*

Framing Effect

This is sometimes thought of as an 'irrational' (in terms of *expected utility theory*) response by subjects in experiments. It occurs when the same question, asked in somewhat different ways, elicits different answers. For example, people respond differently according to whether the choices presented to them are framed in terms of gains or in terms of losses. But, of course, this may not be irrational at all and, indeed, is not in the context of *prospect theory*. Cf. *Reflection Effect*. See *Regret Theory*. See Tversky and Kahneman, 1986. See Ubel et al. (2001) for framing and *equity*.

Framingham

A town in Massachusetts whose residents have been studied by epidemiologists for more than 50 years, especially in connection with diseases of the heart, lung and blood. The data collected in this massive set of data have been enormously influential. For a health economics example of its use and a controversy over peer effects and obesity see Fowler and Christakis (2008) and associated papers in that issue.

Free Good

In economics, a free good is not the same as one that is offered free of charge. 'Free good' is used in economics to describe a good that is not *scarce*; more of which is not demanded than is already available at a zero price – as much is available as anyone wants. It is therefore not an *economic good* and it has no *opportunity cost*. Many goods and services that are offered free of charge are not 'free' in the economic sense, and health care is a classic example (for insured persons). An economic good that is offered free of charge will normally have required scarce resources in its production and there is likely to be an *excess demand* for it.

Free Loader

Same as *free rider*.

Free Lunch

The jaunty double negative 'There ain't no such thing as a free lunch' refers to the depressing fact that things that appear to be free are always paid for in some way and are not, anyway, free in the economist's sense of free. Cf. *Free Good*.

Free Rider

One who consumes a good (especially a *public good*) without contributing to the cost of providing it.

Frequency

The number of times an event occurs over a period. Not the same as 'being regular'!

Frequency Distribution

A distribution of the frequencies with which an event or observation occurs. See *Beta Distribution, Gamma Distribution, Gaussian Distribution, Lognormal Distribution, Normal Distribution, Triangular Distribution, Uniform Distribution*.

Frequentist Approach

This is the approach to *probability* adopted by classical statisticians who estimate the probability of an event (for example, the probability that a given individual *x* will have disease *y*) by taking a suitable sample of the relevant population, discovering the *prevalence* of the disease in that sample, and then inferring that the chances of *x* having *y* are the same as the prevalence rate in the sample. Strictly speaking, the frequentist approach depends upon a 'large' number of samples being taken. This approach is to be contrasted with the *Bayesian approach*. Much heat has been generated as to which approach is more useful (there is agreement about the maths) – as may be expected, given that each approach depends upon particular (subjective) assumptions being made and holding true, though the nature of these assumptions is not the same in each. For example, the frequentist approach involves judgments about how many samples to take, and of what size, and upon a judgment that the sample is a sufficiently faithful representation of the population. Cf. *Bayesian Method*.

Frictional Unemployment

This is that part of total unemployment in an economy caused as people change jobs, engage in job search from a position of not being employed (and therefore perhaps freer to travel to interviews, etc.). Frictional unemployment exists even when there is technically full employment because most people change jobs at some time and many do so frequently in dynamic economies. See *Full Employment, Friction Cost, Involuntary Unemployment, Natural Rate of Unemployment, Structural Unemployment.*

Friction Cost

Friction cost is the name given in *cost–effectiveness* and *cost–utility analyses* to the loss of productive work time that is incurred between the time that an employee is absent from work through accident or sickness and their replacement by another. It is a form of *productivity cost*. Some studies in these genres, particularly early ones, used the *human capital* approach in assessing the benefits of health care and tended to assume that replacement took place only when the injured/sick employee returned to work. The friction cost approach recognizes that there is usually more than merely *frictional unemployment* in any economy – that is, there is *involuntary unemployment* too – and this pool of potential workers may have the effect of substantially reducing the time for which a job is vacant. From a societal *perspective*, these costs, it should be noted, do not include the expenses incurred by firms in paying 'sick pay' and the like, which are *transfers* and not *opportunity costs*. A classic exposition is Koopmanschap et al. (1995) but see Johannesson and Karlsson (1997).

Frontier

A *locus* of combinations of *inputs*, *outputs* or *outcomes* that constitutes the boundary between what is possible with given technologies and resources and what is not. See *Health Frontier*.

FSP

Acronym for *Financial Sustainability Plans*.

F-test

A test based on the *F*-distribution. The *F*-test is used in economics most usually to test whether the *coefficients* in a regression with more than two explanatory variables are significantly different from zero. The decision rule is to reject the null hypothesis when estimated *F* is larger than a critical value, that is, reject the null if the *p-value* of *F* is less than 0.05. For an introduction see Kennedy (2003).

Fugitive Literature

Another term for *grey literature*.

Full Employment

A situation where all who wish to work at going wage and salary rates do so. This is not synonymous with zero unemployment thanks to *frictional unemployment*. Governments generally seek not to exceed the 'natural' rate of unemployment, defined (by Milton Friedman) as the lowest rate consistent with non-accelerating *inflation* (also termed NAIRU to avoid the apparent inevitability or acceptability implied by 'natural'). See also *Structural Unemployment*. On NAIRU see Friedman (1968) and Phelps (1968).

Full Profile Conjoint Analysis

A form of *conjoint analysis* in which the subjects prioritize the full range of the *attributes* of services. The large datasets that can result from considering all attributes can be reduced by using fractional factorial models. Cf. *Adaptive Conjoint Analysis*, *Pairwise Comparison*. See, for an example, Phillips et al. (2002).

Fully Integrated Organizations

A US form of integration of physicians and hospitals. See *Vertical Integration*.

Fundholding

Between 1991 and 1999, *general practitioners* in the UK could become fundholders, an arrangement under which they were given budgets with which they could purchase *elective surgery* for those patients who were registered with them. For an analysis of the impact of fundholding (especially on waiting lists) see Dusheiko et al. (2004).

Funnel Plot

A graph of *sample* size plotted against *effect* size that is often used to investigate *publication bias* or the *heterogeneity* of studies in *systematic reviews*. Each blob in the *scatter plot* indicates the results of one study. The name arises from the fact that precision in the estimation of the true treatment effect increases as the sample size of the component studies increases. Because large studies estimate effect size more precisely than small studies, they tend to lie in a narrow band at the top of the scatter plot, while the smaller studies, with more variation in results, fan out over a larger area at the bottom, thus creating the impression of an inverted funnel. In the absence of *bias* the plot should resemble a symmetrical inverted funnel. See, for one of many examples, Devereaux et al. (2002).

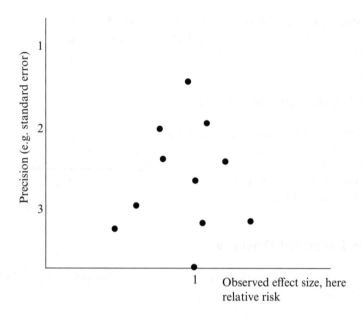

Futility Trial

A *trial* designed to demonstrate a specific *threshold* difference between one treatment and another. Cf. *Equivalence Trial, Non-inferiority Trial, Superiority Trial*.

Future Costs in Cost–Effectiveness Analysis

There is ongoing controversy as to whether future 'unrelated' medical *costs* ought to be included in computations of *cost-effectiveness*. See Nyman (2004). Garber and Phelps (1997) said 'No', Meltzer (1997) said 'Yes'. The issues become somewhat clearer in Lee (2008) and the associated correspondence.

G

Gail and Simon Test

This is used in a *clinical trial* to explore quantitatively and qualitatively the *homogeneity* of the effects of treatment amongst sub-groups and to identify sub-groups of patients with greater or lesser levels of *treatment effect*. See Gail and Simon (1985).

Gambler's Fallacy

The ensnaring but incorrect belief that the *probability* of an event occurring rises the longer the elapsed time since its last occurrence.

Game Theory

Game theory consists of *models* of strategic decisions, as the parties to the game move or propose moves and countermoves. The playfulness implied by the label is by no means a common characteristic either of the game in question (which may be a war) or of the players (who may be criminals). See *Expected Utility Theory*.

Gamma Distribution

This is a *probability distribution* often used to *model* individual heterogeneity, especially in *count data* regression and *duration analysis*. See *Frequency Distribution*.

Gastroenterology

The medical speciality concerned with diseases and abnormalities of the stomach and intestines.

Gatekeeper

A community-based provider (often a *general practitioner*) who, in many *managed health care* plans and public health care systems, coordinates the patient's diagnosis treatment across the various possible disciplines and professions and who refers patients to *secondary care* for specialist treatment. See Scott (2000) and Brekke et al. (2007b).

Gateway Effect

Usually referring to the way in which the *demand* for a legal habit-forming substance leads to the subsequent use of illegal substances. See Pacula (1997) and Pudney (2003).

Gaussian Distribution

Same as *normal distribution*. Named after Carl Friedrich Gauss (1777–1855), the German mathematician and astronomer.

GAVI

See *Global Alliance for Vaccines and Immunization*.

GDP

Acronym for *gross domestic product*.

GDP Deflator

An index of the general price level in the economy: the ratio of *gross domestic product* (GDP) in *nominal* (cash) terms to GDP at *constant prices*.

GE

Acronym for *general equilibrium*.

Gencat

Logo for the *Catalan Agency for Health Technology Assessment and Research*.

General Agreement on Trade in Services

GATS, an international agreement under the World Trade Organization as a part of the General Agreement on Tariffs and Trade (GATT) that regulates trade in services including health care. See R.D. Smith (2004).

General Equilibrium

A state of an entire economy in which there is no *excess demand* or *supply* and no incentive for any actor to change their behaviour. It is modelled by multiple equations describing the relationships between *independent* and *dependent variables* in systems of equations that reflect the behaviour of the actors in the system, the technical possibilities open to them and the nature of any significant interactions between the various sectors. Cf. *Partial Equilibrium*. See *Arrow–Debreu Equilibrium, General Equilibrium Theory*.

General Equilibrium Theory

An extension of *partial equilibrium theory*, in which the feedbacks between sectors and other interactions are explicitly modelled. In general *equilibrium* theory, the consumer is envisaged as being endowed with a bundle of real *goods* rather than 'income'. See *Computable General Equilibrium Models, Nash Equilibrium*.

Generalizability

The extent to which the results or conclusions of one piece of *empirical* evidence may be validly transposed to other situations. It is sometimes referred to as 'transferability'. In statistics the term '*exchangeability*' is sometimes used. A study of variations in the *cost-effectiveness* of Chagas disease control policies illustrates the significance of the issue with respect to geography (Castillo-Riquelme et al., 2008). Cf. *Effectiveness, Efficacy, External Validity, Internal Validity*.

Generalized Least Squares

A generalization of *ordinary least squares* that relaxes the assumption that the error terms are independently and identically distributed across observations.

General Practice

See *General Practitioner*.

General Practitioner

A doctor, dentist or other health care professional who diagnoses and treats the health problems of individuals and families in the community and who may refer more complex or technically demanding cases to a hospital specialist. See also *Gatekeeper*, *Primary Care*. For a review see Scott (2000).

General Surgeon

One whose region of operation normally lies in the abdomen – between the diaphragm and the pelvis.

Generic

Usually used to describe drugs that are no longer patent protected and that are generally sold under a name related to their chemical character rather than their *brand name*. Thus, the generic name for the famous anti-depressant Prozac is fluoxetine and the generic name for the world's best-selling anti-cholesterol medicine, Lipitor, is atorvastatin (global sales $13 thousand million in 2008!).

Genetics

The science of heredity and inherited characteristics.

Geographical Equity

The geographical distribution of health care resources has been much examined by health economists in Western countries, particularly the UK, but also in international comparisons. See *Allocation Formulae, Equity, Inverse Care Law*. Examples include Gravelle and Sutton (2001) for GPs, Maynard (1972) for psychiatrists and Maynard and Ludbrook (1980) for budgets.

Geometric Mean

Like the ordinary average (*arithmetic mean*) this is a measure of the central tendency in a distribution of a *variable*. The geometric mean is the nth root of n positive real numbers multiplied together. It dampens the effect on the mean of extreme values of a *variable* in comparison with the arithmetic mean.

Geriatrics

The medical speciality concerned with the diseases and care of elderly people.

Gerontology

The study (usually multidisciplinary) of old people and *aging* processes.

GHM

Acronym for *Groupe Homogène de Malades*.

Giffen Good

A type of *inferior good*. It is supposed to generate an upward-sloping *demand curve*, though the evidence for its *empirical* validity is contested. Named after the British statistician Sir Robert Giffen (1837–1910), alleged examples are hotly contested and none is known in the health care literature. Cf. *Normal Good*.

Gini Coefficient

The Gini *coefficient* was invented by the Italian statistician Corrado Gini (1884–1965) as a measure of income inequality, though it can be (and has been) used to measure, say, the *distribution* of health or of health care resource consumption. The Gini coefficient is a number between 0 and 1, where 0 corresponds to perfect equality (everyone has the same income, health care, etc.) and 1 is perfect inequality (one person has all the income, health care, etc.). While the Gini coefficient is mostly used to measure income inequality, it can be used to measure wealth inequality as well.

The Gini coefficient is related to the areas in a Lorenz diagram. Let the area between the line of perfect equality and *Lorenz curve* be *A*, and the area underneath the Lorenz curve be *B*, then the Gini coefficient is *A*/(*A* + *B*). See *Lorenz Curve*. See Van Doorslaer et al. (1997) for a classic use of the Gini coefficient.

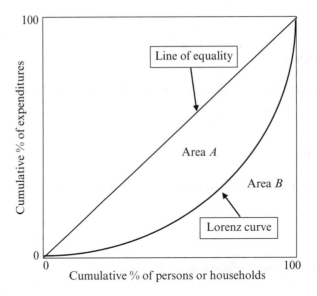

Global Alliance for Vaccines and Immunization

An international partnership of 75 low-income countries for the global purchasing of vaccines. Also known somewhat repetitiously as 'the GAVI Alliance'. Its website is available at: http://www.gavialliance.org/ (accessed 31 October 2009).

Global Budget

An overall financial allocation to a hospital or other health care provider, sector or region, out of which it is expected to provide or purchase health services. It is generally based on a previous year's global allocation with adjustments for inflation and special pleading. See Hurst (1991) for the use of global budgets in Europe.

GLS

Acronym for *generalized least squares*.

GNP

Acronym for *gross national product*.

Gold Standard

In health economics, one is most likely to encounter this term in its sense of an instrument or procedure that is considered to be a valid measure of exemplary good practice against which the validity or goodness of others can be tested.

Gompertz Function

Benjamin Gompertz invented a 'law of mortality' to the effect that the *mortality rate* increases with age in a geometric progression. When death rates are plotted on a logarithmic scale, a straight line known as the Gompertz function is obtained. Benjamin Gompertz (1779–1865) was a self-educated (being denied access to English universities, as was then the wicked rule, by virtue of being Jewish) English mathematician (of Dutch parentage).

Gompertz's Law of Mortality

See *Gompertz Function*.

Goodness of Fit

A measure of the extent to which the values of a *variable* estimated in a *model* agree with the observed data. See R^2.

Government Purchasing of Health Care

See *Commissioning*.

Gradient in Health

The phenomenon that mortality and *morbidity* systematically rise as socioeconomic class falls. See also *Socioeconomic Differences*. See Marmot et al. (1991), Evans et al. (1994), Case et al. (2002, 2008) and Deaton (2002).

Grey Literature

Working papers, internal reports, student theses and other literature that have not been peer-reviewed and that are often available only in obscure places. Also known as fugitive literature.

Gross Domestic Product

The total expenditure by residents and foreigners on domestically produced goods and services in a year.

Gross Investment

An economy's total *investment* before deducting *capital* consumption (or fixed capital formation) before *depreciation* but including the value of any change in physical stocks of goods.

Gross National Product

This is *gross domestic product* plus income earned abroad by residents less income earned in the economy by foreigners: i.e. GDP plus net property income from abroad.

Grounded Theory

Grounded theory is a form of *qualitative analysis* and underpins much *action research*. It is a research process that models a process of discovery – for example, that of discovering hypotheses and theories that may account for empirical observations (quantitative or qualitative) and be predictive of phenomena not previously anticipated. It proceeds initially through data collection (a process that will have probably been informed by some implicit theoretical ideas) and the making of interpretative comments on the data, through comparison of these data with other material (primary or in literature), at which stage tentative hypotheses might suggest themselves and are written down. Reflection on these may then lead to more explicit theorizing, which may generate ideas for further data collection and comparison. See Glaser and Strauss (1967) for its origin. For its application in health economics see Coast (1999).

Groupe Homogène de Malades

The French equivalent of *diagnostic-related group*.

Group Insurance

An *insurance* arrangement under which a group of people is covered by a common policy (as when employees are covered by their employer).

Guidelines

See *Clinical Guidelines*.

Guttman Scale

A method of scaling qualitative entities such that any point on the scale indicates an accumulation of characteristics. Also known as cumulative scaling or scalogram analysis. Suppose there are ten ordered statements. Then a score of six will indicate that a subject agrees with the first six statements and a score of ten indicates that there is agreement with all ten. The scale is *ordinal*. Named after Louis Guttman (1916–87). See Guttman (1944) for the originator, Ryan et al. (2001) for a review of scaling methods including Guttman scales.

Gynaecology

Also 'gynecology'. See *Obstetrics and Gynaecology*.

H

Haematology

The medical speciality concerned with the *physiology* of blood. Also 'hematology'.

HALE

Acronym for *health-adjusted life-expectancy*.

Halo Effect

The effect on recorded observations of the observer's perceptions of aspects that are not part of the study. Not the same as *placebo effect*. See, for an example in *health economics*, Phillips et al. (2002).

Handicap

Disadvantages experienced by an individual arising from *impairment* or *disability*. The extent of handicap may be conditional on environment (for example, the nature of work, the values of co-workers) and may include general deleterious effects on the *quality of life*.

Happiness

The association between *health* and happiness as an empirically measured *attribute* has received some attention from health economists. Cf. *Utility, Welfare*. See, e.g. Blanchflower and Oswald (2008); also Kahneman (1999, 2000).

Harvard Center for Risk Analysis CUA Database/CEA Registry

The database formerly maintained here is now the CEA Registry in the *Center for Evaluation of Value and Risk in Health* at Tufts University. Its website is available at: https://research.tufts-nemc.org/cear/default.aspx (accessed 2 November 2009).

HAS

Acronym for *Haute Autorité de Santé*.

Haute Autorité de Santé

The French organization (High Authority for Health) with responsibility for hospital certification, *clinical guidelines* and *health technology assessment*.

Hawthorne Effect

An improvement in productivity due to its observation. The effect was first noticed in the Hawthorne plant of Western Electric in Cicero, Illinois, where production increased not as a consequence of actual changes in working conditions but because there was a Harvard research team taking an active interest in working conditions in the plant, and management was also taking an interest. A type of *confounding factor* in experiments and *trials* that may lead to *bias*. The term is now used for any situation where the behaviour of the subjects being studied may be affected by the fact of their being studied. Also known as *attention bias* and 'searchlight effect'. See Rothlisberger and Dickson (1939). See also Holden (2008).

Hazard

The *probability* of occurrence of an *outcome*: an estimate of the number of people experiencing the outcome divided by an estimate of the number at risk.

Hazard Function

Closely related to the survival curve, it shows the risk of dying in a very short time interval after a given time (assuming survival to that point).

Hazard Rate

The instantaneous hazard rate is the limiting value of the number of events per unit of time divided by the number at risk as the time interval falls to zero.

Hazard Ratio

Same as *relative risk*.

HBG

Acronym for *health benefit group*.

HCFA

Acronym for *Health Care Financing Administration*.

Health

According to the first principle in the *World Health Organization*'s constitution (revised 2006), this 'is a state of complete physical, mental and social *well-being* and not merely the absence of disease or infirmity'. Less star-gazing notions are usually embodied in practical work (including, mercifully, that of the WHO). See *Health-related Quality of Life*. See http://www.who.int/governance/eb/who_constitution_en.pdf (accessed 2 November 2009) for the WHO definition. See Fuchs (1993). For a comprehensive tour through economic orthodoxy see Brazier et al. (2007).

Health Achievement Index

This is a measure that combines the average level of *health* in a community and the inequality of its distribution in that community. It was originated by Wagstaff (2002b). See *Concentration Index*.

Health-adjusted Life-expectancy

Health-adjusted life-expectancy (HALE) is life expectancy weighted or adjusted for the level of *health-related quality of life*. The average number of years that a person in a given jurisdiction can expect to live in full health by taking into account years lived in less than full health due to *disease* and/or injury. It is the basic indicator of *population health* levels used by the *World Health Organization*. See Wolfson (1991).

Health Benefit Group

Health benefit groups (HBGs) are standard groupings of people who are expected to need similar health care interventions and to derive similar benefits from their treatment. HBGs focus on those at risk from a particular health condition or disease and on people with *acute* or continuing long-term needs. They are developed to complement *healthcare resource groups* (HRGs) in the *National Health Service* (NHS) in England. The objective is to provide the NHS with a standardized presentation of relative needs for health care resources.

Health Benefit Plan

Any programme of directly provided health services or indemnification of medical expenses offered by service providers or *third party payers*, e.g. a *health insurance* policy, a *health maintenance organization, preferred provider organization*, health service contract sponsor, or an approved employee welfare benefit plan. The term does not usually include medical coverage under *workers' compensation* or automobile insurance.

Health Care

Goods and services provided to promote *health*, or prevent, alleviate or eliminate ill-health. Sometimes one sees the Germanic portmanteau: 'healthcare'.

Health Care Expenditures

Same as *expenditures on health care*.

Health Care Financing

Health care is typically financed from a number of sources in any jurisdiction, though the proportions vary greatly from one to another. The usual sources are *direct* and *indirect taxes* (including taxes on employers and employees and special taxes designated or earmarked for health care), social *insurance* contributions, private insurance premiums and direct payments for care (paid by patients or *third party payers*).

Health Care Financing Administration

Now termed *Centers for Medicare & Medicaid Services*, this is the US federal body formerly responsible for these programmes. Its website is available at: http://www.cms.hhs.gov/default.asp? (accessed 2 November 2009).

Healthcare Resource Group

Healthcare resource groups (HRGs) are standard groupings of clinically similar treatments, which use common levels of health care resources in the *National Health Service* of England. They are intended to enable *case-mix* adjusted comparisons between institutions and underpin the national schedule of *reference costs*. They have also been used in setting targets for providers to reach. Cf. the US predecessor: *Diagnostic Related Group*, and *Health Benefit Group*.

Health Care Savings Account

Same as medical savings account and *health savings account*.

Health Care Systems

Systems for financing and providing health care vary substantially across jurisdictions. They are commonly classified (by first world writers) into four (not very well-differentiated) types: sickness *insurance* (private insurance and care provision with often large public subsidies and governmental regulation as in Austria, Belgium, France, Germany, Luxembourg and the Netherlands); national *health insurance* (public insurance with premiums either separate or embodied in the tax structure and mixtures of public and private provision as in Canada, Finland, Norway, Spain or Sweden); national health services (public insurance mostly via the tax structure and mostly public provision as in Denmark, Greece, Italy, New Zealand, Portugal, Turkey and the UK); mixed systems (having the forgoing in varying mixes, as in Australia, Iceland, Ireland, Japan, Switzerland and the US). Some would dispute that the latter group (especially the US) classifies as a 'system'. The greater part of humankind does not live under any kind of health care 'system'. Some of the other features for framing 'systems', without attempting to be all-embracing, might be: traditional health care; *primary, secondary, tertiary* health care; 'Western' health care; health services, public health. See *Comparative Health Systems*.

Health Econometrics

See *Econometrics*.

Health Economic Evaluations Database

This (HEED) is a database of some 28 000 articles that are or purport to be *economic appraisals* of health care technologies. It covers 4500 journals and is produced by the Office of Health Economics. Its website is available at: www.ohe-heed.com (accessed 2 November 2009).

Health Economics

The application of economic theory to phenomena and problems associated with *health*. Topics include, among others, the meaning and measurement of *health status,* the production of health and health services, the *demand for health* and *demand for health services*, the *determinants* of healthy and unhealthy behaviour and the behavioural responses to changes in these determinants, *cost–effectiveness* and *cost–benefit analysis* in the health territory, *health insurance*, the analysis of markets for health services, health service financing, *disease costing, option appraisal* in health services, *manpower planning*, the economics of medical supply industries, *equity* and the determinants of inequalities in health and health care utilization, *hospital economics*, health care budgeting, territorial resource allocation, methods of remuneration of medical personnel, economics of *comparative health systems*.

See *Information Resources in Health Economics, Microeconomics, Postmodernism, Williams' Schematic of Health Economics*. See Maynard and Kanavos (2000) and Wolfe (2008) for short overviews. See Blaug (1998) for an evaluation by a historian of economic thought. Various texts cover specific aspects of health economics, such as cost–effectiveness analysis and these may be referred to under appropriate headwords and phrases. A postmodern view is in Mannion and Small (1999). A 'non-mainstream' view is in Hodgson (2008). Popular general health economics textbooks, written at a variety of levels, include: Cullis and West (1979), R.G. Evans (1984), McGuire et al. (1992), Mooney (2003), Jacobs and Rapoport (2004), Henderson (2004), Donaldson et al. (2005), Feldstein (2005), Phillips (2005), Wonderling et al. (2005), Getzen (2006), Getzen and Allen (2007), Morris et al. (2007), Santerre and Nuen (2007), Folland et al. (2010), McPake and Normand (2008), Palmer and Ho (2008), Phelps (2010), Rice and Unruh (2009) and Zweifel et al. (2009). For texts dealing explicitly with the health economics of the developing world, see Witter and Ensor (1997), Jack (1999) and Witter et al. (2000). On cost-effectiveness methods: Gold et al. (1996) and Drummond et al. (2005).

Health Economists' Study Group

The oldest of the professional associations for health economists, founded in 1972. Its website is available at: http://www.city.ac.uk/economics/research/chec/hesg.html (accessed 2 November 2009). See Croxson (1998) for a history up to 1997.

Health Expenditures

See *Expenditures on Health Care*.

Health Frontier

A *locus* of the maximum health (or gain in health) possible for two or more individuals when resources and technology are given, but the resources going to each individual may be varied. Cf. *Cost–Effectiveness Frontier, Production Possibilities Curve*. See Wagstaff (1986).

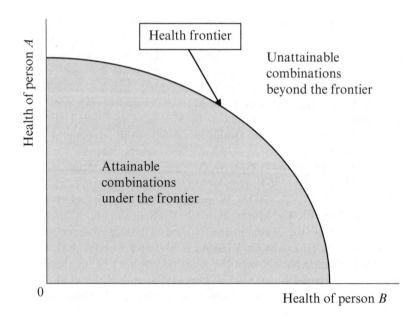

Health Gain

An increase in the *health* of an individual or a *population*. In *health economics*, the term is usually used in the context of an explicit comparator, for example, health gain from having health care rather than not having it, or the health gain to be had from use of a particular technology (perhaps new) compared with another (perhaps the currently standard treatment). It is rarely used in a *'before and after'* sense. Thus, in the figures, let *A* represent health state at time t_0, *B* represent health state at time t_1 after the application of a health care technology and *C* represent health state at time t_1 after the application of another (*comparator*) health care technology. Then, beginning at t_0, a prognosis may follow the trajectory *A* → *B* (using technology 1) or *A* → *C* (using technology 2). Expected health gain (from using technology 1 relative to technology 2) at t_1 is the vertical distance between points *B* and *C*, not the vertical distance between *B* and *A* in either figure. In short, there may be an expected health gain even when health falls, provided that the technology in question entails a less dramatic reduction than the best *alternative*. See *Capacity to Benefit, Cost–Effectiveness Analysis, Health Technology Assessment*.

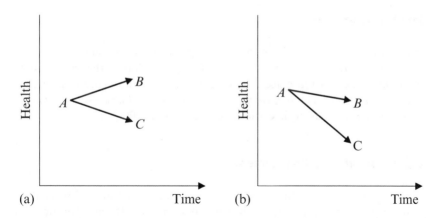

(a) Time   (b) Time

Health Human Resource Planning

See *Manpower Planning*.

Health Impact Assessment

A *World Health Organization* inspired approach to health service planning through which any policy, programme or project is judged in terms of its potential effects on the health of a *population*, the *distribution* of the health effects across the population, and the steps that could be taken to enhance desired and reduce undesired consequences. *Health economics* may or may not come into the analysis. For more detail see the WHO site at http://www.who.int/hia/about/en/ (accessed 2 November 2009).

Health Indemnity Plan

Health insurance that reimburses the insured person retrospectively after paying their own medical expenses, minus any *deductible* or *copayment*.

Health Indicator

A precursor of such instruments as the *quality-adjusted life-year* (QALY). See, e.g., Culyer et al. (1971).

Health Insurance

An arrangement under which the insurer pays contingent sums of money to the insured person or their service provider according to the terms of the *insurance* policy. A more accurate term would be 'health care insurance'. See *Copayment, Deductible, Demand for Health Care, Elasticity, Insurance*. A comprehensive review is Cutler and Zeckhauser (2000).

Health Insurance Experiment

Usually a reference to the largest social science empirical trial of health policy options ever conducted. See Brook et al. (1983) and Manning et al. (1987). For critiques and responses see Newhouse et al. (1987), Welch et al. (1987), Nyman (2007) and Newhouse et al. (2008). For other results that conflict sharply, see Chandra et al. (2007).

Health Maintenance Organization

A health maintenance organization (HMO) is a group of US health care providers that offers an agreed *comprehensive* package of care to a subscriber for a prepaid premium. HMOs are a species of *managed health care* plan. There is a great variety of forms of HMO and great variety in the form of remuneration for physicians but two broad types of HMO are approved by the US Health Maintenance Organization Act. One is the closed panel HMO. Under this type, the HMO employs a group of medical professionals at a central location or contracts with a medical group to provide services exclusively for the HMO's members. Tight control of medical services is maintained because of the close affiliation between the employer HMO and its medical personnel. Another type is the *Independent Practice Association*. Yet another is the *mixed model HMO*. See also *Preferred Provider Organization* and *Jackson Hole Group*. See Luft (1987).

Health Outcomes Assessment

A broad term describing analytical techniques for understanding or predicting the *determinants* of health or changes in health at individual or *population* levels. '*Health*', or a change in a measure of it, is seen as the '*outcome*' in question. For a review see Lipscomb et al. (2005).

Health Production Function

A function showing the maximum impact a variety of variables can have on a person's or people's health. See *Health Frontier, Household Production Function*. See Grossman (1972) for the pioneering study, Rosenzweig and Schultz (1983), Kenkel (1995), Contoyannis and Jones (2004) and Heckman (2007). For wide-ranging review, see Strauss and Beegle (1996).

Health Promotion

Health promotion is defined by the WHO as the process of enabling people to increase control over their health and its *determinants*, and thereby improve their health. This distinguishes it from *primary* or *secondary prevention*, with its focus on *disease* or injury. See the WHO website at http://www.searo.who.int/en/Section1174/Section1458/Section2057.htm (accessed 2 November 2009).

Health Reimbursement Arrangement

A form of income tax deductible employer-operated savings plan for employees who can use the accumulated savings for future medical expenses. Cf. *Health Savings Account*. See Rowe et al. (2008) for some analysis of its effects.

Health-related Quality of Life

There are a large number of empirical measures all measuring a concept related to the idea of '*health*' and in widespread use in *epidemiology* and *cost-effectiveness* work. For a selection of the more generic (i.e. not highly patient or disease-specific) instruments, see *Assessment of Quality of Life, Barthel Index, Child Health Questionnaire, Disability-adjusted Life-years, Duke Health Profile, EQ-5D, 15D®, Health, Health Gain, Health Status, Health Utilities Index, Healthy Years Equivalent, MOS-20, MOS-HIV Health Survey, Nottingham Health Profile, Quality-adjusted Life-year, Quality of Well-being Scale, Saved Young Life Equivalent, SF-6D©, SF-8©, SF-12©, SF-36©, Sickness Impact Profile*. For reviews see Brazier et al. (1999, 2007) and Dolan (2000).

Health-related Societal Value

How to value health and health *outcomes* is a thorny issue involving the making of many social *value judgments*. One issue concerns the source of *value* – whose values ought to be embodied in outcome measures? An approach that has attracted many was devised by Nord et al. (1999). This is a two-stage procedure in which the patients' *preferences* are used to produce *utility* scores, and societal representatives are then used to convert these into units of social value.

Health Research

There has been considerable interest in assessing the value of research in health care given the substantial public and private resources devoted to it. Cf. *Value of Information Analysis*. For an approach based on explicit theoretical consideration of the value of research as information see Claxton and Posnett (1996). A pioneering empirical approach was Buxton and Hanney (1996). On reviews by institutions see Health Economics Research Group et al. (2008) and Canadian Academy of Health Sciences (2009).

Health Savings Account

An income tax deductible form of saving in the US for funding future health care *out-of-pocket* expenses. Also known as 'medical savings account' and 'health care savings account'. Cf. *Health Reimbursement Arrangement*. See, for a proponent, Goodman and Musgrave (1994). See also Remler and Glied (2006).

Health Services/Technology Assessment Text

An internet search facility operated by the National Center for Biotechnology Information (NCBI) of the US National Library of Medicine (which is located at the National Institutes of Health in Bethesda, Maryland). The texts in question are books or reports. Its website is available at: http://www.ncbi.nlm.nih.gov/books/bv.fcgi?rid=hstat (accessed 2 November 2009).

Health Status

A measure of a person's or *population's health*, often via some form of *utility* measure, based on *attributes* of a person's or group's state of health. Normally measured with respect to *activities of daily living* such as freedom from pain, anxiety, ability to feed, dress oneself. See *Health-related Quality of Life*.

Health Technology

A widely used term conventionally relating to the ways in which health services can promote health or prevent/postpone ill-health. The 'ways' in question are in principle very broad and may, for example, extend well beyond the practice of medicine, for example to embrace managerial arrangements and upstream social policy interventions, though it is more common for a narrower range of technologies to be embraced, even as narrow as drugs alone. Because we lack a suitable term for technologies that this narrow interpretation would exclude, it seems desirable to see its scope as even wider, to treat anything as a 'health technology' that promoted health or prevented ill-health, regardless of whether it was located in 'health services' conventionally understood.

Health Technology Assessment

Health technology assessment (HTA) usually addresses the following questions: does the technology in question work? For whom does it work? How well does it work? At what cost does it work? How does it compare with other technologies deemed to be suitable *comparators*? It generally uses insights from economics, *epidemiology* and biostatistics. See Gold et al. (1996), Sculpher et al. (1997) and Drummond et al. (2005) for standard texts.

Health Technology Assessment Database

This is a database managed by the *Centre for Reviews and Dissemination* at the University of York, in the UK, that brings together details of completed and ongoing *health technology assessments* from around the world. The abstracts in the database are descriptive rather than ana-lytical and do not contain critical appraisals of the assessments. The database is produced in collaboration with the *International Network of Agencies for Health Technology Assessment*. Its website is available at: http://www.crd.york.ac.uk/crdweb/Home.aspx?DB=HTA (accessed 2 November 2009).

Health Technology Assessment Programme

This is a comprehensive funded programme of research by the UK's National Institute for Health Research and managed by the *Coordinating Centre for Health Technology Assessments* at Southampton University. Its website is available at: http://www.ncchta.org/ (accessed 2 November 2009).

Health Tourism

See *Medical Tourism*.

Health Utilities Group

This group (HUG) is a group of Canadian economists and decision theorists who have developed the *Health Utilities Index*. Its website is: www.fhs.mcmaster.ca/hug/ (accessed 2 November 2009).

Health Utilities Index

The Health Utilities Index (HUI®) is a generic, preference-scored, comprehensive system for measuring *health status, health-related quality of life* and producing utility scores. It is sponsored (and was essentially created by members of) the *Health Utilities Group* (HUG), which focuses on preference-based measures of health-related quality of life for describing treatment process and *outcomes* in clinical studies, for *population health* studies and economic evaluations of health care services. There are three versions of the Index: HUI Mark1 (HUI1), HUI Mark2 (HUI2) and HUI Mark3 (HUI3). HUI2 has seven *attributes*: Sensation on a scale of 1–4, Mobility (1–5), Emotion (1–5), Cognition (1–4), Self-care (1–4), Pain (1–5) and Fertility (1–3). HUG's website is available at: www.fhs.mcmaster.ca/hug/ (accessed 2 November 2009). See *Health-related Quality of Life*. See Horsman et al. (2003).

Healthy Entrant Effect

A source of possible *bias* in *trials* whereby the health *outcome* of the treatment under investigation is better than would be expected in the general *population* (or the population at risk) on account of the trial's subjects being healthier than average at the beginning of the trial.

Healthy Life Expectancy

See *Life Expectancy*.

Healthy Worker Effect

Age for age, workers generally experience lower *mortality rates* and better health than the general *population* on account of the fact that those who are severely ill or disabled are not usually in employment. This is the original 'healthy worker effect' but it applies to any sub-group from which those at relatively high risk of death or ill-health are excluded. Any sample based on the sub-group would give a biased picture of the general population from which it was drawn unless this effect were compensated for.

Healthy Years Equivalent

The number of years of perfect health followed by instantaneous death that has the same *utility* as a profile of actual health states over an expected lifetime. The experimental method used to derive preference-based values of health states for use in *cost–effectiveness* and *cost–utility* analyses employs both the *standard gamble* and the *time trade-off* methods. The HYE was invented in order to overcome disquiet over some of the assumptions needed to base *quality-adjusted life-years* on individual *preferences*. In particular, HYEs do not depend on 'adding up' QALYs ascribed to periods within an overall period of time (e.g. a life-time); they depend instead on an individual's ability to ascribe a health value to the profile of health states across the whole time period. See *Health-related Quality of Life*. See Mehrez and Gafni (1989) and Gafni and Birch (1993).

HeaLY

The healthy life year (HeaLY) is a composite measure of health loss that combines the amount of healthy life lost due to *morbidity*, plus that attributed to premature mortality. See *Health-related Quality of Life*. See Hyder et al. (1998).

Heckit Model

A two-step estimator designed to deal with *sample selection bias* for which James Heckman was awarded the Nobel Prize for Economics in 2000. Cf. the *Tobit Model*, which is designed to deal with estimation *bias* associated with *censoring*. See Heckman (1979).

Hedonic Prices

These are prices calculated on the basis that the *value* attached to any good is a function of its characteristics, both inherent (such as colour, quality) and external (such as location and environment). The hedonic prices are computed by *regression* techniques and indicate the price of a marginal change in one of the characteristics or the addition of another characteristic, *ceteris paribus*. They are commonly used in economic studies of the quality of goods and services or to adjust for changes in quality over time when calculating price indices. Cf. *Conjoint Analysis*. See for an example of their use in health economics Berndt et al. (2002).

Hedonic Wages

An approach to the valuation of life or the risk of death in workplaces. It is similar to the idea behind *hedonic prices* and proceeds by analysing the extent to which wage differentials compensate for hazards. See Viscusi (1993).

HEED

See *Health Economic Evaluations Database*.

Herd Immunity

The protection offered by vaccines is rarely 100 per cent. Any vaccine will be more *effective* at the *population* level if more people have been vaccinated because some diseases may be able to jump from a vaccinated person to a person who has not been vaccinated but is unlikely to jump from one vaccinated person to another who has been vaccinated. Empirically, when a particular percentage of a population is vaccinated, the spread of the disease is effectively stopped. This critical percentage varies according to the disease, the interactions between members of the population and the vaccine, but 90 per cent is not uncommon. This is herd immunity – the fact that others in the herd or population are vaccinated provides protection to all, whether or not vaccinated themselves. An obvious implication is that 100 per cent vaccination is not normally a technically necessary target that is necessary to obtain effective 100 per cent population protection. Of course, a *cost-effective* rate of vaccination will normally be even lower, depending on the social value of the marginal reduction in risk and the cost of increasing vaccination from a lower to a higher percentage of the population at risk. (It will be lower than the herd immunity level.) The *marginal costs* of increasing vaccination rates may rise quite sharply as one seeks to immunize groups who are reluctant (for a variety of reasons, including religious objections, fear of the needle, imaginary risks, lack of contact with health care services, ignorance, misinformation). See Brisson and Edmunds (2003) for an assessment of herd immunity's impact on economic evaluations.

Herfindahl Index

The Herfindahl index is a measure of the degree to which an industry is concentrated and is the sum of the squares of each firm's market share. The formula for the index (H) is:

$$H = \Sigma_n f_n^2$$

Where f_n is the market share of the nth firm. It has a maximum value of $100^2 = 10\,000$ (which indicates a *monopoly*) and a minimum value of zero. It is sometimes also termed the *Herfindahl–Hirschman Index*. See *Concentration Ratio*. See Nauenberg et al. (2004) for an application to US hospitals.

Herfindahl–Hirschman Index

Abbreviated to HHI. See *Concentration Ratio, Herfindahl Index*. See Nauenberg et al. (2004) for an application to US hospitals.

HES

Acronym for *hospital episode statistics*.

Heterogeneity

The property of being *heterogeneous*. For a study of unobserved heterogeneity in the determinants of health and how it can lead to underestimates of the impact of behaviour on self-assessed health, see Contoyannis and Jones (2004).

Heterogeneous

This exists when there is *variance* in a relevant characteristic of an entity. Cf. *Homogeneous*.

Heteroskedasticity

It is usually assumed in *regression analysis* (for example, *ordinary least squares*) that the *error term* has a constant *variance*. This will be true if the observations of the error term are assumed to be drawn from identical *distributions*. But if the error term were to increase (or decrease) with each observation, this assumption would be invalidated and this is heteroskedasticity. Also appears as 'heteroscedasticity'. Its converse is 'homoskedasticity'.

Heuristic

Assisting in the process of learning or understanding. It is both noun and adjective.

HHI

Acronym for *Hirschman–Herfindahl index*.

HIA

Acronym for *health impact assessment*.

HIE

Acronym for *health insurance experiment*.

Hierarchical Choice

A statistical procedure for deriving *utilities* in *conjoint analysis*. See Ryan et al. (2001).

Hierarchical Data

Data that are organized in classes, with sub-classes beneath them and possibly further subdivisions of the sub-classes.

Hierarchical Modelling

A method of *modelling* systems that exploits the fact that some elements are nested in others and have some causes that are, so to speak, within the nest rather than outside it. For an application in the synthesis of *cost–effectiveness analysis* from several countries see Manca et al. (2007).

Hierarchy of Evidence

A procedure for labelling the strength of the evidence in support of the use of drugs and other medical products and procedures. It is widely used in *systematic reviews* and is a pillar of *evidence-based medicine*. A ranking might be as follows:

Ia   Evidence from systematic reviews or *meta-analysis* of *randomized controlled trials*.

Ib   Evidence from at least one randomized controlled trial.

IIa   Evidence from at least one controlled study without randomization.

IIb   Evidence from at least one other type of *quasi-experimental* study.

III   Evidence from non-experimental descriptive studies, such as comparative studies, *correlation* studies and *case-control studies*.

IV   Evidence from expert committee reports or opinions and/or clinical experience of respected authorities.

Pioneers of such hierarchies include Guyatt et al. (1995). There is much controversy over such classifications, much of which arises because the strength attributed will depend, amongst other things, on the purpose of the review. For example, if the purpose were to minimize *bias* (sometimes called *internal validity*), a hierarchy might serve that would be less useful were the purpose to assess the validity of the research as a predictor of what might happen in real-world practice (sometimes referred to as *external validity*).

Histogram

Same as *bar chart*.

Histology

The study of the structure of cells and tissues. It usually involves the microscopic examination of tissue sections. For example, the histology of a tumour is determined by a biopsy of it, which is examined under a microscope.

Historical Controls

Patients who are not assigned to an *arm* of a *trial* at its start but who received treatment at some time previously and are used as a *comparator*.

HMO

Acronym for *health maintenance organization*.

Holding Gain

The increase over time in the value of an asset merely by continuing to own it.

Hold-up

A rate of reimbursement by a purchaser at which the provider receives the lowest rate they are willing to accept to provide a service but which provides no incentive to invest. See *Purchaser–Provider Split*.

Homogeneous

An entity is homogeneous when there is a lack of variance in its relevant characteristics. (Note that there is a second 'e' in this word.) The opposite of *heterogeneous*.

Homoskedasticity

This exists when the variance of the *error term* is constant across observations. The *homogeneity* of *variance*. Cf. *Heteroskedasticity*.

Homotheticity

This is a property mainly used (in economics) when *production functions* have a constant slope of the *isoquants* along any *expansion path*.

Horizontal Equity

Treating equally those who are equal in some morally relevant sense. Commonly met horizontal equity principles include 'equal treatment for equal need' and 'equal treatment for equal deservingness'. Cf. *Vertical Equity*. See *Equity*.

Hospice Care

See *Palliative Care*.

Hospital-acquired Infection

See *Nosocomial*.

Hospital at Home

An alternative to in-patient care whereby patients receive professional health care in their own homes. See Frick et al. (2009) for a US study and Shepperd et al. (1998a, b) for the UK. Also Campbell et al. (2001).

Hospital Behaviour

Theories of the behaviour of hospitals as institutions generally take their *non-profit* status as given (see *Hospital Economics*) and then explore *models* and their *comparative statics* for purposes of explanation and pre-diction. Despite the potentially complex interactions between the Chief Executive Officer, the Board (of 'trustees') and senior clinical staff, it is generally assumed that 'the hospital' can be characterized as an individ-ual and that it maximizes a *utility function* defined over entities such as quantity of service, quality and net income. This function is maximized subject to a *budget constraint* and to a condition that the net residual ('profit') be zero, so that *average cost = average revenue* and there may be elements of *X-inefficiency* as decision-makers work to ensure that average cost is sufficiently high for the purpose (the hospital is, to some extent, a 'conspicuous producer', using prestigious technologies that are not *efficient* from a societal *perspective* (for some people this may, of course, be an indicator of 'quality'). The limiting case when doctors' incomes are the only *arguments* in the utility function produces a theory in which the hospital is assumed to maximize net revenue per (already on the staff roll) doctor.

Where there is *competition* in the market for hospital services, one predicts that all these utility-maximizing models tend to converge on the general profit-maximizing model of the firm, even though the ownership (shares) of the hospital is not tradable in *capital* markets. This is expected partly because price competition will drive out hospitals (or hospital managements) that inflate costs in order to generate sources of utility for management and partly because new entrants (if there are no significant *barriers to entry*) will tend to cause prices in established institutions to fall and income residuals, whether for spending on on-the-job or take-home sources of utility, will fall. In fact, there is a secular trend in the US for non-profit hospitals to convert to *for-profit* status and in other jurisdictions, private sector providers (whether for profit or non-profit) are increasingly being allowed to compete with public sector hospitals for contracts to provide services for publicly insured patients.

Empirically, it is hard to detect differences that would enable one to discriminate between these rival theories. This is particularly so in markets where competition is limited, where *third party payers* have considerable influence on *caseloads, case-mix* and *reimbursement* rates, and where *exit barriers* may be strong. See *Hospital Costs, Hospital Economics*. For a non-profit theory of hospitals, see Newhouse (1970) and Pauly and Redisch (1973). On the interaction of the physicians and management of hospitals see Harris (1977). On hospitals as competing enterprises, see Dranove et al. (1992), Keeler et al. (1999) and Kessler and McClellan (2000). On hospital networks see Burgess et al. (2005).

Hospital Costs

Hospital cost analysis has been mainly concerned with the use of routine data either to explain apparent differences in unit costs or to inform decisions about what the appropriate 'allowances' might be to compensate hospitals for 'teaching' or 'research'. All studies are beset with the problem of coping with varying degrees of technical *efficiency* and *X-inefficiency* (as when hospitals are not located on *isoquants*), varying degrees of 'difficulty' of patient cases and dating of the endpoint at which the health *output* is assessed (which is often after discharge from hospital), differences in *case-mix*, and imperfect specification of outputs, which leads to problems of *omitted variable bias*. The literature is highly technical and considerable imagination is given to the solution of these and other difficulties. While carefully conducted *econometric* analysis of hospital costs can be of great value in practical decision-making, to use it well requires sophistication and the ability to integrate it into a wider understanding of the hospital world. The classic tour de force in this territory is undoubtedly Feldstein (1967). For an introduction see Lave and Lave (1984) and Butler (1995). On hospitals specifically in a non-competitive environment see Bilodeau et al. (2000).

Hospital Economics

Hospitals are characteristically (though not invariably) *non-profit* institutions that are often also registered charities (or have a similar status). The essential characteristic of a non-profit institution is that its owners (usually either 'trustees' when the hospital is privately owned, or publicly appointed non-executive directors when publicly owned) do not have the right to any residual profit, which may not be taken out of the business. Charitable status also grants them exemption from many of the obligations of *for-profit* organizations, including exemption from corporation tax. These (together with some other characteristics) give rise to the special treatment of hospitals in economics. A puzzle that arises is why this form of organization is so common, whether the hospital be privately owned non-profit (where the owners are effectively the trustees) or publicly owned non-profit (where the owner is a government). Embarrassingly, there is no good answer to this question (in economics). Most attempts run along the lines that hospitals are there to internalize marginal (*Pareto-relevant*) *externalities* and produce services that have in many respects the character of *public goods*. However, while this suggests that hospitals (of any kind) are likely to under-produce without special incentives, it scarcely explains why (or justifies why) they should be publicly owned or be charitable, as distinct from being in receipt of a public *subsidy* in return for providing services of a kind and on a scale they would not otherwise choose.

Another explanation rests on the assertion that non-profit organizations are more trustworthy than *for-profits*. Yet other explanations arise from the historic context in which most hospitals began (as charitable foundations for the poor sick) but then gradually became centres of expertise as medical science progressed, eventually becoming centres for the treatment of all without, however, having shed their legal status.

Besides the for-profit/non-profit issue is the public/private issue. Why are hospitals such popular targets for being publicly owned? There exist popular beliefs that public ownership is somehow more *efficient* than private, or that public ownership in the specific case of medical care is more efficient than private (which is hard to pin down theoretically, desperately difficult to nail empirically and whose advocates – this is largely a world of advocacy rather than analysis – seem less concerned with *primary care* (general practitioners are almost universally private in all systems) than *secondary*. Other explanations are managerial in nature, to the effect that it is easier (cheaper) to manage hospitals in accordance with a set of public objectives if they are directly line-managed from the 'ministry' than if they were private institutions under contract to the same ministry. Again, the theory is unclear and the evidence is absent (which is not, of course, the same as saying there is evidence of absence of a case for the private production plus public subsidy argument).

One set of reasons for the evidence being so difficult to obtain in this area, in addition to the absence of any coherent theory, is that (1) there is a huge variance in the *performance* of hospitals (however judged) within the non-profit groups (and within the public or charitable sectors) as well as across them; (2) hospitals produce multiple *outputs* that are easy to oversimplify (e.g. 'deaths and discharges' – as though the difference did not matter) but difficult to summarize in ways that are conducive to *quantitative analysis*; (3) hospitals also produce widely differing mixes of these outputs (notably varying in their *case-mix*); (4) hospitals are presented with human cases of widely varying 'difficulty' (both in *diagnosis* and treatment); and (5) hospitals also have a widely varying perceived 'quality' independently of the goodness of their clinical *outcomes*. In quantitative analysis it is consequently very easy to fall foul of the problem of *omitted variable bias*.

Amongst the more plausible partial theories of hospitals in economics is a theory that builds on the descriptive historical account alluded to above and sees them essentially as doctors' workshops. This approach utilizes a version of *interest group theory* in which being able to admit patients to hospital became a powerful right through which doctors increasingly acquired control over hospitals – and, in particular, over other doctors and any threat their behaviour might constitute by way of impediment to the private practice of medicine. The non-profit mode suits this interest group by ensuring the dominance of their interests over those of shareholders. The public acquiesce in this arrangement partly because of *asymmetry of information* and partly because, unlike the doctors, they are diffuse and disorganized. See *Hospital Costs, Hospital Behaviour*. A classic is Newhouse (1970). Good reviews are Dranove and Satterthwaite (2000) and Sloan (2000).

Hospital Episode Statistics

Hospital Episode Statistics (HES) provides information on admitted patient care delivered by *National Health Service* (NHS) hospitals in England from 1989. This is used to provide wide-ranging analysis for the National Health Service, government and other organizations and individuals. The HES database is a record-level database of hospital admissions and is currently populated by taking an annual snapshot of a subset of the data submitted by NHS *trusts*. Quarterly information is also collected. A separate database table is held for each financial year containing approximately 11 million admitted patient records from all NHS trusts in England. Its website is available at: http://www.hesonline.nhs.uk/ (accessed 8 November 2009).

Hospital Networks

Hospital networks are formal and informal arrangements that link local hospitals in collaborative ventures. In principle, networking hospitals ought to be able to achieve both *economies of scale* and *scope* through collaboration and specialization, and better prices through collusive activity. The latter effect seems to predominate. See Burgess et al. (2005).

Hospital Separation

A discharge from hospital (dead or alive – as if the difference did not matter!).

Household

Usually defined (pragmatically) as a single person living alone or a family group voluntarily living together, having meals together and having housekeeping shared in common.

Household Production Function

This is the idea that members of families (or households) typically produce commodities through combining goods usually purchased in the market place with their own time. Thus, the purchased goods essentially have a *derived demand*. See Becker (1965). The idea lies at the root of Grossman's (a student of Becker) theory of the demand for health (Grossman, 1972). See also Rosenzweig and Schultz (1983). For wide-ranging review, see Strauss and Beegle (1996). In the context of investment in health, see Heckman (2007). On lifestyle and the production of health see Kenkel (1995) and Contoyannis and Jones (2004).

HRG

Acronym for *healthcare resource group.*

HRQoL

Acronym for *health-related quality of life*.

HTA

Acronym for *health technology assessment*.

HUI®

Acronym for *Health Utilities Index*.

HUI2

See *Health Utilities Index*.

HUI3

See *Health Utilities Index*.

Human Capital

The *stock* of human skills embodied in an individual or group. In value terms it is usually measured as the *present value* of the *flow* of marketed skills (for example, the present value of expected earnings over a period of time). It is determined by basic ability, educational attainment and *health status*, among other things. The 'human *capital* approach' in early *cost–effectiveness analyses* tended to regard increases in human capital, or prevention of reductions in it, as the principal *outcome* of health care. This seemed to be the product of a distressing mental state in which the analysts were incapable of distinguishing people from cart-horses – and is thankfully not an approach much taken today. When an outcome measure such as '*health*' is also used there is also the risk of *double-counting* a benefit already included in the valuation placed upon an additional (quality-adjusted?) life-year. Cf. *Value of Life*. For a review by the concept's chief inventor see Grossman (2000). See also Heckman (2007).

Human Resources

The treatment of human beings as *inputs* in the production of goods and services, in contrast to (though not to the exclusion of) their treatment as the ultimate end-purpose of health policies.

Hybrid Health Plan

Same as *point-of-service plan*. A health benefit plan in the US that combines elements of *managed health care* and traditional *indemnification* for medical fees. Members are encouraged to use a *health maintenance organization* or similar provider network but may also choose a doctor outside the network and be reimbursed for a part of the cost.

HYE

Acronym for *healthy years equivalent*.

Hyperbolic Discounting

This characterizes *time preference* when there is a relatively high *discount rate* over short and early periods but a lower rate on equally short but distant periods. This evidently creates a conflict between today's preferences and those of the future, since in the future what was originally distant and not heavily discounted now becomes near and heavily discounted. Thus, if I decide today to quit smoking next year but, when next year arrives, decide to carry on for a further year, then I am behaving as though I had a hyperbolic discount function. This finding about intertemporal preferences comes mainly from experiments in *cognitive psychology* to the effect that people often prefer low early benefits over high later ones when the low benefits are immanent but, when they are more distant in time, there is a *preference reversal*. Thus, if offered the choice between £90 now and £100 in a year's time one may choose the immediate £90. However, given a different choice of £90 in five years' time or £100 after six, they prefer the £100 even though the benefits are identical and equally postponed. This is inconsistent with the standard analysis of time preference and *discounting*. It seems to be a particular characteristic of addicts. See Laibson (1997) for the approach in general, Van der Pol and Cairns (2002) for a general *health economics* interpretation, Kan (2007) for a specific application in *addiction* and Robberstad and Cairns (2007) for an application in Tanzania.

Hypothecation

Same as *earmarking*.

Hypothesis

A conjecture, preferably with a clear foundation in theory, which can be empirically refuted (at least in principle).

Hysteresis

This is a term in economics that has been borrowed from physics. It refers to a situation in which the past history of a *variable* can affect its current value. For example, the longer the period one has been off work through sickness, the less likely you are to find employment (regardless of your current state of health).

I

Iatrogenesis

An adverse condition induced in a patient through the effects of treatment by a health professional. It can arise in many ways: through clinical errors of *diagnosis* or treatment, through medical negligence, through environmental effects as in *nosocomial* infection, through the careless or deliberate flouting of best practice guidelines (as in the case of extensive prescribing of antibiotics for viral disease leading to antibiotic resistance), poor prevention practice and incompetent follow-up. As many (hospitalized) patients as an estimated 98 000 people die from iatrogenesis in the US each year (Kohn et al. 1999). See *Evidence-based Medicine*. For some examples, see Wright et al. (2002). On prescribing errors and their causes in group practices see Kralewski et al. (2005). See Evans et al. (2007) for many examples of useless or harmful clinical practices that have not been informed by available evidence.

ICECAP

An interval index of *capability* for older people that focuses on *quality of life* rather than health alone for use in decision-making across health and social care. It has five *attributes* of attachment (able to have love and friendship), security (able to think about the future without concern), role (able to do things that make one feel valued), enjoyment (able to have enjoyment and pleasure), control (able to be independent), and with values ranging from 1 (full capability) to 0 (no capability). See Grewal et al. (2006) and Coast et al. (2008c).

ICER

Acronym for incremental cost–effectiveness ratio.

ICER Threshold

A set *incremental cost–effectiveness ratio* above which a technology will not be adopted (or not unless special considerations come into play).

ICF

Acronym for *International Classification of Functioning, Disability and Health*. See *Disability*.

ICUR

Acronym for *incremental cost–utility ratio*.

Identification Problem

This arises in *econometric* attempts to estimate two or more relationships when each shares *variables* with another (for example, *supply* and *demand* share both price and quantity).

Idiography

An approach to (usually psychological) data that emphasizes their individuality and the danger (or impossibility) of making generalizations. The in-depth study of individuals. Cf. *Nomotheticism*. See Allport (1937).

IHE

Acronym for *Institute of Health Economics* at the University of Alberta, Edmonton, Canada. Cf. the *Swedish Institute for Health Economics* in Lund, Sweden.

Immunization

A process of stimulating the immune system through vaccination (inoculation) with weakened or dead viruses in the case of preventing viral disease or dead bacteria in the case of bacterial disease. See *Herd Immunity*. A comprehensive literature is in World Health Organization (2004b).

Impact Statement

A statement of all the identified and significant effects on the health care system of an option in *economic appraisal* and who within the system they affect. Cf. *Health Impact Assessment*. See, for an example, Blackhouse et al. (2008).

Impairment

An impairment is usually taken to be any loss or abnormality of psychological, physiological or anatomical functioning. Cf. *Disability*, *Handicap*.

Imperfect Competition

A market situation in which sellers need to search out the profit-maximizing price for their products. See *Competition*, *Price-searching*.

Implied Value Cue

Hint in questionnaires or interviews that prompts particular and biased responses. See *Starting Point Bias*.

In-area Emergency Services

Emergency medical care rendered within the service area of a *health maintenance organization* (HMO). A typical HMO plan's provision covers members who are treated at any nearby emergency facility, rather than requiring them to go to a specific facility under contract with the HMO. See *Out-of-network Services*. Cf. *Carveouts*.

INAHTA

See *International Network of Agencies for Health Technology Assessment*.

Incentive Contracts

Contracts between insurers or other *third party payers* and the providers of health care that embody incentives and penalties (both usually financial) for failing to meet particular conditions. Such contracts seem significantly to affect the behaviour of (e.g.) *primary care* physicians. See, for examples of empirical cases, Rochaix (1993) and Gruber and Owings (1996).

Incentives

The response of individuals (patients, doctors, etc.) to anything that relaxes any of the various financial and other limits on their ability to act as they prefer. They are positive inducements to act in particular ways. Disincentives are negative inducements. For a study of professional incentives see P.C. Smith and York (2004). For a study of financial inducements to reduce drug dependency see Sindelar et al. (2007).

Inception Cohort

A group of patients assembled at the onset of the *disease* being investigated.

Incidence

This has wholly different meanings in *epidemiology* and economics. In epidemiology, 'incidence' is the number of new cases of a disease identified during a time period. It is usually expressed as the proportion of those who are susceptible or at risk at the beginning or middle of the period.

In economics, 'incidence' concerns who pays taxes and various other costs, that is, who bears the ultimate distribution of the burden after all effects arising from the *elasticities* of *demand* and *supply* have been allowed to work their way out. Unless the elasticities of demand and supply have very extreme low values, economists generally expect there to be what is known as *shifting*. Thus, it may appear self-evident that a tax, like a *payroll tax* to fund *health insurance*, or compulsory *copayment,* is paid by whoever gives up the cash, writes a cheque or pays by credit card. There is, however, a difference between the statutory, or formal, incidence of tax (the persons who initially pays) and the final or economic incidence. Thus, in the case of a general payroll tax, the immediate impact is to reduce the take-home pay of workers; this will cause the supply of labour to fall and generate a (partially) compensating rise in the wage rate (depending on the elasticity of supply) through which a part of the burden of the tax is paradoxically shifted on to the owners of *capital*. The prices of goods will also rise, with goods and services produced in labour-intensive industries rising more than elsewhere (depending on the relative elasticity of demand for them), thereby shifting some of the burden of the tax on to consumers of the more labour-intensive goods. In the economy as a whole, the capital–labour ratio will fall.

Similar sorts of effects will arise when one is analysing the impact of diseases on labour productivity, wages and movements in the *labour market*. It also turns out that the prevalence of a disease is a potentially important *determinant* of such impacts. See DeLeire and Manning (2004). For a health benefit application see Gruber (1994). On incidence in US *health insurance* see Levy and Feldman (2001). For an application of formal incidence to health sector subsidies see O'Donnell et al. (2008) Chapter 14.

Inclusion/Exclusion Criteria

These have two common uses. One refers to the medical or social standards determining whether a person may or may not be allowed to enter a *clinical trial*. The criteria usually include age, gender, type and stage of a disease, previous treatment history and other medical conditions. The aims are to identify experimentally appropriate participants and to avoid harming them.

The other relates to the scientific standards set to determine which items in a literature (journal articles, book chapters, etc.) will be included in a *systematic review* or *meta-analysis*. The criteria usually include quality and specific tests related to the purposes for which the review is being conducted.

Income and Health

The (positive) association between income and *health* has an economic explanation in Grossman's theory of *health capital* (Grossman, 1972). A wider multidisciplinary *'population health'* perspective is in R.G. Evans et al. (1994) and Heymann et al. (2006). While the idea that health and wealth are positively correlated has not been much contested (though there are issues around the direction of causation) the idea that relative income and, in particular, that unequal income distributions tend to lower population health has been much contested and the evidence for it is weak. See *Gradient in Health*.

See Wilkinson (1996) for the unequal income proposition and Gravelle (1998) for the other side. A more recent appraisal is Jones and Wildman (2008). See also Wildman (2003) and McLeod et al. (2003). On the direction of causation see Smith (1999). On the use of estimated *elasticities* to explain rising income and rising income-related health inequality see Van Ourti et al. (2009).

Income Distribution

The way in which total income is divided amongst the *households* in an economy. Usually measured in terms of greater or lesser equality by a statistic such as the *Gini coefficient*. See *Equity*.

Income Effect

The effect on the *demand* for a good or service that arises from the impact on *real income* of a change in its price, *ceteris paribus*. It may be positive or negative. For example, a fall in price means that the same rate of consumption can be maintained at a lower level of expenditure. This is equivalent to an increase in real income (one can now buy more of everything) and this will lead to a rise in demand for all *income-elastic* goods. If the good whose price has fallen is itself an income-elastic good, then there will be a further boost to its own demand deriving from this income effect. Cf. *Substitution Effect*. See *Compensating Variation, Equivalent Variation*. For an example of how income effects seem to matter when measuring the so-called welfare loss from excess insurance see Nyman (1999a).

Income-elasticity

The responsiveness of something (usually *demand*) to a change in income. See *Elasticity*.

Incomplete Data

It is common for the data in clinical studies and *cost–effectiveness analyses* to be incomplete. This may or may not be a significant problem. Examples of types of missing data include single missing items (e.g. failure to record a survey result for one item in an *EQ-5D* schedule), missing whole questionnaires, and missing data due to drop-out. Whether these omissions matter will depend partly on whether they are 'missing completely at random', in which case the *sample* remains representative, 'missing at random', in which case they can be imputed, or whether they are not randomly missing (sometimes termed 'non-ignorable non-response'). Ways of coping (which can hardly be commended) have included *'last observation carried forward'*, *'complete case analysis'* (i.e. using only complete cases with no imputed values, with the risk of *bias* if the sample with omissions is not representative); *'unconditional mean imputation'* (i.e. replacing missing data with the mean value of the data in the sample with omissions), with again evident risk of bias. Better methods include 'regression imputation', 'stochastic regression imputation', and 'multiple imputation' in which missing values are replaced with plausible *alternatives* in a process that takes account of the uncertainty about the right value to impute. See Briggs et al. (2003).

Increasing Returns to Scale

A feature of *production functions*. A production function exhibits increasing returns to scale if increasing all inputs in the same proportion increases outputs by a larger proportion. For an example see Valdmanis et al. (2003).

Incremental Analysis

Same as *marginal analysis* but, in *cost–effectiveness analysis*, it often refers to the differences in *costs* or *outcomes* between two or more technologies.

Incremental Benefit

Same is *marginal benefit* or, in *cost–effectiveness analysis*, the benefit of one option less that of another having lower benefits.

Incremental Cost

Same as *marginal cost* or, in *cost–effectiveness analysis*, the cost of one option less that of another having a lower cost.

Incremental Cost–Effectiveness Ratio

The ratio of the difference between the *costs* of two alternatives and the difference between their *effectiveness* or *outcomes*. Cf. *Cost–Effectiveness Plane*.

Incremental Cost–Utility Ratio

Same as *incremental cost–effectiveness ratio* – though some economists interpret the *outcome* as a measure of *utility* rather than health.

IND

Acronym for *investigation of a new drug*.

Indemnification

The compensation or benefits payable under an *insurance* policy, or a principle of insurance, to the effect that an insured person should be retrospectively restored to the same financial position as before a covered loss.

Indemnity

A sum of money contracted to be paid to one person by another as compensation for a loss whether or not the indemnifier caused the loss.

Indemnity Insurance

Traditional private health care *insurance*, which places few restrictions on the character of service covered or choice of provider.

Independent Practice Associations

An association of physicians and other health care providers, including hospitals, who contract with a *health maintenance organization* (HMO) to provide services to its members but usually still see non-HMO patients and patients from other HMOs. Patients are usually seen in the physicians' own offices. The doctors maintain their own private practices and thus can contract with more than one HMO and see regular *fee-for-service* patients as well. The usual method of remuneration is *capitation*, though the other contracts may be fee-for-service. See *Vertical Integration*.

Independent Variable

A *variable* that affects other variables but is not affected by them. Often called an *outcome* variable in *epidemiology*. See *Argument*. Cf. *Dependent Variable*.

Index Medicus

Catalogue of the United States National Library of Medicine (NLM), and a periodical index to the medical literature. Available in printed form, or electronically as *MEDLINE*®. The website is available at: http://www.ncbi.nlm.nih.gov/pubmed/ (accessed 3 November 2009).

Index Numbers

The most common forms of index met in health economics are price and quantity indices. A price (cost of living) index measures the change in the weighted prices of a (constant) bundle of goods or services over time. It is the standard measure of *inflation*. A quantity index (standard of living) measures the change in the weighted quantities of goods or services when prices are constant. The procedure in each case is basically the same: the current data are compared with those in a 'base' (usually earlier) period and presented either as a ratio or (if multiplied by 100) as a percentage. The weights used may be either those of the current period or those of the base period. Thus:

$$P_L = \Sigma P_n Q_0 / \Sigma P_0 Q_0$$

is the Laspeyres price index, P_n is the price per unit in period n and Q_0 is the quantity produced in base period 0 using base period quantities as weights in both period n and period 0. The Laspeyres price index thus measures the change in cost of purchasing the same basket of goods and services in the current period as was purchased in a specified base period. It is named after German economist, Etienne Laspeyres (he preferred it pronounced Las-pey-res) (1834–1913).

$$P_P = \Sigma P_n Q_n / \Sigma P_0 Q_n$$

is the Paasche price index, which compares the cost of purchasing the current basket of goods and services with the cost of purchasing the same basket in an earlier period. Prices are weighted by current quantities. P_n is the price per unit in period n and Q_n is the quantity produced in period n. It is named after another German economist Hermann Paasche (the 'e' is not silent) (1851–1925).

Quantity indices weight different bundles by the prices obtaining either in period n or period 0.

Other indices include Fisher's ideal index (the *geometric mean* of the Laspeyres and Paasche indices of price or quantity). This is named after the US economist Irving Fisher (1867–1947); the Malmquist index, a method of measuring productivity change that does not depend upon knowledge of the prices of *inputs* or *outputs* provided that a production *frontier* is known. It is used in *data envelope analysis*; and the Törnqvist index, the weighted average change in the log of price or quantity in the measurement of changes in (e.g.) productivity over time. See Laspeyres (1871), Paasche (1874), I. Fisher (1922), Törnqvist (1936) and Malmquist (1953). For a review of medical care price index construction see Berndt et al. (2000).

Indifference

A situation in which the *utility* gained by an individual from either of two entities is the same. See *Indifference Curve*.

Indifference Curve

A *locus* of points in a diagram having two goods, one on each axis, such that an individual is indifferent between all points on the curve. The curve is usually axiomatically taken to be convex to the origin, reflecting a diminishing *marginal rate of substitution*, and indicating that both goods are *economic goods*. If an individual is indifferent between two options, this is generally taken in economics to be equivalent to the statement that the two options have equal *utility*. A family of indifference curves (an 'indifference map') shows successive curves like contours on a geographical map. As

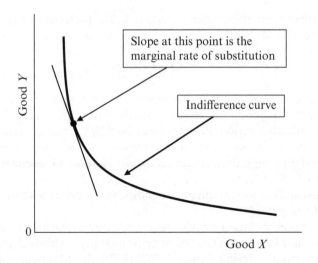

one moves in a north-easterly direction each indifference curve is associated with a higher utility number. An alternative name for an indifference curve is an 'iso-utility curve'. The geometry gets complicated when there are more than two goods, though three dimensions have been used, even in health economics, e.g. Culyer (1971a). See its inventor, Hicks (1939b).

Indirect Cost

In *cost–effectiveness analyses*, this refers usually to the *productivity costs* that may be the consequence of the use of a particular technology. It is also used in the analysis of the overall costs of disease. Cf. *Consumption Cost*. For a third world example, see Popkin et al. (2006).

Indirect Tax

A tax on the production and sale of goods and services. Common taxes of this sort are value-added tax (VAT), sales tax, purchase tax, *excise tax*, customs duty, stamp duty. See *Taxes*.

Indivisibility

An *input* in a production process that cannot be physically subdivided into smaller parts. Given sufficient time, it may be possible to acquire smaller versions of an indivisible input (say, an ambulance) but they, in turn, cannot be physically subdivided without changing their character (as when they are disassembled and become 'spare parts'). When indivisibility presents a problem it may sometimes be avoided by including an explicit time dimension: 'an hour/day/week/year/etc. of a building's use' instead of 'a building'. Cf. *Divisibility*, *Fixed Costs*. For a health economics application see Lord et al. (2004).

Industrial Organization

The branch of economics dealing with the way in which industries and the people who work in them behave under various regimes of *competition* and regulation. For a review see Dranove and Satterthwaite (2000).

Inequalities in Health

Health inequalities are one important aspect of inequities in health, health care and health care financing. See *Equity*. For a comprehensive review see Wagstaff and Van Doorslaer (2000); also Wagstaff (2002b). A general text is Cowell (1995). On some reasons why inequalities often persist despite efforts to reduce them see Contoyannis and Forster (1999).

Infant Mortality Rate

Deaths in one year of infants under one year of age divided by number of live births in that year, all multiplied by 1000.

Infectious Disease

Same as *communicable disease*. See *External Effect, Vector*. For an economic analysis see Philipson (2000).

Inferential Statistics

The type of statistics in which *samples* in a *population* are taken and inferences made from the samples about the character of those populations.

Inferior Good

A good for which a change in income causes an opposite change in *demand*. The *income-elasticity* is negative. In an extreme case and if money income does not change, it is possible to conceive of the demand for a strongly inferior good actually having a positive relationship to price, though alleged examples of this so-called Giffen good, named after the British statistician Sir Robert Giffen (1837–1910), are hotly contested and none are known in the health care literature. Cf. *Normal Good.*

Inflation

Rising prices. Usually measured by the percentage increase in an *index number* of prices. For medical inflation in the US see Cutler et al. (1996).

Influence Diagram

An alternative to the *decision tree* as means of describing the various nodes of a decision problem under uncertainty. It is useful in *value of information analysis*. Also known as 'decision network' and 'relevance diagram'.

Informal Care

Health care given by such (usually professionally unqualified) people as family members. For an economic analysis see Brouwer et al. (2005).

Informatics

The study of information and its management, processing and dissemination.

Informational Rent

The surplus over and above the minimum required by a provider to supply a service that arises because of an informational advantage (say about costs) that they have but to which the purchaser is not privy. See *Purchaser–Provider Split, Rent*. See Galizzi and Miraldo (2008).

Information Asymmetry

The usual asymmetry in *health economics* relates to the difference in the information known to a patient, or member of the public, and that known to a professional such as a doctor or nurse. Another asymmetry is that between insurers and those insured. The information asymmetries in health care have deep-reaching consequences for its organization, regulation and financing, mainly in order that the lay person (patient, potential patient, family carer) is not exploited. For a fuller discussion see *Asymmetry of Information*. For a health economics perspective see Rochaix (1989) and Phelps (2000).

Information Bias

A form of *bias* that occurs when subjects' responses are affected by beliefs and values that colour their responses to questions that are not about such beliefs and values. Also known as 'observational bias'.

Information Cost

A form of *transaction cost* that relates to the cost of acquiring and interpreting information (for example, about the quality of locally provided doctors' services). Originators of the idea were Alchian and Demsetz (1972). A review is Hirshleifer and Riley (1979). A health economics application is Smith and Street (2006). For way information is or is not used in insurance selection see Abraham et al. (2006).

Information Resources in Health Economics

A comprehensive listing can be found at: http://www.york.ac.uk/inst/crd/econ.htm (accessed 3 November 2009). For a comprehensive listing of university departments and institutes of health economics go to http://edirc.repec.org/healthecon.html (accessed 3 November 2009).

Informed Consent

'Consent' in general is usually legally grounded either on the principle that a physician has a duty of care or that a patient has a right to self-determination. In most countries the informed consent of a patient to a treatment is based on the notion of what information a reasonable patient might expect to be told in a given situation. In the UK, informed consent is based upon what professionals regard as reasonable to provide and hence on what information in any given case a physician's peers would provide.

Inframarginal

Whereas most *microeconomics* analyses phenomena at the *margin*, i.e. when there is a small change, positive or negative, in a *variable* and the consequential changes it induces elsewhere in a *model* of the economy, inframarginal values are those that lie at rates of consumption, production, etc. that are lower than the marginal rate. Thus, for example, *consumer's surplus* is the sum of the excess of value over cost of acquisition of all inframarginal units of consumption (those lower than the marginal rate).

Input

Same as *factor of production*. The resources that are used in production processes. See *Production Function*.

Input–Output Analysis

Input–output analysis is a method of quantifying the mutual relationships between various sectors of an economy, the *outputs* of one being the *inputs* of another. An input–output table describes the flows between the sectors (such as industries). The method was invented by Leontief (1941). See *Leontief Production Function*. For an application in *health economics*, see Butler (1995).

In Situ

A Latin tag meaning 'in a particular location' or 'in its original place'. In the treatment of cancer it refers to the original location of a cancer before it has metastasized. When interventions on cells or tissue take place on the living tissue, cells, etc. in the body rather than in the laboratory, the tissue etc. is also said to be 'in situ'.

Instantaneous Rate

A term used by some epidemiologists to mean what economists simply call 'rate'.

Institute for Work & Health

A non-profit research institute in Toronto, Canada, devoted to the analysis of occupational health and health and safety in workplaces. Its website is available at: http://www.iwh.on.ca/ (accessed 3 November 2009).

Institute of Health Economics

A non-profit organization engaged in health economics and health technology assessment in Edmonton, Canada. Its website is available at: http://www.ihe.ca (accessed 3 November 2009). Note also the *Swedish Institute for Health Economics*.

Institut fuer Qualitaet und Wirtschaftlkichkeit im Gesundheitswesen

The German federal organization (Institute for Quality and Efficiency in Health Care) responsible for evaluating clinical interventions, including (since 2007) conducting *cost–benefit analyses* of drugs. Its acronym is IQWiG. Its website is available at: http://www.iqwig.de/ (accessed 3 November 2009).

Instrumental Variables

A method of statistical estimation of *models* with *endogenous* regressors (i.e. regressors that are correlated with the *error term*). It relies on *variables* ('instruments') that are good predictors of an endogenous regressor but that are not independently related to the *dependent variable*. These can be used to purge *bias* caused by *endogeneity*. See Heckman (1997). For an introduction see Kennedy (2003). For a health economics application see Mullahy and Portney (1990).

Insurance

Health insurance consists of a contract between the client and the insurer to the effect that in the event of specified events occurring the insurer will pay certain sums of money either to the insured person or (the usual case) to the health service agency. By pooling risks the insurer is able to select premiums that actuarially (after allowances for other expenses, etc.) make it worthwhile for the purchaser. For the insured person, the advantage of insurance is that the probability of a large financial loss through lost earnings or expenses of medical care is exchanged for the certainty of smaller loss (the payment of a premium). The standard *expected utility* explanation for why people insures is as follows.

The figure shows how *utility* varies with income. *Diminishing marginal utility of income* is assumed. When income is $30 000, utility is 0a, when income is $5000, utility is 0b. Suppose that an uninsured individual would have to pay out $25 000 if they fell ill. Let the probability that this will occur be taken as 0.4. The expected value of income is therefore 0.4 × $5000 + 0.6 × $30 000 = $20 000. The expected utility of this expected income is 0c (0.4× 0b + 0.6 × 0a), assuming that the utility function stays where it is in sickness or in health. Now, however, suppose that insurance can be bought at an actuarially fair premium of $10 000. Paying this sum (for certain) leaves an income of $20 000, whose (certain) utility is 0d. Since 0d > 0c, plainly the expected utility maximizing individual will prefer 0d,

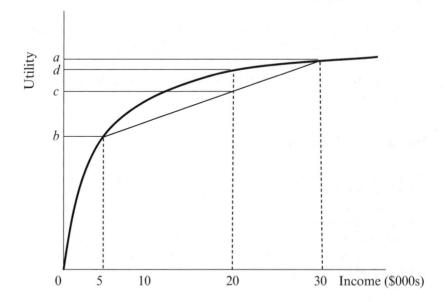

the insurance choice. Such an individual will also still choose to insure even when the premium is actuarially unfair, so long as it is not too unfair. See also *Adverse Selection, Copayment, Creaming, Deductibles, Dumping, Loading, Moral Hazard, Skimping.* For a survey see Cutler and Zeckhauser (2000) and Pauly (2000). For analyses of insurance in the context of low- and middle-income countries see World Bank (1993), Creese and Bennett (1997), Dror and Jacquier (1999), Sachs (2001), Jowett et al. (2004) and Sinha et al. (2007). A review is Ekman (2004).

Intangibles

The literal sense of 'not capable of being touched' is not the general sense in which this term is used in economic analyses. These effects, which are often unfortunately labelled 'intangible costs' in some *cost–effectiveness analyses*, are usually undesired states or consequences of decisions such as pain, disutility, disappointment, etc. that have it in common that they are not quantified or measured. It is not a satisfactory term since few, if any, consequences are truly intangible in this sense. There are, in fact, many quantifying measures of pain, disutility, etc. Nor are they *'costs'* in the economic sense of the term. See *Opportunity Cost, Tangibles, Utility.* See Sloan et al. (1998) for a *willingness to pay* approach to measuring intangibles.

Integrated Care

A medical benefit programme in the US that is provided by an employer and that coordinates *workers' compensation* insurance with group health coverage to provide seamless medical care to the employee. Two sepa- rate insurance policies are issued: one for workers' compensation and one for *health insurance.* See McRae et al. (2008) for a *cost–effectiveness analysis.*

Intellectual Property Right

Intellectual property rights (IPRs) are exclusive private property rights such as copyrights, trademarks or *patents* to use ideas in particular ways and for particular purposes that deny their use to others without agreed compensation of the owner. A senior economist's straightforward view on the matter, especially as regards third world countries, is Stiglitz (2006).

Intensity

Usually refers to the ratio of a *factor of production* to *output*. The higher the ratio the greater the intensity.

Intensive Margin

See *Extensive Margin*.

Intention to Treat

A method of analysis in randomized *clinical trials* in which all patients who are randomly assigned to one of the treatments are analysed together, regardless of whether or not they actually received or completed that treatment. One of the reasons for this type of analysis is to guard against any *bias* that might be introduced when dropping out is related to the outcome. Cf. *Per Protocol* analysis.

Intercept

The point at which a line crosses an axis in a diagram. In an equation such as:

$$X = a + bY$$

the intercept is *a*.

Interdecile Range

The central 80 per cent of (ordered) observations (i.e. excluding the first and tenth *deciles*). See *Quantile*.

Interest

A payment for the use of borrowed money denoted as a percentage of the sum borrowed. See *Discounting, Internal Rate of Return, Time Preference*.

Interest Group Theory

The basic theory comes from the economic approach to political decision-making, in which government activities are viewed as processes through which *wealth* or *utility* is redistributed between individuals and groups. For some, the unit cost of collectively organizing so as to procure a transfer from others is less than the value of the transfer; for others, the contrary is the case. People can thus be seen as demanders and suppliers of transfers. Representative democracy and its agents are seen as the mechanisms through which these interests are played out and equilibria established. The theory's origins were probably Olson (1965) and Stigler (1971). Also Posner (1974). For a *health economics* application see Goddard et al. (2006).

Intergenerational Equity

This concerns the fairness of the treatment of young people relative to old people and the relative weights to be attached to the *health gains* each might make. It can also concern the consequences of decisions today for people as yet unborn. See *Equity*. See Williams (1997).

Interior Solution

An *equilibrium* that is not a *corner solution*. For example, in the figure overleaf, the tangency of the *indifference curve* with the *budget constraint* is an interior solution. Cf. *Corner Solution*.

Intermediate Care

There seems to be no generally agreed definition of intermediate care but it might in a general way be thought of as a group of multi-professional services that do not require the resources of a general hospital but are beyond the scope of a normal (in the UK) *primary care* team. More or less the same as 'continuing care'. There are few economic studies and other evaluative research studies appear to be poorly controlled. For a cost-minimization study see, for example, Jones et al. (1999). Wiener et al. (2004) is a review.

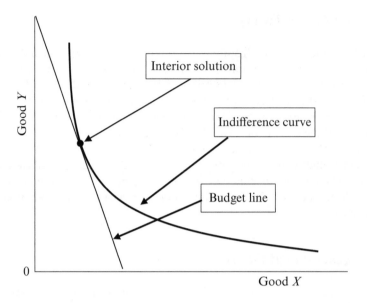

Intermediate Good

A good or service that does not itself yield *utility* to an individual but that might be used to create another good or service that is a *final good* or be used in conjunction with other goods and services to yield utility. Although it is sometimes said that health care does not yield utility (apparently on the ground that illness has negative utility), *cost-effective* health care does – that is, (expected) utility is higher with it than without, even though utility might have been even higher had the *need* for health care not arisen in the first place. Cf. *Intermediate Care*.

Internal Cost and Benefit

A cost or benefit that accrues to the decision-maker in question rather than being thrust upon an external party. Cf. *Externality*.

Internal Market

Market-like arrangements used within publicly provided services like health care. The central characteristic of internal markets is that the players are divided functionally into purchasers (sometimes called *commissioners*) and providers, with the former contracting with the latter to provide services of specified types to a specified group of clients (usually defined on a geographical basis) at an agreed cost and to agreed standards. England's *National Health Service* is essentially organized as the world's largest internal market, in which *Primary Care Trusts* commission (they are also providers of *primary care* services) hospitals to provide *secondary care*. See *Purchaser–Provider Split*. See Gerdtham et al. (1999).

Internal Rate of Return

That *discount rate* that makes the net present value of costs and benefits equal zero. Thus, with B_t and C_t representing costs and benefits in year t, the annual internal rate of return is r^* in the formula:

$$0 = \Sigma_t(B_t - C_t)/(1+r^*)$$

See *Discounting*. Morris and McGuire (2002) is an empirical example of its use.

Internal Validity

The reliability and accuracy of a *trial*'s results thanks to the removal of *bias*. Cf. *External Validity*.

International Classification of Disease

The International Classification of Diseases (ICD) is designed to promote international comparability in the collection, processing, classification and presentation of mortality statistics and is published by the *World Health Organization*. The current classification is the tenth edition (ICD-10). The codes are:

I	Infectious and parasitic diseases
II	Neoplasms
III	Diseases of the blood and blood-forming organs
IV	Endocrine, nutritional and metabolic diseases, and immunity disorders
V	Mental and behavioural disorders
VI–VIII	Diseases of the nervous system and sense organs
IX	Diseases of the circulatory system

X	Diseases of the respiratory system
XI	Diseases of the digestive system
XII	Diseases of the skin and subcutaneous tissue
XIII	Diseases of the musculoskeletal system and connective tissue
XIV	Diseases of the genito-urinary system
XV	Complications of pregnancy, childbirth and the puerperium
XVI	Certain complications originating in the prenatal period
XVII	Congenital malformations, deformations and chromosomal disorders
XVIII	Symptoms, signs and ill-defined conditions
XX	External causes of morbidity and mortality

The classification can be examined on the WHO website: http://www.who.int/classifications/icd/en (accessed 3 November 2009).

International Classification of Functioning, Disability and Health

The *World Health Organization*'s comprehensive definition of *disability*. ICF's website is available at: http://www.who.int/classifications/icf/en (accessed 3 November 2009).

International Comparisons

There is a large *health economics* literature dealing with international comparisons of expenditures, delivery (health care industry) structures, financing methods, *population health, equity* and inequity. See, e.g., on expenditures (monetary) Newhouse (1977), Gerdtham and Jönsson (2000), expenditures (real) Anell and Willis (2000), on cost-effectiveness Rapoport et al. (2009), on objectives Culyer et al. (1982), on processes and their outcomes Anderson (1998), on equity Van Doorslaer et al. (1999), Wagstaff and Van Doorslaer (2000), O'Donnell et al. (2008), on workplace health and safety Hotopp et al. (2008), on cost containment Mossialos and Le Grand (1999).

International Network of Agencies for Health Technology Assessment

The Network aims to accelerate exchange and collaboration among agencies, promote information sharing and comparison, and prevent unnecessary duplication of activities. Its website is available at: http://www.inahta.org/ (accessed 3 November 2009).

International Society for Pharmacoeconomics and Outcomes Research

This is a multidisciplinary and multi-professional international organization for promoting pharmacoeconomics and health outcomes research. Its website is available at: http://www.ispor.org (accessed 3 November 2009).

International Trade

Health care is amongst those services that are traded internationally, though not much analysed by health economists. See *General Agreement on Trade in Services, Global Alliance for Vaccines and Immunization, Parallel Trade, Pharmaceutical Industry*. See Kanavos and McKee (2000), Drager and Vieira (2002), Woodward et al. (2002) and Smith (2004).

Interpersonal Comparisons of Utility

An influential book by Lionel (later Lord) Robbins (1898–1984) (Robbins, 1932) provided not only the most commonly met definition of economics that is still in use (see *Economics*) but also introduced into economics the highly influential distinction between *normative* and positive. In positive economics, making interpersonal comparisons of *utility* has been regarded, at least by economists influenced by *logical positivism*, as 'meaningless' partly on the grounds that one person's utility is not observable to anyone else and partly because making such interpersonal comparisons was held to involve ethics – and ethics, according to logical positivism, is scientifically meaningless. In *welfare economics* a similar ban on making interpersonal comparisons exists amongst staunch users of the *Pareto criterion* but on less clear grounds, since this seemed to deny welfare economics the possibility of addressing most practically relevant ethical issues in public policy (even Pareto himself did not hesitate to make them when necessary – as in policy judgments). Interpersonal comparisons are explicitly disallowed in the *Arrow social welfare function*, and Arrow himself described interpersonal comparisons of utility as having 'no meaning'. Thus, for example, policy measures to alleviate extreme poverty might be agreed to be highly desirable but they could not be *Pareto improvements* if they were to involve involuntary sacrifices by the rich (they might be actual improvements but the criterion could not say whether that was so).

Yet people plainly have empathy and make interpersonal comparisons of subjective feelings and experiences all the time, especially within families and other groups having important things in common, and the 'states of mind' of others are not invariably invisible, though we may sometimes be deceived about them, nor is our objective behaviour uninfluenced by what we perceive others to feel. While several very distinguished economists have provided penetrating analyses involving interpersonal comparisons of utility many, however, still do their best to avoid analysis involving them while others make them, but implicitly.

Health economists have tended to be far less squeamish regarding inter-personal comparisons than other economists, especially those adopting the *extra-welfarist* position, largely because *health* and the *equity* of its *distribution* lie at the heart of so much public policy and a concern on the economists' part that economics be able to contribute to the solution of the enormous resource allocation issues that arise in the field of health. This is not to suggest that it is any economist's business to make distributional value judgments; rather it is to suggest that their orderly discussion (by economists among others) in public policy debate is highly desirable and to the benefit of those whose business it is to make such judgments. See also *Arrow Social Welfare Function, Externality, Perspective, Quality-Adjusted Life-Year, Social Welfare Function, Utility*. On the big philosophical issues involved see Harsanyi (1982) and Elster and Roemer (1991).

Interquartile Range

The central 50 per cent of (ordered) observations, i.e. excluding the first and last 25 percentiles.

Interrater Reliability

An indicator of the consistency of the rating or score assigned to an entity by different judges. Cf. *Intrarater Reliability*.

Interrupted Time Series

A study design in which measurements are taken over time, interrupted on occasions of treatment.

Interval Estimate

The range of a *variable* within which a *value* is predicted to lie.

Interval Regression

A variant of the *ordered probit model* that can be used when *threshold* values are known.

Interval Scale

A scale of measurement in which – like temperature measurement – the ratios of intervals between the points on the scale are the same for each set of possible numbers and the zero point is arbitrary. Each set of possible numbers is a *linear transformation* of another. See *Utility*.

Interviewer Bias

A form of *bias* that arises in social surveys when the expectations or prejudices of the interviewer colour the respondents' responses.

Intrarater Reliability

An indicator of the stability of the rating or score assigned to an entity by the same judge on different occasions. Cf. *Interrater Reliability*.

Inverse Care Law

A generalization to the effect that the availability of good medical care tends to vary inversely with the *need* for it in the *population* served. Originated in Hart (1971).

Inverse Elasticity Rule

Same as *Ramsey pricing*.

Inverse Variance Method

An approach in *meta-analysis* to combining results from more than one study. The average effect size across all studies is computed as a weighted *mean*, where the weights are equal to the inverse *variance* of each study's estimate of effect. Large studies and studies with less random variation have greater weight than small studies.

Investigation of a New Drug

A formal stage of testing a new drug in the US for which approval from the *Food and Drug Administration* is required before *trials* on human subjects may proceed.

Investment

Investment is the change in the *stock* of *capital* over a period. In *national income accounting*, investment (descriptively) consists of expenditures on house building, plant and equipment, and stocks (inventories). In each case, it is only new *output* produced during the accounting period that is included. See *Gross Investment, Net Investment*.

Investment Appraisal

Same as *option appraisal*.

Invisible Hand

Describes the way in which markets apparently coordinate the activities of thousands of people without any evident 'steering'. See *Price Mechanism*.

Involuntary Unemployment

Unemployment that exists when workers are willing to accept jobs at the going wage but cannot find vacancies.

IPA

Acronym for *Independent Practice Association.*

IPR

Acronym for *intellectual property right.*

IQWiG

Acronym for *Institut fuer Qualitaet und Wirtschaftlkichkeit im Gesundheitswesen.*

Isocost

A line in a two-input diagram along which costs are constant. Similar to a *budget constraint.* See *Expansion Path.*

Isoproduct Curve

Same as *isoquant.*

Iso-utility Curve

Same as *indifference curve.*

Isoquant

A contour in a two-*input* diagram showing the lowest combinations of the two necessary in order to produce a given rate of *output.* Being 'on' an isoquant implies that the organization in question is technically *efficient.* Selecting an appropriate point on the isoquant will produce *cost-effectiveness* (the *opportunity cost* of producing that rate of output will be minimized). To achieve this one needs to know the prices (ideally the marginal *opportunity costs*) of the two inputs. The cost-minimizing combination of inputs at each rate of output is where the isoquant for that output rate is tangential to an isocost line. Selecting the appropriate isoquant (and, of course, the appropriate point on it) will produce general *efficiency* in the sense of marginal cost = marginal value. To achieve this one needs to know the marginal social value of the output in question. See *Cost-effectiveness, Expansion Path.*

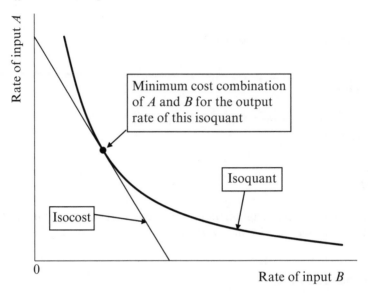

ISPOR

Acronym for *International Society for Pharmacoeconomics and Outcomes Research.*

Item Non-response

Occurs in surveys when a respondent does not provide data for a particular *variable.*

IWH

Acronym for the *Institute for Work & Health.*

J

Jackson Hole Group

The Jackson Hole Group is a US think tank, founded by Paul Ellwood and Alain Enthoven in 1992, which successfully promoted the idea of *managed health care* organizations. It is so-named on account of its annual meeting place in Paul Ellwood's home in Wyoming. See Ellwood and Etheredge (1991).

Jarman Index

An index of social deprivation used mainly in the UK. Cf. *Townsend Index*. See Jarman (1983).

JCAHO

Acronym for *Joint Commission on Accreditation of Healthcare Organizations*.

Job-lock

Reductions in labour mobility that may arise in systems of employment-based *health insurance* – or, indeed, any other benefits that are tied to employment with a particular employer. Can be used to assure employers of a return on their investments in employee *human capital*. See Becker (1962).

Joint Commission on Accreditation of Healthcare Organizations

An independent, not-for-profit US organization, JCAHO is a major standard-setting and *accreditation* body in health care. It evaluates and accredits nearly 16000 health care organizations and programmes in the US. Its mission is 'To continuously improve [*sic*] the safety and quality of care provided to the public through the provision of health care accreditation and related services that support *performance* improvement in health care organizations'. Its website is available at: http://www.jcaho. org/ (accessed 31 October 2009).

Joint Costs

'Is the cost of the animal's feed the cost of the mutton or of the wool?' This is the problem famously posed when a production process (in this case sheep farming) produces joint products. The question as posed is unanswerable (sensibly), though the question 'What is the cost of extra feed?' is answerable when one is considering increasing meat or wool production or changing the combination of the two by slaughtering later or earlier. Fortunately there are few (if any) practical situations that can be usefully informed by asking (let alone trying to answer) the opening question in this entry. In health economics, the classic context for this question has been teaching hospitals, which produce health care services and medical education (and some even produce research output). See also *Overhead Cost, Sunk Cost*. See, for an application, Ma and McGuire (1993) and, on teaching hospitals, Lehner and Burgess (1995).

Joint Health and Safety Committee

A committee consisting of labour and management representatives in a company that meets regularly to deal with *workplace health and safety*. They are statutorily required in some countries.

Judgment

To exercise one's judgment is to bring to bear on a matter one's experience, knowledge, powers of discernment and discrimination in order to make a decision or to determine the merit of something (like an argument). In health economics, judgments are frequently required in deciding (for example) whether the data that are available are good enough for purposes, whether a likely *bias* in one's empirical work is sufficiently important to warrant detailed investigation, whether the literature has been thoroughly enough searched, whether the claims for or against a particular course of action are warranted, or partly warranted, or not at all warranted by the available evidence base and the arguments put up. A particular type of judgment has been much discussed in economics:

judgment of value (usually termed a *value judgment*), which has nothing to do with value in the sense of the price of something but refers instead to the ethical or moral merit in something. *Welfare economics* concerns itself principally with such value judgments. For a comprehensive treatment, see Yates (1990).

Justice

This, along with the principles of *autonomy, beneficence* and *nonmalefi-cence,* comprises the so-called 'four principles' of health care ethics. There is no generally agreed notion of justice in health care ethics or health care policy, though most analysts seem to agree that it has something to do with *'fairness'. Distributive justice* is often equated (by economists) to *'equity'*. See *Equity, Need*. See Beauchamp (2007).

Justification Bias

Economic and other incentives can affect people's responses to surveys. Self-reports of work *disability* are especially prone to *bias*, for example, people who are economically inactive are inclined to under-report their *health status* retrospectively to rationalize their status. Also known as 'state-dependent reporting', it leads to overestimating the effect of health on labour force participation. See, for an economic application, Baker et al. (2004).

K

Kakwani Index

A measure of the *progressivity/regressivity* of health care payment systems. It is the difference between a *concentration index* for payments and the *Gini coefficient* for *prepayment* incomes, equivalent to twice the area between the payments *concentration curve* and the *Lorenz curve*. A positive value indicates progressivity, a negative value regressivity and zero indicates *proportionality*. See Kakwani (1977). For applications see, e.g., O'Donnell et al. (2008).

Kaldor–Hicks Criterion

This is a criterion (*compensation test*) for judging whether a proposed change (say, the introduction of a new drug or the demolition of a new hospital) is *welfare*-enhancing. It is named for Nicholas (Lord) Kaldor (1908–86) and Sir John Hicks (1904–89). The Kaldor criterion says that if the minimum the gainers from the change are willing to pay is more than enough to compensate the losers fully, then the project is welfare-enhancing. The Hicks criterion says that if the maximum amount the losers are prepared to offer to the gainers in order to prevent the change is less than the minimum amount the gainers are prepared to accept as a bribe to forgo the exchange, then the project is welfare-enhancing. The Kaldor compensation test takes the gainers' point of view; the Hicks compensation test is made from the losers' point of view. If both conditions are satisfied, both gainers and losers will agree that the proposed activity will move the economy toward *Pareto optimality*.

There is the possibility that the Kaldor–Hicks criterion might sanction a move from state *A* to state *B* and then from *B* to *A* (ad infinitum and, probably, nauseam). This has led to the explicit ruling out of the reversal possibility, known as the *Scitovsky criterion*, which also needs to be satisfied if a change is to be judged to be welfare-enhancing. Note that the compensation does not actually have to be paid. Note also that there is an implicit assumption that everyone has the same *marginal utility of income*. For true Pareto optimality compensation must actually be paid. See *Compensating Variation, Equivalent Variation, Interpersonal Comparisons of Utility*. See Hicks (1939a), Kaldor (1939) and Scitovsky (1941). See, in *health economics*, Johansson (1995) and Reinhardt (1998).

Kaplan–Meier Method

The Kaplan–Meier method is a method of estimating the proportion of patients still surviving by any given date. See *Survival Function*. See Kaplan and Meier (1958).

Keeler–Cretin Paradox

This is the argument in *cost–utility analysis* that, if health benefits are *discounted* at a lower rate than costs, the *cost–effectiveness ratio* can be improved by delaying the introduction of the technology in question and continue to be improved by further delays ad infinitum. The problem disappears if one uses present values instead of ratios of cost and benefit. See Keeler and Cretin (1983).

Kendall's Coefficient of Concordance

A measure of the degree of agreement (concordance) between different rank orderings of the same set of entities. Cf. *Spearman's Rank Correlation Coefficient*. See Kendall (1938).

Keynesian Economics

An approach to economics whose principal distinctive feature (though not the only one) was perhaps that it supposed that markets did not clear in the manner assumed in *classical economics* so that resources, especially labour, could remain unemployed for lengthy periods of time. See also *Economics, Neoclassical Economics, Postmodernism*. The locus classicus is Keynes (1936). For neo-Keynesian syntheses, see Mankiw and Romer (1991) and Woodford (2003).

Kinesiology

The *physiological* study of muscles and the movement of the human body.

Knowledge Transfer and Exchange

This is collaborative problem-solving between researchers and decision-makers involving both in mutual learning through the processes of planning, disseminating and applying existing or new research. See Lavis et al. (2003) and Barer (2005). For an evaluation see Grimshaw et al. (2005).

Knowledge Translation

Same as *knowledge transfer and exchange.*

KTE

Acronym for *knowledge transfer and exchange.*

Kurtosis

A measure of the peakedness or flatness of a *frequency distribution* compared with a *normal distribution.* It measures the 'fatness' of the tails of a probability distribution compared with measures of skewness that measure the 'fatness' of a single tail.

L

L'Abbé Plot

This is a convenient visual scatter diagram used in *meta-analysis* that compares the risks observed in the *experimental* and *control arms* of *clinical trials*. Each trial is located in the space of a diagram as shown here where the sizes of the circles (three in this case) indicate the sizes of the trials. Trials in which the experimental treatment had a higher risk than the *control* will be in the upper left of the plot. If risk in the both groups is the same the circle will fall on the line of equality. If the control treatment has a higher risk than the experimental treatment then the point will be in the lower right of the plot. It is often used as an indicator of *heterogeneity* and hence as an indicator of the likelihood that results from different trials can be validly combined. Named after Kristin L'Abbé. See L'Abbé et al. (1987). See Song (1999).

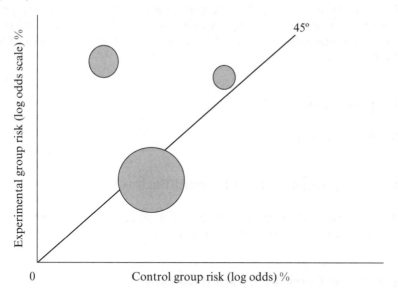

Labour Force Participation

The proportion of a *population* (usually a sub-group of the total non-institutionalized population of a jurisdiction) that is above a certain age (usually 16) and willing to work (i.e. either in work or actively looking for it).

Labour Market

The formal and informal mechanisms through which workers and employers are brought together, wages and working conditions are determined. In some countries (notably the US) *health insurance* is employment based. See *Incidence*. For a *health economics* review see Gruber (2000). On nurse shortages see, e.g. V.L. Phillips (1995) and Shields (2004).

Lagging Indicator

A lagging (or lagged) indicator is a quantitative or qualitative measure of an entity or activity whose changes reflect prior changes in a *determinant*. Its main value lies in audit and other evaluative exercises to test the extent to which planned changes had the hoped for consequences. For example, falling death rates may be a lagging indicator of earlier measures taken to reduce hospital infection rates. Also known as a 'trailing indicator'. Cf. *Leading Indicator*.

Laspeyres Index

See *Index Numbers*.

Last Observation Carried Forward/Backward

A (not very good) method of dealing with *incomplete data*. Sometimes termed 'last value carried forward/backward'.

Last Value Carried Forward/Backward

Same as *last observation carried forward/backward*.

Latent Variable

A latent variable is one that is not directly observed (or observable) but that may be inferred from other observed variables. Also sometimes known as a 'hidden variable' or 'latent construct'. *Health-related quality of life* is a frequently encountered latent variable in *health economics*. For an introduction to the use of latency in statistical analysis see Kennedy (2003). For applications in *health economics* see Jones and O'Donnell (2002) and Van Ours (2003).

Law of Demand

This states that *demand* (in the sense of quantity demanded per time period) rises as price falls. While for some economists the 'law', which states that *demand curves* always slope downwards from left to right is an article of faith, its interpretation really depends on what is held constant along the demand curve. There are conceivable empirical exceptions if income in the sense of money income is held constant and the good in question is an *inferior good*. No empirical exception is permitted if income in the sense of *utility* is held constant for, in this case, the 'law' is merely another way of putting the standard *axiom* of *convexity* (or diminishing *marginal rate of substitution* in consumption). These *ceteris paribus* notions are precisely that, of course – notions. In empirical work they are included amongst the *determining variables* but they still need careful definition (the concept of *'real' income* to be used particularly needs definition). See *Demand Function*. Because the role of price in (Western) health care is much attenuated by *insurance* arrangements most empirical demand analysis has concerned the demand for health (cf. health care) (e.g. Kenkel, 1991), the demand for health care insurance (e.g. Manning et al. 1987), the non-price *determinants* of demand (e.g. Dranove, 1988) and the (apparent) demand for bad health (e.g. Liu et al., 1999).

Law of Diminishing Returns

A somewhat less satisfactory term than an alternative: *law of variable proportions*.

Law of One Price

A regularity that is often predicted by economic theory (though less frequently observed in practice) to the effect that a good that can be cheaply transported (like a pharmaceutical) and that is sold in international markets (like a pharmaceutical) will sell at the same price in all markets (unlike pharmaceuticals despite their trivial transport costs). See Parkin (2008).

Law of Variable Proportions

This 'law' is a generalization about the nature of technology when *factors of production* are substitutable. It states that as the rate of use of one *factor* is increased, the others remaining constant, the *marginal product* (the associated increase in output) will eventually fall and the *average product* too will eventually fall. While this is suggested as a general characteristic of *production functions*, it is particularly applicable in the *short run*. The term 'law of diminishing returns' is sometimes met but ought probably to be discarded in that it focuses attention on the 'constancy' or otherwise of factors of production rather than what is critical: the proportions in which the different factors are used. The element in the definition that runs 'the others remaining constant' is not a literally descriptive characterization but rather an analytical one, describing an essentially mathematical property of a production function. See *Diminishing Returns to Scale, Production Function.*

Leading Indicator

A leading indicator is a quantitative or qualitative measure of an entity or activity whose changes anticipate changes in a *dependent variable*. For example, having effectively functioning health and safety committees in businesses may be a leading indicator of (lower) future workplace accidents. Cf. *Lagging Indicator.*

Lead-time Bias

A *bias* in screening programme evaluation taking the form of increased survival times that arise solely from making a *diagnosis* earlier in the history of the disease.

League Table

The relative *cost-effectiveness* of various health care technologies is frequently presented in the form of 'league tables' based upon literature reviews. A common reason for doing this is the maximizing idea that, provided the data reflect the true incremental cost-effectiveness of each technology and the effectiveness measure is appropriate, then the health budget will have its maximum impact by working down the table until the budget is exhausted (and by not funding anything else). Amongst the dangers in using such tables in other than a broadly indicative way are the following: the list is probably incomplete (and omits some cost-effective technologies); the data are not actually marginal (*incremental cost–effectiveness ratios*) but averages; the *perspective* on cost and benefit may vary from one technology to another; the literature reviews may have had inappropriate *inclusion* or *exclusion criteria*; the cost–effectiveness ratios may be dependent on the scale of use of each technology; the circumstances of the evidence collection in the reviewed studies may make the transfer of conclusions to other settings and circumstances inappropriate.

See Drummond et al. (1993) and Mason et al. (1993). A wide range of cost-effectiveness results (going beyond health care interventions) is tabled in Tengs et al. (1996). A table based on a review of 228 medical studies

Technology	Cost per QALY (£ sterling)
Pacemaker for atrioventricular heart block	700
Hip replacement	750
Valve replacement for aortic stenosis	900
Coronary Artery Bypass Graft (CABG) severe angina; left main disease	1 040
CABG severe angina; triple vessel disease	1 270
CABG (moderate angina; left main disease)	1 330
CABG (severe angina; left main disease)	2 280
CABG (moderate angina; triple vessel disease)	2 400
CABG (mild angina; left main disease)	2 520
Kidney transplantation (cadaver)	3 000
CABG (moderate angina; double vessel disease)	4 000
Heart transplantation	5 000
CABG (mild angina; triple vessel disease)	6 300
Haemodialysis at home	11 000
CABG (mild angina; double vessel disease)	12 600
Haemodialysis in hospital	14 000

Source: Williams (1985).

and using only those meeting stated quality conditions is Chapman et al. (2000). A (famous) example is the table.

Learning By Doing

This is the effect of repetition in tasks on *productivity*. The originator was (as so often) Arrow (1962). For an example in *health economics* see Ho (2002).

Least Squares

A method for estimating *parameters* in a *regression analysis*, so-called on account of its minimizing the sum of the squared differences between each observation and its estimated value.

Length Bias

The mistaken attribution of increased survival times to a *screening* programme that arises from a tendency for insidious, slow-developing diseases to be more easily detected by screening than fast-developing, aggressive diseases. See *Bias*.

Length of Stay

A term usually referring to the time a patient of a particular type (or patients in general) spends in hospital. Mean length of stay (say, by *diagnostic related group* – DRG) is calculated by dividing the sum of in-patient days by the number of patients within the DRG. People entering and leaving a hospital on the same day have a length of stay of zero. For a study of the effect of length of stay on hospital costs see Polverejan et al. (2003).

Leontief Production Function

The Leontief production function has fixed factor proportions, implying zero substitutability between *factors of production*. It is a special case of *constant elasticity of substitution*. The Russian-American Nobel laureate economist Wassily Leontief was the inventor of *input–output analysis*. See

Leontief (1941). For an example of its use in *health economics*, see Li and Rosenman (2001).

Liberty Principle

A principle of social justice associated with the American philosopher John Rawls (1921–2002). It is a schedule of basic rights, including liberty of conscience and movement, and freedom of religion, which ought to be equally distributed and as complete as is consistent with each having the same freedom. See *Fairness*.

Licence

The legal (or other formal) permission granted to a professional person to practise their profession or for a pharmaceutical company to manufacture a product whose *patent* or other *intellectual property right* is owned by someone else.

Life Expectancy

The statistically expected remaining years of life for a representative person (usually in a specific jurisdiction and by sub-group – male, female, by ethnicity, etc.) at a given age (say, at birth, or having already reached 65). The *World Health Organization* publishes 'healthy life expectancy' data, which include an adjustment for time spent in poor health. Healthy life expectancy at birth measures the equivalent number of years in full health that a newborn child can expect to live based on the current mortality rates and prevalence distribution of health states in the population.

Unadjusted life expectancy data show enormous variations across the world. A child born in Japan in 2002 had an expectation of life of 81.9 years (85.3 if female) whereas one born in Sierra Leone had an expectation of life of 34.0 years (35.7 if female). In general, females have a longer expectancy than males. Much of the disparity is attributable to high infant mortality rates. In Africa around 40 per cent of deaths occur amongst infants under five years of age. Poor sanitation and associated disease characteristics of grinding poverty – malnutrition, diarrhoea, malaria and infections of the lower respiratory tract – are principal causes. While the past decades have seen a general rise in expectation of life in all countries, in some regions, especially in Africa (for example Botswana, Lesotho, Swaziland and Zimbabwe) life expectation is actually falling on account of HIV/AIDS. See World Health Organization (2004a). For an economic study assessing the contribution of increasing life expectancy to *welfare* in poor and middle-income countries see Soares (2009).

Life Table

A table showing how many people survive for a variety of periods of time. 'Survive' need not mean 'merely remain alive' (the table may be about surviving in a particular condition) and the periods do not have to be years, though life tables frequently embody both features. Another name for them is survival tables.

Likelihood

Same as *probability* in the *frequentist* sense.

Likelihood Function

A function that represents the joint *probability* of all the points in a dataset.

Likelihood Ratio

The likelihood that a particular test result is expected in a patient with the target condition compared with the likelihood that this same result would be expected in a patient without that condition. The link between the likelihood ratio (LR) and *sensitivity* and *specificity* is as follows:

Positive LR = sensitivity/(1 – specificity)
Negative LR = (1 – sensitivity)/specificity.

Likert Scale

An *ordinal* scaling of health states based upon ordinal rankings derived from surveys. A typical approach will pose a statement and ask the respondent whether they Strongly Agree, Agree, are Undecided, Disagree or Strongly Disagree. See Likert (1932). For an application in *health economics* see Wildman (2003).

Limited Dependent Variable

See *Dependent Variable*.

Lind Library

The James Lind Library is an easily accessible database of well-designed evidence about the *effectiveness* of clinical interventions. It is named after James Lind (1716–94), a Scottish doctor and pioneer of naval hygiene and the treatment of scurvy. Its website is available at: http://www.jameslind library.org/ (accessed 4 November 2009).

Linear

See *Linearity*.

Linearity

A process or equation that can be expressed in a linear equation having the form:

$$X = a + bY,$$

where b, the slope of the straight line relating X and Y, is a constant and a is a constant *intercept*.

Linear Probability Model

A *model* of binary *dependent variables* based on *multiple linear regression*. See *Binary Variable* and *Multiple Linear Regression*.

Linear Programming

A mathematical technique for finding the maximum or minimum value taken by a function (the *objective function*) that satisfies a set of linear *constraints* in the form of equalities and inequalities. For an exposition in *health economics* see Lord et al. (2004).

Linear Structural Relations

A software package often used in economic modelling of systems of equations. For example, see Jones and O'Donnell (2002).

Linear Transformation

The transforming of a variable, A, into another, B, by use of a linear equation of the form:

$$X = a + bY,$$

Where b, the slope of the straight line relating X and Y, is a constant and a is a constant *intercept*. Also 'linear transform'.

Line Item Budget

Same as *global budget*.

Line of Equality

A line on a graph that indicates a completely equal distribution of whatever is measured on the axes. See *Concentration Curve*, *Lorenz Curve*.

LISREL

Acronym for *linear structural relations*.

Living Will

See *Advance Directive*.

Loading

A term indicating that providing *insurance* has administrative and other costs 'loaded' on to a premium over and above the *actuarially fair* premium, which in principle is the expected cost of health care multiplied by the probability of that care being utilized. Because loading is unlikely to be systematically related to the risk of events, one of its consequences is that *for-profit* free market insurers are unlikely to offer policies for either very likely or very unlikely *adverse events*, where potential insurance clients' *willingness to pay* to avoid the consequences of risk is relatively low and the fraction of the premium taken up by loading is consequently higher. See *Insurance*. For a health economics application see Bundorf and Pauly (2006).

LOCF/B

Acronym for *last observation carried forward/backward*.

Locus

A line traced on paper (or on-screen) by a point that moves as some underlying determining variables change.

Logical Positivism

A twentieth-century philosophical movement in which, in its most extreme form (which had considerable impact on economics), the only statements deemed to be meaningful are those that (1) are analytically true and/or (2) can be empirically verified (sometimes, which is not, of course, the same thing, 'refuted') by the evidence of one's senses as in controlled scientific experiments. A major originator was Wittgenstein but, in economics, the main protagonist has been Friedman (1953). See *Positive Economics*.

Logistic Distribution

A *continuous* probability *distribution* that is the basis of the *logit model* of binary choice.

Logistic Regression

Regression between a *binary dependent variable* and one or more *independent variables* using a *logit model*. In *epidemiology* it is often used to *model* an individual's odds of disease or some other outcome as a function of a risk factor or intervention. Cf. *Discriminant Function Analysis*. For an example of its use in *health economics*, see Johannesson and Johansson (1997). Cf. *Multinomial Logistic Regression*.

Logit Model

A *model* with binary *dependent variables* based on the *logistic distribution*. Its use is normally associated with the maximum likelihood estimation procedure instead of *ordinary least squares*. The idea is to posit an underlying *continuous* latent variable, such that, given binary date, whether the score is 0 or 1 depends upon a critical value of the latent variable. Thus, if the binary variable is sick/well, the critical threshold might be a stipulated value of a *quality-adjusted life-year*. The latent variable is then posited to be a linear function of other variables including unobservable ones and the error term is assumed to be standard logistically distributed. Cf. *Probit Model*. Introduced by Berkson (1944). For a *health economics* application see Gertler et al. (1987).

Lognormal Distribution

A *variable* has a lognormal *distribution* if the log of the variable has a normal distribution. It is a frequency distribution that is *skewed* to the right (so the *mean* is larger than the *median*) but whose logarithm is in the form of a *normal distribution*. Like the normal distribution, the lognormal is characterized by two *parameters*: the mean and *standard deviation*. Values cannot be negative.

Longevity

Length of life.

Longitudinal Data

Data that relate to successive periods of time. Cf. *Cross-sectional Data*.

Longitudinal Study

Any study using *time series* data. In econometric studies, the object is often to analyse the *determinants* of (the growth of) income, expenditure (for example, national health care expenditures) or consumption. Increasingly there are micro datasets available as well as macro datasets. *Clinical trials*, when individual people are followed, are called longitudinal *cohort studies* or *follow-up studies* (the two terms are substitutable). If individual people are not followed, but classes of people (usually age classes) are restudied, one has a longitudinal *cross-sectional study*.

Long Run

A theoretical idea that has to do with the speed with which *factors of production* can be adjusted. The 'long run' is a context (rather than a particular time period to which the literal-minded might be attracted) in which all factors are treated as variable. See *Short Run*, *Time*. For estimations of long-run cost functions see Vitaliano (1987).

Long-term Care

Long-term care is usually provided in people's own homes, often with the support of visiting health and social care professionals, or in such institutions as nursing homes, which are typically private organizations, often operating for profit. For a comprehensive review of the economics of many of the issues that arise see Norton (2000).

Lorenz Curve

The Lorenz curve was developed by Max Lorenz (1880–1962), a US economist who developed it to describe income inequalities. It shows the cumulative percentage of income, health care expenditures, etc. held by successive
percentiles of the *population*. The percentage of individuals or *households* is
plotted on the horizontal axis, the percentage of income, health care expenditures, etc. on the vertical axis. A perfectly equal *distribution*, where each has
the same, appears as a straight line called the *line of equality*. A completely
unequal distribution, where one person has everything, appears as a mirror
L shape. This is a line of perfect inequality. See *Concentration Index, Gini
Coefficient.* See Lorenz (1905). For extensive use see O'Donnell et al. (2008).

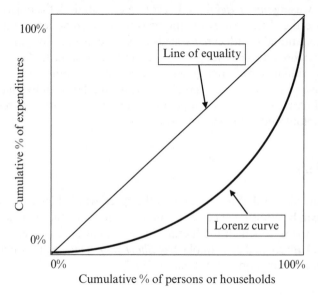

LOS

Acronym for *length of stay*.

Loss Aversion

A feature of *prospect theory*, embodying a *preference* for avoiding losses
over acquiring gains. See Tversky and Kahneman (1991). For a *health
economics* application see Neuman and Neuman (2008).

Loss Function

Also known as 'criterion function'. It is a function that is minimized to achieve a desired objective. For example, econometricians minimize the sum of squared errors in making an estimate of a function or a slope; in this case the loss function is the sum of squared errors.

Loss to Follow-up

A common cause of missing data, especially in long-term studies, loss to follow-up occurs when researchers lose contact with participants in a trial for such reasons as migration or failure to maintain contact prior to the termination of a study or of planned endpoints. Planned data collection is incomplete as a result.

Lottery

In *health economics*, this usually refers to a choice in which the pay-off is uncertain (not necessarily one in which the chances of a good outcome are extremely small). The *standard gamble* is a form of lottery used to elicit experimentally the value individuals attach to various states of health.

Low-income Countries

Regarding insurance, see *Insurance*. See also *Equity*, *Poverty*.

Luxury Good

An *economic good* with an *income-elasticity* greater than 1.0. Because the term has pejorative overtones and also because the elasticity condition defines as 'luxuries' many things (apparently including many forms of health care!) that are not generally regarded as luxuries, it is a term better avoided and 'good with an income elasticity greater than 1.0' used instead, which has the advantage of saying directly what the characteristic is that matters without overtones of approval or disapproval, importance or unimportance. See also *Necessity*. See Parkin et al. (1987) and Getzen (2000).

M

Macroeconomics

The study of aggregate entities in the economy, like money supply, income, exports or unemployment, interest rates, inflation, business cycles, and the links between them. For an empirical study including health effects, see R.D. Smith et al. (2005).

Macroeconomics and Health

The association of *macroeconomic* phenomena like income, its cyclical patterns, or its distribution, with the health of populations has been much argued about. The empirical analysis is assailed by difficulties, including possible *omitted variable bias* and problems of estimating time lags between changes in variables in the economy and their effects on other variables. For a review see Ruhm (2006). The impact of economic shocks in the third world can be massive. See, for physical impact, Frankenberg et al. (2003) and for psychiatric effects Friedman and Thomas (2007). The general macro environment and the constraints it can impose on health care systems is usefully analysed in Ranson et al. (2003). For use of a *computable general equilibrium model* and antimicrobial resistance see Smith et al. (2005).

Magnitude Estimation

A method of deriving a *ratio scale* by asking raters of alternative states of health to think of them in terms of multiples (for example, state *A* may be 'twice as bad' as state *B*). See Rosser and Kind (1978).

Malpractice

Mistaken, careless or unethical (legally negligent) medical practice for which the practitioner may be sued. Unfortunately, not all that is (legally speaking) malpractice is bad practice. See also *Defensive Medicine*. For a tragic US case of *evidence-informed* practice being determined by a jury as culpable see Merenstein (2004). For a review of the economic approaches see Danzon (2000).

Managed Behavioral Health Care

A form of *managed health care* provided in the US for mental health patients and substance abusers. See Bouchery and Harwood (2003) and Frank and Garfield (2007).

Managed Competition

Same as *managed health care*.

Managed Health Care

In the US, managed health care refers to a system of health care in which services are delivered through a network of contracting hospitals, physicians and other providers and financed through a set fee. Some forms of managed health care, such as *preferred provider organizations* (PPOs) and *point-of-service plans* (POSs), allow patients to receive services outside the network but at a higher *out-of-pocket price* than for in-network services. *Closed-panel health maintenance organizations* (HMOs) do not allow this but POSs, which are one form of open-panel HMOs, do. Ideally, the managed health care organization monitors the quality and appropriateness of care to guard against both over- and under-*utilization*, although sometimes *cost containment* or *dumping* the patient on another cost centre are said to be the most tangible motivations. Typically, *primary care* physicians are either salaried or paid *capitation* rates in HMOs and POSs, but in PPOs they generally are paid on a *fee-for-service* basis. HMOs and POSs usually require that patients first see a primary care *gatekeeper* for referrals but this is rarely the case in PPOs. Managed health care organizations rely more on supply-side controls (such as the provision only of services for which there is evidence of *cost-effectiveness*) than on demand-side, although recent years have seen substantial increases in patient *cost-sharing* requirements.

In idealized form, managed health care will effectively control both the *demand* and the *supply* side of a local market, acting as *agent* for members, eliminating demand for ineffective care on the one hand, and negotiating lower prices and restricting provision to services deemed to be cost-effective on the other. In the diagram, for example, the 'normal' *demand curve D* is shifted to the left (D_M) and the price negotiated down from P to P_M so that total expenditure falls from the amount indicated by the larger rectangle to that indicated by the smaller shaded one. Although the diagram does

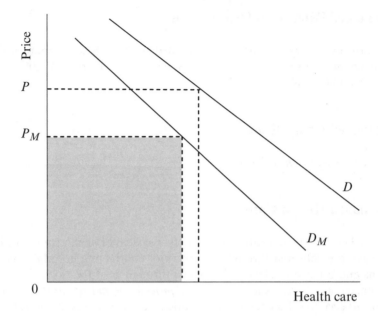

not show the (hoped for) impact on health, it indicates the potential that managed health care has for cost control. Essentially the same reasoning often lies behind arguments for '*socialized*' medical care. See *Jackson Hole Group* for its origins. See Enthoven (1993) for the pioneering account. For a review, see Glied (2000).

Management, Economic, Social and Human Infrastructure

MESH defines an infrastructure designed to improve the *capacity* of communities and other entities to implement health service programmes efficiently. See Thomas et al. (2007).

Management Services Organization

A US form of integration of physicians and hospitals. See *Vertical Integration*.

Mandated Cover

Insurance benefits that are made compulsory by a regulatory or other governmental body.

MANOVA

Acronym for *multivariate analysis of variance*.

Manpower Planning

The art of projecting the future demand and supply of particular types of labour so that appropriate policies may be adopted in the short term as regards training and education to ensure that future supplies are adequate for the demands that are to be met. Also more inclusively known as 'health human resource planning'. It features scarcely at all in the subject indices of textbooks these days, largely because its practice seemed almost completely devoid of economics. Some nails were knocked into its coffin by Maynard and Walker (1978).

Mantel–Haenszel Test

A method of combining *odds ratios* in *meta-analyses*. See Mantel and Haenszel (1959).

Marginal Analysis

An approach to decision-making that focuses on small changes (up or down) in *outcomes* and the changes in other outcomes, resource use or costs that may cause them or be a consequence of them. It is sometimes called 'incremental' analysis but that term suffers from the disadvantage of appearing not to be applicable to decrements (decreases), *disinvestments,* etc. It is also sometime misleadingly described as relating to the 'last' unit of something, which suggests that the idea relates to sequential use or consumption (which it does not). Mathematically it is the first derivative of the consequence with respect to the (*continuous*) determining variable in question. See Neuhauser and Lewicki (1975) for a striking illustration. See *Programme Budgeting and Marginal Analysis*.

Marginal Benefit

The changed *benefit* from increasing or reducing the rate or volume of an activity. Mathematically it is the first derivative of benefit with respect to the (*continuous*) *variable* in question. Cf. *Incremental Benefit*.

Marginal Cost

The changed *cost* from increasing or reducing the rate or volume of an activity. Mathematically it is the first derivative of cost with respect to the (*continuous*) *variable* in question.

Marginal Cost–Effectiveness Ratio

Same as *incremental cost–effectiveness ratio*.

Marginal Intertemporal Rate of Substitution

The rate at which a person will trade present consumption for a small increase in future consumption. It is the slope of an intertemporal

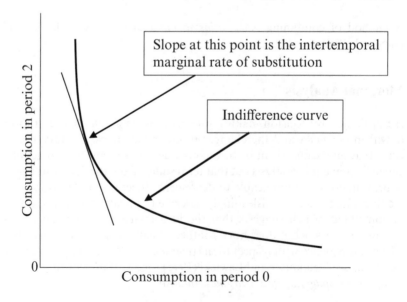

indifference curve showing the amounts of consumption in some future period and (usually) the current period, which yield the same *utility*. Cf. *Marginal Rate of Substitution*, where the trade-off is between types of consumption in a single time period. It is the ratio of the *marginal utilities* of current and future consumption as one is substituted for the other such as to leave the individual in question indifferent (*ceteris paribus*). See *Time Preference*.

Marginal Product

The change in *output* rate obtained by increasing or reducing the rate of use of a single *input* (any other being held constant). Mathematically it is the first derivative of output with respect to the input. See *Production Function*. For some estimates of the marginal product of health expenditure in the UK see Martin et al. (2008). For a (classic) screening example see Neuhauser and Lewicki (1975).

Marginal Rate of Return

The incremental percentage financial gain over time (conventionally a year) from sacrificing a little more current consumption or resource. Cf. *Rate of Return*.

Marginal Rate of Substitution

The marginal rate of substitution in consumption is the (negative) slope of an *indifference curve*. It is the ratio of the *marginal utilities* of two goods as one is substituted for the other such as to leave the individual in question indifferent (*ceteris paribus*).

The marginal rate of substitution in production is the (negative) slope of an *isoquant*. It is the ratio of the *marginal products* of two *inputs* as one is substituted for the other such as to leave the *output* rate constant (*ceteris paribus*). Also known as the 'marginal rate of technical substitution'.

Marginal Rate of Technical Substitution

Same as *marginal rate of substitution* in production.

Marginal Rate of Transformation

The slope of a *production possibilities curve*. It shows the maximum (minimum) increase (decrease) in the rate of *output* of one good that is possible for any reduction (increase) in the rate of output of another, given a fixed stock of resources and a given technology of production.

Marginal Social Cost

The sum of marginal private *cost* (costs internal to the decision-maker) and marginal *external costs*. It is sometimes confusingly identified with the external costs, especially by non-economists.

Marginal Social Value

The sum of individual *marginal values* placed upon a good or service that many must consume if anyone does. See *Public Goods*.

Marginal Utility

The change in *utility* associated with a small increase (fall) in the rate of consumption of the good yielding it. Mathematically it is the first derivative of utility with respect to changes in the consumption of something. See *Diminishing Marginal Utility*, *Indifference Curve, Utility*.

Marginal Utility of Income

The *marginal utility* from a small change in income.

Marginal Value

The maximum *value* attached to a little more or less of a good, service or desired characteristic. See *Demand Curve*.

Marginal Willingness to Pay

Usually met in the context of *willingness to pay* for small reductions in the risk of *adverse events* such as death or injury. See *Value of Life, Willingness to Pay*.

Marker

An indicator, like a diagnostic measure or an observable personal characteristic such as poverty, that is a predictor of ill-health. Also a relatively easily observed indicator that stands in for a more fundamental, latent and hard to observe predictor. Income is often used as a marker for *socioeconomic status*. Cf. *Latent Variable, Surrogate Marker*.

Market

There is a sense in which 'the market' as an abstraction or as a real-world phenomenon lies at the heart of *neoclassical economics*, which has focused greatly on understanding the market's regularities, oddities, successes and injustices, in equal measures of positive and normative theory, sometimes explicit, sometimes implicit, often bits of both. The literature is vast. For a readable romp from one who is no apostle of libertarianism, see Reinhardt (2001).

Marketability

This is the idea that any product or service can be marketed. In practice many cannot be, and are not, and many markets are incomplete, leading to *market failure*. See Arrow (1963) and Chernew (2001).

Market Failure

Markets in health care are notable not because they fail to satisfy any one of the standard assumptions required for competitive markets to achieve *Pareto optimality* but because they pretty well fail every single one of them: there is enormous *asymmetry of information* between producers (medical professionals of all kinds) and consumers (patients actual and potential); the *agency relationship* works imperfectly and can be distorted by systems of physician pay; there is little evidence that patients behave in accordance with the *axioms* of rational *choice theory*; markets, especially those for risk, are incomplete; the medical care industry is riven with monopolistic organizations, from those in the *pharmaceutical industry* through those in the medical professions themselves, to the local *monopolies* held by hospitals and community-based *primary care* practices. In addition, much of health care has the character of a *public good* and generates *externalities* both physical (as with *communicable disease*) and psychic (as when you derive comfort from knowing that your neighbours are insured). Health care is also a field in which *equity* has always been regarded as of at least equal importance to *efficiency* (even if that is not how economists have allocated their effort).

This accounts for (though in logic it scarcely justifies) the extensive public intervention in health care and for the development of more or less economically informed methods of professional and other regulation, allocating resources to regions and institutions and conducting health technology *appraisals*. It also accounts for the substantial demand for health economists in both the private and the public sector beyond secondary and tertiary education! The reason for the qualification in the above is that it is well known that replacements for the market are themselves not 'perfect'. Indeed, perceived imperfections of the interventions of the state are on their own perceived by many as providing an equally unjustified prima facie case for leaving things to the market. See *Second Best*. See Pauly (1986) and Reinhardt (2001).

Market Forces Factor

An adjustment made to the costs in the *national tariff* for the *National Health Service*'s *commissioning* arrangements to allow for local variations in wages and prices. See *Purchaser–Provider Split*.

Market Imperfections

Broadly, the reasons for *market failure*.

Market Mechanism

Same as *price mechanism*.

Market Prices

In *national income accounting*, designating *gross domestic product* or *gross national product* at market prices means that the measure of each includes the effect of *taxes* and *subsidies*. Cf. *Factor Cost*.

Market Segmentation

The act of dividing an overall market into groups, or segments, of consumers with similar characteristics such as age, region of residence or average *health status*. It is usually done in order to engage in *price discrimination* in price-searchers' markets. Prices in the markets with less *elastic demand* tend to be higher. In order to work effectively, the segments need to be such that resale is not possible from low-price to high-price segments (*parallel trade*), so segmentation is likely to be seen when there is *price-searching* and the product is highly perishable, transport costs are high, or where, if segments correspond to jurisdictions, suppliers have managed to 'capture' regulatory agencies and create *barriers to entry*. See Kessel (1958) and Danzon and Towse (2003).

Markov Chain

A Markov chain is a sequence of events whose probabilities in any one time interval depend upon previous values in the *decision tree*. See *Markov Model*.

Markov Model

A type of *model* used in *cost–effectiveness* and *cost–utility* analyses in which the progress of a disease with and without interventions is modelled in a sequence of time periods, each being associated with a particular measure of health, and each having a probability of moving from it to the next state. The method is an extended form of the *decision tree* that is particularly suited to the analysis of chronic conditions when a normal decision tree might become uncontrollably complex. Named after the Russian mathematician Andrei Andreyevich Markov (1856–1922). See Sonnenberg and Beck (1993) and Briggs and Sculpher (1999). Kobelt et al. (2005) is an example of the method in application.

Markov Node

A decision point in a *decision tree*. See *Markov Model*.

Markov System

Same as *Markov Model*.

Masking

Same as *blinding*.

Matching

A process through which pairs of individuals are brought together in order to trade, share or otherwise engage in some mutual activity. There is also matching in biostatistics: selecting a *control* population that is matched on some characteristics that may influence the outcome of interest independently of the disorder in question. See Dow and Philipson (1996).

Matching Law

The matching law is a competing explanatory account of choice behaviour to *utility theory*. It views choice not as a single event or an internal thought process and states that an individual chooses entities in exact proportion to the value derived from each activity. While it is referred to by some health economists it has had no known application in *health economics* to date. Its inventor is Richard Herrnstein (Herrnstein, 1970).

Maternal Mortality Rate

The number of deaths in a year from puerperal causes divided by the number of live births in the same population in that year, all multiplied by 1000.

Matrix

An array of numbers (called 'elements') displayed in *vectors*: rows and columns. There is a special algebra for manipulating matrices.

Matrix Approach

A term sometimes used to describe the way in which the *costs* and *benefits* of an *option* are presented.

Maturation Effect

A change in a *dependent variable* that is due to the passage of time.

MAUT

Acronym for *multi-attribute utility theory*.

Maxillofacial Surgery

A branch of dentistry specializing in the surgery of the jaw and mouth.

Maximand

That which is to be maximized – for example, *health, profit, utility* or *welfare*.

Maximin

An ethical rule of distributive *fairness* that stipulates that one should maximize the *welfare* of the least well-off person in a society. It was invented by John Rawls (1971).

Maximum Difference Design

Same as *best–worst scaling*.

Maximum Endurable Time

A concept in health measurement: that there exist states of health so severe that people would willingly endure them only for a limited time (for example, to allow them to 'put their affairs in order'). See Dolan and Stalmeier (2003).

Maximum Likelihood Estimation

Statistical estimation using the criterion of what is most likely to be the case. A method of estimation that specifies the probability of the observed set of data and finds the *parameter* values that maximize that probability. For example, if the sampled variable in which you are interested is normally distributed, the mean is the maximum likelihood estimator of the population *mean*, and the variance is an approximation to the maximum likelihood estimator of the *population*. The idea was that of the English statistician Sir Ronald Fisher (1890–1962) (see Fisher, 1922).

Maximum Price Law

A system established in 1966 in the Netherlands whereby a maximum price is set for pharmaceuticals of a particular class based on comparisons with prices in a selection of other European countries.

MBHC

Acronym for *managed behavioral health care* in the US. See *Managed Behavioral Health Care*.

MBHO

Acronym for *managed behavioral health organization* in the US.

McCarran–Ferguson Act

The US McCarran–Ferguson Act of 1945 established the primacy of the states in regulating and taxing the *insurance* industry.

MCDA

Acronym for *multiple criteria decision analysis*.

Mean

A measure of the central tendency of a set of numbers. The average of a set of numbers. The sum of the observations divided by their number. Arithmetic mean = $\Sigma X_i / N$, where the X_i are the values of X and N is the total number of observations. The qualifier 'arithmetic' is usually dropped. Cf. *Geometric Mean*.

Mean Survival

The average period for which a person having particular characteristics survives. See *Survival Analysis*.

Measurement

Assigning numbers to entities according to a rule in order to indicate order, size, value, or other characteristics of interest. Cf. *Cardinal Scale, Health-related Quality of Life, Ordinal Scale, Utility Measurement*.

Measurement Bias

Bias arising from inaccuracy in measurements, coding or classification in *trials*.

Median

The middle value of an ordered set of numbers.

Median Voter Model

This is a theorem in *public choice theory* that states that the *median* voter determines the rate of output chosen for *public goods* that are publicly produced (or privately produced but publicly financed). In the diagram there are five *demand curves* for a community of five taxpayers, who each pay the same amount of tax but have different demands for the good (in this case 'health care'). Public output decisions are taken by simple majority vote. The marginal tax rate (exogenously given) is indicated by MT and the demand curves, D_1, D_2, etc. are the *marginal value* curves for the five voters. At the given marginal tax rate, voter 1's preferred output is Q_1, voter 2's is Q_2, etc. If Q_1 is proposed, only voter 1 will support it, the others all preferring larger output rates. If Q_2 is proposed, voters 3, 4 and 5 will outvote voters 1 and 2, preferring more. If Q_4 is proposed voters 1, 2 and 3 will outvote voters 4 and 5 and voters 1, 2, 3 and 4 will outvote voter 5 in opposing output rate Q_5. The rate that commands the majority is Q_3, which just happens to be voter 3's preferred rate and voter 3 is the median voter. See Black (1948) for its origins.

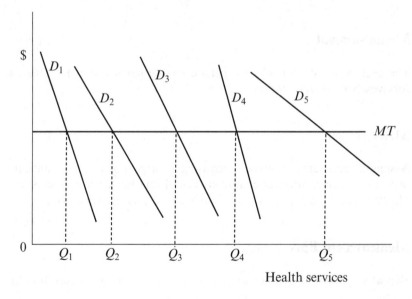

Medicaid

Medicaid is a US health plan developed by the federal government in 1965 as a companion to the *Medicare* programme. The programme is for low-income residents of the US and is addressed particularly to families with children, pregnant women, children, the aged, the blind and the disabled. To be eligible for Medicaid, a person must belong to one of these groups and meet certain financial criteria. There are optional groups also, such as the 'medically needy', which allows states to extend eligibility to others with too much income to qualify otherwise. Eligibility for the programme is through a means test that reviews the income and resources of those applying for coverage. A state qualifies for federal Medicaid matching funds only if its programme meets specific federal requirements such as the inclusion of specific population groups, coverage for certain medical services and medical providers, and adherence to specific rules relating to payment methodologies, payment amounts and *cost-sharing*.

Medicaid provides open-ended federal contributions according to a statutory formula. Each state is reimbursed for a portion of actual computed expenditure from a formula that takes into account the average per capita income for each state relative to the national average. By law, this portion (known as Federal Medical Assistance Percentage) cannot be less than 50 per cent. See *Medicare*.

Medicaid Notch

A discontinuity in the leisure–income trade-off for *Medicaid* beneficiaries that provides a disincentive to work more than a given amount (beyond which substantial benefits are lost). Cf. *Continuity*.

Medical Possession Ratio

The percentage of time a patient has access to a medication.

Medical Savings Account

See *Health Savings Account*.

Medical Services Advisory Committee

An Australian agency that advises the Minister for Health and Ageing on evidence relating to the safety and *cost-effectiveness* of medical technologies. Its website is available at: http://www.msac.gov.au/ (accessed 4 November 2009). See also *Pharmaceutical Benefits Advisory Committee*.

Medical Subject Headings

These (MeSH) are terms used by the US National Library of Medicine to index articles in *Index Medicus* and *MEDLINE*®.

Medical Tourism

A term describing the travel of individuals to countries solely for the purpose of receiving health care. See R.D. Smith et al. (2009).

Medicare

A term used generally to describe publicly funded and provided health care in Australia, Canada and the US. Medicare is the term used in Australia to describe its universal *health insurance* scheme. Introduced in 1984, it provides access to free treatment in a public hospital and free or subsidized treatment by primary practitioners (specified services only). It is funded through taxes and a special Medicare levy based on taxable income. In Canada, the term is used loosely to describe the provincially provided (but in broad terms federally controlled) systems of public health care insurance, providing free access to hospital and doctors' (specialists and general practitioners) services. It is funded through provincial and federal general taxation with occasional provincial premiums.

In the United States the term refers explicitly to a federal programme that is the main *health insurance* programme for people aged 65 and older, the disabled, and people with end-stage renal disease regardless of income. People who qualify for social security benefits are automatically eligible for Medicare. It is funded via *payroll taxes* and members' payments: premiums, *deductibles* and *coinsurance*. Medicare coverage provides for *acute* hospital care, physician services, brief stays in skilled nursing facilities, short-term skilled home care related to a medical problem and prescription drugs. There are two major programmes: Hospital Insurance (Part A) and Supplementary Medical Insurance (Part B). The Medicare coverage for Part A has no premium and pays 100 per cent of hospital costs for the first

60 days after payment of a deductible (currently about $1086). Medicare Part B pays up to 80 per cent of doctors' bills for a monthly premium of $96.40. Doctors may bill beneficiaries for an additional amount (the 'balance') not to exceed 15 per cent of the Medicare approved charge (See *Balance Billing*). Medicare currently has about 45 million beneficiaries. See *Medicaid*.

Medicare Advantage Plans

These are health plan options that are approved by Medicare in the US but run by private companies. They are part of the *Medicare* programme, and sometimes called 'Part C'.

Medicare Payment Advisory Commission

The Medicare Payment Advisory Commission (MedPAC) is an independent Congressional agency that advises the US Congress on issues affecting *Medicare*. The Commission's statutory mandate is broad: in addition to advising the Congress on payments to private health plans participating in Medicare and providers in Medicare's traditional *fee-for-service* programme, MedPAC is also tasked with analysing access to care, quality of care and other issues affecting Medicare.

Medigap

Private insurance programmes that supplement *Medicare* coverage in the US. See, e.g., Ettner (1997) and Fang et al. (2008) for economic analyses.

MEDLINE®

MEDLINE® (Medical Literature, Analysis, and Retrieval System Online) is the US National Library of Medicine's (NLM) premier bibliographic database, containing over 12 million references to journal articles in life sciences with a concentration on biomedicine. MEDLINE® is available on the internet through the NLM home page at www.nlm.nih.gov (last accessed 5 November 2009) and can be searched free of charge. No registration is required.

MedPAC

Acronym for *Medicare Payment Advisory Commission.*

Mental Health

The economics of mental health is much like the rest of health economics in the challenges it poses for standard economic theory – only more so. The particular additional concerns arise from doubts as to the applicability of the usual *axioms* of *utility* theory as a basis either for explaining behaviour or for prescribing what is best for patients. For an elaboration of this theme, see Frank (2000).

Merit Good

A good or service whose consumption is regarded (by someone influential) as being unusually meritorious. It is generally associated with the idea that people are not consuming enough of something and that it would be good for them (or society) if they consumed more. But the claim is not being made on *externality* grounds or because of *market failure* and seems inherently paternalist (for example, a belief that people are myopic or ignorant). Education is often cited as an example of a merit good; health care is rarely so cited. The grounds for this asymmetry are obscure. The term originated with Musgrave (1957).

MeSH

Acronym for *Medical Subject Headings.*

MESH

Acronym for *management, economic, social and human infrastructure.*

Meta-analysis

A statistical method of integrating quantitative research results from several research studies. 'Meta-' has a Greek origin and indicates, amongst other things, that the subject matter (in this case 'analysis') has a second-order character: an analysis of analyses. A meta-analysis is a form of *systematic review* of literature in which the quantitative results of several studies are systematically combined to generate more precise estimates of the effects under investigation, improve on the power of individual studies to detect effects, and to raise and discuss matters that may not have been evident in the individual studies. Meta-analysis cannot correct for any defects that run throughout a literature (for example, the use of the potentially less valid outcome 'change in tumour size' rather than 'postponed death' as the socially relevant outcome of a screening programme).

Meta-analysis has several advantages over traditional *narrative reviews*. It is relatively free of the subjectivity in personally selected samples. It not only shows the direction of the effect (up or down), it also quantifies it and identifies the determining *variables*. It should include all the quantitative empirical studies relevant to the research question. The criteria used for selecting the studies included in the review are explicitly stated. Meta-analyses are usually presented in the form of a *forest plot*. See Glass (1976), Hunter et al. (1982) and Egger et al. (1997).

Meta-regression

Like *meta-analysis*, meta-regression uses multi-level models to combine studies in a way that allows for within and between study variance but with the purpose not of obtaining a single point estimate but of addressing questions about how study findings are influenced by characteristics such as study context and participants. For examples of its use in *health economics* (in relation to *time preference* and health), see Asenso-Boadi et al (2008) and (in measuring elasticities) Gemmill et al. (2007).

MEWA

Acronym for *multiple employer welfare arrangement*.

MFF

Acronym for *market forces factor*.

MHC

Acronym for *managed health care*.

Microeconomics

The economic study of individual units in society like persons, *households* and firms. Cf. *Macroeconomics*.

MIMIC

Acronym for *multiple indicators-multiple causes*.

Mixed Economy

An economy in which the ownership of productive enterprises is variously private, charitable and public.

Mixed Model HMO

A *health maintenance organization* having both its own employed physicians and contracted others.

Mode

The most frequently occurring value of a single *variable* in a dataset.

Model

Models are simplified versions of a complex reality usually where there is considerable interdependence between the *variables* from which they are constructed. Their main use is to predict the effect of *exogenous* changes. Two broad kinds of modelling are done in health economics. One is the general kind employed throughout economics, which might be termed 'theoretical modelling', in which empirical characteristics are assumed (like *transitivity* of preferences) and general implications derived through an essentially analytical process of reasoning. The use of *utility* theory to model individual choices is a good example, from which is derived the implication that *demand curves* have a negative slope. The other is empirical modelling, where empirical relationships are postulated and interest focuses on simulating and quantifying the cause-and-effect relationships, *elasticities* and the like. Some modelling is relatively theory-free and is mainly concerned with forecasting by the extrapolation of past trends, with due allowance for interaction between determining variables but without necessarily any prior notion of the nature of such interactions.

In health economics, empirical modelling has assumed considerable importance in *cost–effectiveness analysis* and related techniques. It is often necessary to construct models that project costs and consequences beyond the *endpoints* of *clinical trials* in order to estimate both *clinical effectiveness* and *cost-effectiveness*. Such a model may be a theoretical decision analytic model using aggregated data or an empirical model using patient-level data. In *epidemiology* a distinction is made between cohort modelling (where all modelled individuals share similar characteristics at the outset) and micropopulation simulation modelling (which can represent the mixed nature of real populations or communities).

Critical issues in empirical economic modelling include relevance (e.g. the embodiment of appropriate *comparators*), having an appropriate time horizon (e.g. consequences that are modelled over a realistic *time horizon*), taking a relevant *perspective* (e.g. one relevant for decision-makers), embodying relevant *outcomes* (e.g. final, intermediate or surrogate), making realistic assumptions (e.g. concerning *adverse events*) and having robust mathematical descriptions and appropriate *modelling* techniques (e.g. using *sensitivity analysis*, *discounting*). See Sheldon (1996) and Buxton et al. (1997).

Model Uncertainty

Variously, uncertainty about the mathematical structure of a *model* (for example, its equations) or, more comprehensively, uncertainty about the general form of the model.

Moment Utility

Same as *experienced utility*.

Monopolistic Competition

A form of market in which sellers with differentiated products have to search out the price that is best for them but in which they take the prices charged by their competitors as given. The description seems to fit many health care markets quite well. See *Competition, Price-searching.* The originator of the term was Chamberlin (1933). See Dranove and Satterthwaite (2000) for a review in health economics.

Monopoly

A market in which there is a single seller. See *Competition, Price-searching.*

Monopsony

A situation in which a resource user is sufficiently dominant in the market for the price of resources to be affected as this user's *demand* rises or falls. Cf. *Monopoly.* See *Competition.*

Monotonicity

The general property of a sequence of numbers that each successive number is greater than or equal to its predecessor (increasing monotonicity) or smaller than or equal (decreasing monotonicity). The ordering is 'strong' if ties are not allowed. In economics, this property of choices generally means that if x is preferred to y, then the *utility* of $x >$ utility of y. In health economics, a special usage is that if the health of one person increases then the level of the community's health (or welfare) also increases (*ceteris paribus*).

Monte Carlo Simulation

A form of simulation used in *cost–effectiveness* and *cost–utility analyses*, in which repeated random numbers drawn from a given probability *distribution* stand for the values of uncertain *variables*. *Confidence limits* are placed on the most likely value after a large number of such *simulations*. Monte Carlo simulation is named after Monte Carlo, Monaco, where roulette wheels, dice, cards and slot machines replace the soberer games of economic modellers. See *Simulation*. For a health economics example, see Macario et al. (2006).

Moral Hazard

This is of two main types. *Ex ante* moral hazard refers to the effect that being insured has on behaviour, generally increasing the *probability* of the event insured against occurring. *Ex post* moral hazard derives from the price-*elasticity* of *demand*: being insured reduces the patient's price of care and hence leads to an increase in demand by insured persons. The basic economics of ex post moral hazard can be elucidated by considering the diagram. The vertical axis shows the price of health care P (assumed – implausibly in health care but expositionally convenient – to be set equal to *marginal cost*) and the *marginal value* placed upon health care consumption by an individual. The horizontal axis indicates the rate of consumption of health care (so much per week, month, etc.). The *demand curve*, or marginal value curve is not perfectly inelastic, indicating that at lower prices more care (longer in-patient stays, for example) are demanded (up to a limit). The horizontal line is the (constant) *marginal cost* curve. In a world of no *insurance*, the individual faces a price $0P$ at which $0C_1$ care will be consumed when ill. Let the individual (while healthy) consider buying insurance. Suppose neither the individual nor the insurer is in any doubt about the probability, p, of illness striking in any period (another tall order). Given that the insured, when uninsured, would consume $P \times 0C_1$ the actuarially *fair premium* (sometimes termed 'risk premium') is p times the cost of this amount of care. We assume (again for simplicity) also that there is zero *loading* – that is, the insurer adds nothing to the premium to cover the administrative costs of operating the insurance serve. Now let the event insured against occur. Assuming that the premium payment has not had an effect on the individual's income sufficient to shift the demand curve, the amount demanded will now be $0C_2$ – being insured reduces the price of consuming care to zero. Expenditure by the insurer will be $0PdC_2$ – much larger than the amount upon which the premium was based. This is ex post moral hazard. It is held to be inefficient because the cost of producing C_1C_2 care is much more than its value to the consumer – there is an *excess burden* or *deadweight loss*, or 'waste' of adC_2. However, before rushing to the conclusion that moral hazard must be controlled through *coinsurance*, *copayments* and other forms of rationing, it needs to be borne in mind that there may be reasons for wanting individuals to consume more care than, given their personal circumstances, they would normally choose (see, for example, *externality*). If such grounds exist, then a *second best* optimum may entail the need to do less to constrain demand (and even to encourage it further!). Even more fundamentally, there may be reasons for entirely eschewing the idea that the demand curve reveals anything worth knowing about the value placed on health care. In that case, even if the behavioural account given of moral hazard may still stand, the ethical accusation of 'waste' entirely fails.

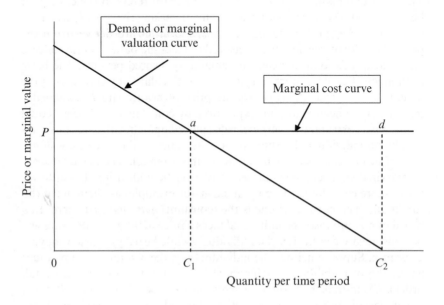

One behavioural effect of moral hazard in a market-based system is evidently to cause premiums to rise – in the example just considered, the increase in the premium is $p(C_1 adC_2)$. Premiums thus reflect both the inherent element of risk (the fair premium) and the additional costs generated through moral hazard. This may be sufficient not only to cause the insured to withdraw from insurance and self-insure, it may, as in the figure, actually exceed the cost of purchasing *out-of-pocket* the original planned consumption of care at price *P*! The welfare effects of moral hazard ought thus to be considered both in terms of its impact on health care *utilization* and on the take-up of health care *insurance*.

Another form of moral hazard has been held to be the effect that being insured in public programmes like the US *Medicaid* has on savings. Thus, because Medicaid will pay for, say, the nursing home care of the elderly with few savings, then the poor have an even smaller incentive to save than they do being poor. As with other forms of moral hazard, one needs to ask again whether the consequence is intended or unintended, desirable or undesirable. See *Market Failure*. The classic is Pauly (1968) but see also Arrow (1968) and Zeckhauser (1970). An empirical study is Gaynor and Gertler (1995). A later review is Zweifel and Manning (2000). Rice (1992) argues against using the demand curve as a reliable indicator of a person's welfare.

Morbidity

A synonym for illness, often proxied by a patient's contact with a physician and the resultant *diagnosis*. Morbidity rates are calculated in a manner similar to that for *mortality rates* – especially cause- (or disease) specific mortality rates.

Mortality Rate

The crude mortality rate is the total number of deaths per year divided by the population at mid-year times 1000 (i.e. number of deaths per 1000 person-years of observation). The age-specific mortality rate is the mortality rate for a specific age group (e.g. 65 years and older). The sex-specific mortality rate is the mortality rate for males or females. The age- and sex-adjusted rates are weighted according to the proportion of each group in the *population*. The disease- or cause-specific mortality rate is the annual number of deaths from the particular disease divided by the mid-year population times 1000. For an example of an economic model in which reductions in mortality are the main force behind economic development see Soares (2005). On *determinants* of mortality reductions in the developing world see Soares (2007).

MOS-20

Derived from Medical Outcomes Study, a RAND project. Better known as *SF-20©*. The Medical Outcomes trust website is available at http://www.outcomes-trust.org/instruments.htm (accessed 5 November 2009).

MOS-36

See *SF-36©*.

MOS-HIV Health Survey

The MOS-HIV is a generic health status measure having ten dimensions (general health perceptions, pain, physical functioning, role functioning, social functioning, energy/fatigue, mental health, health distress, cognitive function and quality of life). The Medical Outcomes trust website is available at http://www.outcomes-trust.org/instruments.htm (accessed 5 November 2009).

Movies

A term coined in Wagstaff and Waters (2005) in which inequalities in health or health care are measured as though they were frames in a projected film. Cf. *Snapshot*.

MPR

Acronym for *medical possession ratio*.

MSAC

Acronym for *Medical Services Advisory Committee*.

MSD

Acronym for *musculoskeletal disorder*.

MTA

Acronym for *multiple technology appraisal*.

MTU-FSIOS

Acronym for Medical Technology Unit, Federal Social Insurance Office.

Multi-attribute Utility Theory

Same as *multi-attribute valuation*.

Multi-attribute Valuation

The method commonly used to calculate *quality-adjusted life-years*. It is multi-*attribute* by virtue of the *latent* concept ('health') being considered to be a function of several attributes (absence of pain might be one). The valuation part relates to the process of combining and scaling the attributes using the principles of *utility* (or *expected utility*) theory. The measurements involved are usually derived from sample surveys or formal experiments involving groups of the public deemed to be relevant for the purposes of the study in question. See *Health-related Quality of Life*.

Multicollinearity

When two or more *independent variables* are linearly related, they both convey essentially the same information in *multiple linear regression* analysis. One is not likely to contribute significantly to the *model* in the presence of the other(s). Together they may, however, contribute a lot. When this happens, the independent variables are said to be collinear and the phenomenon is called multicollinearity. Also spelled 'multicolinearity'. For an introduction see Kennedy (2003).

Multilevel Modelling

The analysis of data that have a *hierarchical* structure and that yield information about the impact each level of the hierarchy has on the *dependent variable* of interest. This is done by decomposing the *error term* in *regression* equations into component parts that are attributed to the various levels. For example, if hospital care is organized hierarchically by region, area and district (descending order) the outcome in any particular district is a linear function, having an *intercept*, a slope and three random *error terms* relating to region, area and district respectively. Cf. *Fixed Effects Model, Random Effects Model*. See Rice and Jones (1997) and Manca et al. (2005).

Multinomial

A mathematical expression for the addition of a series of terms. Similar to a *polynomial*, with a form like $y = a + bx + cx^2 + dx^3 + ex^4 + \ldots$, where a, b, c, etc. are constants and x and y are variables.

Multinomial Logistic Regression

A *logistic regression* method used mainly when the *dependent variable* can take more than two values.

Multinomial Logit Model

A statistical *model* for unordered *multinomial* outcomes. For a third world application see Gertler et al. (1987).

Multiple Correlation

The *correlation* between a *variable* and more than one other variable. Cf. *Partial Correlation*.

Multiple Criteria Decision Analysis

The analysis of complex decision problems using multiple criteria that may conflict with one another. Cf. *Utility Maximization* in which there is but one criterion. A standard text is Belton and Stewart (2002). The method has hardly been applied in *health economics* at all but, for a plea that it ought to be, see Baltussen and Niessen (2006).

Multiple Employer Welfare Arrangement

A US trust arrangement for self-funding a corporate group benefit plan covering medical and dental *insurance* and pensions. MEWAs are usually created by small employers. See Leibowitz et al. (1992).

Multiple Indicators-Multiple Causes

A method in *econometrics* for estimating the *parameters* of a model having multiple indicators and multiple causes of a single *latent variable*. For a *health economics* application see Jones and O'Donnell (2002).

Multiple Linear Regression

A statistical technique based on an assumed linear relationship (i.e. of the form $y = a + bx + cz + \ldots + \varepsilon$) between a *dependent variable* and a variety of explanatory or *independent variables*. ε (epsilon) is an *error term* generated by the fact that the independent variables are unlikely to account for all the changes in the dependent variable. The technique involves finding the line that best fits the data to the hypothetical linear structure. The *least squares* method does this by minimizing the sum of squares of the vertical distances of each actual observation from the fitted line (assuming the dependent variable to be on the vertical axis). The *coefficients* give a quantitative account of the relationship between y and x. Thus, if $b = 7.4$, then this means that a one-unit increase in x (any other variables constant) is associated with a 7.4 increase in the predicted value of y. The method is widely used in health economics as in most other branches of economics. For a classic study of aggregate health expenditures see Newhouse (1977). For use of the method in *cost–effectiveness analysis* see Hoch et al. (2002).

Multiple Technology Appraisal

This is a procedure used by the *National Institute for Health and Clinical Excellence* in England and Wales for the *appraisal* of the *cost-effectiveness* of a single product, device or other technology with several indications; or of several products etc., with one or more indications.

Multiplicative Model

A statistical *model* in which the combined effect of several *factors* is the product of the effects produced by each in the absence of the others. For example, if one factor increases risk by a per cent and another increases it by b per cent, the combined effect of the two factors is $(a \times b)$ per cent. Cf. *Additive Model*.

Multiplicity

In *clinical epidemiological* studies, multiplicity problems of statistical interpretation of the direction and size of effects arise when there are multiple endpoints or sub-groups in a trial.

Multiproduct Cost Function

Cost functions derived for producers (like hospitals) having multiple outputs. Cf. *Joint Costs*. See for example, Butler et al. (1995).

Multi-task Agency

The *agency relationship* in medicine typically operates through the performance of many tasks (as is, for example, vividly revealed in physician fee schedules). Different methods of remuneration tend to produce different mixes of these various tasks and different mixes of quality. The optimal solution as regards mix is elusive and methods of payment (such as *fee-for-service* or *capitation*) tend to be complemented by organizational, legal and social assumptions and values that reinforce the agency relationship. The idea originates with Holmström and Milgrom (1991).

Multivariate Analysis

An analysis in which there is more than one *independent variable*. Non-economists often reserve this term for systems that have multiple *dependent variables* and use 'multivariable' for the case of multiple independent variables.

Multivariate Analysis of Variance

A statistical model that extends the *analysis of variance (ANOVA)* model to situations in which the *dependent variables* are plural and possibly interrelated.

Multivariate Sensitivity Analysis

A form of *sensitivity analysis* that allows for the possibility that factors affecting *incremental cost–effectiveness ratios* are not independent of one another. Same as *scenario analysis, multi-way sensitivity analysis* or (in more restrictive form) *two-way sensitivity analysis*. For an example of its use (in cystic fibrosis treatments) see Van den Akker-Van Marle et al. (2006).

Multi-way Sensitivity Analysis

See *Two-way Sensitivity Analysis*.

Musculoskeletal Disorders

These are amongst the most frequent causes of occupational ill-health and absence from work. They include lower back injuries and low back pain, neck pain, carpal tunnel syndrome, tendonitis, joint strain and repetitive strain injuries. They also cause major expense to insurers and employers in *workers' compensation* schemes or social security systems.

Mutatis Mutandis

A Latin tag meaning the 'necessary changes having been made'. In contrast to *ceteris paribus*, it allows other affected *variables* to change as a consequence of a change in the variable of interest. More commonly used in the law than in economics.

N

Narrative Review

This is the traditional way in which literature reviews have been done, in which the selection of items reviewed, the quality assessments, the data extraction and the conclusions and the extent to which different studies come to the same conclusion, are all subjective, using implicit criteria, and are biased in unsystematic ways. Narrative reviews, in contrast to systematic reviews, are virtually unreplicable. See *Systematic Review*.

NAS

Acronym for *new active substance*.

Nash Equilibrium

A concept used in *game theory* and, in particular, non-zero-sum games. A Nash *equilibrium* is a set of strategies such that no player can benefit by changing their strategy while the other players keep theirs unchanged. Named after John Nash, economics Nobel Laureate, mathematician and *game theorist* (he of the 'beautiful mind'). For a *health economics* application, see Bolin et al. (2001).

National Coordinating Centre for Health Technology Assessment

The research centre through which the *Health Technology Assessment* (HTA) programmes of the government's Department of Health are coordinated for England and Wales. Its website is available at: www.ncchta. org/ (accessed 5 November 2009).

National Health Service

The common name given to the health care systems of the four countries in the United Kingdom (England, Wales, Scotland and Northern Ireland).

Although broadly similar, there are variations in the administrative and managerial arrangements between them and in their funding levels. There are also NHSs in Italy, Spain and several other countries.

National Health Service Economic Evaluation Database

The UK's NHS Economic Evaluation Database (NHS EED) contains over 7000 abstracts of quality assessed economic evaluations (wherever they have been conducted). The database aims to assist decision-makers by systematically identifying and describing economic evaluations, appraising their quality and highlighting their relative strengths and weaknesses. It is maintained at the *Centre for Reviews and Dissemination* at the University of York, UK and the website is http://www.york.ac.uk/inst/crd (accessed 5 November 2009).

National Income

Same as *net national product*.

National Income Accounting

A set of definitions and methods for calculating the aggregate income and production of a jurisdiction (a country or a region), often used as a rough and ready indicator of a jurisdiction's economic *welfare*. There are basically three ways of measuring national economic activity: the *output* approach: the money value of the total production of goods and services during a year; the income approach: total income (wages/salaries, interest, rents, profits) derived from economic activity after allowance has been made for *capital* consumption; and the expenditure approach: the money value of consumption, investment, government expenditure and net exports. In theory, all three methods must yield the same results, because total expenditures on goods and services must equal the total income paid to the producers, which must also equal the total value of the output of goods and services.

A difficult characteristic of the national accounts is that for most of the public sector, output is assumed to be equal to *input*, making public sector productivity growth (or its absence) impossible to measure and discouraging serious consideration of what the non-monetized outputs of this sector are. The practice can also be downright misleading if the accounts are interpreted as an indicator of aggregate welfare: an *exogenous* shock such as an *epidemic* will (ignoring any other effects it may have) increase the use of health care and generate an apparent rise in *gross domestic product*. See *Gross National Product*. On the treatment of public expenditures (including health care) in the national accounts, see Atkinson (2005) and P.C. Smith et al. (2008). On the special problems that arise for health accounting in developing countries see Berman (1997). For specific examples (Latin America and Nepal) see Musgrove (1983) and Rous and Hotchkiss (2003).

National Institute for Health and Clinical Excellence

The Institute (NICE) is a statutory *National Health Service* (NHS) organization for England and Wales whose principal jobs are to identify and recommend *cost-effective* health care technologies and develop authoritative *clinical guidelines* that include economic criteria. It is probably unique in apparently living up to the promise of its acronym. Its website is available at: http://www.nice.org.uk/ (accessed 5 November 2009). See Claxton et al. (2002). For a comparison of NICE and the *Scottish Medicines Consortium*, see Cairns (2006).

National Service Framework

This is a planning mechanism used in the UK *National Health Service* to set national standards and define service *models* for a service or care group, put in place programmes to support implementation and to establish *performance* measures against which progress within agreed timescales can be measured. They currently (2009) cover broad areas like cancer, coronary heart disease, diabetes, mental health, older people and children.

National Tariff

A list of prices per *healthcare resource group* used in *commissioning* health care in the *internal market* of the English *National Health Service*.

Natural Rate of Unemployment

The rate of unemployment that is (just) consistent with a zero inflation rate. Although there may be nothing 'natural' about it, it does appear to be determined by factors outside the conventional fiscal and monetary instruments of government (for example, such 'structural' factors as customary employer and trade union practices). Deregulation and greater flexibility of working practices are argued to be some means by which the natural rate might be reduced. Also sometimes called the 'non-accelerating inflation rate of unemployment' (NAIRU), which does not carry the unfortunate implication of inevitability suggested by 'natural'. See Phelps (1968).

NCCHTA

Acronym for *National Coordinating Centre for Health Technology Assessment*.

NCE

Acronym for *new chemical entity*.

NDA

Acronym for *new drug approval*.

Necessity

Economists frown on loaded terms like luxury and necessity and they generally have no precise meaning in economics. Of course, this has not stopped them being used. See Getzen (2000).

Need

Arguably the most used and the least properly comprehended word in discussions of health and health care. The meanings that attach to it are legion. Its persuasive power probably derives from a combination of two factors: one, the embodied implication that the entity asserted to be needed is actually necessary; the other, that this needed entity ought to be provided/received. To elucidate what any particular writer may be getting at, it is often helpful to ask what the thing said to be needed is needed for, and what the interests are of whoever is specifying that it is needed (given the ever present fact that whenever a professional is deciding what someone needs they are nearly always identifying a source of income for themselves). From this one might enquire as to whether there are other means than the one asserted to be needed – especially ones that may be more *effective*, or more *cost-effective*, and whether the person specifying the need is appropriately qualified (e.g. by training, *accountability* or responsibility). One may also enquire as to the social value, moral worth, etc. of the *outcome* for which the thing said to be needed is necessary (if it is necessary). In this way, some analytical content might be injected into what otherwise is in danger of being mere slogan-mongering.

It is invariably a good procedure to distinguish between a need for health and a need for health care (the latter may be seen as a kind of *derived demand* for the former).

Important and difficult issues remain concerning, for example, whether any particular need ought to be met and how much of it ought to be met. In prioritizing needs, economists naturally reach for the tools of *cost–effectiveness* and *cost–utility analysis*, which can indeed be helpful, not least in exposing the necessity for making *social value judgments* and interpersonal comparisons of health and illness.

The most frequently met practical measures of need at the community level are *morbidity* and mortality data. They plainly imply a need for health though not necessarily a need for health care (which may not be effective in altering either for the better and, even if it is, may not be the most cost-effective general instrument available). Other concepts include *capacity to benefit* from health care (which is an outcome measure if the underlying thing needed is health care) and the resources that are necessary to reduce capacity to benefit to zero (i.e. to the point at which the *marginal benefit* falls to zero). There are manifest and formidable problems of measurement with both of these.

Need is often used as a criterion for adjusting the *distribution* of health care resources in the interests of *fairness* or *equity*. Again, its usefulness in this role would be much enhanced (in proportion to the reduction of its capacity to spread confusion and policy paralysis) if the questions suggested above are probed. For fuller economic discussions building on these points see Culyer and Wagstaff (1993) and Culyer (1995, 2007).

Negative Predictive Value

Negative predictive value (NPV or PV−) is the proportion of individuals with negative test results who really do not have the disease being investigated. In the figure, $PV- = d/(c + d)$. Cf. *Positive Predictive Value, Sensitivity, Specificity.*

| | | Diagnosis | | |
		Present	Absent	Total
Test result	Present	a (true positive)	b (false positive)	$a + b$
	Absent	c (false negative)	d (true positive)	$c + d$
Total		$a + c$	$b + d$	

Negative Rights Good

Opposite of *positive rights good.*

Negbin Model

An extension of the *Poisson regression* model used for *count data*. Short for 'negative binomial'. The *variance* of the *dependent variable* is larger than the *mean*, in contrast to the Poisson regression model, where the variance equals the mean.

Neoclassical Economics

This is the 'modern' (as distinct from *postmodern*) synthesis of *utilitarianism* as applied to economic phenomena that forms the basis for most *microeconomics* and, in turn, most *health economics*. It is not constrained by the extreme assumptions of *classical economics* and has useful analyses of, for example, *market imperfections, non-profit* motivation, *household* behaviour, *industrial regulation, international trade,* and it comes in positive and normative guises. It remains, like *classical economics*, firmly rooted in individualism. The term was coined by Thorstein Veblen in 1899 in a series of articles in the *Quarterly Journal of Economics.*

Neonatal

Concerning the first four weeks of life after birth.

Nephrology

The medical speciality concerned with diseases and abnormalities of the kidneys. Same as renal medicine.

Nested Case-control Study

Same as *cohort case-control study*.

Net Benefit

An approach to *cost-effectiveness* that eschews the *incremental cost–effectiveness ratio* in favour of the net benefit attributed to *alternative* health care technologies. It employs the difference between the present value of (monetized) benefits and costs in a *cost–benefit analysis*. In a *cost–effectiveness analysis*, the *incremental cost–effectiveness ratio* in real terms (e.g. $\Delta costs/\Delta QALYs$) of two interventions can be turned into a net benefit criterion, thus: net benefit = $\lambda\Delta QALYs - \Delta costs$, where λ is the money value of a QALY gained or lost. If λ is set at the *threshold* rate set by some authoritative body a positive net benefit suggests (with a few side-conditions) that the technology in question may be efficient. See Stinnett and Mullahy (1998) and Lord et al. (2004).

Net Benefit Regression

The use of regression analysis of *net benefits* in a sample of patients to estimate *cost-effectiveness*. See Hoch et al. (2002).

Net Exports

A *national income accounting* term: the difference between the value of exports and imports in a time period (usually a year).

Net Health Benefit

See *Net Benefit*.

Net Investment

A *national income accounting* term: it is *gross investment* less *depreciation*. See *Investment*.

Net Monetary Benefit

See *Net Benefit*.

Net National Product

A *national income accounting* term: it is *gross national product* less *depreciation* (or *capital* consumption). This is the entity commonly referred to as 'national income' even though it is computed from the output side of the economy. But NNP can also be computed by adding up the incomes accruing to residents of a jurisdiction in a period and allowing for depreciation: incomes from employment, self-employment, profits (including interest and dividends) and rents. Adding net property income from abroad yields net national product at *factor cost*.

Net Present Value

The *discounted* value of the differences over time between monetary *costs* and *benefits* in each period.

Network

A linked grouping of terminals, computers, servers, etc. More generally, any linked grouping of people in communication with one another, usually with one or more interests held in common.

Network Externality

See *External Effects*.

Network Model HMO

A US consortium of *Independent Practice Associations*.

Neumann–Morgenstern Independence

This is an assumption of *expected utility theory* that means, roughly speaking, that adding a third lottery to two lotteries, whose order of preference has already been determined, will not affect that order.

Neurology

The science of nerve systems.

New Active Substance

A pharmaceutical or similar product that was not on the market in the European Union before a specified date.

New Chemical Entity

A new chemical entity is a drug containing no active molecule or ion that has previously been approved by a regulatory authority.

New Drug Approval

The term applied to approval by the US *Food and Drug Administration* of a new drug for interstate sale.

NHP

Acronym for *Nottingham Health Profile.*

NHS

Acronym for *National Health Service.*

NHS EED

Acronym for the *National Health Service Economic Evaluation Database.* Website: http://www.crd.york.ac.uk/crdweb/ (accessed 5 November 2009).

NHS QIS

Acronym for *NHS Quality Improvement Scotland.*

NHS Quality Improvement Scotland

This organization provides the *National Health Service* in Scotland with advice, guidance and support on effective clinical practice and service improvements.

NICE

Acronym for *National Institute for Health and Clinical Excellence.*

NND

Acronym for *number needed to diagnose.*

NNH

Acronym for *number needed to harm.*

NNT

Acronym for *number needed to treat*.

n-of-1 trial

A type of *trial* in which the patient undergoes pairs of treatment periods wherein one involves the use of the experimental treatment and the other involves the use of an alternative. Treatment periods are replicated until the triallist is convinced that the treatments have different *outcomes* (or not, as the case may be).

Nominal

The use of the adjective 'nominal' in economics distinguishes monetary changes in *value* that are merely inflationary from others corresponding to changes in the *flow* of goods and services. When there is a monetary change but no corresponding change in the flow of goods and services, the change is nominal. Cf. *Real*.

Nominal Income

Income that has not been adjusted for changes in the (usually intertemporal) general price level (*inflation*). Cf. *Real Income*.

Nominal Price

A monetary price that is not adjusted for changes in the (usually intertemporal) general price level (inflation). Cf. *Real Price*.

Nominal Variable

A *categorical variable* like eye colour for which there is no natural ordering. Gender is another categorical variable of which there are two types (male and female) and it is not politically correct (nor indeed is it right) to order them intrinsically.

Nomogram

A two-dimensional diagram (sometimes a table) designed to allow the approximate graphical computation of one value given values for another. Its accuracy is limited by the precision with which physical markings can be drawn, reproduced, viewed and aligned. See *Altman's Nomogram*.

Nomotheticism

The study (usually psychological) of those aspects of individuals about which it is possible – and interesting – to generalize. Cf. *Idiography*. See Allport (1937).

Non-cooperative Game

A type of game in *game theory* in which the players may not cooperate in deciding what each will do. Cf. *Cooperative Game*. See Bolin et al. (2001) for an application in *health economics*.

Non-diversifiable Intertemporal Risk

A risk in providing private long-term *insurance* is that future costs may be far off in time and may be substantially higher than now. This may be held to account for the fact that most insurance policies offer *indemnity* benefits rather than benefits in kind. See, for a health insurance application, Cutler and Zeckhauser (2004).

Non-ignorable Non-response

A problem with some survey instruments when non-responders may differ from responders in relevant ways. See *Incomplete Data*.

Non-inferiority Trial

A trial designed to determine whether one procedure is no worse (it could be equally *effective* or better) than another. Cf. *Equivalence Trial, Futility Trial, Superiority Trial*.

Non-marketed Good

This is a good that is not traded in any market. In health economics the principal good of this type is *health* itself. The absence of observed prices (even imperfect ones) and even the absence of straightforward quantities requires the imputation of *shadow prices* and indirect ways of measuring the entity of interest (health in our case).

Nonmaleficence

The general ethical principle in medicine of not doing harm to patients. Along with the principles of *autonomy*, *beneficence* and *justice*, it completes the so-called 'four principles' of health care ethics. See Beauchamp (2007).

Non-parametric Methods

Nonparametric statistical methods do not assume any particular family of *distribution* (for example, that the distribution is *normal*), for example as defined by mean and standard deviation, for the distribution of the data and so do not estimate any *parameters* for such a distribution. See Briggs et al. (1997) for a *health economics* application.

Non-profit

Organizations whose objective is assumed to be other than profit. Any trading surplus is not available for distribution to owners (or 'trustees'). In economics, it is nonetheless usually assumed that hospitals maximize something (like the utility of managers, or that of the senior doctors who work in them). Being non-profit is a characteristic of health care *insurance* that is sometimes (as in Canada) required by statute. The legitimate role of profit-seeking in health care provision has concerned health economists from the earliest days of the sub-discipline, both in order to understand better why the non-profit organization is so frequently found, even in market-oriented economies, and whether on balance and in what circumstances it can be counted as a good thing. Opinion amongst economists is unlikely, however, to reach a consensus, given the wider political connotations of the issue. The pioneering piece is Newhouse (1970). Some standard references are Pauly and Redisch (1973), Frank and Salkever

(1994), Keeler et al. (1999) and Sloan (2000). A discussion in the third world context is in Patouillard et al. (2007). See *Competition, For-profit, Hospital Economics, Profit*.

Non-satiation

One of the *axioms* of *choice theory*. It means that if, for any amount of a good or service, more is preferred to less, then more will be preferred to less also at all larger amounts of that good or service. See *Utility*.

Normal Distribution

A frequency *distribution* with one *mode*, having the symmetrical shape of a bell. Also known as a *Gaussian distribution*. It is characterized by two *parameters*: the *mean* and the *standard deviation*. Sixty-seven per cent of values lie within one standard deviation on either side of the mean. See *Distribution*.

Normal Good

A good for which a change in income causes a change in *demand* in the same direction. The *income-elasticity* of demand is positive. This is probably the only sense in which health care can be regarded as a 'normal' good! Cf. *Inferior Good*.

Normative

The adjective is usually taken to mean 'containing one or more social value judgments' and hence implying a 'norm' or standard that ought to be aimed at. *Welfare economics* is entirely concerned with normative matters. It is to be compared with *positive economics*. Positive economics is, however, sometimes used as a kind of Trojan horse for the introduction of implicit social value judgments, as when all variety of good or bad things are linked with the operation of 'the market'. See *Extra-welfarism, Interpersonal Comparisons of Utility, Logical Positivism, Welfare*. For a review of normative *health economics* see Hurley (2000).

Norwegian Centre for Health Technology Assessment

The Norwegian Centre for Health Technology Assessment critically reviews the scientific basis for methods used in health care and evaluates their costs, risks and benefits. Its website is available at: www.sintef.no/smm/News/FramesetNews.htm (accessed 5 November 2009).

Nosocomial

Occurring in a hospital. Hospital-acquired disease. As many (hospitalized) patients as an estimated 98 000 people die from *iatrogenesis* in the US each year (Kohn et al. 1999). For some examples, see Wright et al. (2002). On prescribing errors and their causes in group practices see Kralewski et al. (2005). See I. Evans et al. (2007) for many examples of practice that is not informed by evidence contraindicating it. See *Evidence-based Medicine*. Cf. *Iatrogenesis*.

Nosology

The art of producing taxonomies of diseases, for example, by *aetiology*, *pathogenesis* or *symptoms*.

Notifiable Disease

A disease, usually infectious or contagious, whose occurrence is required by law to be made known to a health officer or local government authority.

Nottingham Health Profile

A profile approach to *health status* measurement developed at Nottingham University covering physical mobility, pain, social isolation, emotional reactions, energy and sleep. See *Health-related Quality of Life*. See Hunt et al. (1985).

NPV

Acronym for *net present value* (economics) or *negative predictive value* (epidemiology).

NSAID

An acronym for non-steroidal anti-inflammatory drug.

N3

A *dummy variable* used in studies of health measures like *EQ-5D* to indicate extreme 'severity' in any of the *dimensions* of ill-health, to which subjects are often extremely averse. For an example, see Dolan (1996).

Nuclear Medicine

The medical speciality in which images are produced by administering a radioactive isotope, as in positron emission tomography (PET) or single positron emission computed tomography (SPECT).

Null Hypothesis

The prediction that there is no 'effect' or that the theory being tested is not 'true'. In other words, the presumption is that the prediction, theory, etc. in question needs empirical support before it can be accepted even provisionally. The idea is to try to refute the theory; only if one fails does one's acceptance of it begin to be justified. But note that 'has not been refuted' is not an equivalent statement to 'is true', though it is about as far as scientific method can take one towards 'truth'. See *p-value*.

Number Needed to Diagnose

Number needed to diagnose = $1/[Sensitivity - (1 - Specificity)]$.

Number Needed to Harm

The number of patients required for a specific treatment to cause harm in one of them. It is the converse of the *number needed to treat*. It is often referred to as NNH. It is the reciprocal of the *absolute risk increase* (NNH = 1/ARI). Unlike NNT, with NNH large numbers are better than small, because the adverse effect will occur less frequently.

Number Needed to Treat

The number of patients needed to be treated with a particular therapy in order to prevent one additional bad *outcome*. Often referred to as NNT. The reciprocal of the *absolute risk reduction* (NNT = 1/ARR). Suppose an existing procedure entails a risk of an adverse effect of 0.005 while an alternative has a risk of 0.004, then ARR = 0.001 and NNT = 1000. Switching from the former to the latter procedure yields an expected reduction of one *adverse event* in every 1000 cases.

Nursing Home

See *Long-term Care*.

Nutrition

Usually refers to the dietary materials necessary to support life. For a study of the economic and other *determinants* of nutrition in the elderly in the US, and the effects of federal support programmes, see Akin and Guilkey et al. (1985). For a third world application, see Thomas and Strauss (1997). On the feasibility of subsidies to encourage healthy consumption of grains, see Nordström and Thunström (2009).

O

Oaxaca Decomposition

See *Decomposition*.

Obesity

Generally taken to be a condition of having a body mass index (weight in kilograms/height in metres) in excess of 30. For economic analyses see Lakdawalla and Philipson (2006) and Grossman (2008).

Objective Function

A function that is to be maximized (or minimized) with respect to choice variables of interest (like 'health') and subject to whatever *constraints* (like 'resources') may apply.

Objectives

The aims or end-states that are sought in health systems or parts of systems. They may be cast in rather general forms such as 'to maximize *utility*' or more specifically in terms of directly measurable achievement (e.g. number of patients successfully discharged). Useful statements of objectives are normally cast in terms of *outputs* to be achieved or net *benefits* to be maximized. A characteristic of most planning systems is that objectives are stated, with dates set for their accomplishment, and methods of monitoring progress identified.

Observational Bias

Same as *information bias*.

Observational Cohort Study

Same as *prospective cohort study*. See also *Observational Study*.

Observational Study

A study that depends merely on observing 'what is' without observer intervention, say, in the form of creating *controls* or *blinding* or *randomizing*. Causal relationships may be hypothesized and tested empirically using data from such studies. The great majority of multivariate empirical economics is of this kind.

Observer Bias

A form of *bias* arising from lack of objectivity in those who are recording or measuring subjects' responses in *trials* or social surveys. The cure for this disease is *blinding* (single or, preferably, double).

Obstetrics and Gynaecology

The medical and surgical specialities concerned with midwifery, childbirth (obstetrics) and the reproductive health of girls and women (gynaecology – also spelled gynecology).

Occupational Disease and Injury

Disease and injury attributable to workplace exposures to risks, occupational characteristics or the activity of working. As a field for the systematic application of *health economics* (or any other kind) the topic has been largely starved (but see below). For an assessment of burden see Schulte (2005). For a review of the multi-factorial *determinants* of work-related illness and injury see Mustard (2008). On workplace danger see Dorman (1996). A general and belated economics of interventions to reduce occupational disease and workplace injury and death is Tompa et al. (2006, 2008).

Occupational Therapy

See *Physiatry*.

Odds Ratio

The ratio of two probabilities. In epidemiological *case-control studies* it is an estimate of the *relative risk*. The ratio of the probability, for example, of having a disease in a *population* exposed to certain *risk factors* and the probability of having that disease in another population not so exposed, or the probability that one treatment is more *effective* than another. It is calculated thus: the number of individuals with disease who were exposed to a risk factor (D_e) over those with disease who were not exposed (D_n) divided by those without disease who were exposed (H_e) over those without who were not exposed (H_n). Thus $OR =$

$$(D_e/D_n)/(H_e/H_n) = D_e H_n/D_n H_e.$$

OECD

Acronym for *Organisation for Economic Co-operation and Development*.

Office of Clinical Standards and Quality Programs

See *Centers for Medicare and Medicare Services*.

Office of Health Economics

A group of health economists based in London, providing independent research, advisory and consultancy services on policy implications and economic issues within the pharmaceutical, health care and biotechnology sectors. It is funded primarily by the British *pharmaceutical industry* but has independent Policy and Editorial Boards. Its website is to be found at: www.ohe.org (accessed 6 November 2009).

Official Financing

A component of the *balance of payments*.

Off-label Prescribing

The widespread (legal) clinical practice of prescribing drugs for purposes for which they have not been licensed. The practice is unmonitored and not evidence-informed. See, for its extent, Radley et al. (2006).

OHE

Acronym for *Office of Health Economics*.

OHTAC

Acronym for *Ontario Health Technology Advisory Committee*.

Oligopoly

A market with few sellers, whose interaction may involve mutually dependent strategies and tactics. See *Competition*.

OLS

Acronym for *ordinary least squares*.

Omitted Variable Bias

The difference between the value of an estimated *parameter* and its true value due to failure to *control* for a relevant explanatory (*confounding*) *variable* or variables. It is often possible to assess the direction of the *bias* by using common sense. For example, if a regression of hospital costs finds that the cost per patient episode is higher in teaching hospitals than in non-teaching hospitals, the inference that teaching hospitals are less *cost-effective* than non-teaching hospitals is likely to be false because their costs are in reality increased by the presence of teaching – a variable that was omitted. So the bias is clear. It is probably better on the whole to err on the side of including the wrong variables than to omit the right ones. Trends over time are a potent source of omitted variable bias. Consider the following figure. Kocj discovered the tubercle bacillus in 1882 but effective treatment for respiratory tuberculosis began only in 1947. The fall in the death rate from this disease is manifest.

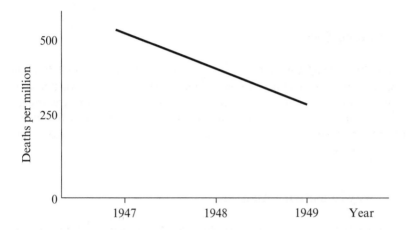

But seen against a longer time frame in the second figure, the impact of treatment appears much less dramatic. Plainly something else was going on besides the new treatment. It seems that curative medical measures played little role in mortality decline. What these factors may have been is

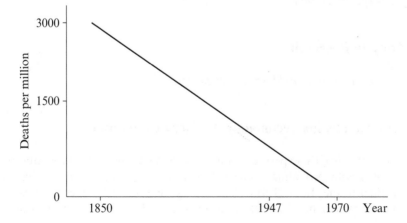

argued about. See McKeown (1976), Szreter (1988) and Colgrove (2002). See *Confounding*.

Oncology

The speciality of medicine concerning the diagnosis and treatment of cancer.

One-tailed Test

A *statistical significance* test based on the assumption that a real difference can occur in only one tail of the *distribution* so that any observations in the other are purely by chance. For example, testing whether one treatment is better than another would be a one-tailed test, being concerned only with the better *outcomes*. Testing whether it was better or worse would be a *two-tailed test*.

One-way Sensitivity Analysis

For the main entry see *Sensitivity Analysis*. A one-way sensitivity analysis systematically examines the impact of each variable in a *cost–effectiveness analysis* (or similar) by varying it across a plausible range of values with all other variables constant at their *baseline value*. Cf. *Extreme Scenario Sensitivity Analysis, Probabilistic Sensitivity Analysis, Two-way Sensitivity Analysis*. For an example of the technique in practice see Bhatti and Baibergenova (2008).

Only In Research

See *Coverage With Evidence Development*.

Ontario Health Technology Advisory Committee

An arm's length expert committee with some patient representation charged with providing evidence-based advice to the Ontario Ministry of Health and Long Term Care on the use of health technologies in that Canadian province. Its website is available at: http://www.health.

gov.on.ca/english/providers/program/ohtac/ohtac_mn.html   (accessed   6 November 2009).

Open Cohort Study

This is a *cohort study* in which the subjects are recruited and enrolled via a procedure that allows for in and out migration of people. Cf. *Fixed Cohort Study*.

Open-ended Questionnaire

An interview schedule that does not restrict the respondent to a specific set of predetermined answers but allows answers to be freely determined. Cf. *Closed-ended Questionnaire*.

Open Enrolment

A designated period when people may enrol in a US *health insurance* plan or *health maintenance organization* or change to an alternative form of coverage. Open enrolment periods generally last for about a month every year or two. See Hill and Wolfe (1997) for a case study in health economics.

Open-panel HMOs

See *Managed Health Care*.

Open Physician-Hospital Organizations

A US form of integration of physicians and hospitals. See *Vertical Integration*.

Open Sequential Design

See *Sequential Trial*.

OPHO

Acronym for *Open Physician-Hospital Organization.*

Ophthalmology

The medical speciality concerned with diseases and abnormalities of the eyes. The word is usually pronounced as though the 'h' were not there.

Opportunity Cost

Economists use the word 'cost' in a particular way that differs from everyday usage and also from accounting concepts of cost. Cost, in economics, is opportunity cost. Opportunity cost is the value of a resource in its most highly valued *alternative* use. In a world of competitive markets, in which all goods are traded and where there are no *market imperfections*, opportunity cost is revealed by the prices of resources: the alternative uses forgone cannot be valued higher than these prices or the resources would have gone to such uses. Where these stringent conditions are not met, opportunity cost and market prices can diverge and *shadow prices* may be estimated to measure the former.

Identification of opportunity cost is a skilled art that can be applied only in the context of a particular decision. It requires one either to identify the consequences of alternative courses of action or to assume that someone else has done so. In general, opportunity cost cannot be defined independently of the context in which the term is being used. There are, perhaps, two main reasons for this. First, if the context is, as it frequently is, one of decision-making, then the cost of a decision will depend upon such factors as the period of time over which the decision is believed to have consequences, which may go either well beyond a conventional accounting period (for example, when one decides to add a particular drug to a reimbursement tariff for the indefinite future) or fall short of it (for example, as when one wishes to know the cost of acquiring – as distinct from owning and operating – an item of equipment). Second, one must ask 'cost to whom?', for example, whether the resource-using consequences of a decision are to be seen as limited to the decision-maker alone, or to a wider set of affected parties.

At best, market prices can reveal the opportunity cost of resources in their most highly valued uses to people other than the decision-taker in question. They do this by showing what the decision-maker must pay to bid resources away from others. The opportunity cost of using resources one already owns is not usually revealed in market prices since the best alternative may be an alternative use in one's own organization (unless there is an *internal market*). In such cases, opportunity costs need to be elicited by discussion and judgment, and may not be readily put in monetary terms.

In some health care applications, opportunity cost is health forgone – as, for example, when there is a fixed budget that can be used only for the promotion of health. In such circumstances, the opportunity cost of using resources one way rather than another is the *health gain* not secured through the other route.

Opportunity costs should not be confused with *transfer payments* or *effort*. Cf. *Opportunity Loss*.

Opportunity Loss

The most highly valued use of resources (cf. the most highly valued alternative use). It is used especially in the context of decision-making under *uncertainty*, when the value attributed to obtaining additional information depends on the opportunities thereby created. It is the cost of not selecting the most highly valued use. See *Expected Value of Information*.

Optimism Bias

This is the tendency to be too optimistic in appraising the outcomes of projects or options. Enthusiasm can, in general, be a dangerous attribute in a scientist – especially enthusiasm for particular results (for example, results that may support a position to which one has previously committed oneself). See *Bias*.

Optimization

The solution to a mathematical problem that satisfies both the *constraints* (e.g. the available budget) and the *objective function* (e.g. *profit, welfare, utility* or *health gain*).

Optimum

Usually defined in economics as a *Pareto optimum*.

Option

An option in financial markets that gives one the right to buy or sell an asset at a specified future date or within a specified period of time. The idea has been used in *health economics* as one way of evaluating uncertainty in health investment decisions. See Palmer and Smith (2000).

Option Appraisal

This is the use of *cost–benefit analysis* or *cost–effectiveness analysis* and related techniques to assess the desirability of one option relative to another, to help decision-makers understand the critical differences between options and to select their preferred one. It is not really distinguishable from these methods of analysis. For a well-conducted study of colorectal cancer screening (described by the analysts at *NHS EED* as a cost–effectiveness and cost–utility analysis) see Tappenden et al. (2007).

Option Demand

Option *demand* is the value being placed on the availability of something, like adequate hospital capacity to meet unexpected demands at some future date, even if it is not directly used. Its availability for use is the thing valued. The mere availability of a local hospital might be valued even if one had no plan to use it and no expectation of ever having to. See *Existence Value*. See Weisbrod (1964).

Ordered Probit Model

A statistical *model* of ordered *multinomial outcomes*. For an introduction see Kennedy (2003).

Order Effects

Order effects occur in studies of patients' and others' choices when the order in which options are presented affects their order of preference. It is a form of *framing effect* and, when it occurs, violates the principle of *procedural invariance*. See Stewart et al. (2002).

Ordering Effects

See *Order Effects*.

Ordinal Scale

This is a numerical measure of a *variable* in which the function of the numbers is no more than to indicate the order of the observations (for example, in order of size). See *Utility*.

Ordinal Utility

A numerical indicator of preference or predictor of choice whose particular characteristic is that the entities amongst which one may choose are simply placed in order: those that are 'more preferred' receiving a higher number. A 'strong' order is one that does not allow ties; otherwise the order is 'weak'. See *Utility*.

Ordinary Least Squares Regression

OLS is the standard statistical method of estimating a *multiple linear regression model*. Its essence is finding *parameter* values that minimize the sum of squared errors. It involves estimating a straight line (in the case of two *variables*) in a scatter diagram such that the sum of the squared differences between the observations and the line are minimized. *Two-stage least squares*, or other more sophisticated techniques, need to be used when systems of equations are interdependent. When the *dependent variable* is *binary*, the *error term* using OLS is *heteroskedastic* and the method of *weighted least squares* may be preferred. For an introduction see Kennedy (2003).

Ordinate

The vertical axis in a two-dimensional diagram commonly referred to as the *y*-axis. Or a point on that axis. Cf. *Abscissa*.

Oregon Experiment

In 1989 the US state of Oregon initiated a controversial reform of its *Medicaid* programme by simultaneously increasing the number of people it covered but reducing the number of services that were insured. The services included were to be based on an explicitly prioritized list after extensive consultation with the public (though not much deliberation that involved them). The scheme was introduced in 1994, having gained federal approval from the *Health Care Financing Administration*. See Tengs (1996).

A Health Services Commission developed a prioritized list of paired *diagnoses* and treatment. The process entailed much public consultation and *focus groups*. Criteria such as the probability of death or *disability*

Prioritized List

Line 1   Diagnosis: severe/moderate head injury, haematoma or oedema with loss of consciousness
Treatment: medical and surgical

Line 2   Diagnosis: insulin dependent diabetes mellitus
Treatment: medical

Line 3   Diagnosis: peritonitis
Treatment: medical and surgical

Line 4   Diagnosis: acute glomerulonephritis, with lesion of rapidly progressive glomerulonephritis
Treatment: medical therapy including dialysis

Line 5   Diagnosis: pneumothorax and haemothorax
Treatment: tube thoracostomy or thoracotomy, medical therapy

Line 576   Diagnosis: internal derangement of the knee and ligamentous disruptions of the knee
Treatment: repair, medical therapy

Line 577   Diagnosis: keratoconjunctivitis sicca, not specified as Sjögren's syndrome
Treatment: punctal occlusion, tarsorrhaphy

Line 578   Diagnosis: noncervical warts
Treatment: medical therapy

Line 579   Diagnosis: anal fistula
Treatment: fistulectomy

Line 580   Diagnosis: relaxed anal sphincter
Treatment: medical and surgical

with and without treatment were used in ranking procedures. The list of approved diagnoses/procedures was subjected to *sensitivity analysis* and eventually had 745 items (in 1995) of which the top five and five around the cut-off point of 578 are in the box.

The creation of this list represents one of the world's most significant excursions into explicit *'rationing'* of health care. Despite its many imperfections, and although *cost-effectiveness* was not an explicit criterion, there would probably be widespread agreement that treatments above the line are more *cost-effective* than ones below it and that the ones ranked highest are properly so ranked. See Eddy (1991) and Hadorn (1991) (who commented on an earlier list).

Organisation for Economic Co-operation and Development

An international data gathering and analysis organization with 30 member countries. As well as collecting data, OECD monitors trends, analyses and forecasts economic developments and researches social changes or evolving patterns in health and many other areas of public policy. Its website is available at: http://www.oecd.org/pages/0,3417,en_36734052_36734103_1_1_1_1_1,00.html (accessed 6 November 2009).

Original Position

A vantage point from which to evaluate the justice of various states of the world. See *Fairness*. See Rawls (1971).

Orphan Drug

A drug developed for rare diseases and conditions that, in the US, affect fewer than 200 000 people or, in the European Union, affect five or fewer per 10 000 people. For an economic discussion of the status of such drugs see McCabe et al. (2005).

Orthogonal

A line that lies at a right angle to another or intersects another at a right angle is said to be orthogonal.

Orthogonal Main Effects Plan

An experimental design used in *discrete choice experiments* and elsewhere that permits the estimation of 'main effects' (i.e. assuming only minor interactions between experimental interventions). See Burgess et al. (2006).

Orthopaedics

The surgical speciality concerned with the correction of deformities of and damage to bones. Also spelled 'orthopedics'.

Orthotics

The speciality of making and fitting devices (orthoses) to correct or stabilize malformed or weak body parts. See *Physiatry*.

Osteopathy

The treatment of disease through the manipulation of people's bones.

OTC

Acronym for *over-the-counter* drugs.

Otolaryngology

The surgical speciality concerning diseases of the ears and throat.

Otorhinolaryngology

The surgical speciality concerning diseases of the ears, nose and throat. Same as *ENT*.

Outcome

This is another term for *output*. It tends to be used in preference to output when the effects in question are not quantitative or when they are characteristics of people, like their ability to perform *activities of daily living*, or changes in such characteristics. See *Health-related Quality of Life*.

Outcomes Program

This is any *managed health care* plan in the US that includes the collection and analysis of information about the results of prescribed treatments and procedures. An outcome is usually defined as the patient's change in *health status* at a particular time following treatment. Surveys of patient satisfaction are sometimes included in the data. The information is used by the plan to determine the most *cost-effective* treatments of specific health conditions and to reduce unnecessary medical interventions.

Outcomes Research

This term has come to embrace a wide range of *outcomes*, both biological and those to do with *quality of life*, of clinical interventions. In the commercial sector, outcomes researchers tend to be those with a wider remit, for example one embracing estimates of all relevant dimensions of a decision problem (outcomes, risks, uncertainties, costs, service impact and manageability). This is largely in response to the growth in the informational demands of regulatory agencies. A professionals' website is available at: http://www.healtheconomics.com/ (accessed 6 November 2009).

Outlier

An observation that lies outside the range of most of the observations in a *distribution*.

Out-of-network Services

These are services by US health care providers that are not employed by or under contract with a *managed health care* plan. Some plans require care to be provided only by doctors approved by the plan and some allow a member to see physicians outside the plan subject to *deductibles* or *coinsurance payments*. Emergency medical care outside of the geographic area of a benefit plan is not considered out-of-network, but is usually specifically covered. See *In-area Emergency Services*. Cf. *Carveouts*. See, e.g., Ma and McGuire (1998).

Out-of-pocket

Refers to payments made at the point of purchase of medical care that is not covered or is only partially covered by *health insurance*. Its growth in the US is charted in Chernew et al. (2006).

Out-patient

Either a patient who is treated by a hospital but not admitted as an in-patient or a patient treated in a community practice setting.

Output

The effects produced by production. Changes in *health status* are the ultimate output of the health service *production function*. However, sometimes more proximate throughput measures are used such as 'patients discharged'. In general, the use of *inputs* as measures of output is not recommended since the practice begs the question as to the nature and amount of output (if any!) that the inputs may generate, particularly at the margin, by assuming essentially that there is a one-to-one correspondence between input and output. Cf. *Outcome*.

Output Budgeting

A method of presenting allocated sums of money in an organization according to the *outputs* or *objectives* that the resources are directed towards. It is in distinction to traditional budgets that focus on *input* classifications like 'wages and salaries', '*capital* expenditure', 'equipment'. Ideally, output budgeting transcends the boundaries of particular agencies, so that a complete picture of the resources devoted to a particular end is obtained. In health care, outputs might relate to intermediate process outcomes like patient discharges from hospital or the number of *finished consultant episodes.* See *Programme Budgeting, Programme Budgeting and Marginal Analysis.*

Overdiagnosis

The detection of conditions that do not progress to clinical disease. This can lead to possibly harmful treatment of no benefit. Even *true positives* can be overdiagnostic as is the case, for example, with some cancers.

Overhead Costs

These are *opportunity costs* resulting from resource use that serve a variety of programmes, departments or activities but that cannot unambiguously be ascribed to any one of them. They pose an attribution problem in any organization if one is interested in discovering the *total cost* of a specific programme, department, etc. that has overhead support along with others in the organization. Any marginal impact on overhead costs arising from a change in the rate of any of the specific activities they support poses less of an intellectual challenge of attribution, though the practical challenges may be considerable.

Overinsurance

Same as *excess health insurance.*

Over-the-counter Drugs

Drugs that may be purchased without a doctor's *prescription* and from a wider range of suppliers than registered pharmacists. Usually abbreviated to OTC drugs. For a study of the effects of *subsidies* on these drugs see Sule et al. (2002).

Overutilization

Too much (somehow defined) use of something. It is not a technical term in economics. See *Utilization.*

P

Paasche Index

See *Index Numbers*.

Paediatric Economic Database Evaluation

PEDE is a comprehensive database of *paediatric* economic evaluations published since 1 January 1980. Its website is available at: http://pede.ccb. sickkids.ca/pede/about.jsp (accessed 7 November 2009).

Paediatrics

The medical speciality concerned with diseases of children. Also spelled 'pediatrics'.

Paired Comparison

An experimental method in which raters compare two states of health at the same time and record one as 'better' than the other. An *interval scale* can be derived using this method together with *Thurstone's Law of Comparative Judgment*. See Magat et al. (1988).

Pairwise Comparisons

A method of eliciting people's preferences for various characteristics of health services. It proceeds through survey instruments that ask subjects to make such (pairwise) comparisons as whether they prefer a *general practitioner*'s surgery to have longer opening times combined with a night-time deputizing service or shorter day-time opening combined with the general practitioners taking their own out-of-hours calls. See *Conjoint Analysis*. See, for a *health economics* application, Torrance (2001).

Palliative Care

Palliative care is mainly directed at providing relief to terminally ill people through symptom and pain management. The goal is not to cure but to provide comfort, emotional ease and to maintain the highest possible quality of life for as long as life remains. Also known as 'comfort care' or 'hospice care'. It seems not to have been much examined by health economists. See Bruera and Suarez-Almazor (1998).

Pandemic

An *epidemic* that is geographically widely dispersed.

Panel

A group of respondents in a survey.

Panel Data

Survey data in which each respondent is observed several times. For an introduction see Kennedy (2003). For *health economics* applications see Rice and Jones (1997) and Contoyannis et al. (2004).

PAR

Acronym for *participatory action research*.

Parallel Export

An outward *flow* of goods in *parallel trade*.

Parallel Group

A design feature of some *trials* in which the treatment being investigated and the *control* are applied simultaneously to two separate groups of subjects. This is different from a *crossover design* where each subject gets the treatment and then the control (or the control and then the treatment) in sequence. Cf. *Crossover Design*.

Parallel Import

An inward flow of goods in *parallel trade*.

Parallel Systems

Health care insurance systems that run in parallel with one another, sometimes in competition, sometimes with exclusive *earmarked* spheres of responsibility and accountability. A common example is that of *workers' compensation*, which covers workers' health care requirements (and also social security) arising from workplace accidents and exposures, and that works alongside other *health insurance* plans. See, e.g. Costa-i-Font and Jofre-Bonet (2008) and Hurley et al. (2008).

Parallel Trade

A kind of *arbitrage* in which drugs are imported without the manufacturer's consent into a jurisdiction from a market having lower prices. Since drug prices are regulated in most countries, parallel trading is unlikely, however, to produce the usual implication of arbitrage – the emergence of a single (or close to single) price for each product overcoming inefficiencies arising from uncompetitive practices – because the price differentials reflect efforts to earn a return on Research & Development investment rather than differences in production costs. Parallel trade, though legal in some jurisdictions (for example, within the EU), is bitterly opposed by the *pharmaceutical industry* because it undermines the value of a patented product and because it effectively imports the results of other countries' regulatory schemes. It is not clear that parallel trade redounds particularly to the benefit of consumers or *third party payers*, as distinct from that of the parallel traders. See Danzon (1998) and Kanavos and Costa-i-Font (2005).

Parameter

Parameters do not relate to the actual measurements or *attributes* of a *variable* but are quantities that define a theoretical *model*. The *coefficients* on the *input* variables in a *production function* are parameters. The *mean* and *standard deviation* of a theoretical *distribution* that might be used to characterize an empirical distribution are likewise parameters, as are the height and slope of a regression line (the regression coefficients) parameters of the regression model.

Parameters can also be values that are altered to see what happens in a *model* or a system. For example, the construction of a *partial equilibrium demand curve* normally assumes constant *real income* but it is often interesting to ask what happens if real income changes. In doing this one is effectively treating real income as a parameter rather than a value in an observed dataset. The *cost-effectiveness* of a screening programme will depend, amongst other things, on the *sensitivity* and s*pecificity* of the screening test. In assuming different values for them in order to discover the consequences for cost-effectiveness, one is treating them parametrically. The term 'parameter' is often misused by, for example, being confused with *variable*, or, even more vulgarly, with 'perimeter', as in the degraded English phrase 'within these parameters'.

Parameter Estimation by Sequential Testing

PEST is a method for eliciting responses from subjects in experimental situations, for example, when measuring *quality-adjusted life-years*. For a *health economics* application see Roberts (1999).

Parametric Methods

Statistical methods for estimating the *parameters* of an underlying theoretical *distribution* of a *variable*.

Parametric Test

A test that makes particular assumptions about *parameters*.

Pareto Efficiency

A state of the world in which no one can have their *welfare* (as they see it) improved without someone else having their welfare (as they see it) reduced. See *Efficiency, Pareto Optimality*.

Pareto Improvement

A change such that at least one person is better off (as judged by them) and no one is worse off (as judged by them). See *Pareto Optimality*.

Pareto Optimality

An allocation of resources such that no one can be made better off without at least one other person being made worse off. In both cases, being better off or worse off is judged from the viewpoints of the individuals in question. Its attraction to economists is three-fold: (1) it does not require the direct comparison of individuals' *utilities*; (2) it is readily applicable to market transactions, where compensation takes place as a matter of course, usually in monetary form; (3) it seems to be relatively uncontroversial – after all if anyone who could conceivably object to a proposed change is adequately compensated (as they see things), then who could – or ought to – possibly object? This gives away the implicit liberal political underpinning of the Paretian approach, which is an attraction to some and unappealing to others.

The Paretian approach is not able to categorize changes as desirable or undesirable when some have uncompensated losses. It is a vulgar error to infer from this that the Pareto criterion rules such changes out. It does not; it is simply silent about them. It is also silent about changes whose purpose is to affect the *distribution* of income, or health (or utilities). It is, in fact, silent on quite a lot of important issues.

Economists have amused themselves (probably not anyone else) by considering awkward cases, like the negotiations that might be successfully concluded between a masochist and a sadist and how they can be regarded in terms of *welfare*-enhancement. They have also examined the situation when transfers of income, otherwise not evaluable in Paretian terms, are themselves sources of utility (for example, to charitably inclined people). Named after Vilfredo Pareto (1848–1923) the Italian economist who was a leader of the Lausanne School of Economics. See *Efficiency, Extra-welfarism, Interpersonal Comparisons of Utility, Pareto Improvement, Welfare Economics*. See Sen (1970).

Pareto Optimum

Same as *Pareto efficiency*.

Pareto-preferred Move

Same as a *Pareto improvement*.

Partial Correlation

The *correlation* between two *variables* controlling for any interaction they may have with a third or other variable. Cf. *Multiple Correlation*.

Partial Equilibrium

The 'partial' element in this term refers to a theoretical ploy used in economics to simplify analysis by focusing on the principal relationships and setting aside feedback effects and other effects deemed to be non-central, even at the price of some compromise in logical coherency. '*Equilibrium*' refers to the solution of a set of simultaneous equations, some of which describe behavioural reactions to *parameter* changes. Thus, a simple *demand* and *supply* analysis might posit linear demand and supply functions, and an equilibrium condition:

$$D = a - bP$$

$$S = c + dP$$

$$D = S.$$

The equilibrium price is thus $(a - c)/(d + b)$. All else is held constant (*ceteris paribus*) notwithstanding the facts that a change in price will affect the purchasing power of money income (so *real* income is strictly speaking not constant and the good may have a positive or negative *income-elasticity*), or that a change in S might affect the demand for labour and hence a person's income (so money income is not constant either). Absence of side-effects such as these can be regarded as stipulations for the circumstances under which the theory in question is applicable (i.e. when the impact of a price change on income is likely to be minute because, say, the good whose demand is being investigated occupies a trivial fraction of an individual's expenditure). When this is not sustainable *a general equilibrium* approach must be taken, or at least one that explicitly takes account of the consequential effects of any initial disturbance to equilibrium. See *Nash Equilibrium*.

Partial Equilibrium Theory

Classic *demand* and *supply* analysis in which each market is treated in isolation from all others. Cf. *General Equilibrium Theory*. See *Partial Equilibrium*.

Participatory Action Research

A form of *action research* in which the researcher and other participants collaborate in experimenting with methods of improving the *performance* of an organization. See Wadsworth (1998).

Part-worth Utility

The part-worth is the element of the *utility* of a service that attaches to a particular *attribute* in *conjoint analysis*. For a *health economics* application see Flynn et al. (2007).

Patent

A patent for an invention is a territorial *intellectual property right* granted by an official agency of the government to the inventor, giving the inventor the right for a limited period to stop others from making, using or selling the invention without the permission of the inventor. It is a temporary *monopoly*. When a patent is granted, the invention becomes the property of the inventor, which – like any other form of property or business asset – can be bought, sold, rented or hired. Patent laws exist in order to reward, and hence encourage, innovation and invention. In *health economics*, they have been particularly important for the *pharmaceutical industry*.

Patent protection is usually for 20 years from the date the patent application was filed. The practical life of most pharmaceutical patents is much shorter than this because it takes many years to bring a product to market, satisfy safety and *efficacy* regulatory agencies and to negotiate prices. Seven to ten years may be a realistic effective patent life over which a product must recoup its development costs (and those of other 'failed' products). Some countries permit extensions to a patent's term for a further term, usually to compensate patentees for delays in securing approval to market a drug.

Some countries allow the production, sale, or use of a patented product, without the patent owner's permission, for the purposes of obtaining permission to market the product. Such an exception to patent rights (known as *springboarding*) is intended to allow generic drugs to enter the market as soon as possible after the patent on the drug expires. See *Effective Patent Life*. See Scherer (2000).

PATH

Acronym for *Program for Assessment of Technology in Health*.

Pathogenesis

The postulated pathway through which an organism (pathogen) such as a bacterium or virus produces disease. Not on any account to be confused with parthenogenesis, which is an asexual form of reproduction.

Pathology

The science of diseases of the body. It is also used to characterize the symptoms of a disease.

PATHOS

An acronym for *Pathways to Healthy Outcomes*.

Pathways to Healthy Outcomes

A proposal of the *Jackson Hole Group* in the US for federal and state governments to collaborate in developing evidence-informed medical practice, empowering patients, institutionalizing the production and dissemination of evidence and clinical guidelines and affording universal *health insurance* coverage to all Americans. See Ellwood (2003).

Patient-reported Outcome Measure

PROMs are measures of a patient's *health status* or *health-related quality of life*. They are typically short, self-completed questionnaires to measure patients' health status or health-related quality of life at a single point in time, as used in the NHS in England *before and after* a clinical intervention since 2009.

Patient Sub-group

A group of patients with a telling characteristic in common but that differentiates them from the larger group. For example, an identifiable sub-group of patients may respond better to a treatment than the wider group of people with the condition in question.

Patient Years of Life Lost

A measure of the *burden of disease*, or of the potential benefit from an *effective* intervention to improve health.

Pay for Performance

A form of reimbursement of physicians or manufacturers under which remuneration moves in part directly in line with their *performance* on a set of indicators. It is being experimented with in the context of paying for costly drugs whose *effectiveness* may vary widely across various sub-groups. See Rosenthal and Frank (2006) for a review of the empirical evidence.

Payment by Results

In the English *National Health Service* this refers to the system, introduced in 2002, of financial controls and rewards through which the central ministry influences providers throughout the care delivery service. Providers are paid for the activity they actually deliver. *Commissioners* will have sufficient funding to look for alternative providers if agreed activity levels are not met. *Primary Care Trusts* commission the volume of activity required to deliver service priorities, adjusted for *case-mix*, from a range of providers using standard *national tariffs* for *healthcare resource groups*. The tariff is adjusted for regional variation in wages and other costs of service delivery using a nationally determined formula. In the US there are at least 31 separate sponsors of similar arrangements, covering more than 20 million enrolees. The incentives relate to both process and structure with some role for patient-related outcomes. The procedure usually rewards good *performance* (including those already performing well) rather than improvement. See *Activity-based Financing, Pay for Performance*. See Rosenthal et al. (2004), Rosenthal and Frank (2006), Maynard (2008) and Sussex and Farrar (2009).

Payment Card

A questionnaire design in *willingness to pay* studies under which a card lists several monetary values from which respondents choose that which corresponds to their maximum willingness to pay. Cf. *Dichotomous Choice*. See Ryan et al. (2004).

Payment Period Effects

An effect in *willingness to pay* studies by which the value elicited for the entity being valued is affected by the period over which weekly, monthly, etc. payments are proposed. It is a form of *framing effect* and when it occurs it is a violation of the principle of *procedural invariance*. It has not been well-studied in *health economics* but see Pinto et al. (2009).

Payment Vehicle

The way in which *willingness to pay* payments are made in *contingent valuation* experiments. Common payment vehicles include direct *out-of-pocket* expenditures or hypothetical premiums.

Payroll Tax

Payroll taxes are proportionate *direct taxes* on labour income, usually imposed to finance public pension schemes, health care *insurance* and unemployment benefits. See *Incidence, Taxes*. For a study of the *incidence* of such taxes in Chile see Gruber (1997).

PBAC

Acronym for *Pharmaceutical Benefits Advisory Committee.*

PBMA

Acronym for *programme budgeting and marginal analysis.*

PBS

Acronym for *Pharmaceutical Benefits Scheme.*

PCAS

Acronym for *primary care assessment survey.*

Peak-end Effect

An event or experience is more likely to be remembered, it seems, when it has a peak before it ends than if it has a continuous intensity. For example, an *acute* pain having a peak just before the end of the overall painful experience scores higher on remembered pain intensity than a *chronic* pain pattern with no peak at the end. See Kahneman (1999).

PEDE

Acronym for *Paediatric Economic Database Evaluation.*

Peer Effect

The impact that imitative behaviour can have on the *demand* for or utilization of health care. For empirical examples see Norton et al. (1998), Lundborg (2006), Fowler and Christakis (2008) and Holla and Kremer (2009).

Percentile

Same as *centile*. See *Quantile*.

Perfect Competition

A market in which the number of competing firms is sufficiently large for none of them to be able individually to affect the price of the products they sell. Similar to *price-taking* in this regard but the *model* of perfect *competition* also usually assumes large numbers of well-informed consumers, none of whom alone can affect prices, *homogeneous* products, low *barriers to entry* and exit, complete information. For a classic analytical study of a competitive *insurance* market see Rothschild and Stiglitz (1976).

Performance

The measurement of the performance (*productivity*) of organizations is beset by problems arising from the difficulty of monitoring the effort of individuals, especially when engaged in team production, and locating incentives appropriately. For early work see Alchian and Demsetz (1972) and in health care Goddard et al. (2000). See *Pay for Performance*, *Payment by Results*.

Performance Bias

A *bias* in *outcomes* found in *clinical trials* without *blinding* and attributable to behavioural responses by subjects or researchers to the knowledge that a subject is in or not in a *control group*.

Performance Prism

A management tool for linking organizational *performance* to strategic objectives and linking with a range of stakeholders. See Neely et al. (2002).

Performance Pyramid

A management tool for linking organizational *performance* to strategic objectives. See Lynch and Cross (1991).

Perinatal

The period between the 28th week of pregnancy and the end of the first week of life.

Period Effect

The difference in the clinical *outcomes* observed in different treatment periods in a *crossover trial*.

Permanent Income

The regular *annuity* for an individual or organization whose *present value* equals the *wealth* of the individual or organization. It is used in economics as an alternative to current income on the grounds that people are more likely to consume, save, etc. in relation to permanent income than *transitory income*, which may have substantial ups and downs. The inventor of the concept was Friedman (1957).

Permuted Block

See *Blocking*.

Per Protocol

A term used to describe a *clinical trial* in which only the subjects who complete the trial are counted and not those who drop out. Regarded as statistically inferior to *intention to treat* analysis.

Personality Bias

See *Therapeutic Personality Bias*.

Person Trade-off Method

Originally called the 'equivalence of numbers' method of creating a '*quality of well-being scale*', this is a method of assigning utilities to health states that works as follows: subjects are asked a question of the following kind: 'If x people have health state A (described) and y have health B, and if you can only help (cure) one group, which group would you choose?' One of the numbers x or y is then varied until the subject finds the two groups equally deserving of their vote. The undesirability (*disutility*) of situation B is x/y times as great as that of situation A and this *ratio* provides the index of the *utility* of one state relative to the other. See also *Standard Gamble*, *Time Trade-off Method*. See Nord (1995).

Perspective

The viewpoint adopted for the purposes of an *economic appraisal* (*cost–effectiveness, cost–utility analysis*, etc.) that defines the scope and character of the *costs* and *benefits* to be examined, as well as other critical features, which may be *social value-judgmental* in nature, such as the *discount rate*. The perspective may be set by a client or determined by the analyst. Most textbooks advocate the use of the social (or 'societal') perspective, according to which all potential *costs* and *benefits* are to be included regardless of who bears or receives them. However, this is merely a value judgment of the authors that the conscientious investigator need feel no scruple in ignoring. It has the virtue of inclusivity but the vice of demanding much work that may be irrelevant in particular circumstances. It also has the more dangerous vice of encouraging a belief that a single perspective, whether inclusive or exclusive, is the appropriate way to perform such analyses. In some cases, particularly where the potential clients for a study are *heterogeneous* in their interests and values, it may be desirable to adopt more than one perspective (for example, the perspective of workers and employers is likely to differ concerning the *cost-effectiveness* of health and safety practices in the workplace). Distributional issues, such as the weights to be attached to *health gains* accruing or denied to different sorts of people (old/young, fit/ill, geographical location, etc.) ought in principle to be settled within any discussion of perspective, but they rarely are. For two contrasting views on perspective, see Appendix A in Gold et al. (1996) and Chapter 5 in National Institute for Clinical Excellence (2004).

PEST

Acronym for *Parameter Estimation by Sequential Testing*.

Peto Method

A method of combining *odds ratios* in *meta-analyses*. A variant of the *Mantel–Haenszel test*. See Yusuf et al. (1985).

P4P

Acronym for *pay for performance*.

PHARMAC

Acronym for *Pharmaceutical Management Agency*.

Pharmaceutical Benefits Advisory Committee

An Australian statutory body that makes recommendations and gives advice to the Minister of Health about which drugs and medicinal preparations should be made available as pharmaceutical benefits. No new drug may be made available as a pharmaceutical benefit unless the Committee has so recommended. The Committee is required by the Act to consider the *effectiveness* and *cost* of a proposed benefit compared with alternative therapies (not just *placebo*).

Pharmaceutical Benefits Scheme

The Australian public support system for subsidizing approved prescription drugs. Its website is available at: http://www.pbs.gov.au/html/home (accessed 7 November 2009). See *Pharmaceutical Benefits Advisory Committee*.

Pharmaceutical Industry

The global industry concerned with the manufacture and distribution of drugs for medical use. For a review of the economics of the industry see Scherer (2000).

Pharmaceutical Management Agency

An agency of the New Zealand government that conducts *economic appraisals* of drugs, maintains a list of approved subsidized drugs and manages the purchasing of hospital pharmaceuticals. Its website is available at: http://www.pharmac.govt.nz/ (accessed 7 November 2009).

Pharmaceutical Price Regulation Scheme

The Pharmaceutical Price Regulation Scheme (PPRS) regulates the overall profitability of pharmaceutical companies with sales of branded prescribed medicines to the *National Health Service* in the UK. Its objects are to secure the provision of safe and *effective* medicines for the National Health Service at 'reasonable' prices; promote a strong and profitable *pharmaceutical industry* capable of sustained research and development; and encourage the efficient supply of medicines to pharmaceutical markets in the UK and elsewhere. It operates through negotiation based on companies' financial records and regulates both the return on *capital* (usually restricted to a range of pre-tax 17–21 per cent on *assets*) and prices. It allows freedom of pricing for all new chemical entities, requires companies to seek permission for any price increases (which have to meet particular criteria), requires companies with NHS sales in excess of a critical amount per annum to submit data on sales, costs, assets and profitability and to repay any excess profits over an agreed return on capital. Its website is available at: http:// www.dh.gov.uk/PolicyAndGuidance/MedicinesPharmacyAndIndustry/ PharmaceuticalPriceRegulationScheme/fs/en (accessed 7 November 2009). See Maynard and Bloor (1997) and Claxton et al. (2008).

Pharmacoeconomics

The economics of drugs (*cost–effectiveness* and *cost–utility analysis* of their effects) and of the *pharmaceutical industry*. See Glick et al. (2007).

Pharmacology

The science of the action and/or mechanism of action of drugs on living tissue.

Phases of Clinical Trials

Clinical trials on humans are conducted in stages, prior to which tests on animals for toxicity will have been completed. Each phase has a different purpose. In Phase I trials, researchers test a new drug or treatment in a small group of healthy people (usually less than 100) for the first time to evaluate its safety, determine a safe dosage range, and identify side-effects. In Phase II trials, the treatment is given to a larger group of people (100+) with the disease to see if it is *effective* (*proof of principle*) and to evaluate its safety further. In Phase III trials, the treatment is given to large groups of people (1000–3000) preferably in *double-blind* trials (sometimes multi-centre) to confirm *effectiveness*, monitor side-effects, compare it to commonly used treatments and collect information that will allow the drug or treatment to be used safely. There are also Phase IV trials: post-marketing studies yielding additional information about the drug's risks, benefits and optimal use. Cf. *Post-marketing Surveillance*.

Physiatry

Same as *rehabilitation medicine*. This is the mainly North American term for a medical speciality centred on physical medicine and rehabilitation medicine. However, rehabilitation usually involves teams including other non-medical specialties such as *audiology, occupational therapy, orthotics, physiotherapy, prosthetics and speech therapy*.

Physical Therapy

Same as *physiotherapy*.

Physician Behaviour

Doctors' behaviour is usually assumed by economists to be *utility-maximizing*, in which the main *arguments* of the *utility function* are patient welfare/health, personal status (professional and social) and personal wealth. The weights attaching to these seem to be highly variable. More in the tradition of *satisficing* theory, some theories posit a target income. Some *models* have boldly assumed that the medical profession seeks to operate as a wealth-maximizing *price-discriminating monopoly*, and some professional behaviour in some jurisdictions seems consistent with this idea. The classic pursuit of this latter idea is Kessel (1958). For a wide-ranging review see Pauly (1981).

Physician Extender

While there is no precise or universally agreed definition of the scope of a physician extender's work, the term always refers to a health care professional, such as a registered nurse practitioner or a physician assistant, whose skills have been enhanced by an appropriate course of training. The idea is to substitute some of the extender for some of the physician. For a literature review see Richardson et al. (1998).

Physician-induced Demand

Same as *supplier-induced demand*.

Physiology

The science of the functions of living organisms and their various parts.

Physiotherapy

The use of physical exercise, massage and manipulation for the prevention and treatment of stress or trauma.

Piechart

A diagram showing the *distribution* of a non-*continuous variable* (e.g. social class) in which the size of the slice for each indicated value is proportional to the relative frequency of observations in that category of the variable. In the diagram, the slices are proportional to the frequency of words of various lengths in the first sentence of the entry for *Bar Chart*. The numbers above the percentages are the lengths of words in letters beginning with the smallest (1) and moving clockwise.

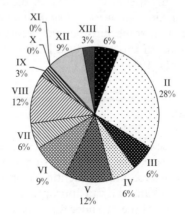

Pigovian Subsidy

See *Pigovian Tax*. (Also 'Pigouvian'.)

Pigovian Tax

A tax designed to change behaviour in such a way as to promote the optimal rate of an activity, whether beneficial or harmful. The idea is most commonly met in the context of harmful *externalities*, when the tax seeks to reduce the activity to the *Pareto optimal* rate. By analogy, a Pigovian *subsidy* encourages the rate of activities that generate beneficial externalities. Also Pigouvian. Named for the Cambridge economist Arthur Cecil Pigou (1877–1959). A *health economics* example of how the subsidy idea can be applied is Geoffard and Philipson (1997).

Ping-Pong Method

A method of ascribing values to entities like health states or the equilibrating probability in a *standard gamble* experiment or *willingness to pay* studies by successive approximations from above and below. See Dolan et al. (1996b) for an example of the method.

Placebo

A non-active apparent treatment used in a *clinical trial* that is in appearance indistinguishable from the active treatment being investigated. The idea is to identify the effect of the specific treatment under investigation as distinct from 'treatment' in a general sense. From the Latin meaning 'I will please'. See *Placebo Effect*.

Placebo Effect

The impact on health that a *placebo* may have even though it is not known (or known not) to contain any active therapeutic ingredient. Cf. *Hawthorne Effect*.

Planning–Programming–Budgeting System

An accounting framework that broadly includes *output budgeting* and *programme budgeting*. For a review see Mitton and Donaldson (2001).

Plumbing Diagram

May refer to Alan Williams' taxonomizing account of the scope of health economics. See *Williams' Schematic of Health Economics*.

Podiatry

Same as *chiropody*.

Point-elasticity

See *Elasticity*.

Point Estimate

A single estimate, as distinct from, say, a range within which the true value is believed to lie.

Point of Inflexion

See *Concavity*.

Point-of service Plan

Point-of-service is a type of plan in the US whose members can choose their services when they need them, either in a *health maintenance organization* (HMO) or from a provider outside the HMO at some cost to the member in the form of a reduced benefit level. The term is also used to describe a plan in which the primary provider directs services and referrals.

Point Prevalence

The *prevalence* of a particular condition at a particular date.

Poisson Distribution

A *distribution* having the characteristic that the *mean* is equal to the *variance*. Named after the French mathematician Siméon Denis Poisson (1781–1840).

Poisson Regression

A statistical *model* for *count data* based on the *Poisson distribution*. Named after the French mathematician Siméon Denis Poisson (1781–1840). See also *Negbin Model*.

Polynomial Regression

A regression procedure for estimating non-linear relationships between *dependent* and *independent variables* (it may be quadratic, cubic, etc.). See *Multinomial*. For a *health economics* application see Zweifel et al. (1999).

Pooling

In *health insurance*, the mixing of insured parties having different risks in a common pool and facing the same premium.

Pooling Equilibrium

An *equilibrium* that may occur in the presence of asymmetrical information and which does not permit differential prices to be charged even though the seller would be able to charge differential prices with better information about relevant characteristics of buyers. Cf. *Separating Equilibrium*. See Rothschild and Stiglitz (1976) and, for a *health insurance* example, Selden (1999).

Population

The total collection of individuals, events, technologies, or other entities of interest (of which the human population of a jurisdiction is the most common example) from which *samples* are often taken in order to understand better the characteristics of the whole and its parts.

Population Health

The *determinants* of the health of whole populations has been largely the province of social epidemiologists rather than that of economists. The empirical difficulties are formidable. The determinants are many and they stretch back in time through genetic inheritance and parental child-rearing. The causal pathways through social conditions have their impacts on health, some of which seem to operate via stresses on the human immune system, are only beginning to be understood and there is much to uncover in this inherently multidisciplinary territory. A notable group has been those working with Michael Marmot at University College London (e.g. Marmot et al., 1991). See also Marmot (2008). Those working with Robert Evans in the (now completed) Canadian Institute for Advanced Research's Population Health Program included several economists besides Evans himself (e.g. Evans et al., 1994, Heymann et al., 2006). See also Heckman (2007). The many international studies led by Wagstaff and Van Doorslaer are the main economic contributions in the fields of *equity* of health care, health care financing and health itself in both the developed world and the developing (e.g. Wagstaff and Van Doorslaer, 2000). See also Deaton (2003). Some recent *econometric* work tends to overturn common presumptions amongst epidemiologists – with respect, for example, to the impact of lifestyle on mortality. See Contoyannis and Jones (2004) and Balia and Jones (2008). For an economic approach to the *determinants* of mortality reductions in the developing world see Soares (2007). See, for studies regarding smoking, Kan (2007), smoking and pregnancy, Grossman (2003), teenage drugs use and sexual behaviour, Grossman (2004), fast food consumption and childhood obesity, Grossman (2008), maternal working and child development, Gregg et al. (2005), schooling and cigarette usage, Farrell and Fuchs (1982). On effects of war (and the population movements it causes) see Montalvo and Reynal-Querol (2007).

Another usage is more strictly epidemiological and distinguishes the causes of *cases* from the causes of *incidence*, with population health being concerned with the latter and population health interventions being those aimed at shifting the distribution of disease rather than compressing its tails. See Rose (2008).

Population Sub-group

Same as *patient sub-group* but referring to a population.

Portability

Refers to the ability of an individual to retain their rights to medical care when they leave one jurisdiction for another or one *insurance* scheme for another. With full portability one's rights move with one. A characteristic of a health care system that is commonly desired or sometimes (as in Canada) required by statute.

Positive Controls

The patients in a trial who receive a therapeutically active treatment (i.e. not *placebo*) as *controls* in a trial of another active therapy.

Positive Economics

An approach to economics that seeks only to explain and predict rather than prescribe or recommend. It thus concerns 'what is' or 'what might be' rather than 'what ought to be'. It is (somewhat extremely) also the doctrine that the descriptive accuracy of theory (and likewise of the assumptions necessarily made in theorizing about anything) is irrelevant compared with its analytical relevance and ability to 'predict' or be empirically testable. Cf. *Normative Economics*. See Friedman (1953) for a classic statement; for an antidote: Hausman and McPherson (2006).

Positive Predictive Value

Positive predictive value (PPV or PV+) is the proportion of individuals with positive test results who really do have the disease being investigated. In the figure, $PV+ = a/(a + b)$. Cf. *Negative Predictive Value, Sensitivity, Specificity*.

		Diagnosis		
		Present	Absent	Total
Test result	Present	a (true positive)	b (false positive)	$a + b$
	Absent	c (false negative)	d (true positive)	$c + d$
Total		$a + c$	$b + d$	

Positive Rights Good

Although it is not a term in economics, the notion of positive rights is closely linked with the notion of a *merit good*. Positive rights are rights or guarantees to have certain things, in contrast to negative rights, which are the rights to be free from certain things, like abuse or coercion. If a right exists at all, it is positive when its realization entails some action on the part of others and it is negative when its realization entails inaction on the part of another. Health care is often cited as an example of a positive rights good.

Positivism

See *Positive Economics*.

Positivity Criterion

Same as *cutoff value*.

POS Plans

Acronym for *point-of-service plans*.

Posterior Distribution

A probability *distribution* that takes account not only of the data but also the *prior distribution*. See *Bayesian Method*.

Posterior Probability

A belief about the likelihood of an event that is a modified *prior probability* as the result of additional information. See *Bayesian Method*.

Post-marketing Surveillance

Routine follow-up studies of the use of drugs after their licensing for public use. A means of discovering effects of long-term use and any undiscovered adverse effects not revealed during earlier trials. See *Phases of Clinical Trials*.

Postmodernism

Postmodernism is easier to define as what it is not rather than the variety of fresh approaches to culture, art and science that it is. Thus, in economics, it is a reaction against the rationalist, consequentialist, essentially optimistic and rather Whiggish zeal of classical and *neoclassical economics*. In *health economics*, see Mannion and Small (1999).

Postnatal

After, but within one year of, giving birth.

Post-test Odds

The odds that the patient has the target condition after a diagnostic test has been carried out (calculated as the *pre-test odds* times the *likelihood ratio*).

Potential Pareto Efficiency

The idea that if gainers from a change could compensate losers and still gain then there is an increase in social welfare (even if the compensation is not actually paid). If they cannot, or will not, then efficiency in this Paretian sense exists. Another version is the idea that if potential losers can offer gainers an equivalent gain sufficient for them to forgo the proposed change and still be better off than with the change, then the change will not enhance welfare (even if the equivalent is not actually paid). These contortions are gone through in order to avoid having to face up to the reality that a dollar of gain may not be of the same value to each person or, even if it were, that it should be so treated in the *social welfare function*. See *Efficiency, Kaldor–Hicks Criterion*.

Potential Pareto Improvement

Similar to *potential Pareto efficiency* but referring to whether a change from one state to another is efficient rather than the state itself. Plainly if a state were Pareto inefficient it would seem to imply that there were potential improvements to be had.

Poverty and Health

Poverty and ill-health are intertwined. Low-income countries tend to have worse health than richer ones. Within either, poor people have worse health than richer ones. Causality runs both ways: poverty breeds ill-health, and ill-health keeps poor people poor and can make well-to-do people poor (mainly in the US). For an economic review see Wagstaff (2002a, b).

Power

See *Statistical Power*.

PPO

Acronym for *preferred provider organization*.

PPP

Acronym for *purchasing power parity*.

PPRS

Acronym for *Pharmaceutical Price Regulation Scheme*.

PPV

Acronym for *positive predictive value*.

Pragmatic Trial

A species of controlled *trial*. Pragmatic trials measure *effectiveness* as distinct from *efficacy* and are not so much concerned with scientific questions of explanation (why something works or does not work) as with the degree of beneficial effect to be expected in real clinical practice. The pragmatic trial thus seeks to maximize *external validity*. A pragmatic trial is much less likely to use *placebo* as a *comparator* procedure than an explanatory trial, since placebo is unlikely in most cases to be a real-world *alternative* to the technology under review. Cf. *Explanatory Trial.*

Preadmission Review

A review of a patient's needs to determine whether admission to hospital is indicated.

Precision

Precision is a measure of how close an estimate is to the true value of a *parameter.* Less precision is usually indicated by a larger *standard error.*

Preclinical Trials

These are trials in the test tube or on animals designed to test such basic characteristics of drugs as toxicity and the strength and frequency of dosages that will be both safe and *effective.* They are a necessary preliminary stage before trials in humans may be carried out. Cf. *Phases of Clinical Trials.*

Predictive Validity

An instrument or measure that permits accurate predictions of future states of the *construct* in question.

Preference

Choices are usually assumed in economics to be the result of an interaction between preferences and *constraints,* where preferences are embodied in a *utility function.* 'Preferred' often means 'chosen rather than' (the *revealed preference* approach) but sometimes can mean a verbal statement of preference (the *stated preference* approach). Most economists take preferences as primitive concepts, about which one need not enquire much (for example, as to their origin, causes or merit). Difficulties start to arise when people have preferences about (other people's) preferences or when they have preferences that everyone agrees are appalling (for example, a preference – taste? – for cannibalism). Preferences are usually also taken as constant over time. This poses particular difficulties when studying processes (like much education and some health care) whose aim (or consequence, regardless of aim) is to change people's preferences. Whether preferences alone are a satisfactory basis for making judgments about *social welfare* is a matter that divides *welfarists* and *extra-welfarists* in *health economics*. See Brouwer et al. (2008).

In *discrete choice experiments*, especially those using *random utility theory*, there has been much discussion of ways of separating the scale of the estimated *parameters* and the magnitude of the random component. See Hensher et al. (1998). On whether preferences are a satisfactory basis for making judgments about health see Hausman (2006).

Preference Function

Same as *utility function*.

Preference Reversal

Preference reversal is a phenomenon widely observed in experiments designed to test the validity of the assumptions usually taken as underlying economic theories of behaviour (see *Utility*) and of *welfare*. In choices between pairs of simple monetary gambles, it has been found that individuals choose bets involving high probabilities of small gains (so-called P-bets) rather than bets offering a smaller chance of a larger prize (so-called $-bets) even though they attach a higher monetary value to the $-bets. This evidence has generated a controversy as to whether the preferences that are assumed to underlie people's choices are better seen as context-free (the usual economic point of view, in which the means through which a preference is elicited is supposed to be irrelevant) or context-sensitive (the usual psychological point of view, in which the experimental means can affect the outcome). See, for some *health economics* examples, Shackley and Donaldson (2002), Oliver (2006) and Bleichrodt and Pinto (2008). Cf. *Framing Effect*.

Preferred Provider Organization

In the US a PPO differs from a *health maintenance organization* (HMO) in that (1) the providers are paid not by the prepaying subscriber as with an HMO but by an *insurance* company or employer on a *fee-for-service* basis, (2) patients are usually able to avail themselves of non-PPO providers, albeit with substantial *copayments* and (3) there is no *primary care gatekeeper*. PPOs can range from a single hospital and its practising physicians contracting with a large employer to a national network of physicians, hospitals and laboratories that contract with insurers or employer groups. PPO contracts typically provide discounts from standard fees, incentives for plan members to use the contracting providers, and other *managed health care* cost containment methods. For a study of a PPO in the developing country context see Ranson et al. (2006).

Prenatal

Same as *antenatal*.

Prepayment

Payment by the individual to the provider in advance of receiving (or needing) treatment. For its effect on *demand* in the US see Manning et al. (1984).

Pre-post Study

Same as *before and after study*.

Prescription Drug

A drug that is available to a member of the public only when prescribed by a physician and obtained by a formally registered pharmacist. Cf. *Over-the-counter Drugs*. On *insurance* for prescription drugs see Grootendorst (2006).

Presenteeism

A term coined to parallel 'absenteeism'. Presenteeism is reduced productivity at work through sickness or accidents. An empirical study of the effects of depression on presenteeism is Berndt et al. (1998). For a third world example see Fox et al. (2004).

Present Value

The value at a particular point in time of a future *flow* of income, health, etc. See *Discounting*.

Preston Curve

A concave graphical relationship between *life expectancy* and *GDP* per capita. See Preston (1975).

Pre-test Probability

In *epidemiology*, the proportion of people with the target condition in the *population* at risk at a specific time (point *prevalence*) or time interval (period prevalence). It is commonly used by practising physicians to refer to the probability that a patient has a particular condition after the application of the physician's intuition or a clinical prediction rule but before ordering a diagnostic test.

Prevalence

The proportion of a *population* in which a particular medical condition prevails at a particular date (point prevalence) or over a period (period prevalence). Cf. *Incidence, Pre-test Probability*.

Prevention

Any procedure taken to stop a disease from either occurring (*primary prevention*) or worsening (*secondary prevention*). Some classifications also have *tertiary prevention*. For an economic review see Kenkel (2000). For actual *cost-effectiveness* results relating to the question 'Is prevention better than cure?' see Cohen et al. (2008). For examples of how *copayments* can deter preventive *screening*, see Ellis et al (2004) and Trivedi et al. (2008). Prevention (e.g. in the form of mass screening) can also be plain ineffective or harmful as well as cost-ineffective (Morris, 2002).

Price Discrimination

A process through which profit-seeking sellers in *price-searchers' markets* charge different prices for different increments of a good or service provided or charge different prices to different groups of buyers in *segmented markets*. In market-oriented systems of health care provision, the fact that rich patients may be charged more than poor ones for the same service has been held to be price discrimination (though the reasons given by its practitioners are of course different!).The diagram below shows the profit-maximizing price and output rate for a price-searcher who charges a single price (*P*). It is where *marginal cost* equals marginal revenue. The *demand curve* shows not only the maximum amount that will be purchased at each price but also the maximum amount that will be paid for each additional unit of the good or service in question. For example, the maximum payable for the very first unit is 0*b* and the maximum payable for an additional unit when consumption is already at *Q* is *Qa*. The segment of the demand curve *ba* indicates the maximum amounts that would be paid by a person with this demand curve for increments of output in the range 0*Q*. So the maximum the seller could obtain, if it were possible to charge the consumer the maximum *willingness to pay*, is the succession of prices in the segment, yielding additional profit *Pba*. In fact, in this case, one may readily see that the profit could be further increased by selling each unit at

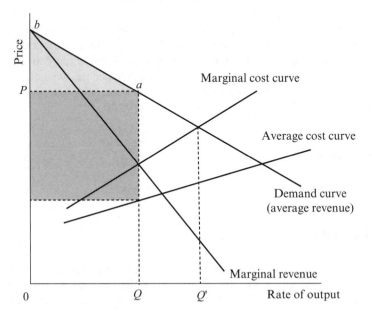

the maximum the buyer will pay up to output rate Q', where marginal cost equals price, which generates the same output rate as under price-taking conditions (though there is a transfer of *consumer's surplus* from consumer to seller, which does not happen under price-taking).

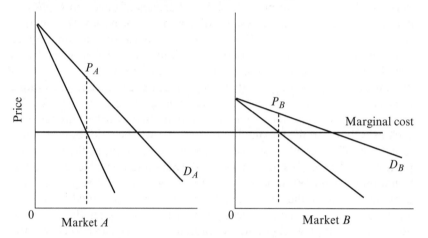

This form of price discrimination is rarely seen in explicit form. *Market segmentation* is, however, widely practised. In this situation, the output is produced, we assume, under identical conditions for two (or more) segmented markets as in the diagrams above. The conventional profit-maximizing price is charged so that in each market the marginal cost is set equal to marginal revenue (whether by careful design or chance) and the prices P_A and P_B are set in market segments A and B respectively. The higher price is charged in the segment with the lower price-elasticity. The classic economic study of price discrimination in medicine is Kessel (1958). For a study of pharmaceuticals see Danzon (1997a).

Price Index

See *Index Numbers*.

Price-making

A somewhat less satisfactory term for *price-searching*. It is less satisfactory because prices cannot be 'made' by firms independently of the demand for their product. Any firm that is not a *price-taker* has to discover (by guessing, searching for, copying similar others, doing market research on, running econometric *models* of, consulting entrails concerning. . .) the price that is most advantageous to it.

Price Mechanism

The market mechanism that sends price signals to producers about what to produce, to labour about whether to work and at what, and that allocates goods and services amongst consumers. Markets and the rules by which they operate are human creations and, in practice, are rarely perfect (not only in design but also in execution, since their operation is itself costly). It is usually assumed (by economists) that prices settle in an *equilibrium* from which they are disturbed by *exogenous* shocks. Provided the system as a whole is stable, a new equilibrium is expected to be established. The remarkable feature of this mechanism is that it works without any general external control or planning mechanism other than the existence (and enforcement) of exchangeable private property rights in goods and services, which define the uses to which the goods and services may be put (the so-called 'invisible hand') and the terms on which they may be traded. There are many reasons why any particular market system may be very slow to adapt to change, which are as fascinating to contemplate as is the 'invisible hand' itself. One should not jump to the conclusion, simply because a particular price mechanism operating in a particular market with its particular set of (human made) rules actually succeeds in allocating resources, that it does so in the best imaginable (or even best practically possible) way. Nor ought one to swing violently the other way and assume that markets are always and everywhere pernicious inventions. See also *General Equilibrium, Market Failure, Partial Equilibrium.*

Price-searching

The market phenomenon that exists when a seller's decision to increase or reduce the rate of supply of a good or service will change its market price. The problem for the seller is to find the *output* rate and price that maximize their *objective function* (usually assumed to be *profit*). Any firm that is not a *price-taker* has to discover (by guessing, searching for, copying similar others, doing market research on, running *econometric models* of, consulting entrails concerning. . .) the price that is most advantageous to it. Since the *demand curve* that confronts the seller will have negative slope (cf. the demand curve under *price-taking*) the point on this curve that is best from the seller's perspective may need to be searched for, it is not given (as under price-taking); hence the name. Whatever the method used by the seller to locate the 'best' price, in logic, the profit-maximizing price and rate of output are determined by equality between *marginal cost* and marginal revenue. This is shown in the diagram.

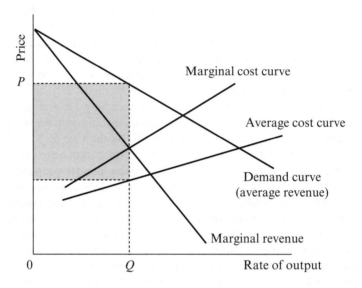

The shaded area shows profit (maximized) at the price P and output rate Q, where marginal cost equals marginal revenue. For a public sector health care analogy see Culyer et al. (2007). For some estimates suggesting that the huge consumer's surplus losses due to price-searching in the *pharmaceutical industry* are more than compensated by the advent of new products see Santerre and Vernon (2006).

Price-taking

A market phenomenon under which the seller of a good or service cannot affect the market price by varying their own rate of *output*. The *demand curve* as it appears to the firm is perfectly *elastic* – a horizontal line – and price is not a choice variable; it is given by the market and so has to be 'taken'. Hence the name.

Primacy Effect

A cognitive *bias* that arises in some experimental psychology and economics whereby subjects attach a disproportionate weight to early compared with later experiences or observations. Opposite of *recency effect*.

Primary Care

Primary care is that care provided by doctors and other generalists, including nurses, who are usually based in the community (as distinct from hospitals) who practise as generalists (see *General Practitioner*). A primary care professional (not always a physician) will frequently coordinate the care of *ambulatory* patients across various clinical (e.g. dental, ophthalmic or nursing care) and other local non-clinical professionals (e.g. social services). They also serve as the first point of contact (*gatekeepers*) to the health care system as a whole. They refer patients judged to be more appropriately diagnosed and treated in other parts of the system. Primary care services commonly include health promotion, disease prevention, vaccination, family planning, health maintenance, counselling, patient education and the initial diagnosis and first-line treatment of *acute* and *chronic* illnesses that are deemed not to require referral to a hospital-based specialist. Cf. S*econdary Care, Tertiary Care*. For some economics of primary care in the UK, see Scott (2000). For a comprehensive review of primary care in the third world, see Akin et al. (1985). On the general *cost-effectiveness* of primary care see Doherty and Govender (2004).

Primary Care Assessment Survey

The PCAS is a 51-item, patient-completed questionnaire embodying seven aspects of *primary care*: *access*; *continuity*; *comprehensiveness*; integration; clinical management; 'whole-person' orientation; and sustained clinical–patient relationship. The website for potential users is: http://160.109.101.132/icrhps/resprog/thi/pcas.asp (accessed 7 November 2009).

Primary Care Trust

PCTs are trusts (since 2002) within the English National Health Service with responsibility both for providing *primary care* services in their areas and for *commissioning* health care from hospitals and other specialist centres. They are required to develop health plans for their areas that are integrated with the plans of other agencies such as social services. PCTs have chief executives, chairs and boards comprising executive and non-executive directors. Cf. *Secondary Care Trust*.

Primary Prevention

Primary prevention entails actions intended to deter, delay or prevent the occurrence or development of disease or injury by reducing *risk factors*. The actions include behaviour-modifying actions such as health education, safety advice and legislation, as well as clinical interventions such as vaccination. Cf. *Secondary Prevention*. See *Prevention*.

Primary Research

This is research that generates the data it uses. It does not use (or mainly use) data, such as administrative data, collected for purposes other than the research purpose at hand. Cf. *Secondary Research*.

Principal

In health economics, this refers to one of the parties in the *agency relationship*. The principal is the party on whose behalf an *agent* acts.

Principal Component

A constructed variable using *factor analysis*, through which many (possibly) correlated *variables* are collapsed into a smaller number of uncorrelated variables.

Principal Component Analysis

A method of analysis that uses *principal components*. Cf. *Factor Analysis*.

Prior Distribution

The *probability distribution* of a *variable* in the minds of analysts before they have collected any data. See *Bayesian Method.*

Prioritarianism

An approach to *social welfare* that embodies both the usual *neoclassical economic* welfarist principles with interpersonal weights, typically to give larger weights (i.e. priority) to the worst off in a distribution of health, income, etc. See Kagan (1997) and Jensen (2003).

Priority Setting

Ordering possible actions, policies or strategies in such a way that those that ought most to be chosen are ranked at the top. For an application of economic methods to research priorities see Claxton and Posnett (1996) and to choice of health care technologies Laupacis et al. (1992).

Prior Probability

A view about the probability of an event (which may be objectively or subjectively based) prior to the receipt of other information pertinent to the *likelihood* of that event. See *Bayesian Method.*

Probabilistic Sensitivity Analysis

A technique in *cost–effectiveness analysis* and *decision analysis* in which *probability distributions* are created for each *factor* about which there is uncertainty. By simulating the consequences of random drawings from these distributions, it enables judgments to be formed about the *robustness* of decisions in relation to each factor. Cf. *Deterministic Sensitivity Analysis.* See Ades et al. (2003) and Claxton et al. (2005).

Probability

The *frequentist* definition is the proportion of times (as a decimal fraction) an event would occur if an experiment were repeated a large number of times. More generally, the chances (however assessed) of an event occurring. It lies between 0 and +1. See *Bayesian Method, Likelihood.*

Probability Distribution

In statistics, this is a mathematical representation of the relative *likelihood* of each of the discrete values that a *variable* might take or the probability of each *value* falling within a particular interval if the variable is *continuous.*

Probit Model

A generalized linear statistical *model* with *binary dependent variable*s based on the cumulative *normal distribution.* Its use is generally associated with the *maximum likelihood estimation* procedure instead of *ordinary least squares* estimation. The idea is to posit an underlying *continuous* latent variable, such that, given binary date, whether the score is 0 or 1 depends upon a critical value of the latent variable. Thus, if the binary variable is sick/well, the critical *threshold* might be a stipulated value of a *quality-adjusted life-year.* The latent variable (QALYs) is then posited to be a linear function of other variables including unobservable ones and the *error term* is assumed to be normally distributed. Cf. *Logit Model.* Introduced in Bliss (1935). For a *health economics* application see Buchmueller and Feldstein (1997) and Contoyannis and Jones (2004).

Procedural Invariance

This is the idea that the rankings or *utility* scores attached to entities like health states in experiments should be invariant with respect to the procedure used to elicit them. It requires that logically equivalent procedures for expressing *preferences* should yield identical results in experiments. If a subject stipulates that 20 years of life in full health is equivalent to 40 years of life with an impairment, procedural invariance requires that the subject display the same *indifference* if asked instead to specify the number of years with the impairment considered to be equivalent to 20 years of good health. Propositions in welfare economics critically depend upon procedural invariance. Unfortunately, empirical research has displayed that people systematically violate procedural invariance. See *Extra-welfarism, Utility, Welfare*. See Tversky et al. (1988). In the context of valuing QALYs, see Pinto et al. (2009). Cf. *Preference Reversal*. For other *health economics* examples, see Lenert et al. (1998) and Lenert and Treadwell (1999).

Process Utility

The idea that *utility* might be gained from a process, like being consulted, rather than a health *outcome* following consultation, or the act of gambling rather than its expected outcome. See *Extra-welfarism*. For an application to the role of informal carers, see Brouwer et al. (2005).

Proctology

A surgical speciality that dealt with disorders of the rectum and anus. Now known as colorectal surgery.

Producer Sovereignty

Not a standard term of art in economics though, on grounds of fairness, it ought to have the same status as *consumer sovereignty*. If the term existed, it would presumably describe a situation in which producers of goods (and services) determined the character and quantity of *outputs*, who would consume them and on what terms. The medical care market would seem an obviously approximate case, driven by the *information asymmetry* that denies (as some seem to believe) non-doctors the ability to know their own *needs*.

Producer's Surplus

The difference between what a producer receives and the minimum required to compensate the producer for producing/selling. In the diagram, the marginal cost curve (supply curve) in a *price-takers' market* defines the lower boundary of the producer's surplus (the shaded area). Cf. *Consumer's Surplus*.

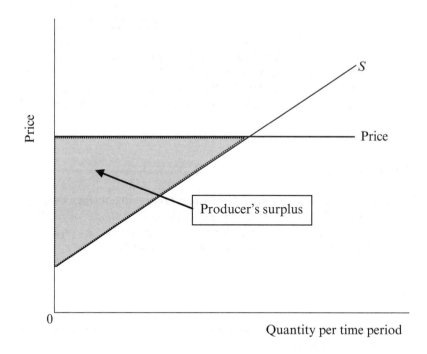

Production Frontier

Same as *production possibilities curve.*

Production Function

A technical relationship between *inputs* and the maximum *outputs* or *outcomes* of any procedure or process. Also sometimes referred to as the 'technology matrix'. Thus a production function may relate the maximum number of patients that can be treated in a hospital over a period of time to a variety of input flows like doctor- and nurse-hours, and beds. For econometric purposes the relationship is usually postulated to be in a particular mathematical form, of which one is the so-called *Cobb–Douglas production function*, $X = kA^{\alpha}B^{\beta}$ where X is the rate of *output* (or throughput of clients), k, α and β are positive constants, and A and B are rates of use of two *inputs*. The production function specifies efficient combinations of inputs required at each rate of output, *viz.*, the fewest of each needed to produce that output (see *Efficiency*). Depending on the values of *parameters* like a and b an equal proportional increase in all inputs may entail either a larger, smaller or equal increase in output. This corresponds to *increasing, decreasing* or *constant returns to scale*. For one of many studies indicating the presence of *diminishing returns to scale* see Doherty (1990). For increasing returns see Valdmanis et al. (2003). For constant returns, see Lohrisch et al. (2006). A pioneering study is Auster et al. (1969). See *Constant Elasticity of Substitution Production Function, Household Production Function, Leontief Production Function, Translog Production Function.*

Production Possibilities Curve

A *locus* indicating the boundary between all the combinations of goods and services that an economy can produce with given resources and technologies, and those it cannot. Its slope is the *marginal rate of transformation*, showing in two dimensions the minimum amount of one good or service that must be sacrificed in order to produce an additional unit of the other (or the maximum that can be produced of one for a given sacrifice of the other). Also known as a production frontier or *transformation curve.*

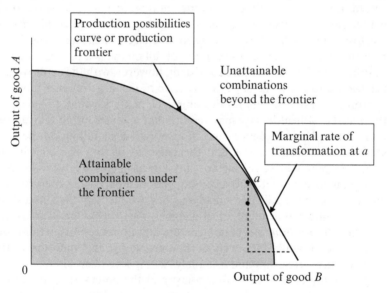

Productivity

This refers to the *output* of goods and services produced by one or more *factors of production. Total factor productivity* is the rate of output divided by the amount of all *inputs* used in production where each input is usually weighted by its share in total cost. The rate of growth of total factor productivity is sometimes also referred to as the *residual* after the contributions of *capital* and labour to the growth of *gross domestic product* have been accounted for. See Smith et al. (2008) for a *health economics* study. The impact of better health on productivity is difficult to measure with precision but nearly everyone agrees that it is positive and marked (though high income also gives rise to better health). On this aspect of productivity in a third world context see Schultz (2005). See also *Average Product, Marginal Product*. See also Martin et al. (2008). A general review is Burgess (2006).

Productivity Cost

A substitute term for *indirect cost* (or for a part of indirect costs) often chosen so as to avoid confusion with the accountants' usage of 'indirect cost'. A productivity cost is the *opportunity cost* of an individual's time not spent in productive work activity and it is generally conceived as including valued uses for leisure time. The status of this category of cost has been a matter of controversy, with some arguing that, if the (*extra-welfarist*) *perspective* from which a study is being conducted considers health as the only relevant outcome, then costs that do not fall on the health sector ought to be disregarded. It seems more consistent, however, with the extra-welfarist perspective to allow the *objective function* to include whatever those with appropriate responsibility for deciding such matters want it to include. So the minister of health (say) may require that analyses are to take account both of health consequences and of resources costs falling on the health services, the social services and the personal sector. The conventional *welfarist* approach would include any effects that directly or indirectly affect individuals' utilities. If a consequence of a particular intervention to improve health actually does increase work productivity then, as a strictly practical matter, this might affect incomes, the *demand for health services* (and health care *insurance*) and generate additional resources to produce health care. It would then seem curmudgeonly for any 'minister' to treat such effects as irrelevant and ask analysts to ignore them.

Most analysts have expressed concern at the potential *equity* implications of including work-related productivity costs, fearing that this might lead to systematic *bias* in technologies that favours the working population over children, the unemployed and the retired, or the very productive over the not so productive. Of course, any procedure that ruled these costs out of all consideration would then deny decision-makers the opportunity of assessing them and forming a judgment about their significance for distributional equity. That would seem politically presumptuous of analysts. See also *Friction Costs, Human Capital*. See, for contrasting views, Brouwer et al. (1998) and Weinstein et al. (1998).

Professional Standards Review Organizations

Professional standards review organizations (PSROs) were mandated under United States Public Law 92-603 to promote *cost containment* in hospitals by reducing '*overutilization*' while maintaining 'proper quality of care'. PSROs are locally based vetting agencies responsible for conducting reviews of the quality and appropriateness of hospital services. See *Utilization*.

Profit

The economic concept of profit differs from the accounting concept by deducting from revenue not only the obvious costs of production but also the *opportunity costs* of owners' time (especially important in small businesses like nursing homes) and the opportunity cost of *capital* (effectively the *rate of return* that could be earned on the *assets* if they were invested in a risk-free asset like a government bond adjusted for the kind of risk of default common to firms of this size and type). Economic profit is always less than accounting profit. In a perfectly competitive economy, profits are zero when it is in *equilibrium*.

The legitimate role of profit-seeking in health care provision has concerned health economists from the earliest days of the sub-discipline, both in order to understand better why the *non-profit* organization is so frequently found, even in market-oriented economies, and whether on balance and in what circumstances it can be counted as a good thing. Opinion amongst economists is unlikely, however, to reach a consensus, given the wider political connotations of the issue. The pioneering piece is Newhouse (1970). Some standard references are Pauly and Redisch (1973), Frank and Salkever (1994), Keeler et al. (1999) and Sloan (2000). A discussion in the third world context is in Patouillard et al. (2007). See *Competition, For-profit, Non-profit*.

Prognosis

A forecast of the future progress and pattern of a disease and its symptoms.

Program for Assessment of Technology in Health

This research unit performs economic evaluations and *health technology assessments* mainly for the Ministry of Health and Long Term Care in Ontario, Canada. It is a part of the Centre for Evaluation of Medicines at McMaster University. Its website is available at: http://www.thecem.net/path.php (accessed 8 November 2009).

Programme Budgeting

Similar to *output budgeting* except that the basis for classification is the targeted client group (the 'programme') rather than the *output* or *outcome* in question. Examples include maternity care, child care and care of the elderly. Cf. *Programme Budgeting and Marginal analysis*.

Programme Budgeting and Marginal Analysis

PBMA combines *programme budgeting* with *marginal analysis* to provide a means of both determining which resources have been allocated to which programme goals and to analyse the opportunity cost of marginal changes in the sizes of programmes and the mix of *inputs* in comparison with the consequential changes in goal *outcomes*. See Cohen (1994), Mitton and Donaldson (2001) and Ruta et al. (2005).

Progressivity

Usually relates to the proportion of *household* or personal income that is taken in taxes; a progressive tax is one for which the proportion of income taken in tax rises as income rises, a *regressive* tax is one for which that proportion falls, and a *proportional* tax is one for which it remains constant. Cf. *Regressivity*. See *Ability to Pay*. For a health care financing example, see O'Donnell et al. (2008) Chapter 16.

PROM

Acronym for *patient-reported outcome measure*.

Prominence Effect

A type of *bias*. In the *willingness-to-pay* and some of the experimental psychological literature it has been found that when people are asked to provide a valuation of something using numerical scales with which they have been provided they tend to select prominent values such as 1, 2, 5, 10, 20, 50, 100. See Fischer and Hawkins (1993).

Proof of Principle

The empirical establishment that a prototype technology has its predicted effect on an appropriate biological marker. With drugs, this is the main purpose of *Phase II trials*.

Propensity Score

In *observational studies*, the propensity score is the *conditional probability* of treatment or exposure, given various background variables. See Rosenbaum and Rubin (1983).

Proportional Hazards Regression Model

Same as *Cox proportional hazards model*.

Proportionality

Usually relates to the proportion of *household* or personal income that is taken in taxes; a proportional tax is one for which the proportion of income taken in tax is constant whatever the size of income. A *regressive* tax is one for which that proportion falls. A *progressive* tax is one for which it rises.

Proprietary Drug

A drug with a trade name and *patent* protection.

Prospective Cohort Study

Same as *observational cohort study*. An observational study of a *cohort* of initially disease-free individuals whose exposure to *risk factors* and whose health is followed over a period of time, or the observational study of a cohort of individuals already having a disease or some risk factor to examine their exposure to different treatments and health over time. It is usually regarded as the design of choice for an observational study. Cf. *Retrospective Cohort Study*.

Prospective Payment System

A mechanism through which US *Medicare* reimburses hospitals on the basis of a given sum per case in a *diagnosis-related group* rather than retrospectively in the light of the actual costs (claimed to have been) incurred. See Ellis and McGuire (1986, 1996) and Cutler (1995).

Prospective Reimbursement

A method of reimbursing health service providers (especially hospitals) by establishing rates of payment in advance, which are paid regardless of the costs in actual individual cases. See *Prospective Payment System*. See Ellis and McGuire (1986, 1996).

Prospective Study

An empirical (usually observational) study in which individuals are followed forward from a particular date and the effect of future events on them is investigated. See *Prospective Cohort Study*.

Prospect Theory

An approach to decisions under uncertainty that provides an alternative account for the phenomenon of *risk aversion* to that of *expected utility theory* and that helps to explain why *framing effects* exist. Prospect theory differs from *expected utility theory* in assigning 'decision weights' rather than probabilities to *outcomes* and in assuming that decision weights tend to overweight small probabilities and underweight moderate and high probabilities. It also differs from expected utility theory in that it replaces the notion of *utility* with 'value', defined in terms of deviations from a reference point. The value function has a different shape for gains and losses. For losses it is convex and steep, for gains it is concave and flatter. Although hardly in current use in *health economics* it is likely to make an appearance in the future, initially, perhaps, in topics that use experimental methods like *health status* measurement. Cf. *Expected Utility Theory, Regret Theory*. See *Reflection Effect, Utility*. See Kahneman and Tversky (1979). See Oliver (2003b) and, for an application which failed see Feeny and Eng (2005).

Prosthetics

The clinical speciality dealing with prostheses or prosthetic devices, or any artificial extension that replaces a missing body part, like artificial limbs. See *Physiatry*.

Protected Values

Values that are not traded-off against other values. A phenomenon that is commonly met in studies of preference elicitation, when people, for example, find it impossible to put a value of reducing the probability of death. It is a direct denial of the *comparison axiom* that underpins most economic theories of choice. See Tetlock (2003).

Protest Zero

A zero score given to an object of choice in an economic experiment that does not reveal the subject's true valuation of the object but reveals instead a need to register a 'protest'.

PSA

Acronym for *probabilistic sensitivity analysis*. (Also prostate-specific antigen.)

PSRO

Acronym for *professional standards review organizations*.

Psychiatry

The medical speciality concerned with mental illness.

PTO

Acronym for *person trade-off method* (as well as for 'please turn over').

Publication Bias

A *bias* in reports on the published literature arising from the criteria (which may in part be arbitrary) used by editors to select articles for journals. The bias includes a preference for 'new' results (rather than confirmation of 'old' ones), 'positive' results (rather than 'we don't know') and familiar languages (rather those that are unfamiliar to the review team). See *File-drawer Problem, Systematic Review*.

Public Choice Theory

Public choice theory is based on the idea that individuals in public positions make decisions according to their own interest rather than voluntarily follow any rules for maximizing *social welfare*. See *Median Voter Model*. Black (1948) was an early pioneer and subsequent developments were much influenced by Buchanan and Tullock (1962). See Goddard et al. (2006) for a *health economics* application.

Public Good

A good or service that it is not possible to exclude people from consuming once any is produced. Clean air is a classic example and clean water another, though one could be avoided by migration to an urban environment and the other (in the UK and in 1999) by swimming off one of the 57 British beaches named by the European Commission as having water too polluted for safe swimming (there were fortunately only two such beaches seven years later!). Public goods are non-rival in the sense that providing more for one person does not entail the other having any less (the marginal *opportunity cost* of provision to another consumer is zero). Most public goods are not wholly public in this sense and whether health care itself has significant public good characteristics is a point of debate. Some programmes (especially those called 'public health') have considerable public good characteristics and even the care consumed by an individual may have a public aspect by virtue of any 'sympathy' that others may feel, so the consumption of one may in this way affect the *utility* of many others. Thus, if the alleviation of someone's ill-health is valued by any other than that individual, and there is more than one such externally affected person, then the *externality* will have the *attribute* of publicness.

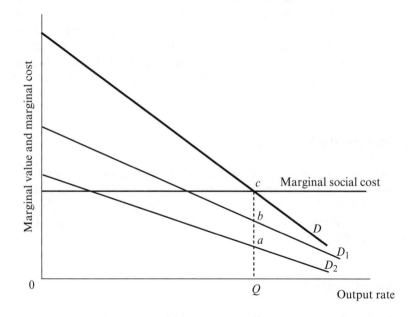

The first-order rule for optimizing the *output* of a public good entails adding the *marginal value* each consumer attaches to the good at a variety of outputs and selecting that output at which the sum of the marginal values (*marginal social value*) is equal to *marginal social cost*. In the diagram, the two *demand curves* D_1 and D_2 are to be interpreted as *marginal value curves* for two individuals, 1 and 2. The boldly drawn curve D is the vertical summation of these two curves. At output rate Q, which is the optimal rate, the individuals value additions to the output rate at amounts Qa and Qb, whose sum, Qc, the marginal social value, is equal to the marginal social cost. Note that, in economics, a public good is not defined by whether it is produced in the public sector – which also produces private goods (i.e. ones that do not have the characteristics described above) – or the private (where the charitable sector often produces public goods). See *External Effects, Median Voter Model, Public Health Medicine.*

Public Health

Public health is similar to *population health*, and draws on social epidemiology to embrace the widest range of *determinants* of health in a society; a broader range of technologies for addressing them than is encompassed in *public health medicine*, such as better parenting for childhood development, better housing, even greater equality of income and wealth; and the broader range of institutional pathways and vectors of influence implied by the forgoing, such as schooling and schools, working and workplace. To tackle health effectively in this fashion plainly involves many disciples and professions.

Public Health Medicine

The practice of disease prevention and health promotion through the use of collective agencies and actions (for example, population vaccination, safety at work, health education, water purification). Virtually the same as *social medicine*. For some economics of public health see Bishai and Adam (2006).

Public–Private Mix

The public–private mix of funding for health care is an inevitable simultaneous source of controversy and passion, with various sides arguing that the one causes great damage to the other. Similar comments apply to the public–private mix in health care delivery (which is not the same as the mix of *non-profit* and *for-profit* agencies on the delivery side of things). For a refreshingly cool look at these matters see Flood et al. (2004) and Maynard (2005). For a study of the interaction of public and private *insurance* see Besley et al. (1998) and of public and private care Propper et al. (2005).

PubMed

The host database for *MEDLINE®* maintained by the US National Library of Medicine, National Institutes of Health.

Pulmonary Medicine

The medical speciality concerned with diseases and abnormalities of the lungs. See also *Respiratory Medicine*.

Purchaser

A term that has acquired a special meaning in the English *National Health Service*, where it denotes various collective agencies such as *Strategic Health Authorities* or *Primary Care Trusts* that have statutory powers and centrally determined budgets to commission health care and related services on behalf of local communities. See *Block Contract*, *Payment by Results*, *Purchaser–Provider Split*.

Purchaser–Provider Split

An aspect of *internal markets* for health care in which the purchasing or *commissioning* of services on behalf of groups of the *population* (often geographically defined) is not done by providers of services. See *Commissioning*.

Purchasing Power Parity

Rates of currency conversion that eliminate the differences in price levels between countries are termed purchasing power parity rates of exchange. Each is the ratio of price levels in two jurisdictions having different currencies, where the prices used are those of a common bundle of goods and services. This is sometimes called 'absolute purchasing power parity' to differentiate it from relative PPP, which states that the rate of appreciation of a currency is equal to the difference in inflation rates between it and that in another jurisdiction. The purpose of PPPs is to obtain more reliable ways of making international economic comparisons (for example, of health care expenditures) than can be done by using *exchange rates* (which are subject to many other *determinants*). The *Organisation for Economic Co-operation and Development* (OECD) publishes PPP rates for OECD countries that are regularly updated and compared with exchange rates. See http://www.oecd.org/document/47/0,3343,en_2649_34357_36202863 _1_1_1_1,00.html (accessed 9 November 2009). For an analysis of the issues at a less aggregated level (comparing international *cost–effectiveness analysis*) see Wordsworth and Ludbrook (2005).

Purposive Sample

A *sample* of a set of subjects chosen not randomly but with particular criteria in mind (for example, they are the children of parents with some genetic characteristic of interest). Often used in *qualitative analysis*. Cf. *Consecutive Sampling, Random Sample*. For an example see Boutin-Foster (2005).

PV+

Another acronym for *positive predictive value, PPV*.

PV–

Another acronym for *negative predictive value, NPV*.

p-value

The probability, when the *null hypothesis* is true, of obtaining a sample result that is at least as unlikely as what is observed. It is often called *statistical significance*. The *p*-value is a statement about the *null hypothesis*. A numerically small value indicates a rejection of the null hypothesis. The convention is to use $p = 0.05$ as the borderline. Hence if a test yields a *p*-value lower than this the result is said to be (statistically) 'significant at the 5 per cent level'.

PYLL

Acronym for *patient years of life lost*.

Q

QALE

Acronym for *Quality-adjusted Life-expectancy*. See Williams (1997).

QALY

Acronym for *quality-adjusted life-year*.

Qualitative Analysis

This term is used in two distinct senses. The first refers straightforwardly to any kind of analysis that focuses on the direction of causation or change (e.g. positive/negative, better/worse) or their relative size, not their absolute magnitude. The second kind is an approach to the understanding of social phenomena that is largely exploratory and interpretive and intended to be a means through which general (usually social scientific) presumptions or high-level general theorizing may be crafted into more specific hypotheses and theories – hypothesis generating rather than hypothesis testing. It produces findings not usually arrived at by means of statistical procedures or other quantitative techniques, and may include in-depth (often deliberately unstructured) interviews, *focus groups*, participant observation, story-telling, use of 'key informants', grounded theory and documentary analysis.

See, for a general text, Marshall and Rossman (2006). Qualitative methods have been used by health economists to develop outcome measures (see, for example, Grewal et al., 2006), to explore the use of techniques for eliciting preferences (see, for example, R. Smith, 2007), and for broader examination of health care organizations, particularly in relation to priority setting (see, for example, Coast, 2001; Bryan et al., 2007). For discussions of the use of qualitative analysis in health economics see Coast (1999), Mannion and Small (1999), Coast et al. (2004) and Small and Mannion (2005). Cf. *Quantitative Analysis*.

Qualitative Effect

The sign (positive or negative) of the effect of one *variable* on another. The magnitude of the effect is quantitative rather than qualitative.

Qualitative Research

Same as *qualitative analysis*.

Quality

The quality of health care is somewhat nebulous, not least as regards the criteria used to judge it (clinical process, hotel services, health outcomes, frequency of *adverse events*, other outcomes. . .). It has nonetheless been embodied in various ways in economic models of hospitals, nursing homes, nurses and physicians, not least because it seems to be widely thought that higher quality entails higher costs. See Newhouse (1970) and Ma (1994). For the insights of a non-economist see Donabedian (1988). On nursing homes: Grabowski and Norton (2006). Effects of *competition* on quality in general: Gowrisankaran and Town (2003). The association between staffing levels and types of staff and patient health has been explored somewhat. See e.g. Lankshear et al. (2005). See, for a depressing view across adult health care in the US McGlynn et al. (2003). On quality-adjusted cost functions see Gertler and Waldman (1992). On competition between hospitals in the UK, see Propper et al. (2004). On low-income countries see, for example, Das et al. (2008) and, for behaviourally revealed quality judgments by clients in Tanzania, Leonard et al. (2002). On unintended consequences of quality control mechanisms see Werner and Asch (2005).

Quality-adjusted Life-expectancy

Life-expectancy using *quality-adjusted life-years* rather than years of life. See Williams (1997).

Quality-adjusted Life-year

The quality-adjusted life-year (QALY) is a generic measure of *health-related quality of life* that takes into account both the quantity and the quality of life generated by interventions. The invention and further development of the QALY was a response to the treatment of health outcomes solely in terms of survival without any weight being given to the quality of the additional years of life. A year of perfect health is scaled to be 'worth' 1 and a year of less than perfect health 'worth' less than 1. Death is commonly indicated by 0, though in some situations there may be states regarded as worse than death and which would have negative numbers attached to them. Thus, an intervention that results in a patient living for an additional five years rather than dying within one year, but where quality of life fell from 1 to 0.6 generates five years extra life with a quality of 0.6 (= 3.0) less one year of reduced quality $(1 - 0.6)$ (= 0.4), so the (net) QALYs generated by the intervention are $3.0 - 0.4$ (= 2.6).

The status of the QALY has been the subject of some debate and not a little confusion. Is it a measure of preference for health states? Is it a measure of health outcome that is independent of health states? Does it possess *construct validity*? Is it a *utility* measure of someone's preferences (the fact that its construction may entail the use of utility theory does not itself necessarily imply that it is a measure of anyone's preference)? Is it *cardinal* or *ordinal*? Is it consistent with the conventions of *welfare economics* or is it inescapably a part of *extra-welfarism*? What *value judgments* does it embody and what is their acceptability? What empirical forms of it exist and how do they differ?

A QALY is customarily generated using one of three empirical (experimental) methods: *expected utility theory* (in particular, the technique known as the *standard gamble*), the *time trade-off* and the *person trade-off*. These methods generate a form of cardinal utility measure that is either on an *interval scale* or a *ratio scale* (usually, the latter is required). The interval scale does not, however, permit interpersonal comparisons of the 'Individual A is twice as ill as individual B' sort.

The extra-welfarist interpretation of QALYs is that they are socially chosen cardinal indicators of health or *health gain* that are interval or ratio scales depending on their method of construction. It is as though the social welfare function is separable into different types of measure, some of which may be utility measures but one of which is, in any event, health or health gain. The outputs of public programmes, of which health is typically one, are determined directly by political decision-makers, as are the budgets allocated to each and, if each budget is efficiently used to maximize its intended outputs, the incremental cost-effectiveness of each programme is indirectly determined by the two decisions about outputs and budgets.

The weights applied to various components of the QALY may reflect *preferences* (for example, of people expected to be beneficiaries) but otherwise are *value judgments* decided in some other way by people deemed to be appropriate judges of such matters. On this interpretation, interpersonal comparisons can be explicitly made, as can (at least in principle) whole *distributions* of health (or health gain), thus enabling questions of *equity* to be addressed directly. This has given rise to various proposals for weighting QALYs according to who gets them (e.g. old vs. young, male vs. female, married vs. single), how many you already have (relatively well vs. relatively sick), and how many you have already had (a life time of *chronic disability* vs. a recently acquired disability). See *Health-related Quality of Life*. See Williams (1974), Torrance (1986), Loomes and McKenzie (1989), Torrance and Feeny (1989), Nord (1992a, b), Broome (1993), Anand (1999), Dolan et al. (1996b) and Brazier et al. (2007). For an interesting attempt to interpret QALYs in a welfarist fashion, see Adler (2006). On the (variable) practice of QALY calculation, see Richardson and Manca (2004). On the use of *utility* theory in health measurement see Hausman (2006).

Quality of Life

An index or profile of the quality of a year of life embodying the value judgments of selected judges, clients or others. See *Health-related Quality of Life*, *Quality-adjusted Life-years*, *Utility*.

Quality of Well-being Scale

The QWB scale is a generic preference-weighted measure combining three scales of functioning with a measure of symptoms and problems on a scale of 0 (death) to 1.0 (full health). This measure is then weighted according to population-based preference weights and combined with expected life-years to generate quality-adjusted life-years. See *Health-related Quality of Life*. See Kaplan and Anderson (1990).

Quantile

When a *continuous variable* is split for convenience into equal-sized chunks of data the cut-off points between them are called quantiles. Thus, if there are four such groups (*quartiles*), each containing 25 per cent of the data, there are three quantile cut-off points, the central one being the *median*. Common divisions are *tertiles* (three groups), *quartiles* (four), *quintiles* (five), *deciles* (ten), *centiles* or *percentiles* (100).

Quantitative Analysis

An analysis dealing in measured quantities of entities. Cf. *Qualitative Analysis*.

Quartile

When a *continuous variable* is split for convenience into four equal-sized chunks of data the cut-off points between them are called quartiles. See *Quantile*.

Quasi-experimental Research

Comparative research in which the assignment of subjects to *comparator* groups is not random or a *control group* is not used.

Quasi-market

Same as *internal market*.

Quasi-random Allocation

Non-random methods of allocating people to the *arms* of a *trial*. Common methods include allocation by date of birth, medical record number and choosing alternate persons. These methods are all subject to *selection bias*.

Queue

Queues seem to be endemic in health care. Most of them are not the standing-in-line type, a major *opportunity cost* of which for the person waiting is the time not available for alternative uses. Queues mostly represent the postponement of care (including diagnostic care), whose consequences can vary from the non-existent (as when restoration to health occurs through natural processes) to the catastrophic (as when a rapidly fatal condition goes undiagnosed or untreated). In most Western countries with waiting lists, people are mainly waiting for *elective surgery*.

In *welfare* terms what probably matters more than the numbers waiting is the time spent waiting, and the hazards to which that might expose the waiter: for example, someone waiting for a hip replacement steadily loses muscle strength, becomes more vulnerable to falls and also suffers pain and reduced mobility while a large number of waiting people may wait only for trivial periods. See *Waiting List*. See Worthington (1991), Hoel and Saether (2003), Siciliani and Hurst (2004) and Willcox et al. (2007).

*Quick*DASH

The *Quick*DASH is a shortened version of the *DASH* Outcome Measure. Instead of 30 items, the *Quick*DASH uses 11 items to measure physical function and symptoms in persons with any or multiple musculoskeletal disorders of the arms, shoulders and hands. Its website is available at: http://www.dash.iwh.on.ca/conditions.htm (accessed 9 November 2009). See *Disabilities of the Arm, Shoulder and Hand*.

Quintile

When a *continuous variable* is split for convenience into five equal-sized chunks of data the cut-off points between them are called quintiles. See *Quantile*.

QoL

Acronym for *Quality of Life*.

Quota Sample

A *sample* chosen in such a way that the proportion of subjects possessing a certain characteristic is the same as in the population from which the sample comes.

QWB

Acronym for *quality of well-being*.

R

Radiography

The diagnostic use of radiation such as X-rays to make images.

Radiology

The science of X-rays and radiation in imaging and treatment processes.

Radiotherapy

The treatment of cancer by X-rays or gamma rays to destroy cancer cells. Cf. *Nuclear Medicine*.

Ramsey Pricing

This is a pricing principle that minimizes the *welfare* loss when production is *monopolistic* and subject to a minimum *profit constraint*. The rule is to set prices so as to exceed *marginal cost* by a sum that is inversely proportional to the *elasticities* of *demand*. Also known as the 'inverse elasticity rule'. See Ramsey (1927). For *health economics* applications see Wedig (1993) and Danzon and Towse (2003). Cf. *Price Discrimination*.

Random Effects Model

This is a statistical way of controlling for *omitted variable bias* when using *panel data*. The method differs from the *fixed effects model* by allowing the fixed differentials between groups to vary at random. See, for an example, Rice and Jones (1997) and Burgess et al. (2005).

Random High

A random high is a kind of *false positive* in clinical trials and it occurs when implausibly high treatment effects are observed – often in small samples. Premature stopping is inherently prone to this *bias*.

Randomized Clinical Trial

Same as *randomized controlled trial*.

Randomized Controlled Trial

A *trial* in which patients (or physicians, or settings of care, etc.) are allocated to interventions (not necessarily clinical ones) and *comparators* in a random fashion. The essential idea is that randomization removes *confounding* effects and reduces *bias* in the result. Also known in strictly clinical circles as a 'randomized clinical trial'.

Randomizing

Allocating patients, subjects, physicians, settings (etc.) to *alternative* interventions in a *controlled trial* in a random fashion (i.e. by chance).

Random Number Generation

Random numbers and pseudo random numbers can be generated in many ways, some old-fashioned, like tossing a fair coin or drawing numbers from an urn; some using computer *algorithms*; some using yet other methods. See Gentle (2003). (Also a song from the sexually ambiguous musical *Hedwig and the Angry Inch*.)

Random Permuted Blocks

A random method of assigning equal numbers of participants to comparison groups. Permuted blocks are used in *trials* using *stratified randomization*. Also called *blocking*.

Random Sample

A *sample* of individuals or observations drawn from a population from which each has an equal chance of being selected.

Random Utility Function

See *Random Utility Theory*.

Random Utility Theory

A procedure in which *utility functions* are modelled as having a random element to reflect uncertainty about such factors as the full characteristics of a service or measurement error that arise from imperfect information. Cf. *Discrete Choice Analysis*. See Luce and Suppes (1965) and Manski (1977). In health economics see Gyrd-Hansen (2004).

Range

The difference between the smallest and the largest in a set of numbers.

Range Bias

The distorting effect that stating the upper and lower ends of a scale can have on subjects' views about the likely *willingness to pay* in a *contingent valuation* study. See *Bias*. See Whynes et al. (2004).

Rank Correlation Coefficient

See *Spearman's Rank Correlation Coefficient*.

Rank Dependence

A type of *model* that is often used in the analysis of decisions under uncertainty. In *health economics* it refers to a system for *equity* weighting *quality-adjusted life-years* (QALYs) in a *social welfare function*. The weight depends on each individual's relative ranking in terms of expected lifetime QALYs. See Bleichrodt et al. (2004).

Rank-dependent Expected Utility

Rank-dependent utility theory models *expected utility* by using non-linear perceptions of *probabilities*. It was introduced in Quiggin (1993).

Ratchet Effect

An effect in *internal market* negotiations between purchasers and providers by which the purchaser utilizes knowledge from previous negotiations to ratchet up the expected level of *performance* at the same price or *global budget*. See *Purchaser–Provider Split*.

Rate of Interest

Interest is the amount of money payable to a lender for lending a given amount for a period. The interest rate is that amount divided by the sum that is lent, usually on the assumption that the period is one year, and expressed as a percentage. See *Discounting*.

Rate of Return

The rate of discount (see *Discounting*) that makes the *present value* of a stream of money *costs* and *benefits* over time equal to zero. See *Internal Rate of Return*.

Rational Addiction

The idea that *addiction* may be explained in terms of the usual economic *axioms* of *utility* or *expected utility theory*. The classic economic theory of addiction is to be found in Becker and Murphy (1988). See also Gruber and Köszegi (2001) and Bernheim and Rangel (2004).

Rational Drug Design

A focused strategy for organizing commercial pharmaceuticals research based on knowledge of the workings of proteins in human biology. Cimetidine, the prototypical H_2-receptor antagonist, was one of the first drugs produced via this method. It was pioneered by the physiologist and pharmacologist Nobel Laureate Sir James Black.

Rationality

Generally used by economists to refer to behaviour that is consistent with the *axioms* of *utility* or *expected utility theory*. This idea of rationality has been pretty well attacked. An early assault was from Keynes on the ground that its axioms were not obeyed by at least some financially successful people who ought not to be dubbed 'irrational' in light of the evidence. It has been attacked also because it is too narrow in excluding the emotional effects of not knowing things ahead of time, effects such as anxiety, disappointment and regret, because it is too demanding, and because its literal pursuit might actually reduce welfare (see *Bounded Rationality*). Moreover, identifying rationality as consistency with the axioms of a theory invites the unhelpful conclusion, every time any of these is actually violated (for example, in a controlled experiment), not that the theory is perhaps wrong but that the human subject in question is an irrational being.

It is useful to keep in mind the distinction between *positive* and *normative* economics. In the former, there is no need to use the word 'rational' at all. The axioms of *utility theory* say it all and one seeks only to account for or predict what actually happens, not what ought to happen if people behaved consistently with any concept of rationality. To the extent that their behaviour flouts the axioms, then the theory is empirically the weaker for it, since any empirical refutation of an axiom is a refutation of the theory (whether one calls it 'rationality' or anything else). Frequent flouting is, of course, of more concern than occasional (and possibly predictable) flouting. Other criticisms of the economic concept of 'rationality' are simply untrue. For example, although it is a popular notion that 'rationality' entails selfishness, this is actually not usually a characteristic assumed in economics nor is it embodied in the axioms.

In the case of normative economics, the issues are more comprehensive and complex, for in normative analysis, one attaches welfare significance to 'rational' behaviour. If the basic axioms of the (positive) behavioural theory are wrong, then it seems hard to conclude that anything normative can be derived from them. But even if they are right, it may well be (as in *extra-welfarism*) that one needs more than mere rational choice making to identify what is in the best interest of society. Quite apart from the fact that subjective preferences hardly amount to a unique basis on which to evaluate social welfare, some individuals may be 'rationally' (i.e. consistently with the axioms) making perfectly ghastly, even evil, choices. If 'rationality' must be used at all, it is probably best, first, to be very clear about the meaning that attaches to it and, second, to use it in such a fashion as to include what the clients on behalf of whom the analysis is being done find ethically acceptable. There are numerous economic studies of behaviour that is apparently rational – but turns out to be inconsistent with the economist's model of rational behaviour, including the risk-laden consumption of hazardous goods that entail a raised probability of death. See also *Addiction, Bounded Rationality, Consistency, Expected Utility Theory, Social Welfare Function, Utility Theory*. For a review, see Rieskamp et al (2006). On hazardous consumption see Ippolito (1981).

Rationing

A general definition is: allocating resources according to a rule or administrative arrangement. One rule might, for example, be 'resources shall go to whoever is willing to pay the highest price'. Such a rule does not much commend itself in health care however, since those most in need of health care are usually those least able to pay for it. The most common general usage of 'rationing' is in connection with (usually war-time) arrangements under which, in exchange for a voucher, individuals (or families) are entitled to purchase fixed quotas of goods at *administered prices*. A lot of tendentious hot air is generated in public debates about whether health care in any jurisdiction is or ought to be 'rationed'. Those with political responsibility are understandably unwilling to concede that health care is rationed in either of the two ways just described but sometimes less understandably unwilling to concede that some form of rationing mechanism does indeed have to be used; the critical question relating not to 'whether?' but to 'which?'. There is also debate about the desirability of being explicit about the criteria to be used in determining the 'rules'. See *Need, Oregon Experiment, Pareto Optimality, Price Mechanism*. See New (1997), Cookson and Dolan (2000) and Ham and Coulter (2001).

Ratio Scale

A property of some measures of *health* and also of some measures of *utility*, such that multiplying any scale by a constant does not affect the ratios between the values assigned to the entities being measured. For example, six kilometres is twice three kilometres and 6000 metres is twice 3000 metres (in this instance the kilometre scale being multiplied by 0.001).

Rawlsian

An approach to questions of social justice named after the American philosopher John Rawls (1921–2002). See *Fairness*. See Rawls (1971).

RBRVS

Acronym for *resource-based relative value scale*.

RCT

Acronym for *randomized controlled trial* or, more restrictedly, randomized clinical trial.

RD

Acronym for *risk difference*.

Readings in Health Economics

Those collections of reprinted articles on health economics that I have been able to trace are: Cooper and Culyer (1973), Culyer (1991b, 2006a) and Cawley and Kenkel (2008).

Real

The use of the adjective 'real' in economics is to distinguish monetary changes in *value* that are merely inflationary from others corresponding to changes in the *flow* of goods and services. *Index numbers* are used to deflate *nominal* values and thereby generate real values. Cf. *Nominal*.

Real Income

Nominal (i.e. money) income adjusted to remove the effect of changes in the price level on purchasing power.

Real Price

Nominal price divided by a general price index.

Recall Bias

A distortion in data that arises from people's imperfect memories of events they are being asked to remember. See *Bias*.

Receiver Operating Characteristic Curve

A plot of the *sensitivity* of a test against 1 minus its *specificity*. It is used to compare tests in *epidemiology* or to select an ideal cut-off value in a particular test. See *Area Under the Curve* (AUC).

Recency Effect

A kind of *cognitive bias* that arises in psychological and economic experiments whereby subjects give a disproportionate weight to more recent experiences and observations. Opposite of *primacy effect*.

Recurrent Cost

Expenditures or *opportunity costs* that occur on a regular (usually annual) basis rather than being incurred once and for all.

Redistributive Impact

The effect on the *income distribution* of the arrangements adopted in a jurisdiction for health care financing. It is generally measured as the difference between the *Gini coefficients* for prepayment and post-payment income distributions and, quantitatively speaking, seems to be determined by the average proportion of *household* income spent on health care, the *progressivity* of the health care financing system, the extent of horizontal inequity, and the extent to which households are re-ranked in the distributions when post- and prepayment distributions are compared. See *Incidence*. On the measurement of the redistributive impact of health care financing see O'Donnell et al. (2008) Chapter 17.

Redlining

An industrial practice in the US of denying access to health care or increasing the cost of services. Employers in redlined industries will not find health insurers willing to sell *insurance* to them. It is illegal when based on race, religion, gender, familial status (if there are children in a family), *disability*, or ethnic origin. The term comes from the marking of red lines on a map to mark areas whose population would be discriminated against. See Light (1992).

Reduced Form

The reduced form of a system of *structural equations* constituting a *model* of economic behaviour is simply the result of solving the system. This considerably cuts down on the visible complexity of a model. For example, take the very simple case of a linear *supply* and *demand* model having three equations, two behavioural for the *endogenous variables* D and S, and one *equilibrium* condition:

$$D = a - bP$$

$$S = c + dP$$

$$D = S.$$

The reduced forms are (with a bit of elementary algebra):

$$P = (a - c)/(d + b),$$

$$Q = (da - bc)/(d + b).$$

Of course, the reduced form's increased simplicity comes at a price – detail is lost and the detail may be important in understanding what is actually causing effects to happen. Then one may need a fuller structural equation approach.

Reference Case

A standard set of methods and assumptions that analysts should follow in performing *cost–effectiveness* or *cost–utility analyses*. For two examples, see Gold et al. (1996) and Chapter 5 in National Institute for Clinical Excellence (2004).

Reference Cost

This is derived from pooled data returned from (English) *National Health Service* (NHS) providers to compute average costs for all *healthcare resource groups* and a *reference cost index* for each NHS provider. It underpins the *national tariff*.

Reference Cost Index

This is an index used in the English *National Health Service* (NHS) of the actual cost for each NHS provider organization divided by national average cost for the same activity multiplied by 100. An 'adjusted index' allows for local price variations.

Reference-dependent Theory

Reference-dependence assumes that people consider *outcomes* as gains and losses with respect to a given reference point, which is often their current position. Reference-dependence in combination with *loss aversion* can lead to violations of *procedural invariance*, which is a fundamental assumption of most *welfare economics*. See Tversky and Kahneman (1991) and Feeny and Eng (2005).

Reference Pricing

A reimbursement mechanism (usually for pharmaceuticals) whereby a *third party payer* or insurer determines the maximum price at which it will reimburse the supplier (the reference price). The consumer pays the difference between the reference price and the market price. The reference price is often set at the price of the lowest priced product in the therapeutic group or is the weighted average of the lowest prices in the market. The market prices are set at the discretion of the supplier. See Danzon (1997b) and Brekke et al. (2007a).

Referral Bias

Particular physicians and centres of *secondary care* that attract individuals with specific disorders or exposures but that are atypical of the general class of referrals or of patients of this type. Also known as centripetal bias. See *Bias*.

Referral Cue

Guidance to help *general practitioners* and their patients decide when a consultation with a specialist, usually at a hospital, is appropriate.

Reflection Effect

Reflection effects in experimental economics and psychology involve gambles whose *outcomes* are opposite in sign, though of the same size, and they can be a problem in identifying people's '*rational*' preferences. Compare two choices, one between a certain gain of $20 or a one-third chance of $60 and the other between a certain loss of $20 and a one-third chance of losing $60. Most people choose the certain gain in the first choice but the one-third chance of loss in the second. The effect is predicted by *prospect theory* as a consequence of the S shape of the *value function*. Cf. *Expected Utility Theory, Framing Effect, Preference Reversal*. See Manski (1993).

Reflective Equilibrium

A set of ethical beliefs that are stable and mutually consistent arrived at through a sequence of personally considered judgments or perhaps through a *deliberative process*. The term (if not the basic idea) comes from Rawls (1971).

Region of Acceptability

That section of a *cost–effectiveness plane* in which the technology under investigation is cost-effective.

Regression Analysis

Same as *multiple regression*.

Regression Coefficients

These *coefficients* give a quantitative account of the relationship between a *dependent variable* and one or more *independent variables* in a regression equation. See *Multiple Regression*.

Regression to the Mean

An empirical phenomenon in which extreme values tend to be followed by more normal ones. For example, parents of exceptional longevity tend to have less long-lived children.

Regressivity

Usually relates to the proportion of household or personal income that is taken in *taxes*; a regressive tax is one for which the proportion of income taken in tax falls as income rises, a *progressive* tax is one for which that proportion rises, and a *proportional* tax is one for which it remains constant. Cf. *Progressivity*. See *Ability to Pay*.

Regret Theory

An approach to decisions under uncertainty that takes account of the possibility that people anticipate the possibility that they will come to regret making a particular decision even at the time of making it. Cf. *Expected Utility Theory, Prospect Theory*. See Loomes and Sugden (1982). For *health economics* examples see Ritov and Baron (1990) and Smith (1996).

Regulation

Usually refers to the supervision and control of private sector activity – both firms and individuals. Regarding firms, regulation can relate to health and safety at work (see e.g. Hotopp et al., 2008), prices and profits in the pharmaceutical industry (see, e.g. Danzon, 1997a, b) and prices and profits in hospitals (see e.g. Salkever, 2000) as well as to other aspects of their working. For some economic theories of regulation see, e.g. *Interest Group Theory*.

Rehabilitation Medicine

This is a physician speciality but rehabilitation usually involves teams including other non-medical specialities such as *audiology, occupational therapy, orthotics, physiotherapy, prosthetics* and *speech therapy*. Same, broadly speaking, as *physiatry*.

Reimbursement

A payment made to someone by an *insurance* agency for *out-of-pocket* expenses that they have incurred or to a provider for expenses incurred on behalf of an insured patient. A study of the optimal balance of prospective and retrospective reimbursement of hospitals is Newhouse (1992). See also Newhouse (1996). A study of the selection of an efficient bundle of services to include in a public insurance package is Griffin et al. (2008).

Relative Hazard

Same as *relative risk*.

Relative Price

A pure number: the price of one good or service divided by the price of another. This is the concept of price most commonly (if not always explicitly) found in *microeconomics* textbooks.

Relative Price Effect

The movement over time of a specific *price index* (e.g. one for health care, or expenditure on physician services) relative to a general price index such as the *GDP deflator*. Alternatively, the consequences of a change in one price relative to another or to the price of a bundle of other goods and services.

Relative Risk

A ratio of two risks, usually the chance of developing a disease if exposed to particular *risk factors* divided by the chance of developing it if one is not so exposed, or the ratio of risk in an *experimental arm* in a *trial* (E) to the risk in the *control arm* (C). It is used in *randomized clinical trials* and *cohort studies* and is calculated as E/C. Relative risk is often abbreviated to RR. Cf. *Absolute Risk, Odds Ratio, Relative Risk Reduction*.

Relative Risk Reduction

A measure of treatment effect in *clinical trials*, calculated as $(C - E)/C$, where C is the risk in the *control arm* and E is the risk in the *experimental arm*. Cf. *Absolute Risk Reduction, Relative Risk*.

Relative Value Unit

A (US) hospital accounting procedure in which each item of service is given a weight showing its relative 'value', which, when multiplied by a *tariff*, yields a cost per item that can then be summed with other such items to calculate a patient's treatment costs.

Relevance Diagram

Same as *influence diagram*.

Reliability

The ability of an instrument, observer or other means of measuring entities to discriminate consistently between different values of the entity under investigation. It is not the same as mere consistency, with which it is sometimes confused: a car may consistently fail to start, which makes it an unreliable means of transport; a broken thermometer may give a consistently wrong reading – neither can be relied upon to do the job for which it was designed. There are many kinds. See *Intrarater Reliability, Interrater Reliability, Test-retest Validity*. See Shiell and McIntosh (2008).

Remembered Utility

As the name implies, this is a subject's recollected evaluation of past experiences. In health measurement, it will usually imply that one is enquiring about what patients think they suffered or gained from past experiences of, for example, a treatment. Cf. *Experienced Utility*. See Fredrickson and Kahneman (1993) and Kahneman et al. (1993).

Renal Medicine

The medical speciality concerned with diseases and abnormalities of the kidneys. Same as nephrology.

Rent

In economics, this is used in two senses: (1) the income accruing to an owner of a *capital* good, like land or machinery, from another person contracting to use it; (2) receipts in excess of the minimum amount necessary to keep a *factor of production* in its present use. That is, receipts in excess of its *transfer earnings*.

Rent Seeking

This is a term used by some economists to describe the processes through which individuals and corporations seek to use government to further their own interests and, in particular, to acquire streams of money (*rents*). An example is members of a regulated industry manipulating the regulatory agency. See *Public Choice Theory*. See Krueger (1974) and for a *health economics* application Cookson and Dawson (2006).

Repeatability

The extent to which the measurements of an observer at one date agree with those the same observer makes in the same circumstances at another date. See *Reliability*.

Replacement Investment

Same as *capital consumption*.

Report Card

A report card is an instrument for recording the *performance* of an individual or organization. It originated with school reports on a child's progress in class. In health care, report cards for hospitals commonly embrace quality of care, patient satisfaction, meeting of financial targets and other such qualitative and quantitative indicators at both broad and more specific levels. They are increasingly used as a management tool within an organization, as a means of addressing aspects of *accountability* to funding and other external stakeholders, and as a means of ranking institutions for patient information purposes. For an analysis of the *effectiveness* of this type of information see Dranove et al. (2003) and Coory et al. (2008).

Reporting Bias

Same as *selection bias*.

Representative Sample

A *sample* that is an acceptable representation of a *population*. *Random* and *stratified samples* are examples.

Reproducibility

The extent to which the same results are obtainable under different circumstances, at another time, in another country, by another researcher, etc.

Reputational Good

Health care is sometimes regarded as a reputational good or service, though the term does not have wide currency or a widely accepted meaning. This term seems to mean that the market for health care is characterized by *price-searching* and by substantial *information costs*, especially as regards the quality of service offered by different providers in the market. One common means of acquiring information about the *attributes* of various local health care providers is to ask the opinions of friends, neighbours and the current clients of various providers, i.e. to seek information about the reputation of the providers. See *Information Cost*.

Reputational Rent

Income to health care professionals that derives from one's reputation and status (to avoid *double counting*, exclude income if income itself determines reputation and status).

Required Rate of Return

A target average *rate of return* for a public sector trading body in the UK.

Reservation Wage

The minimum wage that an employee will accept to take a job.

RESET

A general statistical test for misspecification of the functional form of a *regression* model and for omitted *variables*. See Ramsey (1969).

Residual

The difference between the observed and the fitted values of the *dependent variable* in a *regression analysis*.

Resource-based Relative Value Scale

A method of determining appropriate reimbursement under US *Medicare* based on the value of the estimated resources used per service. The fee paid to the physician is the number of *relative value units* (RVUs) multiplied by the dollar value per RVU (known as the 'conversion factor').

Resources

Variously used to refer to *factors of production*, *inputs* or *goods* that have already been produced that are used in the delivery of health care. It includes human resources.

Respiratory Medicine

The medical speciality concerned with diseases of the lungs and respiratory tract. See also *Pulmonary Medicine*.

Respirology

Same as *respiratory medicine*.

Respite Care

A means of offering informal (e.g. family) carers of patients with *chronic* health problems some temporary relief from the strain of their caring. The respite may take different forms such as temporary caregivers coming to the patient's home or the patient moving to a short-term care home.

Respondent-driven Sampling

Similar to *snowball sampling*. However, whereas in snowball sampling the names of the contacts are handed over to the researcher and they initiate the invitation, in respondent-driven sampling, the participant does not hand over the names but instead passes on the invitation personally – leaving the researcher blind to who has been contacted.

Response Bias

Same as *sample selection bias*.

Responsibility

In *health economics*, this is most likely to be met in the context of considerations regarding the merits or otherwise of subsidising health care or health *insurance*. Some causes of illness are sometimes regarded as essentially matters of individual choice and responsibility (such as lifestyle) while others are thought to be more exogenous (such as health hazards in the workplace). See, e.g., Dias and Jones (2007) and Dolan and Tsuchiya (2009).

Results and Determinants Framework

A framework for measuring organizational *performance* in relation to objectives. See Fitzgerald et al. (1991).

Retirement and Health

Despite its evident importance and quite a large literature, the linkages between retirement decisions and health and even the direction of causation remain unsettled by economists, with many empirical studies in outright contradiction, so little is known with any confidence. An element making for difficulty is how to allow for the endogeneity of retirement decisions. For some beginnings see Coe and Lindeboom (2008) and Neuman (2008).

Retrospective Cohort Study

An *observational study* of a *cohort* of initially disease-free individuals whose health experience following exposure to risk factors is followed over a period of time. Cf. *Prospective Cohort Study*.

Retrospective Payment

Reimbursement of, say, an insured person by an *insurance* company, after they have incurred some health care expense. It is also used to describe the compensation paid to a provider of service after the service has been provided. A disadvantage of both forms of payment is that the reimburser has little control over the factors that have caused the expense to be what it is. Another, from the claimant's point of view, is the delay that occurs between incurring the expense and receiving the reimbursement. Cf. *Prospective Payment*.

Retrospective Review

A review of a patient's past care management.

Retrospective Study

A research study in which individuals are selected and past events investigated for their effects on health.

Return on Investment

Same as *internal rate of return*.

Returns to Scale

These describe what happens to the rate of *output* as all *inputs* are increased in the same proportion. See *Production Function*.

Revealed Preference

A person's (usually marginal) *willingness to pay* for an entity as revealed by (e.g.) market transactions or a controlled experiment. The emphasis is on the preference being revealed through behaviour in the form of a real act of choice or a hypothetical one rather than mere introspection. The theory of revealed preference is a branch of *utility theory* in which one entity is either preferred to another or the other is preferred to the one or, in some versions, neither is preferred to the other – '*indifference*'. It is concerned less with questions about whether choices actually do reveal preferences (sometimes this is taken axiomatically to be the case) than with building a logical structure of consistent *axioms* for *choice theory* and specifically one that yields the implication that an individual's *demand curve* for any good will have a negative slope. Cf. *Indifference Curves*. See *Conjoint Analysis* and *Discrete Choice Experiment* for experimental versions of revealed preference that have become used in *health economics* to evaluate the quality of health services. See Samuelson (1938) for the birth of the idea (not then so-called). See *Willingness to Pay*.

Reverse Causality

Is health a cause or an effect? The answer, depending on the context, can be either or both. 'Reverse' causality refers either to a direction of cause-and-effect contrary to a common presumption or to a two-way causal relationship in, as it were, a loop. Thus, higher incomes are associated with better health. But which causes which? Higher incomes are expected on balance to lead to better health but better health may enhance productivity growth and hence lead to higher incomes. For a review of the literature and some evidence that the relationship, either way, is not strong, see Frijters et al. (2005).

RevMan

Short for 'Review Manager'. It is software developed for the *Cochrane Collaboration* to assist people doing *systematic reviews*.

Rheumatology

The medical speciality concerned with the treatment of diseases of the musculoskeletal system of joints and muscles and some other inflammatory or auto-immune conditions.

Right-censored Data

Data about patients who did not reach the planned *endpoint*. Also known as 'suspended data'. More generally, a dataset in which some entities in a sample had not experienced the event of interest (for example, some machines had not broken down over the experimental time period of the test).

Risk Adjustment

In health economics, this is generally taken to mean the adjustments made to actuarially calculated *health insurance* premiums in order to promote *efficiency* and/or *equity*. The general idea is to strike a balance between the consequences of unbridled profit seeking by insurers and the requirements of equity thus avoiding *cream skimming*, *skimping* and the like. See *Adverse Selection, Cream Skimming, Risk Equalization*. For a review see Van de Ven and Ellis (2000).

Risk Aversion

There are various definitions of this in economics. That most frequently met is the definition from expected utility theory: the extent to which a sure and certain outcome is preferred to a risky *alternative* with the same *expected value*. It is an implication of *diminishing marginal utility* of income. If people had a constant *marginal utility of income* they would be *risk-neutral* and, if an increasing marginal utility, *risk-loving*. In the finance literature on *capital* pricing, a quite different concept of risk aversion is used, in which people are classified as risk-averse if, for a given expected return, they prefer a portfolio with a smaller variance. See *Insurance* for an account of the way the diminishing marginal utility of income produces risk aversion. While most people are probably risk-averse, that does not, of course, mean that they will not accept risks – provided they are adequately compensated. High-risk jobs tend to bring with them higher wages (Viscusi, 1993), sex workers will offer unprotected sex if the fee is right (Gertler et al., 2005). Cf. *Loss Aversion*. See *Expected Utility, Risk-loving, Risk-neutral*. See Quiggin (1981).

Risk–Benefit Analysis

A limited form of *cost–benefit analysis* that examines the benefits and risks of a particular procedure or alternative procedures. The 'risks' are not themselves probabilities or expectations but the negative factors to weigh in a choice. Of course, neither pros nor cons are usually known with certainty but it seems odd to regard only the possibly negative consequences as risky. A more complete mouthful would be 'risk-of-harm with risk-of-benefit analysis' but then it is clear that the 'analysis' has become *cost–effectiveness analysis*, cost–benefit analysis or something rather better defined.

Risk Difference

In a *clinical trial*, the risk difference is the *absolute risk* in the *treatment* group minus the absolute risk in the *control group*. Sometimes called the 'absolute risk difference'. Cf. *Relative Risk*.

Risk Equalization

Similar to *risk adjustment*. In public systems of *health insurance* that seek *competition* between insurance providers, it is common to attempt to eliminate *adverse selection* and *cream skimming* through schemes of risk equalization. For an analysis of risk equalization under the German sickness fund system see Breyer et al. (2003).

Risk Factor

A probabilistic *determinant* of ill-health. An element of behaviour, one's history, genetic inheritance, early parenting, exposure to harmful micro-organisms, environment, etc. that increases the probability of becoming diseased or having an injury. For an economic theory of risky consumption see Ippolito (1981).

Risk-loving

Opposite of *risk aversion*. See *Expected Utility Theory*.

Risk-neutral

Being neither *risk-averse* nor *risk-loving*. See *Expected Utility Theory*.

Risk Pooling

Insurance pools risks. Since the costs of health care can be extremely high, uninsured individuals face possible large losses. By agreeing to contribute a small premium to a common pool held by an insurer for use to compensate whoever actually suffers the loss, individuals may be able to reduce the net costs of risk bearing in a way that increases their welfare. Premiums will normally include elements beyond the expected cost of insured events and their probabilities of occurring in order to cover the operating costs of the insurer and a return on *capital* (so-called *loading*). The advantages of risk pooling may be offset by *moral hazard* (on this see Manning and Marquis, 1996, 2001). See *Adverse Selection*. See Ma and McGuire (1997).

Risk Premium

In general, the reward to one who holds a risky asset as compared with a safer one. See *Moral Hazard*.

Risk Ratio

Same as *relative risk* in *epidemiology*.

Risk Selection

This refers to forms of distortion in the *health insurance* market. Risk selection is usually of two kinds: *adverse selection* and *cream skimming*. Both effects are generated by *competition* and both are harmful to *welfare*. Health insurance thus provides an exception (or ought to) to economists' characteristic predilection for competition. For an application (in Germany) see Nuscheler and Knaus (2005).

Road Safety

See *Environmental Health and Safety*.

Robustness

A test is said to be robust if violations of the assumptions on which it is based do not much affect its *statistical significance*. It is one desideratum by which options may be ranked in *cost–effectiveness* and related types of analysis. Cf. *Sensitivity Analysis*.

ROC

Acronym for *receiver operating characteristic curve*.

Roemer's Law

What has been dubbed 'Roemer's Law' is, according to the late US researcher and public health advocate Milton Roemer 'the notion that under conditions of insurance or other prepaid support, the supply of beds tends to set a minimum utilization rate'. This has been popularly shortened to the adage that, 'a bed built is a bed filled'. See Roemer (1961).

Rosser Index

An early *ratio scale* method of measuring *health*. See Rosser and Kind (1978).

RR

Acronym for *relative risk*.

R²

The proportion of the total variation in the *dependent variable* of a multiple *regression* that is 'explained'. A measure of the goodness-of-fit of the equation. Also known as the 'coefficient of determination'.

Rule of Rescue

This so-called 'rule' is often proposed as an alternative (or supplement) to a *cost-effectiveness* criterion for selecting which treatments ought to be made available and to whom. The rule of rescue reflects, in a general sense, a concern that many people have for those facing the immediate prospect of death (or something else regarded as pretty awful) and, in economic terms, it might be seen as a way of describing a *caring externality*. In situations where cost-effectiveness is being used as the basic criterion for determining the treatments that are to be made available within a health care benefits package, the rule of rescue is suggested as an element to be brought into consideration when the *incremental cost–effectiveness ratio* is highly unfavourable, there is only one treatment option, death is imminent, the situation occurs rarely and the total cost to the *third party payer* is 'small' (these are criteria used by the *Australian Pharmaceutical Benefits Scheme*). It is not altogether clear whether ethical awkwardnesses in the application of cost-effectiveness principles might be better avoided in other ways. The intentions of those advocating the 'rule' might still be realized by weighting *health gains* for those with relatively short life expectancy, or with chronic past and/or prospective disabilities, higher than health gains accruing to others, without needing to supplement the cost-effectiveness *algorithm*. It seems plain however, whatever one may think of its merits, that it is not really a 'rule' at all. See Cookson et al. (2008).

Rule Utilitarianism

Under rule *utilitarianism* the rightness of an action is settled first by establishing the best general rule of conduct in terms of its expected utilitarian consequences and then following it. If the action fits the rule and is followed, it is right. See *Utilitarianism*.

RVU

Acronym for *Relative Value Unit*.

Rx

Doctors' shorthand for prescription drug or recommended course of medical treatment.

S

Saddle-point

A combination of two *independent variables* at which the *dependent variable* is maximized in respect of changes in one independent variable and minimized in respect of changes in the other. So-called on account of its resemblance to a mountain pass or col connecting two mountains but with steep slopes on its other sides. For some applications in *health economics* see Forster (2001) and Levy (2002).

Salami Slicing

The identification of patient sub-groups for whom *cost-effectiveness* is highest and that may make a case for a higher price for the technology in question.

SAM

Acronym for *social accounting matrix*.

Sample

A set of data about individuals or other entities of interest that is smaller than the *population* from which it is drawn. There are many ways in which this may be appropriately done, some involving replacement of subjects already drawn from the population (like drawing a number from a hat and then putting it back before drawing again), others not. Some common types of sample are: *cluster sample, convenience sample, purposive sample, quota sample, random sample, sequential sample, stratified sample.*

Sample Selection Bias

The *bias* created from analysing survey data when non-responders in a survey are systematically different from responders. This is also termed *response bias*. Cf. *Selection Bias*.

Sample Size

The number of entities (subjects, etc.) in a subset of a *population* selected for analysis. The size of the *sample* and the way in which it has been drawn from the population are critical issues in any research study. In some studies, such as *trials*, particularly where one wants the sample to be representative of the population, size is a major indicator of the statistical *power* of the analysis. *Randomizing* the sample selection is necessary for statistical tests to be valid. In other cases, however, as is sometimes the practice in *qualitative analysis*, non-random samples will be taken to reveal other *attributes* of the population.

Sampling Distribution of the Mean

A *distribution* of the *sample means* after taking repeated samples of a given size from a *population*.

Sampling Error

That element of the difference between what is observed in a *sample* and what is in the *population* sampled that can be attributed to the character of the sample.

Sampling Variability

The variation in an *empirical* estimate as a consequence of using a sample rather than the entire population.

Satisficing

A version of *bounded rationality*. Satisficing is behaviour that attempts to achieve a minimum level of a particular objective, but not to maximize it. It has been commonly used in analysing the behaviour of firms (including hospitals), where profit, instead of being the *maximand* is a *constraint* that has to be achieved but, once achieved, enable managers also to choose other goals. Cf. *Target Income Hypothesis, Supplier-induced Demand*. See its originator, Simon (1955).

Saved Young Life Equivalent

This is an alternative health outcome measure to the *healthy years equivalent* or the *quality-adjusted life-year*. It works via the *person trade-off*
method, by asking experimental subjects to determine how many individuals it would take to move from health state X to health state Y (better) for
such a change to be judged equivalent to saving one young person's life.
For example, if the answer to that question proved to be 15 individuals,
then 0.07 (i.e. 1/15) would be the value ascribed to moving one person
from health state X to health state Y. See Nord (1992a).

Scale Compatibility

A form of *bias* in the experimental elicitation of *utility* values. Scale compatibility asserts that respondents tend to give more weight to *attributes*
that are more compatible with the response scale used in the elicitation.
For example, a response scale emphasizing qualitative elements generates
a different preference ordering from one emphasizing quantitative elements. It is a violation of *procedural invariance*. See Bleichrodt and Pinto
(2002).

Scalogram Analysis

See *Guttman Scale*.

Scarcity

The general condition of life that has given rise to the dismal science.
Economics is founded on the proposition that there is scarcity – i.e. that
more is wanted of goods and services than is available (either to individuals or to populations). A scarce good is a good having these characteristics, in contrast to a *free good*.

Scatter Diagram

Same as *scatter plot*.

Scatter Plot

A plot of the values of one *variable* against the corresponding values of another, with the coordinates of each pair marked by a dot. By visually inspecting the plot one can often detect whether the two variables seem to be related and, if so, whether linearly or non-linearly and this may lead further to speculation as to whether there might be a causal relationship between them.

Scenario Analysis

A form of *sensitivity analysis* that allows for the possibility that factors affecting *incremental cost–effectiveness ratios* are not independent of one another. For an example of the technique in practice see Bhatti and Baibergenova (2008).

SCHIP

Acronym for *State Children's Health Insurance Program.*

Scitovsky Criterion

A method of judging whether there is an increase in *social welfare*. See *Kaldor–Hicks Criterion, Pareto Improvement*. Named after Tibor Scitovsky (1910–2002).

Scope Effects

Same as *economies of scope.*

Scottish Intercollegiate Guidelines Network

A body within the Scottish *National Health Service* that develops guidelines for good medical practice that embody research on *cost–effectiveness*. SIGN works in conjunction with the *National Institute for Health and Clinical Excellence*. Its website is available at: http://www.sign.ac.uk/ (accessed 9 November 2009).

Scottish Medicines Consortium

This body provides advice to *National Health Service* in Scotland about the use of all newly licensed medicines. Their advice is based on evidence that includes evidence on *cost-effectiveness*.

Screening

Screening is a means of detecting a disease in its pre-symptomatic stage (i.e. when no symptoms are apparent). Contrary to much popular opinion, screening is not always a good thing. The number of people screened is typically large and those showing evidence of disease will then normally receive further (typically more costly and/or more risky) confirmatory tests and treatment. The theory is that early detection enables early treatment, though whether this is more *effective* (than, say, watchful waiting) or more *cost-effective*, is an empirical matter rather than one of principle (or ideology) and ought to be so treated. Screening programmes are subject to problems with *false positives* and *false negatives*. See also *Sensitivity* and *Specificity*. The evaluation of screening programmes is subject to *bias* (a common one is *lead-time bias*). A screening programme is a *health technology* that is often a suitable subject for a *trial* and for *cost–effectiveness* or *cost–utility analysis*. An example of a cost–effectiveness analysis of a screening technology is Roderick et al. (2003). Some dangers from unthoughtful screening (for neuroblastoma in children) are illustrated by Morris (2002).

SD

Acronym for *standard deviation*.

SE

Acronym for *standard error*.

Search Cost

The costs in money and time of finding and exploiting opportunities to trade, including advertising and purchasing information about possible buyers/sellers. For a *health economics* application see Marini and Street (2007).

Searchlight Effect

Same as *Hawthorne effect*.

Seasonal Variation

A variation in a *variable* that is attributable to the times of the year at which it was measured.

Secondary Analysis

Using data collected for one purpose for another, for example to explore other hypotheses.

Secondary Care

Health care provided in a hospital or institution to which a patient has been referred by a health care professional. Cf. *Primary Care, Tertiary Care*. For a study of the cost-effectiveness of secondary care, see Räsänen et al. (2005).

Secondary Care Trust

In the English *National Health Service*, a hospital or other health care provider to which patients are referred that is also a *trust*.

Secondary Prevention

This term has two slightly different meanings, both of which are widely used. In the public health literature it is used to describe actions taken to prevent disease or injury when other *risk factors* are known to be present but before symptoms or other adverse consequences have become evident. In *clinical epidemiology* it means preventive actions intended to slow or stop the progress of a disease during its early clinical stages or to moderate the adverse consequences of disease or injury, especially through the prevention of recurrence. Screening tests are examples of the 'public health' approach, as these are done on populations at risk of diseases with significant latency periods but without clinical presentation, like hyperlipidemia, hypertension, breast and prostate cancer. The amelioration of adverse consequences or slowing of deteriorations becomes classed as 'tertiary prevention' on this view. Cf. *Primary Prevention*. See *Prevention*.

Secondary Research

Research that uses data (for example, administrative data) collected for purposes other than those to hand. Cf. *Primary Research*.

Second Best

A theorem in welfare economics to the effect that correcting one or more, but not all, *market imperfections* will not necessarily increase *social welfare*. For example, well-conducted *health technology appraisals* may indicate that the use of a particular set of technologies should be encouraged in a publicly funded health care system because the *incremental cost–effectiveness ratio* (ICER) is below a policy threshold, so local health care *commissioners* are instructed by a central authority to commission these services. In doing this, however, unless the budget is adjusted appropriately, the local commissioner will be forced, at least in the *short run*, to reduce expenditures on some other technologies that may have higher ICERs. Thus, removing the one imperfection (underuse as revealed by the *appraisals*) may not enhance outcomes if another (the budget) is left unaddressed. More generally, no real-world market achieves a first-best equilibrium due to a multiplicity of *market failures*, so there is much ingenuity expended (and employment for economists) in identifying ways of improving existing arrangements. The inventors of the concept were Lipsey and Lancaster (1956). For an application in *health insurance* see Blomqvist and Léger (2005).

Second Fundamental Theorem of Welfare Economics

The proposition that any *Pareto optimum* can be achieved, given particular assumptions, through competitive markets and the ability to select the starting distribution of resource *endowments*. Cf. *First Fundamental Theorem of Welfare Economics*. See, for its originator, Debreu (1959).

Second Order Uncertainty

You will not be in any doubt that a head is a head and a tail a tail but you will be in doubt as to which a throw of a fair coin will show (first order uncertainty). If you do in fact doubt the fairness of the coin, then that is second order uncertainty. First order uncertainty refers to variability in data and is reflected in the *standard deviation* and *variance*; second order uncertainty refers to uncertainty about *parameter* values and is reflected in the *standard error*. See *Uncertainty*.

Segmented Market

A *price-searcher*'s market that is divided by a producer or seller in such a fashion as to enhance profitability. See *Price Discrimination*. For an application in the market for pharmaceuticals see Frank and Salkever (1992).

Selection Bias

A *bias* created when using data from a sample that differs systematically in its characteristics from the general population due to a feature of the selection process. Such a bias will enter, for example, if the selection rule is 'take those whose names start with A', or 'those who live on the corner', or 'those who respond to a mailed questionnaire'. It also refers to the selection by patients or physicians of treatments that they believe will confer the greater benefits. It may arise as a direct form of scientific fraud. *Blinding* is no safeguard against this form of bias. Measures taken to prevent it include taking the appropriate steps to minimize specific forms of it (such as *volunteer bias*), to require full disclosure of scientific procedures and possible conflict of interest, or to correct for it by multiplying an observed *odds ratio* by the inverse of the 'selection odds ratio'. In the US, selection bias also relates to the health characteristics of patients in different *insurance* plans and its consequences for premium setting, profit and *equity*. Cf. *Randomizing, Sample Selection Bias, Sample Size*. For an economic review see Polsky and Basu (2006).

Selective Contracting

This is one of the means used by health care insurers to control costs. Selective contracting entails the insuring agency contracting with local providers (doctors and hospitals) to provide specific services at pre-agreed prices and often with agreed quality assurance mechanisms. See *Managed Health Care, Preferred Provider*.

Self-care

Self-care is the care taken by individuals to maintain and improve their own health. The focus is on a healthy lifestyle, the meeting of social, emotional and psychological needs, the management of any long-term conditions, and the prevention of further illness or accidents. For a systematic review of economic evaluations of self-care see Richardson et al. (2005).

Self-referral

This term has two common meanings. One is the ability of patients to refer themselves directly to a specialist without going through a *gatekeeper*. The other is when physicians make referrals to institutions in which they have a direct or indirect financial relationship.

Semantic Differential Technique

A scaling device used in health measurement. A common form, in which the respondent is invited to rate an entity (like 'health' or 'satisfaction') on a scale is to circle a number:

Good   3   2   1   0   1   2   3   Bad

where 0 is neutral and one moves outwards from it towards the extremes of goodness and badness (of 'health' etc.). Cf. *Likert Scale*.

Semi-Markov Model

A type of *Markov model* in which the *transition probabilities* are not constant but are related to the passage of time.

Semiparametric Model

A statistical method that combines parametric assumptions (e.g. that the relation between *dependent* and *independent variables* is linear) and non-parametric assumptions (e.g. that the *distribution* of the *error term* is unknown).

Sensitivity

The proportion of individuals with a condition who are correctly identified as such by a test. It is calculated thus: Sensitivity = $TP/(TP+FN)$, where *TP* is the number of true positives and *FN* is the number of false negatives. The terms 'positive' and 'negative' are used to refer to the presence or absence of the condition of interest. In the figure, sensitivity = $a/(a + c)$. A test that has low sensitivity will not detect all or even most of the people with the condition – the test is not sensitive enough. See *Screening*. Cf. *Negative Predictive Value*, *Positive Predictive Value*, *Specificity*.

		Diagnosis		Total
		Present	Absent	
Test result	Present	a (true positive)	b (false positive)	$a + b$
	Absent	c (false negative)	d (true positive)	$c + d$
Total		$a + c$	$b + d$	

Sensitivity Analysis

Sensitivity analysis is a procedure that adds further information to that derived in clinical research studies and *cost–effectiveness analyses*. There are broadly two kinds: *variable-by-variable analysis* (sometimes called *univariate sensitivity analysis*) and *scenario analysis* (or *multivariate sensitivity analysis*). In variable-by-variable analysis one lists the important factors that affect the size of the costs and outcomes and for each of them a range of plausible values around the *mean* (e.g. 'optimistic', 'most likely', or 'pessimistic') is specified. *Incremental cost–effectiveness ratios* (ICERs) are then calculated for each value of each factor holding all other factors at their expected or most likely values. Thus, if there are three important factors and three estimates for each factor, seven different ICERs will be calculated. In this way one hopes to identify the source(s) of the biggest variations about which decision-makers will have to make a judgment (and which may identify priority areas for future research). Scenario analysis allows for the possibility that factors affecting ICERs are not independent of one another, as is assumed in variable-by-variable analysis. In this case, one selects a variety of gen-eralized states of the world (e.g. worst case, middling case, best case) to calculate the ICERs that would result under the circumstances specified. Typically, this method produces much more extreme variations than the variable-by-variable method. In many cases the price of the product is the single most important *determinant* of relative cost-effectiveness. All the above are examples of *deterministic sensitivity analysis*. Cf. *Probabilistic Sensitivity Analysis*. See *Extreme Scenario Sensitivity Analysis, Modelling, One-way Sensitivity Analysis, Two-way Sensitivity Analysis*. See Briggs (2000) for a general review. For an example of a disease (river blindness) where the cost-effectiveness of the preventive programme critically depended on the price of the drugs see Waters et al. (2004).

Sentinel Event

A serious adverse health event that may have been avoided through appropriate care or *alternative* interventions or one that may indicate an important change in a population's characteristics. In the US the *Joint Commission on Accreditation of Healthcare Organizations* (JCAHO) uses the term to describe serious medical errors.

Separating Equilibrium

An equilibrium that may occur in the presence of asymmetrical informa-tion and that permits differential prices to be charged even though the seller lacks full information about relevant characteristics of buyers. Cf. *Pooling Equilibrium*. See Rothschild and Stiglitz (1976) and, for a *health insurance* example, Selden (1999).

Separation

Hospital separation is a discharge from hospital (alive or dead).

Sequential Dominance

A method of comparing *welfare distributions* when the *populations* being compared are *heterogeneous* and when, for example, their incomes, needs and health all differ. See, for the originators, Atkinson and Bourguignon (1987).

Sequential Sample

A procedure for creating a *sample* by adding subjects drawn from a *population* up to the point at which some predefined requirement for accuracy is satisfied.

Sequential Trial

A *trial* in which the data are analysed as each participant's results become available. An open sequential trial is one in which no upper limit on the number of participants is set. Otherwise the trial continues until a clear benefit is seen in favour of one of the *comparison groups*, or it is judged unlikely that any difference will emerge.

SERC

Acronym for *Service Rendu à la Collectivité*.

Serial Correlation

Serial *correlation* occurs when a *variable* is correlated with itself in successive time periods.

Service Rendu à la Collectivité

A term used by the French *Haute Autorité de Santé* to denote non-clinical *outcomes* of health care interventions.

Severity Adjustment

The estimation of the value of resources used over the course of episodes of treatment. Used in the calculation of *insurance* premiums.

SF-6D©

SF-6D© is a preference-based single index measure of general health that is widely used in economic evaluation, based on the *SF-36©* and *SF-12©*. The SF-6D© enables the calculation of *quality-adjusted life-years* (QALYs). Potential users may contact the owners on: http://www.shef.ac.uk/scharr/sections/heds/mvh/sf-6d (accessed 17 November 2009). For a comparison between EQ-5D and SF-6D© see Brazier et al. (2002, 2004).

SF-8©

The SF-8© is an eight-item version of the *SF-36©* that yields a comparable eight-dimension health profile and comparable estimates of summary scores for the physical and mental components of health. The instrument, in both this and its other versions (SF-36© and SF-12©), is copyrighted. Permissions can be sought at www.qualitymetric.com/products/descriptions/sflicenses.shtml (accessed 9 November 2009).

SF-12©

A 12-item shorter form of *SF-36©*. The instrument, in both this and its other versions (SF-36© and *SF-8©*), is copyrighted. Permission to use it can be sought at www.qualitymetric.com/products/descriptions/sflicenses.shtml (accessed 9 November 2009).

SF-20©

A 20-item short-form health survey covering physical functioning, role functioning, social functioning, mental health, current health perceptions and pain. It was developed for the RAND Health Insurance Experiment, which was probably the most ambitious *health insurance* study ever conducted. Its website is available at www.rand.org/health/hiedescription.html (accessed 9 November 2009).

SF-36©

The SF-36© is a multi-purpose, short-form health survey of 36 questions that yields an eight-scale generic profile of *health status* and psychometrically-based physical and mental health summary measures and a *preference*-based health utility index (*quality-adjusted life-years*). See Ware and Sherbourne (1992). The instrument, in both this and its smaller versions is copyrighted and permission to use it can be sought at www.qualitymetric.com/products/descriptions/sflicenses.shtml (accessed 9 November 2009).

SG

Acronym for *standard gamble*.

Shadow Price

The marginal *opportunity cost* of using a resource as estimated in a situation where there is no market price or the market price is believed to reveal opportunity cost sufficiently imperfectly to warrant the exercise. It may also be the marginal valuation of a service as revealed by methods such as *conjoint analysis*. Often used in *cost–effectiveness* and *cost–utility analyses*. See *Willingness to Pay*.

Shifting

A term describing the way in which the *incidence* of *taxes* or *subsidies* changes as market transactions take place and prices react. It generally implies that those upon whom the burden or initial benefit apparently falls are not those who ultimately bear it or benefit from it. The extent to which this happens will depend upon the various *elasticities* of *demand* and *supply*. See *Taxes*. See, for a *health economics* application, Levy and Feldman (2001).

Shortage

All too frequently 'shortage' is used in an assertive way by people having a vested interest of some sort in the entity asserted to be in short supply. The only technical meaning for 'shortage' in economics (using the test for 'how much' of a resource is 'enough') relates to the value to be attached to the increase (and by whom it is attached) compared with the cost of creating the increase. If the value exceeds the cost, there is a shortage in the sense that (*ceteris paribus*, and given a few other assumptions) more ought to be consumed. Behaviourally, if *demand* exceeds *supply* at the going price there is said to be a shortage. However, it does not follow that this shortage ought to be eliminated (e.g. by allowing price to rise, supply to increase or demand to fall, or any combination of these three) unless there are grounds for believing that the *efficient* (or equitable) allocation of resources would be enhanced thereby. Likewise, in comparing the *marginal value* with the *marginal cost*, the *normative* interpretation given above needs to take account of any illegitimate omissions from marginal cost and marginal value. Cf. *Excess Demand*.

Shortfall Inequality

A term coined by Amartya Sen to denote a way of looking at inequalities between people in terms of the shortfalls that individuals experience with respect to their maximal potential achievements. Cf. *Attainment Inequality*. See Sen (1981).

Short Run

A notional period (rather than a particular time period to which the literal-minded might be attracted) in which some but not all *inputs* or *factors of production* are treated as *variable*. The ones treated as *fixed* may not necessarily be literally fixed in any technological sense (for example, the organization may be bound by a contract not to vary them). A dramatic example (not from health care) of a factor of production that might appear to be quite decidedly technologically 'fixed' – but was not – comes from railway history. When the English Great Western Railway's old broad gauge track was changed to the modern standard narrow gauge in 1892 the entire stretch of 213 miles from Exeter to Penzance was changed in one weekend. Moreover, 177 miles of this had to be altered from the old longitudinal timbers to the modern cross-sleepers (ties). Of course, it took an army of platelayers to do it – 4200 of them (L.A. Smith, 1985)! The point is that almost anything is possible given sufficient resources. The key issue is what is chosen or assumed to be fixed for the purposes of the particular question being addressed. See *Time*.

In general, the faster one seeks to make any change in input use, the more costly such changes will be. Some inputs are costlier, for many reasons, than others to alter and those that are costliest will tend to number amongst those most frequently treated as fixed. The real point, however, is that what to treat as fixed and what variable is itself a choice problem and any decision about this will restrict the scope of inputs to be considered variable. See *Long Run*. For a study of short-run cost functions see Cowing and Holtmann (1983).

Sickness Impact Profile

A pioneering 136-item behavioural measure of *health status* covering sleep and rest, eating, work, home management, recreation and pastimes, ambulation, mobility, body care and movement, social interaction, alertness behaviour, emotional behaviour and communication. See Bergner et al. (1981).

Sick Role

A concept of medical sociology. In contrast to the 'medical model', in which illness is seen as a physical malfunctioning of the body or its microbiological invasion, the sick role is a temporary, medically sanctioned form of deviant behaviour by patients. The role entails being excused one's usual duties and not being held responsible for one's condition. In return, one is expected to seek professional advice and to adhere to treatments in order to 'get well'. Medical practitioners are empowered to sanction temporary absences from work and family duties.

SID

Acronym for *supplier-induced demand.*

Sign

Indications of disease that can be seen or measured by a person other than the one experiencing them (e.g. high blood pressure, fever, or skin rash). Cf. *Symptom.*

SIGN

Acronym for *Scottish Intercollegiate Guidelines Network.*

Significance

Statistical significance is defined under those headwords. Other forms of significance include clinical and policy significance. A result may be statistically significant but, for example, too small or rare to be of major clinical or policy significance. In general, statistical significance probably ought to be regarded as a necessary precondition for results to have either of the other kinds of significance.

Significance Level

A threshold probability that will require the rejection of the *null hypothesis* if the *p-value* is below it. It is generally 0.05, though this is a subjective choice rather than a scientific one.

Simulation

Simulation is an analytical method or model for imitating a real-life system, predicting the course of someone's health or health care costs, etc., usually in order to see the consequences for some *variables* of changes in their *determinants.* See *Monte Carlo Simulation.*

Single Blind Trial

A *trial* in which the patient (or clinician) is aware of which *arm* the patient is in but the clinician (or patient) is not. In some situations it is the adjudicator of the outcome who is blinded to the treatment assignment instead of patients and clinicians. For example, in a trial comparing surgery to watchful waiting, both the patient and the surgeon are likely to be aware of the treatment assignment, but the radiologist-adjudicator may not be. Cf. *Double Blind Trial*. See *Blinding*.

Single Case Report

Same as *case study*.

Single Factor Design

An experimental research design having only one *independent variable*.

Single Technology Appraisal

This is a procedure used by the *National Institute for Health and Clinical Excellence* in England and Wales for the *appraisal* of the *cost-effectiveness* of a single product, device or other technology, with a single indication. See Kaltenthaler et al. (2008).

SIP

Acronym for *sickness impact profile*.

Skew

A *distribution* is said to be skewed if it is asymmetrical, having either a long tail to the left (negatively skewed) or a long tail to the right (positively skewed). In a positively skewed distribution, the *mean* is larger than the *median* (which is larger than the *mode*) and vice versa for a negatively skewed distribution. In *cost–effectiveness analysis* studies, the cost data often display right-skewedness partly because costs cannot be negative and partly because a small fraction of patients often consume a disproportion-ately large amount of health care resources. In the distribution of income (see figure) most people make under $50 000 a year, but some make lots more and a small number make many millions a year. The positive tail therefore stretches out while the negative tail stops at zero. See *Kurtosis*. For a review in *health economics* see Manning (2006). On how to treat skewedness in cost data see Briggs and Gray (1998).

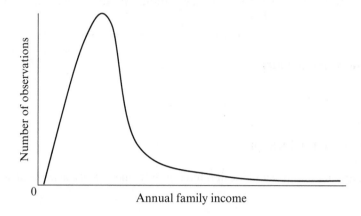

Skimping

Providing less intensive or lower-quality care than that specified in some standard or protocol in order to reduce costs in relation to the reimburse-ment due to the provider. This is believed to be particularly a problem in payment systems that are prospective and when doctors are paid by *capitation* or salary. When skimping is actually detrimental to patient health or welfare is harder to ascertain than to assert. See Ellis (1998).

Small Area Variations

A term usually applied to the observed wide variations in clinical practices within jurisdictions having otherwise similar health care organizational structures and payments systems, and having *populations* with similar demographic, economic, social and *epidemiological* characteristics. These variations appear to be entirely arbitrary and most likely reflect uncer-tainty about or ignorance of best professional practice or the exercise of professional 'freedom' to ignore it (as well as biasing financial incentives).

See Paul-Shaheen et al. (1987), Wennberg (2002) and Wennberg et al. (2002). See *Surgical Signature*.

SMM

See *Norwegian Centre for Health Technology Assessment*.

SMR

Acronym for standardized mortality rate or *standardized mortality ratio*.

Snapshot

A term coined in Wagstaff and Waters (2005) in which inequalities in health or health care are measured as though they were photographs taken at a single point in time. Cf. *Movies*.

Snowball Sampling

This is a method of *sampling* in which existing study subjects recruit future subjects from among their acquaintances. Hence the recruits grow in snowball fashion. The technique is often used with hidden populations of people, such as drug users or prostitutes, who are otherwise difficult for researchers to access. The results can be less subject to *selection bias* than one might suppose. It is similar to *respondent-driven sampling*. However, whereas in snowball sampling the names of the contacts are handed over to the researcher and they initiate the invitation, in respondent-driven sampling, the participant does not hand over the names but instead passes on the invitation personally – leaving the researcher blind as to who has been contacted. See Heckathorn (2002).

Social Accounting Matrix

This is a *matrix* of all the economic flows of resources that take place within an economy. See *Social Accounts*. For an example of its use in *health economics*, see R.D. Smith et al. (2005).

Social Accounts

Used both to describe the formal systems of national accounts that measure economic activity in a country over a period of time and also to describe a wider set of statistics that embrace non-financial entities like *life expectancy, health status*, environmental pollution, crime rates. See *Social Accounting Matrix*.

Social Class

Similar to *socioeconomic status*. In the UK, the National Statistics Socioeconomic Classification (the official definition of social class) is based upon occupation. The occupational categorization since 2001 has been as follows: 1.1 Large employers and higher managerial, 1.2 Higher professional, 2 Lower managerial and professional, 3 Intermediate, 4 Small employers and own-account workers, 5 Lower supervisory and technical, 6 Semi-routine, 7 Routine and 8 Never worked and long-term unemployed.

Social Cost or Benefit

Social costs (or benefits) are the sum of *internal* and *external costs* (or *benefits*). Social costs (or benefits) include internal costs (or benefits) together with any other effects that may create costs (or benefits) for other members of the community. Social costs are all *opportunity costs*. Thus the social cost of a medical procedure will include its effects on the household and other sectors and not just the costs that are private to a hospital or clinic. Social costs do not include *transfers* (transfer payments) since what one gains another loses.

Social Discount Rate

This is the *discount rate*(s) stipulated for use in public decision-making. In evaluating health-related projects, there is controversy as to whether *benefits* ought to be discounted at a lower rate than *costs*. There is also disagreement as to the principles that ought to govern the choice of discount rate even if there is to be but one. One view is that the *opportunity cost* of *capital* for the economy as a whole ought to be used so that health-related investments are costed in similar ways to other investments (some argue that this rate might be modified in the case of public sector health invest-ments to reflect a presumed lower risk; others that risk adjustments ought to be made separately and not confounded with time discounting). There is no agreement on whether a marginal or an average opportunity cost of capital ought to be used. A second view is that the rate ought to cor-respond to the average (or possibly marginal) rate of *time preference* in the community as a whole. A third view is that, because of the high degree of *publicness* of health investments, the social rate ought perhaps to be a rate chosen in a *deliberative* way by society's representatives (effectively, poli-ticians or people appointed by accountable politicians) bearing in mind whatever ethical and other considerations they choose. See *Cost–Benefit Analysis, Cost–Effectiveness Analysis, Cost–Utility Analysis.* Cf. *Social Rate of Time Preference.* See Claxton et al. (2006b, 2010) and Gravelle et al. (2007a).

Social Indicators

Social indicators are intended to provide a macro-social and economic view of the well-being (or otherwise) of a community, usually a country. They pose many problems of measurement, interpretation, reliability and comparability. For a review, see Strauss and Thomas (1996). For a third world context, see Srinivasan (1994).

Social Medicine

See *Public Health Medicine.*

Social Opportunity Cost

Opportunity cost viewed from the standpoint of all members of a society rather than that of a particular group or decision-maker.

Social Rate of Time Preference

The rate at which a social decision-maker trades off increments in present consumption against future consumption or increments in present health against future health. See *Social Discount Rate, Time Preference.*

Social Value Judgment

A *value judgment* made by or on behalf of society as a whole.

Social Welfare

The overall well-being of a society. It is generally assumed by economists to depend upon the welfares (i.e. the satisfied *preferences*) of the individuals who make up that society but how they are linked or added up is a matter for much controversy. See *Arrow Impossibility Theorem, Arrow Social Welfare Function, Bergson–Samuelson Social Welfare Function, Extra-welfarism, Pareto Optimality.*

Social Welfare Function

A function that relates overall *social welfare* to its *determinants,* especially the *preferences* of those individuals taken as members of a society. See *Arrow Impossibility Theorem, Arrow Social Welfare Function, Bergson–Samuelson Social Welfare Function, Extra-welfarism, Pareto Optimality.*

Socialized Health Care

Although it is not a technical term in economics, 'socialized' health care seems generally to be a term used to describe a system in which a *third party payer* like an *insurance* agency (which may be private or public) covers its members (membership will usually be compulsory for people with defined characteristics like area of residence) for a specified list of procedures (usually ones deemed to be *cost-effective*) for a fee that is unrelated to need and that may be part of the tax structure. It is similar to *managed health care* both in terms of its potential for containing *health care expenditures* and in its promotion of *evidence-based medicine,* though managed health care organizations in the US are, with notable exceptions like Kaiser Permanente, generally *for-profit* organizations, and on a smaller scale than most systems described as 'socialized' (for example, restricted to particular employee groups or people with specific eligibilities as under *Medicare* or *Medicaid*). Alternatively, the term may refer to the public ownership of health services. The UK's *National Health Service* is 'socialized' on both counts. Canada's system, being mainly privately owned, is socialized only on the former count.

Societal Perspective

A view often adopted in *cost–effectiveness* and *cost–utility analyses* to the effect that all the costs and outcomes of the use of a technology ought to be taken into account regardless of any characteristics of the person or individual on whom they fall.

Socioeconomic Differences

Persisting differences in mortality and *morbidity* by socioeconomic group have often been noted and described as the 'gradient'. A classic in the genre is Marmot et al. (1991). See *Equity, Gradient in Health.*

Socioeconomic Status

A description of a person or group of people having a similar social, political and economic position in society. Cf. *Social Class.*

Solidarity

The condition of having united or common interests. The principle of solidarity underpins several European systems of health care financing and delivery. Cf. *Externality.* See Chinitz et al. (1998).

Spacing Out Bias

A *bias* that is sometimes met when using instruments for measuring *health status*. It occurs when subjects space out their scores to fill the available range offered and there are grounds for believing that their scores ought to be more concentrated.

Spatial Wage Differentials

The phenomenon of persisting differences in wages for similar jobs in different local labour markets.

Spearman's Rank Correlation Coefficient

Spearman's ρ (Greek rho) (sometimes r_s) is used when the data to be correlated are *ordinal* in character: a means of measuring the strength of the association between ordinally ranked entities. It has limits of +1 and –1. Named after the British psychologist and statistician Charles Edward Spearman (1863–1945).

Specificity

The proportion of individuals without a condition that is correctly identified as such by a test. It is calculated thus: Specificity = $TN/(TN+FP)$, where TN is the number of true negatives and FP is the number of false positives. The terms 'positive' and 'negative' are used to refer to the presence or absence of the condition of interest. In the figure, specificity = $d/(b + d)$. A test that has low specificity will identify too many people as having the condition – the test is not specific enough. See *Screening*. Cf. *Negative Predictive Value, Positive Predictive Value, Sensitivity*.

| | | Diagnosis | | |
		Present	Absent	Total
Test result	Present	a (true positive)	b (false positive)	$a + b$
	Absent	c (false negative)	d (true positive)	$c + d$
Total		$a + c$	$b + d$	

Spectrum Bias

This *bias* exists when the *sensitivity* and/or *specificity* of a test vary in different populations that have different characteristics such as sex ratios, age, or severity of disease.

Speech Therapy

One of the professions that may be a part of a rehabilitation team.

Spillovers

Same as *external effects*.

Springboarding

The production, sale, or use of a patented product, without the *patent* owner's permission, for the purposes of obtaining marketing approval.

STA

Acronym for *single technology appraisal*.

Standard Deviation

The standard deviation (SD) is measure of the dispersion of a set of numbers around the *mean* value of a *variable*. It is the square root of the *variance*. A large value of SD implies a large dispersion about the mean and vice versa.

Standard Error

The *standard deviation* of the sampling *distribution* of the *mean*. In *multiple linear regression* analysis, the *SE* is usually placed beneath the estimated value for each *coefficient* – the smaller it is relative to the coefficient, the more accurate the estimate is likely to be. Sometimes, however, the *Student's t-test* or the *z-test* is placed beneath the estimated value for each coefficient. In these cases, the larger the number the more accurate the estimate is likely to be.

Standard Gamble

A method of measuring *health status* (or some aspects of quality of life) using *expected utility theory*. It proceeds by asking an appropriate panel of judges to rank the entities to be measured. Any two of these are then assigned numbers that preserve their relative ordering (any numbers will do). A less preferred third entity is then offered each judge in uncertain combination with the more preferred entity and each is asked to say whether they prefer the uncertain prospect to the certainty of the less preferred of the initial two entities. The probability in the uncertain prospect is adjusted until the judge is indifferent between it and the certain prospect, at which point the judge will have implicitly assigned a numerical value to the third entity. In this way many entities can be measured on interval scale (see *Utility* for an explanation of this). Thus, if $H(.)$ denotes the index of health status, and three styles of living are ranked $H(A) > H(B) > H(C)$. Then letting $H(A) = 4$ and $H(B) = 2$, the value for $H(C)$ can be found by adjusting p (the probability) until the following equation holds:

$$pH(A) + (1-p) H(C) = H(B).$$

If, in an experiment, $p = 0.4$, then the values are $H(A) = 4$, $H(B) = 2$ and $H(C) = 2/3$. Of course, the set of values ($H(C)$ etc.) obtained in this manner yields valuations of health states only if the subjects of the experiments are people who choose as though they are expected utility maximizers. See *Person Trade-off Method, Time Trade-off Method*. See Torrance (1986), Bleichrodt and Johannesson (1997a, b), Bleichrodt (2002) and Oliver (2003b).

Standardized Mortality Rate

Same as *standardized mortality ratio*.

Standardized Mortality Ratio

The standardized mortality ratio (SMR) is the number of observed deaths in a study population divided by the expected deaths in the study population and multiplied by 100. The expected deaths are the number of deaths that would occur if the study population experienced the same age-specific, sex-specific (and sometimes ethnicity-specific) mortality as the reference population. Thus, if the mortality experience of the study population is lower than expected, then SMR < 100. The statistic enables easy calculation of the 'excess mortality', which is due to variables other than age, sex, or race. Cf. *Crude Death Rate*.

Standard of Living

An economic measure of individuals' *welfare*. Often calculated as an index of the value of an average person's consumption (with suitable weights for children and other dependants). Most economists would argue that savings contribute to welfare, if only for the *utility* of security, so consumption is an underestimate: income as a whole is better. Both income and consumption methods typically also understate or exclude subsidized and free-of-charge goods and services and take no account of *externalities*. In health economics, measures of the standard of living have been important in providing a benchmark for studies of *equity*, for example in comparing the differential health or *access* to health care of people having different standards of living. See Lindelow (2006). For a general review, see O'Donnell et al. (2008) Chapter 6.

Starting Point Bias

A *bias* sometimes found in responses to *contingent valuation* questionnaires and similar instruments. The final amount settled upon is determined in part by the initial amount bid, or prompted. See *Bias*. See, in *health economics*, Stålhammar (1996).

State Children's Health Insurance Program

The State Children's Health Insurance Program (SCHIP) is a US federal programme established in 1997 to fund states for the provision of *health insurance* for families with children. It covers uninsured children in families with incomes that are modest but too high to qualify for *Medicaid*.

State-dependent Utility

The idea that *expected utility* from consumption in general is not the same if one is (say) well as when one is ill or that the value of health care is not the same if one is well as when one is ill. In other words, the *utility* of consumption (or investment) is dependent on one's own state (of health, amongst other things) and external characteristics (an ice cream in the rain is not the same thing as an ice cream in the sunshine). The idea also introduces another role for *uncertainty*, *viz*. uncertainty about one's health state (how high is my 'bad' cholesterol? Am I a carrier of that gene?) or about the weather (etc.). Oddly, the idea is much less used and discussed in *health economics* than one might expect. See, for an exception to this generalization, Evans and Viscusi (1991).

Stated Preference

Willingness to pay for a non-marketed entity as derived from questionnaires or experiments. It is 'stated' verbally or numerically (and orally or in writing) rather than revealed by actual behaviour in experiments or in real life. Another term for it is *contingent valuation*. See *Conjoint Analysis, Revealed Preference*. For a study using this method in respect of health insurance choices see Harris and Keane (1999).

State-preference

Same as *state-dependent utility*.

State Transition Models

Models (economic and *epidemiological*) that allow for patients moving from one health state to another with the passage of time, on account of health care interventions and the like. *Markov models* are the classic type in health economics.

Stationarity

In *time series analysis*, stationarity refers to the tendency of the effects of shocks to disappear after a short while. That is not the case with non-stationary time series.

Statistical Inference

Statistical inference is the inference of the properties of an unknown *distribution* from data that have been generated by that distribution. There are many forms such as graphical analysis and *Bayesian* analysis, as well as more formal methods of hypothesis testing.

Statistical Power

In *health technology assessment*, 'power' most frequently refers to the statistical power of a *trial*. In general, a trial ought to be big enough to have a high chance of detecting a *statistically significant* effect on *cost* or *outcome* and one that is also clinically or biologically significant. *Sample* size is therefore critically important. The researcher needs to decide the degree of difference between two groups being compared that would constitute a minimally clinically significant effect. How large the sample needs to be to deliver statistically significant results can be determined by using a statistical *nomogram*. The power of the study (moderate, high, or very high) is the chance of detecting a pre-specified true clinically relevant difference between the groups at a pre-specified *p-value* (usually $p < 0.05$).

Statistical Significance

In general, a measure of how confidently an observed event or difference between two or more groups can be attributed to a hypothesized cause. The *p-value* is the most commonly encountered way of reporting statistical significance. The (*frequentist*) interpretation of a *p*-value of 0.05 is that if you repeated an experiment that yielded a particular result 100 times, you would expect that particular result or one more extreme five times by chance alone. More formally, one forms a null hypothesis about what the underlying data or relationships are. The null hypothesis is typically that something is not present, that there is no effect, or that there is no difference between the experimental group and the *controls* in an experiment. One then calculates the probability of observing those data if the null hypothesis is correct, using an appropriate statistical test (which will depend on the shape of the *distribution* of the sampled variables). If the *p*-value is small (0.05 is conventionally used) the result is said to be 'statistically significant' (i.e. it is highly unlikely that the null hypothesis is true).

Clinical significance and policy significance are entirely different from statistical significance. One can have highly statistically significant estimates of things that are wholly irrelevant clinically, biologically or in terms of public policy. One reason why it may be irrelevant is that an effect may be highly statistically significant but so small in its absolute effect as to be completely uninteresting. Cf. *Statistical Power*.

Steering

A term used in the US *health insurance* industry. It describes a process by which people who are enrolled in insurance plans are directed by the insurers towards particular providers. See *Managed Health Care, Preferred Providers*.

Stepped Wedge Study Design

A method of assigning subjects to interventions in *clinical trials* that is useful mainly when the presumption of benefit is so strong that it is deemed unethical to have a *control group* whose members do not receive the intervention. Subjects are allocated to the intervention over time but in a random order such that by the completion of the study all subjects will have received it.

Stepwise Regression

This involves adding *independent variables* in a *regression* equation one at a time in order to assess the additional impact each has, given the others. For one of many examples of its use in *health economics* see Hurst et al. (1994).

Stochastic

A synonym for 'random' or 'probabilistic'.

Stochastic Cost–Effectiveness Analysis

Cost–effectiveness analysis based on data from one or more *trials*.

Stochastic Frontier

Econometric attempts to estimate *production possibilities curves* (frontiers) tended to assume that deviations from the frontier implied less than maximum *efficiency* rather than random shocks or other *exogenous* effects. Stochastic frontier analysis is a method for overcoming this problem. Cf. *Data Envelope Analysis*. For examples see Gerdtham et al. (1999), Brown (2003), Street (2003), Ortún and Puig (2004), Hollingsworth (2008) and McKay and Deily (2008).

Stochastic Model

A model that allows randomness in one or more of its *parameters* or *variables*. The predictions of the model give probability *distributions* of possible estimates rather than point estimates. Cf. *Deterministic Models*. For a *health economics* example (stochastic demand for hospital services), see Hughes and McGuire (2003).

Stochastic Regression Imputation

A method of dealing with *incomplete data*.

Stock

The quantity of an entity (like beds, or nurses, or health, or money) that exists at a point in time. Cf. *Flow*.

Stop-loss

The maximum annual *out-of-pocket* payment by an insured person. See *Insurance*.

Stopping Rule

In *randomized controlled trials* and similar systematic research designs, stopping rules define circumstances in which the experiment will cease (perhaps only temporarily), bearing in mind the statistical reliability of the evidence. The evidence might take the form of clear *dominance* of one of the procedures being compared over the other before the trial has been completed.

Strategic Health Authorities

Statutory bodies of the *National Health Service* (NHS) in England, of which there are 28, with responsibility for planning the health care arrangements in their localities and for overseeing the effective functioning of local NHS organizations.

Stratified Randomization

A method used in *clinical trials* to ensure that equal numbers of participants with a characteristic thought to affect prognosis or response to the intervention are allocated to each *arm*. For example, in a trial of women with breast cancer, it might be used to ensure that there are similar numbers of pre-menopausal and post-menopausal women in each comparison group. Cf. *Blocked Randomization*.

Stratified Sample

A *sample* drawn from a *population* that is divided into strata from each of which a random sample is taken. The strata selected may relate to features of the population that are expected to alter the impact of the treatment being investigated. For instance, a vitamin may be anticipated to have smaller effects on families that grow many of their own vegetables compared with ones who do not. If the sample is not stratified to include an adequate proportion from those who do and do not grow their own vegetables, it may turn out, by chance, that all selected by random come almost exclusively from only one of these two groups. This may result in the effect of vitamin supplements being over- or underestimated for the population as a whole, underestimated if there were an unrepresentatively large group of vegetable growers in the sample, overestimated in the reverse case. The problem is reduced if the total sample size is large enough to allow for stratified sampling with respect to factors expected to alter the *effectiveness* of a treatment. In addition, if the stratified sample is large enough, the differential impact of the treatment on the different sub-groups can be estimated.

Structural Equations

Structural equations specify the key causal pathways from cause to effect in economic *models*. A simple example is the 'supply and demand' model, in which *supply* is hypothesized to rise as price rises (*ceteris paribus*), *demand* to fall as price rises (*ceteris paribus*) and in which an *equilibrium* is predicted to be established (instantaneously in the simplest of models) as *excess demand* or *excess supply* at particular non-equilibrium prices pushes price up or down to the equilibrium price. In this model the structural equations are (assuming them to be *linear*):

$$D = a - bP$$

$$S = c + dP$$

$$D = S$$

And the equilibrium price is thus $(a - c)/(d + b)$, where D is the rate of demand, S the rate of supply and P is price. The lower case letters are *parameters*. Cf. *Reduced Form*.

Structural Unemployment

Structural unemployment exists when an individual's *marginal value* to any employer is lower than the minimum wage conventionally or legally payable (in the limit, a person's work value could be zero in which case their value is lower than any wage payable). This is the main constituent of most countries' unemployment statistics. Since being active in searching for work is usually a part of the definition of (involuntary) unemployment, some (perhaps many) who are structurally unemployed are not included in unemployment statistics because after a time these people may have become so convinced that they will not find a job that they stop trying. Structural unemployment frequently accompanies the wholesale decline of industries that are geographically concentrated.

Student's *t*-test

See *t-test*. A test based on the *t*-distribution:

$$t = \frac{\bar{x} - \mu}{s/\sqrt{n}}$$

where $\bar{x}$ is the sample *mean*, μ is the population mean and s the sample *standard deviation*. This is a method of comparing a sample mean with a hypothesized value, or of comparing two sample means, or of testing whether the slope of a *regression* line differs *statistically significantly* from zero. The decision rule is to reject the null hypothesis when estimated t is larger than a critical value, that is, reject the null if the *p-value* of t is less than 0.05. It was invented by William Gossett (1876–1937) a chemist employed by Guinness in Dublin and, later, London. He used the nom-de-plume 'Student' because Guinness employees were not permitted to publish. The only other students in question seem to have been Mr. Gossett's consumers (of his extensive statistical work, of course). Cf. *F-test*.

Study Arm

Refers to the experimental group in a *trial* having a *control* or other comparison group.

Study Boundary

The defined limits in the scope of a *cost-effectiveness* study (for example, the *costs* and *benefits* to be included).

Sub-group Analysis

In *trials* and *cost–effectiveness analyses*, particular interest might focus on particular sub-groups of patients defined by characteristics such as gender, race, age, study centre, country, *comorbidity* or disease *risk factors*. Sub-group analysis is the *epidemiological* and economic analysis of such groups. It can degenerate into *data mining*. Many *confounders* such as sex, age, race, smoking status, stage of disease, or coexistent disorders can affect outcome. When these are examined post hoc, the risk of *false positives* and false inferences is high: there may be statistically significant differences in outcome between sub-groups even when neither *arm* of the study receives any intervention. In one study (the Second International Study of Infarct Survival) there was found to be a slight adverse impact of aspirin therapy on patients born under the star signs Gemini and Libra! See Jönsson (2001) and Drummond et al. (2005).

Subjective Uncertainty

Same as *second-order uncertainty*. See *Uncertainty*.

Subsidy

A subsidy is a negative tax and, like taxes, raises issues of *incidence* (who ultimately receives the benefit) and *welfare* (does overall welfare rise or fall?). See *Taxes* and *Incidence* for the main entries. For (contrary) *health economics* applications see Dowd and Feldman (1987) and Jack and Sheiner (1997).

Substance Abuse

See *Addiction*.

Substitutes

Goods or services whose *demand* rises or falls as the price of another good rises or falls. The *cross-elasticity of demand* is positive. They tend to be goods that serve similar purposes. To take an extreme example, in some markets you can buy 'Aspirin', which is a protected name and is owned by the German company Bayer AG. In other markets, you can get *generic* aspirin under the name 'aspirin'. Aspirin sells at a higher price than aspirin. So chemically identical goods – perfect substitutes (unless you prefer your medicines to be initially capped) – do not always cost the same and the higher-priced version still finds buyers, in the (sometimes mistaken) belief that a higher price signals higher quality as well as for other reasons.

Substitution Effect

The effect on the *demand* for a good or service of a change in its relative price, holding *real income* constant, and *ceteris paribus*. Cf. *Income Effect*.

Substitution in Production

The common property of most health and other *production functions* that some amount of one *input* may be replaced by some amount of another without *output* changing.

Sunk Cost

A cost that has already been incurred. By virtue of their being 'sunk', costs of this kind are not *opportunity costs* at all as they represent no current or prospective sacrifice that is necessarily entailed in a decision. This does not always mean that they are irrelevant to current decision-making, however, for sunk costs may be thought to hold useful lessons for the future or managerial commitment, especially to major investment projects, may be an important element in the future credibility of the people who make major decisions of that sort. It is a common experience that sunk costs often do weigh heavily with firms and households and it seems preferable to explore the possibility that this is not 'irrational' than to assume without exploration that there is no possibility of its actually being rational. Cf. *Fixed Costs*, which, by contrast, are opportunity costs.

Superior Good

Another name for *normal good*.

Superiority Trial

A *clinical trial* designed to test the superiority of one procedure over another, the *null hypothesis* being that there is no difference. Cf. *Equivalence Trial, Futility Trial, Non-inferiority Trial.*

Supplier-induced Demand

The effect that doctors (or some other group of professionals), as providers of services, may have in creating more patient *demand* than there would be if they acted as perfect *agents* for their patients. There appears to be some adjustment of physician behaviour in order to maintain incomes. Supplier-induced demand (SID) has commonly been alleged to arise when there is an increase in the number of doctors; however, the fact that the supply of services increases as doctors increase may be the ordinary result of an increase in supply (demand constant) rather than the result of a shift in both supply and demand. Testing for the presence and extent of SID has been bedevilled by this *identification problem*. Other problems arise through the suspected effects of unmeasured or *omitted variables*. *Fee-for-service* is often held to encourage unnecessary supplier-induced demand, though the evidence for this is hotly contested. The debate is clouded by a number of other mysteries: how 'unnecessary' is any demand that might be induced? Might not inducement be a good thing in the presence of certain kinds of *externality*? See Evans (1974), Fuchs (1978), McGuire and Pauly (1991); also the exchange between: Labelle et al. (1994a, b) and Pauly (1994). For specific case studies see Dranove and Wehner (1994), Scott and Shiell (1997) and Yip (1998). The German system for remunerating doctors has been found to be conducive to inducement (see Benstetter and Wambach, 2006). See *Agency Relationship, Asymmetry of Information, Roemer's Law, Small Area Variations, Target Income Hypothesis*.

Supply Assurance

A term indicating that a health care *provider* is contracted with a specific purchaser to have sufficient *capacity* set aside to deal with peaks in *demand* from that purchaser's patients. See *Purchaser–Provider Split*.

Supply Curve

A bivariate (two-variable) geometrical representation of a *supply function* where the *dependent variable* is quantity supplied per period and the *independent variable* is price. In general, a supply curve shows both the maximum rate of supply per unit of time at a variety of prices, and also the minimum price that must be paid to induce the supplier to provide that amount, *ceteris paribus*. (A so-called 'backward bending' supply curve shows only the maximum that will be supplied at a variety of prices.) Conventionally, the price variable is measured on the y axis and the quantity on the x axis, even when quantity is the dependent variable. Under *price-taking* conditions, the *marginal cost* curve is the supply curve.

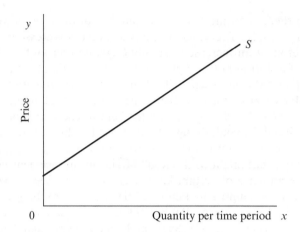

Supply Function

The supply function is a mathematical representation of the rate of supply as the *dependent variable* and its various *determinants*. The *supply curve* is a two-dimensional representation of a supply function, with supply shown as a function of price (*ceteris paribus*). On the supply of labour see, e.g. Antonazzo et al. (2005).

Supply-side Cost-sharing

See *Cost-sharing*.

Surgical Signature

Surgical signature describes the striking and persistent differences in the frequency of *performance* of particular surgical procedures such as prostate operations, back surgery and coronary artery bypass grafting, even among neighbouring regions with very similar demographic, social and economic characteristics and where the health care systems have similar reimbursement mechanisms. The variations seem to be completely arbitrary and are usually conjectured to arise from physician uncertainty, the absence of agreed protocols and other *clinical guidelines*, and/or physicians' ignorance of or unwillingness to adopt best practice as determined by senior professional peers. There are also marked variations across jurisdictions, where to 'surgical signature' get added the variety in reimbursement systems, different demographic characteristics, differences in medical education and so on. See *Small Area Variations, Supplier-induced Demand*. The concept had its birth in Wennberg and Gittelsohn (1973).

Surrogate Endpoint

In *trials*, surrogate *endpoints* are usually specific levels of physiological or biochemical markers, or clinically or economically significant events, that are easily measured and that predict the outcomes of interest. Also called intermediary or surrogate outcomes.

Surrogate Marker

In *cost–effectiveness analyses* of health care interventions, combining an economic *model* (when one is used) with *trial* data poses a problem if the trial *outcome* measures are not suitable *variables* for use in the model, whose outcomes are usually cast in terms of patient *well-being*. The trial outcome is the surrogate marker that needs to be converted into a patient-relevant outcome. Thus, changes in bone mass density might be the surrogate marker as used in a trial and the (empirical) question then needs to be explored as to whether (and in what way) such changes are linked to outcomes in terms of, say, QALYs, via effects on the frequency of hip fractures.

Surveillance Bias

A *bias* in *trials* arising because some groups in a sample are more closely investigated than others (and the consequential discovery of spurious differences between them).

Survival

See *Survival Analysis, Survival Function, Time to Event*.

Survival Analysis

The analysis of *trial* data in terms of time to an *outcome* (such as death). *Mean survival* is the time to the outcome in question divided by the number of subjects in a trial. See *Censored Data, Survival Function, Time to Event.* See Kaplan and Meier (1958).

Survival Curve

Same as *survival function.*

Survival Function

In some *trials*, the *outcome* is the difference in the *distributions* of survival times of an experimental and a *control* group. Survival functions (or curves) plot the proportion of all individuals in a *population* or *sample* surviving at a variety of dates. The term 'survival' sounds like life-and-death, which it sometimes is, but survival curves can be used to study times required to reach any well-defined *endpoint* (e.g. discharge from hospital, return to work).

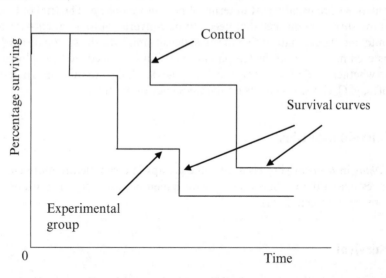

The analysis of survival data in *trials* can pose problems because some observations are censored as the event of interest has not occurred for all patients over the study period. For example, when patients are recruited over, say three years, one recruited at the end of the study may be alive at follow-up after a year, whereas one recruited at the start may have died after two years. The patient who died has a longer observed survival than that for the one who still survives and whose ultimate survival time may be unknown. The *Kaplan–Meier method* is a method of estimating the proportion of patients surviving to any given date, which is also the estimated probability of survival to that time for a member of the population from which the sample is drawn. A survival curve (Kaplan–Meier curve) plots the estimated probability of survival for a sample of data (not the actual proportion surviving) against time on the horizontal axis in such a fashion that the censoring is allowed for and the maximum use is made of the available data. See Kaplan and Meier (1958).

Survival Probability

The probability that a person will be alive at a given future date.

Survival Rate

The number of subjects in a *trial* who have survived at time *t* divided by the number of subjects.

Survivor Costs

It has been a matter of controversy as to whether the predicted regular consumption costs of survivors of a medical intervention and the expected costs of future unrelated health care ought to be included amongst the costs when appraising the *cost-effectiveness* of the initial technology. For what seems to be a sensible resolution, see Nyman (2004).

Swedish Institute for Health Economics

This institute is a non-profit research institute that is a wholly-owned subsidiary of Apoteket AB (the National Corporation of Swedish Pharmacies). It conducts health economics analyses including health technology *appraisals*. Its website is available at: http://www.ihe.se/start-2. aspx (accessed 10 November 2009).

Swiss Network for Health Technology Assessment

Switzerland's national association for people engaged in *health technology assessment*. Its website is available at: http://www.snhta.ch/ (accessed 10 November 2009).

Switching Value

That value of a *variable* that renders the decision-maker indifferent between taking an action and not taking it (or taking another).

Symptom

An indication of a disease or health condition that a patient feels (e.g. pain, dizziness, or nausea). Cf. *Sign*.

Systematic Review

A systematic review differs from other types of review in that it is a comprehensive and relatively unbiased synthesis of the research evidence. Essential features include the prior specification and explicit identification and scoping of research questions, the use of explicit methods for searching the literature, explicit criteria for including or excluding material, explicit criteria for appraising quality and reliability, and a systematic analysis/synthesis of research findings (e.g. by *meta-analysis*). Cf. *Narrative Review*. See Chalmers and Altman (1995). For up-to-date guidance on the conduct of a review, see Moher et al. (2009). On health economics in systematic reviews see Shemilt et al. (2006). A characteristic systematic review of a health economics topic (cardiac rehabilitation) is Papadakis et al. (2005).

T

Tangibles

A term that is sometimes used to describe the outcomes of decisions that are either in the form of priced consequences or in some other measurable and quantifiable form. The term is unsatisfactory (as is its antonym *'intangible'*) on the ground that consequences that are not measured are unmeasured usually because no one has yet invented a measure for them rather than because they are in principle immeasurable. Even 'psychic' effects yield to various forms of *utility measurement*. The critical judgments that need to be made usually concern the adequacy of particular extant measures (for example, prices) or the characteristics that a measure ought to have if it is to be regarded as a good one for a particular set of purposes.

Target Income Hypothesis

A hypothesis that physicians (and possibly others) have a target income (which need not be fixed over time) that their rate and style of work is adjusted to achieve, given a fee schedule specifying the *fee-per-service* provided. Originated in Evans et al. (1973). See McGuire and Pauly (1991) for some clarification. Cf. *Satisficing*.

Tariff

Sometimes used as a term for the weights on 'dimensions' in a measure of *health-related quality of life*.

Tarification à l'Activité

The French *prospective payment system* for hospital financing based upon a common national tariff for *Groupes homogènes de malades*.

TAU

This is an acronym for the Technology Assessment Unit of McGill University. Its website is available at: http://www.mcgill.ca/tau (accessed 10 November 2009).

Taxes

Taxes may be classified in a number of ways. One common distinction is between personal, or direct, taxes on specific individuals, like income, *payroll* or inheritance taxes, and 'in rem', or indirect, taxes on commodities, like purchase taxes. Some taxes are 'ad valorem', where the rate of tax is a proportion of the selling price, like most sales taxes, and others per unit, where there is a fixed amount per unit of the taxed item, like excise duties on tobacco and alcohol. Taxes on commodities may also be classified according as they are general taxes, like retail sales tax or value-added tax, or selective commodity taxes, like excise taxes and import duties. Factor taxes are taxes on *factors of production*, like labour or *capital*, and include property taxes. Examples of economic studies of the effect of taxes on health include: Wasserman et al. (1991), Philipson and Posner (1995), Evans and Ringel (1999), Markowitz and Grossman (2000), Forster and Jones (2001) and Adda and Cornaglia (2006). For studies on whether smokers 'pay their way' see Stoddart et al. (1986) and Manning et al. (1989).

Technical Efficiency

Equivalent to being on an *isoquant*, i.e. not using more of any one *input* than is strictly necessary, given the amounts of others in use. See *Cost-effectiveness*, *Efficiency*.

Technological Change

This refers to new knowledge and inventions (see *Patent*) and generally falls into two classes: 'embodied technological change', when increased productive potential is created by the use of new or upgraded *capital*, and 'disembodied technological change', when the change takes the form of new methods of management, or marketing, or other processes. 'Capital' here includes *human capital* and might also include drugs, which classically embody new technologies. See *Productivity*. See Weisbrod (1991).

Technology Assessment Unit

A research unit of the McGill University, Canada, that conducts *health technology assessment*s and *cost–effectiveness analyses* for hospitals in Quebec. Its website is available at: http://www.mcgill.ca/tau/ (accessed 10 November 2009).

Technology Matrix

A table showing the relationship between *inputs* and the maximum *outputs* or *outcomes* of any procedure or process. See *Input–Output Analysis, Leontief Production Function, Production Function*.

Temporal Monotonicity

Imagine two identical sequences of experiences, to one of which an improvement is added. Temporal monotonicity means that the changed sequence will be preferred to the unchanged one or, while if you worsen part of it, the unchanged sequence will be preferred. Experiments suggest that individuals do not always behave in this apparently rational way. See Kahneman et al. (1993).

Terms of Trade

The ratio of an index of a jurisdiction's export *price index* to its import price index. The terms of trade are said to 'improve' if weighted export prices rise faster or fall more slowly than weighted import prices.

Tertiary Care

Specialized hospital care, usually available only on referral from *primary* or *secondary* medical care personnel, provided by specialists working in regional or national centres having the personnel and facilities for special investigations, treatment and training. Cf. *Primary Care, Secondary Care*.

Tertiary Prevention

This term is sometimes used to describe procedures elsewhere known as *secondary prevention* – the amelioration of the consequences of disease, symptomatic relief and *palliative care*. Secondary prevention, when the tripartite distinction is made, becomes concerned mainly with *screening*. See *Prevention, Primary Prevention*.

Tertile

When a *continuous variable* is split for convenience into three equal-sized chunks of data the cut-off points between them are called tertiles. See *Quantile*.

Test Discount Rate

The *discount rate*(s) required by government to be used in the public service. See *Option Appraisal, Perspective, Social Discount Rate*.

Test-retest Validity

The degree to which scores in a study as assigned by the scorer are the same when the experiment is repeated using the same scorer.

Textbooks

See *Health Economics*.

Theil Index

A measure of inequality:

$$T_T = \frac{1}{N} \sum_{i=1}^{N} \left(\frac{x_i}{\bar{x}} \cdot \ln \frac{x_i}{\bar{x}} \right)$$

where x_i is the income of the ith person, x is the mean income and N is the number of people. It was proposed in Theil (1967).

Therapeutic Personality Bias

This *bias* occurs when the observer is not *blinded*. The observer's beliefs about *effectiveness* may thereby influence *outcomes* and their measurements.

Thermometer

In *health economics*, reference to a thermometer is likely to be to a device known as a *visual analogue scale* resembling a thermometer with the aid of which subjects in an experiment assign numbers to states of health. See Parkin and Devlin (2006).

Third Party Payer

A payer, typically a private or public *insurance* agency, who either compensates the provider for the expense of providing a service to the patient, or the patient after the patient has paid the provider's bill. Patients and providers are the other two 'parties'.

Thoracic Surgery

The branch of surgery concerned with diseases of the chest (between the neck and the diaphragm). The region between the diaphragm and the pelvis is the province of the general surgeon.

Threshold

A test *incremental cost–effectiveness ratio* that sets the upper bound for health care technologies to be deemed to be *cost-effective*. For obscure reasons, a dollar figure of around $50000 per quality-adjusted life-year seems to have acquired benchmark status. See *Cost–Effectiveness Threshold*. On the $50k convention see Grosse (2008).

Threshold Analysis

A type of *cost–effectiveness or cost–utility analysis* study in which estimates are made of the maximum *costs* or minimum *benefits* that would have to be yielded by a technology if it were to meet a predetermined threshold (minimum for acceptability) *incremental cost–effectiveness ratio*. See *Acceptability Curve, Cost–Effectiveness Threshold*. For an example see Coleman et al. (2004).

Thurstone's Law of Comparative Judgment

A procedure used in *pairwise comparisons*, through which descriptions of states of health are scaled by subjects who compare descriptive statements in pairs and to indicate which statement of the pair presents greater 'intensity'. Thurstone's Law is a probabilistic expression for the strength of this intensity. Named after the US psychometrician Louis Leon Thurstone (1887–1955). See Thurstone (1928).

Time

Time plays at least four distinct roles in economics. First, it enters most economic functional relationships either because one is considering rates of consumption (e.g. of drugs per week) or rates of inputs (e.g. so many X-ray machine hours per year) or rates of enjoyment of particular states (e.g. such and such a state of health for one year) or because one is considering entities at a particular point in time, such as *stocks* of health. Second, time enters explicitly as a factor in intertemporal *choice theory*, concerning the optimal pattern of consumption, investment, or the use of a resource over time. Third, time is used to classify 'runs' in production theory, as in *short run* and *long run*. Fourth, time is itself a kind of resource having *opportunity costs* and it can be either efficiently or inefficiently utilized; thus, patient's time is an inherent part of many processes of healing, as it is frequently an inherent part of gaining access to health care (*waiting*). See *Time Preference*.

Time Consistency

See *Time Inconsistency*.

Time Cost

Reflects the idea that people's time has alternative uses that are valuable and are, hence, *opportunity costs*. Not all time costs in health care are, however, costs in this sense. For example, although waiting in a doctor's waiting room may involve some sacrifice of time (whose value will depend on the alternative use to which it would have been put) waiting for admission as a hospital in-patient normally does not and one's time is available for other uses (though it may have other disadvantages and the other uses may be limited by the state of health). See *Queue, Time Price, Waiting List*. For study of adult *obesity* using a time cost variable see Chou et al. (2004).

Time Horizon

A fixed point of time in the future that is an *endpoint* in a *trial* or the point at which consideration of the consequences (*costs* or *benefits*) of an earlier decision is deemed to cease.

Time Inconsistency

This is the idea that individuals' behaviour in the future is not consistent with their stated preferences in the present concerning that future behaviour. Much evidence suggests that people, and governments too, are time inconsistent. The pioneering empirical psychological work is Ainslie (1992). For an application to *health insurance* see Cochrane (1995).

Time Preference

An individual's preference for consumption now rather than consumption later. It is measured by the *marginal intertemporal rate of substitution*: the minimum future sum required to compensate an individual for forgoing a little consumption now. Thus, to use a cash example, if the time preference rate is 3 per cent per annum, the individual will be indifferent between $1.03 next year and $1.00 today. It is also the slope of an *indifference curve* where the horizontal axis shows consumption today and the vertical axis shows consumption at a future date. As the name implies, the usual presumption is that the rate of time preference will be positive.

The distinction between marginal and average time preference rates ought to be borne in mind. The average rate relates to a total bundle of goods and services consumed now or in the future. The marginal rate relates to a small incremental bundle. Quite why future consumption (setting aside all considerations of uncertainty) should be considered less valuable to individuals than the same level of current consumption has never been satisfactorily explained (at least, not by economists), though it seems plausible to accept that people with large current consumption and small and uncertain future consumption may have a negative rate of time preference. The rate of time preference has typically been taken as *exogenous* to the *model* being employed, it being unclear (at least to economists) as to where time preference, patience, or impatience come from. This issue was tackled by Becker and Mulligan (1997). See *Discounting*. For an early discussion of time preference in health affairs see Fuchs (1982). For a study questioning whether time preference can account for harmful consumption patterns see Cutler and Glaeser (2005).

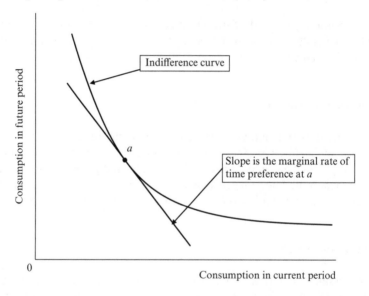

Time Price

This reflects the idea that money prices are not the only access barrier to health services. Just as money price and the rate of use are negatively associated, so is time price – for example, the time spent travelling to a facility – and the rate of use. The *direct cost* of travelling also plays a similar role. These time costs are generally regarded as direct costs in *cost–effectiveness* and *cost–utility analyses* rather than *indirect* or *productivity costs*, which include the value of lost working and leisure time. Note that time spent waiting need not be a cost in the same way as it is when standing in a line or queue: standing in line or sitting in a waiting room represents *opportunity cost* (the time has alternative valuable uses); time on a list waiting for admission to hospital is a postponement of treatment and does not involve current opportunities being forgone. See *Queue*. See Grossman (1972) for its use in *health economics*.

Time Series Analysis

A branch of *econometrics* that uses economic models to analyse the movement or trends of variables over time. For an introduction see Kennedy (2003). For a *health economics* application see Wagstaff (1985).

Time to Event

In *clinical trials* patients are recruited over a period and followed up to a fixed date or possible event such as death or recurrence of a tumour (negative), conception or discharge from hospital (usually positive) or cessation of breast feeding (neutral). The time between recruitment and the event is 'time to event' or survival (even when death is not the event in question). Subjects in the trial who survive to the fixed date but for whom the event has not occurred are said to have a censored survival time.

Time Trade-off Method

TTO is a preference-based method for assigning utilities to health states, in which the subject is asked how much time they are willing to sacrifice from a given lifespan in one health state to have a given number of years in perfect health. Thus, if $H(.)$ denotes the index of *health status*, and two styles of living are ranked $H(A) > H(B)$, one seeks experimentally to find how much shorter the time spent with $H(A)$ should be to be of the same utility as a longer period in state $H(B)$. Let t be the time spent in state $H(B)$ and x in state $H(A)$. One then seeks experimentally to vary x until the subject is *indifferent* between the two states:

$$x.\,U(H(A)) = t.\,U(H(B)).$$

The ratio x/t provides the utility of state $H(B)$ relative to state $H(A)$. If the latter is arbitrarily set at 1.0 (= perfect health), then the *(ratio) scale* for all such states of lower utility may be revealed. The use of TTO values in economic evaluation relies on some key assumptions, notably the acceptability of preference-based measures of health, *constant proportional time trade-off* and *additive separability*. See *Healthy Years Equivalent, Person trade-off Method, Quality-adjusted Life-Year, Standard Gamble.* For the theory see Buckingham and Devlin (2006). For an application in *population health* measurement see Dolan et al. (1996a).

Timing of Costs and Benefits

Dating the occurrence of *costs* and *benefits*, usually as a prelude to their *discounting*. See *Discounting*.

Tobit Model

A procedure for doing *multiple linear regression* when the data are *censored data*. It has nothing to do with the Book of Tobit in the Apocrypha but is named after economics Nobel prize-winner James Tobin (1918–2002). See Tobin (1958). For an introduction see Kennedy (2003). For a *health economics* application (*catastrophic* health care payments) see Skinner and Feenberg (1994).

Top-down Studies

A term used in costing methods for *cost–effectiveness analysis* and similar analyses, according to which sources for costs are pre-collected data, often routine and often gathered for purposes other than the purposes of the study in question, or else designed for a variety of uses (for none of which they may be ideal). Cf. *Bottom-up Studies*.

Tornado Diagram

A graphical way of displaying *one-way sensitivity analyses* placing the variable with the highest sensitivity at the top (with wide extremes) and the lowest at the bottom, so that the resultant diagram resembles the shape of a tornado.

Total Cost

This is the sum of *fixed* (or *overhead*) costs and *variable costs* when output is produced in a technically *efficient* way.

Total Factor Productivity

This is the *productivity* of all factors involved as a whole in a production activity. For an example in *health economics*, see Cromwell and Pope (1989).

Townsend Index

An index of social deprivation used mainly in the UK. Cf. *Jarman Index*. See Townsend et al. (1988).

Toxicology

The science of poisons.

Trade-off

This is the idea that every individual will voluntarily sacrifice some of one good or service in exchange for a sufficient increase in the amount of some other. In *production functions* it is the idea that some of one *input* or *factor of production* can be sacrificed without loss of *output* if there is a sufficient increase in some other input. See *Indifference Curve, Isoquant, Marginal Rate of Substitution*. An early classic on a difficult choice is McNeil et al. (1981). On the equity–efficiency trade-off see Wagstaff (1991), Williams and Cookson (2006) and Culyer (2006b).

Trade-off Matrix

An instrument used in *conjoint analysis*. It presents in matrix form how the subject can have more of one *attribute* of a service only by having less of another. In complex cases, where the attributes are many, the matrices usually reduce the number of comparisons to pairs (*pairwise comparisons*) or some other manageable number. See Lancsar and Louviere (2008).

Trade-related Aspects of Intellectual Property Rights

The World Trade Organization's TRIPS (not TRAIPS!) covers a variety of intellectual property rights such as trademarks, copyright and *patents*. It introduced a greater degree of international uniformity in their treatment, for example, by setting standard patent lives at 20 years.

Traditional Healing

Traditional medicine is commonly practised in parts of the developing world and is paid for by its clients in market transactions. It is frequently dismissed as a trade of charlatans. For a more sympathetic economic account than would be customary from a Western cultural perspective see Leonard and Zivin (2005).

Tragedy of the Commons

A term attributable to the ecologist Garrett Hardin. Common grazing land ('the commons') is of value to farmers, each of whom gain from grazing their flocks on it without charge but, the more each grazes it the less grazing there is. The tragedy arises when the land (or any other common property resource – fisheries are another classic case) is entirely destroyed or used up. One solution may be to substitute private and exchangeable property for public property. Another may be for a public authority to own it and ration its use through prices or some other mechanism. See Hardin (1968).

Trailing Indicator

See *Lagging Indicator*.

Transaction Cost

The cost of making any kind of transaction in a market. It includes the costs involved in searching for possible providers of (or clients for) service, the range of services offered, assessing their quality, their fees and charges, any *agent*'s or broker's charges, any time spent in waiting rooms, and any other cost that is not a part of the money price actually paid for the service.

Cf. *Search Cost*. See, for a *health economics* application, Marini and Street (2007).

Transferability

See *Generalizability*.

Transfer Earnings

The minimum payment required by the owner of a *factor of production* to prevent it from being transferred to another use. Transfer earnings are usually lower than actual earnings (which is why the current owner has not transferred the factor!). Sometimes called 'transfer cost'. See *Rent*.

Transfer Payment

A transfer of purchasing power from one group (for example, taxpayers) to another (for example, health care beneficiaries). It is not to be confused with *opportunity cost* or *transfer earnings* since transfer payments do not measure the most highly valued alternative use of resources, whether human or non-human.

Transfer Price

This is a procedure used in the pharmaceutical and other industries to exploit the differences in tax rates in different countries. For example, when a manufacturer transfers goods to overseas subsidiaries, a high price is charged to those operating under high tax regimes so that the subsidiaries will have relatively low profits and hence low profit tax obligations, and a low price is charged to subsidiaries in low tax regimes, which will have larger profits but involve paying less profits tax. The idea is to achieve a net tax saving to the parent company from its global operation. The classic on the subject is Hirshleifer (1956).

Transformation Curve

Same as *production possibilities curve*.

Transition Matrix

This is a matrix of *transition probabilities* in a *Markov chain*. The rows list the probabilities of moving from one state to another (or remaining in the existing state) and sum to 1.0. The columns list the states.

Transition Probability

This is the probability of transition from one state of health to another in a *Markov model*.

Transitivity

The *axioms* of all utility theories include this one, to the effect that if entity *A* is preferred or indifferent to entity *B,* and entity *B* is preferred or indifferent to entity *C*, then *A* will be preferred or indifferent to *C*. This axiom may seem to characterize something that is *rational* but individuals commonly violate it in experiments. It depends on what you regard as rational. For example, in a series of choices I might choose a large apple over a banana, and a banana over a small apple, but a small apple over a large apple (so as not to appear greedy). It is not clear why such preferences ought to be seen as irrational. See *Utility*.

Transitory Income

Current income in contrast to *permanent income*.

Translog Production Function

Translog is an abbreviation of 'transcendental logarithmic', a form of *production function* having greater generality than the *Cobb–Douglas* or *constant elasticity of substitution* functions. For a *health economics* application to hospital pharmacies see Okunade (2006).

Treadmill Effect

The adjustment of activity by physicians to compensate for loss of or reduction in fees per item of service. Cf. *Supplier-induced Demand*. See Benstetter and Wambach (2006).

Treatment

See *Factor*.

Treatment Effect

Same as *effect size*.

Triage

The word triage comes from the French word 'trier', to sort (not necessarily into threes!). It seems to have originated with a Frenchman, Baron Dominique Jean Larrey (1766–1842), a surgeon in Napoleon's army, who devised a method for evaluating and categorizing the wounded in battle quickly so as to evacuate those most likely to benefit from receiving urgent medical attention. Its usage today varies from place to place and circumstance to circumstance but in general it still involves the classification of patients according to judgments of their *capacity to benefit* and the urgency of their case. For example, people injured and at the site of an accident might be sorted into: the dead for whom one can do nothing; the injured who need immediate transfer to hospital; the injured whose transport can be delayed; and the walking wounded who may need only *primary* rather than *secondary care*.

Triage Nurse

A nurse who first assesses patients in an emergency department or room and decides how urgent their problem is, or who performs a telephone interview and makes an assessment of the *health status* and health service needs of the caller. See *Triage*.

Trial

Trials are generally tests of the *efficacy* of public health or interventions that may or may not be clinical but in which an *experimental* and a *control group* are compared. Cf. *Clinical Trial*. On trial design from an economic perspective see Eckerman and Willan (2009).

Triangular Distribution

A frequency *distribution* with three *parameters*: minimum, maximum and mode. It may be symmetrical, or positively or negatively *skewed*. Cf. *Normal Distribution*.

Triple-blind Trial

A *trial* in which subjects, observers/clinicians and analysts are unaware of patient assignment to the *arms* of the trial. See *Blinding*.

TRIPS

Acronym for *trade-related aspects of intellectual property rights*.

True Negative

A test result indicating that a disease-free individual is disease-free.

True Positive

A test result indicating that a diseased individual is diseased.

Trusts

Trusts were established in 1991 in the English National Health Service (NHS). NHS trusts are created under statute as corporate bodies with legal personalities. Statutes and regulations prescribe the structure, functions and responsibilities of the boards of these bodies and prescribe the way chairs and members of boards are appointed. The function of trusts is to provide hospital and community services on behalf of the Secretary of State for Health. A Trust is managed by a board of directors made up of executive directors and non-executive directors. The non-executive directors are part-time (including the chair) and are paid an honorarium. Foundation trusts are a new (2004) type of NHS hospital having a greater degree of autonomy than conventional trusts. NHS Foundation Trusts have the freedom to decide at a local level how to meet their obligations, and have constitutions that make them accountable to local people, who can become members, directors and governors, and are authorized, monitored and regulated by an independent regulator of NHS Foundation Trusts. See Marini et al. (2008).

t-test

This is a method of comparing a sample mean with an accepted value, or to compare two sample means, or to test whether the slope of a *regression* line differs *statistically significantly* from zero. Cf. *F-test*. See *Student's t-test*. For an introduction see Kennedy (2003).

TTO

Acronym for *time trade-off method*.

2SLS

An acronym for *two-stage least squares*.

Two-stage Least Squares

A method of statistical regression used as an alternative to *ordinary least squares* (OLS) when some of its assumptions are violated. The two stages are: (1) the creation of new *dependent* or *endogenous variables* to replace original ones, and (2) computing the regression OLS fashion, but using the newly created variables. For an introduction see Kennedy (2003). For but one of many *health economics* examples see Auster et al. (1969).

Two-tailed Test

A *statistical significance* test based on the assumption that the data are distributed on either side of a central value. For example, testing whether one treatment is better than another would be a *one-tailed test*, being concerned only with the better outcomes. Testing whether it was better or worse would be a two-tailed test.

Two-way Sensitivity Analysis

For the main entry see *Sensitivity Analysis*. A two-way sensitivity analysis systematically examines the impact of pairs of variables in a *cost–effectiveness analysis* (or similar) by varying them across a plausible range of values and combinations with all other variables constant at their *baseline value*. Varying more than two becomes rather complicated and is termed 'multi-way sensitivity analysis'. Cf. *Extreme Scenario Sensitivity Analysis, One-way Sensitivity Analysis, Probabilistic Sensitivity Analysis*. For an example of the technique in practice see Bhatti and Baibergenova (2008).

Tx

Doctors' shorthand for medical treatment. Cf *Rx*.

Type I Error

Rejection of the *null hypothesis* when it is true, that is, concluding that a relationship exists when it doesn't. Cf. *Type II Error, Type III Error*.

Type II Error

Non-rejection of the *null hypothesis* when it is false, that is, concluding that there is no relationship when there is. Cf. *Type I Error, Type III Error*.

Type III Error

With a somewhat different emphasis from Types I and II, this additional form of error has been suggested and consists in producing right answers to wrong questions, especially when the answer is limited because the scientific methods chosen to answer the question are not well-suited. For example, one might ask the question 'What causes this disease?' but the research actually addresses a (significantly more limited) question 'Why is the prevalence of this disease higher in group A than group B?' Cf. *Type I Error, Type II Error.*

U

ULYSSES

An international collaboration between the universities of Barcelona, Rome (Università Cattolica del Sacro Cuore), Montreal and Toronto to provide a master's level programme of training in *health technology assessment*, including *economic evaluation*, health systems analysis, economics of health care and *equity*. Its website is available at: http://www.ulysses program.net/program.html (accessed 11 November 2009).

Unbalanced Panel

A *panel* in which one or more waves of data are missing for some respondents. In contrast, a *balanced panel* is one in which only respondents with complete data for all waves are included.

Uncertainty

Usually applied to future events, *costs* and *benefits* even though the reliability of *evidence* about past events and their interpretation is also and notoriously subject to many uncertainties. The trouble is that our knowledge can be only finite, while our ignorance must necessarily be infinite (Popper, 2002, p. 38). Sometimes attempts to 'quantify' uncertainty are made by assigning probabilities based on past experience or derived by judgments of various kinds. Sometimes alternative scenarios of the future are devised. Out of the infinity of possible futures, the art lies in trying to narrow down the range to a manageable set of imaginable possibilities that, between them, encompass what are seen as the main characteristics of these possibilities. The reduction of uncertainty about the financial consequences of ill-health (health care expenditures and loss of earnings due to sickness) is the principal advantage of and rationale for *health insurance*.

Analysts distinguish between stochastic uncertainty (sometimes '*first-order uncertainty*') and subjective uncertainty (sometimes '*second-order uncertainty*'). The former is uncertainty arising from randomness in the data studied. The second is uncertainty relating to *parameter* values and is due to insufficient knowledge. See *Bayesian Method, Cost–Effectiveness*

Plane, Expected Utility Theory, Frequentist Approach, Insurance, Prospect Theory, Regret Theory, Sensitivity Analysis. On the treatment of uncertainty in *cost–effectiveness analysis* see O'Hagan et al. (2005).

Uncertainty Aversion

Same as *ambiguity*.

Unconditional Mean Imputation

A method of imputing missing values when there are *incomplete data*.

Unconditional Probability

The probability that something is the case (like the presence of disease) given minimal knowledge of the characteristics of the subject (for example, only that they are a member of the population at large). Cf. *Conditional Probability*.

Unconfounded Comparison

For a comparison to be unconfounded in a *trial* the *arms* must be treated identically and the patients in them similar in all relevant respects, apart from the randomization itself.

Unemployment

The definitions vary from jurisdiction to jurisdiction but most follow the following general character: the number of jobless people who are available for work and are actively seeking it. The fact that unemployment can both be caused by and be a cause of ill-health is, of course, a field of study for health economists. See *Friction Cost, Full Employment, Involuntary Unemployment, Natural Rate of Unemployment, Structural Unemployment*. For a study that examined the direction of causation for Swedes see Gerdtham and Johannesson (2003). For a UK study see Stewart (2001).

Uniform Distribution

A frequency *distribution* having only two *parameters*: the minimum and maximum. All values within the range thus defined are equally probable. Cf. *Normal Distribution*.

Unimodal Distribution

A *distribution* of a *variable* that has one *mode* (peak).

Unintended Consequences

The meaning of unintended consequences of policy is plain but despite this many consequences that could have been anticipated are frequently not anticipated or sought for in *empirical* work. Thus, increasing the legal age for alcohol consumption may have the unintended consequence of increasing marijuana use through a rather obvious (to economists, at least) process of *substitution*. This particular example seems to be real (though the effect size is not large), see Dinardo and Lemieux (2001). Neglect of *opportunity cost* can produce unanticipated consequences that are neither *efficient* nor *fair*, as when special interests plead their cases successfully and obtain a greater share of health care resources – at the expense of health losses to (anonymous) others who may have more valid claims on a fixed pot of resources. On unintended consequences of quality control see Werner and Asch (2005).

Unit Non-response

One of a number of non-sampling sources of potential *bias* in surveys. It occurs when selected subjects fail to respond to a questionnaire. Other errors and possible biases include defective questionnaire wording and format, interviewer errors and coding and/or inputting errors.

Unit of Allocation

The unit that is assigned to the *alternative* interventions being investigated in a trial. Most commonly, the unit will be an individual person but, for example, in a *cluster randomized trial*, groups of people will be assigned together to one or the other of the *arms* of the trial. In some other trials, different parts of a person (such as the left or right eye) might be assigned to receive different interventions. See also *Unit of Analysis Error*.

Unit of Analysis Error

An error made in statistical analysis when it fails to take account of the *unit of allocation*. In some studies, the unit of allocation is not a person, but is instead a group of people, or parts of a person, such as eyes or teeth.

Univariate Analysis

Analysis involving a single *variable*.

Univariate Sensitivity Analysis

A type of *sensitivity analysis* in which there is variable-by-variable adjustment to examine the impact on critical outcomes like *incremental cost–effectiveness ratios*.

Universality

A characteristic of a health care system that is commonly desired or sometimes (as in Canada) required by statute. It refers to the coverage of people with entitlement to use a service. Cf. *Comprehensiveness*.

Unquantified Costs and Benefits

Consequences of decisions that are very costly to quantify, unconvincingly quantified or not worth quantifying. See *Opportunity Cost* and *Benefit*.

Unrelated Future Medical Costs

See *Future Costs in Cost–Effectiveness Analysis.*

Urology

The medical speciality concerned with diseases and abnormalities of the urinary system.

User Charges

These are prices for health care payable by a user at the time of use.

Utilitarianism

This is the ethical doctrine, a variant of which underlies nearly all *welfare* (and some *extra-welfarist*) *economics*, which specifies *utility* as the principal morally good characteristic of society – what humankind as a whole ought to maximize. The moral slogan for a society (of given population) to pursue under utilitarianism is 'the greatest utility for the greatest number'. Under utilitarianism, that which is right is any action or arrangement whose consequences are good in the sense of increasing total utility measured as the sum over all people of each person's individual utility. Hence utilitarianism is a *consequentialist* moral theory. 'Rule utilitarianism' maintains that a code or rule of behaviour is morally right if the consequences of adopting it are more favourable for total utility than not adopting it. 'Act utilitarianism' maintains that the morality of an action is determined by the balance of the favourable or unfavourable consequences in terms of utility that flow from it.

Utility is usually thought of as an indication of the strength of a *preference*. The view that policy ought to be based on individuals' preferences has a long history. Amongst its attractions are the idea that 'everyone counts' in the sense that everyone's utility is treated equally or, in a variant (*maximin*) form, that the social goal ought to be to maximize the utility of the least well off individual. A less attractive feature is that some people have utterly disgusting preferences.

The *classical economists* treated utility as a *cardinal* entity accruing to individuals, which could be added up (like their weights). Since the 1930s welfare economics has tended to shy away from the *interpersonal comparisons of utility* (on the somewhat odd ground that it is 'meaningless' to compare them, when everyone ordinarily compares such things on a daily basis) in favour of the *Pareto criterion* under which a change is judged to be a social improvement only when no one loses utility from it (this does not imply that other changes are not social improvements; only that one cannot say whether they are). Pareto himself, however, used cardinal and interpersonal comparisons of utility whenever he felt it necessary to do so.

Utility theory has also tended to treat utility as measured by linear instruments (like temperature), which enable one to distinguish rising or falling increments of it (*marginal utility*). Considerable controversy attaches both to the question of the people whose utility is to be 'counted', the ways in which the utilities accruing to different people are to be 'added up' or compared, and the character of the entities that are deemed to yield utility or disutility. Goods and services are always 'in' but the following are not always allowed – to illustrate a few possibilities – prospects of consuming goods and services, the relative consumption of goods and services by others, the *distribution* of goods and services generally, characteristics of goods and services, consumption by others, others' utility, the means of acquisition of goods and services, the processes of change as ownership bundles change, characteristics of people such as their health and cognitive skill, and *capabilities* of people like their talent for survival. See *Entitlement Theory, Fairness, Interpersonal Comparisons of Utility, Social Welfare Function, Utility.* The high priests of utilitarianism were Jeremy Bentham (1748–1842) and John Stuart Mill (1806–73) (who may have coined the term 'utilitarianism'). See Bentham ([1789] 1907) and Mill ([1863] 2001).

Utility

Utilities are numbers assigned to entities (usually benefits or things presumed to be the objects of people's *preferences*) according to a rule. This enables the entities to be quantified and ranked according to preference, desirability or choice (these are not, of course, synonyms). There are four common scales of measurement: *categorical*, in which entities belong to a category like 'able to wash self' or 'not able to wash self' (not necessarily only *binary*); *ordinal*, in which rank order is revealed and any numbers will serve that preserve the correct order (e.g. the entity 'dead' is always worse than the entity 'getting along'); *interval*, in which – like temperature measurement – the ratios of intervals between the points on the scale are the same for each set of possible numbers and the zero point is arbitrary; and *ratio*, in which – like measures of weight or distance – zero means 'none' and 'twice as much' is indeed twice as much, whichever set of numbers are being used. The final two just mentioned are both forms of *cardinal* measurement. The sort of measurement normally used in *indifference curve* analysis is ordinal.

The table illustrates three kinds of utility measurement for the four entities that here correspond to health states, or diseases, where high numbers denote better states. The first three columns show some possible numbers (out of an indefinitely large set) that rank the four entities ordinally. Each is equally valid and each ranks them in the same order. The differences between the numbers assigned in each column mean nothing so it is not possible, for example, to speak of increasing or diminishing *marginal* health (nor *marginal utility* of health). The second set of three columns show three sets of numbers that have been assigned to the states according to a different (interval) rule. The same order is preserved but this time column 6 = 10 + twice column 5, and column 7 is –10 + column 5. Each is a *linear transformation* of the other, having the general form $A = a + bB$. With this second set of numbers one can speak of increasing or diminishing marginal health (or marginal utility of health) as each column will show the changes between cells increasing or decreasing. The final three columns are related by a ratio scale as follows: column 9 is as column 8 multiplied by 0.035 and column 10 is column 8 multiplied by 35. Here the form of the equation relating them is $A = bB$, where $b = A/B$, a constant. Not only does this measure rank the entities in the same order, and preserve increasing or decreasing increments or decrements, but we can also say that if 'good health' is 1.67 times as good as 'better health' on one ratio scale, so will it be on any other.

Examples of Utility Scalings

Entity	Ordinal			Cardinal					
					Interval			Ratio	
1	2	3	4	5	6	7	8	9	10
Poor health	1	23	66	1	12	–9	1	0.035	35
Better health	2	24	67	6	22	–4	6	0.210	210
Good health	3	77	68	10	30	0	10	0.350	350
Excellent health	4	987	69	13	36	3	13	0.455	455

The *welfare* connotations of 'utility' are important in economics although, when used simply as an index or preference, utility theory also forms the usual basis of the economist's approach to behaviour: it is predictive, explanatory and conventionally *positive*. The usual *axioms* underlying utility theory are, where the As, Bs and Cs are 'bundles' of goods or services:

- Completeness: either *A* is preferred to *B*, or *B* to *A* or an individual is indifferent between them.
- Transitivity: if *A* is preferred or indifferent to *B* and *B* is preferred or indifferent to *C*, then *A* is preferred or indifferent to *C*.
- Continuity: there is an indifference curve such that all points to its north-east are preferred to all point to its south-west.
- Convexity: the marginal rate of substitution is negative.
- Non-satiation: more is always preferred.

These are essentially positive and experimentally refutable (and have all been more or less frequently refuted empirically!).

The welfare connotations arise in *welfare economics*, when the preferences of individuals form the basic building blocks used to identify improvements or deteriorations in social welfare via a *social welfare function*. Here 'more utility' is a 'good thing', though one might cavil at the idea of a person whose preferences were disgusting having them honoured in the same way as those of a decent citizen. 'More utility' would also, of course, be a good thing if the basic building block consisted of entities ranked by something other than 'preference' but no less value-laden, for example, entities that one was duty-bound to select, or ones that, on some ethical grounding or other, ought, morally speaking, to be ranked higher than the rest. The fact that what one wants to choose is not what one thinks one ought to choose is rarely reflected in discussions of utility, even though there is no reason why the workhorse of utility numbers could not do duty in ranking either. However, 'utility' is so inextricably wedded to 'preference' that it is better to use some other term when assigning numbers to entities that are not to do with preferences (even when the rules of measurement are similar).

In a rather different way that is special to *health economics*, there are welfare connotations arising from the use of utility theory as the analytical framework for constructing indices of health, as in the use of, say, *expected utility theory* in the *standard gamble* approach to *quality-adjusted life-year* (QALY) construction. Here two common, but different, value assumptions may be met. One is that the values embodied in entities (like QALYs) intended to inform public decision-making ought to reflect the preferences of the community on whose behalf the decisions are being made; the other is that the values ought to reflect the preferences (or rankings on other grounds) of decision-makers who are accountable to the public via the usual processes of representative democracy. In either approach, difficulties arise when any of the underlying *axioms* (assumptions) of utility theory are violated. See *Extra-welfarism, Interpersonal Comparisons of Utility, Protected Values, Utility Frontier, Utility Maximizing, Welfarism*.

On the basics of measurement see Alchian (1953). A pioneering use of utility theory in the economic evaluation of health care technologies is Torrance et al. (1972).

Utility Frontier

A utility frontier is a *locus* of points in a diagram that connects the *utility* of all allocations of two goods between two people such that the *marginal rate of transformation* is equal to the *marginal rate of substitution*. Each such point is a *Pareto optimum*. Thus, each of the points *a, b* and *c* on the downward-sloping curve in the diagram is such an optimum: it is not possible to move from one point to any other without one person losing utility even though the other gains, so such points cannot be ranked using the Pareto criterion. The frontier shows the maximum utility attainable by one individual, given the utility level of the other. Point *d* is unattainable, given the resources available and the extant technologies that define the maximum outputs that can be produced from them. These background conditions determine the position of the frontier. *d* cannot be ranked in relation to *a* or *c* using the Pareto criterion, nor *e* in relation to *a* and *c*. Point *e* is not an *efficient* point since it is possible to move from it to a point on the frontier in such a way that both gain utility (or at any

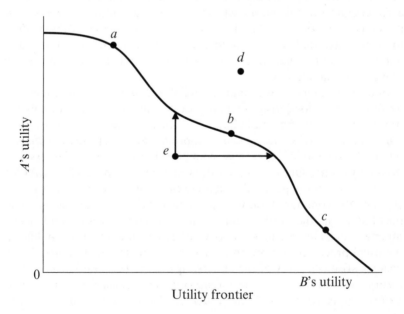

Utility frontier

rate none loses). This is shown by the area enclosed by the two arrows from *e*: any point within this space has more utility for both individuals than point *e* and some point on the frontier in this space is going to be better for at least one of the individuals than some point below it. To choose between points on the frontier requires a *social welfare function* that permits the *interpersonal comparisons of utility*. See *Interpersonal Comparisons of Utility*, *Utility*.

Utility Function

A mathematical function that relates *utility* to the rate of *consumption* of various goods and services or, in some sophisticated cases, to the characteristics of consumer goods and services. The general form of the function is usually:

$$U = U(Q_1, Q_2, Q_3 \ldots Q_N),$$

where the Q_i are goods or services, and where $dU/dQ_i > 0$ is *marginal utility*.

It is possible to model *altruism* in *utilitarian* terms by postulating that some of the *arguments* (the Q_i in the utility function) are entities that accrue to other people. This is to say that the choosing individual derives utility from the consumption, experience, etc. of another person: in a health context, one is, perhaps, pleased to see another person healthier or with greater access to health care than would otherwise be the case. Conversely, of course, a malevolent person by analogy derives negative utility from positive arguments of another's utility. A non-economist may readily imagine what economists make of trading between a sadist and a masochist – a topic treated seriously in Sen (1970)! See *Utility Maximizing*.

Utility Independence

An assumption made in the construction of *quality-adjusted life-years* (QALYs). The *utility* that subjects obtain from the quality of their lives must be independent of the quantity of life, or the utility attaching to a *health-related quality of life* in one time period must be independent of past periods' quality of life and of that anticipated in future periods. First identified by Pliskin et al. (1980). See Broome (1993). But see Bleichrodt and Johannesson (1997a).

Utility Interdependence

A condition in which the *utility* experienced by someone is a function either of the utility of another person or of some more readily perceived characteristic of another (like their health, smell or wealth). See *Externality*.

Utility Maximizing

This (or its variant, *expected utility* maximizing) is the basic motivating drive for human behaviour most frequently used by economists. In some conditions (for example, where there is intense *competition* for the ownership of a firm) profit maximization is used as a good approximation for what motivates managers of firms and this has also been used in health economics. In general, however, economists tend to take it for granted that the behaviour of health care professionals, the health service organizations in which they work and that of their clients is to be examined under the assumption that they maximize some form of *utility function*. This does not imply necessarily that the entities pursued by such decision-makers are selfish ones. See *Utility, Utility Function*. Cf. *Bounded Rationality, Prospect Theory, Regret Theory, Satisficing*.

Utility Measurement

Ascribing numbers systematically to entities so as to indicate *preference*. See *Utility*.

Utility Scales

See *Utility Measurement*.

Utilization

The intensity of use of medical resources per period. Overutilization is use in excess of some optimal, preferred, stipulated (etc.) rate: the benchmark implied varies from context to context and is too frequently left asserted but undefined. The reader should be alert to its ambiguity: it may be propaganda in pursuit of a larger slice of the health resources cake. Utilization has many *determinants,* of which one is income, which has made it the focus of many studies of *equity* (and inequity). For an international study of physician utilization see Van Doorslaer et al. (2004).

Utilization Review

Monitoring programmes in the US that seek to determine the appropriateness of the care delivered and its cost. Reviews, which may be retrospective, current or prospective, usually evaluate the *need*, appropriateness and *efficiency* of health care services, procedures and facilities, including review of the appropriateness of admissions, services ordered and provided, *length of stay*, and discharge practices. Utilization reviews in the US are performed both by peer review groups and public agencies.

V

Validity

In a general sense, the extent to which a measurement instrument measures what it is designed to measure. More specifically, there are *construct validity, convergent validity, criterion validity, discriminant validity, external validity, face validity, internal validity, predictive validity, test-retest validity*.

Value

In economics, *value in use* is usually taken as the maximum amount that an individual or group is willing to pay for a particular good or service rather than go without it. *Marginal value* is the value of *marginal benefit*: the maximum amount an individual is willing to pay for an increment of benefit. *Value in exchange* is a term sometimes used to describe the market value of traded goods or services. The difference between value in use and value in exchange is *consumer's surplus*. See *Demand Curve*.

Value-based Insurance

In *health insurance* this entails keeping the *copayments* for *effective* procedures lower than those for less effective procedures. See Chernew et al. (2007).

Value-based Pricing

A method of pricing pharmaceuticals that links their prices to the estimated value of the health benefits they generate. See Claxton et al. (2008).

Value Function

This is a term used by Kahneman and Tversky (1979) to differentiate discussion of preference orderings from conventional assumptions of *utility functions* having positive and continuously falling slopes (diminishing *marginal utility*). As can be seen from the figure there is a *point of inflection* at which the slope begins to decrease. This characteristic is a feature of *prospect theory*.

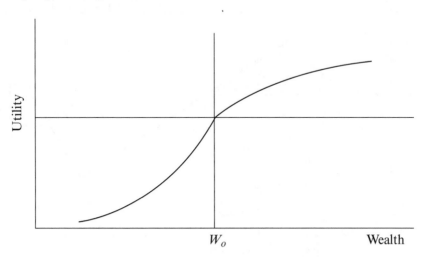

Value in Exchange

The market (exchange) value of a good or service. Illustrated under *Value in Use*. See *Value*.

Value in Use

The maximum amount someone is willing to pay for a particular rate of use of a good or service rather than go without it. Areas $A + B$ in the figure overleaf. See *Value*.

Value Judgment

An ethical opinion made either implicitly or explicitly that a particular course of action, institutional arrangement or method of analysis ought to be implemented, or is itself good. For example, the judgment that consumers' *willingness to pay* ought to determine the allocation of health care services is a value judgment. The judgment that the location and type of services actually provided is determined by willingness to pay is not a

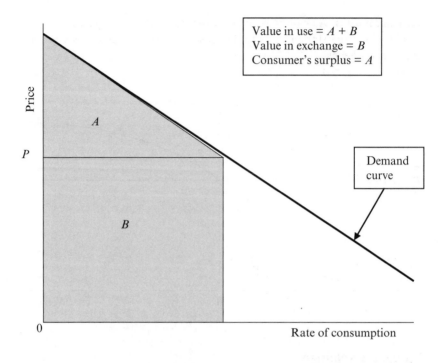

Value in use = $A + B$
Value in exchange = B
Consumer's surplus = A

Demand curve

value judgment (it is a hypothesis about what causes location that can be tested empirically). The judgment that economics ought to be value-free is itself a value judgment. The judgment that economics is value-free is not a value judgment (it is a false statement of fact). *Option apprais-als, cost–effectiveness analyses* and similar evaluative methods typically involve many kinds of judgment, only some of which are judgments of value. A particular class of value judgment is to do with the *welfare* of the members of society: how it ought to be measured, how changes in it or in its *distribution* ought to be assessed, or whether a particular inter-vention or change is likely to have an impact on it for better or worse. A common conflict of values arises in public health policy when mandatory policies (e.g. on no-smoking areas, the wearing of safety helmets and car seatbelt restraints) may enhance health but offend freedom of choice. See *Interpersonal Comparisons of Utility, Welfare Economics*. On some con-flicts in public health see Jones and Bayer (2007) and Homer and French (2009).

Value of a QALY

In *cost–effectiveness* or *cost–utility analysis* studies (CEA or CUA) the nature of the study has often been selected precisely in order not to place a value, such as *willingness-to-pay*, on the *outcome* measure such as the QALY. Not surprisingly, however, there has been interest both in turning a CEA or CUA into a cost–benefit study by monetizing outcomes and in testing the consistency of the political judgments about types of output and the budgets assigned to their production by comparing the *shadow price* of the budget (its *incremental cost-effectiveness*) with what members of the public appear to be willing to pay for incremental QALYs. See Hirth et al. (2000), Gyrd-Hansen (2003), Byrne et al. (2005) and Mason et al. (2009).

Value of Information Analysis

A method from *decision analysis* for evaluating the value of additional (usually research) information in terms of reduced uncertainty about *parameter* values in *health technology assessments*. The expected value of perfect information (EVPI) is the maximum sum one is willing to pay to gain access to perfect information. See, for its use in *health economics*, Claxton (1999) and Claxton et al. (2004, 2006a).

Value of Life

Reduced mortality and increased *life expectancy* are common benefits of health programmes whose *appraisal* will sometimes require a value to be placed on 'life' seen as 'length of life'. There are broadly three approaches to this valuation. The *human capital* approach, which assesses the value as the *present value* of expected future earnings. This has been widely discredited partly for its partial nature (effectively treating people as though they were cart-horses) and partly because of the discrimination it implies against the very young, the old, females, chronic sick, etc. The second, the social decisions approach, infers values from decisions made in the public sector. The third approach enquires experimentally and via surveys about the value placed by individuals on reductions in the size of the risk of death they confront with respect to any particular hazard. Related to this are approaches that seek to explain longevity and the risk of death through the making of rational economic choices. These latter approaches are based on people's *preferences* and are most consistent with the concept of *Pareto efficiency*. They also directly approach the matter in a context of uncertainty, which is the characteristic practical context for most decisions. See Jones-Lee (1989, 1991, 1992), Viscusi (1993) and Viscusi and Aldy (2003). An approach using a life-cycle model of the *demand* for life expectancy and the value of a life saved is Ehrlich (2000). On dangerous work see Dorman (1996). On some *discounting* issues see Alberini et al. (2006).

Value of Statistical Life

See *Value of Life*.

Value Tree Analysis

A procedure used in *multiple criteria decision analysis* in which objectives are arranged hierarchically such that top-level objectives may have other objectives or desired *attributes* within them, which may in turn have other lower-level attributes, etc. See Keeney and Raiffa (1976).

Variable

Characteristics of individuals, usually quantified, such as blood pressure, age, income or region of residence, will vary and, hence, are termed 'variables'. So are other elements in a *model* that can vary but are not characteristics of people, such as *inputs*, price, *GDP*, or industrial concentration. Some variables are *binary*. Such variables usually indicate either the presence or the absence of a feature of interest (such as male or female, black or white, alive or dead). Cf. *Parameter*. See *Binary Variable, Count Variable, Dependent Variable, Independent Variable*.

Variable-by-Variable Analysis

Same as *univariate sensitivity analysis*.

Variable Costs

These are *costs* that vary as the *output* rate varies.

Variable Factor

A *factor of production* that varies as *output* varies. See *Production Function*.

Variable Proportions

See *Law of Variable Proportions*.

Variance

A measure of the dispersion of a set of numbers. It is the *standard deviation* squared. The variance of a *population* is the squared deviations of the measurements from their *mean* divided by the size of the population. The variance of a sample uses the sample means in the calculation of the squared deviations and the sample size minus one as the denominator. In accounting and budgeting practice, 'variance' is the difference between a budgeted amount and the outturn.

Variance Ratio Distribution

Same as *F-distribution*.

Variations in Practice

There are marked international and within national variations in *outcomes* that are frequently attributed to the various financial incentives that characterize different health care systems, the exercise of clinical 'freedom' and the absence of, or failure to follow, best practice guidelines. There are many practical difficulties, however, in establishing the presence or absence of quality variation. See Wennberg (2002) and Wennberg et al. (2002) for two examples from this tireless exposer of (apparently) unwarranted clinical variation in practice, Luft (2003) for variations between *fee-for-service* and *HMO* settings, McPherson et al. (1982) for international variations. See also *Small Area Variations*.

VAS

Acronym for *visual analogue scale*.

Vector

In mathematics, a vector comprises numbers (called 'elements') arranged in a row (row vector) or column (column vector). A vector of n elements is referred to as n-dimensional. There is a special algebra for vectors. In *epidemiology*, a vector is an agent, usually insect or animal, able to carry *pathogens* from one organism to another.

Veil of Ignorance

A device used in moral philosophy, most famously by Immanuel Kant (1724–1804) and, more recently, by John Rawls (1921–2002) in the theory of 'justice as fairness' to eliminate prejudice. See *Fairness*. See Rawls (1971) and Harsanyi (1982).

Verification Bias

Same as *work-up bias*.

Vertical Equity

Treating appropriately unequally those who are unequal in some morally relevant sense. Commonly met vertical *equity* principles include 'higher contributions from those with greater *ability to pay*', 'more resource for those with greater need for resource' and 'lower priority for lower deservingness'. Cf. *Horizontal Equity*. See *Equity*.

Vertical Integration

This entails the bringing together in managed units, activities or firms that were previously separate. It generally comes in one of three forms: backward vertical integration, forward vertical integration and balanced vertical integration. Under backward vertical integration, an organization has subsidiaries producing inputs used in the production of its more 'downstream' products. Under forward vertical integration, an organization has subsidiaries that distribute or market products 'downstream' to customers or use the products themselves. Under balanced vertical integration, an organization has both upstream and downstream subsidiaries.

Health care is characterized by a variety of types of integration (or lack of it). Examples of its absence are the existence (in the US) of doctors contracting with hospitals for use of their beds and provision of professional services to the patients in them, and (in most countries) the complete absence of any kind of coordination between health care services and community-based social care services. For a *health economics* example of its use, see Gaynor (2006). In the US there is a variety of degrees of integration of physicians and hospitals. Some common ones are: *Independent Practice Associations* (IPAs), which contract with *managed health care* plans; *Open Physician-Hospital Organizations* (OPHOs) which, in addition, offer administrative services to physicians; *Closed Physician-Hospital Organizations* (CPHOs), which are similar but have exclusive arrangements with their physicians and claim to coordinate care better; Management Services Organizations (MSOs), which in addition often buy the physicians' assets and manage their financial affairs (billing etc.), and Fully Integrated Organizations (FIOs), which generally also have salaried practitioners. The degree of vertical integration has been rising in the US, probably as a response to the rise of managed care. See Cuellar and Gertler (2006) for an analysis that finds the trend has had a positive impact on prices and no effect on *efficiency*.

Viatical Settlements

A means by which people with terminal disease may access some of the value of their life *insurance*. In a viatical settlement, people with terminal illnesses sell their life insurance policies to 'viatical settlement companies' in exchange for a percentage of the policy's face value. The viatical settlement company may in turn sell the policy to a third party. The purchaser continues to pay the premiums, and collects the face value of the policy when the original policyholder dies. The word comes from the Latin word for 'to travel' and is related to the provisions made for subsistence while travelling, with the metaphorical use in the Roman Church of preparation for the passage from life to death and the last Eucharistic rite or 'viaticum'. The market for viatical settlements developed in the US mainly as a result of the rise of AIDS in the late 1980s, with considerable fraud and *adverse selection*.

Visual Analogue Scale

VAS is a graphical method for rating health states directly. A common instrument is a figure akin to a thermometer, on which are marked two anchor states, and on which the rater is asked to mark their rating of some other state, usually lying between the two anchors. Used in deriving *quality-adjusted life-years* and related measures of *health status*. The instrument may be used to scale hypothetical states of health (as in time trade-off exercises) and as a means for individuals to summarize their own health states. See *EQ-5D*. See Parkin and Devlin (2006).

Vital Statistics

There is an informal definition with which we need not be concerned. The formal definition is statistics at the *population* level relating to key events in and characteristics of life: births, deaths, marriages, migration, *life expectancy* and health. Adoptions, divorces and other population-based 'vital' measures may also be included.

Volunteer Bias

Volunteers in *trials* may exhibit exposures or outcomes that differ systematically from those of non-volunteers. A form of *selection bias*. See *Bias*.

Von Neumann–Morgenstern Utility

vNM utility is a measure of *expected utility* (strength of preference under uncertainty) that is built on the *axioms* developed by the eponymous authors. See the main entry for *Expected Utility*.

Vouchers

An idea borrowed from the economics literature on financing education. It is a scheme that targets low-income households with entitlements like tax credits or certificates (vouchers) exchangeable for health care insurance. It has been supported by the American Medical Association. See Cutler and Reber (1998).

W

Wage-risk Studies

These are *preference*-based studies that value health or reduction in the risk of death through the wage differentials required to induce people to accept jobs having differing degrees of risk to health or death. For example, Viscusi (1993).

Waiting List

A list of people waiting, usually for an *out-patient* examination by a hospital doctor or for admission to hospital as an in-patient. Lists, and the times people spend on them, are often treated as though they were a *rationing* device, akin to a price. However, the length of the queue is a poor indicator of this 'price', since it is the length of time spent waiting that is more likely to be significant. There are crucial differences between waiting times and conventional queues, of which two are that first, although a 'price' of sorts is paid by the patients, it is not received by anyone and so has no (conventional) incentivizing effect on providers; second, the time spent queuing involves postponement of possible benefit rather than any current *opportunity cost* of time, that is, the queuing itself does not reduce the many alternative things one could be doing with one's time, since one doesn't 'stand in line' though any disabling effects of an illness of course may do this. See *Queue*. For a review of the economics of waiting for health care see Cullis et al. (2000); for some implications for efficient resource allocation, see Gravelle and Siciliani (2008). On *effective* strategies for managing lists, see Willcox et al. (2007).

Waiting Time

See *Waiting List*.

Washout Period

The gap between the end of a treatment period and the start of another in a *crossover trial*. The lapsed time 'washes out' the effects of the first period's treatment.

Wayward Use

A term used to describe the prescription of one drug (most likely expensive) when another equally *effective* but cheaper is available.

WB

Acronym for *World Bank*.

Weak Dominance

Same as *extended dominance*.

Wealth

The value of all *assets* owned by an individual or group minus the value of all debts. On the connection between wealth and health see Dollar (2001).

Wealth Effect

The effect that a change in *real wealth* has on consumption of health care or, more generally, the *demand* for goods, services and savings. See, for a *health insurance* application, Lee (2005).

Web of Causation

A term used by some epidemiologists to describe a multi-factorial and multi-layered set of interlinked *determinants* of health (or ill-health) *outcomes*.

Weibull Model

A parametric statistical model for *duration analysis*. Named after the Swedish engineer Waloddi Weibull (1887–1979). See Weibull (1951).

Weighted Least Squares

A method used in *least squares* regression of weighting *dependent* and *independent variables* to correct for *heteroskedasticity*.

Welfare

The quality that is taken by economists to indicate the *well-being* of individuals, of a society or of the arrangements (or changes in them) that a society adopts. It is usually measured as an index. Higher levels of welfare are inherently better for that individual or society – as judged by the economist constructing or using the index. Economists, philosophers, sociologists and psychologists differ among themselves as to what constitutes a higher level of welfare and on whether useful empirical measurements of welfare can be made (*construct validity*). Economists most frequently use per capita GDP (*gross domestic product*) as the index of well-being. Some modify this welfare index with allowance for unpaid activity within households (which GDP excludes) or for environmental and related effects (which GDP treats erroneously from a welfare viewpoint: GDP rises if there is an oil spill and resources need to be used to clean it up). *Extra-welfarists* believe that even with such modifications, GDP is inadequate since policy-makers invariably behave as though welfare involves much more than the mere satisfaction of wants through the consumption of goods and services.

Other words sometimes used by economists for welfare include *utility* and satisfaction. These alternatives are often used, however, without any implication that an individual or society is 'really' better off by having a higher level of either utility or satisfaction. They merely denote that the chooser (the individual or society) has as a goal a higher level of the index, and not necessarily that the economist endorses their goal as an ethically desirable one nor that this is the only or the ultimate goal. Sometimes all that is meant by a utility number is an order of preference; on other occasions it may imply something about a particular level of pain or pleasure, or even 'happiness' for the individual or society in question. According to these views the fundamental element in 'welfare' consists in the satisfaction of *preferences*. Despite its wide currency, this seems a pathetically inadequate and incomplete measure of either individual or societal welfare, particularly when one considers the unappealing (even disgusting) nature of some people's preferences.

Some economists try to avoid the concept of welfare entirely and, indeed, deny that the concept of welfare is meaningful. Such economists are broadly in the *logical positivism* school. Since health economics is largely inseparable from policy issues, in which questions deemed 'metaphysical' by analysts in the positivist tradition are central, those who dodge the welfare implications of economic policies are severely limited in their ability to contribute to health economics. See *Extra-welfarism, Positive Economics, Rationality, Welfare Economics, Welfarism*. See Brouwer et al. (2008).

Welfare Cost

Same as *deadweight loss*.

Welfare Economics

Welfare economics is the branch of economics concerned with identifying the conditions that make for a good society and identifying changes in allocations of goods and services, or arrangements for allocating goods and services, that are better for society. In welfare economics, the noun 'society' is generally taken to encompass all adult rational individuals. How the separate 'welfares' of these individuals are 'added up' to enable an overall judgment of 'good' or 'better' to be reached has been an important part of welfare economics. How the welfare is to be examined of people who do not conform to some definition of 'rational' is less commonly considered. See *Extra-welfarism, Pareto Optimality, Positive Economics, Welfare, Welfarism*. See Culyer (1991a) for a typical example of welfare economics applied to health care.

Welfare Loss

Same as *deadweight loss*.

Welfarism

The approach to evaluating states of society that assumes that *welfare* is the appropriate *maximand*, that (economic) welfare in the form of *utility* is to be had (mainly) from goods and services, that utility depends only on preferences, and that only utilities matter for social welfare. See *Pareto Optimality, Welfare Economics*. Cf. *Extra-welfarism*.

Well-being

An idea related to *utility* but to be distinguished from *health-related quality of life* and the inherent 'worth' of people. See Nord (2001).

What-if-analysis

Same as *sensitivity analysis*.

WHO

Acronym for *World Health Organization*.

WHO-CHOICE

This is a *World Health Organization* project to facilitate the transfer of information on economic evaluation between countries or regions in such a way as to allow it to be modified and applied in another setting. There are regional databases reporting the costs and *effectiveness* of key interventions for 17 sub-regions, grouped together on the basis of *epidemiology*, infrastructure and economic situation. Its website is available at: http://www.who.int/choice/en/? (accessed 10 November 2009).

Wilcoxon Rank-sum Test

This is used to test the hypothesis that two independent *samples* have come from the same *population*. Because it is non-parametric, it makes only limited assumptions about the *distribution* of the data. The method employed is a sum-of-ranks comparison. It is an alternative to the two-sample *t-test*, and is based only on the order in which the observations from the two samples fall. It is of evident use when data are *ordinal* in nature and a comparison of means is meaningless. See Wilcoxon (1945).

Williams' Schematic of Health Economics

A fairly comprehensive taxonomizing framework that systematically embraces the various topics studied by health economists. Its form is as in the accompanying 'plumbing diagram'. The letter labels for each box in the schematic indicate the (approximate) order in which things flow, with various feedbacks etc. indicated by the arrows. Adapted from Williams (2003).

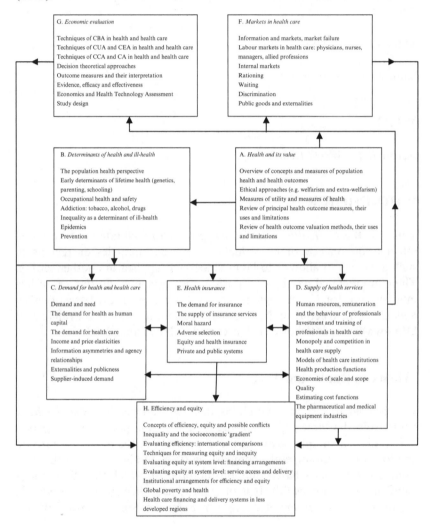

A schematic of health economics

Willingness to Accept

The minimum compensation an individual is willing to accept in exchange for giving up some good or service, or the minimum sum that an individual is willing to accept to forgo a prospective gain. It is usually elicited from *stated* or *revealed preference* experiments. Cf. *Willingness to Pay*. See *Kaldor–Hicks Criterion*. For an application see Van den Berg et al. (2005).

Willingness to Pay

The maximum sum an individual (or a government) is willing to pay to acquire some good or service, or the maximum sum an individual (or government) is willing to pay to avoid a prospective loss. It is usually elicited from *stated* or *revealed preference* experiments. In normative analyses based on user preferences, one should never forget that willingness to pay is highly conditioned by *ability to pay*. Measures of *willingness to accept* typically reveal higher values than measures of willingness to pay. See *Kaldor–Hicks Criterion, Value of a QALY*. See Olsen and Donaldson (1998), Olsen and Smith (2001), Gyrd-Hansen (2003) and Dong et al. (2005).

Withdrawal Bias

A *bias* in trials arising from patients who withdraw from studies being different from those who remain.

Workers' Compensation

A general term to describe the arrangements in many jurisdictions that are designed to ensure that employees who have work-related injuries or disease, or are disabled on the job, receive appropriate medical care and monetary compensations. It is common for schedules to be used that list the compensation available for both economic and non-economic losses on a no-fault basis, thus eliminating the need for litigation. Provision is also often made for dependents of those workers who are killed because of work-related accidents or illnesses. In Australia, Canada and the US, these are state/provincial programmes. In Italy and New Zealand, the system is national. Other jurisdictions, such as the UK, employ mixed systems via national regulation and social security coupled with compulsory private employer liability *insurance*. In Germany, the public insurance agencies are organized by industry. See Dewa and Lin (2000) and Hotopp et al. (2008).

Workers' Compensation Principle

This is a principle underlying most systems of *workers' compensation*. It has two elements: one is 'no fault', so that negligence is not required to be proved in order for a worker to receive compensation for, say, an injury incurred at work, nor can the worker be held responsible for contributory negligence, whereby they may have brought the unwanted event upon themselves. However, the injury is required to be 'work-related'. The other element is that the benefits provided under workers' compensation are the employer's and the insurer's only liability to the employee for workplace injury.

Workplace Health and Safety

See *Occupational Disease and Injury*.

Work-up Bias

Same as *verification bias*. It occurs when patients with negative and positive test results are not evaluated by the same gold standard test. See *Bias*.

World Bank

The World Bank was created in 1944. It consists of two major international organizations: the International Bank for Reconstruction and Development, and the International Development Association. Together with the International Finance Corporation, the Multilateral Investment Guarantee Agency, and the International Centre for the Settlement of Investment Disputes, they form the World Bank Group. The Group's mission is to fight poverty and improve the living standards of people in the developing world. The group is effectively a development bank that provides loans, policy advice, technical assistance and knowledge-sharing services to low- and middle-income countries to reduce poverty. It is the world's largest external source of funding for education and HIV/AIDS programmes.

Its shareholders are nations, with votes proportionate to their *gross domestic products* and it has a Board of Governors made up of national directors (usually ministers of member states). It has major interests in investing in health care facilities in the third world and in measuring international inequalities in health, health care and health care financing. Its web address is: www. worldbank.org/ (accessed 11 November 2009). The World Bank's poverty and health website is a rich source of technical notes on *equity*, equality, and health and poverty: http://web.worldbank.org/WBSITE/EXTERNAL /TOPICS/EXTHEALTHNUTRITIONANDPOPULATION/EXTPAH/0 ,,menuPK:400482~pagePK:149018~piPK:149093~theSitePK:400476,00. html (accessed 11 November 2009).

World Health Organization

The World Health Organization (WHO) is the United Nations' specialized agency for health. It was established in 1948. WHO's objective, as set out in its constitution, is the attainment by all peoples of the highest possible level of *health*. The famous, if unachievable, WHO concept of health in its constitution is 'a state of complete physical, mental and social well-being and not merely the absence of disease or infirmity'.

WHO is governed by 192 member states through the World Health Assembly, which comprises representatives from WHO's member states. The main tasks of the World Health Assembly are to approve the WHO programme and the budget for the following biennium and to decide major policy questions. WHO member states are grouped into six regions, each with a regional office: Africa, the Americas, South-East Asia, Europe, Eastern Mediterranean and Western Pacific.

The WHO is responsible for a host of statistical services; advice, support and training services for member states; international agreements; and broad area strategies for achieving its aims. Its web address is: http://www. who.int/en/ (accessed 11 November 2009).

WTA

Acronym for *willingness to accept*.

WTP

Acronym for *willingness to pay*.

X

X-inefficiency

X-inefficiency is the difference in costs between *efficient* and inefficient firms engaged in essentially the same activity and on the same scale, i.e. it does not arise from differences in product mix and is not a consequence of *economies* (or diseconomies) *of scale* or *scope*. The term was coined by Harvey Leibenstein (1922–94). It generally arises in situations when either or both of the product market or the *capital* market (the market for the firm's ownership) are not *competitive*, resulting in *price-searching* behaviour and an increase in the costs to owners of monitoring and enforcing their own interests within the firm (sometimes referred to as a 'separation' of ownership from control). This enables managers to act in ways that may not be in the interest of owners but that are consistent with *utility-maximizing* by managers in pursuing their own interests. Since most sources of (on-the-job) utility are costly, this necessarily implies that costs will be higher in utility-maximizing firms than in profit-maximizing firms. The difference is X-inefficiency. See *Bounded Rationality, Satisficing*. See Leibenstein (1966) for its origin, Rosko (2001), Brown (2003), Hollingsworth (2008) and Tanya et al. (2008) for some health economics applications.

Y

Yardstick Competition

This is an industrial regulatory procedure under which the regulated price is set at the average of the estimated *marginal costs* of the firms in the industry. See Schut and Van de Ven (2005).

Years of Healthy Life

Life-years adjusted for the level of *health-related quality of life*. Cf. *Health-adjusted Life-expectancy*.

Yellow Card Scheme

A reporting scheme operated by the English National Health Service through which health professionals and members of the public can report side-effects of drugs and other treatments to the Medicines and Healthcare Products Regulatory Agency. It is a form of follow-up or surveillance to supplement *clinical trials*.

Z

Zero-base Budgeting

The principle of creating *budgets* for organizations ab initio, re-establishing basic principles (vision, mission, aims, objectives and the like) and setting the budget accordingly, rather than making marginal adjustments to the budget of a previous (usually last) year.

z-test

A test of the *null hypothesis* that a population *parameter* such as the *mean* is equal to a given value. It assumes that observations have a normal distribution. Cf. *t-test*.

APPENDIX: 100 ECONOMIC STUDIES OF HEALTH INTERVENTIONS

The studies in this catalogue (cost–benefit, cost–consequences, cost–effectiveness, cost–utility studies) are mostly ones that have been entered in the Centre for Reviews & Dissemination (CRD) database (NHS EED) at the University of York, UK, and that have met minimal standards set by CRD or as judged informally by me. Exceptions to these inclusion principles include one or two pioneering studies. I have tried to illustrate the great variety – and the relevance – of the topics addressed. Other criteria include: a clear specification of the study question, a description of the health technology in question, the settings in which it might be used, the population to which it applies, the type of study (CEA, CUA, etc.), the perspective of the study (societal, third party payer, etc.), sources of data, methods of obtaining data, the time period over which data were obtained, measures of benefit, measures of cost, synthesis of benefits and costs, the types of modelling employed, the currency used, dates of measures, the treatment of uncertainty (types of sensitivity analysis), the discounting procedure employed and the rates of discount chosen. It is astonishing how many published studies fail to meet several of these criteria, which many regard as being amongst the hallmarks of high-quality applied research.

I have in general given only one example out of the many that could have been given, for a variety of conditions, technologies or interventions (some clinical, some public health, some managerial or institutional) and for a variety of countries.

Accidents in the home (prevention)

Hendriks, M.R., S.M. Evers, M.H. Bleijlevens, J.C. Van Haastregt, H.F. Crebolder and J.Th. Van Eijk (2008), 'Cost-effectiveness of a multidisciplinary fall prevention program in community-dwelling elderly people: a randomized controlled trial', *International Journal of Technology Assessment in Health Care,* **24**, 193–202.

AIDS (counselling)

Zaric, G.S., A.M. Bayoumi, M.L. Brandeau and D.K. Owens (2008), 'The cost-effectiveness of counseling strategies to improve adherence to highly active antiretroviral therapy among men who have sex with men', *Medical Decision Making*, **28**, 359–76.

AIDS (prevention)

Laufer, F.N. (2001), 'Cost-effectiveness of syringe exchange as an HIV prevention strategy', *Journal of Acquired Immune Deficiency Syndromes*, **28**, 273–8.

AIDS (treatment)

Freedberg, K.A., N. Kumarasamy, E. Losina, A.J. Cecelia, C.A. Scott, N. Divi, T.P. Flanigan, Z. Lu, M.C. Weinstein, B. Wang, A.K. Ganesh, M.A. Bender, K.H. Mayer and R.P. Walensky (2007), 'Clinical impact and cost-effectiveness of antiretroviral therapy in India: starting criteria and second-line therapy', *AIDS*, **21** (Suppl. 4), S117–S128.

Alzheimer's (treatment)

Fuh, J.L. and S.J. Wang (2008), 'Cost-effectiveness analysis of donepezil for mild to moderate Alzheimer's disease in Taiwan', *International Journal of Geriatric Psychiatry*, **23**, 73–8.

Angina angioplasty (treatment)

Sculpher, M.J., D. Smith, T. Clayton, R. Henderson, M.J. Buxton, S. Pocock and D. Chamberlain (2002), 'Coronary angioplasty versus medical therapy for angina (health service costs based on the second Randomized Intervention Treatment of Angina (RITA-2) trial', *European Heart Journal,* **23**, 1291–300.

Angina (treatment)

Campbell, H.E., S. Tait, M.J. Buxton, L.D. Sharples, N. Caine, P.M. Schofield and J. Wallwork (2001), 'A UK trial-based cost-utility analysis of transmyocardial laser revascularization compared to continued medical therapy for treatment of refractory angina pectoris', *European Journal of Cardio-Thoracic Surgery*, **2**, 312–18.

Ankylosing spondylitis

Kobelt, G., P. Sobocki, J. Sieper and J. Braun (2007), 'Comparison of the cost-effectiveness of infliximab in the treatment of ankylosing spondylitis in the United Kingdom based on two different clinical trials', *International Journal of Technology Assessment in Health Care*, **23**, 368–75.

Aortic aneurysm (screening)

Kim, L.G., S.G. Thompson, A.H. Briggs, M.J. Buxton and H.E. Campbell (2007), 'How cost-effective is screening for abdominal aortic aneurysms?', *Journal of Medical Screening*, **14**, 46–52.

Arthritis (treatment)

Wailoo, A.J., N. Bansback, A. Brennan, K. Michaud, R.M. Nixon and F. Wolfe (2008), 'Biologic drugs for rheumatoid arthritis in the Medicare program: a cost-effectiveness analysis', *Arthritis and Rheumatism*, **58**, 939–46.

Asthma, childhood (treatment)

Weiss, K., M.J. Buxton, F.L. Andersson, C.-J. Lamm, B. Liljas and S.D. Sullivan (2006), 'Cost-effectiveness of early intervention with once-daily budesonide in children with mild persistent asthma: results from the START study', *Pediatric Allergy and Immunology*, **17** (Suppl.), 21–7.

Asthma (treatment)

Sullivan, S.D., M.J. Buxton, L.F. Andersson, C.-J. Lamm, B. Liljas, Y.Z. Chen, R.A. Pauwels and K.B. Weiss (2003), 'Cost-effectiveness analysis of early intervention with budesonide in mild persistent asthma', *Journal of Allergy and Clinical Immunology*, **112**, 1229–36.

Automated medical documentation (non-clinical)

Kopach, R., S. Sadat, I.D. Gallaway, G. Geiger, W.J. Ungar and P.C. Coyte (2005), 'Cost-effectiveness analysis of medical documentation alternatives', *International Journal of Technology Assessment in Health Care*, **21**, 126–31.

Bipolar disorder (treatment)

Calvert, N.W., S.P. Burch, A.Z. Fu, P. Reeves and T.R. Thompson (2006), 'The cost-effectiveness of lamotrigine in the maintenance treatment of adults with bipolar I disorder', *Journal of Managed Care Pharmacy*, **12**, 322–30.

Cancer of the breast (screening)

Norman, R.P., D.G. Evans, D.F. Easton and K.C. Young (2007), 'The cost-utility of magnetic resonance imaging for breast cancer in BRCA1 mutation carriers aged 30–49', *European Journal of Health Economics*, **8**, 137–44.

Cancer of the breast (treatment)

Vu, T., S. Ellard, C.H. Speers, S.C. Taylor, M.L. de Lemos, F. Hu, K. Kuik and I.A. Olivotto (2008), 'Survival outcome and cost-effectiveness with docetaxel and paclitaxel in patients with metastatic breast cancer: a population-based evaluation', *Annals of Oncology*, **19**, 461–4.

Cancer of the cervix (screening)

Sherlaw-Johnson, C. and Z. Philips (2004), 'An evaluation of liquid-based cytology and human papillomavirus testing within the UK cervical cancer screening programme', *British Journal of Cancer*, **91**, 84–91.

Cancer of the colon (screening)

Khandker, R.K., J.D. Dulski, J.B. Kilpatrick, R.P. Ellis, J.B. Mitchell and W.B. Baine (2000), 'A decision model and cost-effectiveness analysis of colorectal cancer screening and surveillance guidelines for average-risk adults', *International Journal of Technology Assessment in Health Care*, **16**, 799–810.

Cancer of the colon (treatment)

Aballea, S., J.V. Chancellor, M. Raikou, M.F. Drummond, M.C. Weinstein, S. Jourdan and J. Bridgewater (2007), 'Cost-effectiveness analysis of oxaliplatin compared with 5-fluorouracil/leucovorin in adjuvant treatment of stage III colon cancer in the US', *Cancer*, **109**, 1082–9.

Cardiac angiography (diagnostics)

Barrett, B.J., P.S. Parfrey, R.N. Foley and A.S. Detsky (1994), 'An economic analysis of strategies for the use of contrast media for diagnostic cardiac catheterization', *Medical Decision Making*, **14**, 325–35.

Case management for out-patients (treatment)

Latour, C.H., J.E. Bosmans, M.W. Van Tulder, R. de Vos, F.J. Huyse, P. de Jonge, L.A. Van Gemert and W.A. Stalman (2007), 'Cost-effectiveness of a nurse-led case management intervention in general medical out-patients compared with usual care: an economic evaluation alongside a randomized controlled trial', *Journal of Psychosomatic Research*, **62**, 363–70.

Cataract surgery (treatment)

Rasanen, P., K. Krootila, H. Sintonen, T. Leivo, A.M. Koivisto, O.P. Ryynanen, M. Blom and R.P. Roine (2006), 'Cost-utility of routine cataract surgery', *Health and Quality of Life Outcomes*, **4**, 1–11.

Chagas disease (treatment)

Wilson, L.S., A.M. Strosberg and K. Barrio (2005), 'Cost-effectiveness of Chagas disease interventions in Latin America and the Caribbean: Markov models', *American Journal of Tropical Medicine and Hygiene*, **73**, 901–10.

Chickenpox (vaccination)

Beutels, P., R. Clara, G. Tormans, E. Van Doorslaer and P. Van Damme (1996), 'Costs and benefits of routine varicella vaccination in German children', *Journal of Infectious Diseases*, **174** (Suppl. 3), S335–S341.

Childhood attention deficit (treatment)

Donnelly, M., M.M. Haby, R. Carter, G. Andrews and T. Vos (2004), 'Cost-effectiveness of dexamphetamine and methylphenidate for the treatment of childhood attention deficit hyperactivity disorder', *Australian and New Zealand Journal of Psychiatry*, **38**, 592–601.

Cholera (prevention)

Murray, J., D.A. McFarland and R.J. Waldman (1998), 'Cost-effectiveness of oral cholera vaccine in a stable refugee population at risk for epidemic cholera and in a population with endemic cholera', *Bulletin of the World Health Organization*, **76**, 343–52.

Cholesterol lowering (prevention)

Prosser, L.A., A.A. Stinnett, P.A. Goldman, L.W. Williams, M.G. Hunink, L. Goldman and M.C. Weinstein (2000), 'Cost-effectiveness of cholesterol-lowering therapies according to selected patient characteristics', *Annals of Internal Medicine*, **132**, 769–79.

Circumcision, male (surgical intervention)

Van Howe, R.S. (2004), 'A cost-utility analysis of neonatal circumcision', *Medical Decision Making*, **24**, 584–601.

Contraception for adolescents (prevention)

Wang, L.Y., M. Davis, L. Robin, J. Collins, K. Coyle and E. Baumler (2000), 'Economic evaluation of Safer Choices: a school-based human immunodeficiency virus, other sexually transmitted diseases, and pregnancy prevention program', *Archives of Pediatrics and Adolescent Medicine*, **154**, 1017–24.

Crohn's disease (treatment)

Lindsay, J., Y.S. Punekar, J. Morris and G. Chung-Faye (2008), 'Health-economic analysis: cost-effectiveness of scheduled maintenance treatment with infliximab for Crohn's disease – modelling outcomes in active luminal and fistulizing disease in adults', *Alimentary Pharmacology and Therapeutics*, **28**, 76–87.

CT scanning (diagnostics)

Campbell, K.A., R.P. Berger, L. Ettaro and M.S. Roberts (2007), 'Cost-effectiveness of head computed tomography in infants with possible inflicted traumatic brain injury', *Pediatrics*, **120**, 295–304.

Dengue fever (prevention)

Shepard, D.S., J.A. Suaya, S.B. Halstead, M.B. Nathan, D.J. Gubler, R. Mahoney, D.N. Wang and M.I. Meltzer (2004), 'Cost-effectiveness of a pediatric dengue vaccine', *Vaccine*, **22**, 1275–80.

Depression (treatment)

Peveler, R., T. Kendrick, M.J. Buxton, L. Longworth, D. Baldwin, M. Moore, J. Chatwin, J. Goddard, A. Thornett, H. Smith, M. Campbell and C. Thompson (2005), 'A randomised controlled trial to compare the cost-effectiveness of tricyclic antidepressants, selective serotonin reuptake inhibitors and lofepramine, *Health Technology Assessment*, **9**, 1–134.

Detoxification (treatment)

Parrott, S., C. Godfrey, N. Heather, J. Clark and T. Ryan (2006), 'Cost and outcome analysis of two detoxification services', *Alcohol and Alcoholism*, **41**, 84–91.

Diabetes (screening)

Faronato, P. and G. de Bigontina (1994), 'A cost-benefit analysis of two mass screening strategies for albuminuria in diabetic patients', *Diabetes Nutrition and Metabolism*, **7**, 325–9.

Diabetes (treatment)

Valentine, W.J., J.M. Bottomley, A.J. Palmer, M. Brandle, V. Foos, R. Williams, J.A. Dormandy, J. Yates, M.H. Tan and M. Massi-Benedetti (2007), 'PROactive 06: cost-effectiveness of pioglitazone in Type 2 diabetes in the UK', *Diabetic Medicine*, **24**, 982–1002.

Diabetic retinopathy (screening)

Sculpher, M.J., M.J. Buxton, B.A. Ferguson, D.J. Spiegelhalter and A.J. Kirby (1992), 'Screening for diabetic retinopathy: a relative cost-effectiveness analysis of alternative modalities and strategies', *Health Economics*, **1**, 39–51.

Down syndrome (screening)

Ball, R.H., A.B. Caughey, F.D. Malone, D.A. Nyberg, C.H. Comstock, G.R. Saade, R.L. Berkowitz, S.J. Gross, L. Dugoff, S.D. Craigo, I.E. Timor-Tritsch, S.R. Carr, H.M. Wolfe, D. Emig and M.E. D'Alton (2007), 'First- and second-trimester evaluation of risk for Down syndrome', *Obstetrics and Gynecology*, **110**, 10–17.

Duodenal ulcer (surgery vs medical treatment)

Culyer, A.J. and A.K. Maynard (1980), 'Treating ulcers with cimetidine can be more cost-effective than surgery', *Medeconomics*, **1**, 12–14.

Duodenal ulcer (treatment)

Sintonen, H. and V. Alander (1990), 'Comparing the costs of drug regimens in the treatment of duodenal ulcers', *Journal of Health Economics*, **9**, 85–101.

Embryo transfer (treatment)

Dixon, S., N.F. Faghih, W.L. Ledger, E.A. Lenton, A. Duenas, P. Sutcliffe P. and J.B. Chilcott (2008), 'Cost-effectiveness analysis of different embryo transfer strategies in England', *British Journal of Obstetrics and Gynaecology*, **115**, 758–766.

Fractures (prevention)

Rosner, A.J., D.T. Grima, G.W. Torrance, C. Bradley, J.D. Adachi, R.J. Sebald and D.J.Willison (1998), 'Cost effectiveness of multi-therapy treatment strategies in the prevention of vertebral fractures in postmenopausal women with osteoporosis', *PharmacoEconomics*, **14**, 559–73.

Genetic testing, prenatal (diagnostic)

Heckerling, P.S. and M.S. Verp (1994), 'A cost-effectiveness analysis of amniocentesis and chorionic villus sampling for prenatal genetic testing', *Medical Care*, **32**, 863–80.

Heart disease and statins (prevention)

Johannesson, M., B. Jönsson, J. Kjekshus, A.G. Olsson, T.R. Pedersen and H. Wedel (1997), 'Cost effectiveness of simvastatin treatment to lower cholesterol levels in patients with coronary heart disease', *New England Journal of Medicine*, **336**, 332–36.

Heart disease implants (treatment)

Buxton, M.J., N. Caine, D. Chase, D. Connelly, A. Grace, C. Jackson, J. Parkes and L. Sharples (2006), 'A review of the evidence on the effects and costs of implantable cardioverter defibrillator therapy in different patient groups, and modelling of cost-effectiveness and cost-utility for these groups in a UK context', *Health Technology Assessment*, **10**, 1–164.

Heart disease, non-serum troponin elevation acute coronary syndrome (treatment)

Henriksson, M., D.M. Epstein, S.J. Palmer, M.J. Sculpher, T.C. Clayton, S.J. Pocock, R.A. Henderson, M.J. Buxton and K.A.A. Fox (2008), 'The cost-effectiveness of an early interventional strategy in non-ST-elevation acute coronary syndrome based on the RITA 3 trial', *Heart*, **94**, 717–23.

Heart transplant (bridge to)

Sharples, L., M.J. Buxton, N. Caine, F. Cafferty, N. Demiris, M. Dyer and C. Freeman (2006), 'Evaluation of the ventricular assist device programme in the UK', *Health Technology Assessment*, **10**, 1–119.

Helicopter emergency service

Gearhart, P., R. Wuerz and A. Localio (1997), 'Cost-effectiveness analysis of helicopter EMS for trauma patients', *Annals of Emergency Medicine*, **30**, 500–506.

Hepatitis B (treatment)

Crowley, S.J., D. Tognarini, P.V. Desmond and M. Lees (2000), 'Cost-effectiveness analysis of lamivudine for the treatment of chronic hepatitis B', *PharmacoEconomics*, **17**, 409–27.

Hepatitis C (treatment)

Grieve, R., J. Roberts, M. Wright, M. Sweeting, D. DeAngelis, W. Rosenberg, M. Bassendine, J. Main and H. Thomas (2006), 'Cost effectiveness of interferon A or peginterferon A with ribavirin for histologically mild chronic hepatitis C', *Gut*, **55**, 1332–8.

Hygiene (prevention)

Borghi, J., L. Guinness, J. Ouedraog and V. Curtis (2002), 'Is hygiene promotion cost-effective: a case study in Burkina Faso', *Tropical Medicine and International Health*, **7**, 960–69.

Hypertension (guidelines)

Gaziano, T.A., K. Steyn, D.J. Cohen, M.C. Weinstein and L.H. Opie (2005), 'Cost-effectiveness analysis of hypertension guidelines in South Africa: absolute risk versus blood pressure level', *Circulation*, **112**, 3569–76.

Influenza (treatment)

Postma, M.J., A. Novak, H.W. Scheijbeler, M. Gyldmark, M.L. Van Genugten and J.C. Wilschut (2007), 'Cost effectiveness of oseltamivir treatment for patients with influenza-like illness who are at increased risk for serious complications of influenza: illustration for the Netherlands', *PharmacoEconomics*, **25**, 497–509.

Influenza (vaccination)

Newall, A.T., P.A. Scuffham, H. Kelly, S. Harsley and C.R. MacIntyre (2008), 'The cost-effectiveness of a universal influenza vaccination program for adults aged 50–64 years in Australia', *Vaccine*, **26**, 2142–53.

Kidney disease, chronic (treatment)

Klarman, H., I.O. Francis and G.D. Rosanthal (1968), 'Cost-effectiveness analysis applied to the treatment of chronic renal disease', *Medical Care*, **6**, 48–54.

Leukaemia (treatment)

Bennett, C.L., T.J. Stinson, D. Lane, M. Amylon, V.J. Land and J.H. Laver (2000), 'Cost analysis of filgrastim for the prevention of neutropenia in pediatric T-cell leukemia and advanced lymphoblastic lymphoma: a case for prospective economic analysis in cooperative group trials', *Medical and Pediatric Oncology*, **34**, 92–6.

Liver transplantation

Longworth, L., T. Young, M.J. Buxton, J. Ratcliffe, J. Neuberger, A. Burroughs and S. Bryan (2003), 'Midterm cost-effectiveness of the liver transplantation program of England and Wales for three disease groups', *Liver Transplantation*, **9**, 1295–307.

Low back pain

Eisenberg, D.M., D.E. Post, R.B. Davis, M.T. Connelly, A.T. Legedza, A.L. Hrbek, L.A. Prosser, J.E. Buring, T.S. Inu and D.C. Cherkin (2007), 'Addition of choice of complementary therapies to usual care for acute low back pain: a randomized controlled trial', *Spine*, **32**, 151–8.

Low birthweight babies

Boyle, M.H., G.W. Torrance, J.C. Sinclair and S.P. Horwood (1983), 'Economic evaluation of neonatal intensive care of very low birthweight infants', *New England Journal of Medicine*, **308**, 1330–37.

Lung cancer (diagnosis)

Dietlein, M., K. Weber, A. Gandjour, D. Moka, P. Theissen, K.W. Lauterbach and H. Schicha (2000), 'Cost-effectiveness of FDG-PET for the management of potentially operable non-small cell lung cancer: priority for a PET-based strategy after nodal-negative CT results', *European Journal of Nuclear Medicine*, **27**, 1598–609.

Lung cancer (second line treatment)

Shepherd, F.A., J. Dancey, R. Ramlau, K. Mattson, R. Gralla, M. O'Rourke, N. Levitan, L. Gressot, M. Vincent, R. Burkes, S. Coughlin, Y. Kim and J. Berille (2000), 'Prospective randomised trial of docetaxel versus best supportive care in patients with non-small-cell lung cancer previously treated with platinum-based chemotherapy', *Journal of Clinical Oncology*, **18**, 2095–103.

Lung transplantation

Sharples, L., M. Dyer, F. Cafferty, N. Demiris, C. Freeman, N. Banner, S. Large, S. Tsui, N. Caine and M.J. Buxton (2006), 'Cost-effectiveness of ventricular assist device use in the United Kingdom: results from the Evaluation of Ventricular Assist Device programme in the UK (EVAD-UK)', *The Journal of Heart and Lung Transplantation*, **25**, 1336–43.

Macular degeneration

Hurley, S.F., J.P. Matthews and R.H. Guymer (2008), 'Cost-effectiveness of ranibizumab for neovascular age-related macular degeneration', *Cost Effectiveness and Resource Allocation*, **6**, 1–11.

Malaria (prevention)

Bhatia, M.R., J. Fox-Rushby and A.J. Mills (2004), 'Cost-effectiveness of malaria control interventions when malaria mortality is low: insecticide-treated nets versus in-house residual spraying in India', *Social Science and Medicine*, **59**, 525–39.

Malaria (treatment)

Coleman, P.G., C. Morel, S. Shillcutt, C. Goodman and A.J. Mills (2004), 'A threshold analysis of the cost-effectiveness of artemisinin-based combination therapies in sub-Saharan Africa', *American Journal of Tropical Medicine and Hygiene*, **71**(Suppl. S), 196–204.

Maternal/neonatal health (prevention)

Borghi, J., B. Thapa, D. Osrin, S. Jan, J. Morrison, S. Tamang, B.P. Shrestha, A. Wade, D.S. Manandhar and A.M. de L. Costello (2005), 'Economic assessment of a women's group intervention to improve birth outcomes in rural Nepal', *Lancet*, **366**, 1882–4.

Measles (vaccination)

Shiell, A., L.R. Jorm, R. Carruthers and G.J. Fitzsimmons (1998), 'Cost-effectiveness of measles outbreak intervention strategies', *Australian and New Zealand Journal of Public Health*, **22**, 126–32.

Melanoma (treatment)

Gonzalez-Larriba, J.L., S. Serrano, M. Alvarez-Mon, F. Camacho, M.A. Casado, J.L. Diaz-Perez, E. Diaz-Rubio, L. Fosbrook, V. Guillem, J.J. Lopez-Lopez, J.A. Moreno-Nogueira and J. Toribio (2000), 'Cost-effectiveness analysis of interferon as adjuvant therapy in high-risk melanoma patients in Spain', *European Journal of Cancer*, **36**, 2344–52.

Meningitis (prevention)

Bovier, P.A., K. Wyss and H.J. Au (1999), 'A cost-effectiveness analysis of vaccination strategies against *N. meningitidis* meningitis in sub-Saharan African countries', *Social Science & Medicine*, **48**, 1205–20.

Neural tube defects (prevention)

Kelly, A.E., A.C. Haddix, K.S. Scanlon, C.G. Helmick and J. Mulinare (1996), 'Cost-effectiveness of strategies to prevent neural tube defects', in M.R. Gold, J.E. Siegel, L.B. Russell and M.C. Weinstein (1996), *Cost-Effectiveness in Health and Medicine*, New York: Oxford University Press, 313–48.

Osteoarthritis of the knee (treatment)

Richardson, G., N. Hawkins, C.J. McCarthy, P.M. Mills, R. Pullen, C. Roberts, A. Silman and A. Oldham (2006), 'Cost-effectiveness of a supplementary class-based exercise program in the treatment of knee osteoarthritis', *International Journal of Technology Assessment in Health Care*, **22**, 84–9.

Osteoporosis (screening)

Tosteson, A.N., D.I. Rosenthal, J. Melton and M.C. Weinstein (1990), 'Cost effectiveness of screening perimenopausal white women for osteoporosis: bone densitometry and hormone replacement therapy', *Annals of Internal Medicine*, **113**, 594–603.

Pain relief (treatment)

Rainer, T.H., P. Jacobs, Y.C. Ng, N.K. Cheung, M. Tam, P.K. Lam, R. Wong and R.A. Cocks (2000), 'Cost effectiveness analysis of intravenous ketorolac and morphine for treating pain after limb injury: double blind randomised controlled trial', *British Medical Journal*, **321**, 1247–51.

Polio (prevention)

Thompson, K.M. and R.J.D. Tebbens (2006), 'Retrospective cost-effectiveness analyses for polio vaccination in the United States', *Risk Analysis*, **26**, 1423–40.

Prostate cancer, androgen suppression therapies (treatment)

Bayoumi, A.M., A.D. Brown and A.M. Garber (2000), 'Cost-effectiveness of androgen suppression therapies in advanced prostate cancer', *Journal of the National Cancer Institute*, **92**, 1731–39.

Prostatic hyperplasia (treatment)

Keoghane, S.R., K.C. Lawrence, A.M. Gray, H.A. Doll, A.M. Hancock, K. Turner, M.E. Sullivan, O. Dyar and D. Cranston (2000), 'A double-blind randomized controlled trial and economic evaluation of transurethral resection vs contact laser vaporization for benign prostatic enlargement: a 3-year follow-up', *British Journal of Urology International*, **85**, 74–7.

Psychiatric rehabilitation (treatment)

Beecham, J., M. Knapp, S. McGilloway, S. Kavanagh, A. Fenyo, M. Donnelly and N. Mays (1996), 'Leaving hospital II: the cost-effectiveness of community care for former long-stay psychiatric hospital patients', *Journal of Mental Health*, **5**, 379–94.

Respiratory syncytial viral infection (treatment)

Resch, B., W. Gusenleitner, M.J. Nuijten, M. Lebmeierand and W. Wittenberg (2008), 'Cost-effectiveness of palivizumab against respiratory syncytial viral infection in high-risk children in Austria', *Clinical Therapeutics*, **30**, 749–60.

Schistosomiasis (treatment or prevention)

Kirigia, J.M. (1998), 'Cost-utility analysis of *schistosomiasis* intervention strategies in Kenya', *Environment and Development Economics*, **3**, 319–46.

Schizophrenia (treatment)

Bounthavong, M. and M.P. Okamoto (2007), 'Decision analysis model evaluating the cost-effectiveness of risperidone, olanzapine and haloperidol in the treatment of schizophrenia', *Journal of Evaluation in Clinical Practice*, **13**, 453–60.

Sexually transmitted disease (screening in jails)

Kraut-Becher, J.R., T.L. Gift, A.C. Haddix, K.L. Irwin and R.B. Greifinger (2004), 'Cost-effectiveness of universal screening for chlamydia and gonorrhea in US jails', *Journal of Urban Health*, **81**, 453–71.

Sickle cell anaemia (treatment)

Moore, R.D., S. Charache, M.L. Terrin, F.B. Barton and S.K. Ballas (2000), 'Cost-effectiveness of hydroxyurea in sickle cell anemia', *American Journal of Hematology*, **64**, 26–31.

Small bowel transplantation

Longworth, L., T. Young, S.V. Beath, D.A. Kelly, H. Mistry, S.M. Protheroe, J. Ratcliffe and M.J. Buxton (2006), 'An economic evaluation of pediatric small bowel transplantation in the United Kingdom', *Transplantation*, **82**, 508–15.

Smoking cessation, pharmacist based (prevention)

Thavorn, K. and N. Chaiyakunapruk (2008), 'A cost-effectiveness analysis of a community pharmacist-based smoking cessation programme in Thailand', *Tobacco Control*, **17**, 177–82.

Stroke (treatment)

Casado, A., J.J. Secades, R. Ibarz, M. Herdman and M. Brosa (2008), 'Cost-effectiveness of citicoline versus conventional treatment in acute ischemic stroke', *Expert Review of Pharmacoeconomics and Outcomes Research*, **8**, 151–7.

Syphilis (screening and treatment)

Terris-Prestholt, F., D. Watson-Jones, K. Mugeye, L. Kumaranayake, L. Ndeki, H. Weiss, J. Changalucha, J. Todd, F. Lisekie, B. Gumodoka, D. Mabey and R. Hayes (2003), 'Is antenatal syphilis screening still cost effective in sub-Saharan Africa?', *Sexually Transmitted Infections*, **79**, 375–81.

Tetanus (prevention)

Hutchison, B.G. and G.L. Stoddart (1988), 'Cost-effectiveness of primary tetanus vaccination among elderly Canadians', *Canadian Medical Association Journal*, **139**, 1143–51.

Thromboembolism (treatment)

Perlroth, D.J., G.D. Sanders and M.K. Gould (2007), 'Effectiveness and cost-effectiveness of thrombolysis in submassive pulmonary embolism', *Archives of Internal Medicine*, **167**, 74–80.

Transport of patients

Lee, S.K., J.A.F. Zupancic, J. Sale, M. Pendray, R. Whyte, D. Braby, R. Walker and H. Whyte (2002), 'Cost-effectiveness and choice of infant transport systems', *Medical Care*, **40**, 705–16.

Trauma (treatment)

Nicholl, J., S. Hughes, S. Dixon, J. Turner and D. Yates (1998), 'The costs and benefits of paramedic skills in pre-hospital trauma care', *Health Technology Assessment*, **2**, 1–67.

Trichomoniasis (treatment and prevention)

Price, M., S. Stewart, W. Miller, F. Behets, W. Dow, F. Martinson, D. Chilongozi and M. Cohen (2006), 'The cost-effectiveness of treating male trichomoniasis to avert HIV transmission in men seeking STD care in Malawi', *Journal of AIDS*, **43**, 202–9.

Tuberculosis (childhood screening)

Flaherman, V.J., T.C. Porco, E. Marseille and S.E. Royce (2007), 'Cost-effectiveness of alternative strategies for tuberculosis screening before kindergarten entry', *Pediatrics*, **120**, 90–9.

Tuberculosis (screening travellers)

Tan, M., D. Menzies and K. Schwartzman (2008), 'Tuberculosis screening of travelers to higher-incidence countries: a cost-effectiveness analysis', *BMC Public Health*, **8**, 201.

West Nile virus (screening)

Custer, B., M.P. Busch, A.A. Marfin and L.R. Petersen (2005), 'The cost-effectiveness of screening the US blood supply for West Nile virus', *Annals of Internal Medicine*, **143**, 486–92.

Workplace health and safety (prevention)

Ong, M.K. and S.A. Glantz (2004), 'Cardiovascular health and economic effects of smoke-free workplaces', *American Journal of Medicine*, **117**, 32–8.

Wound management (treatment)

Clegg, J.P. and J.F. Guest (2007), 'Modelling the cost-utility of bio-electric stimulation therapy compared to standard care in the treatment of elderly patients with chronic non-healing wounds in the UK', *Current Medical Research and Opinion*, **23**, 871–83.

Yellow fever (prevention)

Monath, T.P. and A. Nasidi (1993), 'Should yellow fever vaccine be included in the expanded program of immunization in Africa? A cost-effectiveness analysis for Nigeria', *American Journal of Tropical Medicine and Hygiene*, **48**, 274–99.

BIBLIOGRAPHY

Abraham, J.M., R. Feldman, C. Carlin and J. Christianson (2006), 'The effect of quality information on consumer choice of health plans: evidence from the buyers' health care action group', *Journal of Health Economics*, **25**, 762–81.

Acemoglu, D. and S. Johnson (2007), 'Disease and development: the effect of life expectancy on economic growth', *Journal of Political Economy*, **115**, 925–85.

Adda, J. and F. Cornaglia (2006), 'Taxes, cigarette consumption and smoking intensity', *American Economic Review*, **96**, 1013–28.

Ades, A.E., G. Lu and K. Claxton (2003), 'Expected value of sample information calculations in medical decision modelling', *Medical Decision Making*, **243**, 207–27.

Adler, M.D. (2006), 'QALYs and policy evaluation: a new perspective', *Yale Journal of Health Policy, Law, and Ethics*, **6**, 1–92.

Ahituv, A., V.J. Hotz and T.J. Philipson (1996), 'The responsiveness of the demand for condoms to the local prevalence of AIDS', *Journal of Human Resources*, **31**, 869–97.

Ainslie, G. (1992), *Picoeconomics*, Cambridge, UK: Cambridge University Press.

Akerlof, G.A. (1970), 'The market for "lemons": quality uncertainty and the market mechanism', *Quarterly Journal of Economics*, **84**, 488–500.

Akin, J.S., C.C. Griffin, B.M. Popkin and D.K. Guilkey (1985), *The Demand for Primary Health Services in the Third World*, Totowa, New Jersey: Rowman and Allanheld.

Akin, J.S., D.K. Guilkey, P.L. Hutchinson and M.T. McIntosh (1998), 'Price elasticities of demand for curative health care with control for sample selectivity on endogenous illness: an analysis for Sri Lanka', *Health Economics*, **7**, 509–31.

Akin, J.S., D.K. Guilkey, B.M. Popkin and K.M. Smith (1985), 'The impact of federal transfer programs on the nutrient intake of elderly individuals', *Journal of Human Resources*, **20**, 383–404.

Alberini, A., M. Cropper, A. Krupnik and N.B. Simon (2006), 'Willingness to pay for mortality risk reductions: does latency matter?', *Journal of Risk and Uncertainty*, **32**, 231–45.

Alchian, A.A. (1953), 'The meaning of utility measurement', *American Economic Review*, **43**, 26–50.

Alchian, A.A. and H. Demsetz (1972), 'Production, information costs, and economic organization', *American Economic Review*, **62**, 777–95.

Allais, M. (1953), 'Le comportement de l'homme rationnel devant le risque: critique des postulats et axiomes de l'école américaine', *Econometrica*, **21**, 503–46.

Allport, G.W. (1937), *Personality: A Psychological Interpretation*, New York: Holt, Rinehart & Winston.

Altman, D.G. (1991), *Practical Statistics for Medical Research*, London: Chapman and Hall.

Anand, P. (1999), 'QALYs and the integration of claims in health-care rationing', *Health Care Analysis*, **7**, 239–53.

Anand, P. and K. Hansson (1997), 'Disability adjusted life years: a critical review', *Journal of Health Economics*, **16**, 685–702.

Anand, P., G. Hunter, K. Dowding, F. Guala and M. Van Hees (2009), 'The development of capability indicators', *Journal of Human Development and Capabilities*, **10**, 125–52.

Anderson, G. (1998), *Multinational Comparisons of Health Care: Expenditure, Coverage and Outcomes*, New York: The Commonwealth Fund.

Anderson, G.F. and B.K. Frogner (2008), 'Health spending in OECD countries: obtaining value per dollar', *Health Affairs*, **27**, 1718–21.

Anderson, G.F., P.S. Hussey, B.K. Frogner and H.R. Waters (2005), 'Health spending in the United States and the rest of the industrialized world', *Health Affairs*, **24**, 903–14.

Anderson, P., A. Lloyd and G. Grant (2004), 'Pharmacoeconomics: an industry perspective', in T. Whalley, A. Haycox and A. Boland A (eds), *Pharmacoeconomics*, Amsterdam: Elsevier, pp. 55–70.

Andersson, F. and C.H. Lyttkens (1999), 'Preferences for equity in health behind a veil of ignorance', *Health Economics*, **8**, 369–78.

Andersson, H. and G. Lindberg (2009), 'Benevolence and the value of road safety', *Accident Analysis & Prevention*, **41**, 286–93.

Andlin-Sobocki, P., B. Jönsson, H.-U. Wittchen and J. Olesen (2005), 'Costs of disorders of the brain in Europe', *European Journal of Neurology*, **12**, Suppl. 1, 1–90.

Anell, A. and M. Willis (2000), 'International comparison of health care systems using resource profiles', *Bulletin of the World Health Organization*, **78**, 770–78.

Angus, D.C., W.T. Linde-Zwirble, G. Clermont, D.E. Ball, B.R. Basson,

E.W. Ely, P.-F. Laterre, J.-L. Vincent, G. Bernard and B. Van Hout (2003), 'Cost-effectiveness of drotrecogin alfa (activated) in the treatment of severe sepsis', *Critical Care Medicine*, **31**, 1–11.

Antonazzo, E., A. Scott, D. Skatun and R.F. Elliott (2005), 'The labour market for nursing: a review of the labour supply literature', *Health Economics*, **12**, 465–78.

Appleby, J., N. Devlin and D. Parkin (2007), 'NICE's cost effectiveness threshold. How high should it be?', *British Medical Journal*, **335**, 358–9.

Arrow, K.J. (1951), *Social Choice and Individual Values*, New York: Wiley.

Arrow, K.J. (1962), 'The economic implications of learning by doing', *Review of Economic Studies*, **29**, 155–73.

Arrow, K.J. (1963), 'Uncertainty and the welfare economics of medical care', *American Economic Review*, **53**, 941–73.

Arrow, K.J. (1968), 'The economics of moral hazard: further comment', *American Economic Review*, **58**, 537–9.

Arrow, K.J. (1970), *Essays in the Theory of Risk Bearing*, North Holland: Amsterdam.

Arrow, K.J. (1985), 'The economics of agency', in J. Pratt and R. Zeckhauser (eds), *Principals and Agents*, Cambridge, MA: Harvard Business School, pp. 37–51.

Arrow, K.J. and G. Debreu (1954), 'Existence of an equilibrium for a competitive economy', *Econometrica*, **22**, 265–90.

Arrow, K.J., C. Panosian and H. Gelband (Committee on the Economics of Antimalarial Drugs) (eds) (2004), *Saving Lives, Buying Time: Economics of Malaria Drugs in an Age of Resistance*, Washington, DC: The National Academies Press.

Arrow, K.J., M.L. Cropper, G.C. Eads, R.W. Hahn, L.B. Lave, R.G. Noll, P.R. Portney, R. Schmalensee, V.K. Smith and R.N. Stavins (1996), *Benefit-Cost Analysis in Environmental, Health, and Safety Regulation: A Statement of Principles*, Washington: American Enterprise Institute Press.

Asenso-Boadi, F., J. Coast and T.J. Peters (2008), 'Exploring differences in empirical time preference rates: an application of meta-regression', *Health Economics*, **17**, 235–48.

Atkinson, A.B. (1977), 'Optimal taxation and the direct versus indirect tax controversy', *Canadian Journal of Economics*, **10**, 590–606.

Atkinson, A.B. (2005), *Measurement of Government Output and Productivity for the National Accounts*, Basingstoke: Palgrave Macmillan.

Atkinson, A.B. and F. Bourguignon (1987), 'Income distribution and differences in needs', in G.R. Feiwel (ed.), *Arrow and the Foundations of the Theory of Economic Policy*, London: Macmillan, pp. 350–70.

Auld, M.C. (2005), 'Smoking, drinking and income', *Journal of Human Resources*, **40**, 505–18.

Auld, M.C. and P. Grootendorst (2004), 'An empirical analysis of milk addiction', *Journal of Health Economics*, **23**, 1117–33.

Auster, R.D., I. Leveson and D. Sarachek (1969), 'The production of health: an exploratory study', *Journal of Human Resources*, **4**, 411–36.

Baker, L.C. and S.K. Wheeler (1998), 'Managed care and technology diffusion: the case of MRI', *Health Affairs*, **17**, 195–207.

Baker, M., M. Stabile and C. Deri (2004), 'What do self-reported, objective, measures of health measure?', *Journal of Human Resources*, **39**, 1067–93.

Bakker, F.M., R.C.J.A. Van Vliet and W.P.M.M. Van de Ven (2000), 'Deductibles in health insurance: can the actuarially fair premium reduction exceed the deductible?', *Health Policy*, **53**, 123–41.

Balia, S. and A.M. Jones (2008), 'Mortality, lifestyle and socio-economic status', *Journal of Health Economics*, **27**, 1–26.

Baltagi, B.H. (2005), *Econometric Analysis of Panel Data*, 3rd edition, New York: Wiley.

Baltussen, R. and L. Niessen (2006), 'Priority setting of health interventions: the need for multi-criteria decision analysis', *Cost Effectiveness and Resource Allocation*, **4**, 14.

Banting, K.G. and S. Corbett (eds) (2002), *Health Policy and Federalism: A Comparative Perspective on Multi-level Governance*, Kingston and Montreal: School of Policy Studies and McGill-Queen's University Press.

Barer, M.L. (2005), 'Evidence, interests and knowledge translation: reflections of an unrepentant zombie chaser', *Healthcare Quarterly*, **8**, 46–53.

Barros, P.P. (2003), 'Cream-skimming, incentives for efficiency and payment system', *Journal of Health Economics*, **22**, 419–43.

Barros, P.P. and X. Martinez-Giralt (2006), 'Models of negotiation and bargaining in health care', in A.M. Jones (ed.), *The Elgar Companion to Health Economics*, Cheltenham, UK and Northampton, MA, USA: Edward Elgar, pp. 233–41.

Basu, A., W.G. Manning and J. Mullahy (2004), 'Comparing alternative models: log vs Cox proportional hazard?', *Health Economics*, **13**, 749–65.

Bates, L.J. and R.E. Santerre (2005), 'Do agglomeration economies exist in the hospital services industry?', *Eastern Economic Journal*, **31**, 617–28.

Baumol, W. (1967), 'Macroeconomics of unbalanced growth: the anatomy of the urban crisis', *American Economic Review*, **57**, 415–26.

Beaton, D., A.M. Davis, P. Hudak and S. McConnell (2001), 'The DASH (Disabilities of the Arm, Shoulder and Hand) outcome measure: what do we know about it now?', *British Journal of Hand Therapy*, **6**, 109–18.

Beauchamp, T.L. (2007), 'The "four principles" approach to health care ethics', in R. Ashcroft, A. Dawson, H. Draper and J. McMillan (eds), *Principles of Health Care Ethics*, 2nd edition, Chichester: Wiley, pp. 3–10.

Beaulieu, N., D.M. Cutler, K. Ho, G. Isham, T. Lindquist, A. Nelson and P. O'Connor (2006), 'The business case for diabetes disease management for managed care organizations', *Forum for Health Economics & Policy*, **9**, 1072.

Becker, G.S. (1962), 'Investment in human capital: a theoretical analysis', *Journal of Political Economy*, **70** (Suppl.), 9–49.

Becker, G.S. (1965), 'A theory of the allocation of time', *Economic Journal*, **75**, 504–11.

Becker, G.S. and C.B. Mulligan (1997), 'The endogenous determination of time preference', *Quarterly Journal of Economics*, **112**, 729–58.

Becker, G.S, and K.M. Murphy (1988), 'A theory of rational addiction', *Journal of Political Economy*, **96**, 675–700.

Beers, M.H., J.G. Ouslander, J. Rollingher, D.B. Reuben and J.C. Beck (1991), 'Explicit criteria for determining inappropriate medication use in nursing home residents', *Archives of Internal Medicine*, **151**, 1825–32.

Bell, C.M., D.R. Urbach, J.G. Ray, A. Bayoumi, A.B. Rosen, D. Greenberg and P.J. Neumann (2006), 'Bias in published cost effectiveness studies: systematic review', *British Medical Journal*, **332**, 699–703.

Belton, V. and T.J. Stewart (2002), *Multiple Criteria Decision Analysis – An Integrated Approach*, Boston: Kluwer Academic Publishers.

Benstetter, F. and A. Wambach (2006), 'The treadmill effect in a fixed budget system', *Journal of Health Economics*, **25**, 146–69.

Bentham, J. ([1789] 1907), *An Introduction to the Principles of Morals and Legislation*, reprinted in Oxford: Clarendon Press.

Berenson, R. and J. Holahan (1992), 'Sources of the growth in Medicare physician expenditures', *Journal of the American Medical Association*, **267**, 687–91.

Bergner, M.R., A. Bobbitt, W.B. Carter and B.S. Gilson (1981), 'The Sickness Impact Profile: development and final revision of a health status measure', *Medical Care*, **19**, 787–805.

Bergson, A. (1938), 'A reformulation of certain aspects of welfare economics', *Quarterly Journal of Economics*, **52**, 310–34.

Berkman, L.A. and I. Kawachi (2000), 'A historical framework for social epidemiology', in L. Berkman and I. Kawachi (eds), *Social Epidemiology*, New York: Oxford University Press, pp. 3–12.

Berkson, J. (1944), 'Application of the logistic function to bio-assay', *Journal of the American Statistical Association*, 39, 357–65.

Berman, P. (1997), 'National health accounts in developing countries: appropriate methods and recent applications', *Health Economics*, 6, 11–30.

Berndt, E.R., A. Bir, S.H. Busch, R.G. Frank and S.-L.T. Normand (2002), 'The medical treatment of depression, 1991–1996: productive inefficiency, expected outcome variations, and price indexes', *Journal of Health Economics*, 21, 373–96.

Berndt, E.R., D.M. Cutler, R.G. Frank, Z. Griliches, J.P. Newhouse and J.E. Triplett (2000), 'Medical care prices and output', in A.J. Culyer and J.P. Newhouse (eds), *Handbook of Health Economics*, Amsterdam: Elsevier, pp. 119–80.

Berndt, E.R., S.N. Finkelstein, P.E. Greenberg, R.H. Howland, A. Keith, A.J. Rush, J. Russell and M.B. Kelle (1998), 'Workplace performance effects from chronic depression and its treatment', *Journal of Health Economics*, 17, 511–35.

Bernheim, B.D. and A. Rangel (2004), 'Addiction and cue-triggered decision processes', *American Economic Review*, 94, 1558–90.

Bero, L., F. Oostvogel, P. Bacchetti and K. Lee (2007), 'Factors associated with findings of published trials of drug–drug comparisons: why some statins appear more efficacious than others', *Public Library of Science Medicine*, 4, e184.

Besley, T. and M. Gouveia (1994), 'Alternative systems of health care provision', *Economic Policy*, 9, 200–258 (with a commentary by J. Dreze).

Besley, T., J. Hall and I. Preston (1998), 'Social security and health care consumption: a comparison of alternative systems. Private and public health insurance in the UK', *European Economic Review*, 42, 491–7.

Bhatti, T. and A. Baibergenova (2008), 'A comparison of the cost-effectiveness of in vitro fertilization strategies and stimulated intrauterine insemination in a Canadian health economic model', *Journal of Obstetrics and Gynaecology Canada*, 30, 411–20.

Bilodeau, B., P.-Y. Crémieux and P. Ouellette (2000), 'Hospital cost functions in a non-market health care system', *Review of Economics and Statistics*, 82, 489–98.

Birch, S. and A. Gafni (1992), 'Cost effectiveness/utility analyses: do current decision rules lead us to where we want to be?', *Journal of Health Economics*, 11, 279–96.

Birch, S. and A. Gafni (1993), 'Changing the problem to fit the solution:

Johannesson and Weinstein's (mis)application of economics to real world problems', *Journal of Health Economics*, **12**, 469–76.

Birch, S., G.L. Stoddart and F. Beland (1998), 'Modelling the community as a determinant of health', *Canadian Journal of Public Health*, **89**, 402–5.

Birchenall, J.A. and R.R. Soares (2009), 'Altruism, fertility, and the value of children: health policy evaluation and intergenerational welfare', *Journal of Public Economics*, **93**, 280–95.

Bishai, D. and T. Adam (2006), 'Economics of public health interventions for children in developing countries', in A.M. Jones (ed.), *The Elgar Companion to Health Economics*, Cheltenham, UK and Northampton, MA, USA: Edward Elgar, pp. 46–61.

Black, D. (1948), 'On the rationale of group decision-making', *Journal of Political Economy*, **56**, 23–34.

Black, D. (1980), *Inequalities in Health: a Report of a Research Working Group*, London: Department of Health and Social Security.

Black, D., P. Townsend and N. Davidson (1992), *Inequalities in Health: the Black Report*, 2nd edition, London: Penguin.

Blackhouse, G., F. Xie, K. Campbell, N. Assasi, K. Gaebel, M. Levine, D. Pi, M. Giacomini, R. Goeree and R. Banks (2008), *Intravenous Immunoglobulin for Treatment of Idiopathic Thrombocytopenic Purpura: Economic and Health Service Impact Analyses*, Ottawa: Canadian Agency for Drugs and Technologies in Health (CADTH), Brief No. 59.

Blanchflower, D.G. and A.J. Oswald (2008), 'Hypertension and happiness across nations', *Journal of Health Economics*, **27**, 218–33.

Blaug, M. (1998), 'Where are we now in British health economics?', *Health Economics*, **7**, S63–S78.

Bleichrodt, H. (2002), 'A new explanation for the difference between time trade-off utilities and standard gamble utilities', *Health Economics*, **11**, 447–56.

Bleichrodt, H. and A. Gafni (1996), 'Time preference, the discounted utility model and health', *Journal of Health Economics*, **15**, 49–66.

Bleichrodt, H. and M. Johannesson (1997a), 'The validity of QALYs: an experimental test of constant proportional trade-off and utility independence', *Medical Decision Making*, **17**, 21–32.

Bleichrodt, H. and M. Johannesson (1997b), 'Standard gamble, time trade-off and rating scale: experimental results on the ranking properties of QALYs', *Journal of Health Economics*, **16**, 55–175.

Bleichrodt, H. and J.L. Pinto (2002), 'Loss aversion and scale compatibility in two-attribute trade-offs', *Journal of Mathematical Psychology*, **46**, 315–37.

Bleichrodt, H. and J.L. Pinto (2008), 'New evidence of preference reversals in health utility measurement', *Health Economics*, **18**, 713–26.

Bleichrodt, H. and J. Quiggin (1999), 'Life-cycle preferences over consumption and health: when is cost-effectiveness analysis equivalent to cost-benefit analysis?', *Journal of Health Economics*, **18**, 681–708.

Bleichrodt, H., D. Crainich and L. Eeckhoudt (2008), 'Aversion to health inequalities and priority setting in health care', *Journal of Health Economics*, **27**, 1594–1604.

Bleichrodt, H., E. Diecidue and J. Quiggin (2004), 'Equity weights in the allocation of health care: the rank-dependent QALY model', *Journal of Health Economics*, **23**, 157–71.

Bliss, C.I. (1935), 'The calculation of the dosage-mortality curve', *Annals of Applied Biology*, **22**, 134–67.

Blomqvist, A. and T. Léger (2005), 'Information asymmetry, insurance, and the decision to hospitalize', *Journal of Health Economics*, **24**, 775–93.

Bolin, K., L. Jacobson and B. Lindgren (2001), 'The family as the health producer – when spouses are Nash-bargainers', *Journal of Health Economics*, **20**, 349–62.

Bordignon, M. and G. Turati (2009), 'Bailing out expectations and public health expenditure', *Journal of Health Economics*, **28**, 305–21.

Bosworth, R., T.A. Cameron and J.R. DeShazo (2009), 'Demand for environmental policies to improve health: evaluating community-level policy scenarios', *Journal of Environmental Economics and Management*, **57**, 293–308.

Bouchery, E. and H. Harwood (2003), 'The Nebraska Medicaid managed behavioral health care initiative: impacts on utilization, expenditures, and quality of care for mental health', *Journal of Behavioral Health Services & Research*, **30**, 93–108.

Boutin-Foster, C. (2005), 'In spite of good intentions: patients' perspectives on problematic social support interactions', *Health and Quality of Life Outcomes*, **3**, 52.

Box, G. and G. Jenkins (1970), *Time Series Analysis: Forecasting and Control*, San Francisco: Holden-Day.

Bradford, W.D. and A.H.N. Kleit (2006), 'Direct to consumer advertising', in A.M. Jones (ed.), *The Elgar Companion to Health Economics*, Cheltenham, UK and Northampton, MA, USA: Edward Elgar, pp. 306–14.

Bradley, R. (2009), 'Comment – defining health insurance affordability: unobserved heterogeneity matters', *Journal of Health Economics*, **28**, 255–64.

Braveman, P. and S. Gruskin (2003), 'Defining equity in health', *Journal of Epidemiology and Community Health*, **57**, 254–8.

Brazier, J.E., J. Roberts and M. Deverill (2002), 'The estimation of a preference-based measure of health from the SF-36', *Journal of Health Economics*, **21**, 271–92.

Brazier, J.E., J. Ratcliffe, A. Tsuchiya and J. Salomon (2007), *Measuring and Valuing Health Benefits for Economic Evaluation*, Oxford: Oxford University Press.

Brazier, J.E., J. Roberts, A. Tsuchiya and J. Busschbach (2004), 'A comparison of the EQ-5D and SF-6D across seven patient groups', *Health Economics*, **13**, 873–84.

Brazier, J.E., M. Deverill, C. Green, R. Harper and A.A. Booth (1999), 'A review of the use of health status measures in economic evaluation', *Health Technology Assessment*, **3**, 1–164.

Brekke, K.R. and M. Kuhn (2006), 'Direct to consumer advertising in pharmaceutical markets', *Journal of Health Economics*, **25**, 102–30.

Brekke, K.R. and L. Sørgard (2007), 'Public versus private health care in a national health service', *Health Economics*, **16**, 579–601.

Brekke, K.R., I. Königbauer and O.R. Straune (2007a), 'Reference pricing of pharmaceuticals', *Journal of Health Economics*, **26**, 613–42.

Brekke, K.R., R. Nuscheler and O.R. Straume (2007b), 'Gatekeeping in health care', *Journal of Health Economics*, **26**, 149–70.

Brennan, A. and S.A. Kharroubi (2007), 'Efficient computation of partial expected value of sample information using Bayesian approximation', *Journal of Health Economics*, **26**, 122–48.

Brenner, M.H. (1983), 'Mortality and economic instability – detailed analyses for Britain and comparative analyses for selected countries', *International Journal of Health Services*, **13**, 563–619.

Bretteville-Jensen, A.L. (1999), 'Gender, heroin consumption and economic behaviour', *Health Economics*, **8**, 379–89.

Breyer, F., M. Heineck and N. Lorenz (2003), 'Determinants of health care utilization by German sickness fund members – with application to risk adjustment', *Health Economics*, **12**, 367–76.

Briggs, A.H. (2000), 'Handling uncertainty in cost-effectiveness models', *PharmacoEconomics*, **17**, 479–500.

Briggs, A.H. (2001), 'A Bayesian approach to stochastic cost-effectiveness analysis', *Journal of Technology Assessment in Health Care*, **17**, 69–82.

Briggs, A.H. and P. Fenn (1998), 'Confidence intervals or surfaces? Uncertainty on the cost-effectiveness plane', *Health Economics*, **7**, 723–40.

Briggs, A.H. and A. Gray (1998), 'The distribution of health care costs and their statistical analysis for economic evaluation', *Journal of Health Services Research and Policy*, **3**, 233–45.

Briggs, A.H. and B.J. O'Brien (2001), 'The death of cost-minimization analysis?', *Health Economics*, **10**, 179–84.

Briggs, A.H. and M.J. Sculpher (1999), 'An introduction to Markov modelling for economic evaluation', *PharmacoEconomics*, **13**, 397–409.

Briggs, A.H., B.J. O'Brien and G. Blackhouse (2002), 'Thinking outside the box: recent advances in the analysis and presentation of uncertainty in cost-effectiveness analysis', *Annual Reviews of Public Health*, **23**, 377–401.

Briggs, A.H., D.E. Wonderling and C.Z. Mooney (1997), 'Pulling cost-effectiveness analysis up by its bootstraps: a non-parametric approach to confidence interval estimation', *Health Economics*, **6**, 327–40.

Briggs, A.H., T. Clark, J. Wolstenholme and P. Clarke (2003), 'Missing. . . presumed at random: cost analysis of incomplete data', *Health Economics*, **12**, 377–92.

Brisson, M. and W.J. Edmunds (2003), 'Economic evaluation of vaccination programs: the impact of herd-immunity', *Medical Decision Making*, **23**, 76–82.

Brook, R.H., J.R.Ware, W. Rogers, E.B. Keeler, A.R. Davies, C.A. Donald, G.A. Goldberg, K.N. Lohr, P.C. Masthay and J.P. Newhouse (1983), 'Does free care improve adults' health? Results from a randomized controlled trial', *New England Journal of Medicine*, **309**, 1426–34.

Brooks, R., R. Rabin and F. de Charro (2003), *The Measurement and Valuation of Health Status Using EQ-5D: A European Perspective. Evidence from the EuroQol BIO MED Research Programme*, Berlin: Springer.

Broome, J. (1993), 'QALYs', *Journal of Public Economics*, **50**, 149–63.

Brouwer, W.B.F., M.A. Koopmanschap and F.F.H. Rutten (1998), 'Productivity costs in cost-effectiveness analysis: numerator or denominator: a further discussion', *Health Economics*, **6**, 511–14.

Brouwer, W.B.F., A.J. Culyer, N.J. Van Exel and F.F.H. Rutten (2008), 'Welfarism vs. extra-welfarism', *Journal of Health Economics*, **27**, 325–38.

Brouwer, W.B.F., N.J. Van Exel, B. Van den Berg, G.A. Van den Bos and M.A. Koopmanschap (2005), 'Process utility from providing informal care: the benefit of caring', *Health Policy*, **74**, 85–99.

Brown, H.S. (2003), 'Managed care and technical efficiency', *Health Economics*, **12**, 149–58.

Bruera, E. and M. Suarez-Almazor (1998), 'Cost effectiveness in palliative care', *Palliative Medicine*, **12**, 315–16.

Bryan, S., I. Williams and S. McIver (2007), 'Seeing the NICE side of cost-effectiveness analysis: a qualitative investigation of the use of CEA in NICE technology appraisals', *Health Economics*, **16**, 179–93.

Buchanan, J.M. (1963), 'The economics of earmarked taxes', *Journal of Political Economy*, **71**, 457–69.

Buchanan, J.M. and W.C. Stubblebine (1962), 'Externality', *Economica*, **29**, 371–84.

Buchanan, J.M. and G. Tullock (1962), *The Calculus of Consent*, Ann Arbor: University of Michigan Press.

Buchmueller, T.C. and J. DiNardo (2002), 'Did community rating induce an adverse selection death spiral? Evidence from New York, Pennsylvania and Connecticut', *American Economic Review*, **92**, 280–94.

Buchmueller, T.C. and P.J. Feldstein (1997), 'The effect of price on switching between health plans', *Journal of Health Economics*, **16**, 231–47.

Buchmueller, T.C. and S.H. Zuvekas (1998), 'Drug use, drug abuse, and labour market outcomes', *Health Economics*, **7**, 229–45.

Buckingham, K. and N. Devlin (2006), 'A theoretical framework for TTO valuations of health', *Health Economics*, **15**, 1149–54.

Bundorf, M.K. and M.V. Pauly (2006), 'Is health insurance affordable for the uninsured?', *Journal of Health Economics*, **25**, 650–73.

Bundorf, M.K. and M.V. Pauly (2009), 'Reply to Ralph Bradley', *Journal of Health Economics*, **28**, 251–4.

Burgess, J.F. (2006), 'Productivity analysis in health care', in A.M. Jones (ed.), *The Elgar Companion to Health Economics*, Cheltenham, UK and Northampton, MA, USA: Edward Elgar, pp. 335–42.

Burgess, J.F., K. Carey and G.J. Young (2005), 'The effect of network arrangements on hospital pricing behavior', *Journal of Health Economics*, **24**, 391–405.

Burgess, L., D.J. Street and R. Viney (2006), 'Design of choice experiments in health economics', in A.M. Jones (ed.), *The Elgar Companion to Health Economics*, Cheltenham, UK and Northampton, MA, USA: Edward Elgar, pp. 415–26.

Busemeyer, J.R. and J.T. Townsend (1993), 'Decision field theory: a dynamic cognition approach to decision making', *Psychological Review*, **100**, 432–59.

Butler, J.R.G. (1995), *Hospital Cost Analysis*, Dordrecht: Klumer Academic Publishers.

Butler, J.R.G., C.M. Furnival and R.F.G. Hart (1995), 'Estimating treatment cost functions for progressive diseases: a multiproduct approach with an application to breast cancer', *Journal of Health Economics*, **14**, 361–85.

Butler, R.J., R.P. Hartwig and H. Gardner (1997), 'HMOs, moral hazard and cost shifting in workers' compensation', *Journal of Health Economics*, **16**, 191–206.

Buxton, M.J. and S.R. Hanney (1996), 'How can payback from health services research be assessed?', *Journal of Health Services Research & Policy*, **1**, 35–43.

Buxton, M.J., M.F. Drummond, B.A. Van Hout, R.L. Prince, T.A. Sheldon, T. Szucs and M. Vray (1997), 'Modelling in economic evaluation: an unavoidable fact of life', *Health Economics*, **6**, 217–27.

Byford, S. and T. Sefton (2003), 'Economic evaluation of complex health and social care interventions', *National Institute Economic Review*, **186**, 98–108.

Byrne, M.M., K. O'Malley and M.E. Suarez-Almazor (2005), 'Willingness to pay per quality adjusted life year in a study of knee osteoarthritis', *Medical Decision Making*, **25**, 655–66.

Cairns, J. (2006), 'Providing guidance to the NHS: The Scottish Medicines Consortium and the National Institute for Clinical Excellence compared', *Health Policy*, **76**, 134–43.

Campbell, H., J. Karnon and R. Dowie (2001), 'Cost analysis of a hospital-at-home initiative using discrete event simulation', *Journal of Health Services Research & Policy*, **6**, 14–22.

Canadian Academy of Health Sciences (2009), *The Return on Investments in Health Research: Defining the Best Metrics*, Ottawa: Canadian Academy of Health Sciences.

Canadian Institute for Health Information (2007), *Drug Claims by Seniors: An Analysis Focusing on Potentially Inappropriate Use of Medications 2000–2006*, Ottawa: Canadian Institute for Health Information.

Cantor, S.B. (1994), 'Cost-effectiveness analysis, extended dominance and ethics: a quantitative assessment', *Medical Decision Making*, **14**, 259–65.

Cardon, J.H. and I. Hendel (2001), 'Asymmetric information in health insurance: evidence from the National Medical Expenditure Survey', *Rand Journal of Economics*, **32**, 408–27.

Carides, G.W. (2003), 'Methods for analyzing censored cost data', in A.H. Briggs (ed.), *Statistical Methods for Cost-effectiveness Research: A Guide to Current Issues and Future Developments*, London: Office of Health Economics, pp. 65–84.

Carlsson, F. and P. Martinsson (2003), 'Design techniques for stated preference methods in health economics', *Health Economics*, **12**, 281–94.

Carpenter, C. (2004), 'How do zero tolerance drunk driving laws work?', *Journal of Health Economics*, **23**, 61–83.

Case, A., D. Lee and C. Paxson (2008), 'The income gradient in children's health: a comment on Currie, Shields and Wheatley Price', *Journal of Health Economics*, **27**, 801–7.

Case, A., D. Lubotsky and C. Paxson (2002), 'Economic status and health in childhood: the origins of the gradient', *American Economic Review*, **92**, 1308–34.

Castillo-Riquelme, M., Z. Chalbi, J. Lord, F. Guhl, D. Campbell-Lendrum, C. Davies and J. Fox-Rushby (2008), 'Modelling geographic variation in the cost-effectiveness of control policies for infectious disease vectors: the example of Chagas disease', *Journal of Health Economics*, **27**, 405–26.

Cawley, J. (2004), 'The impact of obesity on wages', *Journal of Human Resources*, **39**, 451–74.

Cawley, J. and D.S. Kenkel (eds) (2008), *The Economics of Health Behaviours*, 3 vols, Cheltenham, UK and Northampton, MA, USA: Edward Elgar.

Chalkley, M. (2006), 'Contracts, information and incentives in health care', in A.M Jones (ed.), *The Elgar Companion to Health Economics*, Cheltenham, UK and Northampton, MA, USA: Edward Elgar, pp. 242–9.

Chalkley, M. and J.M. Malcomson (2000), 'Government purchasing of health services', in A.J. Culyer and J.P. Newhouse (eds), *Handbook of Health Economics*, Amsterdam: Elsevier, pp. 847–90.

Chalkley, M. and D. McVicar (2008), 'Choice of contracts in the British National Health Service: an empirical study', *Journal of Health Economics*, **27**, 1155–67.

Chalmers, I. (2004), 'In the dark: drug companies should be forced to publish all the results of clinical trials. How else can we know the truth about their products?', *New Scientist*, **181**, 19.

Chalmers, I. and D.G. Altman (eds) (1995), *Systematic Reviews*, London: BMJ Publishing.

Chaloupka, F.J. and K.E. Warner (2000), 'The economics of smoking', in A.J. Culyer and J.P. Newhouse (eds), *Handbook of Health Economics*, Amsterdam: Elsevier, pp. 1539–627.

Chamberlin, E. (1933), *The Theory of Monopolistic Competition*, Cambridge, MA: Harvard University Press.

Chandra, A., J. Gruber and R. McKnight (2007), 'Patient cost-sharing, Hospitalization Offsets, and the Design of Optimal Health Insurance for the Elderly', National Bureau of Economic Research Working Paper No. 12972, Cambridge, MA: NBER.

Chapman, R.H., P.W. Stone, E.A. Sandberg, C. Bell and P.J. Neumann (2000), 'A comprehensive league table of cost-utility ratios and sub-table of "panel worthy" studies', *Medical Decision Making*, **20**, 451–67.

Chay, K. and M. Greenstone (2003), 'The impact of air pollution on infant mortality: evidence from geographic variation in pollution shocks induced by a recession', *Quarterly Journal of Economics*, **118**, 1121–67.

Chen, Y. and H. Li (2009), 'Mother's education and child health: is there a nurturing effect?', *Journal of Health Economics*, **28**, 413–26.

Chernew, M.E. (2001), 'General equilibrium and marketability in the health care industry', *Journal of Health Politics, Policy and Law*, **26**, 885–97.

Chernew, M.E., P. DeCicca and R. Town (2008), 'Managed care and medical expenditures of Medicare beneficiaries', *Journal of Health Economics*, **27**, 1451–61.

Chernew, M.E., A.B. Rosen and A.M. Fendrick (2006), 'Rising out-of-pocket costs in disease management programs', *American Journal of Managed Care*, **12**, 150–54.

Chernew, M.E., A.B. Rosen and A.M. Fendrick (2007), 'Value-based insurance design', *Health Affairs*, **26**, w195–w203.

Chernichovsky, D. and S. Markowitz (2004), 'Aging and aggregate costs of medical care: conceptual and policy issues', *Health Economics*, **13**, 543–62.

Chinitz, D., A. Preker and J. Wasem (1998), 'Balancing competition and solidarity in health care financing', in R.B. Saltman, J. Figueras and C. Sakellarides (eds), *Critical Challenges for Health Care Reform in Europe*, Buckingham: Open University Press, pp. 55–77.

Chou, S.-Y., M. Grossman and H. Saffer (2004), 'An economic analysis of adult obesity: results from the behavioral risk factor surveillance system', *Journal of Health Economics*, **23**, 565–87.

Clark, D. (1995), 'Priority setting in health care: an axiomatic bargaining approach', *Journal of Health Economics*, **14**, 345–60.

Claxton, K. (1999), 'The irrelevance of inference: a decision making approach to the stochastic evaluation of health care technologies', *Journal of Health Economics*, **18**, 341–64.

Claxton, K. and A.J. Culyer (2006), 'Wickedness or folly? The ethics of NICE's decisions', *Journal of Medical Ethics*, **32**, 373–7.

Claxton, K. and A.J. Culyer (2007), 'Rights, responsibilities and NICE: a rejoinder to Harris', *Journal of Medical Ethics*, **33**, 462–4.

Claxton, K. and A.J. Culyer (2008), 'Not a NICE fallacy: a reply to Dr Quigley', *Journal of Medical Ethics*, **34**, 598–601.

Claxton, K. and J. Posnett (1996), 'An economic approach to clinical trial design and research priority-setting', *Journal of Health Economics*, **15**, 513–24.

Claxton, K., E. Fenwick and M.J. Sculpher (2006a), 'Decision-making with uncertainty: the value of information', in A.M. Jones (ed.), *The Elgar Companion to Health Economics*, Cheltenham, UK and Northampton, MA, USA: Edward Elgar, pp. 514–25.

Claxton, K., M.J. Sculpher and M.F. Drummond (2002), 'A rational framework for decision making by the National Institute for Clinical Excellence (NICE)', *The Lancet*, **360**, 711–15.

Claxton, K., L. Ginnelly, M.J. Sculpher, Z. Philips and S. Palmer (2004), 'A pilot study on the use of decision theory and value of information analysis as part of the NHS Health Technology Assessment programme', *Health Technology Assessment*, **8**, 1–103.

Claxton, K., M. Paulden, H.S.E. Gravelle, W. Brouwer and A.J. Culyer (2010), 'Discounting and decision making in the economic evaluation of health care technologies', forthcoming in *Health Economics*.

Claxton, K., A.H. Briggs, M.J. Buxton, A.J. Culyer, C. McCabe, S. Walker and M.J. Sculpher (2008), 'Value based pricing for NHS drugs: an opportunity not to be missed?', *British Medical Journal*, **336**, 251–4.

Claxton, K., M.J. Sculpher, A.J. Culyer, C. McCabe, A.H. Briggs, R.L. Akehurst, M.J. Buxton and J. Brazier (2006b), 'Discounting and cost-effectiveness in NICE – stepping back to sort out a confusion', *Health Economics*, **15**, 1–4.

Claxton, K., M.J. Sculpher, C. McCabe, A.H. Briggs, R.L. Akehurst, M.J. Buxton, J. Brazier and T. O'Hagan (2005), 'Probabilistic sensitivity analysis for NICE technology assessment: not an optional extra', *Health Economics*, **14**, 339–47.

Coast, J. (1999), 'The appropriate uses of qualitative methods in health economics', *Health Economics*, **8**, 345–53.

Coast, J. (2001), 'Citizens, their agents and health care rationing: an exploratory study using qualitative methods', *Health Economics*, **10**, 159–74.

Coast, J., R. McDonald and R. Baker (2004), 'Issues arising from the use of qualitative methods in health economics', *Journal of Health Services Research & Policy*, **3**, 171–6.

Coast, J., R.D. Smith and P. Lorgelly (2008a), 'Should the capability approach be applied in health economics?', *Health Economics*, **17**, 667–70.

Coast, J., R.D. Smith and P. Lorgelly (2008b), 'Welfarism, extra-welfarism and capability: the spread of ideas in health economics', *Social Science and Medicine*, **67**, 1190–8.

Coast, J., T.N. Flynn, L. Natarajan, K. Sproston, J. Lewis, J.J. Louviere and T.J. Peters (2008c), 'Valuing the ICECAP capability index for older people', *Social Science and Medicine*, **67**, 874–82.

Coast, J., C. Salisbury, D. de Berker, A. Noble, S. Horrocks, T. Peters and T. Flynn (2006), 'Preferences for aspects of a dermatology consultation', *British Journal of Dermatology*, **155**, 387–92.

Cobb, C.W. and P.H. Douglas (1928), 'A theory of production', *American Economic Review*, **8** (Supplement), 139–65.

Cobos, A., J. Vilaseca, C. Asenjo, J. Pedro Botet, E. Sanchez, A. Val, E. Torremade, C. Espinosa and S. Bergonon (2005), 'Cost-effectiveness of a clinical decision support system based on the recommendations of the European Society of Cardiology and other societies for the management of hypercholesterolemia: report of a cluster-randomized trial', *Disease Management and Health Outcomes*, **13**, 421–32.

Cochrane, A.L. (1972), *Effectiveness and Efficiency: Random Reflections on Health Services*, London: Nuffield Provincial Hospitals Trust.

Cochrane, J.H. (1995), 'Time-consistent health insurance', *Journal of Political Economy*, **103**, 445–73.

Coe, N.B. and M. Lindeboom (2008), 'Does Retirement Kill You? Evidence from Early Retirement Windows', IZA Discussion Paper No. 3817.

Cohen, D. (1994), 'Marginal analysis in practice: an alternative to needs assessment for contracting health care', *British Medical Journal*, **309**, 781–4.

Cohen, J.T., P.J. Neumann and M.C. Weinstein (2008), 'Does preventive care save money? Health economics and the presidential candidates', *New England Journal of Medicine*, **358**, 661–3.

Coleman, P.G., C. Morel, S. Shillcutt, C. Goodman and A.J. Mills (2004), 'A threshold analysis of the cost-effectiveness of artemisinin-based combination therapies in sub-Saharan Africa', *American Journal of Tropical Medicine and Hygiene*, **71**, 196–204.

Colgrove, J. (2002), 'The McKeown thesis: a historical controversy and its enduring influence', *American Journal of Public Health*, **92**, 725–9.

Contoyannis, P. and M. Forster (1999), 'The distribution of health and income: a theoretical framework', *Journal of Health Economics*, **18**, 603–20.

Contoyannis, P. and A.M. Jones (2004), 'Socio-economic status, health and lifestyle', *Journal of Health Economics*, **23**, 965–95.

Contoyannis, P., A.M. Jones and R. Leon-Gonzalez (2004), 'Using simulation-based inference with panel data in health economics', *Health Economics*, **13**, 101–22.

Cook, P.J. and M.J. Moore (1993), 'Drinking and schooling', *Journal of Health Economics*, **12**, 411–29.

Cook, P.J. and M.J. Moore (2000), 'Alcohol', in A.J. Culyer and J.P.

Newhouse (eds), *Handbook of Health Economics*, Amsterdam: Elsevier, pp. 1630–73.

Cookson, R. and D. Dawson (2006), 'Hospital competition and patient choice in publicly funded health care', in A.M. Jones (ed.), *The Elgar Companion to Health Economics*, Cheltenham, UK and Northampton, MA, USA: Edward Elgar, pp. 221–32.

Cookson, R. and P. Dolan (2000), 'Principles of justice in health care rationing', *Journal of Medical Ethics*, **26**, 323–9.

Cookson, R., C. McCabe and A. Tsuchiya (2008), 'Public healthcare resource allocation and the Rule of Rescue', *Journal of Medical Ethics*, **34**, 540–44.

Cooper, M.H. and A.J. Culyer (eds) (1973), *Health Economics*, London: Penguin Books.

Coory, M., S. Duckett and K. Sketcher-Baker (2008), 'Using control charts to monitor quality of hospital care with administrative data', *International Journal for Quality in Health Care*, **20**, 31–9.

Costa-i-Font, J. and M. Jofre-Bonet (2008), 'Is there a "secession of the wealthy"? Private health insurance uptake and National Health system support', *Bulletin of Economic Research*, **60**, 265–87.

Costa-i-Font, J. and F. Moscone (2008), 'The impact of decentralization and inter-territorial interactions on Spanish health expenditure', *Empirical Economics*, **34**, 167–84.

Cowell, F.A. (1995), *Measuring Inequality*, London: Prentice Hall/ Harvester Wheatsheaf.

Cowing, T.G. and A.G. Holtmann (1983), 'The multiproduct short-run hospital cost function: empirical evidence and policy implications from cross-section data', *Southern Economic Journal*, **49**, 637–53.

Cowing, T.G., A.G. Holtmann and S. Powers (1983), 'Hospital cost analysis: a survey and evaluation of recent studies', *Advances in Health Economics and Health Services Research*, **4**, 257–303.

Cox, D.F. (1972), 'Cox regression models and life tables', *Journal of the Royal Statistical Society*, B, **34**, 187–220.

Coyle, D., M.J. Buxton and B.J. O'Brien (2003), 'Measures of importance for economic analysis based on decision modeling', *Journal of Clinical Epidemiology*, **56**, 989–97.

Coyle, D., K.M. Lee, D.A. Fergusson and A. Laupacis (1999), 'Economic analysis of erythropoietin use in orthopaedic surgery', *Transfusion Medicine*, **9**, 21–30.

Coyte, P.C., R. Croxford, C.V. Asche, T. To, W. Feldman and J. Friedberg (2001), 'Physician and population determinants of rates of middle-ear surgery in Ontario', *Journal of the American Medical Association*, **286**, 2128–35.

Cragg, J. (1971), 'Some statistical models for limited dependent variables with application to the demand for durable goods', *Econometrica*, **39**, 829–44.

Creese, A. and S. Bennett (1997), 'Rural risk-sharing strategies', in G. Scheiber (ed.), *Innovations in Health Care Financing*, Washington, DC: World Bank, pp. 163–82.

Cromwell, J. and G.C. Pope (1989), 'Trends in hospital labor and total factor productivity, 1981–86', *Health Care Financing Review*, **10**, 39–50.

Cronbach, L.J. (1951), 'Coefficient alpha and the internal structure of tests', *Psychometrika*, **16**, 297–333.

Croxson, B. (1998), 'From private club to professional network: an economic history of the Health Economists' Study Group, 1972–1997', *Health Economics*, Suppl.1, S9–S45.

Csaba, I. and P. Fenn (1997), 'Contractual choice in the managed health care market: an empirical analysis', *Journal of Health Economics*, **16**, 579–88.

Cuddington, J.T. and J.D. Hancock (1994), 'Assessing the impact of AIDS on the growth path of the Malawian economy', *Journal of Development Economics*, **43**, 363–8.

Cuellar, A.E. and P.J. Gertler (2006), 'Strategic integration of hospitals and physicians', *Journal of Health Economics*, **25**, 1–28.

Cullis, J.G, and P.A. West (1979), *The Economics of Health: An Introduction*, Oxford: Martin Robertson.

Cullis, J.G., P.R. Jones and C. Propper (2000), 'Waiting lists and medical treatment', in A.J. Culyer and J.P. Newhouse (eds), *Handbook of Health Economics*, Amsterdam: Elsevier, pp. 1201–49.

Culyer, A.J. (1971a), 'Medical care and the economics of giving', *Economica*, **38**, 295–303.

Culyer, A.J. (1971b), 'The nature of the commodity "health care" and its efficient allocation', *Oxford Economic Papers*, **23**, 189–211.

Culyer, A.J. (1976), *Need and the National Health Service: Economics and Social Choice*, Oxford: Martin Robertson.

Culyer, A.J. (1989), 'Commodities, characteristics of commodities, characteristics of people, utilities and the quality of life', in S. Baldwin, C. Godfrey and C. Propper (eds), *The Quality of Life: Perspectives and Policies,* London: Routledge, pp. 9–27.

Culyer, A.J. (1991a), ' The normative economics of health care finance and provision', in A. McGuire, P. Fenn and K. Mayhew (eds), *Providing Health Care: the Economics of Alternative Systems of Finance and Delivery*, Oxford: Oxford University Press, pp. 65–98.

Culyer, A.J. (ed.) (1991b), *The Economics of Health*, 2 vols, Aldershot, UK and Brookfield, VT, USA: Edward Elgar.

Culyer, A.J. (1995), 'Need: the idea won't do – but we still need it', *Social Science and Medicine*, **40**, 727–30.

Culyer, A.J. (ed.) (2006a), *Health Economics: Critical Perspectives on the World Economy*, 4 vols, Abingdon: Routledge.

Culyer, A.J. (2006b), 'The bogus conflict between efficiency and equity', *Health Economics*, **15**, 1155–8.

Culyer, A.J. (2007), 'Need – an instrumental view', in R. Ashcroft, A. Dawson, H. Draper and J. McMillan (eds), *Principles of Health Care Ethics*, 2nd edition, Chichester: Wiley, pp. 231–8.

Culyer, A.J. and J. Lomas (2006), 'Deliberative processes and evidence-informed decision-making in health care – do they work and how might we know?', *Evidence and Policy*, **2**, 357–71.

Culyer, A.J. and A. Wagstaff (1993), 'Equity and equality in health and health care', *Journal of Health Economics*, **12**, 431–57.

Culyer, A.J., R.J. Lavers and A.H. Williams (1971), 'Social indicators: health', *Social Trends*, **2**, 31–42.

Culyer, A.J., A.K. Maynard and A.H. Williams (1982), 'Alternative systems of health care provision: an essay on motes and beams', in M. Olson (ed.), *A New Approach to the Economics of Health Care*, Washington, DC: American Enterprise Institute, pp. 131–50.

Culyer, A.J., C. McCabe, A.H. Briggs, K. Claxton, M.J. Buxton, R.L. Akehurst, M.J. Sculpher and J. Brazier (2007), 'Searching for a threshold, not setting one: the role of the National Institute of Health and Clinical Excellence', *Journal of Health Service Research & Policy*, **12**, 56–8.

Curnow, W.J. (2006), 'The Cochrane Collaboration and bicycle helmets', *Accident Analysis and Prevention*, **37**, 569–73.

Currie, J. (2000), 'Child health in developed countries', in A.J. Culyer and J.P. Newhouse (eds), *Handbook of Health Economics*, Amsterdam: Elsevier, pp. 1054–90.

Currie, J. and E. Tekin (2006), 'Does Child Abuse Cause Crime?', NBER Working Papers No. 12171, New York: National Bureau of Economic Research, Inc.

Cutler, D.M. (1995), 'The incidence of adverse medical outcomes under prospective payment', *Econometrica*, **63**, 29–50.

Cutler, D.M. (2002), 'Equality, efficiency and market fundamentals: the dynamics of international medical-care reform', *Journal of Economic Literature*, **40**, 881–906.

Cutler, D.M. and E.L. Glaeser (2005), 'What explains differences in smoking, drinking, and other health-related behaviors?', *American Economic Review, Papers and Proceedings*, **95**, 238–42.

Cutler, D.M. and J. Gruber (1996), 'Does public insurance crowd out private insurance?', *Quarterly Journal of Economics*, **111**, 391–430.

Cutler, D.M. and S.J. Reber (1998), 'Paying for health insurance: the trade-off between competition and adverse selection', *Quarterly Journal of Economics*, **113**, 433–66.

Cutler, D.M. and R.J. Zeckhauser (2000), 'The anatomy of health insurance', in A.J. Culyer and J.P. Newhouse (eds), *Handbook of Health Economics*, Amsterdam: Elsevier, pp. 563–643.

Cutler, D.M. and R. Zeckhauser (2004), 'Extending the theory to meet the practice of insurance', in R.E. Litan and R. Herring (eds), *Brookings-Wharton Papers on Financial Services*, Washington, DC: Brookings Institution Press, pp. 1–53.

Cutler, D.M., E.L. Glaeser and J.M. Shapiro (2003), 'Why have Americans become more obese?', *Journal of Economic Perspectives*, **17**, 93–118.

Cutler, D.M., M. McClellan, J.P. Newhouse and D. Remler (1996), 'Are medical prices declining? Evidence from heart attack treatments', *Quarterly Journal of Economics*, **113**, 991–1024.

Daniels, N. (1993), 'Rationing fairly: programmatic considerations', *Bioethics*, **7**, 224–33.

Daniels, N. and J. Sabin (1998), 'The ethics of accountability in managed care reform', *Health Affairs*, **17**, 50–65.

Danzon, P.M. (1997a), 'Price discrimination for pharmaceuticals: welfare effects in the US and EU', *International Journal of the Economics of Business*, **4**, 301–21.

Danzon, P.M. (1997b), *Pharmaceutical Price Regulation: National Policies versus Global Interests*, Washington, DC: AEI Press.

Danzon, P.M. (1998), 'The economics of parallel trade', *Pharmaco-Economics*, **13**, 293–304.

Danzon, P.M. (2000), 'Liability for medical malpractice', in A.J. Culyer and J.P. Newhouse (eds), *Handbook of Health Economics*, Amsterdam: Elsevier, pp. 1339–404.

Danzon, P.M. and A. Towse (2003), 'Differential pricing for pharmaceuticals: reconciling access, R&D and patents', *International Journal of Health Care Finance and Economics*, **3**, 183–205.

Das, J., J. Hammer and K. Leonard (2008), 'The quality of medical advice in low-income countries', *Journal of Economic Perspectives*, **22**, 93–114.

Davidson, B.N., S. Sofaer and P. Gertler (1992), 'Consumer information and biased selection in the demand for coverage supplementing Medicare', *Social Science and Medicine*, **34**, 1023–34.

De Allegri, M., S. Pokhrel, H. Becher, H. Dong, U. Mansmann, B. Kouyaté, G. Kynast-Wolf, A. Gbangou, M. Sanon, J.Bridges and R. Sauerborn (2008), 'Step-wedge cluster-randomised community-based trials: an application to the study of the impact of community health insurance', *Health Research Policy and Systems*, **6** (10).

Deaton, A. (2002), 'Policy implications of the gradient of health and wealth', *Health Affairs*, **21**, 13–30.

Deaton, A. (2003), 'Health, inequality, and economic development', *Journal of Economic Literature*, **41**, 113–58.

Deb, P. and P.K. Trivedi (2006), 'Empirical models of health care use', in A.M. Jones (ed.), *The Elgar Companion to Health Economics*, Cheltenham, UK and Northampton, MA, USA: Edward Elgar, pp. 147–55.

Debreu, G. (1959), *Theory of Value*, New York: Wiley.

Dee, T.S. (1999), 'The complementarity of teen smoking and drinking', *Journal of Health Economics*, **18**, 769–93.

Delea, T.E., J. Karnon, O. Sofrygin, S.K. Thomas, N.L. Papo and V. Barghout (2007), 'Cost-effectiveness of letrozole versus tamoxifen as initial adjuvant therapy in hormone receptor-positive postmenopausal women with early-stage breast cancer', *Clinical Breast Cancer*, **7**, 608–18.

DeLeire, T. and W.G. Manning (2004), 'Labor market costs of illness: prevalence matters', *Health Economics*, **13**, 239–50.

de Meza, D. and D.C. Webb (2001), 'Advantageous selection in insurance markets', *Rand Journal of Economics*, **32**, 249–62.

DerSimonian, R. and N. Laird (1986), 'Meta-analysis in clinical trials', *Controlled Clinical Trials*, **7**, 177–88.

Devereaux, P.J., P.T.L. Choi, C. Lacchetti, B. Weaver, H.J. Schünemann, T. Haines, J.N. Lavis, B.J.B. Grant, D.R.S. Haslam, M. Bhandari, T. Sullivan, D.J. Cook, S.D. Walter, M. Meade, H. Khan, N. Bhatnagar and G.H. Guyatt (2002), 'A systematic review and meta-analysis of studies comparing mortality rates of private for-profit and private not-for-profit hospitals', *Canadian Medical Association Journal*, **166**, 1399–406.

Dewa, C.S. and E. Lin (2000), 'Chronic physical illness, psychiatric disorder and disability in the workplace', *Social Science and Medicine*, **51**, 41–50.

Dias, P.R. and A.M. Jones (2007), 'Giving equality of opportunity a fair innings', *Health Economics*, **16**, 109–12.

Dick, B. (2000), 'Data-driven action research', available at: http://www.scu.edu.au/schools/gcm/ar/arp/datadriv.html (accessed 26 October 2009).

Diener, A., B.J. O'Brien and A. Gafni (1998), 'Health care contingent valuation studies: a review and classification of the literature', *Health Economics*, **7**, 313–26.

Dinardo, J. and T. Lemieux (2001), 'Alcohol, marijuana, and American youth: the unintended consequences of government regulation', *Journal of Health Economics*, **20**, 991–1010.

Dockner, E.J. and G. Feichtinger (1993), 'Cyclical consumption patterns and rational addition', *American Economic Review*, **83**, 256–63.

Doherty, J. and R. Govender (2004), 'The Cost-effectiveness of Primary Care Services in Developing Countries: A Review of the International Literature', background paper commissioned by the Disease Control Priorities Project, Washington, DC: World Bank.

Doherty, N.J.G. (1990), 'Resource productivity and returns to scale in school-based mouthrinsing programs', *Community Dentistry and Oral Epidemiology*, **18**, 57–60.

Dolan, P. (1996), 'Modelling valuations for health states: the effect of duration', *Health Policy*, **38**, 189–203.

Dolan, P. (2000), 'The measurement of health-related quality of life for use in resource allocation decisions in health care', in A.J. Culyer and J.P. Newhouse (eds), *Handbook of Health Economics*, Amsterdam: Elsevier, pp. 1723–60.

Dolan, P. and R. Edlin (2002), 'Is it really possible to build a bridge between cost–benefit analysis and cost–effectiveness analysis?', *Journal of Health Economics*, **21**, 827–43.

Dolan, P. and C. Green (1998), 'Using the person trade-off approach to examine differences between individual and social values', *Health Economics*, **7**, 307–12.

Dolan, P. and P. Stalmeier (2003), 'The validity of time trade-off values in calculating QALYs: constant proportional time trade-off versus the proportional heuristic', *Journal of Health Economics*, **22**, 445–58.

Dolan, P. and A. Tsuchiya (2006), 'The elicitation of distributional judgements in the context of economic evaluation', in A.M. Jones (ed.), *The Elgar Companion to Health Economics*, Cheltenham, UK and Northampton, MA, USA: Edward Elgar, pp. 382–91.

Dolan, P. and A. Tsuchiya (2009), 'The social welfare function and individual responsibility: some theoretical issues and empirical evidence', *Journal of Health Economics*, **28**, 210–20.

Dolan, P., C. Gudex, P. Kind and A.H. Williams (1996a), 'The time trade-off method: results from a general population study', *Health Economics*, **5**, 141–54.

Dolan, P., C. Gudex, P. Kind and A.H. Williams (1996b), 'Valuing health states: a comparison of methods, *Journal of Health Economics*, **15**, 209–31.

Dolan, P., G. Loomes, T. Peasgood and A. Tsuchiya (2005), 'Estimating the intangible victim costs of violent crime', *British Journal of Criminology*, **45**, 958–76.

Dollar, D. (2001), 'Is globalization good for your health?', *Bulletin of the World Health Organization*, **79**, 827–33.

Donabedian, A. (1988), 'The quality of care: how can it be assessed?', *Journal of the American Medical Association*, **260**, 1743–8.

Donaldson, C., H. Mason and P. Shackley (2006), 'Contingent valuation in health care', in A.M. Jones (ed.), *The Elgar Companion to Health Economics*, Cheltenham, UK and Northampton, MA, USA: Edward Elgar, pp. 392–402.

Donaldson, C., K. Gerard, C. Mitton, S. Jan and V. Wiseman (2005), *Economics of Health Care Financing: The Visible Hand*, London: Palgrave Macmillan.

Dong, H.J., B. Kouyate, J. Cairns and R. Sauerborn (2005), 'Inequality in willingness-to-pay for community-based health insurance', *Health Policy*, **72**, 149–56.

Dorman, P. (1996), *Markets and Mortality: Economics, Dangerous Work, and the Value of Human Life*, Cambridge, UK: Cambridge University Press.

Dow, W. and T.J. Philipson (1996), 'An empirical examination of the implications of assortative matching on the incidence of HIV', *Journal of Health Economics*, **15**, 735–49.

Dowd, B.E. and R. Feldman (1987), 'Voluntary reduction in health insurance coverage: a theoretical analysis', *Eastern Economic Journal*, **13**, 215–32.

Drager, N. and C. Vieira (eds.) (2002), *Trade in Health Services: Global, Regional and Country Perspectives*, Washington, DC: Pan American Health Organization.

Dranove, D. (1988), 'Demand inducement and the physician/patient relationship', *Economic Enquiry*, **26**, 281–98.

Dranove, D. (1998), 'Economies of scale in non-revenue-producing cost centers: implications for hospital mergers', *Journal of Health Economics*, **17**, 69–83.

Dranove, D. and M.A. Satterthwaite (2000), 'The industrial organization of health care markets', in A.J. Culyer and J.P. Newhouse (eds), *The Handbook of Health Economics*, Vol. 1B, Amsterdam: Elsevier, pp. 1093–139.

Dranove, D. and P. Wehner (1994), 'Physician-induced demand for childbirths', *Journal of Health Economics*, **13**, 61–73.

Dranove, D. and W.D. White (1987), 'Agency and the organization of health care delivery', *Inquiry*, **24**, 405–15.

Dranove, D., M. Shanley and C. Simon (1992), 'Is hospital competition wasteful?', *RAND Journal of Economics*, **23**, 247–62.

Dranove, D., M. Shanley and W.D. White (1993), 'Price and concentration in hospital markets: the switch from patient-driven to payer-driven competition', *Journal of Law and Economics*, **36**, 179–204.

Dranove, D., D. Kessler, M. McClellan and M.A. Satterthwaite (2003), 'Is more information better? The effects of "report cards" on health care providers', *Journal of Political Economy*, **111**, 555–88.

Dror, D. and C. Jacquier (1999), 'Micro-insurance: extending health insurance to the excluded', *International Social Security Review*, **52**, 71–97.

Dror, D. and A. Preker (eds) (2002), *Social Reinsurance: a New Approach to Sustainable Community Health Financing*, Washington, DC/Geneva: World Bank/International Labour Organization.

Drummond, M.F., G.W. Torrance and J. Mason (1993), 'Cost-effectiveness league tables: more harm than good?', *Social Science and Medicine*, **37**, 33–40.

Drummond, M.F., M.J. Sculpher, G.W. Torrance, B.J. O'Brien and G.L. Stoddart (2005), *Methods for the Economic Evaluation of Health Care Programmes*, 3rd edition, Oxford: Oxford University Press.

Duggan, M. (2004), 'Does contracting out increase the efficiency of government programs? Evidence from Medicaid HMOs', *Journal of Public Economics*, **88**, 2549–72.

Durbin, J. and G.S. Watson (1950), 'Testing for serial correlation in least squares regression I', *Biometrika*, **37**, 409–28.

Durbin, J. and G.S. Watson (1951), 'Testing for serial correlation in least squares regression II', *Biometrika*, **38**, 159–79.

Dusheiko, M., H.S.E. Gravelle and R. Jacobs (2004), 'The effect of practice budgets on patient waiting times', *Health Economics*, **13**, 941–58.

Eckerman, S. and A.R. Willan, (2007), 'Expected value of information and decision making in HTA', *Health Economics*, **16**, 195–209.

Eckerman, S. and A.R. Willan (2009), 'Globally optimal trial design for local decision making', *Health Economics*, **18**, 203–16.

Eddy, D.M. (1991), 'Oregon's methods: did cost effectiveness analysis fail?', *Journal of the American Medical Association*, **266**, 2135–41.

Eddy, D.M. (2005), 'Evidence-based medicine: a unified approach', *Health Affairs*, **24**, 9–17.

Efron, B. and R. Tibshirani (1998), *An Introduction to the Bootstrap*, London: Chapman & Hall.

Egger, M., G. Davey Smith and A.N. Phillips (1997), 'Meta-analysis: principles and procedures', *British Medical Journal*, **315**, 1371–4.

Ehrlich, I. (2000), 'Uncertain lifetime, life protection, and the value of life saving', *Journal of Health Economics*, **19**, 341–67 (with corrections in *JHE*, 2000, **20**, 459–60).

Ehrlich, I. and H. Chuma (1990), 'A model of the demand for longevity and the value of life extension', *Journal of Political Economy*, **98**, 761–82.

Ekman, B. (2004), 'Community-based health insurance in low-income countries: a systematic review of the evidence', *Health Policy and Planning*, **19**, 249–70.

Ellis, J.J., S.R. Erickson, J.G. Stevenson, S.J. Bernstein, R.A. Stiles and A. Fendrick (2004), 'Suboptimal statin adherence and discontinuation in primary and secondary prevention populations', *Journal of General Internal Medicine*, **19**, 638–45.

Ellis, R.P. (1998), 'Creaming, skimping and dumping: provider competition on the intensive and extensive margins', *Journal of Health Economics*, **17**, 537–55.

Ellis, R.P. and T.G. McGuire (1986), 'Provider behavior under prospective reimbursement: cost sharing and supply', *Journal of Health Economics*, **5**, 129–51.

Ellis, R.P. and T.G. McGuire (1993), 'Supply-side and demand-side cost sharing in health care', *Journal of Economic Perspectives*, **7**, 135–51.

Ellis, R.P. and T.G. McGuire (1996), 'Hospital response to prospective payment: moral hazard, selection, and practice-style effects', *Journal of Health Economics*, **15**, 257–77.

Ellsberg, D. (1961), 'Risk, ambiguity, and the Savage axioms', *Quarterly Journal of Economics*, **75**, 643–69.

Ellwood, P. (2003), 'Crossing the health policy chasm: pathways to healthy outcomes', *Progressive Policy Institute Briefings*, available online at: http://www.ppionline.org/ppi_ci.cfm?knlgAreaID=111&subsecID=138 &contentID=251324 (accessed 7 November 2009).

Ellwood, P. and L. Etheredge (1991), *The 21st Century American Health System*, Excelsior, Minnesota: Jackson Hole Group.

Elshaug, A.G., J.E. Hiller, S.R. Tunis and J.R. Moss (2007), 'Challenges in Australian policy processes for disinvestment from existing, ineffective health care practices', *Australia and New Zealand Health Policy*, **4**, 23.

Elster, J. and J.E. Roemer (1991), *Interpersonal Comparisons of Well-Being*, Cambridge, UK: Cambridge University Press.

Engel, E. (1895), 'Die Lebenskosten belgischer Arbeiter-Familien fruher und jetzt', *International Statistical Institute Bulletin*, **9**, 1–74.

Ensor, T. and R. Thompson (2006), 'The unofficial health care economy in low- and middle-income countries', in A.M. Jones (ed.), *The Elgar Companion to Health Economics*, Cheltenham, UK and Northampton, MA, USA: Edward Elgar, pp. 156–63.

Enthoven, A.C. (1980), *Consumer Choice Health Plan: The Only Practical Solution to the Soaring Cost of Medical Care*, Reading: Addison-Wesley.

Enthoven, A.C. (1993), 'The history and principles of managed competition', *Health Affairs*, **12**, 24–48.

Epstein, L.G. (1999), '"A definition of uncertainty aversion"', *Review of Economic Studies*, **66**, 579–608.

Escarce, J.J. (1996), 'Externalities in hospitals and physician adoption of a new surgical technology: an exploratory analysis', *Journal of Health Economics*, **15**, 715–34.

Ettner, S.L. (1997), 'Adverse selection and the purchase of Medigap insurance by the elderly', *Journal of Health Economics*, **16**, 543–62.

Ettner, S.L., R.G. Frank, T.G. McGuire, J.P. Newhouse and E.H. Notman (1998), 'Risk adjustment of mental health and substance abuse payments', *Inquiry*, **35**, 223–39.

Evans, D., A. Tandon, C.J.L. Murray and J. Lauer (2000), 'The Comparative Efficiency of National Health Systems in Producing Health: an Analysis of 191 Countries', Geneva: World Health Organization (Global Programme on Evidence for Health Policy Discussion Paper No 29).

Evans, I., H. Thornton and I. Chalmers (2007), *Testing Treatments: Better Research for Better Health Care*. Available from the authors under a Creative Commons Attribution 3.0 Unported Licence at http://www.jameslindlibrary.org/testing-treatments.html (accessed 30 October 2009).

Evans, R.G. (1971), '"Behavioural" cost functions for hospitals', *Canadian Journal of Economics*, **4**, 198–215.

Evans, R.G. (1974), 'Supplier-induced demand: some empirical evidence and implication', in M. Perlman (ed.), *The Economics of Health and Medical Care*, New York: Wiley, pp. 162–73.

Evans, R.G. (1984), *Strained Mercy: The Economics of Canadian Health Care*, Markham Ontario: Butterworths.

Evans, R.G., M.L. Barer and T.R. Marmor (eds) (1994), *Why are Some People Healthy and Others Not? The Determinants of Health of Populations*, New York: Aldine De Gruyter.

Evans, R.G., E. Parish and F. Sully (1973), 'Medical productivity, scale effects, and demand generation', *Canadian Journal of Economics*, **6**, 376–93.

Evans, W.N. and J.S. Ringel (1999), 'Can higher cigarette taxes improve birth outcomes?', *Journal of Public Economics*, **72**, 135–54.

Evans, W.N. and W.K. Viscusi (1991), 'Estimation of state-dependent utility functions using survey data', *Review of Economics and Statistics*, **73**, 94–104.

Everitt, B.S., S. Landau and M. Leese (2001), *Cluster Analysis*, 4th edition, London: Edward Arnold.

Fang, H., M.P. Keane and D. Silverman (2008), 'Sources of advantageous selection: evidence from the Medigap insurance market', *Journal of Political Economy*, **116**, 303–50.

Farrell, P. and V.R. Fuchs (1982), 'Schooling and health: the cigarette connection', *Journal of Health Economics*, **1**, 217–30.

Farrell, S., W.G. Manning and M.D. Finch (2003), 'Alcohol dependence and the price of alcoholic beverages', *Journal of Health Economics*, **22**, 117–47.

Farrelly, M.C., J.W. Bray, G.A. Zarkin and B.W. Wendling (2001), 'The joint demand for cigarettes and marijuana: evidence from the National Household Surveys on Drug Use', *Journal of Health Economics*, **20**, 51–68.

Feeny, D.H. and K. Eng (2005), 'A test of prospect theory', *International Journal of Technology Assessment in Health Care*, **21**, 511–16.

Feeny, D.H. and G.W. Torrance (1989), 'Incorporating utility-based quality-of-life assessment measures in clinical trials', *Medical Care*, **27**, 190–204.

Feldman, R. and B. Dowd (1991), 'A new estimate of the welfare loss of excess health insurance', *American Economic Review*, **81**, 297–301.

Feldstein, M.S. (1967), *Economic Analysis for Health Service Efficiency: Econometric Studies of the British National Health Service*, Amsterdam: North-Holland.

Feldstein, M.S. (1973), 'The welfare loss of excess health insurance', *Journal of Political Economy*, **81**, 251–80.

Feldstein, P.J. (2005), *Health Care Economics*, 6th edition, Florence, KY: Delmar Learning.

Fenn, P., A. Gray and N. Rickman (2004), 'The economics of clinical negligence reform in England', *Economic Journal*, **114**, F272–F292.

Fenn, P., A. McGuire, V. Phillips, M. Backhouse and D. Jones (1995), 'The analysis of censored treatment cost data in economic evaluation', *Medical Care*, **33**, 851–63.

Fenwick, E., K. Claxton and M.J. Sculpher (2001), 'Representing uncertainty: the role of cost-effectiveness acceptability curves', *Health Economics*, **10**, 779–87.

Fenwick, E., K. Claxton and M.J. Sculpher (2008), 'The value of implementation and the value of information: combined and uneven development', *Medical Decision Making*, **28**, 21–32.

Fetter, R.B., J.D. Thompson and R.E. Mills (1976), 'A system for cost and reimbursement control in hospitals', *Yale Journal of Biological Medicine*, **49**, 123–36.

Fick, D.M., J.W. Cooper, W.E. Wade, J.L. Waller, J.R. Maclean and M.H. Beers (2003), 'Updating the Beers criteria for potentially inappropriate medication use in older adults: results of a US consensus panel of experts', *Archives of Internal Medicine*, **163**, 2716–24.

Fieller, E.C. (1954), 'Some problems in interval estimation', *Journal of the Royal Statistical Society*, Series B, **16**, 175–85.

Fischer, G.W. and S.A. Hawkins (1993), 'Strategy compatibility, scale compatibility, and the prominence effect', *Journal of Experimental Psychology: Human Perception and Performance*, **19**, 580–97.

Fisher, I. (1922), *The Making of Index Numbers: A Study of Their Varieties, Tests, and Reliability*, Boston: Houghton Mifflin Company.

Fisher, R.A. (1922), 'The goodness of fit of regression formulae and the distribution of regression coefficients', *Journal of the Royal Statistical Society*, **85**, 597–612.

Fitzgerald, L., R. Johnston, T.J. Brignall, R. Silvestro and C. Voss (1991), *Performance Measurement in Service Businesses*, London: Chartered Institute of Management Accountants.

Fleurbaey, M. and E. Schokkaert (2009), 'Unfair inequalities in health and health care', *Journal of Health Economics*, **28**, 73–90.

Flood, C., M. Stabile and C. Tuohy (2004), 'How does private finance affect public health care systems? Marshalling the evidence from OECD nations', *Journal of Health Politics, Policy, and Law*, **29**, 359–96.

Flynn, T.N., J.J. Louviere, T.J. Peters and J. Coast (2007), 'Best–worst scaling: what it can do for health care research and how to do it?', *Journal of Health Economics*, **26**, 171–89.

Folland, S., A.C. Goodman and M. Stano (2010), *The Economics of Health and Health Care*, 6th edition, Upper Saddle River: Prentice Hall.

Forster, B.A. (1989), 'Optimal health investment strategies', *Bulletin of Economic Research*, **41**, 45–57.

Forster, M. (2001), 'The meaning of death: some simulations of a model of healthy and unhealthy consumption', *Journal of Health Economics*, **20**, 613–38.

Forster, M. and A.M. Jones (2001), 'The role of tobacco taxes in starting and quitting smoking: duration analysis of British data', *Journal of the Royal Statistical Society*, Series A, **164**, 517–47.

Fowler, J.H. and N.A. Christakis (2008), 'Estimating peer effects on health in social networks', *Journal of Health Economics*, **27**, 1400–405.

Fox, M.P., S. Rosen, W.B. MacLeod, M. Wasunna, M. Bii, G. Foglia and J.L. Simon (2004), 'The impact of HIV/AIDS on labour productivity in Kenya', *Tropical Medicine & International Health*, **9**, 318–24.

Fox-Rushby, J. and J. Cairns (eds) (2005), *Economic Evaluation*, Maidenhead: McGraw-Hill International.

Frank, R.G. (2000), 'Economics and mental health', in A.J. Culyer and

J.P. Newhouse (eds), *Handbook of Health Economics*, Amsterdam: Elsevier, pp. 894–954.

Frank, R.G. and R.L. Garfield (2007), 'Managed behavioral health care carve-outs: past performance and future prospects', *Annual Review of Public Health*, **28**, 303–20.

Frank, R.G. and D.S. Salkever (1992), 'Pricing, patent loss and the market for pharmaceuticals', *Southern Economic Journal*, **59**, 165–79.

Frank, R.G. and D.S. Salkever (1994), 'Nonprofit organizations in the health sector', *Journal of Economic Perspectives*, **8**, 129–44.

Frank, R.G., T.G. McGuire and J.P. Newhouse (1995), 'Risk contracts in managed mental health care', *Health Affairs*, **14**, 50–64.

Frankenberg, E., J.P. Smith and D. Thomas (2003), 'Economic shocks, wealth, and welfare', *Journal of Human Resources*, **38**, 280–321.

Fredrickson, B.L. and D. Kahneman (1993), 'Duration neglect in retrospective evaluations of affective episodes', *Journal of Personality and Social Psychology*, **65**, 45–55.

Frew, E.J., J.L. Wolstenholme and D.K. Whynes (2004), 'Comparing willingness-to-pay: bidding game format versus open-ended and payment scale formats', *Health Policy*, **68**, 289–98.

Frick, K.D., E.W. Gower, J.H. Kempen and J.L. Wolff (2007), 'Economic impact of visual impairment and blindness in the United States', *Archives of Ophthalmology*, **125**, 544–50.

Frick, K.D., L. Burton, B. Clark, S.I. Mader, B. Naughton, J. Burl, W.B. Greenough III, D. Steinwachs and B. Leff (2009), 'Substitutive hospital at home for older persons: effects on costs', *American Journal of Managed Care*, **15**, 49–56.

Friedman, J. and D. Thomas (2007), 'Psychological Health Before, During, and After an Economic Crisis: Results from Indonesia, 1993–2000', Policy Research Working Paper Series No. 4386, Washington, DC: World Bank.

Friedman, M. (1953), 'The methodology of positive economics', in M. Friedman, *Essays in Positive Economics*, Chicago: Chicago University Press, pp. 3–43.

Friedman, M. (1957), *A Theory of the Consumption Function*, Princeton: Princeton University Press.

Friedman, M. (1968), 'The role of monetary policy', *American Economic Review*, **58**, 1–17.

Frijters, P., J.P. Haisken-DeNew and M.A. Shields (2005), 'The causal effect of income on health: evidence from German reunification', *Journal of Health Economics*, **24**, 997–1017.

Fuchs, V.R. (1978), 'The supply of surgeons and the demand for operations', *Journal of Human Resources*, **13**, 35–56.

Fuchs, V.R. (1982), 'Time preference and health: an exploratory study', in V.R. Fuchs, (ed.), *Economic Aspects of Health*, Chicago: University of Chicago Press, pp. 93–120.

Fuchs, V.R. (1993), 'What is health?', in V.R. Fuchs (ed.), *The Future of Health Policy*, Boston: Harvard University Press, pp. 19–27.

Gafni, A. and S. Birch (1993), 'Economics, health and health economics: HYEs versus QALYs', *Journal of Health Economics*, **11**, 325–39.

Gail, M.H. and R. Simon (1985), 'Testing for qualitative interactions between treatment effects and patient subsets', *Biometrics*, **41**, 361–73.

Galizzi, M.M. and M. Miraldo (2008), 'Optimal Contracts and Contractual Arrangements within the Hospital: Bargaining vs. Take-it-or Leave-it Offers', CHE Discussion Paper No. 37, York: University of York.

Gallivan, S., M. Utley, T. Treasure and O. Valencia (2002), 'Booked inpatient admissions and capacity: mathematical modelling study', *British Medical Journal*, **324**, 280–82.

Gandjour, A. (2008), 'Mutual dependency between capabilities and functionings in Amartya Sen's capability approach', *Social Choice and Welfare*, **31**, 345–50.

Garber, A.M. (2000), 'Advances in cost-effectiveness analysis of health care interventions', in A.J. Culyer and J.P. Newhouse (eds), *Handbook of Health Economics*, Amsterdam: Elsevier, pp. 181–221.

Garber, A.M. and C.E. Phelps (1997), 'Economic foundations of cost-effectiveness analysis', *Journal of Health Economics*, **16**, 1–31.

Gates, S.M., K. Kapur and P. Karaca-Mandic (2008), 'Consumer-directed health plans and health savings accounts: have they worked for small business?', *Forum for Health Economics & Policy*, **11**, 1–20.

Gaynor, M. (2006), 'Is vertical integration anticompetitive? Definitely maybe (but that's not final)', *Journal of Health Economics*, **25**, 175–80.

Gaynor, M. and P.J. Gertler (1995), 'Moral hazard and risk spreading in medical partnerships', *RAND Journal of Economics*, **26**, 591–613.

Gaynor, M. and W.B. Vogt (2000), 'Antitrust and competition in health care markets', in A.J. Culyer and J.P. Newhouse (eds), *Handbook of Health Economics*, Amsterdam: Elsevier, pp. 1405–87.

Gaynor, M. and W.B. Vogt (2003), 'Competition among hospitals', *RAND Journal of Economics*, **34**, 764–85.

Gemmill, M.C., J. Costa-i-Font and A. McGuire (2007), 'In search of a corrected prescription drug elasticity estimate: a meta-regression approach', *Health Economics*, **16**, 627–43.

Gentle, J.E. (2003), *Random Number Generation and Monte Carlo Methods*, 2nd edition, New York: Springer.

Geoffard, P.-Y. and T.J. Philipson (1997), 'Disease eradication: private versus public vaccination', *American Economic Review*, **87**, 222–30.

Gerdtham, U.-G. and M. Johannesson (2003), 'A note on the effect of unemployment on mortality', *Journal of Health Economics*, **22**, 505–18.

Gerdtham, U.-G. and B. Jönsson (1992), 'International comparisons of health care expenditure – conversion factor instability, heteroskedasticity, outliers and robust estimators', *Journal of Health Economics*, **11**, 189–97.

Gerdtham, U.-G. and B. Jönsson (2000), 'International comparisons of health expenditure', in A.J. Culyer and J.P. Newhouse (eds), *Handbook of Health Economics*, Amsterdam: Elsevier, pp. 11–53.

Gerdtham, U.-G., M. Löthgren, M. Tambour and C. Rehnberg (1999), 'Internal markets and health-care efficiency: a multiple-output stochastic frontier analysis', *Health Economics*, **8**, 151–64.

Gertler, P.J. and J. Gruber (2002), 'Insuring consumption against illness', *American Economic Review*, **92**, 51–70.

Gertler, P.J. and D.M. Waldman (1992), 'Quality-adjusted cost functions and policy evaluation in the nursing home industry', *Journal of Political Economy*, **100**, 1232–56.

Gertler, P.J., L. Locay and W. Sanderson (1987), 'Are user fees regressive? The welfare implications of health care financing proposals in Peru', *Journal of Econometrics*, **36**, 67–88.

Gertler, P.J., M. Shah and S.M. Bertozzi (2005), 'Risky business: the market for unprotected commercial sex', *Journal of Political Economy*, **113**, 518–50.

Getzen, T.E. (2000), 'Health care is an individual necessity and a national luxury: applying multilevel decision models to the analysis of health care expenditures', *Journal of Health Economics*, **19**, 259–70.

Getzen, T.E. (2006), *Health Economics: Fundamentals and Flow of Funds*, 3rd edition, Hoboken NJ: Wiley.

Getzen, T.E. and B.H. Allen (2007), *Health Care Economics*, Chichester: Wiley.

Giacomini, M., J.E. Hurley and G.L. Stoddart (2000), 'The many meanings of deinsuring a health service: the case of in vitro fertilization in Ontario', *Social Science & Medicine*, **50**, 1485–500.

Glaser, B.G. and A. Strauss (1967), *Discovery of Grounded Theory. Strategies for Qualitative Research*, Mill Valley, CA: Sociology Press.

Glass, G.V. (1976), 'Primary, secondary and meta-analysis of research', *Educational Researcher*, **5**, 3–8.

Glazer, A. and L.S. Rothenberg (1999), 'Increased capacity may exacerbate rationing problems: with applications to medical care', *Journal of Health Economics*, **18**, 669–78.

Glick, H.A., J.A. Doshi, S.S. Sonnad and D. Polski (2007), *Economic Evaluation in Clinical Trials*, New York: Oxford University Press.

Glied, S. (2000), 'Managed care', in A.J. Culyer and J.P. Newhouse (eds), *Handbook of Health Economics*, Amsterdam: Elsevier, pp. 707–53.

Goddard, M., K. Hauck and P.C. Smith (2006), 'Priority setting in health – a political economy perspective', *Health Economics, Policy and Law*, **1**, 79–90.

Goddard, M., R. Mannion and P.C. Smith (2000), 'Enhancing performance in health care: a theoretical perspective on agency and the role of information', *Health Economics*, **9**, 95–107.

Godfrey, C., G. Eaton, C. McDougall and A.J. Culyer (2002), *The Economic and Social Costs of Class A Drug Use in England and Wales, 2000*, London: Home Office Research Study 249, Home Office Research, Development and Statistics Directorate.

Gold, L., A. Shiell, P. Hawe, T. Riley, B. Rankin and P. Smithers (2007), 'The costs of a community based intervention to promote maternal health', *Health Education Research*, **22**, 648–57.

Gold, M.R., J.E. Siegel, L.B. Russell and M.C. Weinstein (eds) (1996), *Cost-effectiveness in Health and Medicine*, New York & Oxford: Oxford University Press.

Goodman, J.C. and G.L. Musgrave (1994), *Patient Power: the Free-enterprise Alternative to Clinton's Health Plan*, Washington, DC: Cato Institute.

Gordon, C.S., G.C.S. Smith and J.P. Pell (2003), 'Parachute use to prevent death and major trauma related to gravitational challenge: systematic review of randomised controlled trials', *British Medical Journal*, **327**, 1459–61.

Gowrisankaran, G. and R. Town (2003), 'Competition, payers, and hospital quality', *Health Services Research*, **38**, 1403–22.

Grabowski, D.C. and E.C. Norton (2006), 'Nursing home quality of care', in A.M. Jones, (ed.), *The Elgar Companion to Health Economics*, Cheltenham, UK and Northampton, MA, USA: Edward Elgar, pp. 296–305.

Grabowski, H.G., D.B. Ridley and K.A. Schulman (2007), 'Entry and competition in generic biologics', *Health Economics*, **28**, 439–51.

Granneman, T.W., R.S. Brown and M.V. Pauly (1986), 'Estimating hospital costs: a multiple output analysis', *Journal of Health Economics*, **5**, 107–28.

Grant, D.M., J.A. Mauskopf, L. Bell and R. Austin (1997), 'Comparison of valaciclovir and acyclovir for the treatment of herpes zoster in immunocompetent patients over 50 years old: a cost–consequence model', *Pharmacotherapy*, **b17**, 333–41.

Gravelle, H.S.E. (1984), 'Time series analysis of mortality and unemployment', *Journal of Health Economics*, **3**, 297–305.

Gravelle, H.S.E. (1998), 'How much of the relation between population mortality and unequal distribution of income is a statistical artefact?', *British Medical Journal*, **314**, 382–5.

Gravelle, H.S.E. and L. Siciliani (2008), 'Ramsey waits: allocating public health service resources when there is rationing by waiting', *Journal of Health Economics*, **27**, 1143–54.

Gravelle, H.S.E. and M. Sutton (2001), 'Inequality in the geographical distribution of general practitioners in England and Wales, 1974–1995', *Journal of Health Services Research & Policy*, **6**, 6–13.

Gravelle, H.S.E., W.B.F. Brouwer, L.W. Niessen, M.J. Postma and F.F.H. Rutten (2007a), 'Discounting in economic evaluations: stepping forward towards optimal decision rules', *Health Economics*, **16**, 307–17.

Gravelle, H.S.E., M. Dusheiko, R. Sheaff, P. Sargent, R. Boaden, S. Pickard, S. Parker and M. Roland (2007b), 'Impact of case management (Evercare) on frail elderly patients: controlled before and after analysis of quantitative outcome data', *British Medical Journal*, **334**, 31–4.

Graves, N., D. Walker, R. Raine, A. Hutchings and J.A. Roberts (2002), 'Cost data for individual patients included in clinical studies: no amount of statistical analysis can compensate for inadequate costing methods', *Health Economics*, **11**, 735–9.

Gregg, P., E. Washbrook, C. Propper and S. Burgess (2005), 'The effects of a mother's return to work decision on child development in the UK', *Economic Journal*, **115**, F48–F80.

Green, R.M. (2001), 'Access to healthcare: going beyond fair equality of opportunity', *American Journal of Bioethics*, **1**, 22–3.

Grewal, I., J. Lewis, T. Flynn, J. Brown, J. Bond and J. Coast (2006), 'Developing attributes for a generic quality of life measure for older people: preferences or capabilities?', *Social Science and Medicine*, **62**, 1891–1901.

Griffin, S., K. Claxton and M.J. Sculpher (2008), 'Decision analysis for resource allocation in health care', *Journal of Health Services Research & Policy*, **13**, 23–30.

Griffiths, R. (1983), *The NHS Management Enquiry Report*, London: Department of Health and Social Security.

Grimshaw, J.M., R.E. Thomas, G. MacLennan, C. Fraser, C.R. Ramsay, L. Vale, P. Whitty, M.P. Eccles, L. Matowe, L. Shirran, M. Wensing, R. Dijkstra and C. Donaldson (2005), 'Effectiveness and efficiency of guideline dissemination and implementation strategies', *International Journal of Technology Assessment in Health Care*, **21**, 1–72.

Groot, W., H.M. Van Den Brink and E. Plug (2004), 'Money for health: the equivalent variation of cardiovascular diseases', *Health Economics*, **13**, 859–72.

Grootendorst, P. (2006), 'Prescription drug insurance and reimbursement', in A.M. Jones (ed.), *The Elgar Companion to Health Economics*, Cheltenham, UK and Northampton, MA, USA: Edward Elgar, pp. 114–25.

Grosse, S.D. (2008), 'Assessing cost-effectiveness in healthcare: history of the $50,000 per QALY threshold', *Expert Review of PharmacoEconomics Outcomes Research*, **8**,165–78.

Grossman, M. (1972), 'On the concept of health capital and the demand for health', *Journal of Political Economy*, **80**, 223–55.

Grossman, M. (2000), 'The human capital model', in A.J. Culyer and J.P. Newhouse (eds), *Handbook of Health Economics*, Amsterdam: Elsevier, pp. 347–408.

Grossman, M. (2003), 'The effect of cigarette excise taxes on smoking before, during and after pregnancy', *Journal of Health Economics*, **22**, 1053–72.

Grossman, M. (2004), 'Get high and get stupid: the effect of alcohol and marijuana use on teen sexual behavior', *Review of Economics of the Household*, **2**, 413–41.

Grossman, M. (2008), 'Fast-food restaurant advertising on television and its influence on childhood obesity', *Journal of Law & Economics*, **51**, 599–618.

Gruber, J. (1994), 'The incidence of mandated maternity benefits', *American Economic Review*, **84**, 622–41.

Gruber, J. (1997), 'Tax incidence of payroll taxation: evidence from Chile', *Journal of Labor Economics*, **15**, 72–101.

Gruber, J. (2000), 'Health insurance and the labor market', in A.J. Culyer, and J.P. Newhouse (eds), *Handbook of Health Economics*, Amsterdam: Elsevier, pp. 645–706.

Gruber, J. and B. Köszegi (2001), 'Is addiction "rational"? Theory and evidence', *Quarterly Journal of Economics*, **116**, 1261–303.

Gruber, J. and M. Owings (1996), 'Physician financial incentives and caesarean section delivery', *RAND Journal of Economics*, **27**, 99–123.

Grytten, J. and D.M. Dalen (1997), 'Too many for too few? Efficiency among dentists working in private practice in Norway', *Journal of Health Economics*, **16**, 483–97.

Guttman, L.A. (1944), 'Basis for scaling qualitative data', *American Sociological Review*, **9**, 139–50.

Guyatt, G. (1991), 'Evidence-based medicine', *ACP Journal Club (Annals of Internal Medicine)*, **14**, Suppl. 2, A-16.

Guyatt, G.H. and the Evidence-based Medicine Working Group (1992), 'Evidence-based medicine. A new approach to teaching the practice of medicine', *Journal of the American Medical Association*, **268**, 2420–25.

Guyatt, G.H. and the Evidence-based Medicine Working Group (1995), 'Users' guide to the medical literature. IX. A method for grading health care recommendations', *Journal of the American Medical Association*, **274**, 1800–804.

Gyrd-Hansen, D. (2003), 'Willingness to pay for a QALY', *Health Economics*, **12**, 1049–60.

Gyrd-Hansen, D. (2004), 'Investigating the social value of health changes', *Journal of Health Economics*, **23**, 1101–16.

Hadorn, D.C. (1991), 'Setting health care priorities in Oregon: cost-effectiveness meets the rule of rescue', *Journal of the American Medical Association*, **265**, 2218–25.

Hall, J., R. Viney, M. Haas and J. Louviere (2004), 'Using stated preference discrete choice modeling to evaluate health care programs', *Journal of Business Research*, **57**, 1026–32.

Ham, C. (1996), 'Contestability: a middle path for health care', *British Medical Journal*, **312**, 70–71.

Ham, C. and A. Coulter (2001), 'Explicit and implicit rationing: taking responsibility and avoiding blame for health care choices', *Journal of Health Services Research & Policy*, **6**, 163–9.

Hardin, G. (1968), 'The tragedy of the commons', *Science*, **162**, 1243–8.

Harris, J. (2005), 'It's not NICE to discriminate', *Journal of Medical Ethics*, **31**, 373–5.

Harris, J. (2006a), 'NICE and not so nice', *Journal of Medical Ethics*, **31**, 685–8.

Harris, J. (2006b), 'NICE is not cost-effective', *Journal of Medical Ethics*, **32**, 378–80.

Harris, J. (2007), 'NICE rejoinder', *Journal of Medical Ethics*, **33**, 467.

Harris, J.E. (1977), 'The internal organization of hospitals: some economic implications', *Bell Journal of Economics*, **8**, 467–82.

Harris, K.M. and M.P. Keane (1999), 'A model of health plan choice: inferring preferences and perceptions from a combination of revealed preference and attitudinal data', *Journal of Econometrics*, **89**, 131–57.

Harsanyi, J.C. (1982), 'Morality and the theory of rational behaviour', in A.K. Sen and B. Williams (eds), *Utilitarianism and Beyond*, Cambridge, UK: Cambridge University Press, pp. 39–62.

Hart, J.T. (1971), 'The inverse care law', *The Lancet*, **1**, 405–12.

Hartwig, J. (2008), 'What drives health care expenditure? – Baumol's model of "unbalanced growth" revisited', *Journal of Health Economics*, **27**, 603–23.

Hauck, K., R. Shaw and P.C. Smith (2002), 'Reducing avoidable inequalities in health: a new criterion for setting health care capitation payments', *Health Economics*, **11**, 667–77.

Hausman, D. (2006), 'Valuing health', *Philosophy and Public Affairs*, **34**, 246–74.

Hausman, D. and M.S. McPherson (2006), *Economic Analysis, Moral Philosophy and Public Policy*, 2nd edition, Cambridge: Cambridge University Press.

Haveman, R. (2000), 'The economics of disability and disability policy', in A.J. Culyer and J.P. Newhouse (eds), *Handbook of Health Economics*, Amsterdam: Elsevier, pp. 996–1051.

Hawthorne, G., J. Richardson and R. Osborne (1999), 'The Assessment of Quality of Life (AQoL) instrument: a psychometric measure of health-related quality of life', *Quality of Life Research*, **8**, 209–24.

Health Economics Research Group, Office of Health Economics, RAND Europe (2008), *Medical Research: What's it Worth? Estimating the Economic Benefits from Medical Research in the UK*, London: UK Evaluation Forum.

Heckathorn, D.D. (2002), 'Respondent-driven Sampling II: deriving valid estimates from chain-referral samples of hidden populations', *Social Problems*, **49**, 11–34.

Heckman, J.J. (1979), 'Sample selection bias as a specification error', *Econometrica*, **47**, 153–61.

Heckman, J.J. (1997), 'Instrumental variables: a study of implicit behavioral assumptions used in making program evaluations', *Journal of Human Resources*, **32**, 441–62.

Heckman, J.J. (2007), 'The economics, technology, and neuroscience of human capability formation', *Proceedings of the National Academy of Sciences*, **104**, 13250–55.

Henderson, J.W. (2004), *Health Economics and Policy with Economic Applications*, 3rd edition, Cincinnati: South-Western Publishers.

Hensher, D., J. Louviere and J. Swait (1998), 'Combining sources of preference data', *Journal of Econometrics*, **89**, 197–221.

Herrnstein, R.J. (1970), 'On the law of effect', *Journal of the Experimental Analysis of Behavior*, **13**, 243–66.

Heymann, J., C. Hertzman, M.L. Barer and R.G. Evans (2006), *Healthier Societies: From Analysis to Action*, Oxford: Oxford University Press.

Hicks, J.R. (1939a), 'The foundations of welfare economics', *Economic Journal*, **49**, 696–712.

Hicks, J.R. (1939b), *Value and Capital: An Inquiry into Some Fundamental Principles of Economic Theory*, Oxford: Oxford University Press.

Hicks. J.R. (1944), 'The four consumers' surpluses', *Review of Economic Studies*, **11**, 31–41.

Hill, S.C. and B.L. Wolfe (1997), 'Testing the HMO competitive strategy:

an analysis of its impact on medical care resources', *Journal of Health Economics*, **16**, 261–86.

Hirshleifer, J. (1956), 'On the economics of transfer pricing', *Journal of Business*, **29**, 172–84.

Hirshleifer, J. and J.G. Riley (1979), 'The analytics of uncertainty and information—an expositional survey', *Journal of Economic Literature*, **17**, 1375–1421.

Hirth, R.A., M.E. Chernew, E. Miller, A.M. Fendrick and W.G. Weissert (2000), 'Willingness to pay for a quality-adjusted life year: in search of a standard', *Medical Decision Making*, **20**, 332–42.

Ho, V. (2002), 'Learning and the evolution of medical technologies: the diffusion of coronary angioplasty', *Journal of Health Economics*, **21**, 873–85.

Hoch, J.S., A.H. Briggs and A.R. Willan (2002), 'Something old, something new, something blue: a framework for the marriage of health econometrics and cost-effectiveness analysis', *Health Economics*, **11**, 415–30.

Hodgson, G.M. (2008), 'An institutional and evolutionary perspective on health economics', *Cambridge Journal of Economics*, **32**, 235–56.

Hoel, M. and E.M. Sæther (2003), 'Public health care with waiting time: the role of supplementary private health care', *Journal of Health Economics*, **22**, 599–616.

Höjgård, S., U. Enemark, C.H. Lyttkens, A. Lindgren, T. Troëng and H. Weibull (2002), 'Discounting and clinical decision making', *Health Economics*, **11**, 355–70.

Holden, J.D. (2008), 'Hawthorne effects and research into professional practice', *Journal of Evaluation in Clinical Practice*, **7**, 65–70.

Holla, A. and M.A. Kremer (2009), 'Pricing and Access: Lessons from Randomized Evaluations in Education and Health', Working Paper No. 158, Washington, DC: Center for Global Development.

Hollingsworth, B. (2008), 'The measurement of efficiency and productivity of health care delivery', *Health Economics*, **17**, 1107–28.

Holmström, B. and P. Milgrom (1991), 'Multitask principal-agent analyses: incentives, contracts, asset ownership, and job design', *Journal of Law, Economics and Organization*, **7**, 24–52.

Homer, J.F. and M.T. French (2009), 'Motorcycle helmet laws in the U.S. from 1990 to 2005: politics and public health', *American Journal of Public Health*, **99**, 3.

Horsman, J., W. Furlong, D. Feeny and G.W. Torrance (2003), 'The Health Utilities Index (HUI®): concepts, measurement properties and applications', *Health and Quality of Life Outcomes*, **1**, 54.

Hotopp, U., J. Mendeloff, S. Sinclair, E. Tompa, B. Koeper and A. Clayton (2008), 'The institutional and regulatory settings for occupational health and safety: an international survey', in E. Tompa, A.J. Culyer and R. Dolinschi (eds), *Economic Evaluation of Interventions for Occupational Health and Safety: Developing Good Practice*, Oxford: Oxford University Press, pp. 93–116.

Hughes, D. and A. McGuire (2003), 'Stochastic demand, production responses and hospital costs', *Journal of Health Economics*, **22**, 999–1010.

Humphrey, L.L., B.K. Chan and H.C. Sox (2002), 'Postmenopausal hormone replacement therapy and the primary prevention of cardiovascular disease', *Annals of Internal Medicine*, **137**, 273–84.

Hunt, S.M., J. McEwen and S.P. McKenna (1985), 'Measuring health status: a new tool for clinicians and epidemiologists', *Journal of the Royal College of General Practitioners*, **35**, 185–8.

Hunter, J.E., F.L. Schmidt and G.B. Jackson (1982), *Meta-analysis: Cumulating Research Findings across Studies*, Beverly Hills, CA: Sage Publications.

Hurley, J. (2000), 'An overview of the normative economics of the health sector', in A.J. Culyer and J.P. Newhouse (eds), *Handbook of Health Economics*, Amsterdam: Elsevier, pp. 55–118.

Hurley, J., D. Pasic, J. Lavis, C. Mustard, A.J. Culyer and W. Gnam (2008), 'Parallel lines do intersect: interactions between the workers' compensation and provincial publicly financed health care systems in Canada', *HealthCare Policy*, **3**, 100–112.

Hurst, J.W. (1991), 'Reforming health care in seven European nations', *Health Affairs*, **10**, 7–21.

Hurst, N.P., P. Jobanputra, M. Hunter, M. Lambert, A. Lochhead and H. Brown (1994), 'Validity of EuroQol – a generic health status instrument – in patients with rheumatoid arthritis', *British Journal of Rheumatology*, **3**, 655–62.

Hutton, G., L. Haller and J.L. Bartram (2007), 'Global cost–benefit analysis of water supply and sanitation interventions', *Journal of Water and Health*, **5**, 481–502.

Hutton, J., P. Trueman and K. Facey (2008), 'Harmonization of evidence requirements for health technology assessment in reimbursement decision making', *International Journal of Technology Assessment in Health Care*, **24**, 511–17.

Hutton, J., P. Trueman and C. Henshall (2007), 'Coverage with evidence development: an examination of conceptual and policy issues, *International Journal of Technology Assessment in Health Care*, **23**, 425–32.

Hyder, A.A., G. Rotllant and R.H. Morrow (1998), 'Measuring the burden of disease: healthy life years', *American Journal of Public Health*, **88**, 196–202.

Ippolito, P.M. (1981), 'Information and the life cycle consumption of hazardous goods', *Economic Enquiry*, **19**, 529–58.

Iversen, T. and H. Lurås (2006), 'Capitation and incentives in primary care', in A.M. Jones (ed.), *The Elgar Companion to Health Economics*, Cheltenham, UK and Northampton, MA, USA: Edward Elgar, pp. 269–78.

Jack, W. (1999), *Principles of Health Economics for Developing Countries*, Washington, DC: World Bank.

Jack, W. and L. Sheiner (1997), 'Welfare-improving health expenditure subsidies', *American Economic Review*, **87**, 206–21.

Jacobs, P. and J. Rapoport (2004), *The Economics of Health and Medical Care*, 5th edition, Sudbury MA: Jones & Bartlett.

Jacobs, R. and A. Street (2005), 'Efficiency measurement in health care: recent developments, current practice and future research', in P.C. Smith, L. Ginnelly and M.J. Sculpher (eds), *Health Policy and Economics: Opportunities and Challenges*, Maidenhead: Open University Press, pp. 148–72.

Jacobsson, F., J. Carstensen and L. Borgquist (2005), 'Caring externalities in health economic evaluation: how are they related to severity of illness?', *Health Policy*, **73**, 172–82.

Jarman, B. (1983), 'Identification of underprivileged areas', *British Medical Journal*, **286**, 1705–8.

Jefferson, T., V. Demicheli and M. Mugford (2000), *Elementary Economic Evaluation in Health Care*, London: BMJ Publishing.

Jelsma, J., K. Hansen, W. De Weerdt, P. De Cock and P. Kind (2003), 'How do Zimbabweans value health states?', *Population Health Metrics*, **1**, 11.

Jensen, K.K. (2003), 'What is the difference between (moderate) egalitarianism and prioritarianism?', *Economics and Philosophy*, **19**, 89–109.

Johannesson, M. and P.-O. Johansson (1997), 'Is the valuation of a QALY gained independent of age? Some empirical evidence', *Journal of Health Economics*, **16**, 589–99.

Johannesson, M. and G. Karlsson (1997), 'The friction cost method: a comment', *Journal of Health Economics*, 16, 249–55.

Johannesson, M. and M.C. Weinstein (1993), 'On the decision rules of cost-effectiveness analysis', *Journal of Health Economics*, **12**, 459–67.

Johansson, P.-O. (1995), *Evaluating Health Risks: An Economic Approach*, Cambridge, UK: Cambridge University Press.

Jones, A.M. (1989), 'A double-hurdle model of cigarette consumption', *Journal of Applied Econometrics*, **4**, 23–39.

Jones, A.M. (2000), 'Health econometrics', in A.J. Culyer and J.P.

Newhouse (eds), *Handbook of Health Economics*, Amsterdam: Elsevier, pp. 265–344.

Jones, A.M. (2007), *Applied Econometrics for Health Economists: A Practical Guide*, 2nd edition, Oxford: Radcliffe Medical Publishing.

Jones, A.M. and O. O'Donnell (eds) (2002), *Econometric Analysis of Health Data*, Chichester: Wiley.

Jones, A.M. and J. Wildman (2008), 'Health, income and relative deprivation: evidence from the BHPS', *Journal of Health Economics*, **27**, 308–24.

Jones, A.M., N. Rice, d'U.T. Bago and S. Balia (2007), *Applied Health Economics*, London: Routledge.

Jones, J., A. Wilson, H. Parker, A. Wynn, C. Jagger, N. Spiers and G. Parker (1999), 'Economic evaluation of hospital at home versus hospital care: cost minimisation analysis of data from a randomised controlled trial', *British Medical Journal*, **319**, 547–1550.

Jones, M.M. and R. Bayer (2007), 'Paternalism & its discontents – motorcycle helmet laws, libertarian values, and public health', *American Journal of Public Health*, **97**, 207–17.

Jones-Lee, M.W. (1989), *The Economics of Safety and Physical Risk*, Oxford: Basil Blackwell.

Jones-Lee, M.W. (1991), 'Altruism and the value of other people's safety', *Journal of Risk and Uncertainty*, **4**, 213–19.

Jones-Lee, M.W. (1992), 'Paternalistic altruism and the value of statistical life', *Economic Journal*, **102**, 80–90.

Jönsson, B. (2001), 'Economics of drug treatment: for which patients is it cost-effective to lower cholesterol?', *Lancet*, **358**, 1251–56.

Joore, M.A., H. Van der Stel, H.J.M. Peters, G.M. Boasand and L.J.C. Anteunis (2003), 'The cost-effectiveness of hearing-aid fitting in the Netherlands', *Archives of Otolaryngology – Head and Neck Surgery*, **129**, 297–304.

Jowett, M., A. Deolalikar and P. Martinsson (2004), 'Health insurance and treatment seeking behaviour: evidence from a low-income country', *Health Economics*, **13**, 845–57.

Kagan, S. (1997), *Normative Ethics*, Boulder: Westview Press.

Kahneman, D. (1999), 'Objective happiness', in D. Kahneman, E. Diener and N. Schwarz (eds), *Well-Being: The Foundations of Hedonic Psychology*, New York: Russell Sage, pp. 3–25.

Kahneman, D. (2000), 'Experienced utility and objective happiness: a moment-based approach', in D. Kahneman and T. Tversky (eds), *Choices, Values and Frames*, New York: Cambridge University Press and the Russell Sage Foundation, pp. 673–92.

Kahneman, D. (2008), *QALYs versus Experience: A Perspective from Experimental Economics*, London: Office of Health Economics.

Kahneman, D. and T. Tversky (1979), 'Prospect theory: an analysis of decision under risk', *Econometrica*, **47**, 263–291.

Kahneman, D. and T. Tversky (1984), 'Choices, values and frames', *American Psychologist*, **39**, 41–50.

Kahneman, D., B.L. Fredrickson, C.A. Schreiber and D.A. Redelmeier (1993), 'When more pain is preferred to less: adding a better end', *Psychological Science*, **4**, 401–5.

Kahneman, D., A.B. Krueger, D. Schkade, N. Schwarz and A.A. Stone (2004), 'A survey method for characterizing daily life experience: the day reconstruction method', *Science*, **306**, 1776–80.

Kakwani, N.C. (1977), 'Measurement of tax progressivity: an international comparison', *Economic Journal*, **87**, 71–80.

Kaldor, N. (1939), 'Welfare propositions in economics', *Economic Journal*, **49**, 549–52.

Kaltenthaler, E., P. Tappenden, A. Booth and R.L. Akehurst (2008), 'Comparing methods for full versus single technology appraisal: a case study of docetaxel and paclitaxel for early breast cancer', *Health Policy*, **87**, 389–400.

Kan, K. (2004), 'Obesity and risk knowledge', *Journal of Health Economics*, **23**, 907–34.

Kan, K. (2007), 'Cigarette smoking and self-control', *Journal of Health Economics*, **226**, 61–81.

Kanavos, P. and J. Costa-i-Font (2005), 'Pharmaceutical parallel trade in Europe: stakeholders and competition effects', *Economic Policy*, **20**, 751–98.

Kanavos, P. and C.M. McKee (2000), 'Cross-border issues in the provision of health services: are we moving towards a European health care policy?', *Journal of Health Services Research and Policy*, **5**, 231–6.

Kant, I. ([1785] 1964), *Groundwork of the Metaphysic of Morals* (trans. H.J. Paton), New York: Harper and Row.

Kaplan, E.L. and P. Meier (1958), 'Nonparametric estimation from incomplete observations', *Journal of the American Statistical Association*, **53**, 457–81.

Kaplan, E.L. and D.P. Norton (1996), *The Balanced Scorecard: Translating Strategy into Action*, Boston: Harvard Business School Press.

Kaplan, R. and J. Anderson (1990), 'An integrated approach to quality of life assessment: the general health policy model', in B. Spiker, (ed.), *Quality of Life in Clinical Studies*, New York: Raven Press, pp. 131–49.

Katz, S., A.B. Ford, R.W. Moskovitz, B.A. Jackson and M.W. Jaffe (1963), 'Studies of illness in the aged. The index of ADL: a standardized measure of biological and psychosocial function', *Journal of the American Medical Association*, **185**, 914–19.

Keeler, E.B. (1995), 'A model of demand for effective care', *Journal of Health Economics*, **14**, 231–8.

Keeler, E.B. and S. Cretin (1983), 'Discounting of life-saving and other non-monetary effects', *Management Science*, **29**, 300–306.

Keeler, E.B., G. Melnick and J. Zwanziger (1999), 'The changing effects of competition on non-profit and for-profit hospital pricing behavior', *Journal of Health Economics*, **18**, 69–86.

Keen, J., S. Bryan, N. Muris, G. Weatherburn and M.J. Buxton (1995), 'Evaluation of diffuse technologies: the case of digital imaging networks', *Health Policy*, **34**, 153–66.

Keeney, R.L. and H. Raiffa (1976), Decisions with Multiple Objectives: Preferences and Value Trade-offs, New York: Wiley.

Kendall, M. (1938), 'A new measure of rank correlation', *Biometrica*, **30**, 81–9.

Kenkel, D.S. (1991), 'Health behaviour, health knowledge, and schooling', *Journal of Political Economy*, **99**, 287–305.

Kenkel, D.S. (1995), 'Should you eat breakfast? Estimates from health production functions', *Health Economics*, **4**, 15–29.

Kenkel, D.S. (2000), 'Prevention', in A.J. Culyer. and J.P. Newhouse (eds), *Handbook of Health Economics*, Amsterdam: Elsevier, pp. 1675–720.

Kennedy, P. (2003), *A Guide to Econometrics*, Boston: MIT Press.

Kessel, R.A. (1958), 'Price discrimination in medicine', *Journal of Law and Economics*, **1**, 20–53.

Kessler, D.P. and M.B. McClellan (1996), 'Do doctors practice defensive medicine?', *Quarterly Journal of Economics*, **111**, 353–90.

Kessler, D.P. and M.B. McClellan (2000), 'Is hospital competition socially wasteful?', *Quarterly Journal of Economics*, **115**, 577–615.

Keynes, J.M. (1936), *The General Theory of Employment Interest and Money*, London: Macmillan.

Kind, P., P. Dolan, C. Gudex and A.H. Williams (1998), 'Variations in population health status: results from a United Kingdom national questionnaire survey', *British Medical Journal*, **316**, 736–41.

Kirigia, J.M. (1997), 'Economic evaluation in schistosomiasis: using the Delphi technique to assess effectiveness', *Acta Tropica*, **64**, 175–90.

Klarman, H., J. Francis and G. Rosenthal (1968), 'Cost-effectiveness analysis applied to the treatment of chronic renal disease', *Medical Care*, **6**, 48–64.

Klein, K., S. Glied and D. Ferry (2005), *Entrances and Exits: Health Insurance Churning, 1998–2000*, New York: Commonwealth Fund.

Kline, P. (1993), *An Easy Guide to Factor Analysis*, London: Routledge.

Kobelt, G., P. Lindgren, A. Singh and L. Klareskog (2005), 'Cost effectiveness of etanercept (Enbrel) in combination with methotrexate in the treatment of active rheumatoid arthritis based on the TEMPO trial', *Annals of the Rheumatic Diseases*, **64**, 1174–9.

Koç, C. (2004), 'The productivity of health care and health production functions', *Health Economics*, **13**, 739–47.

Kohn, L., J. Corrigan and M. Donaldson (eds) (1999), *To Err is Human: Building a Safer Health System*, Washington, DC: The National Academies Press.

Koopmanschap, M.A., F.F.H. Rutten, B.M. Van Ineveld and L. Van Roijen (1995), 'The friction cost method for measuring indirect costs of disease', *Journal of Health Economics*, **14**, 171–89.

Korthals-de Bos, I.B.C., J.L. Hoving, M.W. Van Tulder, M.P.M.H. Rutten-Van Mölken, H. Adèr, H.C.W. de Vet, B.W. Koes, H. Vondeling and L.M. Bouter (2003), 'Cost effectiveness of physiotherapy, manual therapy, and general practitioner care for neck pain: economic evaluation alongside a randomised controlled trial' [with commentary by M Müllner], *British Medical Journal*, **326**, 911–16.

Krahn, M.D., G. Naglie, D. Naimark, D.A. Redelmeier and A.S. Detsky (1997), 'Primer on medical decision analysis: Part 4: analyzing the model and interpreting the results', *Medical Decision Making*, **17**, 142–51.

Kralewski, J.E., B.E. Dowd, A. Heaton and A. Kaissi (2005), 'The influence of the structure and culture of medical group practices on prescription drug errors', *Medical Care*, **43**, 817–25.

Kremer, M. (2002), 'Pharmaceuticals and the developing world', *Journal of Economic Perspectives*, **16**, 67–90.

Kremer, M. and E. Miguel (2007), 'The illusion of sustainability', *Quarterly Journal of Economics*, **112**, 1007–65.

Krueger, A. (1974), 'The political economy of the rent-seeking society', *American Economic Review*, **64**, 291–303.

L'Abbé, K.A., A.S. Detsky and K. O'Rourke (1987), 'Meta-analysis in clinical research', *Annals of Internal Medicine*, **107**, 224–33.

Labelle, R., G.L. Stoddart and T.H. Rice (1994a), 'A re-examination of the meaning and importance of supplier-induced demand', *Journal of Health Economics*, **13**, 347–68.

Labelle, R., G.L. Stoddart and T.H. Rice (1994b), 'Editorial: response to Pauly on a re-examination of the meaning and importance of supplier-induced demand', *Journal of Health Economics*, **13**, 491–4.

Lacey, L., J. Mauskopf, R. Lindrooth, S. Pham, M. Saag and W. Sawyer (1999), 'A prospective cost-consequence analysis of adding lamivudine to zidovudine containing antiretroviral treatment regimens for HIV infection in the US', *PharmacoEconomics*, **15**, Suppl. 1, 23–37.

Lacy, H.P., A. Fagerlin, G. Loewenstein, D.M. Smith, J. Riis and P.A. Ubel (2006), 'It must be awful for them: perspective and task context affect ratings for health conditions', *Judgment and Decision Making*, **1**, 146–52.

Laibson, D. (1997), 'Golden eggs and hyperbolic discounting', *Quarterly Journal of Economics*, **112**, 443–77.

Lakdawalla, D. and T.J. Philipson (2006), 'Economics of obesity', in A.M. Jones (ed.), *The Elgar Companion to Health Economics*, Cheltenham, UK and Northampton, MA, USA: Edward Elgar, pp. 72–82.

Lambert, P.J. and S. Yitzhaki (1997), 'Income tax credits and exemptions', *European Journal of Political Economy*, **13**, 343–51.

Lancsar, E. and J. Louviere (2008), 'Conducting discrete choice experiments to inform healthcare decision making: a user's guide', *PharmacoEconomics*, **26**, 661–77.

Landgraf, J.M. (1999), 'The CHQ and its application to psychological testing and outcomes for the behavioral healthcare practitioner', in M. Maruish (ed.), *The Use of Psychological Testing for Treatment, Planning, and Outcome Assessment*, New Jersey: Lawrence-Erlbaum Press, pp. 665–77.

Lankshear, A.J., T.A. Sheldon and A.K. Maynard (2005), 'Nurse staffing and health outcomes: a systematic review of the international research evidence', *Advances in Nursing Science*, **28**, 163–74.

Laporte, A. (2004), 'Do economic cycles have a permanent effect on population health? Revisiting the Brenner hypothesis', *Health Economics*, **13**, 767–79.

Laspeyres, E. (1871), 'Die Berechnung einer mittleren Waarenpreissteigerung', *Jahrbücher für Nationalœkonomie und Statistik*, **16**, 296–314.

Laupacis, A., D. Feeny, A.S. Detsky and P.X. Tugwell (1992), 'How attractive does a new technology have to be to warrant adoption and utilization? Tentative guidelines for using clinical and economic evaluations', *Canadian Medical Association Journal*, **146**, 473–81.

Lave, J.R. and L.B. Lave (1984), 'Hospital cost functions', *Annual Review of Public Health*, **5**, 193–213.

Lavis, J.N., D. Robertson, J.M. Woodside, C.B. McLeod, J. Abelson and the Knowledge Transfer Study Group (2003), 'How can research organizations more effectively transfer research knowledge to decision makers?', *Milbank Quarterly*, **81**, 221–48.

Lee, K. (2005), 'Wealth effects on self-insurance and self-protection against monetary and nonmonetary losses', *Geneva Risk and Insurance Review*, **30**, 147–59.

Lee, R.H. (2008), 'Future costs in cost effectiveness analysis', *Journal of Health Economics*, **27**, 809–18.

Lehner, L.A. and J.F. Burgess Jr. (1995), 'Teaching and hospital production', *Health Economics*, **4**, 113–25.

Leibenstein, H. (1950), 'Bandwagon, snob, and Veblen effects in the theory of consumers' demand', *Quarterly Journal of Economics*, **64**, 183–207.

Leibenstein, H. (1966), 'Allocative efficiency and *X*-efficiency', *American Economic Review*, **56**, 392–415.

Leibowitz, A., C. Damberg and K. Eyre (1992), *Multiple Employer Welfare Arrangements*, Santa Monica: Rand Report.

Lenert, L.A. and J.R. Treadwell (1999), 'Effects on preferences of violations of procedure invariance', *Medical Decision Making*, **19**, 473–81.

Lenert, L.A., D.J. Cher, M.K. Goldstein, M.R. Bergen and A.M. Garber (1998), 'Effects of search procedures on utility elicitations', *Medical Decision Making*, **18**, 76–83.

Leonard, K. and J.G. Zivin (2005), 'Outcome versus service based payments in health care: lessons from African traditional healers', *Health Economics*, **14**, 575–93.

Leonard, K., G. Mliga and D.H. Mariam (2002), 'Bypassing health centres in Tanzania: revealed preferences for quality', *Journal of African Economies*, **11**, 441–71.

Leontief, W. (1941), *The Structure of American Industry, 1919–1929*, Cambridge, MA: Harvard University Press.

Leung, M.C.M., J. Zhang and J. Zhang (2004), 'An economic analysis of life expectancy by gender with application to the United States', *Journal of Health Economics*, **23**, 737–59.

Levine, P.B., T.A. Gustafson and A.D. Velenchik (1997), 'More bad news for smokers? The effects of cigarette smoking on wages', *Industrial and Labor Relations Review*, **50**, 493–509.

Levy, A. (2002), 'A lifetime portfolio of risky and risk-free sexual behaviour and the prevalence of AIDS', *Journal of Health Economics*, **21**, 993–1007.

Levy, H. and R. Feldman (2001), 'Does the incidence of group health insurance fall on individual workers?', *International Journal of Health Care Finance and Economics*, **1**, 227–47.

Lewis, S. and M. Clarke (2001), 'Forest plots: trying to see the wood and the trees', *British Medical Journal*, **322**, 1479–80.

Li, T. and R. Rosenman (2001), 'Estimating hospital costs with a generalized Leontief function', *Health Economics*, **10**, 523–38.

Lichtenberg, F.R. and S. Virabhak (2007), 'Pharmaceutical-embodied technical progress, longevity, and quality of life: drugs as "Equipment for Your Health"', *Managerial and Decision Economics*, **28**, 371–92.

Light, D.W. (1992), 'The practice and ethics of risk-rated health insurance', *Journal of the American Medical Association*, **267**, 2503–8.

Likert, R. (1932), 'A technique for the measurement of attitude scales', *Archives of Psychology*, **140**, 44–53.

Lindelow, M. (2006), 'Sometimes more equal than others: how health inequalities depend on the choice of welfare indicator', *Health Economics*, **15**, 263–79.

Lipscomb, J., C.C. Gotay and C. Snyder (eds) (2005), *Outcomes Assessment in Cancer: Measures, Methods, and Applications*, Cambridge, MA: Cambridge University Press.

Lipsey, R.G. and K. Lancaster (1956), 'The general theory of second best', *Review of Economic Studies*, **24**, 11–32.

Liu, J.-L., J.-T. Liu, J.K. Hammitt and S.-Y. Chou (1999), 'The price elasticity of opium in Taiwan, 1914–1942', *Journal of Health Economics*, **18**, 795–810.

Lohrisch, D., S. Cabell Shull and M.C. Smith (2006), 'Constant returns to scale for prescription dispensing in U.S. community pharmacy', *Journal of Pharmaceutical Sciences*, **65**, 204–6.

Lomas, J., A.J. Culyer, C. McCutcheon, L. McAuley and S. Law (2005), *Conceptualizing and Combining Evidence for Health System Guidance*, Ottawa: Canadian Health Services Research Foundation.

Longworth, L. and S. Bryan (2003), 'An empirical comparison of EQ-5D and SF-6D in liver transplant patients', *Health Economics*, **12**, 1061–7.

Loomes, G. (2006), '(How) can we value health, safety and the environment?', *Journal of Economic Psychology*, **27**, 713–36.

Loomes, G. and L. McKenzie (1989), 'The use of QALYs in health care decision making', *Social Science and Medicine*, **28**, 299–308.

Loomes, G. and R. Sugden (1982), 'Regret theory: an alternative theory of rational choice under uncertainty', *Economic Journal*, **92**, 805–24.

Lord, J., G. Laking and A. Fischer (2004), 'Health care resource allocation: is the threshold rule good enough?', *Journal of Health Services Research and Policy*, **9**, 237–45.

Lord, J., G. Laking and A. Fischer (2005), 'Non-linearity in the cost-effectiveness frontier', *Health Economics*, **15**, 565–77.

Lorenz, M.O. (1905), 'Methods of measuring the concentration of wealth', *Journal of the American Statistical Association*, **9**, 209–19.

Löthgren, M. and N. Zethraeus (2000), 'Definition, interpretation and calculation of cost-effectiveness acceptability curves', *Health Economics*, **9**, 623–30.

Luce, R.D. and J. Tukey (1964), 'Simultaneous conjoint measurement: a new type of fundamental measurement', *Journal of Mathematical Psychology*, **1**, 1–27.

Luce, R.D. and P. Suppes (1965), 'Preference, utility, and subjective prob-ability', in R.D. Luce, R.R. Bush and E. Galanter (eds), *Handbook of Mathematical Psychology*, Vol. 3, New York: Wiley, pp. 249–410.

Luft, H.S. (1987), *Health Maintenance Organizations: Dimensions of Performance*, New Brunswick, NJ: Transaction.

Luft, H.S. (2003), 'Variations in patterns of care and outcomes after acute myocardial infarction for Medicare beneficiaries in fee-for-service and HMO settings', *Health Services Research*, **38**, 1065–79.

Lundborg, P. (2006), 'Having the wrong friends? Peer effects in adolescent substance use', *Journal of Health Economics*, **25**, 214–33.

Lydon, P., R. Levine, M. Makinen, L. Brenzel, V. Mitchell, J.B. Milstien, L. Kamara and S. Landry (2008), 'Introducing vaccines in the poorest countries: what did we learn from the GAVI experience with financial sustainability?', *Vaccine*, **26**, 6706–16.

Lynch, R.L. and K.F. Cross (1991), *Measure up! Yardsticks for Continuous Improvement*, Oxford: Blackwell.

Lyttkens, C.H. (2003), 'Time to disable DALYs? On the use of disability-adjusted life-years in health policy', *The European Journal of Health Economics*, **4**, 195–202.

Ma, C.-T.A. (1994), 'Health care payment systems: cost and quality incen-tives', *Journal of Economics & Management Strategy*, **34**, 93–112.

Ma, C.-T.A. and T.G. McGuire (1993), 'Paying for joint costs in health care', *Journal of Economics & Management Strategy*, **2**, 71–95.

Ma, C.-T.A. and T.G. McGuire (1997), 'Optimal health insurance and provider payment', *American Economic Review*, **87**, 685–704.

Ma, C.-T.A. and T.G. McGuire (1998), 'Costs and incentives in a behav-ioral health carve-out', *Health Affairs*, **17**, 53–69.

Macario, A., J.L. Chow, and F. Dexter (2006), 'A Markov computer sim-ulation model of the economics of neuromuscular blockade in patients with acute respiratory distress syndrome', *BMC Medical Informatics and Decision Making*, **6**, 15.

Machina, M.J. (2004), 'Nonexpected utility theory', in J.L. Teugels and B. Sundt (eds), *Encyclopedia of Actuarial Science*, Chichester: Wiley, pp. 1173–79.

Machnes, Y. (1979), 'An economic model of mental hospitals', *Empirical Economics*, **14**, 293–401.

Macinko, J.A. and B. Starfield (2002), 'Annotated bibliography on equity in health, 1980–2001', *International Journal for Equity in Health*, **31**, 545–66.

Macpherson, A. and A. Spinks (2008), 'Bicycle helmet legislation for the uptake of helmet use and prevention of head injuries', *Cochrane Database of Systematic Reviews*, Issue 3, Art. No. CD005401.

Magat, W.A., W.K. Viscusi and J. Huber (1988), 'Paired comparison and contingent valuation approaches to morbidity risk valuation', *Journal of Environmental Economics and Management*, **15**, 395–411.

Mahoney, F.I. and D.W. Barthel (1965), 'Functional evaluation: the Barthel Index', *Maryland State Medical Journal*, **14**, 56–61.

Malmquist, S. (1953), 'Index numbers and indifference surfaces', *Trabajos de Estatistica*, **4**, 209–42.

Manca, A., P.C. Lambert, M.J. Sculpher and N. Rice (2007), 'Cost-effectiveness analysis using data from multinational trials: the use of bivariate hierarchical modelling', *Medical Decision Making*, **27**, 471–90.

Manca, A., N. Rice, M.J. Sculpher and A.H. Briggs (2005), 'Assessing generalisability by location in trial-based cost-effectiveness analysis: the use of multilevel models', *Health Economics*, **14**, 471–85.

Mankiw, N.G. and D. Romer (eds) (1991), *New Keynesian Economics. Vol. 1: Imperfect Competition and Sticky Prices, Vol. 2: Coordination Failures and Real Rigidities*, Boston MA: MIT Press.

Manning, W.G. (2006), 'Dealing with skewed data on costs and expenditures', in A.M. Jones (ed.), *The Elgar Companion to Health Economics*, Cheltenham, UK and Northampton, MA, USA: Edward Elgar, pp. 439–46.

Manning, W.G. and M.S. Marquis (1996), 'Health insurance: the trade-off between risk pooling and moral hazard', *Journal of Health Economics*, **15**, 609–39.

Manning, W.G. and M.S. Marquis (2001), 'Health insurance: tradeoffs revisited', *Journal of Health Economics*, **20**, 289–93.

Manning, W.G., E.B. Keeler, J.P. Newhouse, E.M. Sloss and J. Wasserman (1989), 'The taxes of sin: do smokers and drinkers pay their own way?', *Journal of the American Medical Association*, **261**, 1604–9.

Manning, W.G., A. Leibowitz, G.A. Goldberg, W.H. Rogers and J.P. Newhouse (1984), 'A controlled trial of the effect of a prepaid group practice on use of services', *New England Journal of Medicine*, **310**, 1505–10.

Manning, W.G., J.P. Newhouse, N. Duan, E.B. Keeler, A. Leibowitz and M.S. Marquis (1987), 'Health insurance and the demand for medical care: evidence from a randomized experiment', *American Economic Review*, **77**, 251–77.

Mannion, R. and N. Small (1999), 'Postmodern health economics', *Health Care Analysis*, **7**, 255–72.

Manski, C.F. (1977), 'The structure of random utility models', *Theory and Decision*, **8**, 229–54.

Manski, C.F. (1993), 'Identification of endogenous social effects: the reflection problem', *Review of Economic Studies*, **60**, 531–42.

Mantel, N. and W.M. Haenszel (1959), 'Statistical aspects of the analysis of data from retrospective studies of disease', *Journal of the National Cancer Institute*, **22**, 719–48.

Margolis, H. (1984), *Selfishness, Altruism, and Rationality: a Theory of Social Choice*, Chicago: Chicago University Press.

Marini, G. and A. Street (2007), 'A transaction costs analysis of changing contractual relations in the English NHS', *Health Policy*, **83**, 17–26.

Marini, G., M. Miraldo, R. Jacobs and M. Goddard (2008), 'Giving greater financial independence to hospitals – does it make a difference? The case of English NHS Trusts', *Health Economics*, **17**, 751–75.

Markowitz, S. and M. Grossman (2000), 'The effects of beer taxes on physical child abuse', *Journal of Health Economics*, **19**, 271–82.

Marmot, M.G. (2008), *Closing the Gap in a Generation: Health Equity through Action on the Social Determinants of Health*, Final Report of the Commission on Social Determinants of Health, Geneva: World Health Organization.

Marmot, M.G., G.D. Smith, S. Stansfeld, C. Patel, F. North, J. Head, I. White, E. Brunner and A. Feeney (1991), 'Health inequalities among British civil servants: the Whitehall II study', *The Lancet*, **337**, 1387–93.

Marshall, C. and G.B. Rossman (2006), *Designing Qualitative Research*, 4th edition, Thousand Oaks, CA: Sage Publications.

Martin, S., N. Rice and P.C. Smith (2008), 'Does health care spending improve health outcomes? Evidence from English programme budgeting data', *Journal of Health Economics*, **24**, 826–42.

Martin, S., N. Rice, R. Jacobs and P.C. Smith (2007), 'The market for elective surgery: joint estimation of supply and demand', *Journal of Health Economics*, **26**, 263–85.

Mason, H., M. Jones-Lee and C. Donaldson (2009), 'Modelling the monetary value of a QALY: a new approach based on UK data', *Health Economics*, **18**, 933–50.

Mason, J., M.F. Drummond and G.W. Torrance (1993), 'Some guidelines on the use of cost-effectiveness league tables', *British Medical Journal*, **306**, 570–72.

Mauskopf, J.A., S.D. Sullivan, L. Annemans, J. Caro, C.D. Mullins, M. Nuijten, E. Orlewska, J. Watkins and P. Trueman (2007), 'Principles of good practice for budget impact analysis: report of the ISPOR task force on good research practices – Budget Impact Analysis', *Value in Health*, **10**, 336–47.

Maynard, A.K. (1972), 'Inequalities in psychiatric care in England and Wales', *Social Science and Medicine*, **6**, 221–7.

Maynard, A.K. (2005), *The Public-Private Mix for Health*, Abingdon: Radcliffe Publishing.

Maynard, A.K. (2008), *Payment for Performance (P4P): International Experience and a Cautionary Proposal for Estonia*, Geneva: Estonian Health Insurance Fund and World Health Organization Europe.

Maynard, A.K. and K. Bloor (1997), 'Regulating the pharmaceutical industry', *British Medical Journal*, **315**, 200–201.

Maynard, A.K. and P. Kanavos (2000), 'Health economics: an evolving paradigm', *Health Economics*, **9**, 183–90.

Maynard, A.K. and A. Ludbrook (1980), 'Budget allocation in the National Health Service', *Journal of Social Policy*, **9**, 289–312.

Maynard, A.K. and A. Walker (1978), 'Medical manpower planning in Britain: a critical appraisal', in A.J. Culyer, and K.G. Wright (eds) (1978), *Economic Aspects of Health Services*, London: Martin Robertson, pp. 165–90.

McCabe, C., K. Claxton and A. Tsuchiya (2005), 'Orphan drugs and the NHS: should we value rarity?', *British Medical Journal*, **331**, 1016–19.

McGlynn, E.A., S.M. Asch, J. Adams, J. Keesey, J. Hicks, A. DeCristofaro and E.A. Kerr (2003), 'The quality of health care delivered to adults in the United States', *New England Journal of Medicine*, **348**, 2635–45.

McGuire, A., J. Henderson and G. Mooney (1992), *The Economics of Health Care*, Abingdon: Routledge.

McGuire, T.G. (2000), 'Physician agency', in A.J. Culyer and J.P. Newhouse (eds), *Handbook of Health Economics*, Amsterdam: Elsevier, pp. 461–536.

McGuire, T.G. and M.V. Pauly (1991), 'Physician response to fee changes with multiple payers', *Journal of Health Economics*, **10**, 385–410.

McIntosh, E. (2007), *Discrete Choice Literature Review*, London: Office of Health Economics.

McKay, N.L. and M.E. Deily (2008), 'Cost inefficiency and hospital health outcomes', *Health Economics*, **17**, 833–48.

McKenna, M., J. Chick, M.J. Buxton, H. Howlett, D. Patience and B. Ritson (1996), 'The SECCAT survey: I. The costs and consequences of alcoholism', *Alcohol and Alcoholism*, **31**, 565–76.

McKeown, T. (1976), *The Modern Rise of Population*, New York: Academic Press.

McKnight, R. (2007), 'Medicare balance billing restrictions: impacts on physicians and beneficiaries', *Journal of Health Economics*, **26**, 326–41.

McLeod, C.B., J.N. Lavis, C.A. Mustard and G.L. Stoddart (2003), 'Income inequality, household income, and health status in Canada:

a prospective cohort study', *American Journal of Public Health*, **93**, 1287–93.

McNeil, B.J., R. Weichselbaum and S.G. Pauker (1981), 'Speech and survival: trade-offs between quality and quantity of life in laryngeal cancer', *New England Journal of Medicine*, **305**, 982–7.

McPake, B. and C. Normand (2008), *Health Economics: An International Perspective*, 2nd edition, Abingdon: Routledge.

McPherson, K., J.E. Wennberg, O.B. Hovind and P. Clifford (1982), 'Small-area variations in the use of common surgical procedures: an international comparison of New England, England, and Norway', *New England Journal of Medicine*, **307**, 1310–14.

McRae, I.S., J.R.G. Butler, B.M. Sibthorpe, W. Ruscoe, J. Snow, D. Rubiano and K.L. Gardner (2008), 'A cost effectiveness study of integrated care in health services delivery: a diabetes program in Australia', *BMC Health Services Research*, **8**, 205.

Mehrez, A. and A. Gafni (1989), 'Quality adjusted life years, utility theory, and healthy years equivalents', *Medical Decision Making*, **9**, 142–59.

Meltzer, D. (1997), 'Accounting for future costs in medical cost-effectiveness analysis', *Journal of Health Economics*, **16**, 33–64.

Merenstein, D. (2004), 'Winners and losers', *Journal of the American Medical Association*, **291**, 15–16.

Mill, J.S. ([1863] 2001), *Utilitarianism*, Indianapolis: Hackett Publishing Co.

Miller, N.H. (2005), 'Pricing health benefits: a cost-minimization approach', *Journal of Health Economics*, **24**, 931–49.

Mitton, C. and C.A. Donaldson (2001), 'Twenty-five years of using programme budgeting and marginal analysis in the health sector, 1974–1999', *Journal of Health Service Research & Policy*, **6**, 239–48.

Moayyedi, P., S. Soo, J. Deeks, D. Forman, J. Mason, M. Innes and B. Delaney (2009), 'Systematic review and economic evaluation of *Helicobacter pylori* eradication treatment for nonulcer dyspepsia', *British Medical Journal*, **321**, 659–64.

Moher, D., A. Liberati, J. Tetzlaff, D.G. Altman and the PRISMA Group (2009), 'Preferred reporting items for systematic reviews and meta-analyses: The PRISMA Statement', *PLoS Medicine*, **6**, e1000097.

Montalvo, J.G. and M. Reynal-Querol (2007), 'Fighting against malaria: prevent wars while waiting for the "miraculous" vaccine', *Review of Economics and Statistics*, **89**, 165–77.

Mooney, G.H. (2003), *Economics, Medicine, and Health Care*, 3rd edition, Upper Saddle River, New Jersey: Pearson Prentice-Hall.

Mooney, G.H. (2005), 'Communitarian claims and community

capabilities: furthering priority setting', *Social Science and Medicine*, **60**, 247–55.

Mooney, G.H. and S. Houston (2004), 'An alternative approach to resource allocation: weighted capacity to benefit Plus MESH infrastructure', *Applied Health Economics and Health Policy*, **3**, 29–33.

Mooney, G.H. and V. Wiseman (2000), 'Burden of disease and priority setting', *Health Economics*, **9**, 369–72.

Morgan, S.G., B. Mintzes and M.L. Barer (2003), 'The economics of direct-to-consumer advertising of prescription-only drugs: prescribed to improve consumer welfare?', *Journal of Health Services Research & Policy*, **8**, 237–44.

Morris, J.N. (2002), 'Screening for neuroblastoma in children', *Journal of Medical Screening*, **9**, 56.

Morris, S. and A. McGuire (2002), 'The private net present value and private internal rate of return to becoming a nurse in Great Britain', *Applied Economics*, **34**, 2189–200.

Morris, S., N. Devlin and D. Parkin (2007), *Economic Analysis in Health Care*, Chichester: Wiley.

Morton, F.M.S. (2000), 'Barriers to entry, brand advertising, and generic entry in the US pharmaceutical industry', *International Journal of Industrial Organization*, **18**, 1085–104.

Moseley, J.B., K. O'Malley, N.J. Petersen, T.J. Menke, B.A. Brody, D.H. Kuykendall, J.C. Hollingsworth, C.M. Ashton and N.P. Wray (2002), 'A controlled trial of arthroscopic surgery for osteoarthritis of the knee', *New England Journal of Medicine*, **347**, 81–8.

Mossialos, E. and J. Le Grand (eds) (1999), *Health Care and Cost Containment in the European Union*, Aldershot: Ashgate.

Mullahy, J. and P.R. Portney (1990), 'Air pollution, cigarette smoking, and the production of respiratory health', *Journal of Health Economics*, **9**, 193–205.

Mullahy, J. and J.L. Sindelar (1996), 'Employment, unemployment, and problem drinking', *Journal of Health Economics*, **15**, 409–34.

Murray, C.J. and A.K. Acharya (1997), 'Understanding DALYs', *Journal of Health Economics*, **16**, 703–30.

Musgrave, R. (1957), 'A multiple theory of budget determination', *FinanzArchiv*, New Series, **25**, 33–43.

Musgrove, P. (1983), 'Family health care spending in Latin America', *Journal of Health Economics*, **2**, 245–57.

Mustard, C.A. (2008), 'The broad conceptualization of work and health', in E. Tompa, A.J. Culyer and R. Dolinschi (eds), *Economic Evaluation of Interventions for Occupational Health and Safety*, Oxford: Oxford University Press, pp. 3–14.

National Institute for Clinical Excellence (2004), *Guide to the Methods of Technology Appraisal*, London: NICE.

Nauenberg, E., M. Alkhamisi and Y. Andrijuk (2004), 'Simulation of a Hirschman-Herfindahl index without complete market share information', *Health Economics*, **13**, 87–94.

Neely, A., C. Adams and M. Kennerley (2002), *Performance Prism: The Scorecard for Measuring and Managing Stakeholder Relationships*, Harlow: Pearson Education Limited.

Neuhauser, D. and A.M. Lewicki (1975), 'What do we gain from the sixth stool GUAIAC?', *New England Journal of Medicine*, **293**, 226–8.

Neuman, E. and S. Neuman (2008), 'Reference-dependent preferences and loss aversion: a discrete choice experiment in the health-care sector', *Judgment and Decision Making*, **3**, 162–73.

Neuman, K. (2008), 'Quit your job and get healthier? The effect of retirement on health', *Journal of Labor Research*, **29**, 177–201.

Neumann, P.J. and M. Johannesson (1994), 'The willingness to pay for *in vitro* fertilization: a pilot study using contingent valuation', *Medical Care*, **32**, 686–99.

New, B. (ed.) (1997), *Rationing: Talk and Action*, London: King's Fund and British Medical Journal.

Newhouse, J.P. (1970), 'Toward a theory of non-profit institutions: an economic model of a hospital', *American Economic Review*, **60**, 64–74.

Newhouse, J.P. (1977), 'Medical-care expenditure: a cross-national survey', *Journal of Human Resources*, **12**, 115–25.

Newhouse, J.P. (1992), 'Medical care costs: how much welfare loss?', *Journal of Economic Perspectives*, **6**, 3–21.

Newhouse, J.P. (1996), 'Reimbursing health plans and health providers: efficiency in production versus selection', *Journal of Economic Literature*, **34**, 1236–63.

Newhouse, J.P. and A. Sinaiko (2007), 'Can multi-payer financing achieve single-payer spending levels?', *Forum for Health Economics & Policy*, **10**, 1–11.

Newhouse, J.P., R.H. Brook, N. Duan, E.B. Keeler, A. Leibowitz, W.G. Manning, M.S. Marquis, C.N. Morris, C.E. Phelps and J.E. Rolph (2008), 'Attrition in the RAND Health Insurance Experiment: A response to Nyman', *Journal of Health Politics Policy and Law*, **33**, 295–308.

Newhouse, J.P., W.G. Manning, N. Duan, C.N. Morris, E.B. Keeler, A. Leibowitz, M.S. Marquis, W.H. Rogers, A.R. Davies, K.N. Lohr, J.E. Ware Jr. and R.H. Brook (1987), 'The findings of the RAND Health Insurance Experiment – a response to Welch et al.', *Medical Care*, **25**, 157–79.

New South Wales Health Department (2001), *A Framework for Building Capacity to Improve Health*, (State Health Publication No. (HP) 990226), Sydney, Australia: New South Wales Health Department.

Nolte, E. and C.M. McKee (2008), 'Measuring the health of nations: updating an earlier analysis', *Health Affairs*, **27**, 58–71.

Nord, E. (1992a), 'An alternative to QALYs: the saved young life equivalent (SAVE)', *British Medical Journal*, **305**, 875–7.

Nord, E. (1992b), 'Methods for quality adjustment of life years', *Social Science and Medicine*, **34**, 559–69.

Nord, E. (1995), 'The person-trade-off approach to valuing health care programs', *Medical Decision Making*, **15**, 201–8.

Nord, E. (2001), 'The desirability of a condition versus the well being and worth of a person, *Health Economics*, **10**, 579–81.

Nord, E., J.L. Pinto, J. Richardson, P. Menzel and P. Ubel (1999), 'Incorporating societal concerns for fairness in numerical valuations of health programmes', *Health Economics*, **8**, 25–39.

Nordström, J. and L. Thunström (2009), 'The impact of tax reforms designed to encourage healthier grain consumption', *Journal of Health Economics*, **28**, 622–34.

Norton, E.C. (2000), 'Long-term care', in A.J. Culyer and J.P. Newhouse (eds), *Handbook of Health Economics*, Amsterdam: Elsevier, pp. 956–94.

Norton, E.C., R.C. Lindrooth and S.T. Ennett (1998), 'Controlling for the endogeneity of peer substance use on adolescent alcohol and tobacco use', *Health Economics*, **7**, 439–53.

Nozick, R. (1974), *Anarchy, State and Utopia*, New York: Basic Books.

Nuscheler, R. and T. Knaus (2005), 'Risk selection in the German public health insurance system', *Health Economics*, **14**, 1253–71.

Nussbaum, M.C. (2000), *Women and Human Development: The Capabilities Approach*, Cambridge, UK: Cambridge University Press.

Nussbaum, M.C. (2001), 'Compassion and altruism', in M.C. Nussbaum, *Upheavals of Thought: The Intelligence of Emotions*, Cambridge, MA: Cambridge University Press, pp. 335–41.

Nyman, J.A. (1999a), 'The economics of moral hazard revisited', *Journal of Health Economics*, **18**, 811–24.

Nyman, J.A. (1999b), 'The value of health insurance: the access motive', *Journal of Health Economics*, **18**, 141–52.

Nyman, J.A. (2004), 'Should the consumption of survivors be included as a cost in cost–utility analysis?', *Health Economics*, **13**, 417–27.

Nyman, J.A. (2007), 'American health policy: cracks in the foundation?', *Journal of Health Politics, Policy, and Law*, **32**, 759–83.

Oaxaca, R. (1973), 'Male-female wage differentials in urban labor markets', *International Economic Review*, **14**, 693–709.

O'Brien, B.J. (1989), 'The effect of patient charges on the utilization of prescription medicines', *Journal of Health Economics*, **8**, 109–32.

O'Brien, B.J. and A. Gafni (1996), 'When do the "dollars" make sense? Toward a conceptual framework for contingent valuation studies in health care', *Medical Decision Making*, **16**, 288–99.

O'Donnell, O., E.K.A. Van Doorslaer and A. Wagstaff (2006), 'Decomposition of inequalities in health and health care', in A.M. Jones (ed.), *The Elgar Companion to Health Economics*, Cheltenham, UK and Northampton, MA, USA: Edward Elgar, pp. 179–92.

O'Donnell, O., E.K.A. Van Doorslaer, A. Wagstaff and M. Lindelow (2008), *Analyzing Health Equity Using Household Survey Data: A Guide to Techniques and their Implementation*, Washington, DC: World Bank.

O'Hagan, A., C. McCabe, R.L. Akehurst, A. Brennan, A. Briggs, K. Claxton, E. Fenwick, D. Fryback, M. Sculpher, D. Spiegelhalter and A. Willan (2005), 'Incorporation of uncertainty in health economic modelling studies', *PharmacoEconomics*, **23**, 529–36.

Okorafor, O.A. and S. Thomas (2007), 'Protecting resources for primary health care under fiscal federalism: options for resource allocation', *Health Policy and Planning*, **22**, 415–26.

Okunade, A.A. (2003), 'Are factor substitutions in HMO industry operations cost saving?', *Southern Economic Journal*, **69**, 800–821.

Okunade, A.A. (2006), 'Production cost structure of US hospital pharmacies: time-series, cross-sectional bed size evidence', *Journal of Applied Econometrics*, **8**, 277–94.

Oliver, A.J. (2003a), 'A quantitative and qualitative test of the Allais paradox using health outcomes', *Journal of Economic Psychology*, **24**, 35–48.

Oliver, A.J. (2003b), 'The internal consistency of the standard gamble: tests after adjusting for prospect theory', *Journal of Health Economics*, **22**, 659–74.

Oliver, A.J. (2004a), 'Testing the internal consistency of the standard gamble in "success" and "failure" frames', *Social Science and Medicine*, **58**, 2219–29.

Oliver, A.J. (2004b), 'Should we maximize QALYs?', *Applied Health Economics and Health Policy*, **3**, 61–6.

Oliver, A.J. (2006), 'Further evidence of preference reversals: choice, valuation and ranking over distributions of life expectancy', *Journal of Health Economics*, **25**, 803–20.

Olsen, J.A. and C. Donaldson (1998), 'Helicopters, hearts and hips: using

willingness to pay to set priorities for public sector health care programmes', *Social Science and Medicine*, **46**, 1–12.

Olsen, J.A. and R.D. Smith (2001), 'Theory versus practice: a review of
"willingness-to-pay" in health and health care', *Health Economics*, **10**,
39–52.

Olson, M. (1965), *The Logic of Collective Action*, New York: Shocker
Books.

Orphanides, A. and D. Zervos (1995), 'Rational addiction with learning
and regret', *Journal of Political Economy*, **103**, 739–58.

Ortún, V. and J. Puig (2004), 'Cost efficiency in primary care contracting:
a stochastic frontier cost function approach', *Health Economics*, **13**,
1149–65.

Paasche, H. (1874), 'Uber die Presentwicklung der letzten Jahre nach den
Hamburger Bösennotirungen', *Jahrbücher für Nationalökonomie und
Statistik*, **23**, 168–78.

Pacula, R.L. (1997), 'Economic modelling of the gateway effect', *Health
Economics*, **6**, 521–4.

Palmer, G. and M.T. Ho (2008), *Health Economics: A Critical and Global
Analysis*, Basingstoke: Palgrave Macmillan.

Palmer, N. and A.J. Mills (2006), 'Contracting-out health service provi-
sion in resource- and information-poor settings', in A.M. Jones (ed.),
The Elgar Companion to Health Economics, Cheltenham, UK and
Northampton, MA, USA: Edward Elgar, pp. 250–58.

Palmer, S. and P.C. Smith (2000), 'Incorporating option values into the
economic evaluation of health care technologies', *Journal of Health
Economics*, **19**, 755–66.

Papadakis, S., N.B. Oldridge, D. Coyle, A. Mayhew, R.D. Reid, L.
Beaton, W.A. Dafoe and D. Angus (2005), 'Economic evaluation
of cardiac rehabilitation: a systematic review', *European Journal of
Cardiovascular Prevention and Rehabilitation*, **12**, 513–20.

Parkin, D. and N. Devlin (2006), 'Is there a case for using visual analogue scale valuations in cost-utility analysis?', *Health Economics*, **15**,
653–761.

Parkin, D., A. McGuire and B. Yule (1987), 'Aggregate health care expenditures and national income: is health care a luxury good?', *Journal of
Health Economics*, **6**, 109–27.

Parkin, M. (2008), *Economics*, 8th edition, Boston, MA: Addison-
Wesley.

Patouillard, E., C.A. Goodman, K.G. Hanson and A.J. Mills (2007), 'Can
working with the private for-profit sector improve utilization of quality
health services by the poor? A systematic review of the literature',
International Journal for Equity in Health, **6**, 17.

Paul-Shaheen, P., J.D. Clark and D. Williams (1987), 'Small area analysis: a review and analysis of the North American literature', *Journal of Health Politics, Policy and Law*, **12**, 741–809.

Pauly, M.V. (1968), 'The economics of moral hazard: comment', *American Economic Review*, **58**, 531–7.

Pauly, M.V. (1981), *Doctors and Their Workshops: Economic Models of Physician Behavior*, Chicago: University of Chicago Press.

Pauly, M.V. (1986), 'Taxation, health insurance and market failure in the medical economy', *Journal of Economic Literature*, **24**, 629–75.

Pauly, M.V. (1994), 'Editorial: a re-examination of the meaning and importance of supplier-induced demand', *Journal of Health Economics*, **13**, 369–72.

Pauly, M.V. (2000), 'Insurance reimbursement', in A.J. Culyer and J.P. Newhouse (eds), *Handbook of Health Economics*, Amsterdam: Elsevier, pp. 537–60.

Pauly, M.V. and M. Redisch (1973), 'The not-for-profit hospital as a physicians' cooperative', *American Economic Review*, **63**, 87–99.

Payne, G., A. Laporte, R. Deber and P.C. Coyte (2007), 'Counting backward to health care's future: using time-to-death modeling to identify changes in end-of-life morbidity and the impact of aging on health care expenditures', *Milbank Quarterly*, **85**, 13–57.

Payne, J.W., J.R. Bettman and D.A. Schkade (1999), 'Measuring constructed preferences: towards a building code, *Journal of Risk and Uncertainty*, **19**, 243–70.

Pennachio, D. (2003), 'Coding: how to fight bundling', *Medical Economics*, **80**, 65.

Phelps, C.E. (1992), 'Diffusion of information in medical care', *Journal of Economic Perspectives*, **6**, 23–42.

Phelps, C.E. (2000), 'Information diffusion and best practice adoption', in A.J. Culyer and J.P. Newhouse (eds), *Handbook of Health Economics*, Amsterdam: Elsevier, pp. 223–64.

Phelps, C.E. (2010), *Health Economics*, 4th (international) edition, Boston: Pearson Education.

Phelps, E.S. (1968), 'Money-wage dynamics and labor-market equilibrium', *Journal of Political Economy*, **76**, 678–711.

Philips, Z., D.K. Whynes and M. Avis (2006a), 'Testing the construct validity of willingness to pay valuations using objective information about risk and health benefit', *Health Economics*, **15**, 195–204.

Philips, Z., L. Bojke, M.J. Sculpher, K. Claxton and S. Golder (2006b), 'Good practice guidelines for decision-analytic modelling in health technology assessment: a review and consolidation of quality assessment', *PharmacoEconomics*, **24**, 355–71.

Philipson, T.J. (2000), 'Economic epidemiology and infectious diseases', in A.J. Culyer and J.P. Newhouse (eds), *Handbook of Health Economics*, Amsterdam: Elsevier, pp. 1761–99.

Philipson, T.J. and R.A. Posner (1995), 'A theoretical and empirical investigation of the effects of public health subsidies for STD testing', *Quarterly Journal of Economics*, **110**, 445–74.

Phillips, C.J. (2005), *Health Economics: An Introduction for Health Professionals*, Chichester: Wiley (BMJ Books).

Phillips, K.A., T. Maddala and F.R. Johnson (2002), 'Measuring preferences for health care interventions using conjoint analysis: an application to HIV testing', *Health Services Research*, **37**, 1681–705.

Phillips, V.L. (1995), 'Nurses' labor supply: participation, hours of work, and discontinuities in the supply function', *Journal of Health Economics*, **14**, 567–82.

Pinto, J.L., G. Loomes and R. Brey (2009), 'Trying to estimate a monetary value for the QALY', *Journal of Health Economics*, **28**, 553–62.

Pliskin, J.S., D.S. Shepard and M.C. Weinstein (1980), 'Utility functions for life years and health status', *Operations Research*, **28**, 206–24.

Polsky, D. and A. Basu (2006), 'Selection bias in observational data', in A.M. Jones (ed.), *The Elgar Companion to Health Economics*, Cheltenham, UK and Northampton, MA, USA: Edward Elgar, pp. 455–65.

Polverejan, E., J.C. Gardiner, C.J. Bradley, M. Holmes-Rovner and D. Rovner (2003), 'Estimating mean hospital cost as a function of length of stay and patient characteristics', *Health Economics*, **12**, 935–47.

Ponce, N., P.J. Gertler and P. Glewwie (1998), 'Will Vietnam grow out of malnutrition?', in D. Dollar, P. Glewwie and J. Litvack (eds), *Household Welfare and Vietnam's Transition*, Washington, DC: World Bank, pp. 257–75.

Popkin, B.M., S. Kim, E.R. Rusev, S. Du and C. Zizza (2006), 'Measuring the full economic costs of diet, physical activity, and obesity-related chronic diseases', *Obesity Reviews*, **7**, 271–93.

Popper, K.R. (2002) *Conjectures and Refutations: the Growth of Scientific Knowledge*, 3rd edition, Abingdon: Routledge.

Posner, R.A. (1974), 'Theories of economic regulation', *Bell Journal of Economics and Management Science*, **5**, 355–58.

Pratt, J.W. (1964), 'Risk aversion in the small and in the large', *Econometrica*, **32**, 122–36.

Preston, S.H. (1975), 'The changing relation between mortality and level of economic development', *Population Studies*, **29**, 231–48.

Preyra, C. and G. Pink (2006), 'Scale and scope efficiencies through hospital consolidations', *Journal of Health Economics*, **25**, 1049–68.

Propper, C., S. Burgess and K. Green (2004), 'Does competition between hospitals improve the quality of care? Hospital death rates and the NHS internal market', *Journal of Public Economics*, **88**, 1247–72.

Propper, C., J. Eachus, P. Chan, N. Pearson and G. Davey Smith (2005), 'Access to health care resources in the UK: the case of care for arthritis', *Health Economics*, **14**, 391–406.

Pudney, S. (2003), 'The road to ruin? Sequences of initiation to drugs and crime in Britain', *Economic Journal*, **113**, C182–C198.

Quiggin, J. (1981), 'Risk perception and risk aversion among Australian farmers', *Australian Journal of Agricultural Economics*, **25**, 160–69.

Quiggin, J. (1993), *Generalized Expected Utility Theory: The Rank-dependent Model*, Boston: Kluwer.

Quigley, M. (2007), 'A NICE fallacy', *Journal of Medical Ethics*, **33**, 465–6.

Radley, D.C., S.N. Finkelstein and R.S. Stafford (2006), 'Off-label prescribing among office-based physicians', *Archives of Internal Medicine*, **166**, 1021–6.

Raiffa, H. and R. Schlaiffer (1967), *Applied Statistical Decision Theory*, New York: Wiley Interscience.

Ramsey, F.P. (1927), 'A contribution to the theory of taxation', *Economic Journal*, **37**, 47–61.

Ramsey, J.B. (1969), 'Tests for specification errors in classical linear least squares regression analysis', *Journal of the Royal Statistical Society B*, **31**, 350–71.

Ranson, M.K., K. Hanson, V. Oliveira-Cruz and A.J. Mills (2003), 'Constraints to expanding access to health interventions: an empirical analysis and country typology', *Journal of International Development*, **15**, 15–39.

Ranson, M.K., T. Sinha, F. Gandhi, R. Jayswal and A.J. Mills (2006), 'Helping members of a community-based health insurance scheme access quality inpatient care through development of a preferred provider system in rural Gujarat', *National Medical Journal of India*, **19**, 274–82.

Rapoport, J., P. Jacobs and E. Jonsson (eds) (2009), *Cost Containment and Efficiency in National Health Systems: A Global Comparison*, Weinheim: Wiley.

Räsänen, P., H. Sintonen, O.-P. Ryynänen, M. Blom, V. Semberg-Konttinen and R.P. Roine (2005), 'Measuring cost-effectiveness of secondary health care: feasibility and potential utilization of results', *International Journal of Technology Assessment in Health Care*, **21**, 22–31.

Rawlins, M.D. (2008), 'De testimonio: on the evidence for decisions about the use of therapeutic interventions', Harveian Oration, London: Royal College of Physicians.

Rawls, J. (1971), *A Theory of Justice*, Cambridge, MA: Harvard University Press.

Reiffen, D. and M.R. Ward (2005), 'Generic drug industry dynamics', *Review of Economics and Statistics*, **87**, 37–49.

Reinhardt, U.E. (1998), 'Abstracting from distributional effects, the policy is efficient', in M.L. Barer, T.E. Getzen and G.L. Stoddart (eds), *Health, Health Care and Health Economics*, New York: Wiley, pp. 1–52.

Reinhardt, U.E. (2001), 'Can efficiency in health care be left to the market?', *Journal of Health Politics, Policy and Law*, **26**, 967–92.

Reinhardt, U.E., E.P.S. Hussey and G.F. Anderson (2004), 'U.S. Health care spending in an international context', *Health Affairs*, **23**, 10–25.

Remler, D. and S. Glied (2006), 'How much more cost-sharing will health savings accounts bring?', *Health Affairs*, **25**, 1070–78.

Renehan, A.G., S.T. O'Dwyer and D.K. Whynes (2004), 'Cost effectiveness analysis of intensive versus conventional follow up after curative resection for colorectal cancer', *British Medical Journal*, **328**, 81.

Rice, N. and A.M. Jones (1997), 'Multilevel models and health economics', *Health Economics*, **6**, 561–75.

Rice, T.H. (1992), 'An alternative framework for evaluating welfare losses in the health insurance market', *Journal of Health Economics*, **11**, 85–92.

Rice, T.H. and L. Unruh (2009), *The Economics of Health Reconsidered*, 3rd edition, Chicago: Health Administration Press.

Richardson, G. and A. Manca (2004), 'Calculation of quality adjusted life years in the published literature: a review of methodology and transparency', *Health Economics*, **13**, 1203–10.

Richardson, G., H.S.E. Gravelle, H. Weatherly and G. Ritchie (2005), 'Cost-effectiveness of interventions to support self-care: a systematic review', *International Journal of Technology Assessment in Health Care*, **21**, 423–32.

Richardson, G., A.K. Maynard, N. Cullum and D. Kindig (1998), 'Skill mix changes: substitution or service development?', *Health Policy*, **45**, 119–32.

Richardson, J. (1994), 'Cost utility analysis: what should be measured?', *Social Science and Medicine*, **39**, 7–21.

Rico, A. and J. Costa-i-Font (2005), 'Power rather than path dependency? The dynamics of institutional change under health care federalism', *Journal of Health Politics Policy and Law*, **30**, 231–52.

Ried, W. (1998), 'Comparative dynamic analysis of the Grossman model', *Journal Health Economics*, **17**, 383–425.

Rieskamp, J., J.R. Busemeyer and B.A. Mellers (2006), 'Extending the bounds of rationality: evidence and theories of preferential choice', *Journal of Economic Literature*, **44**, 631–61.

Ritov, I. and J. Baron (1990), 'Reluctance to vaccinate: commission bias and ambiguity', *Journal of Behavioral Decision Making*, **3**, 263–77.

Robberstad, B. and J. Cairns (2007), 'Time preferences for health in northern Tanzania: an empirical analysis of alternative discounting models', *PharmacoEconomics*, **25**, 73–88.

Roberts, J. (1999), 'Sensitivity of elasticity estimates for OECD health care spending: analysis of a dynamic heterogeneous data field', *Health Economics*, **8**, 459–72.

Robine, J.M. (1986), *Disability-free Life Expectancy: General Indicators of the Health of the Population*, Scientific Report, Quebec: Conseil des Affaires Sociales et de la Famille.

Robbins, L. (1932), *An Essay on the Nature and Significance of Economic Science*, London: Macmillan.

Robinson, J.C. (2001), 'Theory and practice in the design of physician payment incentives', *Milbank Quarterly*, **79**, 149–77.

Robinson, J.C. and H.S. Luft (1987), 'Competition and the cost of hospital care, 1972 to 1982', *Journal of the American Medical Association*, **257**, 3241–5.

Rochaix, L. (1989), 'Information asymmetry and search in the market for physicians' services', *Journal of Health Economics*, **8**, 53–84.

Rochaix, L. (1993), 'Financial incentives for physicians: the Quebec experience', *Health Economics*, **2**, 163–76.

Roderick, P., R. Davies, J. Raftery, D. Crabbe, R. Pearce, P. Bhandari and R. Patel (2003), 'The cost-effectiveness of screening for Helicobacter Pylori to reduce mortality and morbidity from gastric cancer and peptic ulcer disease: a discrete-event simulation model', *Health Technology Assessment*, **7**, 1–86.

Roemer, M.I. (1961), 'Bed supply and hospital utilization: a natural experiment', *Hospitals*, **35**, 36–41.

Romesburg, C.H. (2004), *Cluster Analysis for Researchers*, available at: http://www.lulu.com/content/paperback-book/cluster-analysis-for-researchers/46479 (accessed 27 October 2009).

Rose, G. (2008), *Rose's Strategy of Preventive Medicine*, with commentaries by Kay-Tee Khaw and Michael Marmot, Oxford: Oxford University Press.

Rosenbaum, P. and D.B. Rubin (1983), 'The central role of the propensity score in observational studies for causal effects', *Biometrika*, **70**, 41–55.

Rosenman, R. and D. Friesner (2002), 'Cost shifting revisited: the case of service intensity', *Health Care Management Science*, **5**, 15–24.

Rosenthal, M.B. and R.G. Frank (2006), 'What is the empirical basis for paying for quality in health care?', *Medical Care Research and Review*, **63**, 135–57.

Rosenthal, M.B., R. Fernandopulle, H.R. Song and B. Landon (2004), 'Paying for quality: providers' incentives for quality improvement: an assessment of recent efforts to align providers' incentives with the quality improvement agenda', *Health Affairs*, **23**, 127–41.

Rosenzweig, M.R. and T.P. Schultz (1983), 'Estimating a household production function: heterogeneity, the demand for health inputs, and their effects on birth weight', *Journal of Political Economy*, **91**, 723–46.

Rosko, M.D. (2001), 'Impact of HMO penetration and other environmental factors on hospital X-inefficiency', *Medical Care Research and Review*, **58**, 430–54.

Rosner, A.J., D.L. Becker, A.H. Wong, E. Miller and J.M. Conly (2004), 'The costs and consequences of methicillin-resistant *Staphylococcus aureus* infection treatments in Canada', *Canadian Journal of Infectious Diseases and Medical Microbiology*, **15**, 213–20.

Rosser, R. and P. Kind (1978), 'A scale of valuations of states of illness: is there a social consensus?', *International Journal of Epidemiology*, **7**, 347–58.

Rothlisberger, F.J. and W.J. Dickson (1939), *Management and the Worker*, Cambridge MA: Harvard University Press.

Rothschild, M. and J.E. Stiglitz (1976), 'Equilibrium in competitive insurance markets: an essay on the economics of imperfect information', *Quarterly Journal of Economics*, **90**, 630–49.

Rous, J.J. and D.R. Hotchkiss (2003), 'Estimation of the determinants of household health care expenditures in Nepal with controls for endogenous illness and provider choice', *Health Economics*, **12**, 431–51.

Rowe, J.W., T. Brown-Stevenson, R.L. Downey and J.P. Newhouse (2008), 'The effect of consumer-directed health plans on the use of preventive and chronic illness services', *Health Affairs*, **27**, 113–20.

Ruhm, C.J. (2000), 'Are recessions good for your health?', *Quarterly Journal of Economics*, **115**, 617–50.

Ruhm, C.J. (2006), 'Macroeconomic conditions, health and mortality', in A.M. Jones (ed.), *The Elgar Companion to Health Economics*, Cheltenham, UK and Northampton, MA, USA: Edward Elgar, pp. 5–16.

Ruta, D., C. Mitton, A. Bate and C. Donaldson (2005), 'Programme budgeting and marginal analysis: bridging the divide between doctors and managers', *British Medical Journal*, **330**, 1501–3.

Rutten, M. and G. Reed (2009), 'A comparative analysis of some policy options to reduce rationing in the UK's NHS: lessons from a general equilibrium model incorporating positive health effects', *Journal of Health Economics*, **28**, 221–33.

Rutten-Van Molken, M.P.M.H., C.H. Bakker, E.K.A. Van Doorslaer and S. Van der Linden (1995), 'Methodological issues of patient utility measurement', *Medical Care*, **33**, 922–37.

Ryan, M. and K. Gerard (2003), 'Using discrete choice experiments to value health care: current practice and future prospects', *Applied Health Economics and Policy Analysis*, **2**, 55–64.

Ryan, M. and J. Hughes (1997), 'Using conjoint analysis to assess women's preferences for miscarriage management', *Health Economics*, **6**, 261–74.

Ryan, M., K. Gerard and M. Amaya-Amaya (2008), *Using Discrete Choice to Value Health and Health Care*, Berlin: Springer.

Ryan, M., D.A. Scott and C. Donaldson, (2004), 'Valuing health care using willingness to pay: a comparison of the payment card and dichotomous choice methods', *Journal of Health Economics*, **23**, 237–58.

Ryan, M., D.A. Scott, C. Reeves, A. Bate, E.R. Van Teijlingen, E.M. Russell, M. Napper and C.M. Robb (2001), 'Eliciting public preferences for healthcare: a systematic review of techniques', *Health Technology Assessment*, **5**, 1–186.

Ryder, H.E. and G.M. Heal (1973), 'Optimum growth with intertemporally dependent preferences', *Review of Economic Studies*, **40**, 1–33.

Sachs, J.D. (2001), *Macroeconomics and Health: Investing in Health for Economic Development*, Commission on Macroeconomics and Health, Geneva: World Health Organization.

Salkever, D.S. (2000), 'Regulation of prices and investment in hospitals in the United States', in A.J. Culyer and J.P. Newhouse (eds), *Handbook of Health Economics*, Amsterdam: Elsevier, pp. 1489–535.

Samuelson, P.A. (1938), 'A note on the pure theory of consumer's behaviour', *Economica*, **5**, 61–71.

Samuelson, P.A. (1947), *Foundations of Economic Analysis*, Cambridge, MA: Harvard University Press.

Santerre, R. and S.P. Neun (2007), *Health Economics: Theories, Insights and Industry*, 4th edition, Cincinnati: South-Western Publishing Company.

Santerre, R. and J.A. Vernon (2006), 'Assessing consumer gains from a drug price control policy in the United States', *Southern Economic Journal*, **73**, 233–45.

Santos Silva, J.M.C. and F. Windmeijer (2001), 'Two-part multiple spell models for health care demand', *Journal of Econometrics*, **104**, 67–89.

Scargle, J.D. (2000), 'Publication bias: the "file-drawer" problem in scientific inference', *Journal of Scientific Exploration*, **14**, 91–106.

Scheffler, S. (ed.) (1988), *Consequentialism and its Critics*, Oxford: Oxford University Press.

Scherer, F.M. (2000), 'The pharmaceutical industry', in A.J. Culyer and J.P. Newhouse (eds), *Handbook of Health Economics*, Amsterdam: Elsevier, pp. 1298–336.

Schulte, P.A. (2005), 'Characterizing the burden of occupational injury and disease', *Journal of Occupational and Environmental Medicine*, **47**, 607–22.

Schultz, T.P. (2005), 'Productive benefits of health: evidence from low-income countries', in G. Lopez-Casasnovas (ed.) *Health and Economic Growth: Findings and Policy Implications*, Cambridge, MA: MIT Press, pp. 257–85.

Schut, F.T. and W.P.M.M. Van de Ven (2005), 'Rationing and competition in the Dutch health-care system', *Health Economics*, **14**, S59–S74.

Schwartz, J.A. and G.B. Chapman (1999), 'Are more options always better? The attraction effect in physicians' decisions about medications', *Medical Decision Making*, **19**, 315–23.

Scitovsky, T. (1941), 'A note on welfare propositions in economics', *Review of Economic Studies*, **9**, 77–88.

Scott, A. (2000), 'Economics of general practice', in A.J. Culyer, and J.P. Newhouse (eds), *Handbook of Health Economics*, Amsterdam: Elsevier, pp. 1175–200.

Scott, A. and A. Shiell (1997), 'Do fee descriptors influence treatment choices in general practice? A multilevel discrete choice model', *Journal of Health Economics*, **3**, 303–21.

Scott, J., S. Palmer, E. Paykel, J. Teasdale and H. Hayhurst (2003), 'Use of cognitive therapy for relapse prevention in chronic depression: cost-effectiveness study', *British Journal of Psychiatry*, **182**, 221–7.

Sculpher, M.J., M.F. Drummond and M.J. Buxton (1997), 'The iterative use of economic evaluation as part of the process of health technology assessment', *Journal of Health Services Policy*, **2**, 26–30.

Sculpher, M.J., E. Fenwick and K. Claxton (2000), 'Assessing quality in decision analytic cost-effectiveness models: a suggested framework and example of application', *PharmacoEconomics*, **17**, 461–77.

Selden, T.M. (1999), 'Premium subsidies for health insurance: excessive coverage vs. adverse selection', *Journal of Health Economics*, **18**, 709–25.

Sen, A.K. (1970), 'The impossibility of a Paretian liberal', *Journal of Political Economy*, **78**, 152–7.

Sen, A.K. (1977), 'Rational fools: a critique of the behavioral foundations of economic theory', *Philosophy and Public Affairs*, **6**, 317–44.

Sen, A.K. (1981), 'Public action and the quality of life in developing countries', *Oxford Bulletin of Economics and Statistics*, **43**, 287–319.

Sen, A.K. (1999), *Commodities and Capabilities*, Oxford: Oxford University Press.

Sen, B. (2002), 'Does alcohol-use increase the risk of sexual intercourse among adolescents? Evidence from the NLSY97', *Journal of Health Economics*, **21**, 1085–93.

Seshamani, M. and A. Gray (2004), 'Ageing and health-care expenditure: the red herring argument revisited', *Health Economics*, **13**, 303–14.

Shackley, P. and C. Donaldson (2002), 'Should we use willingness to pay to elicit community preferences for health care? New evidence from using a "marginal" approach', *Journal of Health Economics*, **21**, 971–91.

Sheldon, T.A. (1996), 'Problems of using modelling in the economic evaluation of health care', *Health Economics*, **5**, 1–11.

Shemilt, I., M. Mugford, M.F. Drummond, E. Eisenstein, J. Mallender, M. McDaid, L. Vale and D. Walker (The Campbell & Cochrane Economics Methods Group [CCEMG]) (2006), 'Economics methods in Cochrane systematic reviews of health promotion and public health related interventions', *BMC Medical Research Methodology*, **6**.

Shen, Y.-C. and G. Melnick (2006), 'Is managed care still an effective cost containment device?', *Forum for Health Economics & Policy*, available online at: http://www.bepress.com/fhep/9/1/3/ (accessed 29 October 2009).

Shepperd, S., D. Harwood, C. Jenkinson, A. Gray, M. Vessey and P. Morgan (1998a), 'Randomised controlled trial comparing hospital at home care with inpatient hospital care. I: three month follow up of health outcomes', *British Medical Journal*, **316**, 1786–91.

Shepperd, S., D. Harwood, A. Gray, M. Vessey and P. Morgan (1998b), 'Randomised controlled trial comparing hospital at home care with inpatient hospital care. II: cost minimisation analysis', *British Medical Journal*, **316**, 1791–6.

Shields, M.A. (2004), 'Addressing nurse shortages: what can policy makers learn from the econometric evidence of nurse labor supply?', *Economic Journal*, **114**, F464–F498.

Shiell, A. and K. McIntosh (2008), 'Subject variation not values clarification explains the reliability of WTP estimates', *Health Economics*, **17**, 287–92.

Shiell, A. and B. Rush (2003), 'Can willingness to pay capture the value of altruism? An exploration of Sen's notion of commitment', *Journal of Socio-Economics*, **32**, 647–60.

Shiell, A., P. Hawe and L. Gold (2008), 'Complex interventions or complex systems? Implications for economic evaluation', *British Medical Journal*, **336**, 1281–3.

Siciliani, L. and J. Hurst (2004), 'Explaining waiting-time variations for elective surgery across OECD countries', *OECD Economic Studies*, **38**, 95–123.

Simon, H. (1955), 'A behavioral model of rational choice', *Quarterly Journal of Economics*, **69**, 99–118.

Simon, H. (1957), *Models of Man, Social and Rational: Mathematical Essays on Rational Human Behavior in a Social Setting*, New York: Wiley.

Sindelar, J.L., T.A. Olmstead and J. Pearce (2007), 'Cost-effectiveness of prize based contingency management in methadone maintenance treatment programs', *Addiction*, **102**, 1463–71.

Sinha, T., M.K. Ranson and A.J. Mills (2007), 'Protecting the poor? The distributional impact of a bundled insurance scheme', *World Development*, **35**, 1404–21.

Sintonen, H. and I. Linnosmaa (2000), 'Economics of dental services', in A.J. Culyer and J.P. Newhouse (eds), *Handbook of Health Economics*, Amsterdam: Elsevier, pp. 1252–96.

Sintonen, H. and M. Pekurinen (1993), 'A fifteen-dimensional measure of health-related quality of life (15D) and its applications', in S.R. Walker and R.M. Rosser (eds), *Quality of Life Assessment: Key Issues in the 1990s*, Dordrecht: Kluwer Academic Publishers, pp. 185–95.

Skinner, J. and D. Feenberg (1994), 'The risk and duration of catastrophic health care expenditures', *Review of Economics and Statistics*, **76**, 633–47.

Slavin, R.E. (1986), 'Best-evidence synthesis: an alternative to meta-analytic and traditional reviews', *Educational Researcher*, **15**, 5–11.

Sloan, F. (2000), 'Not-for-profit ownership and hospital behavior', in A.J. Culyer and J.P. Newhouse (eds), *Handbook of Health Economics*, Amsterdam: Elsevier, pp. 1141–74.

Sloan, F.A., W.K. Viscusi, H.W. Chesson, C.J. Conover and K. Whetten-Goldstein (1998), 'Alternative approaches to valuing intangible health losses: the evidence for multiple sclerosis', *Journal of Health Economics*, **17**, 475–97.

Small, N. and R. Mannion (2005), 'A hermeneutic science: health economics and Habermas', *Journal of Health Organization and Management*, **19**, 219–35.

Smith, J. (1999), 'Healthy bodies and thick wallets: the dual relation between health and economic status', *Journal of Economic Perspectives*, **13**, 145–66.

Smith, L.A. (1985) 'The Broad Gauge Story', available online at:

http://lionels.orpheusweb.co.uk/RailSteam/GWRBroadG/BGHist.html (accessed 9 November 2009).

Smith, N., C. Mitton and S. Peacock (2009), 'Qualitative methodologies in health-care priority setting research', *Health Economics*, **18**, 63–75.

Smith, P.C and A. Street (2006), 'Concepts and challenges in measuring the performance of health care organizations', in A.M. Jones (ed.), *The Elgar Companion to Health Economics*, Cheltenham, UK and Northampton, MA, USA: Edward Elgar, pp. 317–25.

Smith, P.C. and N. York (2004), 'Quality incentives: the case of U.K. general practitioners', *Health Affairs*, **23**, 112–18.

Smith, P.C., N. Black, R. Boyle, A. Coulter, N. Devlin, N. Edwards, M. Richards, A. Towse and A. Vallance-Owen (2008), *Office of Health Economics Commission on NHS Outcomes, Performance and Productivity*, London: Office of Health Economics.

Smith, R. (2007), 'The relationship between reliability and size of willingness to pay values: a qualitative insight', *Health Economics*, **16**, 211–16.

Smith, R.D. (1996), 'Is regret theory an alternative basis for estimating the value of healthcare interventions?', *Health Policy*, **37**, 105–15.

Smith, R.D. (2000), 'The discrete-choice willingness-to-pay question format in health economics: should we adopt environmental guidelines?', *Medical Decision Making*, **20**, 194–204.

Smith, R.D. (2003), 'Construction of the contingent valuation market in health care: a critical assessment', *Health Economics*, **12**, 609–28.

Smith, R.D. (2004), 'Foreign direct investment and trade in health services: a review of the literature', *Social Science and Medicine*, **59**, 2313–23.

Smith, R.D. and J. Coast (1998), 'Controlling antimicrobial resistance: a proposed transferable permit market', *Health Policy*, **43**, 219–32.

Smith, R.D., R. Chanda and V. Tangcharoensathien (2009), 'Trade in health-related services', *The Lancet*, **373**, 593–601.

Smith, R.D., M. Yago, M. Millar and J. Coast (2005), 'Assessing the macroeconomic impact of a healthcare problem: the application of computable general equilibrium analysis to antimicrobial resistance', *Journal of Health Economics*, **24**, 1055–75.

Smith, R.D., D. Woodward, A. Acharya, R. Beaglehole and N. Drager (2004), 'Communicable disease control: a "global public good" perspective', *Health Policy and Planning*, **19**, 271–8.

Smith, V.K., D.H. Taylor, F.A. Sloan, F.R. Johnson and W.H. Desvousges (2001), 'Do smokers respond to health shocks?', *Review of Economics and Statistics*, **83**, 675–87.

Smythe, J.G. (2002), 'Reputation, public information, and physician adoption of an innovation', *European Journal of Health Economics*, **3**, 103–10.

Soares, R.R. (2005), 'Mortality reductions, educational attainment, and fertility choice', *American Economic Review*, **95**, 580–601.

Soares, R.R. (2007), 'On the determinants of mortality reductions in the developing world', *Population and Development Review*, **33**, 247–87.

Soares, R.R. (2009), 'Life expectancy and welfare in Latin America and the Caribbean', *Health Economics*, **18**(S1), S37–S54.

Song, F. (1999), 'Exploring heterogeneity in meta-analysis: is the L'Abbé plot useful?', *Journal of Clinical Epidemiology*, **52**, 725–30.

Sonnenberg, F.A. and R. Beck (1993), 'Markov models in medical decision making: a practical guide', *Medical Decision Making*, **18**, 322–38.

Srinivasan, T.N. (1994), 'Database for development analysis: an overview', *Journal of Development Economics*, **44**, 3–27.

Stålhammar, N.-O. (1996), 'An empirical note on willingness to pay and starting-point bias', *Medical Decision Making*, **16**, 242.

Stearns, S.C. and E.C. Norton (2004), 'Time to include time to death? The future of health care expenditure predictions', *Health Economics*, **13**, 315–27.

Stewart, J.M. (2001), 'The impact of health status on the duration of unemployment spells and the implications for studies of the impact of unemployment on health status', *Journal of Health Economics*, **20**, 781–96.

Stewart, J.M., E. O'Shea, C. Donaldson and P. Shackley (2002), 'Do ordering effects matter in willingness-to-pay studies of health care?', *Journal of Health Economics*, **21**, 585–99.

Stigler, G.J. (1971), 'Theory of economic regulation', *Bell Journal of Economics and Management Science*, **2**, 3–21.

Stiglitz, J.E. (2006), 'Scrooge and intellectual property rights', *British Medical Journal*, **333**, 1279–80.

Stinnett, A. and J. Mullahy (1998), 'Net health benefits: a new framework for the analysis of uncertainty in cost-effectiveness analysis', *Medical Decision Making*, **18**, S68–S80.

Stoddart, G.L., R.J. Labelle, M.L. Barer and R.G. Evans (1986), 'Tobacco taxes and health care costs. Do Canadian smokers pay their way?', *Journal of Health Economics*, **5**, 63–80.

Strauss, J. and K. Beegle (1996), 'Intrahousehold Allocations: A Review of Theories, Empirical Evidence and Policy Issues', Department of Agricultural Economics, Michigan State University International Development Working Papers No. 62.

Strauss, J. and D. Thomas (1996), 'Measurement and mismeasurement of social indicators', *American Economic Review*, **86**, Papers and Proceedings, 30–34.

Street, A. (2003), 'How much confidence should we place in efficiency estimates?', *Health Economics*, **12**, 895–907.

Sugden, R. and A.H. Williams (1978), *The Principles of Practical Cost-Benefit Analysis*, Oxford: Oxford University Press.

Sule, A., T.F. Crossley, P. Grootendorst and M.R. Veall (2002), 'The effects of drug subsidies on out-of-pocket prescription drug expenditures by seniors: regional evidence from Canada', *Journal of Health Economics*, **21**, 805–26.

Sullivan, P.W., S.L. Follin and M.B. Nichol (2003), 'Transitioning the second-generation antihistamines to over-the-counter status: a cost-effectiveness analysis', *Medical Care*, **41**, 1382–95.

Sussex, J. and S. Farrar (2009), 'Activity-based funding for National Health Service hospitals in England: managers' experience and expectations', *European Journal of Health Economics*, **10**, 197–206.

Sutton, M. and P. Lock (2000), 'Regional differences in health care delivery: implications for a national resource allocation formula', *Health Economics*, **9**, 547–59.

Szende, A. and A.J. Culyer (2006), 'The inequity of informal payments for health care: the case of Hungary', *Health Policy*, **75**, 262–71.

Szreter, S. (1988), 'The importance of social intervention in Britain's mortality decline c. 1850–1914: a reinterpretation of the role of public health', *Social History of Medicine*, **1**, 1–38.

Tandon, A., C.J.L. Murray, J. Lauer and D. Evans (2000), 'Measuring Overall Health System Performance for 191 Countries', Geneva: World Health Organization (Global Programme on Evidence for Health Policy Discussion Paper No. 30).

Tanya, G.K., R.M. Bentley, K.P. Effros and E.B. Keeler (2008), 'Waste in the US health care system: a conceptual framework', *Milbank Quarterly*, **86**, 629–59.

Tappenden, P., J. Chilcott, S. Eggington, J. Patnick, H. Sakai and J. Karnon (2007), 'Option appraisal of population-based colorectal cancer screening programmes in England', *Gut*, **56**, 677–84.

Tauras, J.A., P.M. O'Malley and L.D. Johnston (2001), 'Effects of Price and Access Laws on Teenage Smoking Initiation: A National Longitudinal Analysis', NBER Working Papers, Cambridge, MA: National Bureau of Economic Research.

Tengs, T.O. (1996), 'An evaluation of Oregon's Medicaid rationing algorithms', *Health Economics*, **5**, 171–81.

Tengs, T.O., M.E. Adams, J.S. Pliskin, D.G. Safran, J.E. Siegel, M.C. Weinstein and J.D. Graham (1996), 'Five hundred life-saving interventions and their cost-effectiveness', *Risk Analysis*, **15**, 369–90.

Tetlock, P.E. (1999), 'Accountability theory: mixing properties of human agents with properties of social systems', in J. Levine, L Thompson and D. Messick (eds), *Shared Cognition in Organizations: The Management of Knowledge*, Hillsdale NJ: Erlbaum, pp. 117–37.

Tetlock, P.E. (2003), 'Thinking the unthinkable: sacred values and taboo cognitions', *Trends in Cognitive Sciences*, **7**, 320–24.

Theil, H. (1967), *Economic and Information Theory*, Amsterdam: North Holland.

Thomas, D. and J. Strauss (1997), 'Health and wages: evidence on men and women in urban Brazil', *Journal of Econometrics*, **77**, 159–85.

Thomas, S., G. Mooney and S. Mbatsha (2007), 'The MESH approach: strengthening public health systems for the MDGs', *Health Policy*, **83**, 180–85.

Thompson, S.G. and J.A. Barber (2000), 'How should cost data in pragmatic randomised trials be analysed?', *British Medical Journal*, **320**, 1197–200.

Thurstone, L.L. (1928), 'Attitudes can be measured', *American Journal of Sociology*, **33**, 529–54.

Tobin, J. (1958), 'Estimation of relationships for limited dependent variables', *Econometrica*, **26**, 24–36.

Tompa, E., R. Dolinschi and C. de Oliviera (2006), 'Practice and potential of work-place interventions for occupational health and safety', *Journal of Occupational Rehabilitation*, **16**, 375–400.

Tompa, E., A.J. Culyer and R. Dolinschi (eds) (2008), *Economic Evaluation of Interventions for Occupational Health and Safety: Developing Good Practice*, Oxford: Oxford University Press.

Törnqvist, L. (1936), 'The Bank of Finland's consumption price index', *Bank of Finland Monthly Bulletin*, **10**, 1–8.

Torrance, G.W. (1986), 'Measurement of health state utilities for economic appraisal', *Journal of Health Economics*, **5**, 1–30.

Torrance, G.W. (2001), 'Visual analog scales', *Medical Decision Making*, **21**, 329–34.

Torrance, G.W. and D. Feeny (1989), 'Utilities and quality-adjusted life-years', *International Journal of Technology Assessment in Health Care*, **5**, 559–75.

Torrance, G.W., W.H. Thomas and D.L. Sackett (1972), 'A utility maximization model for evaluation of health care programs', *Health Services Research*, **7**, 118–33.

Townsend, P., A. Phillimore and A. Beattie (1988), *Health and Deprivation: Inequality and the North*, London: Croom Helm.

Trivedi, A., W. Rakowski and J. Ayanian (2008), 'Effect of cost sharing on screening mammography in Medicare health plans', *New England Journal of Medicine*, **358**, 375–83.

Tryon, R.C. (1939), *Cluster Analysis*, New York: McGraw-Hill.

Tversky, A. and D. Kahneman (1981), 'The framing of decisions and psychology of choice', *Science*, **211**, 453–8.

Tversky, A. and D. Kahneman (1983), 'Extensional versus intuitive reasoning: the conjunction fallacy in probability judgment', *Psychological Review*, **90**, 293–315.

Tversky, A. and D. Kahneman (1986), 'Rational choice and the framing of decisions', *Journal of Business*, **59**, 251–78.

Tversky, A. and D. Kahneman (1991), 'Loss aversion in riskless choice: a reference-dependent model', *Quarterly Journal of Economics*, **106**, 1039–61.

Tversky, A. and D. Kahneman (1992), 'Advances in prospect theory: cumulative representation of uncertainty', *Journal of Risk and Uncertainty*, **5**, 297–323.

Tversky, A., S. Sattath and P. Slovic (1988), 'Contingent weighting in judgment and choice', *Psychological Review*, **95**, 371–84.

Ubel, P.A., J. Baron and D.A. Asch (2001), 'Preference for equity as a framing effect', *Medical Decision Making*, **21**, 180–89.

Ullman, S.G. and A.G. Holtman (1985), 'Economies of scope, ownership and nursing home costs', *Quarterly Review of Economics and Business*, **25**, 83–94.

Ungar, W.J. (2006), 'Paediatric health economic evaluations: a world view', *Healthcare Quarterly*, **10**, 134–40.

Valdmanis, V., D. Walker and J. Fox-Rushby (2003), 'Are vaccination sites in Bangladesh scale efficient?', *International Journal of Technology Assessment in Health Care*, **19**, 692–7.

Van den Akker-van Marle, M.E., H.M. Dankert, P.H. Verkerk and J.E. Dankert-Roelse (2006), 'Cost-effectiveness of four neonatal screening strategies for cystic fibrosis', *Pediatrics*, **118**, 896–905.

Van den Berg, B., W.F.B. Brouwer, N.J. Van Exel and M.A. Koopmanschap (2005), 'Economic valuation of informal care: the contingent valuation method applied to informal caregiving', *Health Economics*, **14**, 169–83.

Van der Pol, M. and J. Cairns (2002), 'A comparison of the discounted utility model and hyperbolic discounting models in the case of social and private intertemporal preferences for health', *Journal of Economic Behavior & Organization*, **49**, 79–96.

Van de Ven, W.P M.M. and R.P. Ellis (2000), 'Risk adjustment in competitive health plan markets', in A.J. Culyer and J.P. Newhouse (eds), *Handbook of Health Economics*, Amsterdam: Elsevier, pp. 755–845.

Van Doorslaer, E.K.A. and A.M. Jones (2003), 'Inequalities in self-reported health: validation of a new approach to measurement', *Journal of Health Economics*, **22**, 61–87.

Van Doorslaer, E.K. A. Van, X. Koolman and A.M. Jones (2004), 'Explaining income-related inequalities in doctor utilisation in Europe', *Health Economics*, **13**, 629–47.

Van Doorslaer, E.K.A., A. Wagstaff, H. Bleichrodt, S. Calonge, U.-G. Gerdtham, M. Gerfin, J. Geurts, L. Gross, U. Häkkinen, R.E. Leu, O. O'Donnell, C. Propper, F. Puffer, M. Rodríguez, G. Sundberg and O. Winkelhake (1997), 'Income-related inequalities in health: some international comparisons', *Journal of Health Economics*, **16**, 93–112.

Van Doorslaer, E.K.A., A. Wagstaff, H.v.D. Burg, T. Christiansen, G. Citoni, R.D. Biase, U.-G. Gerdtham, M. Gerfin, L. Gross, U. Häkkinen, J. John, P. Johnson, J. Klavus, C. Lachaud, J. Lauritsen, R.E. Leu, B. Nolan, J. Pereira, C. Propper, F. Puffer, L. Rochaix, M. Schellhorn, G. Sundberg and O. Winkelhake (1999), 'The redistributive effect of health care finance in twelve OECD countries', *Journal of Health Economics*, **18**, 291–13.

Van Hout, B.A., M.J. Al, G.S. Gordon and F.F.H. Rutten (1994), 'Costs, effects and C/E ratios alongside a clinical trial', *Health Economics*, **3**, 309–19.

Van Kleef, R.C., K. Beck, W.P.M.M. Van de Ven and R.C.J.A. Van Vliet (2008), 'Risk equalization and voluntary deductibles: a complex interaction', *Journal of Health Economics*, **27**, 427–43.

Van Ours, J.C. (1995), 'The price elasticity of hard drugs: the case of opium in the Dutch East Indies, 1923–1938', *Journal of Political Economy*, **103**, 261–79.

Van Ours, J.C. (2003), 'Is cannabis a stepping-stone for cocaine?', *Journal of Health Economics*, **22**, 539–54.

Van Ourti, T., E. Van Doorslaer and X. Koolman (2009), 'The effect of income growth and inequality on health inequality: theory and empirical evidence from the European panel', *Journal of Health Economics*, **28**, 525–39.

Vernon, J.M. and H. Grabowski (2000), 'Effective patent life in pharmaceuticals', *International Journal of Technology Management*, **19**, 98–120.

Viscusi, W.K. (1993), 'The value of risks to life and health', *Journal of Economic Literature*, **31**, 1912–46.

Viscusi, W.K. and J. Aldy (2003), 'The value of a statistical life: a critical review of market estimates throughout the world', *Journal of Risk and Uncertainty*, **27**, 5–76.

Vitaliano, D.F. (1987), 'On the estimation of hospital cost functions', *Journal of Health Economics*, **6**, 305–18.

von Neumann, J. and O. Morgenstern (1944), *Theory of Games and Economic Behaviour*, Princeton: Princeton University Press.

Wadsworth, Y. (1998), 'What is participatory action research?', *Action Research International*, Paper 2. Available online at: http://www.scu.edu.au/schools/gcm/ar/ari/p-ywadsworth98.html (accessed 7 November 2009).

Wagstaff, A. (1985), 'Time series analysis of the relationship between unemployment and mortality: a survey of econometric critiques and replications of Brenner's studies', *Social Science and Medicine*, **21**, 985–96.

Wagstaff, A. (1986), 'The demand for health: theory and applications', *Journal of Epidemiology and Community Health*, **40**, 1–11.

Wagstaff, A. (1991), 'QALYs and the equity-efficiency trade-off', *Journal of Health Economics*, **10**, 21–41.

Wagstaff, A. (2002a), 'Poverty and health sector inequalities', *Bulletin of the World Health Organization*, **80**, 97–105.

Wagstaff, A. (2002b), 'Inequality aversion, health inequalities, and health achievement', *Journal of Health Economics*, **21**, 627–41.

Wagstaff, A. and N. Nguyen (2004), 'Poverty and survival prospects of Vietnamese children under Doi Moi', in P. Glewwe, N. Agrawal and D. Dollar (eds), *Economic Growth, Poverty and Household Welfare: Policy Lessons from Vietnam*, Washington, DC: World Bank, pp. 313–50.

Wagstaff, A. and E.K.A. Van Doorslaer (2000), 'Equity in health care finance and delivery', in A.J. Culyer and J.P. Newhouse (eds), *Handbook of Health Economics*, Amsterdam: Elsevier, pp. 1803–62.

Wagstaff, A. and E.K.A. Van Doorslaer (2003), 'Catastrophe and impoverishment in paying for health care: with applications to Vietnam, 1993–1998', *Health Economics*, **12**, 921–34.

Wagstaff, A. and H. Waters (2005), 'How were the reaching the poor studies done?', in D. Gwatkin, A. Wagstaff and A. Yazbeck (eds), *Reaching the Poor with Health, Nutrition and Population Services: What Works. What Doesn't, and Why?*, Washington, DC: World Bank, pp. 27–46.

Wagstaff, A., E.K.A. Van Doorslaer and N. Watanabe (2003), 'On decomposing the causes of health sector inequalities, with an application to malnutrition inequalities in Vietnam', *Journal of Econometrics*, **112**, 219–27.

Wakker, P.P. (2000), 'Uncertainty aversion: a discussion of critical issues in health economics', *Health Economics*, **9**, 261–3.

Ware, J.E. Jr. and C.D. Sherbourne (1992), 'The MOS 36-item short-form health survey (SF-36). I. Conceptual framework and item selection', *Medical Care*, **30**, 473–83.

Wasserman, J., W.G. Manning, J.P. Newhouse and J.D. Winkler (1991), 'The effects of excise taxes and regulations on cigarette smoking', *Journal of Health Economics*, **10**, 43–64.

Waters, H.R., J.A. Rehwinkel and G. Burnham (2004), 'Economic evaluation of Mectizan distribution', *Tropical Medicine and International Health*, **9**, a16–a25.

Watson, V. and M. Ryan (2006), 'Exploring preference anomalies in double bounded contingent valuation', *Journal of Health Economics*, **26**, 463–82.

Wedig, G.J. (1988), 'Health status and the demand for health: results on price elasticities', *Journal of Health Economics*, **7**, 151–63.

Wedig, G.J. (1993), 'Ramsey pricing and supply-side incentives in physician markets', *Journal of Health Economics*, **12**, 365–84.

Weibull, W. (1951), 'A statistical distribution function of wide applicability', *Journal of Applied Mechanics*, **18**, 293–7.

Weinstein, M.C. and W.G. Manning (1997), 'Theoretical issues in cost-effectiveness analysis', *Journal of Health Economics*, **16**, 121–8.

Weinstein, M.C. and W.B. Stason (1977), 'Foundations of cost-effectiveness analysis for health and medical practices', *New England Journal of Medicine*, **296**, 716–721.

Weinstein, M.C, J.E. Siegel, A.M. Garber, J. Lipscomb, B.R. Luce, W.G. Manning and G.W. Torrance (1998), 'Productivity costs, time costs and health-related quality of life: a response to the Erasmus Group', *Health Economics*, **6**, 505–10.

Weisbrod, B. (1964), 'Collective-consumption services of individual-consumption goods', *Quarterly Journal of Economics*, **78**, 471–7.

Weisbrod, B. (1991), 'The health care quadrilemma: an essay on technological change, insurance, quality of care, and cost containment', *Journal of Economic Literature*, **29**, 523–52.

Welch, B.L., J.W. Hay, D.S. Miller, R.J. Olsen, R.M. Rippey and A.S. Welch (1987), 'The Rand Health Insurance Study: a summary critique', *Medical Care*, **25**, 148–56.

Wennberg, J. and A. Gittelsohn (1973), 'Small area variations in health care delivery: a population-based health information system can guide planning and regulatory decision-making', *Science*, **182**, 1102–8.

Wennberg, J.E. (2002), 'Unwarranted variations in healthcare delivery: implications for academic medical centres', *British Medical Journal*, **325**, 961–4.

Wennberg, J.E., E.S. Fisher and J.S. Skinner (2002), 'Geography and the debate over Medicare reform', *Health Affairs* (suppl. Web exclusives), W96–W114.

Werner, R.M. and D.A. Asch (2005), 'The unintended consequences of publicly reporting quality information', *Journal of the American Medical Association*, **293**, 1239–44.

Whetten, K., J. Leserman, R. Whetten, J. Ostermann, N. Thielman, M.

Swartz and D. Stangl (2006), 'Exploring lack of trust in care providers and the government as a barrier to health service use', *American Journal of Public Health*, **96**, 716–21.

Whynes, D.K. (2008), 'Correspondence between EQ-5D health state classifications and EQ VAS scores', *Health Quality of Life Outcomes*, **6**, 1–9.

Whynes, D.K., J.L. Wolstenholme and E. Frew (2004), 'Evidence of range bias in contingent valuation payment scales', *Health Economics*, **13**, 183–90.

Wiener, J., D. Brown, B. Gage, G. Khatutsky, A. Moore and D. Osber (2004), *Home and Community-based Services: A Synthesis of the Literature* (Report No. RTI Project 07147.019.003), Waltham, MA: RTI International.

Wilcoxon, F. (1945), 'Individual comparisons by ranking methods', *Biometrics*, **1**, 80–83.

Wildman, J. (2003), 'Modelling health, income and income inequality: the impact of income inequality on health and health inequality', *Journal of Health Economics*, **22**, 521–38.

Wilkinson, R.G. (1996), *Unhealthy Societies: The Afflictions of Inequality*, London: Routledge & Kegan Paul.

Willcox, S., M. Seddon, S. Dunn, R. Tudor Edwards, J. Pearse and J.V. Tu (2007), 'Measuring and reducing waiting times: a cross-national comparison of strategies', *Health Affairs*, **26**, 1078–87.

Williams, A.H. (1974), 'Measuring the effectiveness of health care systems', in M. Perlman, (ed.), *The Economics of Health and Medical Care*, Basingstoke: Macmillan, pp. 361–76.

Williams, A.H. (1985), 'The economics of coronary artery bypass grafting', *British Medical Journal*, **291**, 326–9.

Williams, A.H. (1997), 'Intergenerational equity: an exploration of the "fair innings" argument', *Health Economis*, **6**, 117–32.

Williams, A.H. (2003), 'Health economics: a bird's eye view of the structure of the discipline', in *Health Care Economics for Health Care Professionals: Module 1, Basic Economic Concepts (Module Workbook)*, York: University of York.

Williams, A.H. and R. Cookson (2000), 'Equity in health', in A.J. Culyer and J.P. Newhouse (eds), *Handbook of Health Economics*, Amsterdam: Elsevier, pp. 1863–910.

Williams, A.H. and R. Cookson (2006), 'Equity-efficiency trade-offs in health technology assessment', *International Journal of Technology Assessment in Health Care*, **22**, 1–9.

Williams, I., S. Bryan and S. McIver (2007), 'How should cost-effectiveness analysis be used in health technology coverage decisions? Evidence from the National Institute for Health and Clinical Excellence approach', *Journal of Health Services Research and Policy*, **12**, 73–9.

Windmeijer, F.A.G. and J.M.C. Santos Silva (1997), 'Endogeneity in count data models: an application to the demand for health care', *Journal of Applied Econometrics*, **12**, 281–94.

Witter, S. and T. Ensor (eds) (1997), *An Introduction to Health Economics for Eastern Europe and the Former Soviet Union*, Chichester: Wiley.

Witter, S., T. Ensor, M. Jowett and R. Thompson (2000), *Health Economics for Developing Countries. A Practical Guide*, London: Macmillan Education.

Wolfe, B. (2008), 'Health economics', in S.N. Durlauf and L.E. Blume (eds), *The New Palgrave: A Dictionary of Economics*, 2nd edition, available online at: http://www.dictionaryofeconomics.com/article?id=pde2008_H000031 (accessed 2 November 2009).

Wolfson, M.C. (1991), 'A system of health statistics – towards a new conceptual framework', *Review of Income and Wealth*, **37**, 63–80.

Wonderling, D., R. Gruen and N. Black (2005), *Introduction to Health Economics*, Maidenhead: Open University Press.

Woodford, M. (2003), *Interest and Prices: Foundations of a Theory of Monetary Policy*, Princeton: Princeton University Press.

Woodward, D., N. Drager, R. Beaglehole and D. Lipson (2002), 'Globalization, global public goods and health', in N. Drager and C. Vieira (eds), *Trade in Health Services: Global, Regional and Country Perspectives*, Washington, DC: Pan American Health Organization.

Woolhandler, S., T. Campbell and D.U. Himmelstein (2003), 'Costs of health care administration in the United States and Canada', *New England Journal of Medicine*, **349**, 768–75.

Wootton, D (2006), *Bad Medicine: Doctors Doing Harm Since Hippocrates*, Oxford: Oxford University Press.

Wordsworth, S. and A. Ludbrook (2005), 'Comparing costing results in across country economic evaluations: the use of technology specific purchasing power parities', *Health Economics*, **14**, 93–9.

World Bank (1993), *Investing in Health*, New York: Oxford University Press.

World Bank (2001), *Dynamic Risk Management and the Poor: Developing a Social Protection Strategy for Africa*, Washington, DC: World Bank.

World Health Organization (2004a), *The Word Health Report 2004 – Changing History*, Geneva: World Health Organization.

World Health Organization (2004b), *Economics of Immunization: a Guide to the Literature and Other Resources*, Geneva: World Health Organization.

Worthington, D.J. (1991), 'Hospital waiting list management models', *Journal of the Operational Research Society*, **42**, 833–43.

Wright, C.J., G.K. Chambers and Y. Robens-Paradise (2002), 'Evaluation of indications for and outcomes of elective surgery', *Canadian Medical Association Journal*, **167**, 461–6.

Yamey, G. and M. Wilkes (2002), 'The PSA storm', *British Medical Journal*, **324**, 431.

Yates, J.F. (1990), *Judgment and Decision Making*, Englewood Cliffs: Prentice Hall.

Yeung, S., W. Van Damme, D. Socheat, N.J. White and A.J. Mills (2008), 'Cost of increasing access to artemisinin combination therapy: the Cambodian experience', *Malaria Journal*, **20**, 84, available at: http://www.malariajournal.com/content/pdf/1475-2875-7-84.pdf (accessed 26 October 2009).

Yip, W.C. (1998), 'Physician response to Medicare fee reductions: changes in the volume of coronary artery bypass graft (CABG) surgeries in the Medicare and private sectors', *Journal of Health Economics*, **17**, 675–99.

Yoder, R.A. (1989), 'Are people willing and able to pay for health services?', *Social Science and Medicine*, **29**, 35–42.

Yusuf, S., R. Peto, J. Lewis, R. Collins and P. Sleight (1985), 'Beta-blockade during and after myocardial infarction: an overview of the randomized trials', *Progress in Cardiovascular Diseases*, **27**, 335–71.

Zeckhauser, R. (1970), 'Medical insurance: a case study of the trade-off between risk spreading and appropriate incentives', *Journal of Economic Theory*, **2**, 10–26.

Zweifel, P. and W.G. Manning (2000), 'Moral hazard and consumer incentives in health care', in A.J. Culyer and J.P. Newhouse (eds), *Handbook of Health Economics*, Amsterdam: Elsevier, pp. 409–59.

Zweifel, P., F.H.J. Breyer and M. Kifmann (2009), *Health Economics*, 2nd edition, Oxford: Oxford University Press.

Zweifel, P., S. Felder and M. Meiers (1999), 'Ageing of population and health care expenditure: a red herring?', *Health Economics*, **8**, 485–96.

NAME INDEX

The Name Index refers readers only to names that appear in entries. Names in the Bibliography should be searched for there directly.

Frequency of mention in the Names Index should not be used as an indicator of productivity or fame. To take three famous health economists as examples: neither Ron Akehurst (UK) nor Frans Rutten (Netherlands) appear in the Index but each has five entries in the Bibliography. Morris Barer (Canada) has only one entry in the Index but seven references in the Bibliography. This is mainly the consequence of the system of referencing people's works by first author together with the relative modesty of some senior authors.

SUBJECT INDEX

This list includes some entry headwords but also refers readers to pages on which other useful terms are also to be found, including terms used in the titles of cited works. It does not, however, include the titles of journals cited in the Bibliography.